Young, Corker and Summers on Abuse of Process in Criminal Proceedings

Young, Corker and Summers on Abuse of Process in Criminal Proceedings

Fifth edition

David Young BA (Hons), LLM (London)
of the Middle Temple, Barrister
Red Lion Chambers

Mark Summers QC, LLB (Hons)
of the Inner Temple, Barrister
Matrix Chambers, London

David Corker MA
Oriel College, Oxford and the University of Sheffield
Solicitor, Corker Binning

With (on Chapter 11)
Martin Evans BA (Sussex), Dip Law (City), QC
of the Middle Temple, Barrister
Chambers of Kennedy Talbot QC

With (on Chapter 12)
Sarah Bafadhel LLB (Hons), LLM
of the Inner Temple, Barrister
Chambers of Steven Kay QC

Additional Co-Authors on the 5th Edition:

With (on Chapter 1)
Riel Karmy-Jones QC
Red Lion Chambers

With (on Chapter 3)
Alex Benn
Red Lion Chambers

With (on Chapters 4 and 6)
Aimee Riese
Red Lion Chambers

With (on Chapter 5)
Matthew Fielden
University College London

With (on Chapter 7)
Edmund Vickers QC
Red Lion Chambers

With (on Chapter 8)
Hugo Keith QC
3 Raymond Buildings, and

Tom Davies
Red Lion Chambers

With (on Chapter 10)
Tom Davies

With (on Chapter 11)
David Claxton
Red Lion Chambers

Bloomsbury Professional

LONDON • DUBLIN • EDINBURGH • NEW YORK • NEW DELHI • SYDNEY

BLOOMSBURY PROFESSIONAL
Bloomsbury Publishing Plc
50 Bedford Square, London, WC1B 3DP, UK
1385 Broadway, New York, NY 10018, USA
29 Earlsfort Terrace, Dublin 2, Ireland

British Library Cataloguing-in-Publication Data

A catalogue record for this book is available from the British Library.

ISBN: PB: 978 1 52651 516 2
Epdf: 978 152651 518 6
Epub: 978 152651 517 9

Typeset by Evolution Design and Digital (Kent)

Preface

It is some six years since the last edition of this work. Over that period of time a number of the different strands of the abuse doctrine have developed significantly through new case law. The reshaping or reclarification of the old *Beckford* definition of abuse of process's second limb, which resulted from the important *Maxwell* and *Warren* decisions, has come alive in some of the more recent authorities, where the focus has been on what, in a given case, has been deemed to be necessary to protect the integrity of our criminal justice system.

With disclosure related abuse arguments being the more commonly argued forms of abuse by practitioners, the chapter on the 'Loss or destruction of evidence' introduces interesting new case law. Notable among this are the *R v PR* [2019] EWCA Crim 1225 decision where the Court of Appeal provides further guidance on the approach courts should take where evidence becomes unavailable for criminal trials, as well as the appeal court's observations in the *Hamilton v Post Office* [2021] EWCA Crim 577 proceedings on the level of disclosure failings required to trigger abuse (reaffirming *Ebrahim* principles), and *R v E* [2018] EWCA Crim 2426 which concerned alleged disclosure failings surrounding the downloaded contents of a complainant's mobile telephone.

The Extradition chapter has been comprehensively updated. Within it there is detailed analysis of the courts' gradual clarification of the abuse jurisdiction in extradition proceedings, culminating recently with *Jasvins v General Prosecutor's Office Latvia* [2020] EWHC 602 (Admin). There is also up to date discussion of discrete areas of abuse within the extradition jurisdiction, such as the recent refinement of *Zakrzewski*-type abuse in *Podolak v Poland* [2020] EWHC 2830 (Admin).

The Entrapment chapter analyses the *Syed (Haroon)* [2019] 1WLR 2459 decision which helpfully reviewed the ECHR jurisprudence since *Looseley*, and also reviews the *TL* [2018] EWCA Crim 1821 decision, which considers the potential for an abuse of process doctrine in cases of private entrapment. In the Abuse of power by the executive chapter, the decision of *R v Norman* [2016] EWCA Crim 1564 is highlighted for it comprehensively sets out the state of the current law.

In the revised Double Jeopardy chapter, we review the recent *Wangige* [2020] EWCA Crim 1319 decision, which reaffirmed the *Beedie* and *Phipps* position that second prosecutions in relation to substantially the same facts was unfair and oppressive, and considered the latest guidance on when courts may properly take into account double jeopardy principles in sentence reductions. In the Miscellaneous chapter we introduce some of the interesting new case law surrounding Private Prosecutions. We review the new authorities on the circumstances where courts may infer Prosecutors hold improper motives for bringing private prosecutions, and also consider the *DS* [2020] EWCA Crim 285 and *A* [2020] EWCA Crim 1408 decisions on Modern Slavery Act prosecutions.

The updated Procedural considerations chapter reviews the significant new guidance from the Divisional Court on the challenging of interlocutory decisions by Judicial Review in *R (Parashar) v Sunderland Magistrates Court* [2019] EWHC 514 (Admin), and the appellate guidance in *R v Asiedu* [2015] 2 Cr App R 8 on the circumstances in which entering a guilty plea will not affect a defendant's ability to appeal against a conviction, affirming the *Togher* line of authority. In the renamed Adverse publicity chapter, we detail the recent innovative interventions by the Attorney General to inform the public over the potential legal pitfalls of individuals using the internet and social media, warning against conduct which could adversely affect the fairness of court proceedings.

It is right to acknowledge that certain strands of abuse witnessed little change. While the Delay chapter reviews all the latest case law, such as *R v LG* [2018] EWCA Crim 736 and *R v R* [2015] EWCA Crim 1941, the decisions appear to reaffirm general principles which were previously established in the leading decisions on delay. The Breach of promise chapter similarly saw few significant developments in the case law, as the *Hamza* authority continues to reign. In the Confiscation chapter indeed, one sees a steady decline in the abuse jurisdiction. The significant erosion of the jurisdiction in confiscation cases is analysed in *R v Andrewes* [2020] EWCA Crim 1055.

In stark contrast however to the Confiscation strand, the abuse jurisdiction appears to be growing steadily in the international criminal courts, where international defence practitioners increasingly seek to rely upon abuse arguments on behalf of their clients. The updated International chapter examines this development in three particular international courts. Firstly, in the International Residual Mechanism for Criminal Tribunals (IRMCT), where the cases of *Stanisic*, *Mladic* and *Turinabo* are considered. Secondly, in the Special Tribunal for Lebanon, where the *Sabra* case is reviewed. Thirdly, in the Hague's International Criminal Court itself where abuse arguments featured in the cases of *Al Hasssan*, *Bemba*, *Ntaganda* and *Abd-Al-Rahman*.

We have endeavoured to state the law as of 1st December 2021.

David A. Young

Red Lion Chambers

Acknowledgements

I would like to fully acknowledge and hugely thank, for their considerable assistance in the updating of this fifth edition, the stellar team of barristers, and others, who contributed to the updating of this fifth edition. In addition to the barristers from Red Lion Chambers, I was fortunate to have Hugo Keith QC updating the Extradition chapter, Sarah Bafadhel updating her own international chapter, and, upon the excellent recommendation of Professor David Ormerod QC (Hon), Matthew Fielden from University College London, who took on the updating of the 'Abuse of power by the executive' chapter, and for his additional assistance on chapter six.

From Red Lion Chambers I thank Riel Karmy-Jones QC for her work in updating the 'Delay' chapter (assisted by Tom Jones), Edmund Vickers QC, for his work in updating the 'Double Jeopardy' chapter, Aimee Reese for updating two chapters on 'Entrapment' and 'Miscellaneous abuse', Tom Davies for updating, with Hugo Keith QC, the 'Extradition' chapter, David Claxton for updating the 'Confiscation' chapter and Alex Benn for updating the 'loss or destruction of evidence' chapter. I also thank the pupils and Practice team at RLC for their continued support, and Helena Spector for her research work.

Finally, I thank Kiran Goss and the publishing team at Bloomsbury Professional for their ever-patient and professional assistance in the finalization of this fifth edition, which is now some 22 years after David Corker (of Corker Binning Solicitors) and I wrote the first edition of this textbook.

Contents

Table of Cases

[*All references are to paragraph number*]

B

D

I

J

K

L

M

N

O

Q

R

S

Table of Statutes

[All references are to paragraph number]

BAHAMAS

CANADA

NETHERLANDS

TRINIDAD AND TOBAGO

Table of Statutory Instruments

[All references are to paragraph number]

Table of European Legislation

[*All references are to paragraph number*]

Chapter 1

Delay

INTRODUCTION

1.01 In any system of criminal justice in modern society, delay is an endemic and unalterable characteristic. That there will always be an elapse of time, often substantial, between date of charge and eventual trial is, at least in part, a natural consequence of procedures and processes which are otherwise regarded as hallmarks of fairness. The requirement, for example, of prosecution disclosure of evidence and unused material to the defence pre-trial will, in a complex case, be onerous and protracted in its fulfilment. In some cases, it will be impossible to meet this requirement within the usual timescales. The availability of a court to host the trial, and the availability of trial lawyers are other features which in practice, and absent a perfect world, may inevitably operate to create delay.

1.02 Delay ultimately is in no one's interest and is inimical to fairness; it fades the memory of prosecution and defence witnesses alike; it can cause the inadvertent destruction of relevant documents, or loss of evidence; it allows for lengthy periods of pre-trial imprisonment; and it contributes to anxiety and expense. That the length of any delay should be minimised and its effects ameliorated are clear priorities for any system wishing to dispense justice and to instil public confidence in its processes.

1.03 In broad terms, two remedies have been favoured to combat the evil of delay: first, the imposition of time limits, and second, an overarching requirement of '*reasonableness*' as determined by judicial discretion. To some extent these remedies are mutually inconsistent; whereas time limits impose objective and measurable demands upon the progress of any criminal case passing through pre-defined points, reasonableness prefers a case-sensitive approach, eschewing the imposition of universal formulae, and preferring as yardsticks open-ended concepts such as the 'appropriate' time in the specific circumstances of a case and whether there is an adequate explanation for the delay. As Sopinka J said in the Canadian case of *R v Smith*,[1] '…it is axiomatic that some delay is inevitable. The question is, at what point does the delay become unreasonable?'

1 [1992] 2 SCR 1120 at 1131.

1.04 Our system, via the abuse jurisdiction, has in serious cases lent heavily in favour of the remedy of judicial discretion. This preference is perhaps the result of two factors; history and a mistrust of time limits. History in that the abuse jurisdiction is of course entirely judge-made and thus developed incrementally over decades. It is a creature, like the law on prosecution disclosure was until the advent of the Criminal Procedure and Investigations Act 1996, of the common law. As a result, sudden bold initiatives such as the use of across-the-board time limits, or the imposition of administrative or mathematical formula are unavailable to judges no matter how pioneering. Such initiatives can emanate only from Parliament or, at least, the Lord Chancellor by means of new rules and instruments creating at a stroke new 'black letter' law. As the executive has hitherto largely preferred to allow the abuse jurisdiction to develop organically, so the use of time limits has been overlooked in favour of judicial discretion.

1.05 A general mistrust of time limits as a means of delivering justice is rooted in the embedded notion in our system that judicial discretion is best. In many ways the arguments here are similar to those underlying the implementation of the Human Rights Act 1998 (HRA 1998); that the courts play a critical role in protecting defendants in criminal proceedings,[1] and that a fact-sensitive approach is best, allowing the trial judge to hold the ring between the interests of the accused and that of the wider community. HRA 1998, especially in criminal cases, manifests this doctrine of deference leaving the interpretation of rights in a particular case to the judges.

1 As Lord Steyn argued, especially when public opinion and fair adjudication are at odds, in 'The New Legal System' [2000] EHRLR 549.

THE TEST OF THE COMMON LAW

Introduction

1.06 In contrast to other jurisdictions, neither Parliament nor the common law has sought to confer on an accused any constitutional or absolute right to a speedy trial or to judgment within a specific time. In other words, no overarching limitation period restricting the right of a prosecutor to bring charges against an accused has been imposed.

1.07 A clear illustration of the fact that English criminal law has not imposed any limitation period is the enactment of the War Crimes Act 1991. The legislation was passed principally in order to make it possible in the 1990s to bring to justice persons who were suspected of committing war crimes many years before, during the 1939–45 war. In *R v Serafinowitz*[1] and *R v Sawoniuk*,[2] the defendants were indicted for war crimes committed during the early 1940s. In both cases their submissions, made some 50 years later in 1997 and 1999 respectively, for stays of the proceedings on the basis of abuse based on delay failed, the trial judges holding that the trial process could overcome any prejudice thereby caused. By passing this Act, Parliament had sent out a clear message that its intention was that such crimes should be prosecuted, regardless of massive delay. It should be noted that the principles behind the decisions made in those cases are not restricted to ones brought under this specific Act.

1 (17 January 1997, unreported).
2 [2000] 2 Cr App R 220, CA. This defendant was convicted and sentenced to life imprisonment.

Statutory measures

Limitation period for summary-only offences

1.08 While there is no overarching principle in English law imposing a limitation period on the bringing of criminal charges, Parliament has nonetheless imposed a limitation period for a specific category of alleged offences. These are invariably confined to summary only offences. For example, the Magistrates' Courts Act 1980, s 127 provides that:

> **'Limitations of time**
>
> (1) Except as otherwise expressly provided by any enactment and subject to subsection (2) below, a magistrates' court shall not try an information or hear a complaint unless the information was laid, or the complaint made, within 6 months from the time when the offence was committed, or the matter of complaint arose.'

Via the discipline of this six-month rule Parliament has sought to ensure that summary offences are both charged and tried as soon as reasonably possible after their alleged commission.

1.09 In the exercise of its supervisory jurisdiction over the magistrates' court where all summary offences are tried, the Divisional Court has sought to ensure that this intention behind s 127 is respected both in its letter and spirit. This determination can be illustrated by the authority of *R v Brentford Justices, ex p Wong*.[1] In this case, the prosecutor decided to lay an information against an accused for the summary only offence of careless driving. However, the information was laid only one day prior to the expiry of the six-month period permitted by s 127, and it transpired that the decision by the prosecutor to lay the information had been taken before proper consideration, or any decision had been made as to whether proceedings should, in fact, be continued or not. In other words, the prosecutor had sought to circumvent the six-month limitation period by issuing the information as a holding manoeuvre in order to decide whether to proceed with a prosecution later. The Divisional Court held that such prosecutorial manoeuvring constituted an abuse. Donaldson LJ held that the six-month time limit required prosecuting authorities to act with expedition, and to decide within that time limit finally whether to bring proceedings or not, and said that:

> 'The process of laying an information is, I think, assumed by Parliament to be the first stage in a continuous process of bringing a prosecution. [MCA 1980, s 127] is designed to ensure that prosecutions shall be brought within a reasonable time. That purpose is wholly frustrated if it is possible for a prosecutor to obtain summonses and then, in his own good time and at his convenience, serve them … Here … there was a deliberate attempt to gain further time in which to reach a decision. It is perhaps hard on the prosecutor to characterise that as an abuse of the process of the court because I am sure that there was no intention by the prosecutor to abuse the process of the court. He thought he could legitimately do this … I do not think that he can … it is a matter which has to be investigated by justices.'

1 [1981] QB 445, DC.

1.10 *Ex p Wong* is, therefore, authority that deliberate prosecutorial delay in the context of summary offences will not be tolerated by the courts. The prosecution must decide on the institution of criminal proceedings in good time and also decide upon which factual basis to proceed.

1.11 The principle in *ex p Wong* has also been held to apply where the prosecution lay an information (and so have decided to bring a prosecution) but are undecided between two factual bases upon which the case might proceed. This was the situation in *R v Newcastle-upon-Tyne Justices, ex p Hindle*,[1] the defendant was charged with obstructing a police officer in the execution of his duty, but the information did not specify the nature of the obstruction alleged and, in the circumstances of the case, the prosecution might have been alleging two different senses of objectionable behaviour. When the prosecution refused to resolve this ambiguity, the Divisional Court held that the obstruction summons ought not to proceed. Goff LJ said that the situation was:

> '... at least as objectionable a course as the laying of an information where no decision has been taken to prosecute; for, if permitted, it would allow a prosecution to postpone, until after the expiry of the six month period, their decision whether to prosecute for a particular offence'.[2]

Prejudice had also been caused to the defence because, without knowing how the prosecution intended to put its case, it was unable to properly deal with the question of whether the obstruction charge should be tried before or after other charges against the defendant which arose out of the same incident.

1 [1984] 1 All ER 770, DC.
2 At 778. See also *R v J* [2005] 1 AC 562, HL (the bringing of unsuitable charges because most suitable charges time-barred was capable of constituting abuse even in the absence of dishonesty or improper motive) and *R (Wardle) v Crown Court at Leeds* [2002] 1 AC 754, HL (bringing new charges to avoid custody time limits was capable of constituting abuse even in the absence of dishonesty or improper motive); both discussed in detail in Chapter 4 at para **4.12**.

Implicit limitation periods

1.12 While s 127 is one of very few statutory examples of an explicit limitation period being created on the bringing of criminal proceedings, there are, however, implicit limitation periods which exist by virtue of the obligation being created by the relevant legislation. For example, regs 5 and 12 of the Money Laundering Regulations 1993 make it an offence for a person who conducts 'relevant financial business' not to preserve records of relevant transactions for a period of at least five years after those transactions have been completed. If, therefore, a prosecution were to be mounted against a person for an offence under regs 5 and 12 more than five years after the relevant transactions occurred, the accused would have an absolute defence in that he was entitled to destroy the records once the statutory period had elapsed. A more recent statutory example which also contains such implicit limitation periods on the bringing of proceedings is the Companies Act 2006, which requires the keeping of minutes of meetings of the company directors for a period of at least 10 years (s 248) and the keeping of accounting records (ss 386–389), a copy of the contract or memorandum of a contract for an 'off-market purchase' or a contract for a 'market purchase' (s 702) and the directors' statement and auditor's report for inspection (s 720), all for defined minimum periods of time.

1.13 In this context the practitioner should note the decision of the Court of Appeal in *R v J*.[1] In this case, the defendant had consensual sexual intercourse with a girl under 16. Owing to the fact that the complainant did not report the conduct for three years, a prosecution of an offence of unlawful sexual intercourse with a girl under 16, contrary to s 6(1) of the Sexual Offences Act 1956, would have been time barred by virtue of para 10(a) of Sch 2 to the Act (which has since been repealed by the Sexual Offences Act 2003). So a prosecution was instead brought for indecent assault, under s 14(1), which was not time barred, but was based on the same act of sexual intercourse. The Crown acknowledged the decision to have been motivated by an intention to avoid the statutory time limit.

1 [2005] 1 AC 562 HL.

1.14 The House of Lords (Baroness Hale dissenting) ruled that the conduct of the Crown was not easily accommodated within any of the traditional categories of abuse of process; the delay was not the fault of the Crown, the Crown had not sought to prejudice the conduct of the defence in any improper way, the fairness of the trial had not been imperilled, the Crown had acted without malice or dishonesty and not been guilty of any devious, underhand or manipulative conduct, indeed the decision to prosecute was one that the general public would applaud. But, the House of Lords recalled, the categories of abuse are not closed and defy exhaustive definition. Even if the rationale for the time bar could be regarded as anachronistic, discredited or unconvincing, it remained a statutory time bar that the courts were under a duty to give effect to. Accordingly, when the only evidence relied upon was of consensual sexual intercourse with a girl under 16, a prosecution for indecent assault in respect of that conduct after the 12-month time limit had expired should be stayed.

Practice directions

1.15 Over recent years, efforts have been made to streamline and speed the passage of cases through the Crown Court. As part of this process, practice directions have been promulgated which set down time limits within which cases should be progressed to a specified point. The best example of this is perhaps the Criminal Practice Directions 2015[1] as amended,[2] which dictate that a plea and trial preparation hearing (PTPH) must be held within 28 days of the magistrates sending a case for trial, unless the standard directions of the Presiding Judges of the circuit directs otherwise. The Better Case Management Handbook[3] states that PTPHs may be listed on a day exceeding 28 days, provided the allocated day is not more than 35 days from sending. At the PTPH the court will then ordinarily set four stage dates providing a timetable for the parties to complete their pre-trial preparation. The practice directions further state that after the PTPH there will be no further case management hearings unless one of the conditions in the Criminal Procedure Rules are met.[4] However, it should also be noted that even a breach of statutory time periods regarding case progression (service of papers under ss 51 and 52 of the Crime and Disorder Act 1998 in this case) will not be a ground for the dismissal of proceedings.[5]

1 [2015] EWCA Crim 1567.
2 Criminal Practice Directions Amendment No 11 [2020] EWCA Crim 1347.
3 8 January 2018.
4 CrimPD 3A.21 and CrimPR 3.21(1)(c).
5 *Fehily v Governor of Wandsworth Prison* [2002] EWHC 1295.

1.16 The Criminal Procedure Rules require the court to actively manage the case, including 'discouraging delay, dealing with as many aspects of the case as possible on the same occasion and avoiding unnecessary hearings'[1] and further the court is required at any hearing at which the case cannot be concluded to 'there and then…give directions so that it can be concluded at the next hearing or as soon as possible after that'.[2]

1 Rule 3.2(2)(f).
2 Rule 3.8(1).

CPS Code for Crown Prosecutors

1.17 The Director of Public Prosecutions is enjoined by the Prosecution of Offences Act 1985, s 10, to issue a Code for Crown Prosecutors giving guidance on general principles, inter alia, in determining whether proceedings for an offence should be instituted. The Code is, in practice, an invaluable measure against which to judge abuse. In *Sharma v Browne-Antoine*, PC, Baroness Hale, and Lords Carswell and Mance observed that '… The power to stay for abuse of process can and should be understood widely enough to embrace an application challenging a decision to prosecute on the ground that it was arrived at under political pressure or influence or was motivated politically rather than by an objective review of proper prosecutorial considerations (such as, in England, those set out in the Code for Crown Prosecutors issued under the Prosecution of Offences Act 1985)…'.[1]

That The Code of Conduct in place at the time of writing was published on 26 October 2018, and references to delay are limited. Paragraph 3.5 states that 'Prosecutors should not start or continue a prosecution where their view is that it is highly likely that a court will rule that a prosecution is an abuse of its process, and stay the proceedings'. Paragraphs 5.5–7, deal with the application of the Threshold Test where the evidential part of the Full Code Test has not been met. There it states that in reaching a decision that they are satisfied that there are reasonable grounds to believe that the continuing investigation will provide further evidence within a reasonable period of time, prosecutors must consider:

i. the nature, extent and admissibility of any likely further evidence and the impact it will have on the case;

ii. the charges that all the evidence will support;

iii. the reasons why the evidence is not already available;

iv. the time required to obtain the further evidence, including whether it could be obtained within any available detention period;

v. whether the delay in applying the Full Code Test is reasonable in all the circumstances.

There is a further brief acknowledgement at para 8.2 where it states 'Speed must never be the only reason for asking for a case to stay in the magistrates' court. But prosecutors should consider the effect of any likely delay if a case is sent to the Crown Court, including the possible effect on any victim or witness'.

1 [2007] 1 WLR 780 at para 32.

Police and Criminal Evidence Act Code of Practice

1.18 Code C of the PACE Codes of Practice[1] is entitled 'Code of Practice for the detention, treatment and questioning of persons by Police Officers'. Paragraph 11.6 provides that:

> 'The interview or further interview of a person about an offence with which that person has not been charged or for which they have not been informed they may be prosecuted, must cease when:
>
> (a) the officer in charge of the investigation is satisfied all the questions they consider relevant to obtaining accurate and reliable information about the offence have been put to the suspect, this includes allowing the suspect an opportunity to give an innocent explanation and asking questions to test if the explanation is accurate and reliable, e.g. to clear up ambiguities or clarify what the suspect said;
>
> (b) the officer in charge of the investigation has taken account of any other available evidence; and
>
> (c) the officer in charge of the investigation, or in the case of a detained suspect, the custody officer, see paragraph 16.1, reasonably believes there is sufficient evidence to provide a realistic prospect of conviction for that offence'.

1 Amended version in force from 21 August 2019.

1.19 This provision is designed to ensure that once the substance of a prosecution case is apparent to a police officer/investigator, he should not continue questioning the suspect for the purpose of trying to turn the case into a stronger and better one. Whilst the avoidance of delay is not the primary aim of this provision, it is designed to ensure that once a case is apparent the suspect should be charged and the proceedings should begin at the earliest opportunity. The decision to charge in this context should not be delayed. This point is made even clearer by para 16.1 which reads:

> 'When the officer in charge of the investigation reasonably believes there is sufficient evidence to provide a realistic prospect of conviction for the offence…., they shall without delay inform the custody officer who will be responsible for considering whether the detainee should be charged'.

1.20 It is submitted that several qualifications need to be made to the prescriptions contained in the quoted passages from PACE Code C set out above. First, the custody officer has to know what charge is appropriate, bearing in mind the circumstances of the case. There is in our system no provision for a 'holding charge' to enable a suspect to be charged with an offence merely for the purpose of firstly complying with the Code and secondly for enabling the prosecution to be given some breathing space for the purpose of formulating more specific and appropriate charges. It may therefore be entirely understandable for the police to delay charging in order for their understanding of the case to improve, so as to be able in due course to charge an appropriate offence. It is also understandable to defer charging for the purpose of carrying out certain investigations which may further inform the approach to the case, and / or the proper offence to charge, for example those that have been instigated by the suspect themself in answers given during interview.

1.21 While the wording of the relevant paragraphs of the Code encourages charges to be levelled as soon as the police believe there is sufficient evidence to merit such charges, the courts have been reluctant to adopt this strict approach. Instead, they have preferred a flexible approach allowing investigators not to charge until all relevant evidence is gathered so long as this is achieved within a reasonable period. An example of such judicial tolerance is the judgment of the Lord Chief Justice in *R v Cardiff Magistrates' Court, ex p Hole*.[1] In answer to a specific defence submission that there had been a breach of paras 11.4 (now 11.6) and 16.1 of the Code, Lord Bingham CJ observed that the decision of the police officer to defer charging was reasonable, bearing in mind the complexity of the case and the need to conduct additional enquiries based on what the defendants had said during their respective interviews.

1 [1997] COD 84.

THE CORNERSTONE CASE: ATTORNEY-GENERAL'S REFERENCE (NO 1 OF 1990)[1]

1.22 The decision by the Attorney-General to seek the authoritative guidance of the Court of Appeal regarding delay demonstrated the degree of official concern regarding the then willingness of courts to stay prosecutions. In allowing the Criminal Division of the Court of Appeal a full opportunity to consider delay in the context of abuse it was obviously hoped, by those responsible for criminal prosecutions, that the court would issue clear guidance which would dramatically restrict the extent of trial courts' jurisdiction to stay cases on the ground of delay. In this respect, prosecutors were not to be disappointed. As Lord Lane CJ commented at the end of his judgment:

> 'This judgment will, we hope, result in a significant reduction in the number of applications to stay proceedings on the ground of delay'.[2]

1 [1992] QB 630, [1992] 3 WLR 9; (1992) 95 Crim App R 296, CA; See also *S(SP)* [2006] EWCA Crim 756; [2006] 2 Cr App R. 23 which confirms the principles drawn from the *Attorney-General's Reference (No 1 of 1990)*, stressing the importance of it being for the trial process to ensure all relevant factual issues are placed before the jury, including any reasons for the delay. Unjustified delay alone is not sufficient. The question is whether there is prejudice to a defendant. (Approved in *CPS v F(S)* [2011] EWCA Crim 1844; [2011] 2 Cr App R 28 (see further below at para **1.27**).

2 At [644].

1.23 The facts which gave rise to *Attorney-General's Reference (No 1 of 1990)* concerned a police officer who attended an incident in August 1987, giving rise to subsequent complaint. He was summonsed for an offence in March 1989. At the commencement of his Crown Court trial in December 1989, the trial judge accepted a submission that, because of the August 1987 to March 1989 delay in prosecuting him, this alone constituted an abuse and his trial should accordingly be stayed. The Attorney-General viewed this approach as flawed and pursuant to the Criminal Justice Act 1972, s 36, sought a ruling from the Court of Appeal in relation to the following two questions:

(1) Whether proceedings on indictment may be stayed on the grounds of prejudice resulting from delay in the institution of those proceedings even though the delay had not been occasioned by any fault of the prosecution.

(2) If the answer to (1) is in the affirmative, what is the degree of:

 (a) the likelihood; and

 (b) the seriousness of any prejudice which is required to justify a stay of such proceedings.

1.24 During the hearing of *Attorney-General's Reference (No 1 of 1990)*, the Attorney-General argued that the trial judge had been wrong to hold that the period of delay in the case before him could properly be said to amount to an abuse. Two arguments in support of this were canvassed. First, the delay which did occur was reasonable and justifiable in the circumstances. Secondly, there was no evidence of any specific prejudice to the accused in the preparation of his defence caused by the delay. In reply, the defence submitted that the delay amounted to a breach of Clause 29 of the 1225 version (confirmed by Henry III) and 1297 edition (by Edward I) of Magna Carta;[1] the word 'defer' meaning any period which was longer than that required for proper preparation for the trial.

1 The judgement quotes Clause 29 as: 'No Freeman shall be taken, or imprisoned, or be disseised of his Freehold or Liberties or free Customs or be outlawed, or exiled or any otherwise destroyed, nor will we not pass upon him nor condemn him, but by lawful judgment of his Peers, or by the Law of the Land, we will sell to no man, we will not deny or defer to any man either Justice or Right'. Chapter 29 appears to have been derived from Clauses 39 and 40 of the original 1215 charter, which has been revised on many occasions. It should be noted that Clause 40 of the original reads '… to no one will we sell, to no one deny or delay, right or justice'.

1.25 Lord Lane CJ unhesitatingly rejected this defence submission, holding that the 'deferment' meant wrongful deferment or delay, about which Chapter 29 of Magna Carta could not even begin to offer any guidance. Lord Lane CJ answered the first question as follows:

> 'On the basis of the decision in *R v Telford Justices, ex p Badhan* … the Attorney-General, felt constrained to concede that the answer to the Attorney-General's first question is a qualified "Yes". As it is not possible to anticipate in advance all the infinitely variable circumstances which may arise in the future, we feel ourselves, albeit reluctantly, forced to agree to a limited extent with that concession. However, we remind ourselves

of the principles outlined earlier in this judgment and the observation of Lord Morris in *Connolly*, 48 Cr App Rep 183, [1964] AC 1254 at page 211 and page 1304 that: "... generally speaking a prosecutor has as much right as a defendant to demand a verdict of a jury on an outstanding indictment, and where either demands a verdict a judge has no jurisdiction to stand in the way of it". Stays imposed on the grounds of delay or for any other reason should only be employed in exceptional circumstances .... If they were to become a matter of routine, it would be only a short time before the public, understandably, viewed the process with suspicion and mistrust ... In principle, therefore, even where the delay can be said to be unjustifiable, the imposition of a permanent stay should be the exception rather than the rule. Still more rare should be cases where a stay can properly be imposed in the absence of any fault on the part of the complainant or prosecution. Delay due merely to the complexity of the case or contributed to by the actions of the defendant himself should never be the foundation for a stay'.

1.26 In answer to the second question, Lord Lane CJ said:

'... no stay should be imposed unless the defendant shows on the balance of probabilities that owing to the delay he will suffer serious prejudice to the extent that no fair trial can be held: in other words, that the continuance of the prosecution amounts to a misuse of the process of the court. In assessing whether there is likely to be prejudice and if so whether it can properly be described as serious, the following matters should be borne in mind: first, the power of the judge at common law and under [PACE] to regulate the admissibility of evidence; secondly, the trial process itself, which should ensure that all relevant factual issues arising from delay will be placed before the jury as part of the evidence for their consideration, together with the powers of the judge to give appropriate directions to the jury before they consider their verdict'.

1.27 Turning to the facts of the case as set out above, Lord Lane CJ held that the trial judge was wrong in agreeing to stay the proceedings:

'The delay, such as it was, was not unjustifiable; the chances of prejudice were remote; the degree of potential prejudice was small; the powers of the judge and the trial process itself would have provided ample protection for the respondent; there was no danger of the trial being unfair; in any event the case was in no sense exceptional so as to justify the ruling'.

In CPS v F(S)[1] Lord Judge CJ commented on the *Attorney-General's Reference (No 1 of 1990)*, observing:

'Lord Lane expressed the hope that the judgment would significantly reduce the number of applications for proceedings to be stayed on the ground of delay. The exceptional nature of the jurisdiction was repeated and emphasised. It all proved to be something of a forlorn hope. In 2000, in a trial before the Crown Court, no less than 27 so-called authorities (they were mainly fact-specific decisions) were drawn to the attention of the trial judge in support of an application for a stay on the ground of delay: *R v MacKreth* [2009] EWCA Crim 1849, [2010] Crim LR 226. And so it has continued, the proliferation of decisions cited to the Crown Court, and then in this court, obscuring the principles and eliding the distinct questions whether the trial should be stopped as an abuse of process and whether the case should be withdrawn from the jury on *Galbraith* principles. Yet just as *Galbraith* unequivocally established that the question whether the verdict of the jury was "unsafe" was vested exclusively in this court after conviction, and that no corresponding jurisdiction to bring the trial to an end on some equivalent basis before conviction exists, so *Attorney-General's Reference (No 1 of 1990)* established the principles to be applied in the context of delay, whether in cases involving delayed complaints of sexual abuse, or delays arising for any other reason when the delays were alleged to constitute an abuse of process'.

1 [2011] EWCA Crim 1844, approving *S(SP)* [2006] EWCA Crim 756; [2006] 2 Cr App R 23 (above at para **1.22**, fn.1).

Analysis of Lord Lane CJ's judgment

1.28 Bearing in mind that Lord Lane CJ's judgment has remained the cornerstone of the law on delay, it is necessary to consider it in some detail. It is submitted that the following points are pertinent:

(1) *Some prejudice must be tolerated by the defence.* The hurdle to be surmounted by defendants seeking a stay is a high one. The prejudice must be serious to the extent that no fair trial can be held. A defendant must therefore tolerate some prejudice or unfairness to his case caused by delay even if this is no fault of his own. This unfortunate predicament, Lord Lane CJ contended, can however be largely eliminated, as faith can be placed in the flexibility of the trial process to eliminate residual unfairness caused by delay.

(2) *The remedial effects of the trial process.* Lord Lane CJ urged trial judges to recognise the existence of their other powers to ensure a fair trial as alternatives to the exercise of a stay, i.e. excluding evidence and ensuring that the jury are made aware of the facts concerning delay. In Lord Lane CJ's view, the exercise of such powers would, in most cases where there had been significant delay, be a sufficient remedy and so would ensure that the proceedings were fair.

    However, against this it is difficult to see how the use of such powers and protections will be effective in many delay cases. How, for example, is a jury, when it retires to consider its verdict, to deal with the issue presumably raised by the defence and echoed by the judge as to what the evidence might have been but for the delay? It would appear that this is an open-ended issue which can only be resolved by speculation rather than by fact. How, in a concrete case, can a tribunal of fact seek to resolve this issue based only on the evidence presented to it?

(3) *The culpability of the prosecution.* In his answer to the first question, Lord Lane CJ suggests that judges should be more reluctant to stay proceedings on account of delay if there has been no fault on the part of the prosecution than if there has been such fault. It is submitted, however,

that this distinction creates an immediate uncertainty because in answer to the second question, Lord Lane CJ held that the criterion to be followed is always to be the same, that of serious prejudice to the accused. What then is the relevance of considering the extent of the prosecution's culpability for the delay? Unless Lord Lane CJ meant to suggest that if the prosecution has been culpable then the threshold for imposing a stay should be lower than if it has not, this consideration has no legitimate role. But as Lord Lane CJ did not suggest this, it is submitted that there is an inconsistency between his answers to the two questions vis-à-vis the relevance of prosecution fault. Despite Lord Lane CJ's insistence that there is only one criterion, he appears to concede that the issue of any fault on the part of the prosecution for delay is to be included in the equation, although unfortunately does not explain how. It would appear that Lord Lane CJ accepts that the courts have a role in disciplining the prosecution in this regard.

(4) *Causes of delay to be excluded from consideration.* In his answer to the first question, Lord Lane CJ makes plain that two factors should never militate in favour of the exercise of a stay:

(i) *Complexity*: where delay is due to the complexity of the prosecution's allegations or genuine difficulty in investigating the alleged crime. Delay may be inevitable in complicated cases especially in those involving allegations of fraud. Lord Lane CJ's view here was reflected earlier in *Holyoake*[1] where the defendant was tried in 1990 for offences alleged to have occurred between 1983 and 1986. It was submitted on appeal that this prolonged delay was prejudicial to the defendant. The defence submitted that a material witness had died and an important part of the prosecution case related to a conversation between defendant and victim which had occurred four years previously and where there was a conflict of recollection. Farquharson LJ, however, did not agree either that the delay had caused an unfair trial or that the prosecution delay had been unjustifiable:

> 'These are matters which might give rise to some degree of prejudice it is true …It must be perfectly obviously to everybody concerned that it was a case which required consideration and investigation in depth. Everybody is aware that these company fraud cases (a) take a long time to prepare, (b) generally arrive at the Crown Court at a late date because of the commitments of the people concerned in the case.'

(ii) *The culpability of the defendant.* Unsurprisingly Lord Lane CJ held that when the accused is responsible for the delay he cannot then complain about possible prejudice arising therefrom. Accordingly, a defendant who flees the jurisdiction in order to avoid criminal proceedings against him is in effect estopped from arguing that he cannot receive a fair trial on the grounds of delay.[2] This principle, easy to explain and apply in straightforward situations, has called for qualification when, in the light of a defence complaint about delay, the prosecution riposte that the delay was caused by the defendant's conduct, which itself is to be an issue of dispute in the trial. For example, where the defence complain about delay and deny guilt and the prosecution contend that the accused committed subsequent offences to conceal his principal offence and such attempted concealment caused delay in discovery of the principal offence. In *A-G of Hong Kong v Wai-bun*[3] the question arose as to the accused's responsibility for the delay. The prosecution argued that the defendant was primarily responsible for the delay because he had sought to hinder and delay the investigation by falsifying accounts, the subject of the charge against him. On behalf of the Privy Council, Lord Woolf rejected this argument (upholding the trial judge's decision to stay proceedings). It presupposed the defendant's guilt for the offence alleged against him, which was of course a matter of fact to be decided by a jury necessarily subsequent to any application to stay. Lord Woolf held that prosecutors could not argue, on the strength of Lord Lane CJ's judgment, that in this sense the defendant had contributed to delay. Lord Woolf held that what Lord Lane CJ was referring to in *Attorney-General's Reference (No 1 of 1990)* were acts of the defendant outside the subject of the trial, for example absconding.

(5) *Oral versus documentary evidence cases.* Lord Lane CJ emphasised that a distinction must be drawn between cases which turn largely on contemporaneous documentary evidence and those which do not. Lord Lane CJ perhaps had in mind *R v Buzalek and Schiffer*[4] where the Court of Appeal held that a distinction should be drawn between cases where the prosecution is dependent on available documents, as in most fraud cases, and where it is dependent on a late complaint and oral testimony, as in many sexual offence cases. The court held that generally speaking only in the latter may it be inferred from a long delay that a fair trial would not be possible. This approach was followed by Watkins LJ in *R v Central Criminal Court, ex p Randle and Pottle*[5] where the defendants were in 1990 to be tried for offences that they had allegedly committed in 1963. Watkins LJ rejected the defence submission that the delay between the offence and the trial was sufficiently extreme to warrant a stay on the ground of abuse. Watkins LJ held that, as the defendants had virtually admitted their offence in a book which they had written in 1989, which the prosecution sought to rely on as part of its case, the trial should proceed; fading memory could not realistically be suggested.

1 (24 August 1990, unreported), CA.

2 See, to similar effect, albeit in a different context, *Kakis v The Republic of Cyprus* [1978] 1 WLR 779, HL, discussed in Chapter 8 at paras **8.13–8.15**.

3 [1994] 1 AC 1, PC.

4 [1991] Crim LR 115, CA. See *R v Telford Justices, ex parte Badhan* [1991] 2 QB 78, DC.

5 [1992] 1 All ER 370, CA. It should be noted that this case has received 'Negative judicial consideration' and was overruled by the House of Lords in *Ashton* [1994] 1 A.C. 9. However, *Ashton* appears to have ruled that the decision to strike out charges on the grounds of delay was not subject to judicial review. It is therefore submitted that the dicta of Watkins LJ is still applicable, particularly in light of subsequent cases involving extreme delays such as *R v Serafinowitz* and *R v Sawoniuk* (see above at para **1.07**).

Attorney-Generals Reference (No 2 of 2001)[1]

1.29 Lord Woolf CJ identified two questions of principle:

'(i) Whether criminal proceedings may be stayed on the ground that there has been a violation of the reasonable time requirement in article 6(1) of the European Convention for the Protection of Fundamental Rights and Freedoms ("the Convention") in circumstances where the accused cannot demonstrate any prejudice arising from the delay.

(ii) In the determination of whether, for the purposes of article 6(1) of the Convention, a criminal charge has been heard within a reasonable time, when does the relevant time period commence?'

1.30 Lord Woolf CJ added:

> 'The first question deals with the remedy where there has been a violation, and the second question deals with the commencement date for the computation of the time which has lapsed so as to ascertain whether or not a reasonable time has passed'.

1 [2001] 1 WLR 1869 (CA); [2004] 2 AC 72 (HL).

The Court of Appeal ruling

The commencement date

1.31 Dealing with the second question first, Lord Woolf CJ provided the following answer:

> '... in the great majority of situations the date that a defendant is charged (in the sense we use that term in our domestic jurisprudence) will provide the answer. Ordinarily therefore the commencement of the computation in determining whether a reasonable time has elapsed will start with either a defendant being charged or being served with a summons as a result of an information being laid before the magistrates.'

Accordingly, when called upon to examine the length of any complained of delay, absent some exceptional circumstance the court should measure it from the date of charge or issuance of summons.

1.32 Lord Woolf CJ accepted, however, that in an exceptional case, the test of substantial affectation as established in *Eckle v Germany*[1] and *Deweer v Belgium*[2] might lead to the moment of charge occurring at an earlier point:

> 'There will, however, be situations where a broader approach is required to be adopted in order to give full effect to the rights preserved by article 6(1) of the Convention... For the purposes of that article there could be a period prior to a person formally being charged under English law *if the situation was one where the accused has been substantially affected by the actions of a state so as a matter of substance to be in no different position from a person who has been charged.* The importance of the approach that Mr Perry concedes the court has to adopt is that it takes account of the fact that there may be some stage prior to an accused being formally charged in

accordance with our domestic law where, *as a result of the actions of a state linked to an investigation, when he has been materially prejudiced in his position*'. [Emphasis added]

1 Application no: 8130/78, 15 July 1982.
2 Application no: 6903/75, 27 February 1980.

1.33 As can be seen from the second highlighted passage above, Lord Woolf CJ sought to redefine the concept of substantial affectation as akin to that of material prejudice. Unless this existed at the antecedent date, then the date of commencement would be date of charge. Unfortunately, in stipulating this new concept, Lord Woolf CJ offered no elucidation of its meaning and no illustrative examples were provided.

1.34 The efficacy or helpfulness of 'material prejudice' can be considered in relation to an obvious practical issue: whether the actions of the State in conducting a caution interview of a suspect subsequently prosecuted would constitute such prejudice? In our domestic system, 'charge' has a very distinct meaning and it is a clearly defined moment marking the transition from investigation to prosecution. However, especially in complex cases, interviews of suspects can precede by many months their being charged. In *Attorney-General's Reference (No 2 of 2001)* the trial judge had held that the interview stage did mark the commencement of the proceedings and thus concluded that there had been unreasonable delay. But Lord Woolf CJ disagreed:

> 'In the ordinary way an interrogation or an interview of a suspect by itself does not amount to a charging of that suspect for the purpose of the reasonable time requirement in article 6(1)'.

1.35 In reaching this conclusion, Lord Woolf CJ made no reference to any of the recent Strasbourg cases on the subject, especially *Howarth*[1] where, in relation to a serious fraud investigation, the European Court reached the opposite conclusion. If, it is submitted, Lord Woolf CJ, via the articulation of a new concept of material prejudice, was seeking to distinguish this from the European Court concept of substantial affectation, this required at least some analysis of the purported difference(s) and a justification of why the decision in *Howarth* can be distinguished. As it is there seems no substance to a claim of difference here.

1 [2001] 31 EHRR 37.

The appropriate remedy

1.36 Lord Woolf CJ described the approach of the trial judge as follows:

> '... if there has been unreasonable delay, to go on and proceed to try a defendant results in the court acting in a way which is incompatible with that defendant's rights. There is no discretion about the matter. Once the court has come to the conclusion that the reasonable time requirement in article 6(1) has been contravened, the court has to stay the proceedings'.

In other words, the view of the trial judge was that the right to trial within a reasonable time conferred a correlative right not to be tried after the expiry of a reasonable time.

1.37 Lord Woolf CJ, however, expressed strong disagreement with this approach, holding it to be nonsensical. In his view there was no such correlative right and it was erroneous to hold that the Art 6(1) right was a right not to be tried after a reasonable time:

> 'If a person complains of a contravention of the reasonable time requirement in article 6, and if the court comes to the conclusion that there has been a contravention, then at the request of the complainant the court is required to provide the appropriate remedy. If the court is willing and able to provide the appropriate remedy, then the court is not compelled to take the course of staying the proceedings. That is a remedy which the court can grant, but it is certainly not a remedy which it is required to grant'.

1.38 Alternative remedies to a stay would include reduction of sentence or an award of compensation. Commenting upon the impact of the HRA 1998, Lord Woolf CJ said:

> 'The difference which the Human Rights Act 1998 makes is that the remedies available to a court can be greater than they were hitherto. In particular, it is now in appropriate circumstances open to the courts to make awards of compensation'.

1.39 Having thus held that a trial could proceed even after an unreasonable delay and that a stay was only the last resort, Lord Woolf CJ went on to consider when this remedy should be applied. Here Lord Woolf CJ sought to provide fresh impetus to the judgment in the *Attorney-General's Reference (No 1 of 1990)*,[1] Lord Woolf CJ held that the remedy of a stay should only be granted in the circumstances as outlined there by Lord Lane CJ, saying:

> 'It seems to us in general that the approach that previously existed as to the provision of the remedy of staying the proceedings should be confined, as it was prior to the Convention becoming part of our domestic law, to situations which in general terms can be described as amounting to an abuse of the process of the courts.'
>
> 'As we have already indicated, if there has been prejudice caused to a defendant which interferes with his right to a fair trial in a way which cannot otherwise be remedied, then of course a stay is the appropriate remedy. But in the absence of prejudice of that sort, there is normally no justification for granting a stay'.

1 See above, at para **1.22**.

Analysis of Woolf CJ's judgment

1.40 Lord Woolf CJ wished to ensure that the advent of the HRA 1998 did not cause (as had happened in that case) the staying of prosecutions which under Lord Lane CJ's test in *Attorney-General's Reference (No 1 of 1990)* would not have been stayed. Consequently he confirmed that rigorous adherence to Lord Lane CJ's judgment should remain. In other words, that only where the test of serious prejudice was satisfied should the remedy of a stay be applied. The cornerstone of prejudice being an essential prerequisite for a stay was not to be disturbed. To Lord Woolf CJ, the principal significance of the advent of the HRA 1998 was that it increased the range of remedies available to a trial judge who was satisfied that there had been an unreasonable delay in breach of Art 6(1): the use of a declaration, of awarding compensation etc. All of these remedies were available as appropriate except a stay whose use was governed by Lord Lane CJ's judgment. Lord Woolf CJ sidestepped the issue of whether an English court has jurisdiction to try a defendant in circumstances where it has already acknowledged that his right to a fair trial under Art 6(1) has been violated. Can a court preside over a trial which axiomatically it has already declared unfair?

The House of Lords ruling

1.41 The Court of Appeal referred the same two questions as it had been required to consider to the nine-judge constitution of the House of Lords. In argument there, counsel for the acquitted person did not maintain the argument advanced below, and accepted by the trial judge, that breach of the reasonable time requirement must necessarily lead to a stay of proceedings. Instead, counsel contended for a more flexible approach on the following terms; where the effect of delay or the conduct of the executive is such as to render continuation of the proceedings an abuse of the process of the court, then a stay of the proceedings must be ordered. Otherwise, the court must grant such remedy as is proportionate to the demonstrated breach of the reasonable time requirement. In some cases, a stay may be the proportionate remedy, in others it will not.[1]

1 At para 4.

1.42 The House of Lords upheld the ruling of the Court of Appeal on both issues of principle. The House unanimously approved the Court of Appeal on the issue of the commencement date, and, by a 7:2 majority[1] on the question of remedy for violation of the reasonable time requirement of Art 6(1).

1 Lords Bingham, Nicholls, Steyn, Hoffmann, Hobhouse, Millett and Scott (Lords Hope and Rodger dissenting).

Commencement point

1.43 The House of Lords unanimously affirmed the Court of Appeal's decision on this point that the point of interview does not necessarily commence time for the purposes of Art 6, rather time commences at the point of charge:

> 'In the determination of whether, for the purposes of Art.6(1) of the Convention, a criminal charge has been heard within a reasonable time, the relevant time period commences at the earliest time at which a defendant is officially alerted to the likelihood of criminal proceedings against him, which in England and Wales will ordinarily be when he is charged or served with a summons'.[1]

1 At para 29 (per Lord Bingham). But see *Burns v HM Advocate* [2008] UKPC 63 (defendant 'substantially affected' – such that time commenced when, following interview in England, defendant bailed pending decision as to whether he should be charged in England or Scotland).

Violation and the appropriate remedy

1.44 Giving the leading judgment of the majority of the House of Lords, Lord Bingham of Cornhill recalled that, whilst the rights in the Convention were singled out for protection because they were recognised to be of overriding importance:

> 'the Convention also recognised, implicitly and often explicitly, that "No man is an Island". In the exercise of individual human rights due regard must be paid to the rights of others, and the society of which each individual forms part itself has interests deserving of respect. As pointed out in *Brown v Stott*'.[1]

1 At para 9.

1.45 In making further general observations in respect of Art 6, Lord Bingham also considered that 'the focus of the article is on achieving a result which is, *and is seen to be*, fair [Emphasis added]'.[1]

He observed that in a criminal case 'the issue usually arises between a prosecutor, who may be taken to represent the public interest, on one side and an individual defendant on the other', before drawing a comparison with the application of the Convention in the civil field, where it cannot '… be so interpreted and applied as to protect the Convention right of any one party while violating the Convention right of another'.[2]

1 At para 10.
2 At para 11.

1.46 Lord Bingham went on to observe that it is:

> 'a powerful argument that, if a public authority causes or permits such delay to occur that a criminal charge cannot be heard against a defendant within a reasonable time, so breaching his Convention right guaranteed by Art.6(1), any further prosecution or trial of the charge must be unlawful within the meaning of s.6(1) of the 1998 Act.'[1]

1 At para 20.

1.47 He appreciated that it was not surprising that such an argument has been accepted by respected courts around the world.[1] However, he took the view that there were four reasons which, cumulatively, compelled its rejection:

(1) It would be anomalous if breach of the reasonable time requirement had an effect more far-reaching than breach of the defendant's other Art 6(1) rights (for example, if a hearing took place before a tribunal which lacked independence or a judgment was not given publicly, a conviction would be quashed and a retrial ordered if a fair hearing could still take place) when (as must be assumed) the breach does not taint the basic fairness of the hearing at all, and even more anomalous that the right to a hearing should be vindicated by ordering that there be no trial at all.[2]

(2) As the Court of Appeal recognised, at para 19 of its judgment, a rule of automatic termination of proceedings on breach of the reasonable time requirement cannot sensibly be applied in civil proceedings. An

unmeritorious defendant might no doubt be very happy to seize on such a breach to escape his liability, but termination of the proceedings would defeat the claimant's right to a hearing altogether and seeking to make good his loss in compensation from the state could well prove a very unsatisfactory alternative.[3]

(3) A rule of automatic termination on proof of a breach of the reasonable time requirement has been shown to have the effect in practice of emasculating the right which the guarantee is designed to protect. There is a very real risk that if proof of a breach is held to require automatic termination of the proceedings the judicial response will be to set the threshold unacceptably high since, as La Forest J put it in *Rahey v R* (1987) 39 DLR 481, 516: 'Few judges relish the prospect of unleashing dangerous criminals on the public'.[4]

(4) The Strasbourg jurisprudence gives no support to the contention that there should be no hearing of a criminal charge once a reasonable time has passed. In its interpretation and application of the Convention it has never treated the holding of a hearing as a violation or a proper subject of compensation.[5]

1 At para 20.
2 At para 20.
3 At para 21.
4 At para 22.
5 At para 23.

1.48 The first reason given by Lord Bingham in rejecting the argument that a delayed trial would automatically lead to a stay of proceedings was supported by Lord Millett, who considered the reasonable time guarantee to be different from the other rights contained in Art 6(1), in that a failure to hold a hearing within a reasonable time does not automatically cast doubt on the verdict:

> 'The defendant cannot and does not challenge the propriety of the verdict on this ground. He can only say in effect: "you were right to convict me, but you should have done so sooner." The vice lies in the delay itself, with all its harmful consequences to the defendant. This is what Art.6 prohibits and for which a remedy must be found. The vice does not lie in the holding of the trial itself.'[1]

1 At para 135.

1.49 Lord Millett observed that the authorities *ought* to hold the trial within a reasonable time, but they remain *entitled* to do so after the reasonable time has expired, subject to making adequate reparation for the failure to hold it sooner.[1]

1 At para 138.

1.50 Lord Nicholls formulated the issue to be decided in the case with regard to violation of Art 6 as follows: 'does the breach lie in the holding of a trial after the lapse of a reasonable time? Or does it lie solely in the state's failure to hold the trial within a reasonable time?'[1] By the first hypothesis, holding a trial would itself amount to a violation of Art 6 once the reasonable time period had passed. In the second of Lord Nicholls's hypotheses, a breach in those terms would not be continuing so as to render the holding of a trial, following the lapse of reasonable time, a breach of Art 6 in and of itself. Lord Nicholls preferred the latter interpretation of the Art 6(1) right. Therefore, whilst he accepted that the holding of the trial would itself amount to a violation in circumstances where the pre-trial delay became so protracted that a fair trial could no longer be held (thus necessitating a stay), Lord Nicholls concluded that under any other circumstances:

> 'Just recompense is needed in respect of the pre-trial delay, which resulted in the defendant being exposed for longer than he should have been to the undesirable consequences of pending proceedings. Recompense is not needed in respect of the holding of the trial itself.'[2]

1 At para 36.
2 At para 40.

The settled law on delay

1.51 The Court of Appeal in *R v F(S)*[1] reiterated that the law on delay is settled and that the relevant principles are those laid down in *Attorney General's Reference (No 1 of 1990)*, stating that 'the appropriate test was directly addressed and answered in *Attorney General's Reference (No 1 of 1990)* ... It continues to provide the benchmark'.

1 See above, para **1.27**.

1.52 In *F(S)*, the defendant was charged with committing sexual offences against his stepbrother some 16 years earlier. At the outset of the trial the defendant gave notice of an application to stay the trial as an abuse of process on the grounds of delay, but the judge declined to rule on the application at that stage, and the trial proceeded. At the conclusion of the prosecution case the judge acceded to the abuse application. This was a terminating ruling and the prosecution appealed under s 58 of the Criminal Justice Act 2003.

1.53 The Court in *F(S)* went so far as to state that, where an application is made that a prosecution should be stayed as a result of delay arising from the timing of the complaint, the court should only have regard to the principles in four cases: (1) *R v Galbraith*[1]; (2) *Attorney General's Reference (No 1 of 1990)*; (3) *R v S(P)* [aka *R v Stephen Paul*][2] and (4) 'the present decision' (i.e. *R v F*).

Any consideration of further authorities is superfluous. Lord Judge CJ stated at (47):

> 'When abuse of process submissions on the grounds of delay are advanced, provided the principles articulated in *R v Galbraith*... and *Attorney General's Reference (No 1 of 1990)* ... are clearly understood, it will no longer be necessary or appropriate for reference to be made to any of the decisions of this court except [*R v S (Stephen Paul)*] and the present decision. These four authorities contain all the necessary discussion about the applicable principles. Their application, whether in the Crown Court, or in this court, is fact specific, and is to be regarded, unless this court in any subsequent

judgment expressly indicates the contrary, as a fact specific decision rather than an elaboration of or amendment to the governing principles'.

1 [1981] 1 WLR 1039.
2 [2006] EWCA Crim 756.

1.54 In the case of *R v S (Stephen Paul)* – to which reference is made in the above dicta from Lord Judge CJ, the Court of Appeal, having referred to the earlier authorities, observed that the determination of whether a stay should be granted on the ground of delay is a discretionary decision and sought to further refine the correct approach for a judge to whom such application is made is to consider, laying down the following principles:[1]

(a) Even where delay is unjustifiable, a permanent stay should be the exception rather than the rule.

(b) Where there is no fault on the part of the complainant or the prosecution, it will be very rare for a stay to be granted.

(c) No stay should be granted in the absence of serious prejudice to the defence so that no fair trial can be held.

(d) When assessing possible serious prejudice, the judge should bear in mind his or her power to regulate the admissibility of evidence and that the trial process itself should ensure that all relevant factual issues arising from delay will be placed before the jury for their consideration in accordance with appropriate direction from the judge.

(e) If, having considered all these factors, a judge's assessment is that a fair trial will be possible, a stay should not be granted.

1 per Rose LJ at [21].

1.55 Rose LJ stated in *S* that:

> 'the discretionary decision whether or not to grant a stay as an abuse of process, because of delay, is an exercise in judicial assessment dependent on judgment rather than on any conclusion as to fact based on evidence. It is, therefore, potentially misleading to apply to the exercise of that discretion the language of burden and standard of proof, which is more apt to an evidence based fact-finding process.'[1]

1 At [20].

1.56 Therefore a judge hearing an application to stay a prosecution as an abuse of process need only have recourse to the principles laid down in *Attorney General's Reference (No 1 of 1990)*, *R v S* and *R v F* and seek to apply those principles to the specific factual matrix of the instant case. Consideration may also need to be given to the principles laid down in *Galbraith* should the abuse application fail and a half time submission of 'no case to answer' be made.

More recent cases have continued to restate and affirm the general principles. In *R v LG*,[1] where the prosecution appealed a terminatory ruling on the grounds of abuse of process, the delay complained of was found not to have caused sufficient prejudice to warrant a stay of proceedings. The case related to a single count of causing death by careless driving on an evening when the respondent had been almost exactly twice over the drink-drive limit. Six months after the incident the Crown Prosecution Service decided that no further action should be taken and no charges were brought, however that decision was not communicated to the respondent himself. Various events followed that led to the matter being re-considered, and as a result, six and a half years after the original incident, a summons was issued against the respondent. The trial judge stayed the case as an abuse of process on the basis that all the evidence had been available when the first decision not to prosecute had been made, and in his view the respondent had been entitled to conclude after a number of years had gone by without notification that he was not going to be prosecuted. The Court of Appeal disagreed, and revered the decision, Davis LJ saying that the trial judge 'had failed to assess whether there was significant prejudice, over and above the natural disappointed expectations of the [accused], such that a fair trial could no longer be had…'[2] and that "[t]he rights and interests of victims and their families are not simply to be subordinated to those of a defendant in any given case. Further, … the public interest in prosecuting offences transcends any considerations of punishing the prosecution for delay — always, of course, we add, subject to the delay not having given rise to any significant prejudice to the defence which cannot be accommodated by the trial process".[3]

In *R v R*,[4] the prosecution appealed a decision by the trial judge to stay a complex case as an abuse on the basis of delay. The case had been in the stages of initial disclosure for five years owing to the large quantity of electronic documents involved. The Court of Appeal reviewed the relevant leading authorities and found that the delay complained of was not such as to mean that the defendants could not receive a fair trial. Further, that if there had been a breach of Articles 5(3) or 6(1) ECHR, that could be cured by a reduction in sentence.[5] The Court of Appeal also concluded, as an issue separate for the delay, that there was no deliberate misconduct or bad faith on the part of the prosecution. The judgment, handed down by Sir Brian Leveson P, highlighted that in either scenario 'it is important that conduct or results that may merely be the result of state incompetence or negligence should not necessarily justify the abandonment of a trial of serious allegations. As has been observed, there is no bright line and a broad-brush approach is likely to be necessary',[6] and also observed:

> 'To allow successful abuse of process applications where neither prosecutorial misconduct of the type identified in the authorities nor delay such as would prejudice a fair trial can be established would… provide a perverse incentive for those charged with criminal offences to procrastinate and seek to undermine the prosecution by creating hurdles to overcome all in the hope that, at some stage, a particular hurdle will cause it to fail.'[7]

1 [2018] EWCA Crim 736.
2 At para 29.
3 At para 30.
4 [2015] EWCA Crim 1941.
5 At para 70, and see also *Spiers (Procurator Fiscal) v Ruddy* [2008] AC 873.
6 At para 72.
7 At para 74.

Loss of Evidence Cases

1.57 In practice, one of the principal ways a defendant may be prejudiced by delay is by the loss of evidence that may result from it, which includes the defendant's ability to gather evidence in support of their case. The issue is the extent of the prejudice to the defence case, and whether any disadvantage to the defendant can be dealt with in the trial process. The bar is set very high, and it is rare for such arguments to succeed, absent bad faith on the part of the prosecuting authorities, and even that will not necessarily be determinative. See further *R v RD* and *R v Halahan* (both below at para **1.60**), both of which related to allegations of sexual abuse long past, and concerned the issue of loss of key evidence caused as a result of the passage of time, and Chapter 3.

Sexual allegations arising from events long past

1.58 Numerous defendants in cases involving allegations of sexual offences long past have contended for a stay of proceedings as an abuse of process on the ground of delay. That might not be surprising, given the clear potential for prejudice against the defendant who is accused of engaging in sexual misconduct years prior to the allegations being made against him, and the inherent potential for lack of forensic evidence, one way or the other. But equally, the justification for delayed complaint in such cases is generally more readily understandable.

1.59 The case of *F(S)* was itself a case involving allegations of sexual offences. The Court stated in *F(S)* that:

> 'In the overwhelming majority of historic sex allegations the reasons for the delayed complaint, and whether and how the delay is explained or justified, bear directly on the credibility of the complainant. They therefore form an essential part of the factual matrix on which the jury must make its decision. That is the principal and, in the overwhelming majority of cases, the only relevance of the evidence on these issues. When, in the authorities to which we have referred, it is clearly stated that an abuse of process argument cannot succeed unless prejudice has been caused to the defendant, the principles do not normally encompass the explanation for the delay, nor do they extend to the explanation or explanations which the judge himself or herself may regard as inadequate or unsatisfactory or inconsistent. Indeed features like these are revealed by and become apparent through the ordinary processes of trial, and these questions remain pre-eminently for the jury… it is difficult to conceive of circumstances in which they have any relevance to an abuse of process argument, unless in some manner they impact on the question of whether there can be a fair trial.'[1]

1 At [40]. See also *R v RD* [2013] EWCA Crim 1592 and *R v Halahan* [2014] EWCA Crim 2079 at para **160** below.

1.60 *R v F(TB)*[1] as a case concerning a 62-year-old man who had been convicted of committing sexual offences against two children 30 and 40 years earlier. The court reviewed the previous authorities, and at para 37 Jackson LJ giving the judgement, set out the following five propositions in relation to abuse of process applications based upon delay:

1.60 *Delay*

(i) The court should stay proceedings on some or all counts of the indictment for abuse of process if, and only if, it is satisfied on balance of probabilities that by reason of delay a fair trial is not possible on those counts.

(ii) It is now recognised that usually the proper time for the defence to make such an application and for the judge to rule upon it is at trial, after all the evidence has been called.[2]

(iii) In assessing what prejudice has been caused to the defendant on any particular count by reason of delay, the court should consider what evidence directly relevant to the defence case has been lost through the passage of time. Vague speculation that lost documents or deceased witnesses might have assisted the defendant is not helpful. The court should also consider what evidence has survived the passage of time. The court should then examine critically how important the missing evidence is in the context of the case as a whole.

(iv) Having identified the prejudice caused to the defence by reason of the delay, it is then necessary to consider to what extent the judge can compensate for that prejudice by emphasising guidance given in standard directions or formulating special directions to the jury. Where important independent evidence has been lost over time, it may not be known which party that evidence would have supported. There may be cases in which no direction to the jury can dispel the resultant prejudice which one or other of the parties must suffer, but this depends on the facts of the case.

(v) If the complainant's delay in coming forward is unjustified, that is relevant to the question whether it is fair to try the defendant so long after the events in issue. In determining whether the complainant's delay is unjustified, it must be firmly borne in mind that victims of sexual abuse are often unwilling to reveal or talk about their experiences for some time and for good reason.

In *RD*[3] the appellant had been convicted of a number of sexual offences relating to allegations made by four complainants in respect of events between 1949 and 1973. The delay in bring the matters to trial was described as 'extreme' and ranged from 39 to 63 years. The appellant alleged that the delay in bringing the case had led to serious prejudice, including that important documents were missing, or had been destroyed that would have shown that he was elsewhere at the time of a given allegation, and revealed inconsistent statements. Also that a number of potential witnesses who could have given evidence about relevant facts were now deceased or unavailable through infirmity. Treacy LJ giving the judgement of the Court of Appeal said:

> 'In considering the question of prejudice to the defence, it seems to us that it is necessary to distinguish between mere speculation about what missing documents or witnesses might show, and missing evidence which represents a significant and demonstrable chance of amounting to decisive or strongly supportive evidence emerging on a specific issue in the case. The court will need to consider what evidence directly relevant to the appellant's case has

> been lost by reason of the passage of time. The court will then need to go on to consider the importance of the missing evidence in the context of the case as a whole and the issues before the jury. Having considered those matters, the court will have to identify what prejudice, if any, has been caused to the appellant by the delay and whether judicial directions would be sufficient to compensate for such prejudice as may have been caused or whether in truth a fair trial could not properly be afforded to a defendant.'[4]

The court carried out a careful analysis of the missing material and the evidence given at trial and concluded that 'the appellant had received a fair trial, and was not disadvantaged in a way that could properly be described as amounting to serious prejudice to his ability to mount a proper defence'.[5]

Treacy LJ's reasoning was adopted in the case of *R v. Halahan*,[6] where the appellant, aged 84, had been convicted of three offences of indecent assault against dating back to the 1970's. At that time, he had been an Anglican priest and the victim a resident in a children's home. Amongst the evidence said to be lost were records from the church, home, parish and from a previous police investigation. Relevant witnesses were also deceased. The Court of Appeal accepted that contemporaneous documents were missing, but did not accept that those would necessarily have cast light on the reliability of the victim's evidence. Rather, there was no way of knowing what may have been within them, and as such they did not consider this to be one of the exceptional cases in which a fair trial was no longer possible. The trial judge had not sought to undermine the defence's arguments before the jury by suggesting that they were speculation, but left them to assess the strength of the arguments and to apply it when judging whether the prosecution had proved its case. That, they concluded, 'was the appropriate response to the lacuna in evidence'.[7]

1 [2011] EWCA Crim 726, [2011] 2 Cr App R 13 (145).
2 However, note that in *F(S)* it was recognised that there may be some cases where application should be made at the start of the proceedings, for example where it is contended that the trial should not take place at all. See at para 45.
3 [2013] EWCA Crim 1592.
4 At para 15.
5 At para 31.
6 [2014] EWCA Crim 2079.
7 At para 25.

Timing of an abuse application

1.61 The Court of Appeal in *Smolinski*[1] directed that any application to stay a trial as an abuse of process on the grounds of delay should not be made at the beginning of the trial, but rather should be made after the Crown has put its case. Lord Woolf concluded his judgment at [13]:

> 'We hope to have made clear two things in the court of hearing this appeal. One is that we discourage applications based on abuse in cases of this sort. Secondly, where evidence is given after so many years, the court should exercise very careful scrutiny at the end of the evidence to see whether or not the case is safe to be left to the jury'.

1 [2004] 2 Cr App R 40.

1.62 The approach in *Smolinkski* is an attractive one to the extent that it allows the judge to consider the complainant's evidence and cross examination in light of the defence submission to stay. However, that approach was heavily criticised in the case of *F(S)*[1] where Lord Judge CJ recognised that there may be circumstances where the application is, by its very nature, a preliminary one, rather than as part of the trial process, i.e. where the contention is that the trial should not take place at all.[2]

1 See above, para **1.27**.
2 At para 45.

1.63 The Court in *F(S)* laid down the following principles:

(a) An application to stay a prosecution as an abuse of process on grounds of delay and a submission of 'no case to answer' are two distinct matters which require separate consideration.[1]

(b) Any such application must be determined in accordance with *Attorney General's Reference (No 1 of 1990)*. That application should not succeed unless, exceptionally, a fair trial is no longer possible owing to prejudice to the defendant occasioned by the delay which cannot fairly be addressed in the normal trial process. The presence or absence of explanation or justification for delay is relevant only insofar as it bears on that question.[2]

(c) An application to stop the case on the grounds that there is no case to answer must be determined in accordance with *R v Galbraith*. For the reasons there explained, it is dangerous to ask the question in terms of whether a conviction would be safe, or the jury can safely convict, because that invites that judge to evaluate the weight and reliability of the evidence, which is the task of the jury. The question is whether the evidence, viewed overall, is such that the jury could properly convict.[3]

(d) There is no different *Galbraith* test for offences which are alleged to have been committed some years ago, whether or not they are sexual offences.[4]

(e) An application to stay for abuse of process ought ordinarily to be heard and determined at the outset of the case, and before the evidence is heard, unless there is a specific reason to defer it because the question of prejudice and fair trial can better be determined at a later stage.[5]

1 At [39]–[40].
2 At [38]–[40].
3 At [36]–[37].
4 At [41].
5 At [43]–[45].

1.64 Lord Judge CJ stated:

> 'Where there are genuine grounds for an application to stay on the basis that a fair trial will be impossible because of incurable prejudice to the defendant caused by delay, that application is, by its nature, preliminary to rather than part of the trial process. The contention is that the trial should not take place at all. If it is to be made, notice should be given before the

trial begins.... If the ruling is deferred, there is, as this case demonstrates and as Lord Lane CJ envisaged, a significant danger that the submissions to the judge would conflate *R v Galbraith* principles with the issue of abuse of process. If the application succeeds, it will almost inevitably appear that the judge has usurped the function of the jury.... But perhaps most important of all, as all the authorities underline, it is only in the exceptional cases where a fair trial is not possible that these applications are justified on the grounds of delay, even when the precondition to a successful application, serious prejudice, may have occurred. The best safeguard against unfairness to either side in such cases is the trial process itself, and an evaluation by the jury of the evidence'.[1]

1 At [45].

1.65 It is therefore now settled law that an abuse application to stay a prosecution on the grounds of delay should be made during a preliminary hearing before the trial commences. This approach avoids placing a potentially unnecessary financial and emotional burden on defendants, witnesses and complainants. A complainant, who, even in the event of a successful application to stay, may be telling the truth, will not have to go through the distress of giving evidence at trial only to subsequently have the case stayed as an abuse of process. There are also financial advantages to this approach, in that the legal costs of prosecuting or defending the trial would not be wasted as they would in the event of a subsequent application to stay.

Judicial directions on delay

1.66 As has been discussed in this Chapter, there is a need to demonstrate real prejudice to the defence before any abuse application will succeed. In most cases, any potential prejudice can be ameliorated by the trial process itself. One way in which the trial process seeks to protect the defence in this respect is by the trial judge having a responsibility to confront the exigencies of delay in his or her summing up.[1] In particular, cases affected by delay where the allegations relate to sexual offences will require a clear judicial direction to the jury as to the effects of delay. Before a conviction following a trial in these types of cases can appear to be safe, 'it is necessary to be satisfied that the judge has confronted the jury with the fact of delay and its potential impact on the formulation and conduct of the defence and on the Prosecution's fulfilment of the burden of proof'.[2]

1 See the Judicial College Crown Court Compendium, 22.12.20, Chapter 10-4 on Delay.
2 *R v Percival*, 19 June 1998.

1.67 In the case of *Percival*, the conviction was quashed on appeal after specific criticisms were made of the judge's summing up. The Court observed in *Percival* that it was not appropriate to diminish the impact of delay on the fairness of the trial by implying only that there were disadvantages to both sides: although each side has problems which arise from delay, they are different in both nature and importance. A short, self-contained direction that focuses on the defendant, rather than amalgamating it with other aspects of the relevance of delay (such as regards victims) is preferable: 'the risk of combining and interweaving the potential consequences of delay for the accused with the other delay-related considerations ("putting the other side of the coin") is that the direction, as the principle means of protecting the defendant, is diluted and its force diminished'.[1]

1 *R v PS* [2013] EWCA Crim 992.

1.68 Although it would be unusual for a conviction to be safe in a case where there has been no direction on difficulties for the defence arising from delay, the lack of such a direction will not necessarily be fatal.[1] Whether the conviction is safe in the absence of a direction to the jury on delay will depend on the particular circumstances of the case, including the length of the delay and the cogency of the evidence.[2] To that extent, comparison with the facts in other cases will be unlikely to be decisive in deciding whether or not the absence of a direction on delay is fatal to a conviction. In *Henry* (*H*), the verdict was held to be safe despite the judge's failure to give a direction on delay, as the evidence of the complainant was cogent and the question of credibility was clearly outlined to the jury. Furthermore, the jury was well aware of the period of delay in the case and the problems it had raised in the context of the burden of proof.

1 In *PS*, at [38].
2 *R v Henry H* [1998] 2 Cr App R 161; *R v, John E* [1996] 1 Cr App R 88.

1.69 The Court stated in *Henry* that 'a direction is not to be regarded as invariably required except in cases where some significant difficulty or aspect of prejudice is aired or otherwise becomes apparent to the judge in the course of the trial. Equally, such a direction should be given in any case where it is necessary for the purposes of being even handed as between complainant and defendant'.[1]

1 Per Potter LJ at p 168.

THE REQUISITE CONTENT OF A DIRECTION ON DELAY

1.70 If, as a result of delay there has been some disadvantage to the defendant, this should be identified and explained to the jury by reference to the burden of proof.[1] The Court in *Percival* made clear that the jury should be confronted with the impact of the delay on the preparation and conduct of the defence, and on the prosecution's discharge of the burden and standard of proof. However subsequent cases have sought to aver that the judgment in *Percival* was directed to the summing-up in that particular case. Rose LJ stated in the case of *Brian M*:[2]

> 'We find in [*Percival*] no attempt by the Court to lay down principles of general application in relation to how judges should sum up in cases of delay and we accordingly would wish to discourage the attempts being made, with apparently increasing frequency, in applications and appeals to this court to rely on *Percival* as affording some sort of blueprint for summings-up in cases of delay. It affords no such blueprint. Indeed in this area, as in so many others, prescription by this Court as to the precise terms of a summing-up is best avoided. Trial judges should tailor their directions

to the circumstances of the particular case. In a case where there has been many years of delay between the alleged offences and trial, a clear warning will usually be desirable as to the impact which this may have had on the memories of witnesses and as to the difficulties which may have resulted for the defence. The precise terms of that warning and its relationship to the burden and standard of proof can be left to the good sense of trial judges with appropriate help and guidance from the Judicial Studies Board. In some cases, however, such a warning may be unnecessary and its absence, where the evidence is cogent, will not necessarily render a conviction unsafe, particularly when counsel's submissions at trial have not highlighted any specific risk of prejudice'.

1 See the Judicial College Crown Court Compendium, 22.12.20, Chapter 10-4 on Delay.
2 *R v Brian M* [2000] 1 Cr App R 49 at p 57.

1.71 Thus it can be seen that the courts have been keen to avoid laying down overly prescriptive rules or curb the judicial discretion when it comes to jury directions on delay, in order both to allow the judge to tailor any direction to the particularly circumstances of the case, and to avoid providing defendants with a route to appeal which could be easily abused.

1.72 This point was stressed by the Court of Appeal in *Percival*, a case in which the defendant was convicted of sexual offences after a delay of 34 years since the offences were alleged to have been committed. The Court did, however, detail a list of what it saw as the requisite elements of a direction on delay on the facts of the instant case. These were:

- Delay can place a defendant at a material disadvantage in challenging allegations arising out of events that occurred many years before, and this is particularly so in a case when the defence is essentially a simple denial.
- The longer the delay, the more difficult meeting the allegation often becomes because of fading memories and evidence is no longer available.
- When considering the central question whether the prosecution has proved the defendant's guilt, it is necessary particularly to bear in mind the prejudice that delay can occasion.
- A summary of the main elements of prejudice that were identified during the trial.[1]

1 At [35] per Fulford LJ.

1.73 It is not appropriate for the judge to merely recite the submissions of both counsel regarding delay in a balanced manner: he or she should put the imprimatur of the bench behind directions as to the effect of delay.[1] Nor should the judge presume that because such submissions have been made by counsel before the jury, there is no need for him or her to include the subject of delay in summing up. The court observed in the case of *Dutton*[2] – which involved uncorroborated allegations over a period of between 14 and 20 years prior to the complaint being made – that 'there is a difference between the point being made by counsel and the submission which has been made by counsel being endorsed by the judge…if a judge is silent in relation to a topic such as that when it has been advanced and canvassed extensively by the defendant, then in a case such as this the very silence of the learned judge may tend to devalue what was in effect perhaps the most important point which could be advanced from an adversarial point of view on behalf of the appellant'.

In R v Hewitt[3] the Court of Appeal considered in detail the way the judge at first instance had dealt with delay, and the case is sited in the Crown Court Compendium 2020. One ground of appeal was that the judge's directions to the jury in relation to delay and missing documentation were inadequate, and failed to identify particular aspects of prejudice arising from the missing documentation, and so rendered the conviction unsafe. The Court disagreed, ruling that they were satisfied that the judge conveyed sufficiently clearly to the jury the general prejudice which the appellant was likely to have suffered from the delay and any missing documentation, approving this passage from the trial judge's summing up:

> 'A lengthy delay between the time when an incident is said to have occurred and the time when the complaint is made and the matter comes to trial, is something that you should bear in mind when considering whether the Crown has proved its case or not. Necessarily, the longer the delay the harder it may be for someone to defend themselves because, as I have already said, memories will have faded and material that might have been of assistance may have been lost or destroyed. If you find that the delay in the case [has placed] Mr Hewitt at a material disadvantage in meeting the case against him, that is something that you should bear in mind in his favour.'

1 See *Percival* above, para **1.67**.
2 *R v Dutton* [1994] Crim LR 910.
3 [2020] EWCA Crim 1247.

ECHR JURISPRUDENCE

Article 6(1): Right to be tried within a reasonable time

The status of this Art 6 right

1.74 The terms of Art 6 are well known. Article 6(1) deals with the right to a fair trial. It provides that:

> 'In the determination of his civil rights and obligations or of any criminal charge against him, everyone is entitled to a fair and public hearing *within a reasonable time* by an independent and impartial tribunal established by law'.[1] [Emphasis added]

1 Article 5(3) similarly provides that 'Everyone arrested or detained in accordance with the provisions of paragraph 1 (c) of this Article shall be brought promptly before a judge or other officer authorised by law to exercise judicial power and shall be entitled to trial within a reasonable time or to release pending trial…'.

1.75 Trial within a reasonable time is thus an explicit guarantee of fairness laid down in Art 6(1). Moreover it is an independent or freestanding right separate from the others established by the article. This was confirmed by Lord Hope of Craighead in *Porter v Magill*:[1]

> 'The protections which article 6(1) lays down are that, in the determination of his civil rights and obligations, everyone is entitled to a fair and public hearing within a reasonable time by an independent and impartial tribunal established by law. As I shall explain later when dealing with delay, I consider that this sentence creates a number of rights which, although closely related, can and should be considered separately. The rights to a fair hearing, to a public hearing and to a hearing within a reasonable time are separate and distinct rights from the right to a hearing before an independent and impartial tribunal established by law. This means that a complaint that one of these rights was breached cannot be answered by showing that the other rights were not breached'.

1 [2002] 2 AC 357, HL at para 87.

1.76 Lord Hope added in *Montgomery v HM Advocate*,[1] as regards the status of Art 6 rights:

> 'Article 6, unlike articles 8 to 11 of the Convention, is not subject to any words of limitation. It does not require, nor indeed does it permit, a balance to be struck between the rights which it sets out and other considerations such as the public interest'.

1 [2003] 1 AC 641, PC at p 670.

The purpose of the right

1.77 In *Dyer v Watson*[1] Lord Rodger of Earlsferry described the purpose as follows:

> 'In the case of article 6(1) its principal purpose at least is to prevent an accused being left too long in a state of uncertainty about his fate. Such a protection is, of course, of very real interest to an innocent person who has been charged with an offence or even to a person who has in fact committed an offence but whose guilt the prosecution cannot establish. The accused's whole life, both private and professional, may be thrown into turmoil, doubt and confusion until he is acquitted. Especially for the innocent and for their families the time spent awaiting trial must indeed be 'exquisite agony' (*R v Askov* [1990] 2 SCR 1199, 1219 per Cory J)'.

1 [2004] 1 AC 379, PC, at para 156.

1.78 However he added:

> 'That is not, however, the whole story. The reality is that, especially when they are on bail, many accused who are in fact guilty may prefer to dwell in the interim state of uncertainty rather than to march steadily to the end of their case where that state of uncertainty may well be replaced with a considerably more agonising state of prolonged imprisonment. Delay may indeed bring positive advantages to such persons: prosecution witnesses may die, leave the country, lose interest or forget. The right conferred by article 6 is therefore somewhat unusual. Not infrequently, accused persons may appear to have an interest in invoking it not in order to benefit from its fulfilment but rather in the hope of benefiting from its breach'.[1]

1 At para 157.

The Strasbourg case law – criteria for determining reasonableness

1.79 Many challenges to the length of proceedings have been brought before the court and it is fair to say that there are now a vast number of judgments concerned with this topic. Accordingly, an exhaustive survey of this jurisprudence is beyond the scope of this work. There are, in addition, a large number of what may be termed 'leading decisions', a survey of which, owing to their number, is also beyond this work. The specialist reader is referred to the speech of Lord Bingham of Cornhill in *Dyer v Watson*[1] for a comprehensive review.

1 See above para **1.77**, at paras 30–55.

1.80 However, in the relevant cases the Court has confined itself to repeatedly confirming and applying a small number of core principles, however voluminous the case law. Having espoused these principles, they have then been applied in case after case with the Court sometimes finding a violation and sometimes not.

In *Eckle v Germany*[1] the court stated:

> 'The reasonableness of the length of the proceedings must be assessed in each instance according to the particular circumstances. In this exercise, the Court has regard to, among other things, the complexity of the case, the conduct of the applicants and the conduct of the judicial authorities'.

1 (1982) 5 EHRR 1, at para 80. Also see *Howarth v United Kingdom* [2001] 31 EHRR 37 at [25]; *Frydlender v France* [2000] ECHR 30979/96 at [43] and *Pelissier v France* [1999] ECHR 25444/94 at [67].

1.81 As summarised by Lord Bingham in *Dyer v Watson*,[1] the Strasbourg Court has consistently and firmly rejected any laying down of a tariff or set of minimum periods. The emphasis is always on the word 'reasonable', which the Court has determined can only be understood by reference to the facts.

1 See above para **1.77**, at paras 52–55.

1.82 Three essential criteria are thus propounded:

(1) complexity;

(2) the applicant's conduct; and

(3) the conduct of the State authorities.

Complexity

1.83 The court will permit greater periods of delay in a complex prosecution allowing for the time and resources required to investigate especially economic crimes. In *Eckle v Germany*[1] the court stated:

> 'The court realises that initially the specific forms of economic crime caused the judicial authorities a variety of problems, notably in relation to the speedy and smooth conduct of criminal proceedings'.

1 See above para **1.80**, at para 85.

1.84 In *IJL, GMR and AKP v United Kingdom*[1] the Court held that a period of 4½ years to complete a complex fraud case was not an unreasonable delay. The Court has also recognised that complexity may arise from the need to obtain foreign evidence,[2] the volume of evidence[3] or because of the need to obtain expert evidence.[4] The Court is simply affirming the realistic or self-evident fact that the more complex a case, the longer the time which must necessarily be taken to properly prepare it for trial.

1 (2001) 33 EHRR 11; [2001] Crim LR 133.
2 *Neumeister v Austria* (1968) 1 EHRR 91.
3 *Wemhoff v Germany* (1968) 1 EHRR 55.
4 Ibid.

Conduct of the defendant

1.85 The Court will consider whether the applicant is in part responsible for the delay. In *Eckle v Germany* the court described the applicants' conduct as follows:

> 'Far from helping to expedite the proceedings, Mr and Mrs Eckle increasingly resorted to actions—including the systematic recourse to challenge of judges—likely to delay matters; some of these actions could even be interpreted as illustrating a policy of deliberate obstruction'.[1]

1 See above para **1.80**, at para 82.

1.86 In answer to the defence argument that such manoeuvring should not count against the applicants, as they were simply exercising their legal rights, the Court held:

> '...their conduct referred to above constitutes an objective fact, not capable of being attributed to the respondent State which is to be taken into account when determining whether or not the proceedings lasted longer than the reasonable time referred to in article 6, para 1'(at 82).

The defendant cannot complain of delay of which he is the author; procedural time-wasting must not be used to assist any complaint of delay.

1.87 An applicant cannot, however, be required to cooperate actively with the judicial authorities, nor can he or she be criticised for having made full use of the remedies available under domestic law in the defence of his or her interests. In *Novikov v Russia*,[1] the court stated in this respect:

> '...the Court observes that the defence's insistence on ensuring the possibility for prosecution witnesses to be examined in open court, as well as on calling and ensuring the attendance of witnesses on behalf of the defence, cannot be regarded in the present case as being frivolous, vexatious or an abuse of process in any other way' (at 64).

1 [2013] ECHR 7087/04.

1.88 A defendant is entitled to put the prosecution to proof and caution should be exercised in criticising a defendant for running an unmeritorious defence when considering the reasonable time requirement.[1] Furthermore the fact that the defendant is content to postpone the day of judgment cannot excuse the failure to adhere to the reasonable time requirement.[2]

1 *Rummum v State of Mauritius* [2013] 1 WLR 598, PC at para 18.
2 *Celine v State of Mauritius* [2012] 1 WLR 3707, PC at para 23.

Whether the authorities can excuse or justify the delay

1.89 Again, in *Eckle v Germany*, the Court having examined in detail the various periods of delay and the Respondent State's explanation for them, stated:

> 'The court, like the Commission, has come to the conclusion that the competent authorities did not act with the necessary diligence and expedition'.[1]

1 See above para **1.80**, at para 92.

1.90 The question here is what is the degree of diligence and expedition that must be shown? In other words, was the delay justifiable or not? In *Dyer v Watson,* Lord Bingham of Cornhill provided the following analysis:

> 'It is plain that contracting states cannot blame unacceptable delays on a general want of prosecutors or judges or courthouses or on chronic under-funding of the legal system. It is,generally speaking, incumbent on contracting states to organise their legal systems as to ensure that the reasonable time requirement is honoured'.

But he observed:

> '…it is not objectionable for a prosecutor to deal with cases according to what he reasonably regards as their priority, so as to achieve an orderly dispatch of business. It must be accepted that a prosecutor cannot ordinarily devote his whole time and attention to a single case'.[1]

1.91 However in *Novikov* the Court held that there had been **a breach of the reasonable time requirement** due to failures on the part of the prosecution; namely the failure to secure the attendance of prosecution witnesses (and the failure to provide a satisfactory explanation as to what action had been taken by bailiffs to enforce the judge's orders for compelling witnesses to attend), and the reassignment of the case between judges adversely affecting the length of the proceedings.

1 See above para **1.77**, at para 55.

Evidence of prejudice

1.92 The above analysis shows that the Strasbourg Court has not identified prejudice as a specific factor when determining unreasonableness. In the above articulation of the principles which guide its approach, it is clear that the presence or absence of prejudice is not determinative. Thus, it is not necessary when asserting a breach of Art 6(1) here to establish prejudice. Whilst proof of prejudice is not an essential or necessary prerequisite to the concept of unreasonable delay, it will often be a highly material factor when assessing reasonableness.

The threshold of inordinate or excessive delay

1.93 Whilst the Court has eschewed any approach laying down minimum periods of delay, it has emphasised that, for it to be even presumptively unreasonable, delay must first cross a threshold of being, in the particular circumstances, inordinate or excessive. For 'inordinate' see *Eckle v Germany*[1] and for 'excessive' see *Stögmüller v Austria.*[2] See also *Mansur v Turkey.*[3]

1 See above para **1.80**, at para 80.
2 (1969) 1 EHRR 155, para 5, where it is observed that the purpose of the guarantee is to prevent a person charged remaining too long in a state of uncertainty about his fate. See also *Burns v HM Advocate* [2008] UKPC 63.
3 (1995) 20 EHRR 535, paras 52 and 68.

1.94 Whilst demonstration of prejudice is not essential, the Court has, in reality, imposed a filter on complaints of delay by setting a relatively high threshold to be satisfied before it will conduct any inquiry into the delay and request the prosecutor to supply a justification. In *Dyer v Watson,* Lord Bingham of Cornhill said:

> 'In any case in which it is said that the reasonable time requirement (to which I will henceforward confine myself) has been or will be violated, the first step is to consider the period of time which has elapsed. Unless that period is one which, on its face and without more, gives grounds for real concern it is almost certainly unnecessary to go further, since the convention is directed not to departures from the ideal but to infringements of basic human rights. The threshold of proving a breach of the reasonable time requirement is a high one, not easily crossed'.

1.95 A relevant factor in determining whether delay has been inordinate or oppressive is whether the defendant in question was remanded in custody and, if so, for how long. The European Court stated in *Novikov* that:

> 'An accused in criminal proceedings, especially when he remains in detention pending investigation or trial, should be entitled to have his case conducted with special diligence and Article 6, in criminal matters, is designed to ensure that a person who has been detained is not kept in a state of uncertainty about his fate for a prolonged period' [60].

1 See above para **1.80**, at para 52. See also Lord Hope of Craighead at para 85 and Lord Rodger of Earlsferry at para 154.

How is 'reasonable time' to be measured?

1.96 As Lord Hope of Craighead said in *Montgomery v HM Advocate*:[1]

> 'The requirement that the hearing be "within a reasonable time" predicates that there has been a charge from the date of which the reasonableness of the time can be measured'.

1 See above para **1.76** at p 678.

1.97 In criminal proceedings, the concept of 'charge' has been applied by the European Court as the start-point for the measurement of delay. In *Eckle v Germany*[1] the Court stated:

> 'In criminal matters, the "reasonable time" referred to in article 6 para 1 begins to run as soon as a person is "charged"; this may occur on a date prior to the case coming before the trial court'.

1 See above para **1.80**, at para 73.

1.98 Having identified the concept of charge as the start-point for measurement purposes, the Court in *Eckle v Germany* then sought to explain the meaning of this. Significantly the court held that for this definitional purpose, a person may be charged in either of the two following situations:

> '"Charge", for the purposes of article 6 para 1, may be defined as "the *official notification* given to an individual by the competent authority of an allegation that he has committed a criminal offence", a definition that also corresponds to the test whether "the situation of the [suspect] has been *substantially affected*".'[1] [Emphasis added]

1 At para 73. The 'substantial affectation' test recited here is drawn from an earlier decision, *Deweer v Belgium* (1980) 2 EHRR 439.

1.99 The significance in our jurisdiction of this dual definition of charge, one very different to our domestic understanding, is borne out by the practice of the Court to use its own definitions of legal terms, called 'autonomous meanings', when considering whether there has been a breach of the Convention. Accordingly, what the Court regards as the moment of charge will have primacy over any conflicting domestic definition. In *Porter v Magill*[1] Lord Hope said, in relation to the dichotomy between civil and criminal proceedings and autonomous meanings:

> 'For the purposes of the Convention the category into which the proceedings are placed by domestic law, while relevant, is not the only consideration. The court is required to look at the substance of the matter rather than its form, to look behind the appearances and to investigate the realities of the procedure'.

1 [2001] UKHL 67 at [84].

1.100 This emphasis upon the character or reality of the case, 'is it criminal?', is best demonstrated by the Court's findings in *Funke v France*.[1] Whilst the investigation into the applicant's tax affairs was classified under French law as administrative, not criminal, the Court held that as he was suspected of criminal tax offences then a de facto criminal investigation was being undertaken.[2]

1 [1993] 1 CMLR 897, 16 EHRR 297.
2 For a further analysis of how the English courts have determined what is a criminal investigation see *Attorney-General's Reference (No 7 of 2000)* [2001] 1 WLR 1879, CA.

Official notification and substantial affectation

1.101 On the above definition of 'charge', criminal proceedings are deemed to commence when State agents inform the suspect that they contend that he has committed a criminal offence and a criminal trial will ensue. This is precisely the equivalent of our jurisdiction. A distinction, however, may arise in relation to who are State agents for this purpose. Here, pursuant to the PACE Codes of Practice, only a custody officer as defined may prefer a charge[1] and so there is no ambiguity. However, it is submitted that the use of the expression 'official notification' permits a wider category of agent who may give the necessary notification. For example it encompasses, but is not coterminous with, law enforcement officials, ie police officers or prosecutors. It appears that so long as the agent making the allegation is clothed with a sufficient element of relevant authority then even if his function is not primarily concerned with criminal investigation or prosecution, his allegation may be a sufficient trigger. An example here may be a local authority social worker seeking a care order against the parents of a child on the basis of their suspected child abuse. Thereafter criminal proceedings get underway.

1 Code C, para 16.1.

1.102 The second limb of the definition of charge, that of 'substantial affectation', is a much more vague concept than that of official notification. It relates to the degree of interference by State authorities in a suspect's life which is then deemed to be sufficient to constitute a substantial interference. Does this concept of interference entail the existence of either prejudice or damage to the suspect? It seems plain that a person may be charged, criminal proceedings being deemed to have commenced, whilst he is still unaware of any such proceedings, the test being an objective one independent of the accused's knowledge.

The European Court has, on various occasions, held that a suspect was substantially affected prior to the moment of charge,[1] but on other occasions has held that only a formal charge was sufficient.[2]

1 See, for example, *Howarth v United Kingdom* [2001] 31 EHRR 37, *Heaney and McGuinness v Ireland (Application No 34720/97)* [2001] 33 EHRR 12, *Murray v United Kingdom* [1995] 19 EHRR 193, *Teixeira de Castro v Portugal* [1998] 28 EHRR 101.
2 See, for example, *IJL, GMR and AKP v United Kingdom* [2000] 9 BHRC 222.

Remedies for violation of Art 6(1)

1.103 If there is found to be a breach of the reasonable time requirement, what remedy should a court award to mark this? In the context of our abuse jurisdiction, should a breach here lead to a permanent stay or discontinuance? In other words, does the right to a trial within a reasonable time entail a correlative right not to be tried at all after a reasonable time has elapsed? The Convention itself does not prescribe what the consequence or effect should be of any breach of this right. This is left to Contracting States to determine. Thus the court is not here concerned with remedies, other than in relation to awards of compensation under Art 41. From this, it follows that a number of remedies may be awarded at domestic level.

1.104 In surveying the European jurisprudence on this point in *Dyer v Watson,* Lord Hope of Craighead observed that:

> 'The European Court has repeatedly held that unreasonable delay does not automatically render the trial or sentence liable to be set aside because of the delay (assuming that there is no other breach of the accused's Convention rights), provided that the breach is acknowledged and the accused is provided with an adequate remedy for the delay in bringing him to trial (though not for the fact that he was brought to trial), for example by a reduction in the sentence'.[1]

1 See above para **1.80**, at para 129.

CONCLUSION

1.105 If a criminal case is not heard and completed within a reasonable time, that will constitute a breach of a defendant's Art 6(1) rights, whether or not a defendant has been prejudiced by the delay.[1] That breach will need to be declared and remedied but will not, unless the defendant suffers prejudice, or the delay would bring matters into disrepute on a *Bennett*-style basis, give rise to a stay of the proceedings.

1 See above para **1.92**.

1.106 The defendant who applies to have the proceedings against him permanently stayed as an abuse of process on this ground, therefore, faces the difficult task of establishing that he can no longer receive a fair trial, or that it offends the court's sense of justice and propriety to be asked to try him, if he is to succeed in having the proceedings discontinued. Nonetheless, the applicant who fails in having the proceedings against him stayed might gain redress by other means, such as compensation or a reduction in sentence, so long as he is able at least to establish that his right to a hearing within a reasonable time has been violated.

Chapter 2

Breach of promise

2.01 If in a criminal case the prosecution reneges on a promise it has given to an accused not to prosecute, should a breach of this promise *ipso facto* give rise to unfairness and an abuse of process? The law concerned with breach of promise would be easy to state if the answer to this question was an unequivocal yes. However, the answer is equivocal. Breach of promise not to prosecute does not necessarily give rise to abuse. It depends on the circumstances and each case should be judged on its merits. All that the Court of Appeal has held is that where a defendant has been induced to believe that he will not be prosecuted, this is capable of founding a stay for abuse.

2.02 The authorities concerned with this head of abuse will necessarily touch on a number of issues which must be resolved in order that the parameters of this head are determined. Furthermore, the parties should know when it is permissible for a prosecution to proceed despite a defendant contending that he received a promise that this would not occur. The issues to be resolved are outlined in paras **2.03–2.05**.

The promise

2.03 Must a promise not to prosecute be an explicit unequivocal undertaking by the prosecutor? Alternatively, can a 'promise' be inferred from something lesser such as, for example, an indication or statement of intent? Furthermore, to be binding, must the promise come only from the prosecutor directly or can it instead emanate from someone who is simply a member of the prosecution team, or from what a prosecutor has said to a third party which is known about or overheard by the defendant?

Prejudice

2.04 If a promise has been made, can it nonetheless be withdrawn? For a court to hold the prosecution to its word, is the uttering of a promise enough, or must there in addition be some prejudice which would be caused to the defence were the prosecution to be allowed to renege? In other words, using the terminology of the law of contract, must there be an offer, an acceptance and consideration? By 'consideration' is meant prejudice to the defence; the defendant has relied on the promise and, as a direct consequence, has done some act or abstained from doing some act, which has prejudiced or been detrimental to his defence.

2.05 The heart of the issue here is the difference of approach between the judgment of Lord Lane CJ in *A-G's Reference (No 1 of 1990)*[1] where he emphasised the need to prove prejudice before an abuse submission can be sustained, versus the approach of the House of Lords in *R v Horseferry Road Magistrates' Court, ex p Bennett*[2] which emphasised prosecution impropriety over prejudice – quoting Lord Lowry in *Bennett*, whether to try the case in a circumstance of breach of promise would 'offend the court's sense of justice and propriety to be asked to try the accused'.[3]

1 [1992] QB 630.
2 [1994] AC 42.
3 At p 74.

2.06 The Court of Appeal decision of *R v Abu Hamza*[1] highlighted the competing, but not mutually inconsistent, approaches in *Bennett* and the *A-G's Reference*, as it attempted to lay down guideline criteria. It, arguably however, created further ambiguity over the correct test to apply in a breach of promise situation, which test the courts have struggled to define. While what was described as the second limb of the *Bennett* test for abuse of process[2] (appears alive and well in a string of cases, such as *Bloomfield*[3] and in the 2006 House of Lords decision in *Jones v Whalley*,[4] *Hamza* could be interpreted as marking a potential narrowing of the principles established in the earlier case law, with its emphasis on proof of prejudice through detrimental reliance on a promise. The overall significance of this judgment is considered below at paras **2.41–2.53**.

1 [2007] QB 659.
2 Which description was developed in *R v Beckford* [1996] 1 Cr App R 94, then further reshaped by later decisions in the *Warren* and *Maxwell* authorities, where the central issue on the second limb became an assessment as to whether a stay was necessary to protect the integrity of the criminal justice system.
3 [1997] 1 Cr App R 135.
4 [2007] 1 AC 63.

2.07 How the courts have resolved these difficult issues is the subject of this chapter. The categories of breach of promise are considered in the following sections, namely:

(1) promises not to prosecute;

(2) promises to offer no evidence;

(3) promises on acceptable pleas; and

(4) other promises.

PROMISES NOT TO PROSECUTE

2.08 In England, the cornerstone of the law on breach of promise remains the authority *R v Croydon Justices, ex p Dean*.[1] Before analysing the significance of *Dean*, a brief review of some of the earlier authorities may help to place it in a better context.

1 (1993) 98 Cr App Rep 76.

Pre-Dean authorities

2.09 While some of the most relevant authorities emanate from the Privy Council and from Hong Kong, it is interesting that the English authority of *Lund v Thompson*[1] was not apparently cited in *Dean.*

1 [1959] 1 QB 283.

2.10 In *Lund*, Diplock J, giving the judgment of the High Court, said, albeit with some reluctance, that a statement by police that they had no intention to prosecute did not nullify a prior notice of intended prosecution which had been issued in relation to a road traffic offence. The court acknowledged that in certain cases, where the police indicate an intention not to prosecute and subsequently change their mind (as occurred in *Lund*), this may lead to considerable injustice to the person prosecuted. However, strict statutory construction was said to militate against *Lund*. The fact that a citizen was entitled to mount a private prosecution and permitted to act on the basis of the original notice, whatever subsequent representations were made by the police, was deemed to be an overriding factor. For that reason, the suggested concept of some loose form of 'estoppel', binding a police officer to keep another person's promise not to prosecute, was dismissed by the court.

2.11 In *Chu Piu-Wing*[1] the appellant had been subpoenaed to attend a police disciplinary tribunal to give evidence of certain payments of 'protection money' he had made to police officers in respect of gambling establishments. The appellant had refused to do so because of the conditions on which he had given the information in the first place. The three conditions were first, that he would give the information only once, secondly, that he would only provide information and not give evidence against the policeman in court, and thirdly, that the information would not be used against him. In due course, he was assured by the interrogating International Commission Against Corruption officers that, if any information which he gave verified the material which they already had (which it apparently did), he would not be prosecuted. Notwithstanding such promise, he was charged, convicted and sentenced to imprisonment in respect of the matters on which he had given information. When the appellant was subsequently subpoenaed before the police disciplinary tribunal, he attended, but refused to give evidence of the matters concerned. For this refusal, he was committed to six months' imprisonment for contempt by the High Court. In the light of the circumstances in which the information had been given to the authorities, the Hong Kong Court of Appeal held that the issuance of the subpoena was an abuse of the process of the court.

1 [1984] HKLR 411.

2.12 McMullin VP giving the judgment of Hong Kong's Court of Appeal stated that there was:

> 'a clear public interest to be observed in holding officials of the state to promises made by them in the full understanding of what is entailed by the bargain'.

Further, it was held (at para 417E) that '... it matters not that the police may have been blameless in this regard'. The authorities had reneged on a solemn promise where there was no doubt the appellant must reasonably have believed he had kept his side of the bargain. The theme of holding officials to account for promises or representations runs through the subsequent case law up to the present day.[1]

1 See *Postermobile plc v Brent London Borough Council*, paras **2.37** and **2.38**.

2.13 In *Bell v DPP*[1] the Privy Council considered what was ostensibly a 'delay' case, but which had a bearing on the principles relating to implicit promises or expectations. The case concerned an appellant who had been arrested in Jamaica and charged, inter alia, with firearm offences. Having been convicted in the Crown Court, and successful in an appeal against conviction, a retrial was ordered. On several occasions thereafter, the prosecution were not ready on the due trial dates. Finally, after more adjournments, he was discharged by a judge, the Crown having offered no evidence against him. Three months later, however, he was re-arrested and a retrial was ordered.

1 [1985] AC 937, PC; The court's reasoning in the Bell decision, in relation to the issue of delay, has subsequently been disapproved of, and effectively overruled, by the Privy Council in *Mills v HM Advocate* [2004] 1 AC 441.

2.14 The Board allowed the appeal. It held that the Jamaican courts had overlooked the significance of the order of the retrial and of his being discharged on the basis that further delay would then be unfair to him, his constitutional rights having been infringed (to a fair hearing within a reasonable time). Where the defence submitted that the appellant had been given great hope when no evidence was offered, Templeman LJ said that in a proper case the court could treat the renewal of charges, even after the lapse of a reasonable time, as an abuse of process of the court. For, as the Board noted '… the appellant's complaint is that he was discharged and told to go free …' before being re-arrested.

2.15 In line with the courts' avowed duty to secure 'fair treatment' for those before them, the Privy Council in *Bell* acknowledged, inter alia, the public interest in minimising the '*anxiety and concern of the accused*'[1] in the context of delays awaiting trial. In practice, while there are no doubt many occasions where defendants ought to be aware of the possibility of re-arrest (having been discharged in criminal proceedings), nevertheless, this case illustrates an instance where a legitimate expectation that there would be no further prosecution was foiled.

1 Per Powell J in *Barker v Wingo* 407 US 514 (1972).

2.16 The decisions of *Bell* and *Chu Pui-Wing* were later considered in the 1990 *Harris* decision of the Hong Kong Court of Appeal,[1] which court helpfully reviewed the state of the law in relation to the common law jurisdictions on this topic. Harris was a member of the Attorney-General's Chambers who, while at the time personally responsible for the section dealing with vice prosecutions, was himself later convicted of procuring a girl for unlawful sexual intercourse. The defendant appealed on the basis, inter alia, that, having assured him in May 1989 that he would not be prosecuted, the Attorney-General should not be permitted to change his mind in October 1989, following what was said to be increased pressure from the mass media.

1 [1991] 1 HKLR at 389.

2.17 In dismissing the appeal, Faud VP ruled that the Attorney-General was quite entitled to change his mind in the light of the changing public interest, notwithstanding that it may entail a possible erosion of confidence in his individual decisions. While Silke VP found that: 'There was no "promise" made to the appellant other than in the widest of layman's terms', and albeit that it came from a colleague, can one easily ignore the fact that it came from the Attorney-General himself? Indeed, as one commentator has noted,[1] Harris's counsel posed an interesting question which was left unresolved by the court, counsel perhaps having the facts of *Chu Piu-Wing* in mind, namely, 'Why should the recipient of an unqualified assurance be in a worse position than the recipient of one that is qualified?'

1 Sze Ping-Fat, 'Resiling from Assurances not to Prosecute' [1998] 162 JP 604.

2.18 In *A-G of Trinidad and Tobago v Phillip*,[1] the Privy Council held that the prosecution of offenders, after a pardon had been granted and an order of habeas corpus made, could constitute an abuse of process even if the pardon was in fact legally invalid. In 1990, Phillip participated in an armed insurrection intending to overthrow the lawful Government of Trinidad and Tobago. People were killed and injured and property was damaged. The Acting President decided to negotiate with the insurgents to try to seek a peaceful solution. The Acting President signed a document which stated that he granted an amnesty to all those involved in acts of insurrection and that the amnesty was granted for the purpose of avoiding physical injury to them and was therefore subject to the complete fulfilment of the obligation safely to return them. The hostages were not then released. Shooting outside continued and the insurgents made additional political demands. After further negotiations the insurgents surrendered and were arrested and charged with treason, murder, and other offences committed during the insurrection. Relying on the pardon, they sought and obtained a writ of habeas corpus.

The Privy Council observed, at p 410, that '... It is an executive act of the state. Both under English law and under the Constitution of Trinidad and Tobago, a pardon should not be treated as being analogous to a contract. It does not derive its authority from agreement. It is not dependent upon acceptance of the subject of the pardon. In England, its authority is derived from the prerogative and in Trinidad and Tobago its authority is dependent upon the Constitution...'. It was held, however, that the pardon in that case had not been lawfully issued (it could cover only past acts, not future offending).[2] Nor could it be treated as a statement of intention to grant a pardon since no pardon had subsequently been granted; that although the pardon might be valid as being a pardon subject to a condition to be fulfilled promptly or as soon as practicable, the insurgents had not complied with the condition and their eventual compliance could not bring it into effect; and that, accordingly, the respondents had not been granted a valid pardon.

1 [1995] 1 AC 396, PC. For further analysis of the status of amnesties in this context, see *Azanian Peoples Organization (AZAPO) v President of the Republic of South Africa* (CCT17/96) 1996 (4) SA 672 and, in the context of international law, the judgment of the Special Court for Sierra Leone in *Prosecutor v Morris; Decision on Challenge to Jurisdiction: Lome Accord Amnesty* [2004] SCSL 3.

2 See to similar effect, *R (Pretty) v DPP* [2002] 1 AC 800.

2.19 However, the Privy Council went on to consider, at pp 417–418, the implications of the offer or promise of the pardon. Lord Woolf held that:

> '…In common law jurisdictions there exists a separate ground of protection for those who surrender in reliance on a conditional offer or promise of a pardon. The common law has now developed a formidable safeguard to protect persons from being prosecuted in circumstances where it would be seriously unjust to do so. It could well be an abuse of process to seek to prosecute those who have relied on an offer or promise of a pardon and complied with the conditions subject to which that offer or promise of a pardon was made. If there were not circumstances justifying the state in not fulfilling the terms of its offer or promise, then the courts could well intervene to prevent injustice: see Reg. v. Milnes and Green [1983] 33 S.A.S.R. 211…
>
> The possibility of abuse of process arises on the facts of this case. On the findings of the judges in the courts below the Muslimeen in all the circumstances acted reasonably after the pardon was granted. On any view of the facts, as was pointed out in the judgments in the courts below, the Acting President thereafter prior to the surrender did not give any indication that the validity of the pardon was in question. On the contrary the negotiations which resulted in the ultimate surrender of the Muslimeen and the release of the hostages unharmed were conducted on the basis that they were entitled to the benefit of the pardon. However whether the facts give rise to an abuse of process would have been a question for the trial judge in the event of further criminal proceedings
>
> The result therefore of the decision of the Board is that the pardon was and is invalid. That means that it was not unlawful to initiate a prosecution of the Muslimeen in relation to the events arising out of the insurrection and to arrest them for the purposes of that prosecution. However in those proceedings the Muslimeen could well have been in a position to raise a plea in bar on the basis of abuse of process. The Board does not venture an opinion as to whether that plea would have succeeded; it would have been a decision for the court before whom the trial was to take place…'

The court's policy of holding officials to their promises was shown in extremis in *Phillip*, where this promise was upheld, albeit it was obtained by coercion and in circumstances where a trial could be fairly held. As Lord Woolf, in identifying this particular form of abuse of process, stated:

> 'The common law has now developed a formidable safeguard to protect persons from being prosecuted in circumstances where it would be seriously unjust to do so.'

R v Croydon Justices, ex p Dean[1]

2.20 The facts were as follows. The applicant, aged 17, along with two other men, were arrested by police in respect of a murder investigation. He denied taking part in the killing but admitted that, after it had taken place, he had assisted in destroying the victim's car. At the end of a police interview, he was informed by the officers that he was regarded as a prosecution witness and had the protection of the police. Five days after the co-defendants had been charged, the applicant further assisted and co-operated and admitted that the co-defendant had driven him to the scene of the crime and shown him the victim's body. Later, however, after the CPS had taken charge of the prosecution and reviewed the evidence, it decided that Dean should be charged. The CPS decided, after a conference with the police, to charge him with assisting in the destruction of the car.

1 (1993) 98 Cr App Rep 76. See para **2.08**.

2.21 Following the committal, where the justices rejected an application for abuse, Dean sought a judicial review. The Divisional Court held that the prosecution of a person who had received a promise, undertaking or representation from the police that he would not be prosecuted earlier was capable of being an abuse of process. On the undisputed evidence, the applicant was given to understand, for a considerable time, that he was to be a prosecution witness, from which it almost certainly followed that he was not himself to be prosecuted.

2.22 There was a dispute between the parties concerning the number of occasions when more specific assurances were said to have been given by police that there would be no prosecution, such assurances allegedly given when the tape recorder was switched off. A passage in the CPS representative's affidavit, which contradicted the police position, was accepted by the court as being truthful.

2.23 The CPS argument against the application for judicial review was a constitutional one since the police, in any event, did not have the requisite authority to tell the applicant that he would not be prosecuted and, therefore, such police conduct could not amount to an abuse of process. Staughton LJ, however, was not persuaded and held that, whether or not the promisor had the power to decide,[1] or whether or not it was a case of bad faith or something akin, these were not essential requirements:

> 'The effect on the applicant, or for that matter his father, of an undertaking or promise or representation by police was likely to have been the same … whether or not it was authorised by the CPS… The prosecution of a person who has received a promise, undertaking or representation that he would not be prosecuted is capable of constituting an abuse of process…'

What was found to be in Dean's mind was adjudged highly significant for, as the court noted, '… the impression created was not dispelled for over five weeks, during which period he gave repeated assistance to the police'. The timing of the police promise to use him as a witness, and rule him out as a defendant, was also a feature, given that the promise (which the court accepted) was given at an early stage before he provided the important information. Staughton LJ pointed out that the applicant and his father could have taken legal advice as to the binding effect, or not, of such statements by police, but considered it unreasonable to expect that, in the particular circumstances of the case (ie the applicant's young age, the nature of assistance he had provided and the length of time involved).

1 See to like effect *McDonald v The Queen* [1983] UKPC 13 per Lord Diplock at pp 3–4.

2.24 While no doubt a combination of factors affected the court's decision, the immense prejudice he inflicted on his own position, which was largely irremediable, must have surely been the greatest consideration before the court in opting to stay proceedings. In answer to the CPS's constitutional argument, Staughton LJ held that the remedy 'must surely be a greater degree of liaison at an early state'.

2.25 It is apparent that this case was decided very much on its own particular facts. One can readily foresee a different outcome in circumstances where, for example, an unrealistic promise is either made or implied, by a young police officer to an experienced criminal, who indeed would have realised as much. Further, it is submitted that in practice certain individuals who provide witness statements to the police, having themselves been arrested and charged, expect and/or agree to testify for the Crown not because they expect an immunity, but in the hope (or promise sometimes) of a reduced sentence.

2.26 The central importance of *Dean* is that it explored the interrelationship between the police and the CPS and their respective roles in the prosecution of crime. The CPS argument was that if the Prosecution of Offences Act 1985 is to make any sense, then they ought to be unfettered in decision-making where prior police action is unauthorised. The court, while pronouncing that the CPS succeeded, in that they alone are entitled and bound to decide who shall be prosecuted, granted a somewhat hollow victory, given the police's recognised ability to, in effect, tie their hands. While it follows that the police have no authority to tell a suspect that he will not be prosecuted in connection with an offence (save where the CPS authorise such action), nevertheless, the police will have to conduct themselves with restraint, for their conduct, even inadvertent or unintentional, may lead to a stay of proceedings.

2.27 Police officers will need to be especially wary of having informal unrecorded discussions with the suspect or his solicitor where an impression is conveyed by the officers that, if the suspect co-operates as desired, others, but not him, will be charged. If, in reliance on this vague indication, the suspect confesses and/or implicates the others, he will certainly feel aggrieved, if not betrayed, if charges follow. As this case bears out, informing a suspect that he will be a Crown witness might be construed as an implied promise that no prosecution will take place. Practitioners whose clients complain about being charged, or prosecuted, and who state they genuinely believed they were only to act as witnesses, ought carefully to inquire into the circumstances which led to that belief. Did the client have a legitimate, as opposed to a fanciful, expectation that there would be no prosecution? Was the client justified in holding such a belief or did it simply result from gossip, hearsay, or informal observation or comment? Which officer made or implied such a promise not to prosecute? Was the client entitled reasonably to rely on an indication given by an officer only marginally connected to the case, and perhaps of very junior rank? These are perhaps some of the practical questions with which the courts will have to grapple in deciding the bona fides of alleged unfairness. Lessons will hopefully be learned from *Dean*, which serves well to illustrate that a greater liaison between CPS and police is essential for both branches to function more effectively in the interests of justice.[1]

1 Fionda, 'The Crown Prosecution Service and the Police: A Loveless Marriage?' [1994] LQR 376.

2.28 As Julia Fionda succintly observed, when comparing *Dean* with the earlier decision in *Lund*:

> 'The only possible means of distinguishing that authority [*Lund*] from the circumstances of the recent case [*Dean*] were that in 1958 the court was seeking to prevent the promises of the police being binding on any citizen as a potential prosecutor (that is, third party), whereas in the present case the promise was merely held to be binding on the CPS, a body acting in its official capacity as public prosecutor to whom the police are obliged to refer cases'.[1]

1 Fionda, 'The Crown Prosecution Service and the Police: A Loveless Marriage?' [1994] LQR 376.

2.29 The judgment in *Dean* also relied on Commonwealth cases which had considered whether a stay should be granted in such circumstances. An example is the Australian case of *R v Milnes and* Green,[1] which confirmed that a stay could be granted in relation to a breach of promise to grant a pardon when the grounds for one were clearly made out. Additionally, in the Canadian case of *R v Betesh*,[2] the court stayed proceedings where, as part of an agreement to resolve a strike, the prosecution reneged on its promise not to prosecute strikers for acts of violence.

1 (1983) 33 SASR 211, pp 225-6 and *R v Georgiadis* [1984] VR 1030. See also *Williamson v Trainor* [1992] 2 Qd R 572 which was not mentioned in the *Dean* case.
2 (1975) 30 CCC (2d) 233. See also *R v Crneck, Bradley and Shelley* (1980) 116 DLR (3d) 675.

Post-Dean authorities

2.30 *Dean* has been considered and applied in a number of subsequent cases which are discussed below. The most notable cases include *R v Horseferry Road Magistrates' Court, ex p Bennett*,[1] *R v Townsend, Dearsley and Bretscher*,[2] *R v Abu Hamza*[3] and *R v Downey.*[4]

1 [1994] AC 42.
2 [1997] 2 Cr App R 540.
3 [2007] QB 659.
4 BAILII Citation Number: [2014] EW Misc 7 (CCrimC).

2.31 Before considering these authorities, it should be noted that the principle that a breach of promise can constitute an abuse of process has been similarly developed in a variety of Commonwealth jurisdictions.[1] For example, in *R v Mohi*, a case from the Supreme Court of South Australia, proceedings were stayed when an accused gave two detailed and uncautioned statements during a murder investigation after the police informed him that he was a witness, not a suspect.[2] He made admissions about assisting the offenders and was charged despite promises to the contrary. Martin J. held that 'the administration of justice will be brought into disrepute if, without good reason, the investigating and prosecuting authorities are permitted to decline to comply with the undertakings or assurances given to such persons that they will not be charged and to pursue prosecutions against those to whom such undertakings or assurances are given'.[3] Similarly, in the New Zealand case of *Delellis v R*, the court ordered a stay of proceedings when the police reneged on a promise not to proceed with drug importation charges against an accused if he told them where to find the stash of cocaine.[4] In granting a stay for abuse of process, the court held that, if the police entered into such deals, they should not depart from them.

1 See the Australian cases of *Nolan v Curby* 1995 (unreported) No. 40757 of 1995 (Supreme Court of New South Wales Court of Appeal), *Rona v District Court of South Australia* (1995) 77 A Crim R 16, *R v Mohi* [2000] SASC 384, *Director-General v Epacris Pty Ltd.* [2009] NSWLEC 42. In *Epacris*, a stay was ordered where the defendant company received written notice implying that there would be no prosecution for environmental crimes should they perform certain remedial action, which they did to their detriment. Lloyd J. held (at paras 81–83) that 'the prosecutor is acting unfairly and unjustly in leading the defendants to believe that, by complying with a remediation order, they can thereby save a prosecution… The balancing exercise persuades me that the prosecution must be stayed. The circumstances in this case are sufficiently exceptional, giving rise to an unfairness and an injustice to the defendants amounting to an abuse of process…(a) the prosecutor has gained the advantage of…remediation works …in circumstances where Epacris was reasonably induced to believe that a full and final settlement had been achieved having regard to the parties' respective statements of issues; (b) this had the effect of satisfying the public interest, at least in part; since it achieved a more acceptable ecological outcome; and (c) the unfairness and prejudice caused to the defendants was a direct consequence of the prosecutor's conduct…'. See also the New Zealand case of *Delellis v R* [1989] NZHC 711 where the accused entered into an agreement with the police that he would tell the police of the whereabouts of cocaine on condition that they would not lay any charge of importing against him. The police subsequently laid a charge of importing on the basis that the applicant had not been completely honest with them over the way the drug came to New Zealand. In granting a stay for abuse of process, Sinclair J of the High Court of New Zealand held that '…if the police arrogate unto themselves the right to enter into "deals" which are not conditional in any way, then they ought not to be allowed to depart from the arrangement and any attempt to do so would be regarded as oppressive and an abuse of process of the court…'. Likewise, in Canada, see *R v Bursey* (1991) 109 NSR 402 (2d) (CoCT) where the police had undertaken to drop a fraud charge in return for the accused testifying against his friends, and he did so, but the Crown proceeded with the charge. Proceedings were stayed as an abuse.

2 [2000] SASC 384.

3 At para 47.

4 [1989] NZHC 711.

2.32 In respect of domestic cases, *Townsend* was a case of a suspect in fraud proceedings being treated as a prosecution witness for a considerable period, before the prosecution eventually decided to abandon him as a witness and prosecute instead. While being treated as a witness, Bretscher had made a statement implicating his future co-defendant, Townsend. At the trial, however, an abuse submission was rejected, the judge holding that no prejudice had been suffered.

2.33 At the appeal, the prosecution emphasised that in *Dean,* Staughton LJ had made it plain that the facts in that case were exceptional and therefore *Dean* could easily be distinguished. In this case, during the period that Bretscher was treated as a witness, the CPS were unaware of the true extent of his central role in the fraud. Rose LJ held that, where a defendant has been induced to believe he would not be prosecuted, this is capable of founding a stay for abuse. But such a breach of promise did not necessarily and *ipso facto* give rise to abuse. Considering the circumstances of this case, the court held that there had been nothing improper in interviewing the appellant first as a witness and, further, that he had not changed his position in reliance on his treatment as a prosecution witness or volunteered incriminating information. However, the conviction was held to be unsafe given that the appellant had seriously prejudiced his chances of a fair trial. For, while still acting in the capacity qua witness, the CPS had served on the co-defending lawyers the appellant's witness statement (as unused material), which heavily implicated the co-defendant. This led to the co-defendant giving evidence against him at a joint trial, where a severance application had failed, and to a hostile situation which might well have been avoided.

2.34 Situations in which witnesses metamorphose into defendants are obviously fraught with potential problems and the courts no doubt will have to remain on guard as to the *bona fides* of certain abuse claims. Caution ought to be applied in *Townsend*-type scenarios for the reasons noted by Professor Birch:[1]

> 'It is perfectly possible to imagine a case of a dishonest witness who is happy to implicate another; the other may have been content not to implicate the witness as long as the witness did not become involved. But if his attitude were to change on being served with a lying statement made by the witness, it would not only be understandable, but it would be a charter for the dishonest and unscrupulous witness if it were to be held that his "co-operation" had effectively earned him immunity.'

1 [1997] Crim LR 128.

2.35 The concept of fairness and breach of promise arose in *R v Liverpool Magistrates' Court, ex p Slade*.[1] A dog owner was prosecuted for allowing a pitbull terrier in a public place. Under the relevant legislation this was an offence and, if it was proved, then the magistrates' court was bound to order the destruction of the dog. The issue in the case was therefore whether the dog was of this breed or not. At the trial, the prosecution dog expert failed to appear and the magistrates accordingly dismissed the charge. The next day, the dog owner duly went to the police station to retrieve his dog which was released to him by the police. However, it appears that the police still felt aggrieved at the situation and immediately re-arrested him for possession of (what they then sought to re-prove was) a pitbull terrier.

1 [1998] 1 WLR 531; see also *R v Haringey Magistrates' Court, ex p Cragg* (1996) 161 JP 61.

2.36 The dog owner argued breach of promise. His argument was that by releasing the dog to him at the police station, the police had not only created a legitimate expectation in his mind that having the dog in a public place was perfectly lawful, such that they had also connived with him in continuing to commit the offence. In the Divisional Court this argument found favour. Pill LJ, in holding that there was an abuse here, categorised it as falling under the second limb as delineated by Neill LJ in *R v Beckford*:[1] '… it was unfair to try the accused for the offence and offensive to the court's sense of justice and propriety'.

1 [1996] 1 Cr App R 94.

2.37 In *Postermobile plc v Brent London Borough Council*,[1] the Divisional Court also applied the second limb of *Beckford*. In this case, 25 separate Informations were laid against the appellants by Brent Council for displaying advertisements without obtaining the necessary planning consent. The appellants did not deny the charges but alleged that, at a meeting between a planning consultant employed by the appellants, a director of the appellants and officers of the council, they were told that planning consents would not be required for the advertisements in question. Immediately after the advertisements were erected, the council commenced prosecutions against them.

1 (1997) Times, 8 December; see also *R v Aylesbury Justices, ex p Kitching* [1997] Env LR D16; and *R v DPP, ex p Duckenfield* [1999] 2 All ER 873.

2.38 Schiemann LJ held that the prosecutions were an abuse of process, on the basis that it would be unfair for the defendants ever to be tried. He emphasised the importance of citizens being able to rely on the statements of public officials and commented, with wry humour, that it was not as if they requested 'planning advice from one of the council's gardeners'.

2.39 Equally, in the decision of *R v D*,[1] the Court of Appeal found that a prosecution should have been stayed as an abuse when the police 'went back on their word' and re-instituted proceedings which had been dropped in 1986. In 1986 a Chief Inspector of Police wrote to the defendant in relation to a police investigation against him alleging gross indecency towards a child, thus:

> 'Police enquiries have now been completed and having regard to the circumstances and insufficient evidence, I have decided that no further police action will be taken in this matter.'

In 1997, the prosecution told the defendant's solicitors (now dealing with a second complainant making a similar allegation) that the original decision in 1986 had been taken in view of the then rule of evidence which required corroboration of a child's unsworn testimony. The Court of Appeal did not consider the prosecution's stated reason for reviving proceedings to be an 'adequate explanation or justification'. The court was satisfied that the police had 'misused their powers' by reneging on an unequivocal statement that the prosecution was at an end. In addition, by virtue of the antiquity of proceedings, the defence had been deprived of vital documentation (destroyed in the passage of time) which was found to have caused obvious and substantial prejudice to the preparation of the case.

1 (2000) 1 Archbold News 1, CA: 9 July 1999.

2.40 In the decision of *R v Sevenoaks Magistrates Court*,[1] the Divisional Court reviewed a number of the earlier 'promises not to prosecute' cases. In quashing a decision of the justices to stay proceedings for abuse in relation to a Planning Act prosecution, the court easily distinguished the case on the facts from the 'very special circumstances' present in the *Dean* and *Bloomfield* decisions. Sullivan J, however, clearly stated:

> 'that, in principle, an implicit promise may be sufficient to found a submission that there has been an abuse of process, but as a matter of common sense the

less explicit the promise, the less likely it will be that the court's sense of propriety and justice will be offended by the prosecution.'

1 *R (on the application of Tunbridge Wells Borough Council) v Sevenoaks Magistrates' Court* [2001] EWHC Admin 897.

R v Abu Hamza[1]

2.41 Hamza was the imam of a mosque, who had been convicted of various counts of solicitation to murder, using threatening, abusive or insulting words or behaviour with intent to stir up racial hatred, and counts relating to his possession of various sound recordings and documents. The counts related to public speeches made by him at the mosque, and in other places between 1997 and 2000. In March 1999 Hamza was arrested on suspicion of involvement in a terrorist incident which occurred in the Yemen in 1998. Upon his arrest, the police seized from his home a large number of audio and video cassettes, as well as ten volumes of an Afghani Jihad Encyclopaedia. The police kept this material for some nine months before returning it to him in December 1999. He was informed that no further action would be taken against him.

1 [2007] QB 659.

2.42 A number of grounds of appeal were argued in the Court of Appeal, one of which related to the trial judge's rejection of an application for a stay on this discreet aspect of abuse of process. The defence contended that the actions of the police, in returning the material after scrutiny, naturally and reasonably created in the appellant the clear impression, and an implied promise, that the contents of the returned videos and the Encyclopaedia were not criminal. The police were said to have given the appellant a legitimate expectation that he would not be prosecuted for possession of these items. Against that background, it was contended to be an abuse of process five years later to prosecute him for possession of the same. The Court of Appeal disagreed, and, in dismissing the appeal, found the specific facts relied on to fall a long way short of satisfying the 'criteria' required to succeed.

2.43 Lord Phillips, the then Lord Chief Justice, reviewed the earlier authorities of *ex p Dean*, *Townsend* and *Bloomfield*, and held;

> 'These authorities suggest that it is not likely to constitute an abuse of process to proceed with a prosecution unless (1) there has been an unequivocal representation by those with the conduct of the investigation or prosecution of a case that the defendant will not be prosecuted and (2) that the defendant has acted on that representation to his detriment. Even then, if facts come to light which were not known when the representation was made, these may justify proceeding with the prosecution despite the representation.'[1]

While the Court was rightly critical of the delay in taking the decision to prosecute, it held that the fact the police had not done so for five years could not be 'taken as an assurance, let alone an unequivocal assurance, that they would not do so in the future'. It was deemed to be significant that the context of the seizing of the materials related much more to the specific allegations of alleged involvement in the Yemen, as opposed to some general investigation into his criminality. The court noted that the appellant had been aware of this distinction, and held that:

> 'There is no reason to conclude that the appellant placed any reliance on the reaction, or lack of reaction, of the police to the cassettes and the Encyclopedia when deciding to retain them in his possession. He was simply continuing a course of conduct that had commenced before the police had intervened.'

1 See para 54 of the judgment.

2.44 Both elements of the *Hamza* judgment, which, in fairness to the court, dealt with a whole host of different grounds of appeal, have attracted criticism in relation to this single discreet topic from respected academic commentators. Professor Ormerod has raised a number of issues in relation to the judgment.[1] First, the point is made that, whereas the court found no assurance to have been given, there would appear to have been an explicit assurance that no further action would be taken against him. Secondly, that it would be too fine a distinction to make to suggest that any assurances given could only have been relevant to the Yemen incident. Thirdly, given that Hamza was being prosecuted for possession of materials subjected to police scrutiny for some nine months, which were then returned to him with an assurance of no further action, and with no subsequent arrest for five years, the appellant's expectation that he could continue lawfully to possess the items was reasonable. Fourthly, there would not appear to have been any material change in the circumstances surrounding his possession between 1999 and the date of his arrest.

1 See [2007] Crim LR 320 at 324.

2.45 Professor Choo, in his work on this doctrine,[1] additionally warns of the dangers of courts misinterpreting the second criteria in *Hamza*, in relation to detrimental reliance:

> 'What, then, does the requirement of "detriment" entail? In *Dean* the defendant clearly acted on the representation to his detriment, as "he gave repeated assistance to the police". Equally, a defendant may have acted to his detriment by providing, as a potential prosecution witness, a witness statement implicating someone else.[2] In *Bloomfield*, however, it does not seem possible to isolate from the decision any hint of what tangible "detriment" the defendant may have been considered to have suffered. Perhaps the best approach may be to treat the "detriment" requirement as superfluous and to remove it altogether, since otherwise there is a danger that in time it may come to be misinterpreted as a requirement for a showing of forensic prejudice or disadvantage.'

The authors see force in the critical commentaries of the *Hamza* decision on this one aspect, but suggest that, in spite of the apparent ambiguity, it is inconceivable that the court actually meant to take away a defendant's right to argue abuse of process on the basis of a breach of promise in a *Bloomfield* situation, for example, where there was no forensic prejudice to the defendant. Indeed, in a number of the cases considered in this chapter, there was no detrimental reliance on a representation, nor any forensic prejudice, albeit that the cases merited stays of the proceedings. None of those cases were disapproved by *Hamza*. In fact, one of them, *Bloomfield*, was expressly referred to with approval by Lord Phillips. This is because these cases were stayed on the basis of considerations immersed, not in prejudice, but in the protection of the integrity of the courts' process, and the avoidance of the administration of justice being brought into disrepute.

1 Andrew L-T Choo, *Abuse of Process and Judicial Stays of Criminal Proceedings* (2nd Edn) (Oxford University Press, 2008).
2 *R v Townsend* [1997] 2 Cr App R 540.

2.46 It is is submitted that *Hamza* is perhaps best read, in the light of the later cases below, as requiring some evidence of detriment *unless* the exceptional circumstances set out in *Bloomfield* exist: ie unless there is evidence of an affront to the integrity of the justice system.[1] This can only be decided on a case-specific basis: there is no single, inflexible test. This approach is in keeping with the Lord Chief Justice's position as set out in paragraph 50 in the *Hamza* judgment. Lord Phillips acknowledged the difficulties in formulating a single test, as follows:

> 'As the judge held, circumstances can arise where it will be an abuse of process to prosecute a man for conduct in respect of which he has been given an assurance that no prosecution will be brought. It is by no means easy to define a test for those circumstances, other than to say that they must be such as to render the proposed prosecution an affront to justice. The judge expressed reservations as to the extent to which one can apply the common law principle of "legitimate expectation" in this field, and we share those reservations. That principle usually applies to the expectation generated in respect of the exercise of an administrative discretion by or on behalf of the person whose duty it is to exercise that discretion. The duty to prosecute offenders cannot be treated as an administrative discretion, for it is usually in the public interest that those who are reasonably suspected of criminal conduct should be brought to trial. Only in rare circumstances will it be offensive to justice to give effect to this public interest.'

1 See paras **2.64–2.67**.

2.47 The general need to establish detriment or prejudice to the accused was considered at first instance in Northern Ireland in *R v Brown and Taylor (No.2)* where Hart J held that 'Lord Phillips did refer in detail to several of the relevant authorities, and that his conclusion at [54] that the authorities suggest, inter alia, that the defendant has to have acted upon the representation to his detriment is in keeping with *Ex parte Bennett, Ex parte* Dean and *Townsend*'.[1] The court noted this reasoning was further adopted in *Tsang*[2] and *H v Guildford Youth Court*.[3]

1 [2009] NICC 58 at para 19.
2 [2008] NIQB 135.
3 [2008] EWHC 506 (Admin).

2.48 The case of *R v McGeough* is a recent example of both the fact-specific nature of the power to stay for breach of promise and the exceptional nature of the remedy.[1] In *McGeough*, the appellant was convicted in 2011 of serious offences committed in Northern Ireland in 1981. The appellant had fled to Sweden and tried to claim asylum. This had been rejected and he was later arrested and imprisoned for offences committed in Germany. In 1991, he was visited in a German prison by an inspector of the Royal Ulster Constabulary who informed him that he was being investigated for attempted murder. Extradition was contemplated by the UK but he was instead extradited by the US to serve a sentence for weapons offences in 1992. In 1996 he returned to Ireland. He intended to return to Northern Ireland and claimed that, following a conversation in 2000 with a member of Sinn Fein who had been involved during peace negotiations in discussions about the liability of those who had committed past terrorist acts, he understood that he would not be prosecuted for past crimes. He argued, inter alia, that this 'assurance' was an unequivocal and binding promise on behalf of the executive.

1 [2013] NICA 22.

2.49 The Court of Appeal rejected this argument, confirming, at paras 24 and 25:

> 'There was no issue about the test which should be applied in relation to the submission. The learned disclosure judge dealt with the issue at paragraph 16 of his judgement.
>
> "In R v Abu Hamza [2007] QB 659 Lord Phillips emphasised that it is only in rare circumstances that it would be offensive to justice to give effect to the public interest that those who are reasonably suspected of criminal conduct should be brought to trial. After a review of the relevant authorities he went on to say, at paragraph 54:
>
> > '54 These authorities suggest that it is not likely to constitute an abuse of process to proceed with a prosecution unless; (i) there has been an unequivocal representation by those with the conduct of the investigation or prosecution of a case that the defendant will not be prosecuted and (ii) that the defendant has acted on that representation to his detriment. Even then, if facts come to light which were not known when the representation was made, these may justify proceedings with the prosecution despite the representation.'"
>
> Like the disclosure judge, we do not consider that the evidence indicates any basis for the conclusion that Mr Kelly was a representative of those responsible for the conduct of investigations or prosecutions. We further agree that in any event the statement attributed to Mr Kelly, who did not give evidence, did not contain any representation, never mind one which could be said to be unequivocal for the purpose of this test.'[1]

On the facts of this case, the nature of the alleged promise was simply not unequivocal nor did it bind the relevant authorities.

1 At para 25.

2.50 The courts have also acknowledged the need for a connection between the promise and the actions of the defendant to his/her own detriment. In *R v Gripton*,[1] the defendant was convicted of perjury. She was a prosecution witness in a rape trial. She had said in her witness statement, and at trial, that she could not recall seeing any physical contact in her flat between the complainant and the defendant before the alleged incident. This contradicted the defendant's evidence. He was convicted. One year later, she stated that her original statement to the police had not been true. The defendant was retried and she appeared as a defence witness. Prosecution counsel confirmed during the retrial that defence witnesses would not be prosecuted if the defendant was convicted. Gripton applied to stay her indictment for perjury on the grounds that this representation made her prosecution an abuse of process. Her application was refused and she appealed.

1 [2010] EWCA Crim 2260.

2.51 Her appeal was dismissed. The Court of Appeal noted that an unequivocal statement had been made on behalf of the Crown that Gripton would not be prosecuted for perjury and that it was clearly undesirable, and a matter of concern, that the Crown should change its stance on a matter of such importance without good reason. However, this did not mean the prosecution was an abuse of process. It was not suggested that she had relied on the representation to her detriment, and she did not even become aware of the representation until after her arrest.[1]

The Court of Appeal also commented on previous cases of breach of promises noting the fact sensitive nature of the authorities:

> 'so far as the approaches propounded in Bloomfield and Abu Hamza are concerned, we note that neither was intended by the court adopting it to be a comprehensive binding rule. In Bloomfield Staughton LJ expressly stated that the court was not seeking to establish any precedent or any general principle in regard to abuse of process. Similarly in Abu Hamza Lord Phillips CJ emphasised the difficulties of propounding a test of abuse of process, and the formulation adopted in that case is expressed in terms that conduct would be unlikely to constitute an abuse of process unless certain criteria were satisfied. He was certainly not laying down requirements which would be indispensable in any case. The reason for this is clear: the courts are here concerned with considerations of fairness and they must be free to respond to the circumstances of each case'.

1 Para 27.

2.52 However, this approach clearly does not exclude the possibility of a stay being granted in the absence of detriment. It was acknowledged by the Court of Appeal in *R v Gripton* that the power to order a stay where there has been no detriment persists even though it is exceptional power:

> 'It is not difficult to see why, exceptionally, in the particular circumstances of Bloomfield, the court concluded that to continue with the prosecution would be an abuse of process, notwithstanding the absence of any detrimental reliance on the part of that appellant. The ultimate question will be whether to proceed with the prosecution would be an affront to justice.'[1]

1 *R v Gripton* [2010] EWCA Crim 2260 at para 28.

2.53 Thus, since *Hamza*, the courts have simply reiterated, and re-emphasied, the exceptional nature of the application of the circumstances which would lead to a *Bennett* limb two-strand of abuse of process where a stay is granted because it amounts to an affront to the administration of justice. Any concerns there may have been as to whether Hamza may have led to the narrowing of the principles appear to be ill-founded. Whilst there is no doubt a judicial trend towards 'requiring proof of detrimental reliance'[1] courts must be wary not to see this as a prerequisite for a stay. The cases will clearly continue to be fact-specific. In the 2021 case of *R v Jones (Sally Ann)*[2] for example, which followed the Hamza authority, where an issue arose as to whether a defendant to whom an assurance of immunity from prosecution had been given had acted on that assurance to their detriment, that fact had to be proved by evidence.

1 See Professor Ormerod's commentary on the *Hamza* decision, [2007] Crim LR 324.
2 [2021] EWCA Crim 1195.

2.54 It has been said that the stance that 'fairness must be done to the defendant, the prosecution and the wider public militates against a firm rule and in favour of a flexible approach which maintains the integrity of the court process, but also ensures wherever possible that those suspected of serious crimes are brought to trial'.[1] There will be cases in the future where there is no obvious, tangible, or discernible prejudice, which nevertheless strike at the core of justice and the heart of unfairness. In these instances, the Judiciary will have the ever-continuing challenge of exercising their judgment as to whether the 'exceptional' threshold has been breached.

1 Nick Taylor [2011] Crim LR 388-392.

R v Downey

2.55 The court's current approach is also demonstrated in the recent case *R v Downey*.[1] Here, the court considered again the authorities on breach of promise not to prosecute and ordered a stay of proceedings against Downey, who had been charged with four counts of murder and one of doing an act with intent to cause an explosion. The charges related to the 1982 Hyde Park bombings.

1 BAILII Citation Number: [2014] EW Misc 7 (CCrimC). For further discussion see R. Ekins, 'Amnesty and Abuse of Process' UK Const. L. Blog (3 April 2014).

2.56 Four reasons were put forward as to why the prosecution was an abuse of process. Mr Justice Sweeney stayed proceedings on the third ground, namely that it would be unfair for Downey to be tried because he was given a clear written assurance on behalf of the Secretary of State for Northern Ireland and the Attorney General that there was no outstanding direction for prosecution in Northern Ireland in relation to him. The misconduct in the case consisted of gross incompetence.

Downey was one of the so-called 'on the runs' (or 'OTRs'). These were people either suspected (but not charged) with offences relating to the 'Troubles' in Northern Ireland, or who were charged (or charged and convicted) and who escaped. They were not covered by the Good Friday Agreement implemented by the Northern Ireland (Sentences) Act 1998 ('the 1998 Act'). The Government developed an 'administrative scheme' to address their situation which looked at whether individuals should be prosecuted, a legislative attempt at an amnesty scheme having been rejected by Parliament.[1]

1 Northern Ireland (Offences) Bill 2005.

2.57 As part of the administrative scheme, some individuals were sent a letter which confirmed:

> 'The Secretary of State for Northern Ireland has been informed by the Attorney General that, on the basis of the information currently available, there is no outstanding direction for prosecution in Northern Ireland, there are no warrants in existence nor are you wanted in Northern Ireland for arrest, questioning, or charge by the police. The Police Service of Northern Ireland are not aware of any interest in you from any other police force in the United Kingdom. If any other outstanding offence or offences come to light, or if any request for extradition were to be received, these would have to be dealt with in the usual way'.[1]

1 At para 123.

2.58 Downey was sent such a letter in 2007. However, it was sent in error because he was still wanted by the police in relation to the Hyde Park bombings. On receipt of the letter, Mr Downey travelled within the United Kingdom until he was arrested for the offences in May 2013 at Gatwick airport. Sweeney J considered the case law on abuse of process in some detail, referring to recent judgments:

> '... it is well established that the Court has the power to stay proceedings in two categories of case, namely (i) where it will be impossible to give the accused a fair trial and (ii) where it offends the court's sense of justice and propriety to be asked to try the accused in the particular circumstances of the case. In the first category of case, if the court concludes that an accused cannot receive a fair trial, it will stay the proceedings without more. No question of the balancing of competing interests arises...'.[1]

1 At para 143.

2.59

> The judgment of Lloyd Jones LJ in *SSHD v CC and CF*[1] was referred to as a 'helpful summary of the general principles to be applied'.[2] However, it was recognised, at para 147, that additionally 'there is a distinct body of case law in relation to alleged breach of promise cases'.

1 [2013] EWHC 2837 (Admin), paras 91-101. See Chapter 5, para **5.143**.
2 At para 146.

2.60 Noting[1] *Gripton* para 27,[2] and its treatment of *Abu Hamza* para 54,[3] Sweeney J held that the main question to be addressed was whether 'it offends the court's sense of justice and propriety to try the accused in the particular circumstances of the case' (*R v Maxwell* [2011] 1 WLR 1837, per Lord Dyson at para 13). This required a balancing exercise of competing public interests to be undertaken as in any abuse of process case (see further discussion in **Chapter 5**). Sweeney J, noted:

> 'In conducting the necessary balancing exercise (in which there is an obvious overlap between the public interest in ensuring that executive conduct does not undermine public confidence in the criminal justice system and bring it into disrepute, and the public interest in holding officials of the state to promises they have made in full understanding of what is involved in the bargain) I recognise that the threshold for a stay is a very high one, and that it involves an evaluation of what has occurred in the light of the competing public interests involved. It is not a disciplinary jurisdiction, is untrammelled by rigid rules, and all depends on the particular facts of the case viewed in its entirety.'[4]

1 At paras 148–149.
2 See para **2.51**.
3 See para **2.49**.
4 At para 167.

2.61 Sweeney J considered the facts of the case in detail, focussing on what he described as 'catastrophic' error by the authorities. He noted that '[t]he assurances given in the letter were not only given in the name of the Government in the course of an international peace process, but were intimately connected with the criminal justice system in respect of very serious offences.'[1] This particular promise was of significant import in light of its context and wider political significance.

1 At para 173.

2.62 Sweeney J concluded that the accused had suffered detriment 'by way of arrest, the loss of his freedom for a time, the imposition of strict bail conditions, and being put at risk of conviction for very serious offences (albeit that the latter is tempered, to some extent, by the fact that even if convicted of all the offences he would, in consequence of the 1998 Act, serve no more than two years in prison).'[1] Consequently, he granted a stay for breach of promise, confirming:

> 'Given the core facts as I have found them to be, and the wider undisputed facts, I have conducted the necessary evaluation of what has occurred in the light of the competing public interests involved. Clearly, and notwithstanding a degree of tempering in this case by the operation of the 1998 Act, the public interest in ensuring that those who are accused of serious crime should be tried is a very strong one (with the plight of the victims and their families firmly in mind). However, in the very particular circumstances of this case, it seems to me that it is very significantly outweighed in the balancing exercise by the overlapping public interests in ensuring that executive misconduct does not undermine public confidence in the criminal justice system and bring it into disrepute, and the public interest in holding officials of the state to promises they have made in full understanding of what is involved in the bargain. Hence, I have concluded that this is one of those rare cases in which, in the particular circumstances, it offends the court's sense of justice and propriety to be asked to try the defendant.'[2]

1 At para 173.
2 At para 175.

PROMISES TO OFFER NO EVIDENCE

2.63 In a handful of decisions, the courts have found abuse to apply where, post-charge, the Crown have reneged on promises to offer no evidence. Many of these cases engage the wider public interest in the sense that reneging on a promise becomes an affront to the administration of justice and the court process itself rather than solely causing prejudice to the defendant personally.

2.64 *Bloomfield*[1] was an example of a *volte face* by the prosecution. At a plea and directions hearing in the Crown Court, the prosecution counsel indicated to defence counsel that the Crown wished to offer no evidence. It was accepted that the defendant had been the victim of a set-up. Prosecution counsel confirmed this intention in the trial judge's room. However, it was said that it would be embarrassing to the police and prosecution if no evidence were offered that day, and so the judge was invited, in open court, to adjourn the case and re-list it 'for mention'. The judge duly obliged with the agreement of the defence. However, in the intervening period the CPS arranged a conference with a new prosecution counsel who advised differently and then declared its intention to proceed with the prosecution.

1 [1997] 1 Cr App Rep 135, CA.

2.65 In the Court of Appeal the prosecution counsel, save for stating that the first prosecuting counsel's indication was unauthorised, did not attempt to demonstrate that the original decision was wrong. It would appear that the only hint as to CPS thinking was reference being made first to the fact that the CPS representative was not present in court when the original action was taken and secondly, that the first prosecutor was 'inexperienced'.

2.66 Staughton LJ, in allowing the appeal on an abuse submission, held:

> '... whether or not there was prejudice to the defendant, it would bring the administration of justice into disrepute to allow the Crown to revoke its original decision without any reason being given as to what was wrong with it, particularly as it was made coram judice ... [and] ... That neither the court nor defendant could be expected to enquire whether prosecution counsel had authority to conduct a case in court in any particular way and they were therefore entitled to assume in ordinary circumstances that counsel did have such authority'.

2.67 It is clear that, what particularly offended the court's sense of propriety in *Bloomfield*, was the stark manner in which the CPS appeared to treat the court. Staughton LJ emphasised that the statement by the first prosecution counsel was not merely a statement to the defendant or to his legal representative, it was also made in the presence of the judge. This point, in Staughton LJ's opinion, was so significant that considerations of prejudice became immaterial:

> 'it seems to us that, whether or not there was prejudice it would bring the administration of justice into disrepute if the Crown Prosecution Service were able to treat the courts as if it were at its beck and call, free to tell it one day that it was not going to prosecute and another day that it was'.

This mirrors the approach taken in the New Zealand Court of Appeal case *Moevao v Department of Labour* where the court noted that:

> '...The yardstick is not simply fairness to the particular accused. It is not whether the initiation and continuation of the particular process seems in the circumstances to be unfair to him. That may be an important consideration. But the focus is on the misuse of the court process by those responsible for law enforcement. It is whether the continuation of the prosecution is inconsistent with the recognised purposes of the administration of criminal justice and so constitutes an abuse of the process of the court.'[1]

1 [1980] 1 NZLR 464 at para 482.

2.68 *Bloomfield* was applied by Auld LJ in *R v Wyatt*[1] where prosecuting counsel informed the judge that, 'depending on the results of the DNA evidence, the Crown may be in a position to take a different view which would be in the defendant's favour'. In other words, prosecuting counsel had made plain that if the DNA evidence was found not to incriminate the defendant, the case would be dropped. Eventually, the DNA analyses was forthcoming which was not incriminatory. However, the CPS decided that, rather than discontinue the proceedings against the defendant, a new but less serious count to the indictment should be added. The trial judge held that the proceedings should not be stayed because there was no evidence that the defendant could not have a fair trial in relation to the new lesser charge.

1 (1997) 3 Archbold News 2, CA.

2.69 In his judgment, Auld LJ emphasised that an abuse of process may arise, 'even though it may not affect the fairness of the trial, but is so unfair or wrong that the court should mark it by not allowing the prosecution to proceed'. Applying the facts of the case to this principle, Auld LJ held:

> 'it seems to us in the circumstances that the prosecution's very late change of tack when the matter came before the court was very unfair to the defence ... we take the view that the intervention by the CPS at that late stage, prevailing over counsel for the prosecution's better judgment, was unfortunate.'

2.70 In *Mahdi*[1] a stay was deemed appropriate where a change of judge on the adjourned hearing of a trial left a defendant to face a trial, which he should not have had to do, because of some confusion as to certain indications previously given to counsel. The assistant recorder, before whom the trial was re-listed, was not fully and properly informed as to the case history. Two senior judges had previously made plain their firm views as to whether the trial should proceed. Lord Taylor CJ, in quashing the conviction, found that '... an injustice was inadvertently done to this appellant by reason of the lack of accurate information placed before the assistant recorder'. It should be added that the Court of Appeal stated, *per curiam*, that the case did not fall within the scope of the well-known authorities on abuse of process.

1 [1993] Crim LR 793.

2.71 In contrast to the principles embodied in *Bloomfield*, it is, at first blush, difficult to reconcile the Divisional Court judgment in *R v DPP, ex p Burke*,[1] where an applicant was refused an application for judicial review of the DPP's decision to reinstate a prosecution, the CPS having expressly discontinued proceedings. In *Burke* the applicant had been charged with indecent assault on a 13-year-old child. After the Senior Crown Prosecutor, the Principal Crown Prosecutor and a further prosecutor reviewed the case and agreed that there should be no prosecution, the CPS informed the applicant's solicitor that they had decided to discontinue the prosecution, albeit that the formalities of preparing a notice of discontinuance would take a little while. This information was passed on to the applicant on or about March 1996.

1 [1997] COD 169, DC.

2.72 In April 1996, the Senior Crown Prosecutor received a complaint from the complainant's mother about the decision to discontinue. While the Branch Crown Prosecutor, to whom the matter had been referred, concluded that the Senior Crown Prosecutor had made the wrong decision, nevertheless it was decided to issue a notice of discontinuance, given that the applicant had already been so informed. The standard form discontinuance letter included the words: 'Exceptionally, if further significant evidence were to become available at a later date this decision may be reconsidered'. While no further significant evidence apparently came to light, significant further discussions took place. The complainant's mother complained to the Prime Minister and her complaints were passed on to the Attorney-General and then to the Director of Public Prosecutions. The outcome was that the DPP decided to reinstate the prosecution, the applicant was informed, and a fresh summons issued. While no submissions as to abuse of process were made, the applicant sought judicial review of the DPP's decision, inter alia, on the grounds that he had a legitimate expectation that the prosecution would not be reinstated unless fresh evidence emerged (which it had not).

2.73 While Phillips LJ acknowledged that 'legitimate expectation' was an aspect of fairness, he concluded that the terms of the discontinuance letter were not designed to lead the applicant to believe that he was free of jeopardy. A simple question arises however. What would any ordinary person conclude on receipt of such a letter? Leaving aside the question of a new evidence situation, would one not reasonably conclude that that was the end of the case? Should one be expected to anticipate that the CPS may well, as occurred here, take a different decision at a later date? Would the same decision have been reached had unfairness been considered in the context of the abuse of process authorities, as opposed to the administrative law ones which were apparently argued before the court? In the more recent case of *R v Killick*, the breach of promise authorities were considered in a case in which the defendant was told, via an email to his solicitor, that his prosecution would be discontinued.[1] The decision was reversed over two years later on review. The Court of Appeal approved and applied *Hamza* but found that the email was not an 'unequivocal representation' because of the possibility for review. The court held that the appellant's solicitors would have been well aware of the rights of complainants to seek a review and the Court assumed they would have told the defendant of that possibility. There had been delay in the case that did not in itself amount to an abuse of process or cause prejudice or detriment. The Court of Appeal held that:

> 'We accept the evidence that there was clear strain, but it did not amount to prejudice or detriment.'[2]

1 [2012] 1 Cr App R 10.
2 At para 55.

2.74 The court in *Killick* accepted that detriment was not always required.[1] However, in this case, it could not be contended that the prosecution was 'an affront to public conscience'.[2] In their email, the police had said nothing in relation to the possibility of the matter being reviewed, but the decision rested on the assumption that the defendant solicitor 'must be taken to have been aware of the various rights of review' and to have passed them on to the defendant,[3] a significant inference which needed no evidence to support it.

1 At para 53.
2 At para 55.
3 At paras 22 and 44.

2.75 Even where the court accepts that a promise constitutes a representation, the important case of *R v Horseferry Road Magistrates' Court, ex p DPP*[1] serves to highlight the fact that not all broken promises will be sufficient to justify a stay. In that case, a 'relatively junior' police officer told a representative of the defendant's solicitors (so the magistrate found) that he would not be charged in relation to an alleged fraudulent conspiracy. A year later, he was told he would be charged. The magistrate stayed the proceedings as an abuse of process, in apparent reliance on the principles of *Dean*. However, the Divisional Court subsequently concluded that she had been wrong so to do. The court held that it was not possible to say that a breach of an assurance not to prosecute necessarily justified a stay. Earlier cases were distinguished on the facts by reason of their special features, such as the youth of the defendant, and the assistance he had given to police in *Dean* and in *Bloomfield*, and the fact that the assurance had been given in the presence of a judge.

1 (1999) 7 Archbold News, 8 March 1999.

2.76 In the course of their respective judgments in *ex p DPP*, Kennedy LJ and Blofeld J emphasised the exceptional nature of the abuse jurisdiction. Blofeld J quoted Lord Lowry's judgment in *Bennett* where he said:

> 'the jurisdiction to stay must be exercised carefully and sparingly and only for very compelling reasons. The discretion to stay is not a disciplinary jurisdiction and ought not to be exercised in order to express the court's disapproval of official conduct'[1].

1 *R v Horseferry Road Magistrates' Court, ex p Bennett* [1994] AC 42 at 74.

2.77 In the course of his judgment, Kennedy LJ clearly implied that, for a breach of assurance-type abuse submission to succeed, the defence must pass the high hurdle of 'special circumstances' or 'special features', which were found to be lacking in that particular case.

2.78 In the case of *R*,[1] the Court of Appeal were required to consider the unusual circumstances of an appellant who, having been convicted of offences of conspiracy to rob and kidnapping, received a letter from the CPS expressing the opinion that the convictions were unsafe. The case was duly listed on the understanding that the Crown would not contest the appeal. However, shortly before the date of hearing, the Crown withdrew the concession in the light of advice from counsel. Whilst recognising this highly unsatisfactory position, the court rejected the appellant's argument that the withdrawal constituted an abuse of process. The court distinguished the *Bloomfield*-type authorities on the basis that, whereas they concerned the control of the Crown's power to pursue a criminal prosecution, this case concerned the Court of Appeal's own duty to determine the safety of convictions. It appears that the appellant, having learnt of the CPS's earlier stance, was specifically advised that the final decision over the quashing of the convictions remained with the Court of Appeal itself.

1 *R* (2000) 4 Archbold News, 12 November 1999, CA.

2.79 A further example of a revised or re-visited prosecution opinion is apparent in the decision of *R v Murphy (Graham)*,[1] where the defence sought to argue *Bloomfield/Dean* on appeal. On the facts, it was an argument with little merit, which does not even appear to have been made at trial. In the Magistrates Court the appellant had faced two charges alleging sexual assaults, one on a boy, the other on a girl. At the Magistrates stage, the prosecution decided to proceed solely on the charge relating to the girl. However, when the case reached the Crown Court, Counsel added a second count reinstating the charge on the boy. This was done at a plea and directions hearing without any objection from the defence. Subsequently, the appellant was acquitted of the charge in relation to the girl, but convicted on the count concerning the boy. The court held that there could not be a rule which meant that an early decision in the Magistrates Court not to proceed on one charge, absent further evidence, could never be re-visited by Prosecution Counsel in the Crown Court, even in circumstances where there was no fresh evidence. This was not a situation where no evidence was offered, but instead one where a charge was withdrawn. The court pointed out that the withdrawal of a summons or charge was not a bar to the issue of a further summons in the same matter.

1 [2003] Crim LR 471.

2.80 In the 2004 decision of *R v Mulla*,[1] one has an example of a case which is easily distinguishable on the facts of *Bloomfield*. In this matter, the appellant's case was listed for trial on a charge of causing death by dangerous driving. However, on the morning of trial, prosecuting counsel indicated that they were prepared to accept a plea to the lesser offence of careless driving. When the prosecution counsel told the Judge of his intention to accept the plea to careless driving, the Judge required him to refer the matter back for reconsideration by a senior member of the Crown Prosecution Service. By 2.15pm the same day, prosecution Counsel, having acted as requested, indicated he proposed to proceed with the original, more serious, charge. The Court of Appeal subsequently dismissed the appeal which followed, with little difficulty. First, the appellant had been aware from the outset that the Judge had not been content with the position, which was clearly some way from being determined or resolved. Secondly, the period of time over which it took prosecution counsel to change his position was very short. Thirdly, there had been no apparent prejudice to the appellant by reason of the change of course.

1 [2004] 1 Cr App R 6, at p 72.

2.81 In the course of his judgment, Rose LJ (Vice President)[1] held that the fact the prosecution had indicated to the Court what its view was, was only one of the factors to be considered, and then helpfully added:

> 'Other factors include what view is expressed by the judge when the prosecution gives its indication, the period of time over which the prosecution reconsiders the matter before they change their mind, whether or not the defendant's hopes have been inappropriately raised, and whether there has been, by reason of the change of course by the prosecution, any prejudice to the defence.'

1 See p 77 of the CAR report.

2.82 The importance of the principle that an accused should, as a general rule, be able to rely on a prosecutorial decision was further underlined in the 2004 decision of *Taylor*.[1] This case involved a prosecution appeal by case stated against a Magistrates Court's decision to stay an Information for careless driving. The case concerned a tragic motor accident, involving Taylor, a bus driver, and another driver who was killed, where both drivers were apparently at fault. On 12 June 2003, Taylor was notified in writing that he would not be prosecuted. However, on 18 July 2003, he was told that he would be so prosecuted. Mitting J, in ruling in favour of the defence on appeal, took the view that the original decision to prosecute, which had been reviewed by three prosecutors, must have been based, at least in part, on public interest grounds. The court found that the Magistrates were entitled to stay the proceedings on the basis of *Bloomfield*, which was accepted to be an authority for the proposition that no prejudice was required to be shown for a case to be abusive. This was not a case where there was found to be a mistaken prosecution approach to the review of their evidential test, which would have justified a change of decision under the CPS Code. The change of decision appears to have followed representations from the family of the deceased driver, which is akin to the situation in the *Burke* case cited previously.

1 *Director of Public Prosecutions v Taylor* [2004] EWHC 1554 (Admin).

2.83 Finally, the 2008 decision of *R (on the application of H) v Guildford Youth Court* is reviewed.[1] This is a decision which is also commented upon under a promise not to prosecute above at para **2.47**. H's appeal, against the Youth Court's decision to refuse to stay a prosecution against him for an offence of assault,[2] was not contested. Before his police interview, the 15-year-old, H, was told that it was possible to resolve the matter, which concerned a fellow school pupil, by way of a final warning. During the interview itself, H went on to admit the offence, and put forward his account of events, whereupon the officer explained he would seek to have the matter resolved that day, and that, on the date he was due to return on bail, the matter would be dealt with by way of a final warning. Some three months later, he was formally charged with the offence, the police having indicated in the intervening period, that a final warning might not be appropriate. In allowing the appeal, Silber J, taking account of the principles set down in *Chu Piu-Wing* and *Bloomfield*, considered that there was a clear public interest in upholding the promise made by an officer of the state. Significant factors were no doubt the fact that the officer who made the promise was, at that key stage, in charge of deciding whether or not to prosecute, and also the young age of the appellant. There are similar authorities from Commonwealth jurisdictions which involve defendants making statements or giving evidence following promises not to proceed to prosecution.[3]

1 [2008] EWHC 506 (Admin).
2 Offences Against the Persons Act 1861, s 20.
3 See for example, *R v Mohi* [2000] SASC 384, *Delellis v R* [1989] NZHC 711 and *R v Bursey* (1991) 109 NSR 402 (2d) (CoCT).

PROMISES ON ACCEPTABLE PLEAS

2.84 While formal American-style plea-bargaining is not part of our system, it is an everyday licit practice by the prosecution and defence to broker pleas in order to 'carve the indictment' and so avoid a trial. A considerable amount of time and money is no doubt saved as pragmatic considerations impact on the criminal justice system. Judges are routinely asked to provide sentence indications for specific guilty pleas. It is a practical balancing task, carried out in the public interest, where consideration is keenly given to sentencing levels in respect of various different offences. In the 2005 decision of *R v Goodyear*,[1] a five-Judge Court of Appeal provided detailed guidance in relation to the giving of advance indications of sentence. The procedure should take place in public in open court, where both prosecution and defence are represented, and with full recording of proceedings. Prosecutors should now be well-versed in the Attorney General's Guidelines on the Acceptance of Pleas, which were revised in 2009, and in the 2018 revised Code for Crown Prosecutors.

1 [2005] 2 Cr App R 20.

2.85 For any system of plea negotiations to work, of course, it is expected that the prosecution will keep their side of the bargain, particularly where they agree on acceptable pleas. *R v Thomas*[1] is one such case where the Crown failed to keep their side of a bargain. In *Thomas* at a pleas hearing, the defendant pleaded not guilty to offences of s 18 wounding, ABH and affray, but pleaded guilty on a qualified basis to the alternative s 20 charge. Prior to such a hearing, the CPS had indicated in unequivocal terms, in response to a letter from defence solicitors, that such a proposed plea was acceptable to the Crown. At the Crown Court hearing, the plea having been so entered, the counsel for the Crown then told the court that the plea was not acceptable to him and that he sought a trial.

1 [1995] Crim LR 938.

2.86 In this first instance decision, the court, in holding that there was an abuse, re-emphasised the principle of holding officials of the State to promises made. Whether or not the CPS indication was justifiable, the fact was that the defendant had seriously prejudiced his position by tendering a guilty plea to the s 20 offence. The defendant, of course, may not have tendered a guilty plea at all had it not been for the CPS correspondence.

2.87 This principle was re-affirmed by the Divisional Court in the recent decision of *DPP v Edgar*.[1] In that case the defendant was charged with three road traffic offences, namely, excess alcohol, failing to stop and failing to report. When she pleaded guilty to the latter two offences, the prosecution applied to withdraw the excess alcohol charge. Having retired to consider sentence, the justices returned into court, at the invitation of the prosecutor, who now wished to reinstate the alcohol charge! Whilst the charge was reinstated, the defence subsequently succeeded on an abuse submission, and the prosecutor duly appealed by way of case stated.

1 *DPP v Edgar* (2000) 164 JP 471, DC: see also the critical commentary at [2000] 31 CLW, 14 August.

2.88 In dismissing the prosecutor's appeal, Schiemann LJ stated that:

> 'For my part, the consideration that is uppermost in my mind, and one suspects was uppermost in the justices' minds, is that compromises of this kind between prosecution and defence, where the defence agrees to plead to some charges in return for the prosecution dropping others, are a commonplace of our criminal proceedings and they occur in magistrates' courts and Crown Courts. It is important in principle that such compromises should generally be stuck to and the integrity of the criminal process requires that they should be'.

2.89 Similarly, in *CPS v Mattu*,[1] it was held that, where a detailed 'basis of plea' has been agreed upon and approved by the court, it would be an abuse of process to prosecute related matters where the case advanced by the prosecution was wholly inconsistent with that basis of plea. Pill LJ confirmed that:

> 'A carefully prepared and detailed basis of plea was agreed between prosecution and defence, and approved by the court, first, for the purpose of giving an indication as to sentence and, secondly, for deciding upon sentence. It achieved a status which renders a prosecution attempt to go behind it in the blatant way contemplated here an abuse of process.'[2]

1 [2009] EWCA Crim 1483.
2 At para 19.

2.90 However, it was also noted that:

> 'There will be cases, where, for example, fresh evidence emerges and circumstances change, in which it may be possible for the prosecution to circumvent a basis of plea they have agreed but what the prosecution attempted in this case is not acceptable. Change of counsel and of venue does not remedy the situation.'[1]

1 At para 20.

2.91 Such a case arose in *R v Dowty*.[1] Here, the Court of Appeal held that reneging on promises in relation to pleas was not an abuse of process. The defendant was informed that if he pleaded to two counts of sexual grooming of a young girl, two other charges of making indecent photographs would be dropped. However, after entering pleas, another prosecutor disagreed with his colleague's opinion and proceeded to try the defendant for the photographic offence too. The defendant's argument that this was an abuse of process based on breach of promise failed as he could not establish serious prejudice and there were clear public interest issues at stake. The Court of Appeal referred to para 12 of the CPS Code for Prosecutors (2010), which states that occasionally there may be special reasons why the CPS overturn a decision not to prosecute or when it will re-start a prosecution, particularly if the case is serious. The initial decision had not been wrong and the judge had considered all the competing considerations. The judge had not erred and was entitled to reach the decision he had.

1 [2011] EWCA Crim 3138.

OTHER PROMISES

2.92 In addition to the three above-mentioned areas where this category of abuse has been deemed applicable, there are a number of other areas worthy of attention:

(1) Prosecution promises not to call a witness.

(2) The prosecution code for 're-starting a prosecution'.

(3) Police cautions.

(4) Crown divisibility.

(5) Implied promises.

Prosecution promises not to call a witness

2.93 In the decision of *R v Drury, Clark*[1] the defence made a bold, albeit unsurprisingly unsuccessful, attempt to extend this abuse jurisdiction to include a failure by the Crown to keep its promise to call a particular witness at trial. The case concerned police officers who were indicted for offences of conspiracy to supply Class B drugs and perverting the course of public justice. One of the key witnesses against them was a co-accused, 'F', who had pleaded guilty, and was due to give evidence for the Crown prior to her sentence, the witness being a registered police informant. Upon the discharge of the jury at trial (due to difficulties with F giving evidence), the prosecutor made an unequivocal promise in court that the witness would not be called at the re-trial, 'under any circumstances'. Upon the re-trial, however, the Crown called the witness (who, by then, was willing to give evidence) and the defendants were convicted.

1 *R v Drury, Clark* [2001] EWCA Crim 975, [2001] Crim LR 847.

2.94 In dismissing the appeals, the Court of Appeal highlighted the fundamental difference between calling a witness in support of a count, as against proceeding on the count in the first place. Whilst the Crown had stated that F was not to be called, nevertheless there was seemingly no suggestion that it would be improper to proceed even if she were content to give evidence. Indeed, there was no real detriment caused to the defendants on account of the witness's altered position. Accordingly, the authors agree with David Ormerod's commentary that:

> 'It would have been a significant extension of existing case law to hold that reneging on such a limited promise renders it unfair to try the accused or that a fair trial was impossible.'[1]

1 [2001] EWCA Crim 975, [2001] Crim LR 847.

The prosecution code for 're-starting a prosecution'

2.95 The 2018 edition of the code for Crown Prosecutors is a public document and available on the CPS website.[1] The code, as was previously pointed out by Staughton LJ in *Bloomfield,* is not law, nor is it delegated legislation. It is simply a code which gives guidance on general principles for Crown Prosecutors. Part 10 is entitled 'Reconsidering a Prosecution Decision' and reads as follows:

> 10.1. People should be able to rely on decisions taken by the CPS. Normally, if the CPS tells a suspect or defendant that there will not be a prosecution, or that the prosecution has been stopped, the case will not start again. But occasionally there are cases where the CPS will overturn a decision not to prosecute or to deal with the case by way of an out-of-court disposal or when it will restart the prosecution, particularly if the case is serious.
>
> 10.2. These cases include:
>
> - cases where a further review of the original decision shows that it was wrong and, in order to maintain confidence in the criminal justice system, a prosecution should be brought despite the earlier decision;
> - cases which are stopped so that further anticipated evidence, which is likely to become available in the fairly near future, can be collected and prepared. In these cases, the prosecutor will tell the defendant that the prosecution may well start again;
> - cases which are not prosecuted or are stopped because of a lack of evidence but where more significant evidence is discovered later; and
> - cases involving a death in which a review following the findings of an inquest concludes that a prosecution should be brought, notwithstanding any earlier decision not to prosecute.

1 See www.cps.gov.uk; it is also found at Appendix A of this work.

The Crown Prosecution Service Legal Guidance on 'Reconsidering a Prosecution Decision'

2.96 Further recent CPS guidance explains their position on the circumstances where prosecutors consider that they may institute or reinstitute criminal proceedings after the CPS has told a suspect or defendant that there will not be a prosecution, or that the prosecution has been stopped. The following are relevant excerpts from this guidance:

> '*Principles*
>
> Victims of crime and the public have a legitimate expectation that those who commit offences will be brought to justice. This expectation and the rights of victims cannot be overridden by a suspect's belief that they will not be prosecuted, including where the suspect has been told that there will not be a prosecution or where a prosecution has been stopped. These rights and expectations need to be balanced so that they are fair to all parties. Accordingly, in appropriate circumstances the CPS may:
>
>> Overturn a decision not to prosecute or to deal with the case by way of an out-of-court disposal; or
>>
>> Restart a prosecution.
>
> Victims have a right to seek a review of a decision not to prosecute, without having to seek recourse to judicial review proceedings in the first instance. The Victims Right to Review (VRR) scheme enables victims to seek a review of certain CPS decisions not to start a prosecution or to stop a prosecution. Further details on this scheme are contained in Victims Right to Review – CPS Policy and Guidance. The statutory right of the prosecution to institute / re-institute proceedings is qualified by two important protections for the suspect / defendant, to ensure that there is no injustice done:
>
>> The right of the defendant to revive proceedings in the magistrates' court (see above); and
>>
>> The court's power to stay any proceedings that it views as an abuse of the court's process
>
> *Nature of the review*
>
> When reviewing a case where a suspect or defendant was previously told that there will not be a prosecution, or where the prosecution was stopped, the review should determine:
>
>> Whether the case meets the Full Code Test; and
>>
>> Whether it is highly likely that a court will rule that a prosecution is an abuse of its process: see the section below on Abuse of Process.
>
> If the Full Code Test is met and it is not highly likely that a court will rule that a prosecution is an abuse of its process, the case should be reinstituted.
>
> *Wrong decision cases*
>
> In cases where the review is on the basis that the original decision may have been wrong, including reviews under the VRR scheme, additional considerations apply. In accordance with Section 10.2 of the Code, the review is twofold:

Was the decision not to prosecute wrong?

If so, should a prosecution now be brought in order to maintain confidence in the criminal justice system?

1. Was the decision not to prosecute wrong?

A review of the case will be conducted independent of those who made the original decision. The review will determine whether the case meets the Full Code Test. Having reached a decision that a case passes the Full Code Test, the reviewer will go on to consider the original review and to identify the basis upon which it could be described as 'wrong'. The issue on review is not whether the decision not to prosecute was unreasonable, but whether it was wrong.

It is expected that in the majority of cases where the reviewer decides that the Full Code Test is met, the reviewer will conclude that the original decision was wrong. However, this will not always be the case, as a decision is not necessarily wrong simply because the reviewer disagrees with it. The reviewer should allow a margin of individual prosecutorial discretion when determining whether a decision was wrong, as it is understandable that two prosecutors might differ, particularly when making difficult decisions on complex evidence or on the public interest. Accordingly, there will be some cases where the reviewer concludes that, although they disagree with the original decision, it is not wrong. It is expected that in such cases the original review will have been conducted thoroughly, the prosecutor will have considered all relevant issues and come to a well-reasoned and justifiable decision.

When considering the basis upon which the original decision could be described as 'wrong', the reviewer should determine whether any of the following non-exhaustive list of factors had a significant impact on the decision (either on its own or in combination with other factors):

A misinterpretation of the evidence. For example:

A failure to take into account relevant evidence, or an erroneous decision to take into account irrelevant evidence.

Disproportionate weight attributed to factors such as: victim or witness credibility; initial reluctance of the victim to report the allegation; potential defences not actually raised by the suspect; or the inability of the prosecution to completely rebut the account of the suspect.

An incorrect application of the law.

An incorrect application of the public interest stage.

For example: disproportionate weight attributed to one or more public interest factors tending against prosecution; or insufficient weight attributed to one or more public interest factors tending in favour of prosecution.

A failure to consider, or a decision to not follow, relevant CPS policy that cannot be properly justified.

> Note that: CPS policy may be set out in The Code, Director's Guidance, Legal Guidance or Guidelines. A failure to properly apply or comply with policy includes situations where irrelevant considerations have been taken into account. It remains open to the prosecution in an individual case, for good reason, to disapply its own policy or guidance: *R v A (RJ)* [2012] EWCA Crim 434 [84].

2. Should a prosecution now be brought in order to maintain confidence in the criminal justice system?

If it is determined that the case meets the Full Code Test and the original decision not to prosecute was wrong, prosecutors must then consider whether a prosecution should be brought in order to maintain public confidence.

Prosecutors should consider whether it is highly likely that a court will rule that a prosecution is an abuse of its process: see the section below on Abuse of Process.

If it is not highly likely that a court will rule that a prosecution is an abuse of its process, a prosecution should be brought, in order to maintain confidence in the criminal justice system.'

2.97 In the Guidance the CPS cite the 2019 decision of *R v Cole*[1] as an example of a case where the Crown had discontinued proceedings following a failed application for an adjournment for a witness to attend from overseas. A VRR Review concluded that the decision was wrong, as a hearsay application should have been made to read the witness' evidence, and the proceedings were subsequently reinstated. The court held on the facts that the decision to discontinue the case was not made in bad faith, and the subsequent reinstitution of proceedings did not constitute executive misconduct and was not an abuse of process.

1 [2019] EWCA Crim 1033.

2.98 Practitioners may also need to consider the operation of the Prosecution of Offences Act 1985, s 22B, which was inserted into the Act by virtue of the Crime and Disorder Act 1998, s 45. Section 22B confers the power on Chief Crown Prosecutors to institute fresh proceedings in circumstances where the original proceedings have been stayed under s 22(4), as a result of the expiry of the initial stage time limit.

2.99 The Crime and Disorder Act 1998 had also inserted a specific power in respect of offenders under the age of 18 under s 22B, which has since been repealed by the Policing and Crime Act 2009. The nature of re-instituted proceedings was considered under this section in *R (on the application of the DPP) v Croydon Youth Court*[1] where a prosecution against a young person had been stayed in the light of an expired 99-day time limit [now revoked], in circumstances where an extension had been refused because the Crown had failed to act with 'all due diligence and expedition'. The Crown re-instituted proceedings under s 22B and the justices duly stayed them as an abuse of process. The Divisional Court, in quashing the justices' decision to stay, did so in spite of the fact that the trial date was listed 300 days after the first court appearance, thus holding that a fair trial was still possible. One curious omission from Poole J's judgment in this decision is the lack of any reference to the alternative basis for a stay, namely the second limb, whereby in spite of the fact a fair trial was possible, it was unfair in the circumstances to try him. As James Richardson noted, in his commentary on the case:

> 'Where proceedings have been stayed on the expiry of a time limit, there must be some scope for some such argument, otherwise the time-limit provisions will be rendered completely pointless. To take an extreme example, if the facts justified the inference that the prosecution had made no effort to comply with the time-limit provisions in the knowledge that, in the event of a stay, the prosecution could be re-instituted, there would surely be the basis of an argument that this constituted such a manipulation of the processes of the court as to warrant a stay.'[2]

1 (2001) 165 JP 181, DC.
2 See [2001] 4 CLW, 29 January.

Police cautions

2.100 In the two decisions discussed below, the Courts have been required to consider cases where private prosecutions were brought against individuals who had previously accepted police cautions in relation to the same charges. Firstly, we consider the *Hayter* decision.[1] In *Hayter*, the police took the view that two 16-year-old defendants, who had been arrested for threatening unlawful violence and assault, could properly be cautioned for the offences as a means of disposing of the prosecution. Each defendant received legal advice, admitted his involvement in the offences, signed a form indicating that a caution did not preclude the commencement of proceedings against him by an aggrieved party, and was then duly cautioned. The victim's father proceeded to bring a private prosecution against the defendants in the Youth Court. In due course, the Youth Court ordered that the proceedings be stayed as an abuse of process and dismissed the Informations. The prosecutor appealed by way of case stated to the Divisional Court. It was held, allowing the appeal, 'that it was not an abuse of process to prosecute a defendant after he had been cautioned by the police unless the particular circumstances of a case disclosed an abuse'.

1 *Hayter v L* [1998] 1 WLR 854, QBD.

2.101 In *Hayter*, the defendants were apparently well aware that further criminal proceedings were not precluded, and the court found no unfairness to result from the private prosecution. Indeed, Poole J pointed out that the trial process contained sufficient 'common law and statutory mechanisms to ensure fairness' in reference to the defence's opportunity to apply for exclusion of the evidence of the caution in the event of the Crown seeking to admit it as evidence of an admission. This was a reference to the court's discretion, at common law, and under PACE, s 78, to exclude evidence.

2.102 In the 2006 House of Lords decision of *Jones v Whalley*,[1] the appellant, Whalley, had assaulted and injured Jones. Having admitted the offence of assault in interview, the police officer decided that he should be formally cautioned rather than prosecuted. He was informed that the effect of a caution was that he would not have to go before a Criminal Court in connection with the matter. However, sometime later, Jones brought a private prosecution against him in respect of the assault. The CPS declined to take over the prosecution of the case. In due course, the Justices, on hearing of the circumstances, stayed the proceedings as an abuse of process. Jones's appeal by case stated to the Divisional Court succeeded, but, in turn, Whalley's appeal to the House of Lords was allowed, thus reversing the Divisional Court's decision.

1 [2007] 1 Cr App R 2.

2.103 In the House of Lords, Lord Bingham agreed with the justices' conclusion, and held:

> 'The abuse complained of is not abuse impairing the fairness of the trial, since evidence of the admission and caution should be excluded. The abuse complained of goes, as in … *Ex parte Bennett* … to the fairness of trying Mr. Whalley at all in the circumstances.'

2.104 The appeal was decided on what was termed, the 'narrower issue', namely as to whether a private prosecution may or should be regarded as an abuse of process of the Magistrates' Court where the defendant has agreed to be cautioned formally by the police on the assurance that, if he agrees, he will not have to go before a criminal court. The 'broader issue', which was not decided upon, related to an arguable challenge to the *Hayter* decision, and was put forward by Counsel for Whalley.

2.105 Whalley's Counsel questioned whether, irrespective of what may be said to, or stated in a form given to, a person who is cautioned, conditionally cautioned, reprimanded or warned, it can ever be other than an abuse of process for a court thereafter to entertain a private prosecution against him. Lord Brown and Lord Mance were of the view that, until this broader issue was finally resolved, either by litigation or legislation, some form of modified *Hayter* warning would be helpful, to the effect that the police told an individual receiving a caution, that: 'the caution may not preclude a private prosecution and will not preclude a civil action'. Lord Mance added that the individual should further be advised of the court's power to stay a private prosecution in the event that it finds, despite the warning, it would be abusive for them to continue. Finally, both Lord Bingham and Lord Rodger went on to question the surviving right of private prosecution. Lord Rodger held that:

> ' … it seems to me that allowing private prosecutions to proceed, despite an assurance that the offender would not have to go to court, would tend to undermine not only the non-statutory system of cautions, but also the schemes for cautioning young offenders and adult offenders which Parliament has endorsed in the Crime and Disorder Act 1998 and the Criminal Justice Act 2003. A court is entitled to ensure that its process is not misused in this way.'[1]

1 See ss 22 and 23, CJA 2003; See the Code of Practice on Conditional Cautioning, and the Ministry of Justice Simple Caution for Adult Offender guidance issued on 8 April 2013 and amended on 14 November 2013.

2.106 An increasing reliance on 'out of court' disposals has led to similar challenges and a Government review of the disposal system.[1] For example, in *Guest v DPP*, a man was cautioned for an offence of assault occasioning actual bodily harm in the complainant's home.[2] The complainant had sustained injuries and the alleged attacker wrote a letter of apology. The CPS allowed the police to administer a conditional caution that required him to pay £200 compensation to G. The CPS initially justified the decision not to prosecute in response to a request for an explanation but later stated that the decision not to prosecute was erroneous but that it had no power to rescind the caution. The Crown subsequently conceded that the decision not to prosecute fell to be quashed.

1 See the 'Initial findings from the review of the use of out-of-court disposals' https://www.gov.uk/government/publications/out-of-court-disposals. The review was brought to an end by the Coalition Government. See also Padfield, 'Out-of-court (out of sight) disposals', CLJ 2010, 69(1), 6-8.
2 [2009] 2 Cr App R 26.

2.107 The Court held that the quashing of the conditional caution would not amount to an affront to the public interest but rather the very reverse, given the serious nature of the offence. Goldring LJ explained that:

> 'Criminal litigation is not a game ... It does not seem to me that ... a further prosecution would necessarily amount to an affront to public justice ... Indeed, many might think that what so far has happened deserves that description.'[1]

1 At paras 51–52.

2.108 The court noted that the caution in *Jones v Whalley* had been accepted by the defendant on the basis that it discharged liability for the offence. It could not be said that, where a conditional caution in respect of an alleged offence was quashed, any subsequent prosecution in respect of that alleged offence would inevitably amount to an abuse of proceedings. Sweeney J confirmed:

> '...[a]buse of process involves a judgment by a court, based on well-defined principles, on the particular facts of a case. A decision to stay proceedings is a rare outcome. In a case in which, in accordance with the Code for Crown Prosecutors, the evidential and public interest tests are otherwise met, it will thus be in only the most exceptional case, where the prosecutor can say with a high degree of certainty that a court will rule that a prosecution is proved to be an abuse of its process, that a decision not to prosecute is likely to be valid...'[1]

1 At para 58.

2.109 Unsurprisingly, the courts have also confirmed that being subject to an 'out of court' disposal for one type of offence in relation to an incident will not result in proceedings being stayed for prosecution on other grounds in relation to the same conduct. In *R v Gore and Maher*,[1] the court permitted convictions for GBH to stand despite the fact that the defendants had previously accepted 'on the spot' fixed penalty notices under the Criminal Justice and Police Act 2001 for respectively being involved in an altercation in a public place while drunk and behaviour likely to cause harassment, alarm, or distress. Fixed penalty notices could not be issued for offences under s 18 or s 20 of the Offences against the Person Act 1861. After the police reviewed the CCTV footage and learnt of the severity of the complainant's injury, they concluded that the notices were inappropriate. Gore and Maher were charged with inflicting GBH. Applications to stay the indictment as an abuse of process were refused. Gore pleaded guilty and Maher was convicted after trial. Both argued that the refusal to stay the indictment as an abuse of process was wrong in law.

1 [2009] EWCA Crim 1424. Followed in *R (on the application of Gavigan) v Enfield Magistrates' Court* [2013] EWHC 2805 (Admin).

2.110 The Court of Appeal held that the conviction was for a different offence than the ones for which the fixed penalty notices were imposed. The prosecution for the more serious offences had arisen because the officers had not known the full extent of the facts at the time. It was also clear that the notices did not suggest that by paying the fixed penalty, the defendants had discharged their liability to be convicted of a different, and more serious violent offence. Lord Judge CJ concluded:

> 'There was here no improper escalation of charge, nor any departure from any reasonable expectation that either appellant would not be prosecuted, if any more serious consequences of their conduct, and evidence justifying prosecution for an offence of violence, came to light after the issue of the notice. The reality is that on the night in question the defendants must have been thanking their lucky stars that they got away with the serious violence they had perpetrated. It was not an abuse of process for justice to catch up with them.'[1]

The legislation here is clear and the defendants can have had no reasonable expectation that a caution for low-level anti-social behaviour can discharge liability for a different and much more serious offence based on a different set of facts.

1 At para 16.

2.111 In the 2016 decision of *R (Lowden) v Chief Constable of Northumbria Police* it was re-iterated that the existence of a simple caution administered by the police or the CPS is not in itself a bar to a private prosecution being brought, but it may be an abuse of process for a private prosecution to be brought if an assurance was given in the course of administering the caution that there would be no prosecution.

1 [2016] EWHC 3536 (Admin).

2.112 In their published legal guidance the CPS have properly acknowledged that the administration of a caution may lead to a subsequent prosecution being held to be an abuse of process, citing the decision of *DPP v Alexander*[1] where the Divisional Court considered the effect of a caution in the context of the doctrine of autrefois:

> 'A caution is not a conviction for the purposes of those defences, notwithstanding that a caution will only be administered if the accused person admits his guilt. The principles of autrefois convict and autrefois acquit are applicable only where there has been a finding by a court of guilt

or innocence. They have no application to an extra-judicial procedure, such as the administration of a simple caution'.

However, the Court went on to say that, where criminal conduct has been the subject of an agreed caution, in the absence of good reason for it to be the subject of a subsequent prosecution, such a prosecution will generally constitute an abuse of the process of the court.

Crown divisibility

2.113 The concept of 'the Crown' or of 'the prosecution' has been in a state of evolution. The ambit of the concept became important in the area of criminal law in connection with the prosecution's common law duty of disclosure. Here the courts were concerned in particular cases to expand the concept so that, for example, forensic scientists were covered. In *R v Liverpool Crown Court, ex p Roberts*,[1] Glidewell LJ referred to the 'total apparatus of prosecution'. In *Blackledge*,[2] Taylor CJ referred to the Crown as an 'indivisible unity.'

1 [1986] Crim LR 622.
2 [1996] 1 Cr App R 326.

2.114 The concept of an indivisible Crown or, in reality, an indivisible State has not taken especially firm root in criminal law, perhaps recognising that the State is composed not only of separate government departments with their separate and possibly conflicting aims and policies, but is also composed of an increasing variety of semi-autonomous bodies and agencies. These bodies are the Crown Prosecution Service, the HMRC, the Health and Safety Executive and so on, all of which carry out the public function of criminal investigation and prosecution. Even within these bodies, however, there may be a disparity of function: for example the Inland Revenue is not primarily a prosecutorial agency and the investigation and prosecution of tax fraud is not one of its highest priorities.

2.115 In *R v W*[1] the two applicants were facing trial for conspiracy to defraud. At a preparatory hearing the defence submitted that the Crown was not empowered to prosecute and, further, that the proceedings were an abuse of process. The applicants appealed to the Court of Appeal to challenge the trial judge's first preparatory ruling that the Crown was so empowered. The prosecution case alleged a time-share fraud whereby large amounts of corporation and income tax were said to have been evaded. While the criminal proceedings commenced in 1996, in 1997 the former Inland Revenue (now Her Majesty's Revenue and Customs [HMRC]) agreed to accept a large settlement in relation to the company's tax liability.

1 [1998] STC 550, CA.

2.116 The defence argued that if the Crown, through the Inland Revenue, had elected not to prosecute for tax evasion but instead to accept tax, penalties and interest, then it followed that the Crown, through the CPS, were not empowered or entitled to ignore that election. The defence sought to stress the apparent fact that the Inland Revenue, in deciding not to prosecute, had liaised with the DTI, the Police Commercial Fraud Squad, and the CPS. At some stage, however, whereas the Inland Revenue took the view that a £3.5m transfer on bogus invoices could be regarded as a loan, the CPS took the view that the transfers gave rise to theft!

2.117 The question posed was whether, given that two linked government departments took different views, a criminal prosecution could proceed. Rose LJ, while dismissing the appeal for jurisdictional reasons, gave a ruling on Crown divisibility, albeit obiter. The court held that the Crown was divisible, in essence, because both branches were pursuing separate agendas and policies.

2.118 While this was not an abuse case on the facts, Rose LJ commented:

> 'Of course, Crown indivisibility may well be pertinent to a claim for abuse of process if, for example, the CPS were to prosecute when the Revenue, in accepting settlement from a taxpayer, had told him with the concurrence of the CPS, that he would not be prosecuted by anyone.'

2.119 In so commenting, Rose LJ was rightly acknowledging that, in certain cases, one can readily contemplate the Revenue binding the CPS, in the same way that police officers bound the CPS in *Dean*: see paras **2.20–2.28**. On the facts, it is submitted that the court adopted a realistic approach, given that the applicants had not been misled. Grey areas will no doubt continue to flourish, however, particularly in relation to cases of suspected serious tax fraud where HMRC's 'Hansard' policy comes into play.[1] It has been said:

> 'Although the statement makes it clear that the Board reserves to itself full discretion as to which course of action it takes, and the statement does not guarantee immunity from prosecution, in practice, once the Hansard statement is given, prosecutions are rare'.[2]

1 The Hansard policy is the system whereby, where serious fraud is suspected, the Board may in certain circumstances accept a money settlement instead of instituting legal proceedings in respect of fraud alleged to have been committed by a taxpayer.

2 See Elwes and Clutterbuck 'Tax and Criminal Prosecutions' [1999] Crim LR 139.

2.120 Where taxpayers have co-operated with the HMRC, perhaps having made confessions or declarations against their interest, only to find themselves being prosecuted, practitioners ought carefully to consider whether any express or implied assurances are evidenced, or even legitimate expectations breached. Where no argument lies as to abuse of process, consideration ought to be given to an application for judicial review in the rare circumstances where the decision of the CPS, to bring criminal proceedings, may be attacked on the basis that it was both unfair and contrary to the legitimate expectations of the taxpayer.[1]

1 See in particular the decisions of *R v IRC, ex p Mead* [1993] 1 All ER 772, and *R v IRC, ex p Allen* [1997] STC 1141; see also *R v IRC, ex p MKF Underwriters Agents Ltd* [1990] 1 WLR 1545. See also *R v Board of Inland Revenue, ex p Unilever* [1994] STC 841 and the *Postermobile* case in paras **2.37** and **2.38**.

Implied promises

2.121 The difficulties in mounting a challenge based on implied, as opposed to unconditional, express, promises, have been seen above, most notably in

Hamza. In *Hinchliffe*[1] the defendant had faced CDDA proceedings launched against him by the DTI prior to his prosecution by the SFO. In the course of agreeing a settlement with the DTI, he signed an agreed statement of facts. However, the admissions made by him in this court document were expressed as being made only for the purpose of the CDDA proceedings. Whilst the fact of his admissions did not play any part in the SFO's case, one of the co-accused nonetheless sought to introduce them and cross-examine him on them. Objection to this was made on the basis that H had only made the admissions on the basis of an implied promise that they would only be relevant as regards the CDDA proceedings. However, both the trial judge and Court of Appeal allowed the admissions, dismissing this objection.

1 [2002] EWCA Crim 837.

CONCLUDING REMARKS

2.122 For the practitioner, who is considering the question as to whether or not a breach of promise point arises, there are a number of practical steps to follow. The first, logically, is to determine whether there is, or is not, a 'promise'. It need not simply be a promise in the strict sense, for an 'undertaking' or 'representation' will also suffice. The promise may either be a clear, unequivocal, express promise or one which is sufficiently clear as to be robustly implied and inferred from the particular circumstances of a case.

2.123 The second step is to identify whether there is any evidence of a breach of the said promise. Needless to say, where there is no breach, there is no abuse.

2.124 As a third step, the practitioner may wish to determine whether any significant prejudice has been suffered by the accused. If such prejudice has been sustained that may well go to the fourth question, which relates to issues surrounding the 'fairness' of the proceedings. In certain abuse cases, however, the absence of prejudice will not be fatal to a successful submission. Evidence of prejudice to the individual has been declared unnecessary in cases involving unfairness, in the sense of the prosecution process bringing the administration of justice into disrepute.[1]

1 Per Staughton LJ in *Bloomfield* [1997] 1 Cr App Rep 135, CA.

2.125 The fourth step is arguably to identify whether or not a fundamental 'unfairness' has resulted, and this may involve a nuanced and complex assessment over the ramifications of the injustice, within our system of justice, balanced against the public interest in the prosecution of a particular defendant. In drawing together the strands identified in the case law, it is submitted that the courts have considered, what was previously described as a form of 'unfairness' test, from three particular perspectives, albeit there is a degree of overlap.

Unfairness to the accused

2.126 Was the act (or breach) manifestly unfair to the particular defendant or party to litigation? Was their position seriously prejudiced? These questions relate directly to whether or not a fair trial is possible and whether a stay should be granted under the first limb of the *Bennett* test.

Unfairness in the public perception

2.127 Would the act (or breach) bring the administration of justice into disrepute amongst right-thinking people? Is doubt cast on the bona fides of the prosecution? Lord Oliver, in the House of Lords decision in *Bennett,* considered this an important point when considering the *Dean*[1] authority.[2]

1 See the judgment of Lord Oliver in *R v Horseferry Road Magistrates' Court, ex p Bennett* [1993] 3 WLR 90 at 112F–H.

2 See Dean at p 132.

Unfairness from the judicial perspective

2.128 Does the act complained of offend the court's own sense of propriety and injustice? Using the language of the *Warren* decision, does the court consider a stay is necessary to protect the integrity of the criminal justice system? In breach of promise cases, it is likely that this particular second limb abuse consideration will be the most relevant one for the courts when assessing the merits of individual applications to stay, for the arguments are significantly less considered with forensic prejudice, or the injustice of the case from the Accused's perspective, and far more concerned with wider considerations such as ensuring public confidence in the criminal justice system.

Chapter 3

The loss or destruction of evidence

BACKGROUND

3.01 At the cornerstone of our adversarial system is a belief that the search for the truth in any criminal trial is best procured by combat between the two sides. The role of the criminal justice system through the provision of the various Codes of Practice, and availability of public funding for example, is to ensure that such combat is fair to both sides. If, therefore, the police enjoy a virtual monopoly over the investigation stage of a criminal offence, this advantage is to be ameliorated by an onerous obligation of disclosure to the defence post-charge. The Criminal Procedure Rules state clearly that the overriding objective is that criminal cases be dealt with justly, which includes dealing with the prosecution and the defence fairly.[1] In ECHR jurisprudence, the need to ensure a level playing field, is summed up by the 'equality of arms' principle: despite unequal resources, no party should be allowed an unfair advantage over the other.[2]

1 See r 1.1(1) and (2)(b) of the Criminal Procedure Rules 2020.
2 See *Regner v the Republic* (App No. 35289/11, 19 September 2017 (GC)), at [146].

3.02 In the English system, we strive to achieve the right balance between the opposing sides in order that the wrongly accused are acquitted and the guilty are convicted. This elusive balance and optimum state are ultimately the responsibility of judges who, in a concrete case, are obliged to do justice and serve fairness. An awareness of the recent celebrated miscarriage of justice cases, however, reveals that often judges are prevented from securing such noble objectives, prior to the trial, because evidence has been suppressed, lost, destroyed or perverted. This has the inevitable consequence that a trial, which in all appearances is scrupulously fair and dignified, is reduced to a charade where the search for the truth is an unachievable goal.

3.03 This chapter analyses the circumstances whereby the prosecution's failure to obtain and/or retain material evidence has led to applications to stay proceedings. This particular strand of the abuse of process jurisdiction has developed rapidly over the last few years, having regard both to the defining case law and the increased importance of the revised CPIA Codes in the light of the Attorney General's Guidelines on Disclosure. In this chapter, we first consider the current state of the common law (with emphasis on the guideline decision in *R (on the application of Ebrahim) v Feltham Magistrates*[1]); second, trace back briefly over the historical development of the case law, and finally review the important CPIA Codes of Practice (the most recent being the CPIA 1996 Code of Practice Order 2020) and the Attorney-General's guidelines.

1 [2001] EWHC Admin 130, [2001] 1 All ER 831.

3.04 It will be within the experience of many practitioners, when preparing a case for trial, that they discover something is 'missing' from the case. Whether it is a witness who becomes untraceable, an exhibit which disappears, or an item of unused material one discovers has been destroyed, all manner of things can, and do, go wrong within the system. The simple question then arises, as to what to do? More often than not a solution will be at hand, or at least a feasible damage limitation exercise will arise, which will not compromise a fair trial.

3.05 If the problem is remediable, that is the end of the matter. If it is not, the practitioner logically should go on to question what damage, if any, it will necessarily cause to the client's case. If, for example, the damage related to the prosecution's accidental destruction of a prosecution exhibit (of vital importance to the defence case), three questions may assist the practitioner in determining the extent of the issue:

(1) Does it seriously prejudice the preparation and conduct of the defence?

(2) Is the problem remediable within the trial process? For example, by suitable judicial directions or by the regulation of admissibility of evidence.

(3) Or is the dilemma so exceptional that the practitioner considers an abuse of process has been identified?

3.06 The above questions are relevant in determining whether the defence has sustained such serious prejudice that a fair trial is no longer possible. This is now described as a 'Category 1 case' in *Ebrahim*, the reference being derived from the first limb of Neil LJ's test in *Beckford.*[1] In the light of the *Ebrahim* decision, the courts will have a further consideration to take into account when considering certain prosecution failures to obtain and/or retain material evidence. They may also have to consider whether the defence have proved 'either an element of bad faith or at the very least some serious fault on the part of the police or the prosecution authorities'. These issues will be relevant to the courts' determination as to whether a 'Category 2 case' arises, namely a circumstance where it would be unfair for a defendant to be tried, irrespective of whether a fair trial was possible. Again, from the above, it will be clear that this description is taken from the second limb of Neil LJ's definition. Indeed, when looking at Category 2 cases, practitioners should now have regard to the revised definition of Neil LJ's second limb of abuse of process, because it is now clear that, whilst fairness to an accused may be a factor, the new test of limb 2 abuse, by virtue of the *Maxwell* and *Warren* decisions, applies where the particular circumstances of the case offends the court's sense of justice and propriety to be asked to try the accused.[2]

1 [1996] 1 Cr App Rep 94.
2 *R v Maxwell* [2011] 1WLR 1837, Dyson JSC, para 13 and *Warren and others v Attorney General for Jersey* [2012] 1 AC 22.

CONTEXT

3.07 One concomitant of the prosecution's duty of disclosure of both evidence and unused material is an obligation to preserve such material so that in due course it can be served on, or disclosed to, the defence. An obligation of disclosure which did not also presuppose an obligation to retain material would be rendered otiose. This obligation to retain material also arises as a matter of practical necessity. It is the police who invariably conduct the first investigation into the circumstances of the alleged offence, gathering witness statements and collecting forensic samples and so on.

3.08 Our criminal justice system has not adopted the European model of an independent judge or magistrate supervising and directing a police investigation in an inquisitorial and even-handed manner. Accordingly, in most criminal cases, by the time the defendant has instructed lawyers and such lawyers have become familiar with the issues in the case, the evidential trail has gone cold. This virtual monopoly enjoyed by the police over the gathering and retention of material, however, also carries with it a problem when the question of the obligation to retain material is considered. Clearly, bearing in mind, for example, the rights of third parties to retain their property, the police cannot be expected to seize and retain everything that might possibly be of relevance and therefore judgements of relevance in the field during the course of an inquiry are inescapable. The practical problem, therefore, is always to determine on the basis of limited information what ought to be preserved, even seized, and what need not. A legal obligation of preserving relevant material is easy to accept and understand in the abstract, but the question of relevance in a concrete case may be very hard to determine.

3.09 Inevitably, from time to time, instances have occurred whereby the police and/or prosecution have lost or failed to preserve material which could have had a bearing on a defendant's case at trial. It can easily be understood how this lapse can lead to prejudice being caused to the defence. The line of cases, to be considered below, traces how the common law has grasped this problem in an abuse context. Increasingly, over the last 20 years, both the Court of Appeal and the Divisional Court have had to consider a number of cases where the defence has, at first instance, made a failed abuse application relating to the destruction or loss by the prosecution of allegedly material evidence. On appeal, it has been contended that the trial judge wrongly refused the application and, because of the loss of potentially exculpatory material, the defendant did not receive a fair trial. Unsurprisingly, however, these courts of review have been concerned to ensure that unscrupulous and opportunist defendants are prevented from either successfully making false claims concerning the purported prejudice suffered because of the loss by the prosecution or constructing false defences ex post facto, based on knowledge of the unfortunate loss. This attitude of scepticism towards defence complaints of prejudice in these circumstances is consistent with that concerning defence complaints arising out of prosecutorial delay. In Chapter 1, the approach of Bingham CJ in *R v Cardiff Magistrates' Court, ex p Hole* was considered.[1] There Bingham CJ insisted that the defence, in arguing abuse, would have to establish precisely how in relation to the defence(s) to be advanced at trial prejudice was suffered, '… it is necessary to look at the charges and see exactly what defence it is that they are impeded from advancing'.

1 See para **1.21**.

3.10 In the light of *Ebrahim*'s focusing of initial attention on the question of investigating authorities' and the prosecutor's 'duties', this chapter closes with scrutiny of the true nature and extent of such 'duties'. We end by considering the more proactive disclosure duties and pose the question as to whether a failure to investigate a case properly can lead to an application to stay proceedings. Let us first consider the state of the common law as it now stands.

THE CURRENT STATE OF THE COMMON LAW

3.11 In *R (on the application of Ebrahim) v Feltham Magistrates*, and the linked case of *Mouat v DPP* (hereinafter called simply *Ebrahim*), the Divisional Court delivered the first clear and authoritative guideline judgment on the circumstances where lost or destroyed video material may lead to an abuse of process application. This important decision was partly motivated by the courts' ever-increasing workload of cases based on defence complaints of lost or unavailable CCTV footage. The authors suggest, however, that the principles contained in Brooke LJ's judgment in *Ebrahim* will not simply be limited to video cases. We suggest that, by analogy, they will have a far more general application to all manner of lost or destroyed material, whether it be used or unused.

3.12 Ebrahim's case involved his application for judicial review of a magistrate's decision to stay, on grounds of abuse of process, a prosecution against him for assault. Mouat's was an appeal by way of case stated from a Crown Court judge's decision to dismiss his appeal from his conviction in the magistrates for driving in excess of the speed limit. The facts of the respective cases can be stated briefly.

Mouat

3.13 Mouat had been stopped by police officers whilst driving his car, informed that he had been exceeding the speed limit, and given a fixed penalty ticket. The officers, who had been following him on the dual carriageway, took him into their vehicle and showed him a video recording of the incident. During his magistrates' court trial, he contended that, having initially not exceeded the speed limit, there came a time when, by reason of duress, he felt compelled so to do. At trial, the officers said that if Mouat had done or said anything to dispute the video evidence it would have been retained (for, in this case, the recording was destroyed).

3.14 The Divisional Court held that the videotape contained material which might have been relevant to the police investigation, and should have been retained at least until the end of the suspended enforcement period.[1] As it was the police acted in breach of their duty both under the Criminal Procedure and Investigations Act 1996 to preserve relevant material, and also by virtue of local police policy. The appeal was allowed.

1 At para 49.

Ebrahim

3.15 Ebrahim was charged with assaulting another customer in a Tesco superstore. At trial, he contended that he had only grabbed the man in self-defence, believing that he himself was about to be struck, having regard to an earlier incident when he first entered the store. At a preliminary hearing, the defence requested the CPS' help in obtaining any videotapes that may have shown the earlier incident. When it became apparent the police did not possess the tape in question, the defence applied successfully for a witness summons against Tesco for its production. When it transpired that the superstore had destroyed the tape some weeks after service of the summons, the defence complained that no effort appeared to have been made to preserve the tape or to comply with the summons.

3.16 At trial, the police officer in the case explained, however, that before arresting Ebrahim, he had gone to the CCTV room, and discovered that the location of the alleged assault had not been recorded on film. In those circumstances, he did not seize any of the large number of available videotapes. The Divisional Court found that, on the evidence, the officer had made a reasonable investigation in the circumstances; hence there was no breach of the previous CPIA Code, paras 3.4 or 3.5 (now paras. 3.5 and 3.6 in the 2020 revised code), pursuant to the CPIA 1996. Even if the police could have done more to ensure the retention of material, the court was persuaded by the district judge's statement that it was still possible, on the facts of this case, for the accused to receive a fair trial.[1] Ebrahim's application was dismissed.

1 At para 71.

Analysis of Brooke LJ's judgment

3.17 In the course of his judgment, Brooke LJ reviewed the development of the common law in this area, restated the principles underlying the abuse of process jurisdiction, and highlighted the salient features of the then 1997 version of the CPIA Code of Practice and the Attorney-General's 2005 guidelines (which, since December 2013, were replaced by the 2013 guidelines and, since December 2020, have now been replaced by the 2020 guidelines). The end product was a commendably clear and succinct statement as to how a court 'should structure its inquiries' when facing a defence submission on abuse of process in the light of lost or destroyed videotape evidence, namely:

> 'We would suggest that in similar cases in future, a court should structure its inquiries in the following way. (1) In the circumstances of the particular case, what was the nature and extent of the investigating authorities' and the prosecutors' duty, if any, to obtain and/or retain the [videotape] evidence in question? Recourse should be had in this context to the contents of the 1997 Code and the Attorney-General's guidelines. (2) If in all the circumstances there was no duty to obtain and/or retain that [videotape] evidence before the defence first sought its retention, then there can be no question of the subsequent trial being unfair on this ground. (3) If such evidence is not obtained and/or retained in breach of the obligations set out in the 1997 Code and/or the guidelines, then the principles set out in paras 25 and 28

of this judgment should generally be applied. (4) If the behaviour of the prosecution has been so very bad that it is not fair that the defendant should be tried, then the proceedings should be stayed on that ground. The test in para 23 of this judgment is a useful one.' [The above square brackets are inserted by the authors.]

3.18 By simply removing the bracketed words 'videotape' from the above passage, we are left with an approach worthy of general application to lost or destroyed evidence cases. Whether the case involves a lost videotape, a lost carpet (as in *Gajree*[1]), or a lost car (as in *Beckford*[2]), surely the principle must remain the same? We suggest that the courts will apply the same or a similar test, irrespective of the factual matrix of a given case, for the simple reason that issues of fairness and prejudice are of universal application, and are clearly not uniquely limited to videotapes. Indeed, the same point applies to investigators and prosecutors' duties generally in relation to the retention and preservation of material evidence, whatever it may be.

1 (20 September 1994, unreported).
2 [1996] 1 Cr App Rep 94.

3.19 Brooke LJ suggests an approach, therefore, which may be broken down into three distinct stages.

The first stage

3.20 What was the nature and extent of the investigating authorities and prosecutors' duty, if any, to obtain and/or retain the evidence? In determining that question, the court reasoned that regard should be paid to their duties, both under the CPIA Code and under the Attorney-General's guidelines on disclosure. Thus, in a given case, a court must first decide whether or not a particular videotape, for example, should have been retained. If the court decides there was no such duty, then any argument that a fair trial cannot be held will fail.

3.21 The key question for a court, when determining whether material should have been retained, depends upon the court's view as to whether the videotape, for example, was or may have been 'relevant to the investigation'.[1] The CPIA Code of Practice 2020 defines material which may be relevant in wide terms,[2] thus imposing an onerous obligation on investigators or prosecutors to retain material. Under the CPIA Code, para 2.8 the following definition is given:

> 'material may be *relevant to the investigation* if it appears to an investigator, or to the officer in charge of an investigation, or to the disclosure officer, that it has some bearing on any offence under investigation or any person being investigated, or on the surrounding circumstances of the case, unless it is incapable of having any impact on the case'.

1 See CPIA Code, para 5.1.
2 See CPIA Code, para 2.8.

3.22 This broad approach to retention decisions is in line with the Attorney-General guidelines to investigators[1] whereby they should 'exercise considerable caution' when concluding is not relevant and therefore need not be retained. It is submitted that the definition of 'relevance' is effectively the same as the *Keane*[2] disclosure test. The Code and guidelines are considered in more detail at paras **3.80–3.96**; however, it is important to remember that the investigating authorities and prosecutors' duty is not simply to retain; it is also, in certain circumstances, to obtain. The question then arises as to when it is appropriate to expect them to be proactive and seek out, for example, a given videotape? Each case will, of course, depend on its own particular facts. However, guidance is provided by the CPIA Code, para 3.5, namely:

> 'In conducting an investigation, the investigator should pursue all reasonable lines of inquiry, whether these point towards or away from the suspect. What is reasonable in each case will depend on the particular circumstances'.

1 See Guidelines, para 23.
2 [1994] 2 All ER 478, 99 Cr App Rep 1.

3.23 If a police officer, for example, palpably failed to make any attempt to acquire a known and highly material videotape which was subsequently destroyed, the first stage of Brooke LJ's test may well be met. The duty to investigate, however, is clearly proportionate to the issues involved,[1] relevant considerations being factors such as disclosure requests made and information supplied by a suspect.[2] The importance of the statutory duty, which disclosure officers and investigators have, to gather and record unused material is underlined by its inclusion in the Judicial Protocol on Unused Material 2013.[3]

1 See *R v Sahdev* [2002] EWCA Crim 1064, [2002] 166 JP 19.
2 See the commentary generally on *Ebrahim* [2001] Crim LR 741 at 743.
3 Judicial Protocol on the Disclosure of Unused Material in Criminal Cases, December 2013.

The second stage

3.24 If the material evidence is not obtained and/or retained, in breach of the CPIA Code obligations and/or the Attorney-General's guidelines, the court must go on to consider whether the defendant could nevertheless receive a fair trial, or whether this was a 'Category 1' abuse of process case.

3.25 The above statement is drawn from Brooke LJ's invitation to apply generally the principles set out in paras 25 and 28 of his judgment. Whilst the first of these paragraphs highlights the principle that the trial process itself is equipped to deal with the bulk of abuse complaints, the second restates Lane CJ's important dictum in *A-G's Reference (No 1 of 1990)*[1] that no stay should be imposed:

> 'unless the defendant shows on the balance of probabilities that owing to delay he will suffer serious prejudice to the extent that no fair trial can be held, in other words that the continuance of the prosecution amounts to a misuse of the process of the court'.

1 [1992] 3 All ER 169.

3.26 In this context, the simple test for a defendant will be whether or not he has proved, more likely than not, that, owing to the 'serious prejudice' caused by the lost or destroyed material, he cannot receive a fair trial. The 'serious prejudice' test in *Ebrahim* has since been followed by the Court of Appeal in a number of cases, including a recent judgment issued in 2014 (discussed below). It follows therefore that an element of prejudice will not suffice and must be tolerated. Only where the defence can successfully demonstrate a sufficient level of seriousness to the prejudice will a stay be considered, and this will depend on the facts of the particular case.

The third stage

3.27 If the behaviour of the prosecution has been so very bad that it is not fair that the defendant should be tried, then proceedings should be stayed under Category 2 of the abuse of process doctrine. In order to succeed, the defence must prove that there was either an element of bad faith or at the very least some serious fault on the part of the police or the prosecution authorities in their failing to obtain and/or retain the relevant material.

3.28 This third stage serves as a clear warning to the police and prosecuting authorities that certain levels of bad conduct on their part may well lead to a stay of proceedings. As a recent commentator on the *Medway* decision noted:[1]

> 'where a videotape is not available at trial, a key issue will be the degree of likelihood that it actually recorded anything of any consequence. The greater the likelihood that it did, the more significant will be the inquiry as to what happened to it'.

1 See commentary at [2000] 20 Cr LW, 29 May.

3.29 In the light of the extended disclosure obligations on the police, by virtue of the CPIA Code, the Judicial Protocol on Unused Material, and the Attorney-General's guidelines, significantly greater scrutiny may be placed on their actions and inactions. Findings by individual officers that videotapes contained 'nothing relevant' (which were then returned to third parties), instances of persistent non-disclosure and examples of the deliberate destruction of material evidence may well fall within this category. Even where police officers disregard or dispose of material in perfectly good faith they may well have to justify their decisions. In deciding whether 'serious fault' has been proven, the courts will presumably have 'to assess how likely it is that the particular evidence would have made a difference'.[1]

1 See Professor Smith's commentary also on the *Medway* decision, at [2000] Cr LRev 415.

Post-Ebrahim case law

3.30 The guidelines laid down in *Ebrahim* appear to have been generally followed in the subsequent case law. In *R v Dobson*[1] the Court of Appeal had to consider an abuse of process appeal mounted on the basis of police officers' admitted failings in their duty to obtain and retain certain closed circuit television footage. The court adopted the *Ebrahim* approach of separately considering both 'Category 1' considerations of 'serious prejudice' and also 'Category 2' considerations of 'serious fault'. On the facts in Dobson's case, the appeal was dismissed, for the court held that:

> 'Whilst there was plainly a degree of prejudice in *Dobson* being deprived of the opportunity of checking the footage in the hope it supported his case, that prejudice was not "serious prejudice", given the uncertainty of the likelihood that it would assist'.

A secondary factor that the court considered relevant to their finding of insufficient prejudice concerned the fact that Dobson's solicitors had not requested that the tapes be preserved. Further, the court drew the obvious distinction between 'malice or intentional omission, as opposed to oversight' and consequently found no element of bad faith (paragraph 37).

1 [2001] EWCA Crim 1606, [2001] All ER (D) 109 (Jul).

3.31 We now turn to the Court of Appeal decisions in *R v Howell*[1] and *R v Elliot.*[2] These decisions suggest, as contended above, that the principles in *Ebrahim* are generally applicable to any kind of lost or destroyed evidence argument, not simply to those relating directly to lost videotapes. In *Howell*'s case, which involved a motor vehicle destruction argument, the court, in dismissing the appeal, found insufficient prejudice and only 'minimal' fault on the part of the Crown. In *Elliot*, relating to the loss of various drugs exhibits, again the court found no evidence of undue prejudice or bad faith, nor reason to suspect that the loss of the exhibits 'had been due to anything other than an accident or as a result of incompetence'. The authors foresee the courts, in future cases, having to make difficult decisions in their attempts to distinguish between 'incompetence' and 'serious fault'. When does a 'fault' become a 'serious fault'? This will no doubt be answered by margins of fact and degree in individual cases, where paramount considerations relate to both the alleged materiality of the missing evidence and the conduct of the police or prosecuting authority. While the courts can expect difficult cases to come their way, the post-*Ebrahim* decision of *R v Sadler*[3] was not one of them. Keene LJ's judgment in *Sadler* (at paras 15–27), which adopts the test of Brooke LJ in *Ebrahim*, highlights the rarity of the circumstances required before the courts will stay cases on grounds of the 'serious misbehaviour' of the police or prosecution. Whilst the Court of Appeal in *Sadler* thus acknowledged the 'thoroughly reprehensible' negligent failings of the police (in relation to disclosure, and the retention of material exhibits), nevertheless, it held that these 'fell far short of making it unfair to try' the appellant.

1 [2001] EWCA Crim 3009, [2001] All ER (D) 250 (Dec).
2 [2002] 166 JP 18.
3 [2002] EWCA Crim 1722, [2002] All ER (D) 151 (Jun).

3.32 In the decision of *Boyd,*[1] the Court of Appeal touched on some of the differences between CCTV and non-CCTV destruction abuse cases. On the facts, a blood sample taken from the defendant, and later analysed by the prosecution, had been allowed to decompose, for it had not been properly preserved in a refrigerator or freezer. The court found that, if a sample had been examined by the defence, it may have established that there was no heroin materially affecting the appellant at the time she drove. Accordingly, the prosecution had deprived the defence of the opportunity of establishing a defence which might have been open to them. The case should have been stayed. Rose LJ held that: 'The situation where the scientific examination of samples is concerned, although subject to the same sort of principles as those enunciated …in *Ebrahim*, is very different from that where, as in that case, a videotape is not available but other lay witnesses may be able to speak of the events which occurred' (para 19).

1 *R v Boyd* [2004] RTR 2.

3.33 The 2007 case of *Ali v Crown Prosecution Service*[1] is an example of a recent decision where the Court had to consider the effect of missing evidence. The two appellants had been convicted at trial of false imprisonment, rape, and aiding and abetting rape. As a result of a seven-year delay, a number of documents were missing, including a copy of one of the victim's applications to the Criminal Compensation Authority, the credibility of which had been questioned, for the other victim admitted to having lied in her application. In addition, a police notebook which contained details of a police interview with the two complainants was missing, as was the evidence of the victims' first accounts of the incident. Moses LJ found that the prejudice flowing from the loss of the evidence was not capable of being cured by any judicial directions at trial, and allowed the appeals:[2]

> 'The mere fact that missing evidence might have assisted the defence will not necessarily lead to a stay. But in considering such powers to alleviate prejudice, Brooke LJ [referring to para 23 of the *Ebrahim* judgment] emphasised the need for sufficiently credible evidence, apart from the missing evidence, leaving the defence to exploit the gaps left by the missing evidence. The rationale for refusing a stay is the existence of credible evidence, itself untainted by what has gone missing. In the instant appeals, the missing evidence and the evidence which the jury had to believe cannot be distinguished in that way. That which was missing, T's application to the CICA, was part of the material by which her credibility could be assessed.'

1 [2007] EWCA Crim 691.
2 See paras 29–31 of the judgment.

3.34 By way of contrast to the *Boyd* decision above, we now consider the case of *DPP v Cooper*[1] where the Administrative Court allowed a prosecution appeal by case stated against a stay for abuse of process. The defendant was charged with possession of both diamorphine and criminal property, having been said to possess bank notes, which a prosecution forensic scientist said were overly contaminated with heroin. The magistrates stayed the case in the light of two principal defence complaints: first, the fact that the scientist's treatment of the notes with the Ninhydrin spray rendered them useless for further testing; and, secondly, due to the loss of a video tape which showed the various tests carried out by the scientist on the notes. Silber J., whilst acknowledging the defence were impeded to a certain extent by the missing evidence, nevertheless held that there were adequate alternate means to challenge the prosecution case, for example, by cross-examination of the scientist's methodology. The Administrative Court may well have been of the view that this was a defence argument based upon what Brooks LJ in *Ebrahim* described as a reliance on 'holes' in the prosecution case,[2] where there was sufficient other credible evidence with which the case could be tried.

The *Ebrahim* issue as to whether a fair trial is impossible, where such is in fact raised by a party as an issue at trial, was observed in *Foulser v Revenue and Customs Commissioners*.[3] In this case, the tribunal had proceeded on the basis that the applicant's case did not include a contention that the events in question had made a fair hearing of the tax appeal impossible. The tribunal therefore understood that the applicant was arguing instead that the commissioners were guilty of an abuse of process in the sense of unlawful behaviour in public law. On that basis, the tribunal had been right to hold that such a contention was not within its jurisdiction. However, it had now been established that the applicant's case did involve the contention that the relevant events had made a fair hearing of the tax appeal impossible. Therefore, the tribunal did have jurisdiction to deal with and determine that contention. The appeal was thus allowed and the case remitted to the tribunal.

The approach in *Cooper* was also applied in *R v Taylor (Paul Barry)*[4] where on appeal it was held that the judge was fully justified in refusing the application to stay the indictment. The nature of the 'error' in assessment of the original prosecution case in 1980 in deciding not to pursue a prosecution then did not bear on the question of whether a fair trial could take place. While the considerable interval between the events covered by the indictment and the trial created disadvantages for the defendant, the trial process was nonetheless capable of making due allowance for those difficulties and, properly directed, the jury was able, if appropriate, to reflect their judgment on those difficulties in their verdicts. Further, the absence of the trial papers from the court and the defence solicitors did not of itself render the admission of that evidence unfair. The fairness of the proceedings before a jury would be secured by a judicial direction pointing out that where holes existed, the burden was on the prosecution to remove any doubt created, which was the effect of the direction in the instant case on the impact of delay. This reinforces the original principle set out in *Ebrahim* that abuse of process would only be considered where a defendant could demonstrate on the balance of probabilities that it was no longer possible to conduct a fair trial.

In the recent case of *Clay v Clerk to the Justices*,[5] it was reiterated that where relevant evidence had been lost, the question was whether that disadvantage could be accommodated to ensure a fair trial. In the instant case, the defendant had been interviewed at the scene. He did not suggest that the victim (with whose vehicle his HGV had crashed) had been driving erratically and said that he had no explanation for the crash. However, the prosecution should have preserved the evidence (the victim's car) until the defendant had inspected it. It was undisputed that the victim had been making his way off the motorway because of a damaged tyre. However, evidence from two drivers who had been overtaking the victim at the time of the collision was that the victim had slowed down 'quickly' and without brake lights. The defendant argued that he had been deprived of the opportunity to see if the tyre had been safe and the brake lights had been in working order. It was not doubted that the police had acted in good faith but the justices had been wrong to find that the police had acted within normal and reasonable practice in allowing the car to be destroyed.

Nevertheless, the trial had been able to cope with any disadvantage that arose from the loss of evidence.

1 [2008] EWHC 507 Admin.
2 See para 27 of the judgment.
3 [2013] UKUT 38 (TCC).
4 [2013] EWCA Crim 2398.
5 [2014] EWHC 321 (Admin).

THE HISTORICAL DEVELOPMENT OF THE COMMON LAW

3.35 The Divisional Court in *Ebrahim* laid down a clear set of guiding principles, which courts and practitioners have since adopted as recent case law demonstrates (discussed above). A better understanding of exactly how the court arrived at its conclusions is gleaned by briefly reviewing the somewhat haphazard development of the common law. We do so, in chronological order, by considering on a case-by-case basis instances of lost or destroyed evidence generally, not confining ourselves to unavailable video/ CCTV footage cases.

3.36 By conducting this review, we can see how courts have previously scrutinised, and responded to, defence complaints of prejudice. It reveals how and when courts have sought to deal with prejudice within the trial process and, conversely, demonstrates the thresholds required before granting stays or allowing appeals.

3.37 The authors suggest that the year 1997 marked a significant turning point in the common law as a result, first, of the advent of the coming into force of the first CPIA Code of Practice and, second, in the light of the important judgment in *Reid*[1] which, ironically, was unreported. Where previously the courts had almost exclusively focused attention on the consequential effect of prejudice on a fair trial, from 1997 the equation entertained additional factors involving concepts of 'fault' and 'duty'. It became akin to some sort of quasi-criminal tort of negligence, where a 'duty of care' was owed. The new-found responsibilities on investigators and prosecutors (albeit with little or no statutory sanction for breaches of the Code) soon began to make their mark on the common law.

1 (10 March 1997, unreported).

R v Sadridin

3.38 In *R v Sadridin*,[1] the appellant had been convicted of a shoplifting offence and appealed on the basis of a failed abuse submission, having allegedly been deprived of vital evidence at trial, namely certain till rolls (which had been routinely destroyed by the store in question). The day after his arrest for theft he handed certain receipts to his solicitor and claimed he had found them subsequent to his arrest in a shopping bag. The receipts, which were in evidence at trial, were for the correct amount of the goods, but did not indicate either the type of goods or the identity of the purchaser. The defence asserted that in order to establish that these receipts really were for the allegedly stolen goods, the till rolls were required.

1 (11 July 1985, unreported).

3.39 In dismissing the appeal, Hirst J held that, on the evidence at trial, it was clear the till rolls were only of limited value and, in effect, could not have authenticated the receipts produced by the appellant, which point the appellant's appeal had depended on. The court also found that there was ample other evidence supporting the prosecution case. However, Hirst J stated that:

> 'If at sometime it had become clear that the absence of the destroyed documents was palpably of such crucial significance that a fair trial could not be conducted without them, it would always have been open to the judge, in the exercise of his discretion, to direct an acquittal'.

3.40 The above dictum is a reminder to practitioners to be ever-vigilant of an abuse submission emerging into a position of significance as proceedings continue. The fact that the submission fails on a pre-trial hearing, or at the outset of trial may not necessarily be the end of the matter for, of course, during a trial the significance of an exhibit can vary as the evidence emerges.

R v Sofaer

3.41 In *R v Uxbridge Justices, ex p Sofaer*,[1] the applicants were alleged to have attempted to export parts of aircraft, assembled or dismantled, to South Africa in 1983 at a time when such export was forbidden by the Export of Goods (Control) Order 1981. When interviewed, the applicants had claimed they were not in contravention of the export ban, for they had attempted to export scrap, as opposed to usable or serviceable parts. By the time of the committal proceedings, the customs officers, albeit acting within their powers, had disposed of the seized goods, in what was described by Pain J as 'a somewhat clumsy manoeuvre'.

1 (1987) 85 Cr App Rep 367.

3.42 Having made a failed abuse submission at the committal, the applicants applied for judicial review, alleging a breach of natural justice, stating they had been prejudiced in their defence by the disposal of the parts. The application was refused largely on the basis that there was in existence a full set of detailed photographs of the destroyed parts. Croom-Johnson LJ held that the photographs, as secondary evidence, were sufficiently adequate for the jury to reach a conclusion as to whether the aircraft parts were in fact usable parts, or scrap, as the applicants had asserted. A further difficulty which the applicants faced was that their own defence expert on committal proceedings made a damaging concession under cross-examination. While the expert stated that, in his view the parts did not appear to be serviceable ones, nevertheless he conceded that, given the availability of all the photographs, an actual inspection of the parts would not have taken the matter any further! Considerable doubt was thus cast on the weight which might have attached to any examination, had such examination been possible.

3.43 On the principle of preserving evidence Croom-Johnson LJ cited with approval the case of *R v Lushington, ex p Otto,*[1] wherein Wright J reasoned that:

> '… it is undoubted law that it is within the power of, and is the duty of "constables"—and for "constables" here read "Customs"—to retain for use in court things which may be evidences of crime, and which have come into the possession of the constables without wrong on their part'.

1 [1894] 1 QB 420.

3.44 In commenting on the above, Croom-Johnson LJ noted:

> 'That indeed is a general and very desirable standard which should be maintained and almost always is maintained. Unfortunately it is not always possible to apply it. Exhibits which are part of the evidence do go astray. Sometimes they are tested to destruction. In some cases it is only by testing them to destruction that you obtain the evidence in the first place … but where you cannot produce the original, you rely on secondary evidence …'.[1]

1 (1987) 85 Cr App Rep 367 at 377.

R v Sunderland Magistrates' Court, ex p Z

3.45 In *R v Sunderland Magistrates' Court, ex p Z,*[1] in 1988 the applicant, Z, was committed for trial on a charge of rape, the allegation being that he raped 'X' in 1979. At the committal hearing, Z made an abuse application submitting that, first, the delay in proceeding with the charge against him was excessive and, second, that this delay had resulted in prejudice to him. Examples of such prejudice were the destruction of various documents, clothing and vaginal swabs which made it impossible for the defence to have them forensically examined. However, the magistrates rejected the submission and indicated their intention to proceed with the committal. In response, the defence sought an order of prohibition to prevent the committal taking place.

1 [1989] Crim LR 56.

3.46 The Divisional Court granted the application, agreeing that in the circumstances a fair trial was no longer possible. The court also held that the delay in bringing proceedings against Z was unacceptable. This was on the grounds, first, that the applicant had not contributed to the delay, and, second, that the police had decided in 1979 not to proceed against Z on the grounds of insufficient evidence.

R v Birmingham

3.47 Following *Z* came the (then) most celebrated case on this subject, *R v Birmingham.*[1] The significance of *Birmingham* over, say, *Z* is that for the first time a successful abuse submission was based solely on the ground of destruction of evidence by the prosecution. It was not, for example, bound up with a submission relating to unconscionable delay in bringing the prosecution. While *Birmingham* has undoubtedly become an often-quoted authority on this subject, it is important to bear in mind that it was a first instance decision made by HH Judge Bromley sitting at Wood Green Crown Court.

1 [1992] Crim LR 117.

3.48 The facts in *Birmingham* were briefly as follows: seven defendants were charged with violent disorder at or outside a nightclub, and with various assaults on police officers who were called to the scene. Before the jury was sworn, the judge agreed to a voir dire in order to hear 'evidence from two of the prosecution witnesses on the existence and whereabouts of evidence believed to have been in existence at the time and of relevance to the case and possible use to the defence'. This evidence was a video recording of the locus in quo which had been created by an operational camera within the nightclub. After the incidents in question, the recording had been seized by the police and subsequently viewed by them. However, having done so, the recording was then returned to the nightclub and apparently lost (thrown into a skip). At the voir dire, it was discovered that the recording videotape had been viewed by the officers in the case, but that its existence had not been revealed to the defence even after specific requests for unused material. To make matters worse, the officers candidly admitted that they had taken no steps to preserve the recording because they had decided that it would not be helpful to the prosecution's case (although this was later corrected and said to mean not to help either side's case).

3.49 Sensibly, in order to attain a full understanding of the likely relevance of the recording, the judge attended the nightclub and surveyed the locus in quo for himself.

3.50 The reasons given by the judge for staying the prosecution were as follows:

(1) the prosecution had breached its duty of disclosure in relation to the recording which should have been disclosed to the defence;

(2) the recordings would have been relevant to the defendants' case. The fact that the police had apparently decided otherwise was not only erroneous but also misguided;

(3) in relation to the defence of alibi run by some of the defendants, the recording would have been relevant to this issue;

(4) the recordings could have assisted the defence in tracing potential defence witnesses.

For these reasons, the judge concluded that a fair trial was now impossible.

3.51 For its part, the prosecution had contended that the defence submission of abuse was, in reality, a matter to be determined by a jury and hence the trial should not be stayed. The judge, who was initially attracted to this view, held that the defence had been wrongfully deprived of material which should have been available during defence preparation. Furthermore, it did not, in the final analysis, relate to issues of guilt or innocence of the defendants, but to whether they could be fairly tried. Accordingly, the trial judge declined to follow *Heston-Francois*[1] as prosecution counsel had suggested.

1 For a full consideration of *Heston-Francois*, see paras **10.136–10.142**.

R v Gajree

3.52 Following *Birmingham* was the case of *R v Gajree*[1] where the appellant was convicted in 1994 of raping a 14-year-old girl, the offence allegedly having been committed in 1987.

1 (20 September 1994, unreported).

3.53 The appellant and the victim worked together at a shop. The victim alleged that, after the shop closed, she was taken by the appellant to the rear of the shop and there raped. She alleged that, after raping her, the appellant ejaculated onto the floor, which was carpeted. The victim did not make any complaint about this assault for a period of three weeks and, when she reported the matter to the police, there was a dispute between her and the police as to what exactly she told them. In any event, the police did not carry out any investigation of the locus in quo. There the matter remained undisturbed until 1991 (four years later) when an investigation commenced leading to the trial of the appellant. At the trial, an abuse application was made, which was rejected.

3.54 The Court of Appeal held that the abuse application should have succeeded in the Crown Court because of the destruction of evidence, in this case the shop premises where the alleged rape occurred. During the intervening period, there had been a fire at the shop and there was substantial damage to the premises and the carpet in question had also been destroyed. It was also important that a proper plan of the layout of the shop be taken but owing to the fire and lack of recollection this could not now be done. Sachs J asked, 'Was it possible for this appellant, at the time he stood trial, to obtain a fair trial?'

3.55 In quashing the conviction, Sachs J went on to add:

> 'We are satisfied that because of the passage of time and the inertia of the police officers, this appellant was deprived of evidence that might have otherwise been available to him and that … renders the verdict unsafe and unsatisfactory'.

R v Beckford

3.56 Our attention can now be turned to what was then regarded as the leading case on this subject, the judgment of Neil LJ in the Court of Appeal in *R v Beckford*.[1]

1 [1996] 1 Cr App Rep 94.

3.57 The facts were that the appellant was charged with causing death by careless driving when under the influence of drink or drugs. The appellant, who was driving, crashed his car into a concrete block killing his passenger. In terms of the cause of the accident the principle of res ipsa loquitur seemed to apply, the driver being to blame. Following this fatal accident, police examined the scene and the car, apparently finding no evidence of anything which might have caused the accident. Subsequently, the car was examined by a police forensic expert who also found nothing defective with the car. By a process of elimination, therefore, the police reached the conclusion that the driver must be to blame. When questioned about what had happened, the appellant refused to provide an explanation. Seven months after the accident, the appellant was summonsed. However, during the intervening period the car had been scrapped, the police having given no instructions for it to be preserved.

3.58 At the trial, an abuse application was made on the ground that if the car had not been scrapped it might have provided vital evidence for the defence. The defence complained it had had no opportunity to examine the car and to discover whether there was any defect in it which caused the accident. It submitted abuse but the trial judge said this was a matter for the jury and rejected the application.

3.59 During the trial, the defence also called an expert whose evidence was to the effect that the cause of the accident was probably due to mechanical failure (steering-wheel lock) and not, as the prosecution contended, that the appellant fell asleep while driving. The appellant again, however, did not give evidence of what he claimed had happened, he being the only witness. In the event, the appellant was convicted and appealed. The central issue was whether the proceedings should have been stayed because of the premature destruction of the car. Could the defendant receive a fair trial, despite the wrongful deprivation of the opportunity to test the findings of the prosecution as to there being no evidence of mechanical fault?

3.60 When considering the law on abuse, Neill LJ analysed it[1] as follows:

> 'The jurisdiction to stay can be exercised in many different circumstances. Nevertheless two main strands can be detected in the authorities:
>
> (1) cases where the court concludes that the defendant cannot receive a fair trial;
>
> (2) cases where the court concludes that it would be unfair for the defendant to be tried'.

1 [1996] 1 Cr App R 94, 100-101. As noted previously, the second limb has since been revised by the *Maxwell* and *Warren* decisions.

3.61 Neill LJ considered *Gajree*, which the defence argued was analogous to this case. Without reasoning that *Gajree* was of no use to his consideration, Neill LJ emphasised that 'each case has to be considered on its own facts'. Having stated this, he concluded that the judge was correct to reject the abuse application. According to Neill LJ, there was no evidence to support the defence hypothesis as to the cause of the accident and that the trial was fair:

> 'There had been no evidence of problems of steering the car in the past, no marks on the road that the brakes had been applied, and the prosecution witnesses were of the opinion that the position of the car did not accord with the defence hypothesis of a steering-wheel lock'.

3.62 At the end of his judgment, Neill LJ said:

'It is to be hoped that procedures have been put in place to ensure that cars are not scrapped before express permission has been given by the police and that permission will never be given where serious criminal charges are to be brought which may involve the possibility of some mechanical defect in a car'.

3.63 Are the decisions in *Gajree* and *Beckford* reconcilable? In the light of the clear similarities between the cases of *Gajree* and *Beckford*, at first it is difficult to comprehend the court's finding in the *Beckford* case that no unfairness resulted. On the face of it, is this not yet another clear case in which the defence were wrongly deprived of the opportunity to either put forward a defence or discredit the Crown's case? The difference and the distinguishing feature between these two cases is that in *Gajree* it was accepted that there had been in existence evidence which was relevant to the defence, ie the carpet. In both these cases, the defence had positively asserted that such evidence, if obtainable, would have assisted their cases. But in *Beckford* the relevance of the scrapped car arose only because of a defence expert advancing a hypothesis at the trial. No positive assertion of mechanical failure could be made because the defendant, who could have provided such evidence, had nonetheless chosen not to provide a version of events specifically. He had declined to answer any questions on arrest and interview detailing exactly how the steering-wheel had locked.

3.64 It is submitted that the Court of Appeal (and probably the trial judge) took great cognisance of the fact that the defendant himself had chosen not to give an explanation and not to allow this to be tested by cross-examination. Almost certainly to the court, such a decision had all the hallmarks of a defence being concocted as a result of the discovery of the failure of the police to preserve the car. In such a circumstance, despite the obvious failure by the police and its obvious prejudicial affect, it seems that the court was determined to ensure that the defendant did not unfairly profit from this. It is also to be borne in mind that the burden of proving an abuse lies on the defendant and, in the final analysis, the court was not satisfied that this burden had been satisfied by the mere fact of the premature destruction of the car and the advancing of a hypothesis by the defence expert at the trial.

3.65 The paradox of the situation in *Beckford* is, of course, that, in satisfying the burden on him, the appellant's job was made more difficult because of the loss of evidence. It is interesting to note that the decision in *Beckford* (while different on the facts) reflects to some extent the recent case of *Clay v Clerk to the Justices* (discussed in para **3.34** above) which similarly involved an argument of abuse of process due to destruction of a vehicle where it was submitted by the defendant that the (victim's) vehicle could have established an alternative account of how the accident actually happened had it not been destroyed. One might well share the view of an author who commented:

'The court [in *Beckford*'s case] declined to draw the inference proposed by the appellant, because he produced little or no evidence in support of it. But was that not precisely what he was telling the courts at the trial and on appeal—that he could produce little or no evidence because he had been deprived of it by police inaction'.[1]

1 See (1995) J Cr L 59. See also the commentary on *Beckford* by John Arnold, in *Building on the Decade of Disclosure in Criminal Procedure* (2001), at p 155.

R v Northard

3.66 In *R v Northard*[1] the Court of Appeal allowed an appeal based on another video destruction abuse submission. A jeweller's employee was robbed of a bag containing a quantity of cash, while en route to the bank in a town's shopping centre. The prosecution case was that the appellant had been the 'getaway driver' of a motor car into which the robber had fled. One prosecution witness had an opportunity to observe the driver of the car for some three minutes or so at close range, and took a note of the registration number, at about 11.30 am. The owner of the vehicle was traced and gave evidence that, between 10 and 11 am on the same day, the appellant borrowed his car. That same evening, the car was found abandoned, some three miles away from the scene of the robbery. When the owner looked at it, he found a flat battery, burned wiring and a missing radio. Further, police officers at trial conceded that the state of the car was consistent with it having been stolen. At 2.15 pm that day, some hours after the robbery, the appellant visited the town's police station and reported that the car he had borrowed was stolen. He was duly arrested.

1 (19 February 1996, unreported).

3.67 In police interviews, he repeated that he had borrowed the car and had spent the material time shopping in the town centre (noting the particular shops he had been in or looked in), before visiting a public house between noon and 12.30 pm, which visit several witnesses confirmed at trial in statements which were read. Further, in interview he agreed to stand on an identification parade, gave a detailed account of his movements, and challenged the police to verify his movements by viewing shop video films. At a later stage, he withdrew the offer to stand on an ID parade, but nevertheless invited officers to show photographs to the witnesses who claimed to have seen the robbers.

3.68 On appeal, the appellant argued the failed abuse submissions in the lower court, which consisted of numerous complaints into the police and/or prosecution investigation or conduct of the case. It was claimed that the defence had been led to believe that the police would make every effort to trace and preserve any available video evidence that might have supported the alibi. In reality, the police did obtain and view the videotape evidence but neither the police nor the CPS disclosed its existence to the defence. The officer in the case stated that having viewed the videos of the shopping centre, which showed large crowds of shoppers, it had not been possible to identify any individuals. Twenty-eight days after the incident, the videos had been re-used and the recordings lost. A second defence complaint was that the investigating officer failed to adequately instruct other officers to check the appellant's alibi, by visiting two particular shops. Additionally, there were further alleged failures to check security videos, arrange ID parades and failures to conduct expert examination of the vehicle in question.

3.69 Auld LJ held that the trial judge should either have stayed the prosecution as an abuse or withdrawn it from the jury. The court was concerned by a number of deficiencies and unsatisfactory features and identified 'an accumulation of lost opportunities to the defence to vouch for the alibi, if a true one'. The failure of the prosecution to disclose the existence of the video until it was too late was held to deprive the defence of the opportunity to check the video for themselves, to see if it supported the defence account. Auld LJ wisely noted that the appellant and his solicitor may have examined the video with 'keener eyes' than the police officer. The police were further found to have failed to act on the appellant's initial offer to stand on an ID parade in respect of the only witness who apparently had a good opportunity to observe the robbers. As Auld LJ noted, 'her evidence would have damned or exonerated the appellant'.

R v Reid

3.70 In *R v Reid*[1] Owen J considered some of the above authorities in the context of yet another video destruction case. Reid had faced robbery and assault charges arising out of an incident in a chemist's shop. The dispute at trial was as to whether the appellant had been acting by way of self-defence. While both complainants had knife wounds (from the appellant's knife), the appellant had suffered acid burns, and the simple issue was who had started to use force first. A police officer testified that there had been a recording of the interior of the shop (from an internal security video) but that it had not been preserved. The officer stated that he watched it and nothing on it appeared relevant. By the time of trial, the recording, for reasons that are not clear, had been destroyed. The defence apparently requested, and were granted, a voir dire before the jury were empanelled, for evidence to be heard. In that hearing, the judge accepted the officer's account that having scanned the video, nothing of relevance arose.

1 (10 March 1997, unreported).

3.71 In dismissing the appeal, Owen J sought to distinguish the facts in *Reid*'s case from those of *Birmingham* and *Northard*. The Court of Appeal found itself unable to conclude, either that the video had been relevant, or that the circumstances in which it had disappeared were so unfair as to make the conviction unsafe. It is submitted that the case might, of course, have been decided differently if the cameras had been trained on a more relevant part of the premises, or in circumstances where the officer had made concessions as to relevance of the video.

3.72 Taking the opportunity available to him in *Reid*, Owen J clearly enunciated the existence of the abuse of process jurisdiction in circumstances where there has been a failure to preserve relevant material in criminal proceedings:

> 'There is now a clear duty to preserve material which might be relevant, and nothing in this judgment is meant in any way to cast a doubt on that duty. However, clearly there must be a judgment of some kind by the investigating officer. He must decide whether material may be relevant, and if he does not preserve material which may be relevant, then for sure in the future he may be required to justify his decision, and he may find that, if the breach of his duty is sufficiently serious, that somebody who is in fact a guilty man has to go free because there has been an abuse of process … The position is that

if there has been a failure to preserve relevant material then it may be found that to proceed with a prosecution in those circumstances would be an abuse of process'.

3.73 It is interesting to note that Owen J's judgment in *Reid* was delivered a few weeks before police officers acquired a statutory duty, pursuant to para 5 of the CPIA Code of Practice, to retain material which may be relevant to a police investigation. The wording of the judgment may not, in these circumstances, have been entirely coincidental. This unreported decision of *Reid*, referred to in *Ebrahim*, appears to be the first occasion where the Court of Appeal has openly acknowledged this discrete category of abuse of process, that is, where there has been a failure to preserve relevant material.

R v McNamara[1]

3.74 In this case, police officers had searched the family home and allegedly found quantities of drugs. As the search continued, an officer recorded items of interest and the appellant's comments, some of which amounted to admissions to possession of cannabis. The same were recorded in the pro forma Book 101, being the search record. The appellant later denied making the admissions and, by the time of trial, the Book 101 had been lost, apparently due to 'poor exhibit management'. The defence argued at trial, and on appeal, that the loss of the Book 101 rendered the proceedings an abuse of process. A variety of authorities were relied on, principally *Birmingham*.

1 [1998] Crim LR 278.

3.75 The Court of Appeal unsurprisingly rejected the appellant's argument that the *Birmingham* situation was analogous. First, the court noted that unlike *Birmingham*, the Book 101 was not deliberately destroyed by any officer. Second, the loss of the exhibit would only be of detriment to the Crown and, last, unlike the video film example, the Book 101 was not an item of original evidence.

R v PR

3.76 The appellant appealed against his convictions in respect of four counts of indecency with a child, contrary to the Indecency with Children Act 1960, s 1(1). The allegations stemmed from 2002, with the complainant making a report to the police in the same year. At that time, the police undertook a video-recorded interview with the complainant. Due to the absence of forensic evidence, it was only after the complainant urged the police to re-open the matter in 2016 that the appellant was tried for the offences. The video-recorded interview made in 2002 had been lost. There was, however, other evidence, including records from social services and a copy of the transcript of the appellant's initial police interview. At trial, the appellant submitted that the prosecution ought to be stayed on the ground of abuse of process, contending that there could not be a fair trial. The judge did not order a stay of proceedings, instead directing the jury as to the missing material and its implications for the burden and standard of proof.

The Court of Appeal dismissed the appeal. In doing so, the court made some general observations as to the unavailability of evidence in criminal trials:

> 'It is important to have in mind the wide variations in the evidence relied on in support of prosecutions: no two trials are the same, and the type, quantity and quality of the evidence differs greatly between cases. Fairness does not require a minimum number of witnesses to be called. Nor is it necessary for documentary, expert or forensic evidence to be available, against which the credibility and reliability of the prosecution witnesses can be evaluated. Some cases involve consideration of a vast amount of documentation or expert/forensic evidence whilst in others the jury is essentially asked to decide between the oral testimony of two or more witnesses, often simply the complainant and the accused. Furthermore, there is no rule that if material has become unavailable, that of itself means the trial is unfair because, for instance, a relevant avenue of enquiry can no longer be explored with the benefit of the missing documents or records. It follows that there is no presumption that extraneous material must be available to enable the defendant to test the reliability of the oral testimony of one or more of the prosecution's witnesses. In some instances, the opportunity exists; in others it does not. It is to be regretted if relevant records become unavailable, but when this happens benefit of the missing documents or records. It follows that there is no presumption that extraneous material must be available to enable the defendant to test the reliability of the oral testimony of one or more of the prosecution's witnesses. In some instances, this opportunity exists; in others it does not. It is to be regretted if relevant records become unavailable, but when this happens the effect may be to put the defendant closer to the position of many accused whose trial turns on a decision by the jury as to whether they are sure of the oral evidence of the prosecution witness or witnesses, absent other substantive information by which their testimony can be tested.'[1]

In the particular circumstances of *PR*, the Court of Appeal held that, though relevant records had been destroyed, the appellant was in possession of a substantial amount of material, which could be used to challenge the complainant's reliability and credibility.[2]

1 At para 65.
2 At para 72.

Hamilton v Post Office[1]

3.77 Forty-two employees of the Post Office (or its predecessors) were all prosecuted by their employer for, and convicted of, crimes of dishonesty. Years later, the Criminal Cases Review Commission referred their cases to the Court of Appeal. The convictions largely rested on inaccurate data drawn from the Horizon system, an electronic point-of-sale and accounting system. Once that inaccuracy become known, the CCRC considered that the appellants had two grounds of appeal, one based on the impossibility of a fair trial and the other based on the affront to the public conscience for the trial process to have proceeded.[2]

The Court of Appeal reasoned that, despite the private prosecuting authority's duty to consider reasonable lines of inquiry and make disclosure accordingly, the authority did not adequately consider the concerns about Horizon. Indeed, the authority 'consistently asserted that Horizon was robust and reliable'.[3] Such 'pervasive failures went in each case to the very heart of the prosecution'.[4] The failings were enough to justify a finding of both category 1 abuse of process and category 2 abuse of process, given the deliberate failure to comply with prosecutorial obligations, the clear evidence of systemic failures, the human costs and consequences of the failures, the direct implication of the courts, and the importance of public confidence in the criminal justice system.[5]

1 [2021] EWCA Crim 577.
2 At para 59.
3 At para 121.
4 At para 123.
5 At paras 129–135.

Miscellaneous cases

3.78 Finally, in the two years or so immediately preceding the *Ebrahim* decision, came a number of mainly unreported video destruction cases, which were possibly responsible for prompting the court in *Ebrahim* itself to conduct such a thorough review of the previous authorities. The first of these, *R v Swingler*,[1] concerned a lost video film in the context of a rape investigation. Whilst the Court of Appeal accepted that the lost evidence had been 'of potentially great significance', it dismissed the appeal on the basis that the defence had been unable to point to any significant fault on the part of the police investigating. What was described as a useful test for deciding 'Category 2' abuse submissions, by Brooke LJ in *Ebrahim*, was the same approach suggested earlier by Rougier J in *Swingler*, albeit there in relation generally to arguments based on the disappearance of evidence. The two subsequent decisions of *R v Chipping*[2] and *R v Medway*[3] add little to the development of principle in this area. What can be noted, however, is in both *Swingler* and *Medway* the Court of Appeal appeared to move away from the classic dual fairness test in *Beckford* and towards a narrower more restrictive interpretation. In *Medway*, the court held that there would need to be something wholly exceptional about the circumstances of a case to justify a stay on the ground that evidence had been lost or destroyed, citing as an example, a malicious interference with evidence.

1 (10 July 1988, unreported), CA.
2 (11 January 1999, unreported), DC.
3 [2000] Crim LR 415, CA.

3.79 In the last pre-*Ebrahim* decision which we consider, *R v Stallard*,[1] the pendulum swung back in favour of the broader dual approach, to be later adopted in *Ebrahim* itself. In *Stallard* the Court of Appeal, in yet another video destruction case, considered both whether a fair trial was possible (a Category 1 decision) and also whether the police were seriously at fault (a Category 2 decision).

1 (13 April 2000, unreported), CA.

CRIMINAL PROCEDURE AND INVESTIGATIONS ACT 1996 CODE OF PRACTICE

3.80 This Code of Practice was promulgated pursuant to the Criminal Procedure and Investigations Act 1996, s 23(1) ('CPIA 1996'). There have been various iterations of the Code of Practice since 1996. The most recent version came into force on 31 December 2020. It applies in respect of all criminal investigations conducted by police officers which began on or after 1 April 1997. One highly significant aspect of the Code is that for the first time the way in which police or other investigators conduct a criminal investigation generally is governed by a public Code of Practice. In comparison with the PACE Code of Practice which is concerned only with a narrow area of police operation, mainly the treatment and questioning of suspects post-arrest, this Code is directed at all police conduct, pre- and post-arrest, and is designed to impose clear standards of fairness and accountability.

3.81 In general terms, the Code of Practice sets down detailed regulations in respect of:

(1) the presentation of material by an 'investigator';

(2) the revelation of such material by the investigator to the prosecutor.

3.82 In the light of the focusing of attention in *Ebrahim* and the cases that have since followed on the duties of investigators and prosecutors to obtain and/or retain evidence, it becomes essential to understand fully the nature and extent of these important duties.

3.83 Under the heading 'Responsibilities', in relation to Investigators and Disclosure Officers, the Attorney-General (at para 8 of the guidelines) makes the following emphatic statement:

> 'Investigators and disclosure officers must be fair and objective and must work together with prosecutors to ensure that disclosure obligations are met. Investigators and disclosure officers should be familiar with the CPIA Code of Practice – in particular their obligations to **retain and record** the relevant material, to **review** it and to **reveal** it to the prosecutor (see paragraphs 3–7 of the Code).'

3.84 The authors submit that the above description of 'a failure to take action leading to inadequate disclosure' may well encompass a failure to obtain and/or retain material evidence. The Attorney-General is correctly acknowledging that, at common law, the judicial remedy of a stay is a possible sanction in relation to disclosure failures. Proven breaches of the Act, Code or guidelines, for that matter, may form the basis of an abuse of process application, or, indeed, an application to exclude evidence under PACE, s 78.

3.85 In contrast to the position under PACE, however, where the most effective remedy lies within the Act itself, there is an almost complete absence of sanctions either within the CPIA 1996 or its Code of Practice. The remedy lies within the common law discretion to stay proceedings as an abuse of process. Whereas a practitioner in a PACE case may apply for exclusion of evidence, very serious breaches of the CPIA Code, which might well prejudice an accused's ability to defend himself, do not attract any built-in statutory sanction. The passage of the Criminal Procedure and Investigations Bill through Parliament did indeed see calls for the provision of specific sanctions for non-compliance with the Code, but these were vehemently resisted by the then government.[1] The government's argument was to the effect that serious breaches could, in any event, trigger possible criminal or disciplinary proceedings against the offending police officers. The few sanctions which do exist are not related to the context of this chapter, having regard to prosecutors' observing of time limits (CPIA 1996, s 10(2)) and inferences against an accused (CPIA, s 11(2), (3) and (4)).

1 There is some related commentary by David MacLean in Hansard, HC Deb (8 December 1995, vol 268), cc 603–78, 614.

THE DUTY TO OBTAIN AND/OR RETAIN MATERIAL UNDER THE CPIA CODE

3.86 The following are relevant extracts taken from the Code, which is set out in full at Appendix C to this work:

> 'General Responsibilities
>
> 3.4 The officer in charge of an investigation may delegate tasks to another investigator, to civilians employed by the police force, or to other persons participating in the investigation under arrangements for joint investigations, but they remain responsible for ensuring that these have been carried out and for accounting for any general policies followed in the investigation. In particular, it is an essential part of their duties to ensure that all material which may be relevant to an investigation is retained, and either made available to the disclosure officer or (in exceptional circumstances) revealed directly to the prosecutor.
>
> 3.5 In conducting an investigation, the investigator should pursue all reasonable lines of inquiry, whether these point towards or away from the suspect. What is reasonable in each case will depend on the particular circumstances. It is a matter for the investigator, with the assistance of the prosecutor if required, to decide what constitutes a reasonable line of inquiry in each case.
>
> 3.6 If the officer in charge of an investigation believes that other persons may be in possession of material that may be relevant to the investigation, and if this has not been obtained under paragraph 3.5 above, they should ask the disclosure officer to inform them of the existence of the investigation and to invite them to retain the material in case they receive a request for its disclosure. The disclosure officer should inform the prosecutor that they may have such material. However, the officer in charge of an investigation is not required to make speculative enquiries of other persons; there must be some reason to believe that they may have relevant material. That reason may come from information provided to the police by the accused or from other inquiries made or from some other source.

3.7 If, during a criminal investigation, the officer in charge of an investigation or disclosure officer for any reason no longer has responsibility for the functions falling to them, either their supervisor or the police officer in charge of criminal investigations for the police force concerned must assign someone else to assume that responsibility. That person's identity must be recorded, as with those initially responsible for these functions in each investigation.

Recording of Information

4.1 If material which may be relevant to the investigation consists of information which is not recorded in any form, the officer in charge of an investigation must ensure that it is recorded in a durable or retrievable form.

4.2 Where it is not practicable to retain the initial record of information because it forms part of a larger record which is to be destroyed, its contents should be transferred as a true record to a durable and more easily-stored form before that happens.

4.3 Negative information is often relevant to an investigation. If it may be relevant it must be recorded. An example might be a number of people present in a particular place at a particular time who state that they saw nothing unusual.

4.4 Where information which may be relevant is obtained, it must be recorded at the time it is obtained or as soon as practicable after that time. This includes, for example, information obtained in house-to-house enquiries, although the requirement to record information promptly does not require an investigator to take a statement from a potential witness where it would not otherwise be taken.

Retention of material

(a) Duty to retain material

5.1 The investigator must retain material obtained in a criminal investigation which may be relevant to the investigation. Material may be photographed, video-recorded, captured digitally or otherwise retained in the form of a copy rather than the original at any time, if the original is perishable: the original was supplied to the investigator rather than generated by them and is to be returned to its owner; or the retention of a copy rather than the original is reasonable in all the circumstances.

5.3 If the officer in charge of an investigation becomes aware as a result of developments in the case that material previously examined but not retained (because it was not thought to be relevant) may now be relevant to the investigation, they should, wherever practicable, take steps to obtain it or ensure that it is retained for further inspection or for production in court if required.

5.4 The duty to retain material includes in particular the duty to retain material falling into the following categories:

- Records which are derived from tapes or recordings of telephone messages (for example, 999 calls) containing descriptions of an alleged offence or offender;

- Any incident logs relating to the allegation;
- Contemporaneous records of the incident, such as:
  - –crime reports and crime report forms;
  - an investigation log;
  - any record or note made by an investigator (including police notebook entries and other handwritten notes) on which they later make a statement or which relates to contact with suspects, victims or witnesses;
  - an account of an incident or information relevant to an incident noted by an investigator in manuscript or electronically;
  - records of actions carried out by officers (such as house-to-house interviews, CCTV or forensic enquiries) noted by a police officer in manuscript or electronically;
  - CCTV footage, or other imagery, of the incident in action;
- The defendant's custody record or voluntary attendance record;
- Any previous accounts made by a complainant or any other witnesses;
- Interview records (written records, or audio or video tapes, of interviews with actual or potential witnesses or suspects);
- Any material casting doubt on the reliability of a witness e.g. relevant previous convictions and relevant cautions of any prosecution witnesses and any coaccused;
- Final versions of witness statements (and draft versions where their content differs from the final version), including any exhibits mentioned (unless these have been returned to their owner on the understanding that they will be produced in court if required);
- Material relating to other suspects in the investigation;
- Communications between the police and experts such as forensic scientists, reports of work carried out by experts, and schedules of scientific material prepared by the expert for the investigator, for the purposes of criminal proceedings;
- Records of the first description of a suspect by each potential witness who purports to identify or describe the suspect, whether or not the description differs from that of subsequent descriptions by that or other witnesses.'

5.5 The duty to retain material where it may be relevant to the investigation also includes in particular the duty to retain any material which may satisfy the test for prosecution disclosure in the Act, such as:

- information provided by an accused person which indicates an explanation for the offence with which they have been charged;

- any material casting doubt on the reliability of a confession;
- any material casting doubt on the reliability of a prosecution witness.

5.6 The duty to retain material falling into these categories does not extend to items which are purely ancillary to such material and possess no independent significance (for example, duplicate copies of records or reports).

Relevant material

3.87 Paragraphs 5.7 to 5.10 of the Code proceed to outline the length of time for which material is to be retained in given circumstances. Clearly, the list of categories of material to be retained, as set out in para 5.4 above is a non-exhaustive one. The task on the ground for investigators who routinely have to make hard and fast individual decisions as to relevance, for the purposes of deciding whether or not to retain particular material, will no doubt continue to be challenging. The investigators should be only too aware, however, that prosecutors cannot do their job properly without satisfactory recording and retention of material',[1] and errors of judgement at critical moments in an investigation may well compromise future prosecutions down the line. No doubt with these considerations well in mind the Attorney-General issued a number of practical guidelines to prosecutors, encouraging them to liaise closely with investigators and disclosure officers.[2] Prosecutors are told they have to be alert, proactive and prepared to do 'all that they can to facilitate proper disclosure'. For an example of a recent decision where the Court of Appeal rejected defence claims over the alleged necessity to retain material (in the course of an arson investigation), see *R v Parker*[3] where the court again adopted the *Ebrahim* approach to determining such abuse applications.

In the 2007 decision of *Leatherland v Powys CC*[4] the High Court considered an appeal by case stated, on the basis of a refusal by a magistrates' court to stay proceedings, arising out of an argument over the retention of relevant material. The appellants were convicted of charges under the Animal Health legislation, the relevant material being sheep carcasses. In essence, Leatherland, a farmer, discovered that some of his sheep at market had been assessed by a veterinary surgeon and DEFRA inspector, as in such poor condition they had to be slaughtered. In due course, he went on to be prosecuted, in circumstances where he had generally not been made aware of the decision to slaughter the sheep; consequently, his own veterinary surgeon never had the opportunity to assess the sheep, whose carcasses were all destroyed, and where only a few inconclusive photographs of the sheep existed. Owen J thoroughly reviewed the Ebrahim principles, and the statutory duty to retain material obtained in a criminal investigation, and found that the destruction of the carcasses had so severely handicapped the appellant, a fair trial had not been possible. The appellant was left in no realistic position to mount a challenge to the prosecution veterinary surgeon's evidence as to the condition of the sheep. The court considered that a representative selection of the sheep should have been preserved for at least a sufficient time to inform the appellant of the position, which had not been remedied by the few photographs taken. There should have been a stay of proceedings. For an example of a case, where there was found to be no duty on the facts to preserve material, see *Focus (DIY) Ltd v Hillingdon LBC*.[5]

1 See the Commentary to the previous AG's Guidelines, p 1.
2 See the AG's Guidelines, paras 14–25.
3 [2002] EWCA Crim 90, [2003] All ER (D) 300 (Jan).
4 [2007] EWHC 148.
5 [2008] EWHC 1152 (Admin).

DUTY TO 'PURSUE ALL REASONABLE LINES OF INQUIRY'

The CPIA Code of Practice 1996

3.88 Paragraph 3.5 of the Code contains arguably the most significant and wide-ranging obligation cast on criminal investigators. The CPIA Code is set out in full at Appendix C of this work. Practitioners are urged to carefully consider this obligation when determining whether or not the prosecution have fulfilled their duty 'to obtain' or 'retain' material evidence. It is submitted that never before has an explicit legal obligation been imposed on a criminal investigator to act in the manner stipulated. Paragraph 3.5 states as follows:

> 'In conducting an investigation, the investigator should pursue all reasonable lines of inquiry, whether these point towards or away from the suspect. What is reasonable in each case will depend on the particular circumstances.'

Significance of para 3.5

3.89 Previously in our adversarial system of criminal justice, it was a respectable argument for a prosecutor to make that it was the duty of the accused and his legal team to investigate any matter which was inconsistent with the prosecution's case. If the defence failed to do so and the prosecution were not on notice of any defect or undermining factor so far as their case was concerned, then responsibility for pursuing an exculpatory line of enquiry rested squarely on the defence. Such an argument in the light of para 3.5 is, it is submitted, no longer tenable.

3.90 The significance of para 3.5 can further be emphasised by taking into account that it was presumably inserted into the Code as a quid pro quo for the curtailment under CPIA 1996 of the defence's common law rights to prosecution disclosure. If the original object of the statutory disclosure regime created by CPIA 1996 was to place the prosecution squarely in a management role in so far as decision making concerning disclosure was concerned, then this paragraph, acting as a counterweight, created a clear responsibility to act fairly and impartially while exercising that role.

3.91 Paragraph 3.4 of the Code largely reflects the language used in the CPIA 1996, s 23(1)(a) itself. Interestingly, the duty attaches to the 'investigator' as opposed to, for example, the officer in charge of the case. An 'investigator' is defined as 'any police officer involved in the conduct of a criminal investigation'. The 'officer in charge' of an investigation, who is defined as 'the police officer responsible for directing a criminal investigation', takes on an additional investigative duty, by virtue of para 3.6 of the Code, where it is believed that 'other persons' may be in possession of relevant material. The officer in charge is not obliged to make 'speculative' enquiries of the third parties, but is required to make enquiries where information suggests further action is required. The information which causes them to act may come from a variety of sources, be it the accused, other police inquiries or 'from some other source'.

3.92 So, what exactly does the para 3.5 investigator's duty actually mean? It certainly does not mean that the investigator should pursue every conceivable line of inquiry. Neither does it mean that vast resources have to be applied to the simplest of investigations. We suggest it does mean, however, that the investigator is obliged to investigate all case theories fairly, not just the one pointing to the guilt of the accused.

3.93 In the context of this chapter, we submit that the following three propositions are fundamental. First, that the investigator should be expected to recognise where there is material that may be relevant to an investigation. Secondly, that, having determined what may be relevant, the investigator must make a reasonable effort to obtain it and/or retain it. Thirdly, that where the material to be obtained or retained is within the knowledge of the accused or his legal advisors, yet unknown to the investigator, and in circumstances where the investigator could not reasonably be expected to know about it, then the defence should put the investigator properly on notice before they may legitimately complain about an alleged failure to investigate. The defence are now specifically encouraged to play their part in the new culture of disclosure which is intended to pervade our system. The defence has a critical role in ensuring that the prosecution is directed to material that meets the disclosure test.

3.94 The above three propositions largely relate to the 'duty' of the investigator to actually make an investigation, which goes to the first stage of the *Ebrahim* test. As to the shape of the investigation or the extent of the duty, para 3.5 states: 'What is reasonable in each case will depend on the particular circumstances.' The case law, which is considered below, suggests that the 'reasonableness' or otherwise of a given investigation will depend on a multitude of factors. The guiding principle, however, is that the investigator's inquiries should be proportionate to, or commensurate with, what is required.

The Attorney-General's Guidelines (2020)

3.95 The Attorney-General's Guidelines on Disclosure 2020 replace the existing Attorney General's Guidelines on Disclosure issued in 2013.

3.96 The tenor of the 2020 Guidelines (which are set out at Appendix B to this work), consistent with the duty to pursue all reasonable lines of inquiry, is to demand a proactive approach by investigators who seek to obtain material evidence. This is perhaps best exemplified by the provisions which relate to material held by third parties which is set out below:

Third party material

3.97 The following are relevant extracts taken from the Attorney-General's Guidelines on Disclosure 2020, which are set out at Appendix B to this work:

> '26. Third party material is material held by a person, organisation, or government department other than the investigator and prosecutor, either within the UK or outside the UK. Third parties are not directly involved in the case in question, but may hold information relevant to it.
>
> 27. The CPIA Code and these guidelines make clear the obligation on the investigator to pursue all reasonable lines of inquiry in relation to material held by third parties within the UK.
>
> 28. It is for investigators, in consultation or discussion with prosecutors where appropriate, to pursue all reasonable lines of inquiry. Prosecutors can advise on additional reasonable lines of inquiry and should satisfy themselves that such reasonable lines of inquiry have been pursued.
>
> 29. If as a result of the duty to pursue all reasonable lines of inquiry, the investigator or prosecutor obtains or receives material from a third party, then it must be dealt with in accordance with the CPIA 1996, (i.e. the prosecutor must disclose material if it meets the disclosure tests, subject to any public interest immunity claim). The person who has an interest in the material (the third party) may make representations to the court concerning public interest immunity (see section 16 of the CPIA 1996). Material not in the possession of an investigator or prosecutor falls outside the CPIA. In such cases these guidelines prescribe the approach to be taken to disclosure of material held by third parties.
>
> **Material held by Government departments**
>
> 31. During an investigation or prosecution it may become apparent that a Government department or another Crown body has material that may be relevant to an issue in the case.
>
> 32. The investigator or prosecutor should inform the Government department or Crown body at the earliest opportunity of the nature of the case and the relevant issues in the case, and ask whether it has any relevant material. They should assist the Government department or Crown body in understanding what may be relevant in the context of the case in question.
>
> 33. Crown Servants have a duty to support the administration of justice and should take reasonable steps to identify and consider such material. This extends to revealing to the investigator or prosecutor the extent of the searches conducted and the existence of any information which they believe may be relevant to the issues in the case, to supply them with that information unless it is protected to the issues in the case, and to supply them with that information unless it is protected in law, subject to legal professional privilege or attracts public interest immunity.
>
> 34. If access is denied to relevant material, the investigator or prosecutor should consider the reasons given by the Government department or Crown

body and what, if any, further steps might be taken to obtain the material. The final decision on further steps rests with the prosecutor.

35. Investigators and prosecutors cannot be regarded to be in constructive possession of material held by Government departments or Crown bodies simply by virtue of their status as Government departments or Crown bodies.

36. The steps taken to identify and obtain relevant material held by a Government department or Crown body should be recorded by the investigator and the prosecutor.

37. Where appropriate, the defence should be informed of the steps taken to obtain material and the results of the line of inquiry.

Other domestic bodies

38. An investigator, disclosure officer or a prosecutor may believe that a third party (for example a local authority, social services department, hospital, doctor, school, provider of forensic services, or CCTV operator) has material or information which might be relevant to the case. If so, then reasonable steps should be taken to secure and consider the material held by the third party where it appears that such material exists and that it may be relevant to an issue in the case.

39. The investigator, disclosure officer or prosecutor should follow the steps in paragraphs 32, 34 and 36 above when engaging with the relevant domestic body.

40. A third party has no obligation under the CPIA to reveal material to investigators or prosecutors. There is also no duty on the third party to retain material which may be relevant to the investigation and, in some circumstances, the third party may not be aware of the investigation or prosecution.

41. If access to the material is refused and, despite the reasons given for refusal of access, it is still believed that it is reasonable to seek production of the material or information and that the requirements of a witness summons11F 12, 12F 13 are satisfied (or any other relevant power), then the prosecutor or investigator should apply for the summons causing a representative of the third party to produce the material to court.

42. When the third party material in question is personal data, investigators and prosecutors must refer to paragraphs 11 – 13 of these guidelines to ensure that there is no unjust intrusion of privacy.

43. Further guidance and best practice on obtaining third party material can be found in the Joint Protocol on Third Party Material and Chapter 5 of the CPS Disclosure Manual. 44. The defence should be informed of what steps have been taken to obtain material and what the results of the inquiry have been.'

3.98 When judges are called upon to decide whether an investigator has pursued all 'reasonable lines of enquiry' in a given case, they should take into account the guiding principle that investigators should err on the side of caution in concluding that information is not relevant and therefore need not be retained.[1] The guidelines make it clear, however, that it is not simply the investigators and disclosure officers who should be alive to these important evidential considerations. At para 133 of the guidelines, it states: 'Prosecution advocates must consider, in every case, whether they can be satisfied that they are in possession of all relevant documentation and that they have been fully instructed regarding disclosure matters. If the advocate considers that further information or action is required then written advice should be provided setting out the aspects that need clarification or action'.

1 See the guidelines, para 23.

The position at common law

3.99 At the time of writing there are few authorities on the para 3.5 duty, albeit the authors predict a significant development in this area. The first important statement of principle, however, emerges from Brooke LJ in *Ebrahim* itself wherein he stated:

> 'That the extent of the duty of investigation should be proportionate to the seriousness of the matter being investigated is evident from para 3.4 [ie the previous version of 3.5] of the 1997 Code'.

3.100 By these words, we suggest Brooke LJ did not mean the duty should be assessed in terms of the gravity of the allegation, but rather should be proportionate to the relevance of the inquiry in the context of the issues in the case. There is certainly no mention of 'seriousness' playing a part in the actual wording of this paragraph. The following questions are perhaps more significant to the para 3.5 test: Was there a serious lead or inquiry that should have been followed up? Was there a material issue that should have been investigated given its bearing on the case?

3.101 In *Ebrahim* itself, for example, which concerned a lowly charge of common assault, their Lordships did consider it significant that the officer had made a reasonable investigation to see if there was any video evidence of the assault in question. The court found that the officer 'had no reason to believe that his investigations should encompass what had occurred elsewhere in the store an hour earlier', which meant no breach of then para 3.5 of the Code. The reason why the police were unaware of the significance of the earlier video appears to relate to the fact that Ebrahim was never interviewed. The authors suggest that, in a different case, perhaps against a background of a more serious allegation, police officers could attract legitimate criticism under para 3.5 where they fail to interview an accused. It could well be argued that officers have not pursued lines of inquiry pointing 'away from the suspect' where they have chosen not to even interview the suspect or seek a response to the allegation.

DPP v Metten

3.102 In the earlier decision of *DPP v Metten*[1] the defence alleged a breach of para 3.4 (now 3.5) of the Code in a failure by the police to make any effort to ascertain the identities of potential witnesses to a public order incident for which the defendant was being prosecuted. It is submitted that on the facts of this case there appeared a clear breach of what is now para 3.5, the officers having singularly failed at the only possible moment to speak to those who may have assisted or undermined the prosecution's case. Buxton LJ sitting in the Divisional Court was, it is submitted, nonetheless determined to ensure that despite a clear breach of this paragraph, the defence did not profit from it. While the terms of his judgment are beyond the scope of this chapter, Buxton LJ adopted a highly technical approach to the wording of the Code of Practice holding that there was no breach because the police had not conducted any criminal investigation. As the editor of *Criminal Law Week* observed concerning Buxton LJ's judgment, 'the decision does indeed drive a coach and four through the legislation'.[2]

1 (1999) 13 CLW. See also *R v Roberts* [1998] Crim LR 682, and the commentary at 683.
2 (1999) 13 CLW para 5.

3.103 The principles set out in *Ebrahim* have been followed in the two unreported decisions of *R v Eccleston* and *R v Sahdev*. In *R v Eccleston*[1] the Court of Appeal concluded on the facts of the case that there was no para 3.4 (now para 3.5) duty incumbent on the police to retain a motor car for forensic examination based on a mere 'hint in interview' about the presence of blood on the car. In reaching this decision the court had particular regard to the lack of any 'clear request from either the appellant or his legal advisor' to examine the car, and the fact that the presence or absence of blood on the car was not central to the real issue in the case, which was whether or not the appellant acted in self-defence. It was less than clear that even the proven presence of blood on the car would have materially assisted the defence. On the facts of *Eccleston*, the abuse argument fell at the first hurdle of the *Ebrahim* test, in the sense that there was no duty to obtain or retain the material. Had there been such a duty, it is clear that the court found no serious prejudice in any event, which meant that the abuse argument would similarly have been defeated at the second stage. In contrast, we suggest that the pre-CPIA 1996 case of *Beckford* and most recently in the case of *Clay v Clerk to the Justices*, where, in both instances, the police allowed the motor car to be scrapped, would have passed the first hurdle of *Ebrahim* in the sense that there was a duty to retain, albeit it may not have passed the second stage 'serious prejudice' test.

1 [2001] EWCA Crim 1626, [2001] All ER (D) 118 (Jul).

3.104 In *R v Sahdev*[1] the Court of Appeal similarly endorsed the approach of *Ebrahim* when faced with an appeal based on an abuse of process argument which was said to arise out of an alleged breach of the previous para 3.4 duty. The facts concerned an incident outside a London tube station, whereby the defendant was alleged to have been unlawfully in possession of a knife and committing assaults on police officers. The police retained certain film footage from the scene, which was disclosed to the defence, albeit it did not show the incident. A year later, after a site visit, the defence contended that there were other cameras which may have revealed the incident. The defence arguments unsurprisingly received short shrift from Goldring J, who found that the investigating officer had done 'all he reasonably could have been expected to do'. The officer seized, retained and disclosed the film from one set of cameras, whilst being unaware of any other video cameras. The defence could not produce any cogent evidence that a second set of cameras were present at the material time, or indeed, working. Goldring J emphasised that the extent of the duty to investigate 'must be proportionate to the seriousness of the issues being investigated', and that in this straightforward case the officer had investigated it 'reasonably and proportionately'.

1 See [2002] EWCA Crim 1064, [2002] 166 JP 19.

3.105 In the course of his judgment, Goldring J cited approvingly the cautionary words of Brooke LJ in *Ebrahim*:

> 'It must be remembered that it is a commonplace in criminal trials for a defendant to rely on "holes" in the prosecution case, for example, a failure to take fingerprints or a failure to submit evidential material to forensic examination. If, in such a case, there is sufficient credible evidence, apart form the missing evidence, which, if believed, would justify a safe conviction, then a trial should proceed, leaving the defendant to seek to persuade the jury or magistrates not to convict because evidence which might otherwise have been available was not before the court through no fault of his. Often the absence of a video film or fingerprints or DNA material is likely to hamper the prosecution as much as the defence'.[1]

Brooke LJ's words will serve as a warning to trial judges and magistrates to scrutinise closely opportunistic defence complaints over alleged failures to investigate.

1 At para 20 of *Sahdev* (citing para 27 of *Ebrahim*).

E v E[1]

3.106 The defendant was charged with assault by penetration, contrary to the Sexual Offences Act 2003, s 2, and sexual assault, contrary to s 3 of the same Act. The defence became aware of a screenshot of a text message sent by one of the complainants to another family member, despite that complainant's evidence that she did not communicate with anyone about the incident (though the text message did not explicitly mention the incident). The defence argued that the police had a duty to seize the complainant's phone and, later on, applied under CPIA 1996, s 8 to have a download of the complainant's phone disclosed. The prosecution initially responded that the seizure of the phone had not been a reasonable line of inquiry.[2] By the time of trial, prosecution counsel conceded that, once the police became aware of the existence of the text message, seizure would have been a reasonable line of inquiry.[3] When finally examined, it was discovered that no material remained from the relevant time period.[4] The trial judge ruled that there had been 'a clear contravention of the Director's current guidelines'.[5]

On application for leave to appeal by the prosecution, the Court of Appeal reasoned that the proper approach to consideration of a fair trial was to look at the fairness of the trial generally, not just from the perspective of the defence (or the prosecution).[6] The trial judge ought to have given more detailed consideration to what safeguards could render the trial process fair.[7] The Court of Appeal further reasoned that there was unlikely to be material of relevance on the phone.[8] The court emphasised that *Ebrahim* remained the law and that a stay of proceedings 'should be a last resort and only (in relation to this category of abuse) in circumstances where a defendant cannot receive a fair trial'.[9]

1 [2018] EWCA Crim 2426.
2 At paras 8–9.
3 At para 10.
4 At para 11.
5 At para 13.
6 At para 32.
7 At paras 34–35.
8 At para 37.
9 At para 41.

R v Hewitt[1]

3.107 The appellant appealed against a conviction of rape, committed thirty-seven years previously. One of the issues at trial was the nature of the prosecution disclosure process and the lack of contemporaneous material.[2] Prosecution counsel accepted that there had been serious shortcomings, but submitted that any errors had been remedied by the close of the evidence at trial.[3] Having considered both oral and written submissions on the issue, the trial judge ruled that this was not a rare and exceptional case in which a stay was justified.[4] What followed was late disclosure during the course of the trial, with far more extensive medical records for relevant complainants.[5] The trial judge made a further ruling, noting the amount of material that defence counsel had to use and the degree of speculation about what other material might have shown.[6]

The Court of Appeal held that the trial judge had been entitled to give those rulings, with no serious prejudice such as to make a fair trial impossible.[7] The trial judge had rightly focused on 'the need for a proportionate approach to disclosure, tailored to the issues in the case applying the statutory test for disclosure'.[8] The court emphasised the better placement of the trial judge to assess the fairness of the trial, having regard to the process' ability to compensate for any prejudice.[9]

1 [2020] EWCA Crim 1247.
2 At para 3.
3 At para 27.
4 At para 39.
5 At para 55.
6 At para 77.
7 At para 129.
8 At para 140.
9 At para 141.

R v Warren[1]

3.108 The appellants appealed against their convictions, which arose from trade union-related public order allegations. The central issue in relation to disclosure and destruction of evidence was that some of the civilian eyewitnesses' statements had been destroyed in the early stages of the proceedings, so that so-called replacement statements were provided. The prosecution had assured both the appellants and the original trial judge that they had access to all the relevant statements.[2]

The Court of Appeal held that the convictions were unsafe. In particular, the court noted that:

> 'Critically … none of the surviving statements indicates it is a replacement document, in the sense described in paragraph 16 of the note of 17 September 1973, namely that an earlier statement, or a version of it, had been destroyed leading to a replacement statement. We note that the committal proceedings were delayed because the statements "were still being amended and signed following Counsel's advice".'

In the court's view, there was 'no basis for concluding that the content of a destroyed witness statement would necessarily have been preserved in its replacement'. Indeed, 'in all probability', the court considered that the original statements had 'a different focus than their later iterations' before other evidence was available and before the officers knew what the prosecution sought to prove.[3] Basing its analysis on the development of the common law over the last half-century and the CPIA Code's obligation of retention, the court stressed the importance of retention of material when it might cast doubt on the reliability of a witness.[4]

See para **3.34** above for a discussion on the most recent post-*Ebrahim* case law.

1 [2021] EWCA Crim 413, para 1.
2 At para 15.
3 At para 79.
4 At para 87.

LOST EVIDENCE AND HEARSAY

3.109 Although an original piece of evidence may no longer exist, or cannot be found, all may not be lost. This is particularly so in the case of written material where the evidential value lies in the record of what was written rather than in the writing itself. In such cases, subject to compliance with the rules, hearsay evidence may be admissible as to what the missing writing said. In *Maher v Director of Public Prosecutions*,[1] the defendant was seen reversing her Mini, in a car park, into an Astra car. The witness noted the registration number of the Mini and left it, with her own contact details, on the windscreen of the damaged Astra. When the victim returned to his Astra, he found the note and telephoned the police who recorded the information on an incident log. When interviewed by the police, the defendant admitted being the driver of the Mini at the relevant time and place but denied driving into the Astra. By the time of the defendant's trial, the original note was lost but the magistrates admitted the third-hand evidence of it in the form of the police log holding that it was admissible as a business record. The defendant was convicted and appealed. The appeal was dismissed on the basis that hearsay evidence can be admitted in reliance on s 121(1)(c) of the CJA if the court was satisfied that 'the value of the evidence in question, taking into account how reliable the statements appear to be, is so high that the interests of justice require the later statement to be admissible for the purpose.' Scott Baker LJ considered that the information was very reliable.

In the case of *R v Carmelita Anderson*[2] the Court of Appeal considered yet another case concerning copies of missing documents. There the defendant, who was the proprietor of 'Canway Health Care College', sought leave to appeal against her conviction under s 14(1)(a) of the Trade Descriptions Act 1968 for making false statements in certificates issued to her students that her college was 'in association with City and Guilds'. Her case was that she was the victim of a conspiracy by former students who had created the false certificates to discredit her. The original certificates had been lost but copies thereof were admitted at her trial despite her challenge that to proceed without the originals was an abuse of process. Lord Justice Scott Baker found the defendant's application for permission to appeal to be a hopeless one.

1 [2006] EWHC 1271 (Admin).
2 [2004] EWCA Crim 1112.

THE PROTOCOL ON UNUSED MATERIAL (2013)

3.110 This protocol replaced that first issued by the Court of Appeal in 2006, and is set out in full at Appendix D to this work. Its full title is the protocol for 'Judicial Protocol on Disclosure of Unused Material in Criminal Cases' and the most recent version dates from December 2013. It sets out the duties and responsibilities of investigators, prosecutors and the defence to ensure that disclosure issues are managed effectively and fairly.

EUROPEAN COURT OF HUMAN RIGHTS CASE LAW

3.111 Finally, in this chapter, we turn to some ECHR decisions and consider whether any parallels exist between the domestic abuse of process doctrine and the 'Equality of Arms' provisions applicable to Art 6 of ECHR. Article 6(3)(d) of the Convention provides:

> 'Everyone charged with a criminal offence has the following minimum rights;
>
> (d) to examine or have examined witnesses against him and to obtain the attendance and examination of witnesses on his behalf under the same conditions as witnesses against him;'

In *Sofri v Italy*[1] the Court found a complaint under Art 6 inadmissible as manifestly ill-founded, in circumstances where the complaint had been based on the destruction of a certain evidence relating to a murder trial concerning the killing of a public prosecutor. The dead prosecutor's clothing had gone missing, the bullets from the body were destroyed, as was the car used by the killers. Administrative error, on the part of the Italian authorities, was said to be the likely explanation for the lost material. The destruction of the items did not on the particular facts, however, give rise to any inequality of arms which was to the detriment of the defendants. The court found that the defence were at no significant disadvantage by the loss of the car and bullets, for they had access to forensic reports and photographs which had been made shortly after the killing. Furthermore, the defence were wholly unable to explain how the loss of the clothing had been relevant to their case. The prosecution were adjudged to have laboured under the same difficulties as the defence.

1 Application No 37235/97, May 27, 2003; [2004] Crim LR 846.

3.112 In *Papageorgiou v Greece*[1] however, the Court did find a violation of Art 6(3)(d) in circumstances where 'vital items of evidence were not adduced', or made available to the defence, in spite of repeated disclosure requests. The applicant was a bank clerk charged with a fraud, where it was alleged he and others had used false cheques to withdraw significant sums of money from one of the bank's client's account. For reasons that are not immediately apparent, the domestic court of first instance ordered the destruction of the forged cheques, which were fundamental items of evidence in the proceedings against the applicant. Indeed, the applicant's conviction for fraud was, to a large extent, based on photocopies of the cheques allegedly forged, which cheques the defence claimed had been altered. The court found that it was essential to the applicant's defence for the cheques to have been produced, for they would have enabled him to show that the persons who gave the instructions to make the payments were bank employees and not himself. He had lost the opportunity to use evidence which was potentially exculpatory.

1 (2004) 38 EHRR 30.

3.113 As Professor Ashworth noted in his commentary on *Sofri*, the Strasbourg Court 'is not concerned with the detailed rules of evidence and procedure in domestic law, but rather with the overall fairness of the proceedings'. The different decisions reached by the ECHR in both *Sofri* and *Papageorgiou* are readily understandable on the facts. Had the Court been using the language of abuse of process, the authors suggest that, in *Sofri*'s case, it would have found that a fair trial was possible, in the absence of the lost material, whereas in *Papageorgiou* the conclusion would have been reached that a fair trial was no longer a possibility. In conclusion, the authors agree with the analysis of Professor Choo,[1] that: 'The approach of the courts in England and Wales seems consistent with what appears to be the approach of the European Court of Human Rights'. In both jurisdictions, the Courts are looking to analyse the impact of the lost or destroyed evidence upon the overall fairness of the trial proceedings.

1 See Andrew L-T Choo, *Abuse of Process and Judicial Stays of Criminal Proceedings* (2nd Edn, Oxford University Press) p 101.

Chapter 4

Miscellaneous abuse

4.01 In *R v Derby Crown Court, ex p Brooks*[1] Sir Roger Ormrod defined the jurisdiction of abuse of process as follows:

> 'The power to stop a prosecution arises only when it is an abuse of the process of the court. It may be an abuse of process if either (a) *the prosecution have manipulated or misused the process of the court so as to deprive the defendant of a protection provided by the law or to take unfair advantage of a technicality,* or (b) on the balance of probability the defendant has been or will be, prejudiced in the preparation or conduct of his defence by delay on the part of the prosecution …' (Emphasis added)

1 (1985) 80 Cr App Rep 164 at 169.

4.02 There are an infinite number of situations in which an allegation of prosecutorial manipulation or misuse of the process of the court can be made. This chapter considers only a number of miscellaneous instances in which the abuse jurisdiction has been invoked. It is emphasised that the cases considered below are but mere examples of this head of abuse; the situations in which such an abuse can arise cannot be fully predicted. Fairness is obviously a concept for which parameters cannot be fixed.

PROOF OF PREJUDICE NOT REQUIRED

4.03 One of the characteristics of the law on abuse, as defined by manipulation or by misuse of procedure, is that the court does not require any evidence of actual prejudice caused to the defendant. Manipulation or misuse, if established, tends to be regarded so gravely that the courts will stay the proceedings without further consideration. This approach differs from that in relation to delay where there is an insistence by the courts of the need to establish prejudice even when there has been significant delay.[1]

1 See Chapter 1.

STATUTORY TIME LIMITS

4.04 The cases under this heading can be conveniently divided into two parts: first, those concerned with the Magistrates' Court Act 1980, s 127(1), which states that summonses must be issued within six months of the commission of the alleged offence, and second, those concerned with alleged circumvention of custody time limits.

Magistrates' Court Act 1980, s 127

4.05 The leading case is *R v Brentford Justices, ex p Wong.*[1] Here the defendant was summonsed for driving without due care and attention. The summons was applied for and issued two days before the expiry of the six-month time limit. The defence solicitor, whose suspicions were aroused by the timing of this manoeuvre, made inquiries. Ultimately the prosecution disclosed that the information (the prerequisite for the issuance of the summons) was laid in order that more time be obtained pending a decision as to whether the defendant should be prosecuted with this offence or not. The prosecution admitted therefore that the information was laid before any decision had been made in relation to prosecution. The magistrates held that they had no jurisdiction to consider an abuse application based on an allegation of misuse of process and the case went to the Divisional Court. The court held that it would be an abuse for the prosecutor to lay an information when he has not reached a decision to prosecute. This judgment in this case is considered in paras **1.09–1.11**.[2]

Ex parte Wong was distinguished, in questionable circumstances, by the Queen's Bench Division (Northern Ireland) in *Re Molloy's Application*[3] on the basis that the magistrate had found that there was no improper reason for laying the complaint before the DPP decided to prosecute. On the facts the complaint was laid on 4 February 1997, just inside the six months' period prescribed,[4] however the DPP did not decide to prosecute until 28 February 1997. The fact that the investigation into the alleged offence had been delayed or that there was no improper reason on the part of the prosecution should not be persuasive in allowing information to be laid prior to a decision to prosecute. In *ex parte Wong* Donaldson LJ held that the 'purpose [of the time limit] is wholly frustrated if it is possible for a prosecutor to obtain summonses and then, in his own good time and at his convenience, serve them.'[5] This should be sufficient to constitute abuse.

1 [1981] 1 All ER 884.
2 See also *R v Newcastle upon Tyne JJ ex parte Hindle* [1984] 1 All ER 770.
3 [1998] NI 78.
4 Magistrates' Courts (Northern Ireland) Order 1981 Art.19(1)(a).
5 [1981] 1 All ER 884, per Donaldson LJ at 210.

4.06 The courts are nonetheless prepared to endorse prosecutions launched just before the expiry of a time limit if one then ensues. In *Wei Hai Restaurant v Kingston City Council*[1] a prosecution was brought just before the expiry of a one-year limit under the Food Safety Act 1990. The court held that this was permissible.

1 [2001] EWHC Admin 490, (2001) 166 JP 185.

Expiry of limitation period

4.07 In *R v J*[1] the appellant was convicted on three counts of indecent assault under s 14(1) of the Sexual Offences Act 1956 in circumstances where the conduct charged was that of unlawful sexual intercourse with a girl under the age of 16, which was then an offence under s 6(1) of the 1956 Act. The defence submitted that it was an abuse of process for the Crown to prosecute under s 14 so as to avoid the 12-month statutory time limit applicable to s 6 offences.

In the Court of Appeal, Potter LJ rejected the defence arguments, holding that there was no misuse of the court's process on the particular facts. The prosecution had acted promptly once the complaints had been brought to their attention, in relation to circumstances where the sexual conduct took place over several years, where the appellant had exploited the relationship of a family friend and employer. Commenting on the decision, Professor J C Smith wrote at the time:

> '... it is not surprising that the court was unwilling to rule that every charge of indecent assault after the expiry of 12 months from an event that would have justified a charge under s 6 must be an abuse of process. The "public conscience" is a somewhat vague concept but it is difficult to imagine that it would be affronted by the bringing of a prosecution in the circumstances of the present case. Indeed it is more likely that the public would be outraged to learn that a prosecution was not possible.'[2]

The House of Lords allowed the appeal. Parliament's intention where the 12-month limit is concerned is clear, as also is the intention of the prosecution in charging indecent assault to get around it. If Parliament has provided a protection for a defendant, it is not for any court to sanction a device by which such protection is denied. If the public conscience is affronted, or the integrity of the criminal justice system undermined, that is a consequence of legislation passed and maintained by Parliament and Parliament must provide the remedy.

In the leading opinion, Lord Bingham held that the prosecution ought to have been stayed or dismissed.[3] He held:

> 'It is the duty of the court to give full and fair effect to the meaning of a statute. [...] If a statutory provision is clear and unambiguous, the court may not decline to give effect to it on the ground that its rationale is anachronistic, or discredited, or unconvincing.'[4]

Lord Steyn concurred, adding:

> 'In the present case the intent to avoid the statutory time limit is freely acknowledged and, in any event, manifest. In these circumstances the conclusion is inescapable: as a matter of construction of the Act the time limit cannot be circumvented by the manipulation of the indictment to charge conduct falling squarely within section 6(1) as an offence under section 14 solely in order to avoid the time limit under the former provision.[5] [...]
>
> The CPS as an independent law enforcement agency carry out duties of a public character. It must act fairly and within the law. It must observe statute law as Parliament framed it. [...] And it is plain as a pikestaff that the CPS policy under challenge in the present appeal was intended to circumvent the intent of Parliament in creating a time limit for prosecutions under section 6(1). It is, of course, true that the CPS has acted in good faith and in what it considered the public interest. But the particular policy it adopted

unquestionably fell beyond its powers. It was ultra vires. [...] The decision of the CPS to charge the defendant under section 14 in order to avoid the time limit under section 6(1) was unlawful.'[6]

In 2007 the Court of Appeal considered the implications of the House of Lords' decisions in two appeals brought as *a direct consequence of R v J*. The Court was called to examine the problematic situation of alternative charges of indecent assault *of under-age girls* in the joint appeal in *R v Steven Cottrell, R v Joseph Fletcher.*[7] The first defendant had been convicted of indecent assault where acts amounted to unlawful sexual intercourse; the second of indecent assault as alternative to rape. In the first case, the Court refused the application: but for the practice now considered impermissible following *R v J*, the applicant could on the facts have been indicted for indecent assault and not the two instances of intercourse. It would be a manifest injustice to the complainant if the applicant were able to take advantage of that part of a change in the law which suited him without having to accept the inevitable consequences of the process which would have applied to the case if the erroneous practice had been recognised earlier, and the necessary adaptations to it adopted. On the facts, the case fell well within the long-established principle of the Court of Appeal of refusing applications for extensions of time where, if the appeal was effectively based on a change of law, and nothing else, but the conviction was properly returned at the time, after a fair trial, it was unlikely that a substantial injustice had occurred. Refusal of the application in this case would produce no injustice.[8] In the second case, where on the facts the count in issue was added, rather than left as an alternative to rape, the Court was bound by authority to allow the appeal against conviction on that count.[9]

1 [2004] UKHL 42; [2005] 1 AC 562.
2 See [2003] Crim LR 393.
3 [2004] UKHL 42 per Lord Bingham at 575A.
4 [2004] UKHL 42 per Lord Bingham at 571F.
5 [2004] UKHL 42 per Lord Steyn at 577E.
6 [2004] UKHL 42 per Lord Steyn at 577H-578A.
7 [2007] EWCA Crim 2016, [2008] 1 Cr App R 7.
8 [2008] 1 Cr App R 7 at 108.
9 [2008] 1 Cr App R 7 at 109.

Custody time limits

4.08 Pursuant to the Prosecution of Offences Act 1985, s 22 the Home Secretary may impose by regulation time limits in relation to completion by the prosecution of a particular stage of the proceedings. This section has been amended, most notably in relation to cases sent for trial under ss 51 or 51A(3)(d) of the Crime and Disorder Act 1998. Subject to the prosecution completing that stage within the relevant time limit, the accused may be held in custody. Under s 22(3) a court may extend such limits provided that it is satisfied that the prosecution 'has acted with all due diligence and expedition'. The maximum periods of incarceration will depend upon the nature of the offence (i.e. whether it is a summary offence, triable either way, or indictable only, for example) and whether the case involves a sending for trial. The various time limits may be found in the amended SI 1987/299. If the prosecution fail to satisfy the respective limit or fail to persuade the court to grant an extension then the accused must be granted bail.

4.09 Clearly the underlying policy of custody time limits is to minimise the period spent by the accused in custody awaiting trial, to oblige the prosecution to prepare cases diligently and to allow the court power to determine whether there should be any extension to the maximum period.

4.10 On occasions an accused held in custody is originally charged with one offence but subsequently another is substituted. The Regulations state that time begins to run when an accused is charged and is thus relevant to a particular offence. Accordingly, the charging of a new offence causes a fresh time limit to start, thus enabling overall an accused to be held in custody for a period exceeding the particular set number of days, without the prosecution having to seek the permission of the court to grant an extension.

4.11 Immediately this situation can give rise to a complaint of prosecution manipulation and abuse; by allowing such latitude to the prosecution to substitute and/or charge additional offences it can ensure not only that an accused be kept in custody far longer than intended but also that the requirement to show due diligence can be avoided altogether. Taking this possibility into account it may be alleged that the prosecution have improperly exploited it for the above reasons; that fresh charges have later been added for the purpose of retaining an accused in custody, for example, in excess of the 70 days.

4.12 This situation was considered by the House in *R (Wardle) v Crown Court at Leeds*[1] where a complaint of abuse of process was made. Here the appellant was originally charged with murder and remanded in custody. On the day his limit was to expire, the prosecution substituted a charge of manslaughter and the magistrate ruled a fresh limit of 70 days started that day in respect of the new charge.

1 [2001] UKHL 12, [2002] 1 AC 754.

4.13 Lord Slynn considered the complaint of abuse and held:

> '27. It is accepted that where to add or substitute a new charge amounts to an abuse of process, a new custody time limit does not begin. It has been said that where the new charge is brought in bad faith or dishonestly, that would amount to an abuse of process. In my view the ambit of "abuse of process" is not so limited. If a new charge is brought simply to keep the accused in custody for a longer period, that is clearly contrary to the intention of the legislation and constitutes an abuse of process. As Professor Smith said in his commentary to *R v Great Yarmouth Magistrates', ex p Thomas, Davis and Darlington* [1992] Crim LR 116, at p 117:
>
> "Perhaps the more specific question to be asked is whether the charges of possession with intent were brought solely for the purpose of retaining the applicants in custody".
>
> 28. Equally if the court is satisfied that the way in which and the time at which the new charge is added or substituted, indicates that it is not done for

the genuine purpose of introducing a new charge on a revised assessment of the case, but is done primarily to keep the accused in custody on the initial charge, then this will constitute an abuse of process. Of course on the other hand if the purpose is genuinely to introduce a new charge on such a revised assessment the fact that the accused begins a new custody period does not in itself constitute an abuse of process.'

On the facts Lord Slynn held no abuse. The new charge was brought on the basis of a substantial body of evidence which had been disclosed prior to the charge of manslaughter being laid. He also held that the appellant's Art. 5 right to liberty had similarly not been violated.

PRE-INTERVIEW DISCLOSURE

4.14 Generally there is no right to pre-interview disclosure and ordinarily a failure to effect such disclosure would not enable a suspect to refuse to answer questions in interview and be sure that no adverse inference could be drawn from it pursuant to the Criminal Justice and Public Order Act 1994, s 34, as amended. This would all depend on the circumstances.

4.15 In *DPP v Ara*[1] the Administrative Court was, however, willing to lay down a general principle. Here the applicant had been offered a caution prior to interview on the condition he admitted the offence during it. Perhaps fearing a trap, the applicant's solicitor sought disclosure of the transcript of the applicant's previous interview so that he could assess the strength of the prosecution case and advise his client, in an adequate and informed manner, whether to accept the caution. His request was refused. The court held that advice to a person whether to accept a caution was linked to their right to legal advice. Thus it was an abuse to refuse disclosure of the transcript. Rose LJ said:

> 'the justices were fully entitled to conclude that the proceedings should be stayed as an abuse of process, the police having refused to disclose the terms of the interview, without which informed advice and informed consent to a caution could not properly be given'.

1 [2001] EWHC Admin 493, [2001] 4 All ER 559.

4.16 Rose LJ was anxious to avoid attempts to extrapolate his reasoning into a general right to pre-interview or charge disclosure, and added:

> 'I make it clear that this does not mean that there is a general obligation on the police to disclose material prior to charge. That would, in many cases, be impracticable and, in some cases, (for example where there is an ongoing investigation) highly undesirable, as well as being outwith the contemplation of the legislation, the Code or anything to be implied therefrom. But, in the present case, the failure to disclose the terms of the interview followed by the institution and pursuit of a criminal trial in the circumstances described amply justified the justices in reaching the conclusion which they did.'[1]

1 [2001] EWHC Admin 493, [2001] 4 All ER 559, para 24.

PROSECUTOR'S IMPROPER MOTIVE

4.17 Allegations of improper motive normally arise in relation to the bringing of private prosecutions where the defendant alleges that the underlying motive of the prosecutor is either revenge, obsession or some wholly collateral motive to cause embarrassment to the defendant. The attitude of the Divisional Court to such allegations is a permissive one, generally permitting the bringing of private prosecutions unless there is very clear evidence of improper motive. There are perhaps three reasons explaining this reluctance to intervene: first, the court does not wish to bear the burden of inquiring into the detail of the facts of a case including the alleged underlying motive of the prosecutor; secondly, the court knows that where there is a flagrant abuse then the Crown Prosecution Service has the statutory power to take over and discontinue the proceedings; thirdly, the policy of the courts has generally been to facilitate the bringing of private prosecutions. The legal principles applying to stay on the ground of abuse apply in the same way to private prosecutions as they do to public prosecutions.[1] Indeed in *D. Ltd v A*, the court in applying these principles affirmed the high threshold of bad faith or dishonesty that is required to issue a stay on the grounds of prosecutorial conduct, referencing how this should be balanced against 'the public interest in upholding a person's statutory right to initiate and pursue a private prosecution and the public interest in alleged serious criminality'.[2]

1 Dacre v City of Westminster Magistrates' Court [2008] EWHC 1667 (Admin); D Ltd v A [2017] EWCA Crim 1172.
2 *D Ltd v A* [2017] EWCA Crim 1172 at [94].

Bow Street Metropolitan Stipendiary Magistrates, ex parte South Coast Shipping[1]

4.18 In this case the defendant alleged that the bringing of this private prosecution was an abuse because it was being used as a means of drawing publicity to the 'Marchioness' shipping disaster and as a means of creating political pressure in favour of a public inquiry. The prosecution was alleged to be a mere device to achieve a collateral purpose. The Divisional Court held that even if this attribution of motive to the prosecutor were true, the prosecution would not be an abuse unless this was the prosecutor's sole or dominant motive. That the prosecutor has an ulterior motive other than to bring criminals to justice is not therefore necessarily fatal or open to objection on the grounds of abuse or oppression.[2]

1 [1993] Crim LR 221.
2 *Dacre v City of Westminster Magistrates' Court* [2008] EWHC 1667 (Admin).

4.19 In *Dacre*,[1] the editor of a newspaper, and Associated Newspapers, the publishers, sought judicial review of a District Judge's refusal to stay a prosecution for an alleged breach of the Children Act 1989 (s 97(6)). The Court held that, when determining whether a private prosecution was an abuse of process on *ex parte Bennett* type grounds,[2] the motive and conduct of the prosecutor could be relevant. In considering the issue of 'motive', proceedings tainted by mala fides or spite, or some other oblique motive could amount to an abuse.[3] The mere presence of an indirect or improper motive, however, did not necessarily vitiate a private prosecution. The court further held it would be slow to halt a prosecution where there were mixed motives, unless the prosecution's conduct was genuinely oppressive.[4]

1 [2009] 1 Cr App R 6; [2008] EWHC 1667 (Admin) 16 July 2008.
2 *R v Horseferry Road Magistrates' Court, ex parte Bennett* [1994] 1 AC 42.
3 *Raymond v Attorney General* [1982] 1 QB 839; see also *R v Baines* [1909] 1 KB 258.
4 *R v Bow Street Metropolitan Stipendiary Magistrates, ex p South Coast Shipping Company Ltd* [1993] QB 645.

4.20 The court held that the correct approach was to decide whether there was a primary motive, and one which was so removed from the proceedings that it rendered the prosecution a misuse or an abuse of process.[1] The court held, on the facts of the case, that the District Judge was permitted to conclude the mixed motives of the prosecutor were unobjectionable (given that they were partly concerned with protecting her child's identity in the context of a newspaper in apparent breach of the law). However, he ought to have found that her willingness to disclose information about her affairs to the newspaper's journalist, which would have led to the child's identification, rendered the prosecution an abuse of process.

1 *R v Leeds Magistrates Court, ex p Serif Systems Ltd*, unreported, October 9, 1997.

R v Durham Magistrates Court, ex parte Davies[1]

4.21 A similar approach was also taken in this case. Here, the private prosecutor was alleged to be obsessed with achieving the successful prosecution of the defendant. Accordingly, his motives were improper, they tainted the prosecution and it should be stayed as an abuse. The Divisional Court disagreed, holding that the motivation of a prosecutor was irrelevant to consideration of the abuse claim. It is submitted that the decision in this case is consistent with the cautionary words expressed by Lord Salmon in *DPP v Humphrys*:

> 'I respectfully agree that a judge has not and should not appear to have any responsibility for the institution of prosecutions; nor has he any power to refuse to allow the prosecution to proceed merely because he considers that, as a matter of policy, it ought not to have been brought. It is only if the prosecution amounts to an abuse of the process of the court and is oppressive or frivolous that the judge has the power to intervene.'[2]

Echoing this opinion, Lord Edmund-Davies said: 'Judges should pause long before staying proceedings which on their face are perfectly regular'.[3]

Accordingly, this decision holds that the fact that a prosecutor/complainant may be unreliable as a witness and obsessive about his cause does not of itself justify a decision to stay.

1 (1993) *Times*, 25 May.
2 [1977] AC 1 at 46.
3 [1977] AC 1 at 55.

R v Gloucester Crown Court, ex parte Jackman[1]

4.22 This was another private prosecution, where the criminal prosecution and a civil claim were being run in tandem by the same person against the same defendant. The solicitors acting for the prosecutor/claimant offered to settle both proceedings with the defendant provided that the defendant paid compensation to the prosecutor/claimant. When settlement negotiations broke down, the defendant asserted that the prosecution was oppressive because it was being used as a means of pressuring the defendant to accept settlement terms in relation to the civil proceedings. The court held that the evidence to support this claim was insufficient although it expressed its disapproval of the proposed terms of settlement which included an offer to discontinue the prosecution.

1 [1993] COD 100. See also *R v Horseferry Road Magistrates' Court, ex p Stephenson* [1989] COD 470.

R v Milton Keynes Magistrates, ex parte Roberts[1]

4.23 This was a prosecution brought by the Trading Standards Department of Buckinghamshire County Council for breach of the Trade Descriptions Act 1968. It was alleged that the defendant was dealing in counterfeit parts for Ford cars. The defendant alleged abuse on the ground that the prosecutor was a mere puppet of the Ford Motor Company who had provided the resources for the investigation. The prosecutor had allegedly not exercised independent judgment and Ford were the real prosecutors. The Divisional Court held that the Trading Standards Department had exercised independent judgment. A stay would only be imposed 'if a prosecutor did indeed make himself the creature of a private interest in exercising his powers, then that conduct would at least be *prima facie* abusive'. Furthermore, a prosecution would only be stopped if to allow it to continue would be 'tantamount to endorsing behaviour which undermines or degrades the rule of law' or 'is an affront to justice'.

1 [1995] Crim LR 224.

R v Adaway[1]

4.24 This case involved local authority instituted proceedings, which also related to the Trade Descriptions Act 1968. The local authority had a policy whereby, for a prosecution to be justified, there had to be evidence of fraudulent activity or deliberate or persistent breaches of the proposed defendant's legal obligations. In the Court of Appeal it became clear that the defence contentions at trial, and on appeal, were well founded, for there was no material to suggest that the local authority's criteria had been met.[2] The trial judge ought to have allowed the defence application to stay proceedings as an abuse of process, on the grounds that the prosecution was oppressive.

Adaway was cited in *London Borough of Wandsworth v Rashid*[3] in which the Divisional Court held that where according to the prosecuting authority's policy, prosecution was but one option, it was not an abuse to prosecute in spite of the absence of a clear explanation as to why alternative enforcement action had not been taken. The fact that it would have been reasonable for the local authority to take another course of action did not necessarily lead to a conclusion that the course of action it did take amounted to an abuse of process.[4]

Even where there has been a breach of a prosecuting authority's clear and settled policy, the court will only intervene where to allow the proceedings to continue would bring the administration of justice into disrepute.[5] However, a prosecution that did not constitute an abuse at the date of the conviction could not then become one on the basis of new or amended guidance or policy issued subsequently.[6]

1 [2004] EWCA Crim 2831; *Times*, 22 November, 2004, CA.
2 Applied in *R (on the application of Mondelly) v Commissioner of Police of the Metropolis* [2006] EWHC 2370 (Admin); [2007] Crim LR 298.
3 [2009] 173 JP 547; [2010] Env LR 22.
4 At 383.
5 *Jones v DPP* [2012] RTR 3.
6 *R v A (R.J.)* [2012] 2 Cr App R 8, at 101.

R (on the application of G) v S[1]

4.25 This was a successful appeal against a ruling which stayed a private prosecution as an abuse of process. The factors that the trial judge considered in deciding that there had been an abuse, specifically the fact that alleged fraud had not been pleaded in civil proceedings and the fact that the Applicant had not asked for the police/CPS to take over the prosecution were of insufficient weight and as such the decision to stay the proceedings was not a reasonable one. The Court of Appeal distinguished mixed and ulterior motives clarifying that 'mixed motives are to be distinguished from an oblique motive which is so dominant and so unrelated to the proceedings that it renders them an abuse of process'.[2]

1 [2017] EWCA Crim 2119.
2 [2017] EWCA Crim 2119 at 27.

R (Wokingham Borough Council) v Scott[1]

4.26 This case involved a local authority applying to appeal a Crown Court judge's decision to stay proceedings against the respondents. The trial judge had stayed the proceedings in part due to concern that the local authority's decision to prosecute had been influenced by the financial benefit they would obtain from the subsequential confiscation order. The stay was upheld: where there is a potential conflict between a financial interest in the outcome of the prosecution and the objectivity required of a prosecutor, the prosecutor must be scrupulous in avoiding any perception of bias.[2] However, it does not follow that where the prosecuting agency will stand to benefit from a subsequent confiscation order, that the prosecution will always be stayed for abuse. In *R (on the application of Kombou) v Wood Green Crown Court*,[3] the court held:

> 'It is not however the case that a decision to prosecute will inevitably be open to successful challenge if it might eventually lead to a confiscation order from which the prosecuting authority will benefit. It will often be necessary, before a decision to prosecute is taken, for someone within the authority to consider the possibility that confiscation proceedings might be

brought: it may for example be necessary to consider an application for a restraint order pursuant to s.40(2) of the POCA during the investigation, and it may be necessary to consider the allocation of limited resources as between a number of investigations. There is a crucial distinction between investigators legitimately considering the possibility of confiscation proceedings, and the decision-maker being improperly motivated to decide in favour of prosecution by the prospect of financial gain to the authority.'

1 [2019] EWCA Crim 205; [2020] 4 WLR 2.
2 See also *R v Knightland Foundation* [2018] EWCA Crim 1860.
3 [2020] EWHC 1529 (Admin); [2020] 2 Cr App R 28 para 85.

D. Ltd v A1[1]

4.27 In *D. Ltd v A*, the applicant, a limited company, appealed a terminating ruling staying a private prosecution alleging fraud against a number of individuals. The proposed defendants had succeeded in staying the proceedings at first instance relying on fierce criticism of the motives and conduct of the applicant, specifically that it had 'a lack of open mind, bias, prejudice and vindictiveness'.[2]

The Court of Appeal, in upholding the appeal, set out the key distinction between improper motive, recognising that seeking retribution is not an improper motive, and improper conduct, for which any prejudice must be considered.

In applying these principles, the court affirmed the high threshold of bad faith or dishonesty that is required to issue a stay on the grounds of prosecutorial conduct, referencing how this should be balanced against 'the public interest in upholding a person's statutory right to initiate and pursue a private prosecution and the public interest in alleged serious criminality'.[3]

1 [2017] EWCA Crim 1172; [2018] Crim LR 993.
2 [2017] EWCA Crim 1172; [2018] Crim LR 993 at 53.
3 [2017] EWCA Crim 1172; [2018] Crim LR 993 at 94.

REMOVAL OF RIGHT TO A PARTICULAR TYPE OF TRIAL

R v Rotherham Justices, ex parte Brough[1]

4.28 The defendant was alleged to have committed the offence when aged 16. Pursuant to s 24 of the Magistrates' Court Act 1980, if when the issue of mode of trial was dealt with by the magistrate, the defendant was under 17, then the case could only be remitted to the magistrates for trial. However, the charge was indictable only if the defendant was aged 17. In the event, the return date of the applicant's summons was fixed for the day after his 17th birthday. His suspicious defence solicitor inquired with both the court and the CPS why this should be so and after initial denials from the CPS, ascertained that the timing of the defendant's hearing was not a matter of chance but because the CPS felt that the case should only dealt with by the Crown Court. The applicant alleged misuse of process. The Divisional Court held that manipulation of the date in this way by the CPS was an unacceptable way of advancing the interests of justice. However, the court declined to attribute any element of misconduct or mala fides to anyone within the CPS. The court held that this was not a case where there was 'some element of bad faith or sharp practice or oppressive or overreaching behaviour or, to use a colloquialism some form of dirty trick'. Furthermore, the court held that the defendant was not prejudiced.

1 [1991] Crim LR 522.

R v Redbridge Justices and Fox, ex p Whitehouse[1]

4.29 The defendant was charged with an either way offence and expressed a preference for summary trial. This was opposed by the prosecution, who wished for a Crown Court trial. Subsequently, an additional more serious charge was laid, making the case indictable only. The defendant alleged that this additional charge was motivated by a desire to deprive the defendant of his right to elect for summary trial. The Divisional Court held that such a motive by a prosecutor was permissible provided that on the facts disclosed the court is satisfied that the course proposed by the prosecution is 'proper and appropriate' in the light of the evidence before them.[2]

Applied in *DPP v Hammerton* [2009] EWHC 921 (Admin) H had been charged, along with others, with attempted theft. He pleaded not guilty and elected a jury trial. At the committal the Crown sought to substitute the lesser charge of motor vehicle interference in respect of H only. H contended this would amount to an abuse of process. The magistrates declined to allow the new charge to be laid. On appeal by the DPP, Davis J upheld the decision by the Magistrates' Court decision. The CPS was not entitled to substitute a lesser charge for a more serious charge unless to do so was proper and appropriate to the facts of the case; its application had been made promptly; and considerations of the good administration of justice and the wider picture, for example the situation of any co-accused, had been properly considered.[3]

1 (1992) 94 Cr App R 332.
2 (1992) 94 Cr App R 332 per Neill LJ at 338.
3 per Davis J at 30.

R v Martin[1]

4.30 The appellant was charged with murder and convicted. The conviction was awarded by a court-martial which had been convened in Germany. What was exceptional about this case was that the appellant had been brought from England, where he was eligible to trial by jury, to stand trial by a court-martial in Germany. The reason for this was because when the alleged murder occurred, the appellant was subject to military law. The appellant argued that the court-martial procedure was unfair principally for two reasons: first, the trial of a young civilian by court-martial was inherently unfair and oppressive; secondly, the decision to try the appellant by court-martial in Germany rather than allow him to be tried in England constituted an abuse.

1 [1998] 1 All ER 193.

4.31 The House of Lords dismissed this appeal. It construed the relevant provisions of the Army Act 1955 to hold that Parliament had approved trial by court-martial as an appropriate mode of trial for young civilians in certain circumstances. Furthermore, the decision not to allow a trial in England on the grounds of *forum conveniens* was not inherently unfair or an abuse.

REMOVAL OF A POTENTIAL DEFENCE

4.32 In *R v Asfaw* the Court of Appeal[1] noted its concern over the apparently standard prosecutorial practice, when an asylum seeker seeks to leave the country for another place of refuge using false documents, to combine a charge of infringement of the Forgery and Counterfeiting Act with a charge of attempting to obtain air services by deception. On the facts, the defendant was acquitted of the forgery count (count 1), but pleaded guilty to the deception count (count 2), there being no statutory defence (under s 31 of the Immigration and Asylum Act 1999) to the new count 2, which was added to the indictment. The court considered the different policy considerations. The prosecution suggested that the second count may have been added out of concern for the financial position of the airlines. However, the sentencing judge hinted other factors were at play. The Court of Appeal held that, if the second count had been added in the interests of immigration control, in order to prevent the asylum seeker from relying on the s 31 defence, there would be strong grounds for contending that the practice amounted to an abuse of process. The decision suggests that there may well be occasions where the defence can call into question prosecutorial policy which leads to unfairness. The Appeal Court substituted the sentence of nine months' imprisonment with an absolute discharge.

On appeal to the House of Lords,[2] it was held that if the count was included in the indictment to prevent Ms Asfaw from relying on the defence which s 31 would otherwise provide, there would be strong grounds for arguing that that was an abuse of process. The trial judge could not be criticised for acting in accordance with binding authority[3] in rejecting Ms Asfaw's preliminary objection to the count, however, he should have stayed further prosecution of the count, and if the jury acquitted the defendant on the count of using a false instrument with intent, the stay should have been maintained. It was an abuse of process to prosecute her to conviction.

1 [2006] Crim LR 906; [2006] EWCA Crim 707.
2 [2008] UKHL 31.
3 *R (on the application of Pepushi) v Crown Prosecution Service* [2004] EWHC 798 (Admin), [2004] Imm AR 549 cited.

PROSECUTION OVERCHARGING

4.33 In *Hui Chi-Ming v R*[1] the defendant was alleged to have been an accomplice to murder. Two years before his trial, the alleged killer had been acquitted of the murder and convicted of manslaughter. The prosecution offered the defendant a plea bargain: the murder count would be dropped in return for a plea of guilty to manslaughter. This was rejected and ultimately the defendant was convicted of murder. He submitted that his trial for murder was an abuse. Considering the previous acquittal of the alleged principal for murder it was unfair for this trial to proceed. Furthermore, the prosecution should only have charged manslaughter. The Privy Counsel held that there was no evidence of deliberate overcharging by the prosecution and that on the evidence the prosecution were entitled to bring a charge of murder despite the earlier acquittal of the alleged principal offender. In Lowry LJ's view there was nothing which could credibly be described as an abuse of process:

> 'that is, something so unfair and wrong that the courts should not allow a prosecutor to proceed with what is in all respects a regular proceeding. There can be no suggestion that the appellant was the victim of a plea bargaining situation … there was no sign of fraud or deceit as between the Crown and the appellant'.[2]

In *R v Forsyth (Elizabeth)*[3] the appellant was charged with two offences of handling stolen goods. It was alleged that knowing or believing that £400,000 had been stolen from a company by a fugitive Asil Nadir, she had disposed of or assisted in the disposal of the money by arranging for it to be sent from Switzerland to England. As part of her defence, it was contended that the judge ought to have stayed the appellant's trial as being an abuse of the Court's process: the prosecution had abandoned the trial of another man, T, who was accused of greater criminal involvement with Nadir, on the ground that he could not have a fair trial in Nadir's absence. The Court of Appeal held that it was not an abuse for the Serious Fraud Office to press home the prosecution of one person who 'appears to have been involved at short notice in assisting in an isolated transaction on the fringe of an immense misuse of company funds', after the principal defendant fled the jurisdiction and proceedings against others more centrally involved had been abandoned on the ground that they could not be dealt with fairly in his absence.[4]

1 (1991) 94 Cr App R 236.
2 At 251.
3 [1997] 2 Cr App R 299.
4 At 310.

4.34 In *R v Harlow Magistrates' Court, ex p O'Farrell*[1] the prosecution sought to add an additional and more serious charge based on the same facts after the bench had retired to consider its verdict on the original charge. The bench accepted this addition. The Administrative Court held that it was an abuse to add a charge at this stage in the proceedings as it would prejudice the defence case which had already been pleaded in relation to the original charge. This case thus constitutes authority that any changes to a prosecution case after it has closed can only be made in such a way as to not prejudice the defence.

1 [2000] Crim LR 589.

DISPARITY OF TREATMENT ARGUMENTS

4.35 In *R v Petch and Coleman*[1] a somewhat anomalous situation arose whereby the appellants' murder convictions were upheld, albeit that two co-defendants, who had previously also been charged on a joint enterprise murder, had their pleas to manslaughter and other offences accepted. This left the co-defendants, who had previously fled the jurisdiction, with substantially reduced sentences, and the appellants with a significant sense of grievance. The appellants contended that the resulting unfairness amounted to an abuse of process.

1 [2005] 2 Cr App R 40.

4.36 Pill LJ held:

> 'The prosecution's alleged lack of consistency, resulting from pragmatic considerations, which has resulted in an anomaly different from, but in its way as striking as, that in *Hui Chi-ming*, does not open the door to a finding that the verdicts upon the appellants were unsafe. The law does not permit the court to take an overall view of the situation retrospectively and, in the interest of even-handedness, to declare the convictions of the appellants unsafe.'[1]

1 At para 47.

4.37 The court, however, went on to acknowledge that a review might be called for:

> 'Subsequent developments in the law may, with respect, encourage a review of the approach in *Hui Chi-ming* to how prosecutions in second trials based upon the same events as earlier trials are to be conducted. The prosecution were consistent in that case but to proceed against a secondary party for murder when the principal offender has already been convicted only of manslaughter creates a particular sense of grievance absent in the present situation.'[1]

1 At para 49.

4.38 In *R v L*[1] the appellant had been charged with his baby's murder, which led to concerns for the family's other child. In the ensuing proceedings under the Children Act 1989, the judge held that the cause of the baby's death had not been established, and that he was unable to decide whether one parent was more likely to have caused the injuries suffered by the baby than the other. The appellant sought to stay the subsequent murder trial proceedings as an abuse of process, on the basis that the judge's decision and findings in the Children Act proceedings were conclusive of the criminal proceedings. The Court of Appeal dismissed the appeal, holding that the decision in the care proceedings, in which the prosecution took no part, was not, and could not be, a final determination of the criminal proceedings.[2]

1 [2007] 1 Cr App R 1.
2 Applied in *R v IK* [2007] EWCA Crim 971; [2007] 2 Cr App R 15.

TRIAL IN ABSENCE OF A CO-ACCUSED

4.39 In *R v Forsyth*[1] the defendant was charged with handling stolen goods. Her prosecution arose out of allegations concerning the fugitive Asil Nadir. Her prosecution was exceptional in the sense that, following the absconding of Nadir, the prosecution (Serious Fraud Office) had conceded that the trial of the second defendant should not proceed because, in Nadir's absence, it could not be fair to that defendant. However, in relation to Forsyth the SFO pressed ahead despite accepting that she was a peripheral defendant on the fringe of an immense fraud allegedly committed by Nadir and the second defendant. Beldam LJ held that the decision of the SFO to prosecute Forsyth in the circumstances 'seems a strange decision' but nonetheless:

> 'the decision to do so is the prerogative of the SFO and does not in our judgement itself amount to an abuse of process. It is not for us to say whether such a choice accords with ordinary notions of even handedness, or is likely to enhance the public perception of the fairness of a prosecuting authority'.[2]

1 (1997) 2 Cr App Rep 299.
2 (1997) 2 Cr App R 299 at 311.

REPEATED COMMITTAL PROCEEDINGS

4.40 In *R v Manchester City Stipendiary Magistrate, ex p Snelson*[1] Widgery CJ held that a criminal prosecution could be restarted against a defendant by way of fresh committal proceedings or voluntary bill of indictment even where the original proceedings against the defendant at committal had been dismissed. Lord Widgery, however, considered the danger which his judgment might create as vexatious repeated committal proceedings for the same offence against the same defendant. He said:

> '... the only aspect of the whole case which has troubled me is the feeling that if the prosecution are right in their argument there seems to me to be a risk that a defendant might be prejudiced by repeated committal proceedings all failing, resulting in a committal being repeated time after time ... I am satisfied that this particular difficulty is overcome ... by saying that this court has a discretionary power to see that the use of repeated committal proceedings is not allowed to become vexatious or an abuse of the process of the court'.[2]

1 [1977] 1 WLR 911.
2 At 913.

4.41 This issue arose in *R v Horsham Justices, ex p Reeves*[1] where Ackner LJ held that the repeated committal in that case was an abuse. He said:

> 'should the prosecution be entitled as they see it, to treat the first committal proceedings for all practicable purposes as a dummy run and, having concluded that they over-complicated them, from virtually the same proceedings but in a form which they should have been brought if proper thought had been given by the prosecution to them in the first place? In my judgment, to allow such a course in the particular circumstances of this case would be vexatious to the applicant, and for that reason it would, in my judgment, be an abuse'.

Ackner LJ held that the second set of proceedings, although simplified and shortened compared to the first, were vexatious and an abuse.

1 [1981] Crim LR 566.

4.42 However, in *R v Grays Justices, ex p Graham*[1] the Divisional Court held that the proceedings were not vexatious, the defendant having been discharged in the original proceedings on the grounds of delay.

1 (1982) 75 Cr App R 229.

THE RULE IN HUNTER

4.43 In *Hunter v Chief Constable of the West Midlands*[1] the Birmingham Six, following their conviction for terrorist offences, initiated a civil action against the police for assault. Their statement of claim alleged that during their interviews with individual police officers, in which they made alleged confessions, they were beaten and sustained physical injuries. At their criminal trial, the circumstances in which their confessions were obtained was a central issue. A major plank of each of the defendants' case was the assertion that the confessions were untrue, unreliable and coerced. The jury however must have disbelieved this because they convicted all six. At the hearing of this civil action, the defendant police officers contended that the initiation of the civil action was an abuse of process as the action effectively sought to refute or throw into doubt the finding of both the trial judge and the jury at the criminal trial that the Birmingham Six had not been assaulted by the police. In holding that this action constituted an abuse of process, Lord Diplock articulated a rule which has subsequently come to be known as 'The rule in *Hunter*':

> 'The abuse of process which the instant case exemplifies is the initiation of proceedings in a court of justice for the purpose of mounting a collateral attack on a final decision against the intending plaintiff which has been made by another court of competent jurisdiction in previous proceedings in which the intending plaintiff had a full opportunity of contesting the decision in the court by which it was made'.[2]

1 [1982] AC 529.
2 At 541.

4.44 The rule in *Hunter* was exclusively applied in a criminal context in *R v Belmarsh Magistrates' Court, ex p Watts*.[1] The facts of this case are recounted in **Chapter 10** and are not repeated here. One of the matters to be decided in *Watts* was whether the rule in *Hunter* extended to criminal rather than simply civil proceedings. In his judgment Buxton LJ held that the rule in *Hunter* did apply to criminal proceedings. However, he was careful to restrict its application to where the second proceedings 'must in fact and in effect, and not merely in intention, be a challenge to the finding in the first proceedings'. In other words if the second proceedings were successful, this would contradict the judgment in the earlier proceedings. Buxton LJ also relied on the judgment of Bingham MR in *Smith v Linskills*:

> 'The main considerations of public policy which underlie the existing rule are, as we understand, threefold; (i) the affront to any coherent system of justice which must necessarily arise if there subsist two final but inconsistent decisions of courts of competent jurisdiction … (ii) the virtual impossibility

of fairly retrying at a later date the issue which was before the court on the earlier occasion … (iii) the importance of finality in litigation'.[2]

1 [1999] 2 Cr App Rep 188.
2 [1996] 1 WLR 763 at 773.

4.45 Turning to the merits of the case before him Buxton LJ held that the intention of the prosecutor was to undermine his earlier conviction. However, he should have followed the route of appeal rather than initiate collateral criminal proceedings for the same purpose.

4.46 As to the jurisdiction of the Divisional Court to rule that the rule in *Hunter* applied to exclusively criminal proceedings, Buxton LJ cited Lord Lowry in *ex parte Bennett*[1] that it should offend the courts' sense of justice and propriety to be asked to try the accused in the circumstances of this case.[2] Buxton LJ held that this prosecution fell within that category and could therefore be stayed. This, it is submitted, is a novel application to domestic proceedings of *ex parte Bennett* which hitherto had been regarded as applying only with regard to international executive lawlessness.

1 [1994] 1 AC 42.
2 [1994] 1 AC 42 at 74.

FAILURE TO CONDUCT A FAIR INTERVIEW

4.47 Interviews under caution are governed by PACE Code of Practice C. Most abuse or s 78 applications relating to interviews are in connection with some allegation of unfairness or oppression which was said to have occurred during the defendant's interview. However, the courts have also recognised that an abuse can arise where the police/investigators failed to interview the defendant at all or failed to interview him fairly.

4.48 In *R v Trustham*[1] the accused stood trial for drug-money laundering. Following his arrest he was never interviewed but simply charged. The trial judge held that this had prejudiced the defendant in the following way: 'A defendant who does not give evidence having answered questions in interview is nevertheless entitled to have that explanation considered by the jury'. The trial judge also found that the defendant was further prejudiced as follows:

> 'To deprive a suspect of the right to give an explanation at the earliest opportunity, despite him having been cautioned, that anything he did say would be written down and may be given in evidence, must be a breach of a person's human rights and is clearly an abuse'.

1 (27 November 1997, unreported), Southwark Crown Court.

4.49 In the circumstances of *Trustham*, the trial judge held that the defendant had a right to be interviewed and had a right during such interview to provide an explanation as to his state of mind. Depriving the defendant of an interview deprived him from setting out at the earliest opportunity his defence/innocence which the judge held was unfair because this meant that at his subsequent trial, the defendant could not point to what he said immediately after his arrest.

RETRIALS

4.50 Submissions of abuse have occurred in two situations in retrials. First, in the situation where the prosecution's case on the alleged role of the defendant in the offending had changed between his trial and retrial, as exemplified in *R v Mercer*.[1] Second, in *Bowe v R*,[2] where it was proposed to try the defendant a third time after two juries had been unable to agree. It should also be considered that a re-trial may be ordered even in circumstances where an abuse of process was found in the original trial.[3]

1 [2001] EWCA Crim 638, [2001] All ER (D) 187 (Mar).
2 [2001] UKPC 19, [2001] 4 LRC 372.
3 *R v Maxwell (Appellant)* [2010] UKSC 48, [2011] 2 Cr App R 31 (448).

4.51 In *Mercer* the essence of the complaint was that the prosecution should not be permitted to present one set of alleged facts to a court on one occasion and then alter this on a subsequent occasion. This argument almost amounts to a claim that an estoppel arose once the prosecution had set out its case in front of one court. The submission was dismissed by the Court of Appeal. There was no principle of law or fairness which prevented the prosecution from calling new evidence at a retrial and so altering its case. If unfairness had resulted this would have to be based on another complaint arising out of the fact of there being a retrial.

4.52 In *R v Swaine*[1] at the commencement of the retrial, the judge permitted the prosecution to add an additional count to the indictment and it was thus amended. The Court of Appeal held that as a matter of law it was permissible to amend an indictment at the stage of a retrial provided no injustice was done to the defendant.

1 [2001] Crim LR 166.

4.53 Whilst not a retrial, the situation in *DPP v Jimale*[1] is relevant. Here the prosecution opened its case before the justices and the court adjourned before it was completed. At the adjourned hearing the prosecution sought to call a witness whom previously it had not intended to call. A complaint of unfair advantage arising out of the adjournment was made; the prosecution should not be permitted to call a witness whose existence was known about when its case was opened. The justices agreed and stayed the case. The Administrative Court disagreed and held that the obtaining of new witnesses between hearings was both proper and, in many cases desirable. In any event if some unfair advantage had been taken in relation to a particular witness this could be dealt with by exclusion under s 78 rather than a stay.

1 [2001] Crim LR 138.

4.54 In *Bowe* a submission was made before the Privy Council that a second retrial in these circumstances amounted to an abuse as it was an established practice that a prosecution should not seek a conviction after two failed attempts to persuade a jury of the defendant's guilt. The Board however declined to agree and held that ipso facto a second retrial did not amount to an abuse. However, it made plain its view that in this situation it was incumbent on a prosecutor to consider very carefully whether either the interests of justice or the public interest would be served by a third attempt. Clearly here the Board was sending a message that repeated attempts to convict an accused might well amount to oppression and so an abuse.[1]

1 *Bowe* was also applied in *R v Benguit* [2005] EWCA Crim 1953.

4.55 A similar judgment was given in *R v Henworth (Frank)*,[1] where it was held that the practice against a second retrial was only a convention not a proposition of law. However, any prosecutor contemplating this was duty-bound to assess carefully the interests of justice, this to include the defendant's interests taking into account the effect of delay and prejudice. Whilst the retrial did not amount to an abuse of process, nevertheless the length of the proceedings overall, was adjudged to violate the ECHR Art. 6 reasonable time requirements.[2]

1 [2001] EWCA Crim 120, [2001] 2 Cr App R. 4.
2 *Henworth v UK* (2005) 40 EHRR 33.

WITNESSES: CONTACT WITH WITNESSES AND DUTY TO CALL WITNESSES

4.56 Within our system is it not permitted to coach or rehearse witnesses.[1] In *R v Evans*[2] an allegation was made by the defence, of police impropriety in relation to their approach to and meetings with potential defence witnesses. The police in the course of such meetings said that what the witnesses had stated could not be correct. Consequently, some of the witnesses retracted their statements, which they had made previously to the defence solicitors. An allegation that undue pressure had been put upon them by the police was made at the trial, this being the explanation for why the witnesses had suddenly withdrawn their evidence. In essence it was claimed that the abuse was the police contacting the witnesses with the intention of persuading them to withdraw their evidence.

1 *R v Momodou & Limani* [2005] EWCA Crim 177, [2005] 2 All ER 571, [2005] 2 Cr App R 6.
2 [2001] EWCA Crim 730, [2001] All ER (D) 289 (Mar).

4.57 The Court of Appeal held that it was proper for either the defence or prosecution to meet with witnesses who were intended to give evidence for the opposite side. Moreover, arranging such a meeting for the purpose of seeking changes in witness evidence was also permissible so long as no 'undue pressure' was applied which, if this happened, would amount to a contempt of court as well as an abuse. Here there was no evidence that the police had sought to apply such pressure and so the complaint of abuse was dismissed. Waller LJ held:

> 'There was nothing improper in the police revisiting the witnesses. It would be quite improper for the police to put inaccurately the evidence in order to obtain a statement or a change in a statement from a witness. However, in this case it must be remembered it is not the statement which is important, it is the evidence which is ultimately given at the trial. In the circumstances of this case original statements had been obtained, the police had revisited and possibly obtained changes in those statements, but, the defence solicitors

> were in a position to visit those witnesses themselves and put to those witnesses any aspect on which they had been misled by the police'.

In this regard it would obviously be an abuse for a potential witness to be threatened or offered any inducement in return for them changing their evidence. In *R v Schlesinger*[1] machinations to prevent potential witnesses from giving evidence were held to be an abuse.

1 [1995] Crim LR 137. This case is considered further at para **5.150**.

4.58 In *R. v Haringey Justices*,[1] failure by the prosecution to call a particular witness was held not to be an abuse. The court re-affirmed that the prosecution had an unfettered discretion as to which witnesses to call, though in this case it was preferable for the justices to have exercised their power to call the witnesses themselves rather than dismissing the case as an abuse of process.

1 [1996] 2 Cr App R 119.

SELECTIVE PROSECUTION

4.59 Prosecutors are always permitted to exercise a choice over who to prosecute. There is no obligation to treat all suspects equally, in the sense that where the evidence is the same against all it follows that all must be similarly prosecuted. However, decisions on whether to prosecute or not prosecute are amenable to judicial review and are assessed using judicial review principles.

4.60 In criminal trials it is sometimes alleged that a prosecution witness has fabricated or embroidered his evidence as a means of escaping prosecution himself. Accordingly, his evidence should be disregarded. In most cases the credibility of this accusation is a matter for the jury and no abuse arises. An abuse may arise, however, where it is alleged that there has been collusion between the suspect-turned-witness and the investigators; the suspect was in effect offered an inducement to give false evidence by the investigators, this being a promise of immunity for himself, a friend or relative. It is alleged that the prosecution is therefore tainted by this impropriety and is unfair.

4.61 This situation arose in *R v Bigley*[1] where several individuals were arrested for drugs offences. Each was interviewed under caution and some, during their interviews, incriminated the defendant. Having done so, those individuals were then offered immunity in return for agreeing to become prosecution witnesses against the defendant. This offer was taken up. The defendant alleged abuse of power and unfairness. The Court of Appeal held that as a matter of principle it was acceptable for a prosecutor to decide not to prosecute those guilty of less serious offences in order to prosecute those guilty of more serious offences. In itself the means here justified the end. What the court attached great importance to in dismissing the claim of improper inducement was that before there was any consideration of whether anyone should be charged or not, each suspect had been formally interviewed and their version of events obtained. Accordingly, the versions were given without any promise of reward held out by the investigators. Only after this stage was there any discussion about inducements, ie. assistance in return for immunity.

1 [2001] EWCA Crim 3012; [2001] All ER (D) 253 (Dec).

4.62 Keene LJ stated:

> 'If the more significant criminals are to be prosecuted, it may be necessary to get lesser offenders to come to court and give evidence against them and that may require the prosecuting authorities, in some instances, to agree not to prosecute. There may be situations where the continuing pressure or inducement on a witness or witnesses to give evidence against the defendant is so strong, even by the stage of trial, that the judge forms the view that it would be wrong for a jury to place any reliance on such evidence. He would then exclude the evidence and might, in appropriate cases, stay the proceedings. There will be other cases where the situation is less extreme, and where the jury can properly hear the evidence of such a witness, and hear evidence also about the circumstances in which that witness came to make a witness statement, and then make up their minds about the honesty of the witness.
>
> In the present case we are not persuaded that the police abused their powers. The procedure generally adopted was one where the person arrested was interviewed on tape, before a caution was discussed. That, in our judgment, is an important safeguard and one which accords with the national guidance on this matter. Once that situation has been reached, there is no reason why the willingness of a suspect to co-operate with the police should not be taken into account by the police, when deciding whether to caution or not'.

4.63 Investigators and prosecutors will need always to be mindful of allegations of collusion and improper inducement in a trial where an important prosecution witness against whom there was sufficient evidence of criminality to mount a prosecution has nonetheless never been prosecuted.

NON-DISCLOSURE ABUSE

Non-disclosure and unfairness

4.64 An accused must be in a position to fairly advance his arguments by way of fair disclosure of material in the Crown's possession. In *R v Kenneth Togher, Brian Peter Doran, Robert Parsons*[1] the Court of Appeal held that where an accused's right to a fair trial was vitiated, for example because of non-disclosure, this would almost invariably result in the quashing of the conviction. Woolf CJ held 'If they could establish an abuse, then this court would give very serious consideration to whether justice required the conviction to be set aside'.[2] However, it should be considered that non-disclosure itself is not an abuse of process and in most cases the remedy for material non-disclosure would be for the disclosure of the material, rather than ordering a stay.[3]

1 [2001] 1 Cr App R 33.
2 At 468.
3 *R v Asiedu (Manfo Kwaku)* [2015] EWCA Crim 714.

4.65 The Attorney-General's Guidelines on disclosure were originally issued in 2005, updated in December 2013 and again in December 2020. The first paragraph of the new 2020 Guidelines declares:

'Every accused person has a right to a fair trial. This right is a fundamental part of our legal system and is guaranteed by Article 6 of the European Convention on Human Rights (ECHR). The disclosure process secures the right to a fair trial.'

4.66 The only reference to abuse of process in the new 2020 guidelines is a reminder of the prosecutorial obligations to disclose material in circumstances outside of the statutory scheme, for example, material that may allow the defence to advance an abuse of process argument.[1] There is no explicit reference to failures of disclosure leading to potential abuse of process arguments.

1 https://assets.publishing.service.gov.uk/government/uploads/system/uploads/attachment_data/file/946082/Attorney_General_s_Guidelines_2020_FINAL_Effective_31Dec2020.pdf at para 28.

The CPIA 1996; prosecution failures to comply with their disclosure obligations

4.67 The statutory framework for criminal investigations and disclosure is contained within the Criminal Procedure and Investigations Act 1996. This sets out a staged approach with initial prosecution disclosure, disclosure by the defence and a continual review by the prosecution. Part II (ss 22–27) sets out a detailed code of practice in relation to the police's recording and retaining of material which has been obtained during a criminal investigation, and in relation to the provision of material to prosecutors, who are required to make decisions on disclosure. Section 10 of the Act sets out that the prosecution failure to observe time limits does not on its own constitute grounds for staying the proceedings for abuse of process (except if it involves such delay that the accused is denied a fair trial).

4.68 Before even contemplating an abuse of process application, defence practitioners should first exhaust all the CPIA 1996 disclosure routes, and, in particular, the opportunity to make s 8 applications. The applications are founded upon the basis that there is reasonable cause to believe there is prosecution material which, under s 7A of the Act, has not been disclosed to the defence. Adverse findings against the prosecution, on such an application, may also become a factor for a judge to take into account on a subsequent abuse application. For example, the judge may conclude that the prosecution's non-sensitive disclosure schedule was incomplete in material respects.

The problems encountered

4.69 Unfairness can, of course, result in many ways. Examples of disclosure-related problems have included:

(a) failures by the prosecution to comply with their obligations to provide proper disclosure;

(b) exceptionally late disclosure of material;

(c) failures by investigators and/or disclosure officers to properly advise prosecuting solicitors and/or prosecution advocates as to the proper state of disclosure;

(d) the inadvertent or deliberate misleading of prosecuting solicitors and/or prosecution advocates, in relation to non-sensitive, sensitive or public interest immunity material;

(e) the consequent inadvertent misleading of judges tasked to determine the disclosure to which the defence may be entitled.

4.70 In practice, most of the above defects are capable of cure within the trial process, without resort to a stay of proceedings. Some complaints of non-disclosure will be met with disclosure, others by the granting of adjournments to the defence when faced with very late disclosure, or by the exclusion of evidence or suitable judicial directions. Non-disclosure and abuse will generally only be intertwined where there is a complaint of deliberate violation of the accused's right to disclosure.

The case of *Salt*[1] gave guidance on when prosecution non-disclosure may amount to abuse.

Some of the relevant factors to be taken into account when deciding whether non-disclosure amounts to abuse of process included:

- the gravity of the charges;
- the denial of justice to the complainants;
- the necessity for proper attention to be paid to disclosure, the nature and materiality of the failures;
- the conduct of the defence;
- the waste of court resources;
- the effect on the jury; and
- the availability of sanctions other than halting proceedings.

In this case the Court of Appeal, in balancing these factors, despite describing the conduct of the police and CPS as 'reprehensible', instead attached weight to the strong public interest in the grave crimes being tried and the fact that the undisclosed material had limited materiality. The court concluded that it would not be in the interest of justice to stay the proceedings.

However, in *DPP v Petrie*,[2] Lord Justice Gross noted that in some cases:

> 'A wholesale failure on the part of the prosecution to comply with its disclosure obligations may require the prosecution to offer no evidence, in accordance with the professional code for prosecutors and the guidance set out in the CPS/ACPO Disclosure Manual.
>
> The possibility of such an outcome serves to illuminate that only rarely will recourse to an abuse of process argument be necessary or appropriate'.

This demonstrates how each case will be determined upon its own facts and the rare circumstance where the abuse jurisdiction will be successful in relation to non-disclosure issues.

In the guidance case of *R v R*[3] the Court of Appeal gave guidance on the proper approach to disclosure in criminal proceedings involving large quantities of documents, in particular electronic documents, and on the approach to abuse of process where there was delay because of the disclosure exercise. The court summarised the key principles:

1) the prosecution is and must be in the driving seat at the stage of initial disclosure;

2) the prosecution must then encourage dialogue and prompt engagement with the defence;

3) the law is prescriptive of the results, not the method;

4) the process of disclosure should be subject to robust case management by the judge, utilising the full range of case management powers; and

5) flexibility is crucial.

In relation to abuse of process, the Court concluded in this case, that the delay in disclosure was not sufficient to warrant a conclusion that the defendants could not now receive a fair trial. In considering the second limb of abuse, the Court weighed up the gross misconduct that the criminal justice system could not approbate, against the importance that conduct that may merely be the result of state incompetence or negligence should not necessarily justify the abandonment of a trial of serious allegations: 'there is no bright line and a broad brush approach is likely to be necessary'.[4]

The Court decided in this case that there was no deliberate misconduct, no deliberate disregard for a clear direction of the court (as in *Boardman*[5]) and that to allow a successful abuse application in these circumstances would in fact provide a perverse incentive for those charged to undermine the prosecution by creating hurdles to overcome. Again, the case-by-case approach is evident. It is submitted that prosecutorial disclosure failures that might be sufficient to bring a prosecution to an end through an abuse application would require an element of deliberate misconduct or bad faith.

1 [2015] EWCA Crim 662.
2 [2015] EWHC 48 (Admin) at 39.
3 [2015] EWCA Crim 1941.
4 [2015] EWCA Crim 1941 at 72.
5 *R v Boardman* [2015] 1 Cr App R 33.

4.71 Separately, in considering the disclosure of material that would allow for an abuse application to made, the case of *R (on the application of Kay) v Leeds Magistrates' Court* is important.[1] In this case, the court quashed a District Judge's decision to issue summonses for offences of fraud which had been issued on the application of a private prosecutor. The prosecutor had failed to comply with his duty of candour by not disclosing material which would have enabled the court to consider whether the application was an abuse of process or otherwise improper, to consider whether to make further enquiries and to require the party that he sought to prosecute to be notified of the application and to hear that party. The application was granted. The court held that the withholding of material information was in itself a critical factor in determining whether a summons should be set aside as an abuse of the process of the court.

1 [2018] EWHC 1233 (Admin).

RELEVANT ECHR JURISPRUDENCE

4.72 The practitioner submitting on abuse of process may also seek to draw upon the duties of disclosure imposed upon the prosecution by the European Convention on Human Rights ('ECHR'), Art 6 (which are also reflected under the CPIA 1996). Indeed, the making of parallel abuse and Art 6 submissions is now commonplace, given the inevitable overlap in the arguments.

4.73 In addition to the fair trial guarantee under the ECHR, Art 6 subsection (1), subsection (3)(b) provides a guarantee that is frequently relied upon, for it states the right 'to have adequate time and facilities for the preparation of his defence'. In *Kaufman v Belgium*[1] the Commission stated that:

> 'everyone who is a party to... proceedings should have a reasonable opportunity of presenting his case to the court under conditions which do not place him at a substantial disadvantage vis-à-vis his opponent...'

1 (1986) 50 DR 98.

4.74 The ECtHR has been prepared to condemn lack of defence access to prosecution papers in the most inferior courts, notably in the decision of *Foucher v France.*[1] In *Foucher* the applicant and his father were prosecuted for insulting behaviour towards public service employees. The case was tried in the local police court where they chose to represent themselves and the prosecutor refused them access to their files on the basis it could only be supplied to a lawyer not a private individual. The ECtHR found a violation of Art 6(1) and Art 6(3)(b).

1 (1997) 25 EHRR 234.

4.75 Whilst the ECtHR has made it clear in its decision in *Edwards v United Kingdom*[1] and in a string of subsequent cases, that Art 6 generally requires the prosecution to disclose to the defence all material evidence for or against an accused, it is nevertheless also clear that the entitlement to disclosure of relevant evidence is not an absolute right. This principle was further emphasised by the Court in the 2008 decision of *Botmeh and Alami v United Kingdom.*[2] In *Van Mechelen v Netherlands*[3] the court adopted a principle of 'strict necessity' in this regard; one which permits on necessity grounds some non-disclosure of otherwise disclosable material. Justifications which have been accepted as falling within this remit include national security, the protection of vulnerable witnesses and the keeping secret of police methods of investigation.[4] Clearly this principle is analogous to our domestic doctrine of public interest immunity. It should be noted that *Edwards* was a case decided before the House of Lords established the governing principles and safeguards which apply to public interest immunity hearings in *H and C.*[5] In the context of electronic data, the ECtHR has considered that an important safeguard in the sifting process is to ensure that the defence is provided with an opportunity to be involved in the laying-down of the criteria for determining what might be relevant for disclosure.[6]

1 (1992) 15 EHRR 417.
2 (2008) 46 EHRR 31.
3 (1997) 25 EHRR 647.
4 See *PG and JH v United Kingdom* [2002] Crim LR 308; and *Rowe and Davis v United Kingdom* (2000) 30 EHRR 1.
5 [2004] 2 Cr App R 10.
6 *Sigurður Einarsson and Others v Iceland* Application no. 39757/15.

PUBLIC INTEREST IMMUNITY

4.76 The general principles underlying public interest immunity are well-known. Where the prosecution contend that it would be detrimental to the public interest for certain otherwise disclosable material to be disclosed to the accused, they may seek judicial permission for such non-disclosure. The circumstances where prosecutors should consider the necessity of seeing the judge *ex parte*, however, have now become heavily proscribed as a result of the leading House of Lords judgment in *R v H and C*.[1] The forum for such an application for non-disclosure is known as a public interest immunity hearing where, as a general rule, only the prosecution are represented and make submissions. In exceptional cases, a 'Special Counsel' may be instructed to make submissions on the material, which is said to fall into the 'sensitive' category.

1 [2004] 2 Cr App R 10.

4.77 In order that the prosecution do not abuse their right to seek a public interest immunity/ non-disclosure order concerning material it is obviously vital that true and full representations concerning the material's relevance and sensitivity are made to the judge. The motivation for such a hearing should never be to withhold material from the defence which might embarrass the prosecution or strengthen a defence application or worse still, to prevent the accused from receiving a fair trial. In essence, if the sole or dominant motive for the making of such an application is to gain a forensic advantage then it should never be made. Without doubt if any or similar motivation influences the prosecution and leads it to seek non-disclosure this will amount to a serious abuse of power falling squarely within the abuse doctrine.

4.78 The Court of Appeal's dicta in *R v Davis, Johnson and Rowe* remains applicable to prosecution *ex parte* applications for orders for non-disclosure, under the rules and the legislation. In this decision, the court set out the correct procedure to be followed, where the prosecution attempt to withhold material on the basis of public interest immunity. There may be occasions where, on the basis of the *Davis* decision, a judge will require a prosecutor to provide the defence with notice of an intended PII application and/or the nature of the material, so as to allow the defence to make the most informed submissions *inter partes*. Following the House of Lords decision in *R v H*, there is now no obligation upon the prosecution to disclose material which might not reasonably be viewed as capable of undermining the prosecution's case, or of assisting the case for the defence. Further, neutral material or material damaging to the accused is not required to be disclosed, and should not therefore be brought to the court's attention. On the decision of *H*, it will only be in truly borderline cases that the prosecution should seek a ruling from the judge on the disclosable nature of material in their possession.

4.79 An *ex parte* or one-sided application in an adversarial regime confers a heavy responsibility upon the prosecution to ensure that the judge hearing it is furnished only with accurate information and all points of relevance are clearly made. Inevitably a judge, who may not be the trial judge, in such a hearing is heavily dependent upon the prosecutor's submissions and if they are inaccurate, either accidentally or deliberately, then an injustice results. As one commentator noted:

> 'It is well established that the judge's role in overseeing disclosure of such material is vital in guaranteeing a fair trial, and this depends on there being scrupulously accurate information provided to the judge ... The effect of the trial judge being denied the true picture is to render meaningless any assessment of whether that material should be disclosed to the defence'.[1]

1 See *R v Patel* [2002] Crim LR 304.

4.80 The duty on the Crown to ensure that only accurate information is presented to the judge during an *ex parte* application, was underlined in *R v Jackson*.[1] In that case, prosecuting counsel, relying on inaccurate information supplied by the officer in the case, misled the trial judge in an *ex parte* public interest immunity hearing. The extreme danger of this was demonstrated in *Jackson* because it was purely fortuitous that the error was uncovered when, post-conviction, the error came to the attention of the prosecuting counsel in the course of a different case.

1 [2000] Crim LR 377; see commentary to the report.

4.81 *Jackson* illustrates that the inherent danger of the, generally speaking, one-sided public interest immunity hearings is that if wrong information is conveyed to the court during one, there is a substantial danger that it will never be identified as such. The defence are excluded and the trial judge may be ill-equipped to probe what is said to him/her. It is obviously a matter of concern that absent the appointment of an *amicus* acting in the interests of the defence, there are inadequate safeguards to either prevent or identify mistakes of the kind which happened in *Jackson* from recurring. The only practical remedy is for the courts to constantly remind the prosecution of their onerous duties of fairness and accuracy and that if the court is misled, this will be treated very seriously via the abuse jurisdiction.

Patel and Early; misleading the judiciary and prosecution bad faith

4.82 In the cases of *R v Patel*[1] and *R v Early*,[2] the Court of Appeal was faced with a situation where it appeared that a number of Crown Court judges had been consistently misled during different public interest immunity hearings by officers of Customs and Excise. Both of these cases involved allegations of massive alcohol diversion against the two groups of appellants concerning the same bonded warehouse, London City Bond. At their individual trials some of the appellants had pleaded guilty whereas others had been convicted by juries. In all of these appeals the complaint of non-disclosure and misleading of judges was the same; that Customs had misled the court as to their relationship with and the status of participating informants who were, in addition, prosecution witnesses.

1 [2001] EWCA Crim 2505.
2 [2002] EWCA Crim 1904, [2002] All ER (D) 419 (Jul).

4.83 In *Patel,* Customs largely conceded that the above complaints were valid. The prosecution counsel when appearing for Customs at the public interest immunity hearings had, because they had been misled themselves, misled the court. Further when giving evidence in support of the public interest immunity applications, various Customs officers had also given false information. Moreover, in view of having been misled, when presenting their case to the jury, prosecution counsel had also put forward a false case. Faced with such an appalling situation Longmore LJ concluded:

> 'This failure was so far reaching in nature as to have led, not to those uncomfortable and arguably disturbing omissions that may be the inevitable consequence of considered and proper applications and decisions in relation to non-disclosure but, to both counsel and judge presenting the case to the jury in significant respects on a false basis'.

4.84 The court held there was a serious failure on the part of the prosecution, not simply to disclose the true status of the two individuals in question, but also 'the extent of their participation in the offences with Customs' encouragement'.

4.85 Whilst admitting the catalogue of misconduct by officers, Customs nonetheless submitted that the convictions of the appellants should not be quashed as they were clearly guilty of the offences they had either pleaded to or been convicted of. Thus they had not had an unfair trial and the convictions were safe. Accordingly, the court ought not to quash the convictions on the ground of abuse of process. The court was not persuaded by this submission, holding on the ground of public policy that the misleading of the judges below was an unconscionable act for which the censure of quashed convictions was appropriate. In quashing the convictions in *Patel* the court was influenced by that fundamental consideration for the courts, namely maintaining the integrity of the criminal process itself. On that theme, Longmore LJ cited the words of Roch LJ in *R v Hickey*:[1]

> '... the integrity of the criminal process is the most important consideration for courts which have to hear appeals against conviction. Both the innocent and the guilty are entitled to fair trials. If the trial process is not fair: if it is distracted by deceit or by material breaches of the rules of evidence or procedure, then the liberties of all are threatened'.

1 (30 July 1997, unreported) p 371 of the transcript.

4.86 In *Early* eight appellants successfully appealed against their convictions on the ground that they had pleaded guilty, first, on the false assumption that full and proper disclosure had been made to them by the prosecution and, second, in the light of the non-disclosure of the existence and/or roles of the informants. In two of their cases it was further argued that the lying evidence of the prosecution witnesses had precluded them from making an effective application to stay proceedings as an abuse of process.

4.87 The eight appellants' conjoined appeals arose from three different, albeit related, sets of Crown Court proceedings (in Wood Green, Southwark and Kingston-upon-Thames). The Kingston proceedings revealed, first, that lies had been told to the trial judge by prosecution witnesses, both in the course of public interest immunity hearings and on a 'voir dire' and, secondly, that the lies were part of a deliberate concealment policy operated on the part of Customs and Excise officers. The court noted that the trial judge may have acceded to the defence abuse argument had he not been so misled on disclosure. Similar conclusions were drawn in relation to the two other proceedings. Consistent with the Court of Appeal's approach in *R v Mullen,*[1] as approved in *R v Togher*[2] Rose LJ found that the guilty pleas were no bar to preventing the quashing of the convictions.

1 [1999] 2 Cr App Rep 143.
2 [2001] 1 Cr App Rep 33.

4.88 The lessons to be learned from *Early* and *Patel* should be clear, for Rose LJ made it plain the courts will not tolerate such injustice. He held:

> 'Judges can only make decisions and counsel can only act and advise on the basis of the information with which they are provided. The integrity of our system of criminal trial depends on judges being able to rely on what they are told by counsel and on counsel being able to rely on what they are told by each other. This is particularly crucial in relation to disclosure and public interest immunity hearings … Furthermore, in our judgment, if, in the course of a public interest immunity hearing or an abuse argument, whether on the voir dire or otherwise, prosecution witnesses lie in evidence to the judge, it is to be expected that, if the judge knows of this, or this court subsequently learns of it, an extremely serious view will be taken. It is likely that the prosecution case will be regarded as tainted beyond redemption, however strong the evidence against the defendant may otherwise be'.[1]
>
> 'It is a matter of crucial importance to the administration of justice that prosecuting authorities make full relevant disclosure prior to the trial and that prosecuting authorities should not be encouraged to make inadequate disclosure with a view to defendants pleading guilty'.[2]

Taking a number of considerations into account, the court in *Early* did not consider it in the interests of justice to order retrials for any of the eight appellants.

1 [2002] EWCA Crim 1904, para 10.
2 [2002] EWCA Crim 1904, para 18.

4.89 The consequences of the decision in *Early* have reverberated. In *R v Gell*[1] the court quashed a further seven convictions of all those accused in another Customs operation called Stockade. Here it was conceded by Customs that the Crown Court judge in that case had been misled by prosecution counsel in the context of a defence abuse application. However, in *R v Lawless*,[2] it was held that despite the potential for the judge to have been misled by an officer in a public interest immunity hearing, the officer's conduct had not affected the strength of the Crown's evidence and nor had it strengthened the defence's case and the conviction was not found to be unsafe.

1 [2003] EWCA Crim 123, [2003] All ER (D) 221 (Feb).
2 [2016] EWCA Crim 2185, [2016] 12 WLUK 591.

ABUSE OF PROCESS IN CASES INVOLVING VICTIMS OF TRAFFICKING OR MODERN SLAVERY

4.90 The prosecution of victims of trafficking or modern slavery is a further important area to consider the doctrine of abuse of process. Prior to the Modern Slavery Act 2015, abuse of process was a possible remedy to fill the lacuna in the law, which appeared to allow victims to be prosecuted.[1]

1 *R v LM* [2010] EWCA Crim 2327, [2011] 1 Cr App R 12 (135); *L, HVN, THN & T v R* [2013] EWCA Crim 991, [2014] 1 All ER 113; *R v DS* [2020] EWCA Crim 285.

4.91 Since the Modern Slavery Act 2015, and the availability of the defence pursuant to s 45 of that Act the position has shifted. In *DS*,[1] the court held the abuse of process doctrine could no longer immunise a defendant who claimed to be a victim of modern slavery from prosecution, the responsibility for deciding the facts relevant to the status of an individual as a victim of trafficking is a question for the jury. A victim of modern slavery, even if recognised as a victim through the National Referral Mechanism (NRM), may therefore still be prosecuted. The Court concluded (at [40]):

> 'Cases to which the MSA 2015 applied should proceed on the basis they will be stayed only if an abuse of process as conventionally defined is found. This involves two categories of abuse, as is well known. The first is that a fair trial is not possible and the second is that it would be wrong to try the defendant because of some misconduct by the state in bringing about the prosecution.'

The position was confirmed in *A*,[2] where the court concluded that the CPS guidance on prosecution, in particular the application of the public interest stage test, was an adequate safeguard for preventing victims of trafficking being prosecuted

1 [2020] EWCA Crim 285.
2 [2020] EWCA Crim 1408.

Chapter 5

Abuse of power by the executive

GENERAL PRINCIPLES

5.01 As has been seen above, the modern law of abuse of process allows the court to stay proceedings where it is impossible to give the accused a fair trial *or* where trying the accused would be an affront to the integrity of the criminal justice system. The latter limb of this common law abuse jurisdiction has no equivalent in the jurisprudence of the ECtHR and so this domestic right is not addressed there. Under the ECHR, trials can be halted only if it is unfair to try a defendant or if a defendant cannot receive a fair trial. Section 11 of the HRA 1998, however, makes plain that such a domestic right is preserved despite incorporation and the House of Lords held in *R (Daly) v Secretary of State for the Home Department*[1] that incorporation did not lessen a legal protection already enjoyed by an accused under domestic law. This is because the protection of the ECHR is to provide a minimum floor of fundamental rights: it does not stop states from providing a more extensive ceiling.

1 [2001] 2 AC 532, see paras 30–31.

5.02 The second limb of abuse as established by the House in *ex parte Bennett*,[1] namely that, where a court is aware of a serious abuse of power by the executive, it may refuse to allow the police or prosecuting authority to take advantage of such by regarding it as an abuse of process, also goes significantly further than the test of fairness as established by s 78 of the Police and Criminal Evidence Act 1984. The s 78 discretion is exercised inside, and presupposes, a trial and it concerns the fairness of that trial. It is solely concerned with the impact of the admissibility of evidence on the overall fairness of proceedings whereas abuse seeks to consider whether a trial should be held at all. Where, in particular, there is an allegation of bad faith or oppression, there is no symmetry between the test of fairness of proceedings in s 78 and abuse.

1 *R v Horseferry Road Magistrates' Court, ex p Bennett* [1994] AC 42.

5.03 This point is clearly illustrated by the submissions made in *R v Stapleton*.[1] Here, the accused were charged with VAT fraud following a very lengthy and intrusive surveillance operation mounted by the police. The defence argued abuse on the ground of bad faith and abuse of power; that the authorities were determined to apprehend one of the accused for some crime and that, in reality, the real motive for the surveillance was not suspicion of ongoing criminal activity but an arbitrary and wholesale investigation of the accused. As such, this *ad hominem* investigation was impermissible and in any event in this particular case was wholly disproportionate. It also constituted a violation of Art 8. Thus, it was argued that the trial ought to be stayed for *Bennett*-type abuse as an affront to the criminal justice system itself.

1 [2002] Crim LR 584.

5.04 A similar argument was developed in *R v Khachik.*[1] There was, in that case, no challenge to the integrity of the evidence produced by a covert probe, which formed a fundamental part of the prosecution case against the applicant for conspiring to supply class A drugs. There was, however, a 'root and branch attack' upon the credibility and behaviour of the police officers, who gave evidence against the defendants at their trial in relation to the covert surveillance aspect of the case.[2] The applicant argued that the proceedings should have been stayed as an abuse of process on the basis that the police had dishonestly created the application form under Pt II of the Regulation of Investigatory Powers Act 2000 for the authorisation of the probe and intentionally flouted the rules relating to its use. The applicant contended that the police had thereby manipulated the process of justice such that the prosecution should have been stayed.

1 [2006] EWCA Crim 1272.
2 See judgment paras 36 et seq.

5.05 The trial judge concluded that, whilst the police officers had behaved improperly, they had not been dishonest (in the way in which the application form under RIPA had been completed) and had not set out deliberately to deceive. The Court of Appeal found that it could not go behind the trial judge's findings in that regard and, on the basis of the finding that they had not been dishonest, the police were entitled to the authorisation they had sought in respect of the covert surveillance. As a result, the proceedings were rightly not stayed as an abuse. Nonetheless, the Court observed that if the judge had found that the authorisation had been obtained by deception, 'that would have been a proper basis for staying the proceedings as an abuse of process',[1] notwithstanding the fact that no issue was taken with the integrity of the evidence obtained in itself.

1 At para 39.

5.06 The power to stay proceedings in such circumstances constitutes what has been called a 'very broad discretion indeed'.[1] However, it must be remembered that this is an exceptional power and that an application to stay proceedings will have to cross a high threshold to be successful. In *Warren v Attorney General of Jersey*, it was held that, even where the police were *'unquestionably guilty of grave prosecutorial misconduct'*,[2] it was not necessarily irrational for a court to refuse to stay proceedings. The *Warren* and *Maxwell* cases similarly conclude that, where there is no evidence of error of law or fact, or of irrationality, the judge's decision will not be interfered with by appellate courts.[3] Both cases emphasised the discretion judges possess to decide whether to issue a stay for abuse of process to protect the integrity of the system. The judgments are set out and considered below.

1 *Warren v Attorney General* [2012] 1 AC 22, at para 80, per Lord Brown. See discussion at paras **5.14–5.29**.
2 At para 45.
3 *Warren* [2012] 1 AC 22 at para 43 and *Maxwell* [2011] 1 WLR 1837 at paras 19 and 44.

R v Maxwell[1]

5.07 In *R v Maxwell*, the appellant had been convicted of the murder of an elderly man during a robbery. The evidence against him came largely from an informer. A Criminal Cases Review Commission investigation found that the police had engaged in widespread and sustained misconduct which included the concealment of evidence, perjury, and the provision of improper payments and benefits to the informer in exchange for his evidence. The appellant's convictions were quashed but the Court of Appeal ordered a retrial under s 7 of the Criminal Appeal Act 1968. The tainted evidence would not be used at the retrial and Maxwell had made confessions about his guilt whilst in prison. The Supreme Court had to decide whether it was appropriate to order a retrial in the light of the executive misconduct which had taken place. Lord Brown noted the enormous extent of the malfeasance:

> 'To describe police misconduct on this scale merely as shocking and disgraceful is to understate the gravity of its impact upon the integrity of the prosecution process. It is hard to imagine a worse case of sustained prosecutorial dishonesty designed to secure and hold a conviction at all costs.'[2]

1 [2011] 1 WLR 1837.
2 At para 83.

5.08 However, despite acknowledging the scale of the misconduct, the Supreme Court upheld the Court of Appeal's decision to order a retrial. In so doing, it noted the lack of any precedent covering a situation where the court had to consider the relevance of prosecutorial misconduct in the original proceedings on the question of a retrial. The decision is analysed here because the Supreme Court concluded that the decision to retry was analogous (although not coterminous) with the decision to stay for abuse of process[1] and their Lordships extensively considered the pre-existing case law in relation to abuse of process. Lord Dyson confirmed:

> 'It is well established that the Court has the power to stay proceedings in two categories of case, namely (i) where it will be impossible to give the accused a fair trial and (ii) where it offends the court's sense of justice and propriety to be asked to try the accused in the particular circumstances of the case. In the first category of case, if the court concludes that an accused cannot receive a fair trial, it will stay the proceedings without more. No question of the balancing of competing interests arises'.[2]

However, Lord Dyson further noted that:

> 'In deciding whether or not the interests of justice require a retrial, it is surely clear that the Court of Appeal would be entitled to disregard the earlier misconduct since it would have no effect at the retrial. The only justification for refusing a retrial on the grounds of the misconduct in such a case would be to mark the court's disapproval of that historical misconduct and to discipline the police. But that is not the function of the criminal courts.'[3]

1 At para 21.
2 At para 13.
3 At para 24.

5.09 Thus, despite the fact that this was not an easy case and despite the fact that 'the egregious and persistent nature of the police misconduct involved invite[d] a forceful response',[1] a retrial was permitted. The conclusion reached by the Supreme Court, on a 3-2 majority, was that the appellate court should only get involved where there was evidence of an error of law or irrationality in the judge's decision. Lord Dyson confirmed that:

> 'The interests of justice is not a hard-edged concept…I do not believe it to be controversial that a decision under section 7 of the 1968 Act as to whether the interests of justice require a retrial calls for an exercise of judgment which should only be upset on appeal if it was plainly wrong in the sense that it is one which no reasonable court could have made or if the court took into account immaterial factors or failed to take into account material factors.'[2]

Similarly, Lord Rodgers noted:

> 'Of course, if the Court of Appeal reached a decision on retrial which no reasonable Court of Appeal could have reached, then doubtless this court could intervene to put matters right. But that is not the position in this case'.[3]

1 At para 53.
2 At paras 19 and 38.
3 At para 44.

5.10 The Supreme Court held that the Court of Appeal had adopted the correct approach and had appropriately balanced all the relevant factors. In undertaking the requisite balancing exercise, Lord Mance noted that:

> 'the court is entitled to bear in mind the effect on public confidence in the administration of justice if persons who have on the face of it admitted to very serious crimes (and who, if their admissions are true, perjured themselves at the original trial) are not retried (as they in fact said they wished when making the admissions) in order to establish the truth.'[1]

1 At para 54.

5.11 The court found it significant that the retrial would not be based on evidence resulting from the misconduct, although, clearly, the confessions made by the appellant would not have been made but for the misconduct which had led it his conviction. However, the court concluded that the so-called 'but for' test was simply one relevant factor to be considered. It was not a determinative test.[1] Lord Brown, with whom Lord Collins agreed, confirmed that he would have allowed the appeal, placing reliance on the 'but for' test:

> 'this case can be seen to come within the same category of "but for" situations as the wrongful extradition and entrapment cases: but for the prosecutorial misconduct which initially secured the appellant's conviction and then ensured the failure of his appeal, he would never have made the series of admissions upon the basis of which it is now sought to prosecute him afresh.'[2]

1 At para 26.
2 At para 102.

5.12 For Lord Brown, to allow the trial to proceed would mean that:

> 'Either way, the likelihood is that were a trial now to take place and a conviction to be obtained on the basis of these admissions, those responsible for corrupting the original process would still be seen thereby to have achieved their ends and in the long term to have engineered the appellant's conviction. That to my mind is the critical consideration in this case. The court should be astute to avoid giving the impression that it is prepared, even in this limited way, to condone such unforgivable executive misconduct as occurred here.'[1]

Lord Collins focus was similarly on the integrity of the criminal justice system:

> 'In my judgment, the level of misconduct is such that the interests of justice demand that, after a conviction procured by such misconduct, and after the accused has served a substantial sentence, and would not have made the admissions but for the conviction so procured, there be no retrial. I would find that the interests of justice demand the application of the integrity principle. In this case it means that there should be no retrial on evidence which would not have been available but for a conviction obtained (and upheld) as a result of conduct so fundamentally wrong that for the criminal process to act on that evidence would compromise its integrity.'[2]

1 At para 102.
2 At para 115.

5.13 What lessons can be drawn from *Maxwell*? First, it is important to recall that it was not strictly an abuse of process case but one concerning the power of the court to order a retrial on finding that the original trial had been tainted by prosecutorial misconduct. The test applied in such circumstances is not coterminous with an abuse of process test. Secondly, their Lordships were prepared to note that this was a decision which could have gone either way but that the discretion is very broad so that appellate courts will not interfere with a determination unless it is obviously legally irrational or erroneous. Thirdly, the facts of the case were rather unique, emphasising again the importance of the case-by-case approach. Beyond this, wider lessons may be difficult to draw, save for a re-affirmation of the importance of correctly identifying and balancing competing public interests.

Warren v the Attorney General of Jersey

5.14 The *Maxwell* decision, though liberally quoted in *Warren v the Attorney General of Jersey*,[1] was embargoed until the conclusion of the re-trial. However, the Judicial Committee of the Privy Council (the Board) had the benefit of reading the decision prior to making its own determination in *Warren*, which did concern abuse of process. In *Warren*, the defendants had been involved in a conspiracy to import cannabis worth millions of pounds from Holland, through Belgium and France, to Jersey. The Jersey police had asked the authorities in those countries for permission to track the defendants and to use an audio device attached to their Jersey-registered vehicle. The French, Belgian and Dutch authorities consented to installation of the tracking device but the French and Dutch refused permission for audio monitoring. The police proceeded to install the audio devices after receiving advice from their Legal Office that the evidence was unlikely to be excluded even if it had been obtained unlawfully. After it emerged that the defendants intended to hire a car in France, the French authorities permitted the Jersey authorities to liaise with the car hire firm about installing a tracking device. However, the Jersey authorities also installed an audio device on the pretext that it was a 'back up' tracking device. The conversations recorded while the vehicle was on route led to the arrest and prosecution of the defendants who argued that they were entitled to a stay because of this prosecutorial misconduct. It was clear that, 'but for' this unlawful misconduct of the police, the prosecution could not have succeeded evidentially.

1 [2012] 1 AC 22.

5.15 The Board recognised that the prosecutorial misconduct was extensive: it involved the planned deception of three foreign authorities and the Attorney-General. However, the Commissioner in Jersey had refused to stay proceedings, emphasising that this was a case concerning a 'serious and organised international drug trafficking conspiracy' so the actions 'were not disproportionate'. The Board condemned the actions of the police, noting that the authorities were 'unquestionably guilty of grave prosecutorial misconduct'.[1] Indeed, Lord Hope acknowledged:

> 'The line between effective policing and illegal conduct may be a fine one, and in some cases it may be necessary for the police to work very close to the margin that divides what is legitimate from what is illegitimate...The margin between what was legitimate and what was illegitimate was well known, and it was crossed deliberately in defiance of the laws of the foreign states.'[2]

1 At para 45.
2 At para 61.

5.16 However, the Board upheld the Commissioner's refusal to stay proceedings as being within the reasonable bounds of judicial discretion as there were other significant factors to be balanced against the argument for a stay including the urgency of the decision, the fact that the defendant was a convicted drug dealer, the poor advice given to the police by the Crown Advocate and the fact that the police had not attempted to mislead the Jersey Court about their actions.[1]

1 At paras 47–50.

5.17 Lord Dyson delivering the lead judgment confirmed that there are two categories of case in which a stay may be justified: (i) where a fair trial could not be held; and (ii) where continuing the proceedings would offend the court's sense of justice. The protection provided by the latter limb involved an act of judicial discretion:

> 'In *Latif*, at p 112G, Lord Steyn said that the law in relation to the second category of case was "settled". As he put it, at pp 112G–113B: "The law is settled. Weighing countervailing considerations of policy and justice, it is for

the judge in the exercise of his discretion to decide whether there has been an abuse of process, which amounts to an affront to the public conscience and requires the criminal proceedings to be stayed: *R v Horseferry Road Magistrates' Court, Ex p Bennett* [1994] 1 AC 42." *Ex p Bennett* was a case where a stay was appropriate because a defendant had been forcibly abducted and brought to this country to face trial in disregard of extradition laws. The speeches in *Ex p Bennett* conclusively establish that proceedings may be stayed in the exercise of the judge's discretion not only where a fair trial is impossible but also where it would be contrary to the public interest in the integrity of the criminal justice system that a trial should take place. An infinite variety of cases could arise. General guidance as to how the discretion should be exercised in particular circumstances will not be useful. But it is possible to say that in a case such as the present the judge must weigh in the balance the public interest in ensuring that those that are charged with grave crimes should be tried and the competing public interest in not conveying the impression that the court will adopt the approach that the end justifies any means.'[1]

1 At para 23.

5.18 Lord Kerr set out the principles regarding the abuse of process protection which have emerged from recent jurisprudence as follows:

'(i) the principal purpose of the examination, in the second category of cases, of the question whether proceedings should be stayed is to determine whether this is necessary in order to protect the integrity of the criminal justice system – see R v Maxwell, at para 13. This principle has been expressed in various, slightly differing ways in a number of judgments on the subject. Thus, in *R v Horseferry Road Magistrates' Court, Ex p Bennett* [1994] 1 AC 42, 74g Lord Lowry said that a stay will be granted where a trial would "offend the court's sense of justice and propriety". In *R v Latif* Lord Steyn stated, at p 112f, that a stay should be granted where to allow the trial to proceed would "undermine public confidence in the criminal justice system and bring it into disrepute". In *R v Mullen* [2000] QB 520, 534c–d Rose LJ said that a stay should be granted notwithstanding the certainty of an accused's guilt where to refuse it would lead to "the degradation of the lawful administration of justice". I consider that it should now be recognised that the best way to describe this basis for a stay is that chosen by Lord Dyson JSC in *R v Maxwell* – that it should be granted where necessary to protect the integrity of the criminal justice system.

(ii) A balancing of interests should be conducted in deciding whether a stay is required to fulfil this primary purpose. As Lord Steyn observed in *R v Latif*, the various factors that might arise in the range of cases in which this issue may have to be considered are potentially extensive and it is unwise to attempt to list these exhaustively or, as Lord Dyson JSC has said in para 26 of his judgment in this appeal, to rigidly categorise those cases in which a stay will be granted. But where a stay is being considered in order to protect the integrity of the criminal justice system, "the public interest in ensuring that those that are charged with grave crimes should be tried" will always weigh in the balance: Lord Steyn in *R v Latif* at p 113 a–b. Lord Steyn mentioned that a possible countervailing factor was that the impression should not be created that the court is giving its sanction to an approach that the end justifies any means. With the emphasis that is given in this and other cases to statements that prosecutorial or police misbehaviour will never be condoned, this may not be as significant a consideration as heretofore. Other factors that will commonly call for evaluation are those referred to in the passage from the book by Professor Choo, *Abuse of Process and Judicial Stays of Criminal Proceedings*, 2nd ed (2008), quoted by Lord Dyson JSC in para 24 of his judgment but, again, these should not be regarded as exhaustive.

(iii) The "but for" factor (ie where it can be shown that the defendant would not have stood trial but for executive abuse of power) is merely one of various matters that will influence the outcome of the inquiry as to whether a stay should be granted. It is not necessarily determinative of that issue.

(iv) A stay should not be ordered for the purpose of punishing or disciplining prosecutorial or police misconduct. The focus should always be on whether the stay is required in order to safeguard the integrity of the criminal justice system.'[1]

1 At para 83.

5.19 The Board concluded that it was impossible to lay down hard and fast rules for the type of case that would give rise to a stay under this ground as it would be a matter for the judge in each case although:

> '…in abduction and entrapment cases, the court will generally conclude that the balance favours a stay'.[1]

1 At para 26.

5.20 Indeed, the suggestion in the case of *R v Grant*[1] that there are some types of cases where a stay was mandatory was rejected. The Board confirmed:

> 'Nevertheless, the Board respectfully considers that the decision in *R v Grant* was wrong. The statement at para 54 suggests that the deliberate invasion of a suspected person's right to legal professional privilege is to be assimilated to the abduction and entrapment cases where the balancing exercise will generally lead to a stay of the proceedings. The Board agrees that the deliberate invasion by the police of a suspect's right to legal professional privilege is a serious affront to the integrity of the justice system which may often lead to the conclusion that the proceedings should be stayed. But the particular circumstances of each case must be considered and carefully weighed in the balance. It was obviously right to hold on the facts in *R v Grant* that the gravity of the misconduct was a factor which militated in favour of a stay. But as against that, the accused was charged with a most serious crime and, crucially, the misconduct caused no prejudice to the accused. This was not even a case where the "but for" factor had a part to

> play. The misconduct had no influence on the proceedings at all. In these circumstances, surely the trial judge was entitled to decide in the exercise of his discretion to refuse a stay and the Court of Appeal should not have held that his decision was wrong.'[2]

1 *R v Grant* [2005] EWCA Crim 1089.
2 At para 36.

5.21 The Board reiterated that the discretion to grant a stay of proceedings was a protection to be applied in exceptional circumstances. It required a balancing test between competing public interests. Lord Dyson confirmed that:

> 'It is clear from *Latif* and *Mullen* that the balance must always be struck between the public interest in ensuring that those who are accused of serious crimes should be tried and the competing public interest in ensuring that executive misconduct does not undermine public confidence in the criminal justice system and bring it into disrepute. It is true that in *Bennett* the need for a balancing exercise was not mentioned, but that is no doubt because the House of Lords considered that the balance obviously came down in favour of a stay on the facts of that case (the kidnapping of a New Zealand citizen to face trial in England).'[1]

1 At para 26.

5.22 But of what is this balancing test constituted? Approving of comments made by Professor Andrew Choo in *Abuse of Process and Judicial Stays of Criminal Proceedings*,[1] the Board considered that the balancing exercise:

> 'takes into account such factors as the seriousness of any violation of the defendant's (or even a third party's) rights; whether the police have acted in bad faith or maliciously, or with an improper motive; whether the misconduct was committed in circumstances of urgency, emergency or necessity; the availability or otherwise of a direct sanction against the person(s) responsible for the misconduct; and the seriousness of the offence with which the defendant is charged.'[2]

1 (2008) at p 132.
2 At para 24.

5.23 It was further noted that the balancing test was not about ensuring the fairness of proceedings. It was about the integrity of the process itself as Lord Kerr concluded that:

> 'I think that there is much to be said for discarding the notion of fairness when considering the second category of stay cases. Fairness to the accused, although not irrelevant in the assessment of whether it is fair to allow the trial to continue, is subsumed in the decision whether to grant a stay in second category cases based on the primary consideration of whether the stay is necessary to protect the integrity of the criminal justice system.'[1]

1 At para 84.

5.24 Consequently, it was open to the Commissioner to exercise his discretion not to stay this particular case:

> 'The Commissioner had to undertake a difficult balancing exercise. Some judges might have granted a stay; others, like the Commissioner, would have refused one. The Board finds it impossible to characterise the decision to refuse a stay in this case as perverse or one which no reasonable judge could have reached.'[1]

1 At para 51.

5.25 It is clearly the case that the seriousness of the defendants' criminal conduct played a hugely significant part in the decision that was reached by the Commissioner. But was too much reliance placed upon the gravity of the offence or the nature of the defendant's criminal conduct? What is the relationship between the defendant's criminal conduct and executive misconduct? It has been said: 'If the irregularity is of such seriousness that the court thinks it [the executive] should not do this, it is not clear why the gravity of D's own conduct should be relevant.'[1] That is to say that the ends may sometimes justify the means. The judgment suggests that even the gravest malfeasance will not necessarily result in a stay and that the decision will always depend on the specific facts of the case and whether a legally appropriate balancing exercise has been undertaken.

1 Rogers, 'Abuse of process reconsidered', [2011] Arch. Rev. 6, at p 8.

5.26 How significant is the *Warren* judgment? It is a re-clarification of the general principles in this area of the law. It also demonstrates a seemingly restrictive approach. It should be noted, however, that the Board itself acknowledged (at para 76) that this case was actually at the most complex end of the decision-making spectrum. Lord Brown explained:

> 'I regard the judgments which the commissioner had to reach here (the judgments, as it seems to me, both on the abuse of process application and on the related article 76 application) as very finely balanced indeed. It would certainly have been open to the commissioner to decide one or other of these closely related applications in favour of the defendants and, were the Jersey Police to act in this sort of fashion in future, realistically the court might have no alternative but to strike the balance decisively in favour of indicating the rule of law, however undeserving the accused.'[1]

1 At para 78.

5.27 The decision has been described as permitting the executive a 'yellow card' in circumstances where it is acknowledged that the conduct was wholly unacceptable.[1] However, it has also been said that 'it is worth repeating that the outcome in *Warren* is defensible on its facts and that the decision not to stay the case need not be seen as a green light for routine malpractice of this kind'.[2]

1 O'Connor, '"Abuse of Process" after Warren and Mitchell', *Criminal Law Review* (2012) 672 at 680.
2 Rogers, 'Abuse of process reconsidered', [2011] Arch. Rev. 6 at p 9.

5.28 Finally, it should be noted that the *Warren* judgment, along with the decision in *Maxwell*, seems to have definitively rejected the 'but for' test as determinative of a stay for abuse of process with Lord Dyson concluding that:

'The Board does not consider that the "but for" test will always or even in most cases necessarily determine whether a stay should be granted on the grounds of abuse of process.'[1]

The view taken seems at odds with that set out in *Bennett* and *Basdeo Panday v Senior Superintendent Wellington Virgil*[2] which suggests the test has some independent doctrinal relevance. It seems that the 'but for' test will now be merely one relevant factor to consider when determining whether there should be a stay. The ultimate determination will be left to the judge, and the appellate courts will not get involved unless the judge erred on the facts or the law or acted irrationally.[3]

1 At para 30.
2 [2008] UKPC 24.
3 See discussion in O'Connor, '"Abuse of Process" after Warren and Mitchell', *Criminal Law Review* (2012) 672 and Rogers, 'Abuse of process reconsidered', [2011] Arch. Rev. 6.

Secretary of State for the Home Department v CC

5.29 The impact of *Warren* and *Maxwell* were summarised by the Administrative Court in *Secretary of State for the Home Department v CC*.[1] The facts of the case are considered below at para **5.30**. At paras 92–97, Lloyd-Jones, LJ summarised the current law as follows:

> '92 The threshold for the second category of abuse is very high. The question for the court will be whether the court's sense of justice and propriety or public confidence in the justice system would be offended if the proceedings were not stayed. I do not understand Lord Dyson JSC in *Warren v Attorney General for Jersey* to qualify this very high threshold in any way. On the contrary his speech reaffirms it.
>
> 93. To establish an abuse of process under the second category involves more than the satisfying of a threshold condition. It requires an evaluation of what has occurred in the light of competing public interests…
>
> 94. The abuse jurisdiction is not of a disciplinary character. Thus in *Bennett* Lord Lowry observed (at p.47 H):
>
>> "Discretion to stay is not a disciplinary jurisdiction and ought not to be exercised in order to express the court's disapproval of official conduct.
>>
>> Accordingly, if the prosecuting authorities have been guilty of culpable delay but the prospect of a fair trial has not been prejudiced, the court ought not to stay the proceedings merely 'pour encourager les autres'".
>
> The same theme is taken up by Lord Dyson in his speech in *Maxwell* at paragraph 24 where he refers to Lord Lowry's speech in *Bennett*. Similarly in *Warren* the Board implicitly endorsed the observation of Lord Lowry in *Bennett* while adding, with reference to the decision of the Court of Appeal in *R v Grant* [2006] QB 60 to refuse to order a retrial, a decision which it considered incorrect:

"[I]t may not always be easy to distinguish between (impermissibly) granting a stay in order to express the court's disapproval of official conduct 'pour encourager les autres' and (permissibly) granting a stay because it offends the court's sense of justice and propriety. But it is difficult to avoid the conclusion that in Grant the proceedings were stayed in order to express the court's disapproval of the police misconduct and to discipline the police" (at para 37).

95. It is possible to identify factors which are often taken into account by the courts in performing this balancing exercise. However, Lord Steyn's words of caution against general guidance as to how the discretion should be exercised remain of critical importance. As Lord Dyson observed in *Warren* (at paragraph 36), the exercise of the discretion depends on the particular circumstances of each case and rigid classifications are undesirable. In the context of criminal proceedings the balance must always be struck between the public interest in ensuring that those that are accused of serious crime should be tried and the competing public interest in ensuring that executive conduct does not undermine public confidence in the criminal justice system and bring it into disrepute. With those warnings firmly in mind, it is appropriate to consider what factors have been considered in the authorities to be indications of abuse of process.

96. The connection between the abuse of executive power and the proceedings which are said to be an abuse of process is likely to be a highly relevant consideration. Thus it will often be the case that but for the wrongful conduct the defendant would not be before the court at all. However, the existence of such a causative link is neither a pre‑condition nor a conclusive demonstration of abuse. It is simply a relevant consideration. Thus in *Maxwell* the majority considered that the fact that the confessions on which a retrial would be based would not have been made but for the misconduct was not determinative of whether there should be a retrial. Similarly in *Warren* [per Lord Dyson at para 30]…

97. Clearly the gravity of the misconduct and the degree of culpability on the part of the wrongdoers will be highly relevant in determining whether the threshold test has been satisfied and in which direction the balancing exercise should be resolved…'

1 [2012] EWHC 2837 (Admin).

5.30 *CC v Secretary of State for the Home Department* also emphasises the highly fact-sensitive nature of the post-*Warren* abuse determination and the difficulties of making such determinations in the context of national security where a significant portion of the consideration of the pertinent facts may be contained in a closed judgment. The Administrative Court initially considered an abuse of process argument in relation to the question of unlawful rendition whilst conducting statutory reviews of the control orders/terrorism prevention and investigation measures (TPIM) notices made in respect of the respondents. CC and CF alleged that British security forces and British Special Forces had colluded with the administration of Somaliland to secure their unlawful seizure and interrogation there. They asserted that they had then been unlawfully deported to the UK in order to be made subject to control orders and TPIMs. Given the background of the allegations, Lloyd-Jones, LJ handed down an open and closed judgment and concluded in his open judgment that the allegations raised did not meet the high threshold to constitute an abuse of process.[1]

CC (referred to as MAM in the Court of Appeal's judgment) and CF appealed against this decision on two main grounds: first, as the abuse allegations had been dealt with in closed proceedings, they had been denied even the gist of the Secretary of State's case on their abuse allegations and therefore could not adequately instruct counsel, and second, because detailed consideration of the abuse allegations had been contained in Lloyd-Jones, LJ's closed judgement, they did not know to what extent their allegations of collusion and mistreatment were accepted or rejected, or whether their failure was based on a point of law.[2]

The Court of Appeal considered whether the case attracted the principles set out in *AF (No 3)*[3] that would require the gist of the Secretary of State's arguments on the abuse allegations to be set out to CC (MAM) and CF:

> '14. The case for MAM and CF is that, once it is accepted that there is an abuse of process jurisdiction in control order and TPIM cases (as it now is), it attracts the principles expounded in the *AF (No 3)* case, and El-Masri's case and, to an extent, the common law requirement of reasons as explained in *English v Emery Reimbold & Strick Ltd (Practice Note)* [2002] 1 WLR 2409. As to the latter, whilst it is accepted that the requirement is modified by a statutory closed material procedure, the complaint is that that does not permit the entire reasoning on a fundamental issue to be contained in a closed judgment.
>
> 15. On behalf of the Secretary of State, Mr James Eadie QC makes a number of submissions, of which the following seem to be the most important. *First*, as I have related, he submits that the *AF (No 3)* case is concerned only with allegations *against* the suspected terrorist and not with the Secretary of State's case in opposition to an allegation of abuse of process. *Secondly*, it is said that, by reason of the Secretary of State's duty of candour within the closed material procedure, those in the position of MAM and CF are adequately protected because the court will not countenance an abuse of its process. *Thirdly*, the Secretary of State, when dealing with serious allegations made by suspected terrorists, ought not to be put in the position of having to elect between disclosing the essence of the case on the abuse issue and discontinuing reliance on that case. In this regard, Mr Eadie emphasises the seriousness of the unappealed findings of national security risk posed by MAM and CF, particularly the "overwhelming" case against MAM. *Fourthly*, he refers to *Tariq v Home Office (JUSTICE intervening)* [2012] 1 AC 452 as an example of a case in which the Secretary of State has succeeded in resisting being put to her election. *Fifthly*, he seeks to limit the scope of El-Masri's case on the ground that it was not concerned with a closed material procedure and, more grandiloquently, "it ought not to be bandied about too freely".
>
> 16. I have come to the conclusion that these submissions fail and that, with the greatest respect, the judge ought not to have countenanced such a radical

> departure from procedural and constitutional normality. It is no answer that terrorism is horrendous and that the unappealed factual findings against MAM and CF are of considerable gravity. That was the subtext which prevailed prior to *A v United Kingdom* 49 EHRR 625 and the *AF (No 3)* case [2010] 2 AC 269. However it was not permitted to prevail in, for example, *R v Mullen* [2000] QB 520, where the conviction and 30-year sentence were quashed, notwithstanding the appellant's undisputed involvement in terrorism. However grave the case, there can come a point where "the court's sense of justice and propriety is offended": see *Warren v Attorney General for Jersey* [2012] 1 AC 22, para 35, per Lord Dyson JSC. In my judgment, to differentiate between allegations *against* a suspected terrorist and the case *for* the Secretary of State in opposition to an abuse of process application, is too fine a distinction. The abuse of process application, if successful, would have resulted in the quashing of the control orders and the TPIMs, notwithstanding the gravity of the findings against MAM and CF. The existence of the statutory closed material procedure had the effect of limiting the obligation of disclosure to MAM and CF and of permitting much of the detail to be dealt with only in a closed judgment. However, that does not give rise to tolerance, in relation to a potentially dispositive issue, of the total withholding of the Secretary of State's case on collusion and mistreatment or the total confinement of the reasons for rejecting MAM's and CF's case on those issues to the closed judgment.
>
> 17. I do not accept that there is a principle which protects the Secretary of State from being required to elect between a modicum of disclosure and withdrawing from reliance on the wholly undisclosed material in circumstances such as this. Election might well be required in relation to the criminal prosecution of an alleged terrorist or, for that matter, in relation to a control order or TPIM in relation to which the Secretary of State would be required to make disclosure under the *AF (No 3)* case or elect not to rely on the material in question. It would be no answer in those situations to say that there is sufficient protection in the duty of candour to the court. Nor is it an answer that, in the present case, MAM and CF, in the instigation of the abuse of process application, have had every opportunity to set out their positive case on abuse when they know nothing of the Secretary of State's case on collusion and mistreatment and nothing of the judicial reasoning which resulted in the rejection of their case.'

The Court of Appeal concluded that:

> '20. …In the present case I do not consider that MAM and CF or the public should be denied all knowledge of the extent to which their factual and/or legal case on collusion and mistreatment was accepted or rejected. Such a total denial offends justice and propriety. It is for these fundamental reasons that I consider MAM's and CF's principal ground of appeal is made out. The approach to their abuse of process applications was largely flawed…'

Having rejected the approach taken by the Administrative Court, the Court of Appeal ordered that the case be remitted to the Administrative Court so that the abuse of process issue could be reconsidered.[4] The Secretary of State won permission to appeal to the Supreme Court against the Court of Appeal's decision in 2014 but, possibly due to CC's absconsion prior to the Court of Appeal judgment and likely subsequent death in Somalia,[5] this appeal has not been taken up. In CC's absence it appears that CF has not pursued a rehearing in the Administrative Court.

1 [2012] EWHC 2837 (Admin) at 134–138.
2 [2014] EWCA Civ 559 at 10.
3 [2010] 2 AC 269.
4 [2014] EWCA Civ 559 at 48.
5 https://www.theguardian.com/world/2018/oct/10/al-shabaab-says-it-has-killed-british-spy-in-somalia.

5.31 Although the Court of Appeal remitted the decision back to the Administrative Court, Lloyd-Jones, LJ's discussion regarding whether proof of actual knowledge of illegality on the part of the State is not a legal requisite of this limb of abuse of process was not doubted by the Court of Appeal. The relevant text at paras 98–101 is set out below:

> '98. I accept that actual knowledge has often been a key element in establishing an abuse of process. For example, in *R v Mullen* [2000] QB 520 the Court of Appeal recorded with approval the defendant's concession that proof of actual knowledge of illegality was required.
>
> > "Mr Mackay accepted that the burden of proving abuse of process is on the defendant and that knowledge on the part of the English authorities that local or international law was broken must be shown" (at p. 529D).
>
> Similarly in *Bennett* Lord Griffiths stated the principle as follows:
>
> > "In my view your Lordships should now declare that where process of law is available to return an accused to this country through extradition procedures our courts will refuse to try him if he has been forcibly brought within our jurisdiction in disregard of these procedures by a process to which our own police, prosecuting or other executive authorities have been a knowing party" (at p 62G.)
>
> 99. However, it does seem to me that Mr O'Connor's approach in this regard is over-prescriptive. A case involving actual knowledge of illegality will necessarily be regarded as a particularly serious matter. However, the objective of maintaining the integrity of the legal system can be achieved only by a consideration of the entirety of the conduct in question and untrammelled by any rigid rules. Moreover, as Mr O'Connor himself submits, there are many gradations of states of mind including actual knowledge, wilful blindness, constructive knowledge and recklessness. The court should be free to reflect these matters in its examination of each case in the round. There may be situations in which reckless or possibly even negligent conduct could justify a stay on grounds of abuse of process. Everything will depend on an analysis of the particular features of each case in its entirety.
>
> 100. On behalf of the Secretary of State Mr O'Connor further submits that in a case of an alleged "disguised extradition" the party seeking to

establish the abuse is required to prove not only a flagrant and knowing disregard of the law but also that the authorities colluded in or procured the deportation for some ulterior or wrongful purpose. I accept that it will usually be necessary to show that the UK authorities acted so as to procure the individual's removal to the United Kingdom. (*R v Staines Magistrates' Court ex parte Westfallen* [1998] 1 WLR 652.) However, I consider that here once again Mr O'Connor's suggested approach is unduly prescriptive. Clearly, the existence of a wrongful ulterior motive will be a highly relevant consideration. However the court must be free to consider the conduct in its entirety.

101. In *Warren* the Board recognised that in abduction and entrapment cases the court will generally conclude that the balance favours a stay. However, it was at precisely this point in his speech (paragraph 26) that Lord Dyson warned against the undesirability of rigid classifications and emphasised the need to balance competing interests. Clearly it is insufficient to label a case as falling within a particular category. A challenge on grounds of abuse of process calls for a more refined analysis of the facts and the balancing of the competing interests. It is, however, instructive to observe the approach of the courts to abduction cases given the Respondents' contention that it is in substance what has happened to them in this case.'

R v CB

5.32 In *R v CB*[1] the defendant had been convicted of several counts of assault and sexual assault. CB appealed on several grounds including that the complainant had manipulated the disclosure process in such a way that it amounted to an abuse of process. During proceedings the complaint admitted: lying to investigators about the existence of Facebook messages, destroying evidence and withholding evidence that was only disclosed once the trial had begun. The trial judge ruled that 'the inconvenience and frustration caused by the way that these events had unfolded did not amount to an abuse of the process of the court'.[2]

The Court of Appeal agreed with the trial judge. The court noted that the actions of complainant could not be attributed to the police or prosecutors[3] and therefore did not involve any malfeasance by the state.[4] The court did note that complainant's actions may have affected whether it was possible to give the defendant a fair trial before concluding that procedural steps had been implemented to ensure the defendant was not prejudiced by the complainant's actions.

1 [2020] EWCA Crim 790,
2 At para 26.
3 At para 97.
4 At para 114.

R v Norman

5.33 Lord Thomas, CJ provides a helpful summary of the current law concerning executive abuse of power in *R v Norman*.[1] The facts of the case centred around a prison officer who had repeatedly leaked information concerning the prison system to a journalist in return for payment. This relationship came to light as a result of the phone hacking investigations carried out as part of Operation Elveden. Seeking to avoid corporate charges two newspaper groups made voluntary disclosures to the police which identified payments made to the defendant prison officer. The defendant alleged that the manner in which this evidence was brought to light was the result of improper pressure and was thus an abuse of process. The court rejected the submission that the voluntary disclosure by newspapers was due to improper pressure being applied by the state,[2] but the court went further and held that, even if the state's conduct did amount to improper pressure, the level of misconduct was not so severe as to be an abuse of power.[3] Lord Thomas CJ summarised the current law as follows:

> '21. It is well established that the court has the power to stay proceedings in two categories of case, namely (i) where it will be impossible to give the accused a fair trial, and (ii) where it offends the court's sense of justice and propriety to be asked to try the accused in the particular circumstances of the case (*R v Maxwell* [2010] UKSC 48; [2011] 1 WLR 1837, per Lord Dyson SCJ at para 13). We are concerned with the second category. It is not suggested that the defendant's trial was in any way unfair.
>
> 22. Within the second category fall cases where the police or prosecuting authorities have been engaged in misconduct in bringing the accused before the court for trial. In such cases the court is concerned to protect the integrity of the criminal justice system. A stay will be granted where the court concludes that in all the circumstances a trial will offend the court's sense of propriety and justice (per Lord Lowry in *R v Horseferry Road Magistrates' Court, Ex p Bennett* [1994] 1 AC 42, 74G) or will undermine confidence in the criminal justice system and bring it into disrepute (per Lord Steyn in *R v Latif* [1996] 1 WLR 104, 112F).
>
> 23. This involves a two-stage approach. First it must be determined whether and in what respects the prosecutorial authorities have been guilty of misconduct. Secondly it must be determined whether such misconduct justifies staying the proceedings as an abuse. This second stage requires an evaluation which weighs in the balance the public interest in ensuring that those charged with crimes should be tried against the competing public interest in maintaining confidence in the criminal justice system and not giving the impression that the end will always be treated as justifying any means. How the discretion will be exercised will depend upon the particular circumstances of each case, including such factors as the seriousness of the violation of the accused's rights; whether the police have acted in bad faith or maliciously; whether the misconduct was committed in circumstances of urgency, emergency or necessity; the availability of a sanction against the person(s) responsible for the misconduct; and the seriousness of the offence with which the accused is charged. These are merely examples of factors which may be relevant. Each case is fact specific. These principles were reaffirmed by the Privy Council in *Warren v Attorney General for Jersey* [2011] UKPC 10; [2012] 1 AC 22, in which the Board upheld a

refusal to stay a prosecution for serious drugs offences where the police had acted unlawfully in foreign jurisdictions and deliberately lied to the foreign authorities, the Attorney General and Chief of Police, in order to obtain incriminating recordings of conversations in a car without which no prosecution would have been possible.'

1 [2016] EWCA Crim 1564.
2 At para 27.
3 At para 40.

DISGUISED EXTRADITION

5.34 With those general principles firmly in mind, we consider some specific recognised examples of executive misconduct, beginning with disguised extradition. Here lies the beating heart of the modern law of abuse of process: *R v Horseferry Road Magistrates' Court, ex p Bennett.*[1] An indicator, perhaps, of the good health of that heart comes from Parliamentary attempts to stop it beating in 2007,[2] and to preclude the Court of Appeal from overturning a conviction because of an abuse of process if there was no reason to doubt the defendant's guilt, were met with such universal outrage that they were quietly abandoned.

1 [1994] AC 42, HL.
2 Clause 26 of the Criminal Justice and Immigration Bill, inserted following a joint review in 2006 by the Home Secretary, the Lord Chancellor and the Attorney-General expressing concern in particular about the implications of the decision in *R v Mullen* [2000] QB 520, CA, discussed below at paras **5.79–5.84**, which was perceived by those who promoted the Bill to have been decided on 'purely procedural grounds'.

The issues raised

5.35 The formal process of extradition of a fugitive from another state can be time-consuming and inconvenient, if available at all. Extradition provides the individual with certain safeguards (rule of speciality, double criminality, human rights norms). The motive for circumvention of extradition procedures may be the absence of extradition arrangements between the foreign State and the UK.[1] Alternatively, it may be that such extradition arrangements exist but are unavailable for the particular offence in question, would fail,[2] perhaps because of a technicality or the application of safeguards, or are simply deemed too lengthy or 'bogged down'.[3] It may be that the UK officials were aware that the evidence would be insufficient to obtain extradition from any State.[4] It may even be simple expedience[5] or 'an excess of enthusiasm'[6]. But, whatever the motivation, the problem of state-endorsed 'disguised extradition' has been a long-standing one which has significant implications for the rule of law. Indeed, Bassiouni notes that such action 'circumvents the intent of states who enter into extradition treaties for the specific purpose of avoiding disguised extradition' and as a result it 'detrimentally affects the international rule of law'.[7]

1 *R v Horseferry Road Magistrates' Court, ex p Bennett* (above para **5.34**); *R v Plymouth Justices, ex p Driver* [1986] QB 95, DC; *Sinclair v HM Advocate* (1890) 17 R (J) 38; *In re Schmidt* [1995] 1 AC 339, HL.

2 *R v Mullen* [2000] QB 520; *Bozano v France* (1986) 9 EHRR 297.
3 *R v Mullen* (above) at p 526.
4 *R v Plymouth Justices, ex p Driver* [1986] QB 95, DC at p 107.
5 *R v Hartley* [1978] 2 NZLR 199 per Woodhouse J at pp 216–217.
6 *R v Bow Street Magistrates' Court, ex p Mackeson* (1981) 75 Cr App R 24, DC per Lane LCJ at p 33.
7 M. C. Bassiouni, *International Extradition: United States Law & Practice* (2002) Vol. IV, at 29.

5.36 The circumstances in which disguised extradition may arise are as varied as the motives that can prompt it. A defendant may have been unlawfully arrested abroad by UK officials.[1] He or she may have been unlawfully arrested abroad by foreign officials and handed over to the UK outwith applicable extradition arrangements.[2] He or she may be the subject of a bogus deportation order made at the behest of UK authorities and in breach of local laws and procedures.[3] He or she may have been lured or tricked from a State with whom the UK has no extradition arrangements into a third State with whom it has for the purposes of onward extradition to the UK.[4] He or she may have been lured from the sanctuary of the foreign State by deceit or trick operative upon him,[5] by deceit or trick operative upon the foreign State,[6] or worse still, by forcible abduction.[7]

1 *Ex parte Susannah Scott* (1829) 9 B & C 446, CA; *R v Officer Commanding Depot Battalion RASC Colchester, ex p Elliot* [1949] 1 All ER 373, DC.
2 *Sinclair v HM Advocate* (above para **5.35**); *R v Hartley* (above para **5.35**).
3 *R v Bow Street Magistrates' Court, ex p Mackeson* (above para **5.35**) per Lord Lane CJ at 30; *R v Plymouth Justices, ex p Driver* (above para **5.35**); *R v Mullen* (above para **5.35**) per Rose LJ; *Bozano v France* (above para **5.35**).
4 *Somchai Liangsirisprasert v Government of the United States of America* [1991] 1 AC 225, PC; *In re Schmidt* (above para **5.35**).
5 *Somchai Liangsirisprasert v Government of the United States of America* [1991] 1 AC 225, PC; *In re Schmidt* (above para **5.35**); *R v Latif & Shazad* [1996] 1 WLR 104, HL and alleged in *R v Gokal* (11 March 1999, unreported), CA transcript pp10–15. See also *Bat v Germany* [2011] EWHC 2029 (Admin) where the appellant had not established that he had been lured into the jurisdiction for the purpose of arresting him (at paras 47–54).
6 Also alleged in *R v Gokal* (11 March 1999, unreported), CA transcript pp 10–15.
7 *R v Horseferry Road Magistrates' Court, ex p Bennett* (above para **5.34**); *Ker v Illinois* 119 US 436 (1986); *Frisbie v Collins* 342 US 519 (1952); *United States of America v Sobell* 142 F Supp 515 (1956); *United States v Toscanino* 500 F 2d 267 (1974); State *v Ebrahim* 1991 (2) SA 553; *United States v Alvarez-Machain* 504 US 655 (1992); *Bozano v France* (above para **5.33**); *Dzhurayev v Russia* (2013) 57 EHRR 22.

5.37 Where a defendant is returned to the UK from a foreign State for trial, should the jurisdiction of the courts extend to either or both of the following situations:

(i) where there has been bad faith on the part of the relevant UK authorities in that they have colluded in obtaining the defendant's return other than through regular extradition procedures? or

(ii) extradition was obtained in violation of the domestic law or the requested State, or in violation of international law?

If either of the above apply, then should the trial court have power to stay the proceedings against the defendant as an abuse of process?

Pre-Bennett decisions regarding jurisdiction

5.38 Prior to the House of Lords decision in *R v Horseferry Magistrates' Court, ex p Bennett*,[1] there existed two conflicting lines of authority on the issue of whether[2] or not[3] the trial court possessed any *power* to inquire into the circumstances in which a person, lawfully before the court, had come to be within the jurisdiction. The conflict of authority was brought to a head in *R v Plymouth Justices, ex p Driver*[4] where it was held that the trial court had no power to inquire, and that prior decisions to the contrary[5] were decided *per incuriam.*

1 Above para **5.34**.
2 To the effect that such a power existed; see *R v Hartley* (above para **5.35**); *R v Bow Street Magistrates' Court, ex parte Mackeson* (above para **5.35**); *R v Guildford Magistrates' Court, ex p Healy* [1983] 1 WLR 108, DC.
3 To the effect that such a power did not exist; see *Ex parte Susannah Scott* (above para **5.36**) per Lord Tenterden CJ at p 448; *Sinclair v HM Advocate* (above para **5.35**) per Lord Justice-Clerk MacDonald at pp 41–42, Lord Adam at pp 42–43, Lord M'laren at pp 43–44; *R v Officer Commanding Deport battalion RASC Colchester, ex p Elliot* (above para **5.36**) per Lord Godard CJ at pp 376–378. This continues to be the approach of the US courts; see *United States v Alvarez-Machain* (above para **5.36**).
4 Above para **5.35**.
5 Above fn 2.

Ex parte Bennett

5.39 Bennett, a New Zealand citizen, was charged in England with offences of dishonesty relating to his purchase of a helicopter. After the charges were laid, he had entered South Africa (via Australia) on a false passport, along with his helicopter. He was detained by the South African authorities as an illegal immigrant and a South African court ordered his deportation (to New Zealand). However, there was at that time no direct flight from South Africa to New Zealand and, despite the obvious geographical factors, it was decided to fly him to New Zealand via London. He was placed on a flight to Heathrow, handcuffed to the seat, and on arrival there was immediately arrested by the English police (who had received advance notice of the route from the South African authorities).

5.40 When he appeared before the Magistrates' Court, Bennett applied for a stay on the grounds of abuse of process. He argued that the facts disclosed that, having taken the decision not to employ the extradition process, the English police colluded with the South African police to have him arrested in South Africa and forcibly deported against his will. The application was refused by the Magistrates' Court and he sought judicial review. The Divisional Court,[1] following *R v Plymouth Justices, ex p Driver*,[2] held that, even if there was evidence of collusion between the two police forces in kidnapping Bennett and securing his enforced illegal removal to England from South Africa, the criminal courts had no jurisdiction to inquire into the circumstances by which he came to be within the jurisdiction. Accordingly, it dismissed his application for review. The Divisional Court held that the role of the judge is confined to the forensic process, to see that the accused has a fair trial, and that the process of the court is not manipulated to his disadvantage so that the trial itself is unfair. It held that the wider issues of the rule of law and the behaviour of those charged with its enforcement, be they police or prosecution authority, are not the concern of the judiciary unless such issues impinge directly on the trial process.

1 [1993] 2 All ER 474, DC. See discussion in Andrew L-T Choo, 'International Kidnapping, Disguised Extradition and Abuse of Process', *Modern Law Review*, (1994) Volume 57, Issue 4 pp 491–679.
2 Above para **5.35**.

5.41 In support of this view, the Divisional Court relied on the House of Lords case of *R v Sang,*[1] where Lords Diplock and Scarman emphasised that it is no part of the judge's function to exercise disciplinary powers over the police or the prosecution. Lord Diplock had said that:

> 'the function of the judge at a criminal trial as respects the admission of evidence is to ensure that the accused has a fair trial according to law. It is no part of a judge's function to exercise disciplinary powers over the police or prosecution as respects the way in which evidence to be used at the trial is obtained by them.'

1 [1980] AC 402, HL, at p 436.

5.42 Bennett appealed to the House of Lords who, by a majority of four to one,[1] held that, in a situation of illegal extradition (as the House was obliged to assume on the facts of the case before it, there having been no factual determinations), the courts did have a power to stay domestic criminal proceedings for abuse. The ability of the accused to obtain a fair trial was distinguished from the issue of whether it was appropriate to try the accused. This rested on whether the executive misconduct constituted such a serious affront to the criminal justice system that the trial should not be allowed to proceed. Lord Griffiths perceived the issues posed before the House to be as follows:

> 'In the present case there is no suggestion that the appellant cannot have a fair trial, nor could it be suggested that it would be unfair to try him if he had been returned to this country through extradition procedures. If the court is to have the power to interfere with the prosecution in the present circumstances it must be because the judiciary accept a responsibility for the maintenance of the rule of law that embraces a willingness to oversee executive action and to refuse to countenance behaviour that threatens either basic human rights or the rule of law.'[2]

1 Lords Griffiths, Bridge, Lowry and Slynn (Lord Oliver dissenting).
2 [1994] AC 42, at p 61H.

5.43 Having clearly set out the significance of the issues to be confronted, Lord Griffiths was clear that the courts should widen their abuse jurisdiction:

> 'I have no doubt that the judiciary should accept this responsibility in the field of criminal law …If it comes to the attention of the court that there has been a serious abuse of power it should, in my view, express its disapproval by refusing to act on it.'[1]

1 At p 62B.

5.44 In conclusion Lord Griffiths said that:

> 'In my view your Lordships should now declare that where process of law is available to return an accused to this country through extradition procedures our courts will refuse to try him if he has been forcibly brought within our jurisdiction in disregard of those procedures by a process to which our own police, prosecuting or other executive authorities have been a knowing party.'[1]

1 At p 62G.

5.45 Lord Bridge observed that:

> 'When it is shown that the law enforcement agency responsible for bringing a prosecution has only been able to do so by participating in violations of international law and laws of another State in order to secure the presence of the accused within the territorial jurisdiction of the court, I think that respect for the rule of law demands that the court take cognisance of that circumstance. To hold that the court may turn a blind eye to executive lawlessness beyond the frontiers of its own jurisdiction is, to my mind, an insular and unacceptable view. Having then taken cognisance of the lawlessness it would again appear to me to be a wholly inadequate response for the court to hold that the only remedy lies in the civil proceedings at the suit of the defendant or in disciplinary or criminal proceedings against the individual officers of the law enforcement agency who were concerned in the illegal action taken. Since the prosecution could never have been brought if the defendant had not been illegally abducted, the whole proceeding is tainted.'[1]

1 At p 67G.

5.46 Lord Lowry said:

> 'I consider that a court has a discretion to stay any criminal proceedings on the ground that to try at those proceedings would amount to an abuse of its own process; either (1) because it would be impossible (usually by reason of delay) to give the accused a fair trial or (ii) because it offends the court's sense of justice and propriety to be asked to try the accused in the circumstances of a particular case … So far as existing authority is concerned … the court, in order to protect its own process from being degraded and misused, must have the power to stay proceedings which have come before it and have only been possible by acts which offend the court's conscience as being contrary to the rule of law. Those acts by providing a morally unacceptable foundation for the exercise of jurisdiction over the suspect taint the proposed trial and, if tolerated, would mean that the court's process has been abused.[1]

1 At pp 74F and 76C.

5.47 In answer to the counter-suggestion that the seriousness of an offence alleged against a defendant, or even incontrovertible evidence of guilt, meant that there was an overriding public interest in trying him no matter under what circumstances he had been brought before a court, Lord Lowry was unpersuaded. He said:

'It may be that a guilty accused finding himself in the circumstances predicated is not deserving of much sympathy, but the principle involved goes beyond the scope of such a pragmatic observation and even beyond the rights of those victims who are or may be innocent. It affects the proper administration of justice according to the rule of law and with respect to international law …'.[1]

1 At para 76G.

5.48 Lord Lowry in his speech was also concerned to deal with two other connected issues; first, whether, via its abuse jurisdiction, the court should exercise disciplinary powers over the police, and secondly, whether, by its preparedness to penalise unworthy conduct on the part of investigators, the House was encouraging a flood of abuse applications. In common with Lords Diplock and Scarman in *R v Sang,*[1] Lords Lowry and Bridge both emphasised that the abuse jurisdiction was not a disciplinary one. Lord Lowry said:

'… the discretion to stay is not a disciplinary jurisdiction and ought not to be exercised in order to express the court's disapproval of official conduct … The court ought not to stay the proceedings merely "pour encourager les autres".'[2]

The significance of this disavowal of any disciplinary jurisdiction should be understood. Were such a jurisdiction to be asserted, it would represent a shift towards an automatic or mandatory exclusionary approach following police impropriety. As *Maxwell* and *Warren* have amply shown, the courts are determined not to eschew their traditional discretionary or 'public interest' approach. They have consistently emphasised the discretionary nature of this power and the balancing test between competing public interests which must be undertaken by the trial judge.

1 Above para **5.41**.
2 At p 74H.

5.49 In answer to the 'floodgates' argument, Lord Lowry observed that:

'… if proceedings are stayed when wrongful conduct is proved, the result will not only be a sign of judicial disapproval but will discourage similar conduct in future and thus would tend to maintain the purity of a source of justice. No "floodgates" argument applies because the executive can stop the flood at source by refraining from impropriety.'[1]

1 At p 77A.

5.50 In relation to complaints of basic unfairness, *Bennett* therefore established that courts have a wider supervisory jurisdiction – to protect persons from being prosecuted in circumstances where it would be seriously unjust to do so. However, as the judgments of Lords Griffiths, Bridge and Lowry make plain, the House in *Bennett* was concerned with a particular instance of illegality and abuse of power, namely breach of extradition procedures. The presence of that fact was crucial, as Lord Griffiths said: '… If extradition is not available, various considerations will arise on which I express no opinion'[1]. Moreover, for a court to stay criminal proceedings as an abuse under *Bennett*, it must be satisfied that there was active collusion between the foreign and

English authorities to avoid the defendant being extradited. In the absence of such evidence, the burden being on the defence, an application for a stay could not succeed.

1 At p 62G.

5.51 A reading of the speeches of the majority of the House of Lords in *Bennett* reveals a clear determination that courts should not countenance 'executive lawlessness' (per Lord Bridge). To fail to do so would result in a '... degradation of the court's criminal process' and be an 'affront to the public conscience'. When, therefore, a court is confronted by executive lawlessness, it is entitled to stay the trial for abuse of process.

5.52 While the attitude of the House in *Bennett* to executive lawlessness is unambiguous, the speeches do not clarify whether a rule or merely a principle was being pronounced. Did the House in *Bennett* support an absolutist or mandatory stance whereby any prosecution based on illegal extradition should always be stayed? Or, alternatively, should a court in such a situation exercise a discretion in deciding whether or not such lawlessness should result in a stay? The only speech which dealt with this subject directly was that of Lord Lowry who said:

> '... it is not jurisdiction which is in issue but the exercise of a discretion to stay proceedings, whilst speaking of "unworthy conduct", I would not expect a court to stay the proceedings of every trial which has been preceded by a venial irregularity. If it be objected that my preferred solution replaces certainty by uncertainty, the latter quality is inseparable from judicial discretion.'[1]

1 At pp 77A–77C.

5.53 In *R v Latif and Shahzad*,[1] the House, three years on from its decision in *Bennett,* took the opportunity to reconsider its stance. The sole speech in that case was delivered by Lord Steyn, who held that the House had concluded in *ex p Bennett* that, in a proven situation of executive lawlessness, the trial judge had a discretion to decide whether there had been an abuse of process. Lord Steyn thereby made plain that executive lawlessness should not automatically result in a stay; the court had to exercise a more flexible and pragmatic case-by-case approach:

> '... weigh[ing] in the balance the public interest in ensuring those that are charged with grave crimes should be tried and the competing public interest in not conveying the impression that the court will adopt the approach that the end justifies any means ...Weighing countervailing considerations of policy and justice, it is for the judge in the exercise of his discretion to decide whether there has been an abuse of process, which amounts to an affront to the public conscience and requires the criminal proceedings to be stayed.'[2]

1 [1996] 1 WLR 104. Above para **5.36**.
2 At pp 112–113.

5.54 The primary importance of this balancing exercise has consistently been emphasised in abuse of process cases. As noted above, it was considered again recently by the Supreme Court and the Privy Council when revisiting the courts' broader abuse of process jurisdiction in respect of executive misconduct. In the cases of *R v Maxwell* and *Warren v Attorney General of Jersey*, the wide and exceptional discretion a judge possesses to stay proceedings was confirmed.[1] The absence of mandatory rules was emphasised. Of particular relevance to disguised extradition cases was the recognition that, in abduction and entrapment cases, the court will generally conclude that the balance favours a stay, although 'rigid classifications are undesirable'.[2] Each decision will ultimately turn on its facts. The judge's responsibility is to balance the competing public interests: the public interest in prosecuting those accused of serious offences and the public interest in protecting the integrity of the criminal justice system from executive misconduct. The appellate courts will not interfere save where there is evidence of legal or factual error or irrationality on the part of the judge.[3]

1 *R v Maxwell* [2011] 1 WLR 1837 at para 3 and *Warren v Attorney General of Jersey* [2012]. 1 AC 22 at paras 24–5, 48, 40.
2 *Warren*, at para 26.
3 For example, *Warren* at para 43, *Maxwell* at para 38.

5.55 The details of the cases are considered above. Both are examples of significant executive misconduct which necessitated the appellate courts' consideration of the doctrine of abuse of process. However, the seeming lack of guidance around the application of the principle has raised criticism from commentators that the cases represent a 'shift of tone' which may lead to the possible dilution of the protection in all abuse of process arguments.[1]

1 O'Connor, '"Abuse of Process" after Warren and Mitchell', *Criminal Law Review* (2012) 672. Rogers, 'Abuse of process reconsidered', [2011] Arch. Rev. 6.

APPLICATION OF THE BENNETT ABUSE JURISDICTION IN CASES OF DISGUISED EXTRADITION

Pre-Bennett authorities

5.56 As noted above,[1] the pre-*Bennett* authorities were by no means consistent as to the issue of jurisdiction. Consequently, a number of pre-*Bennett* authorities were considered on their merits on the assumption that such a jurisdiction existed, and therefore remain instructive as to the circumstances in which the jurisdiction, which *Bennett* confirmed to exist, would be exercised.

1 At para **5.38**.

R v Hartley

5.57 In *R v Hartley*,[1] following a retaliatory murder carried out by members of a motorcycle gang, one of the gang (Bennett) fled to Australia. The police had not obtained a warrant for Bennett's extradition and had merely asked the Melbourne police by telephone to put Bennett on the next plane to New Zealand; a request with which they had complied. Bennett appealed against his conviction for manslaughter on the ground that the court had no jurisdiction to try him because he had been illegally brought back to New Zealand. The New Zealand Court of Appeal ruled that the New Zealand court had jurisdiction to try Bennett on the indictment but also had a discretion to discharge the accused under its inherent jurisdiction to prevent abuse of its own process. On the facts of that case, Woodhouse J found that the New Zealand police had deliberately ignored the requirements of the extradition statute and observed that;

> 'Some may say that in the present case a New Zealand citizen attempted to avoid a criminal responsibility by leaving the country: that his subsequent conviction has demonstrated the utility of the short cut adopted by the police to have him brought back. But this must never become an area where it will be sufficient to consider that the end has justified the means. The issues raised by this affair are basic to the whole concept of freedom in society. On the basis of reciprocity for similar favours earlier received are police officers here in New Zealand to feel free, or even obliged, at the request of their counterparts overseas to spirit New Zealand or other citizens out of the country on the basis of mere suspicion, conveyed perhaps by telephone, that some crime has been committed elsewhere? … we are … satisfied that the means which were adopted to make that trial possible are so much at variance with the statute, and so much in conflict with one of the most important principles of the rule of law, that if application had been made at the trial on this ground and the facts had been established by the evidence on the voir dire, the judge would probably have been justified in exercising his discretion.'[2]

1 [1978] 2 NZLR 199.
2 At p 217.

Ex parte Mackeson

5.58 In *R v Bow Street Magistrates' Court, ex p Mackeson*,[1] the applicant, Sir Rupert Mackeson, a British citizen, was resident in Rhodesia (later Zimbabwe), when allegations of fraud were levelled against him in the UK. The Metropolitan Police did not then ask the Rhodesian authorities to extradite him because at that time the de facto government of Rhodesia was in rebellion against the Crown and considered illegal. Subsequently, the Metropolitan Police informed the Rhodesian authorities that the applicant was wanted in England. He was thereupon arrested in Rhodesia as a prohibited immigrant. That determination was accepted to have been based principally upon the existence of the UK fraud charges. A deportation order was thus made against him. His passport was returned to the Metropolitan Police and sent back to the applicant with authorisation for one journey only, to return to the UK. He brought proceedings in Rhodesia for the deportation order to be set aside, which succeeded at first instance (Gubbay J finding that the true purpose of the deportation order was an ulterior one, namely his disguised extradition to the UK). But that decision was set aside on appeal (on a point of law which left the factual findings of the first instance court intact).

1 (1981) 75 Cr App R 24.

5.59 The applicant was escorted back to the UK under the deportation order and handed over to the Metropolitan Police. He applied for judicial review by way of an order of prohibition to prevent the hearing of committal proceedings against him in the Magistrates' Court in respect of those other charges. The Divisional Court (Lord Lane CJ) found that the applicant had been brought back to this country because of the Metropolitan Police persuading the authorities in Rhodesia to deport him for no reason other than that he was wanted for trial in this country. The Court thus found that the applicant had been removed from Rhodesia with ulterior motive. Lord Lane CJ concluded that:

> '... the object of this exercise was simply to achieve extradition by the back door. It seems equally plain to me that the English police authorities were, to say the least, concurring in that exercise[1] ... the Metropolitan Police, no doubt due to an excess of enthusiasm, certainly not due to any conscious intent to do wrong, have in fact transgressed the line.'[2]

1 At p 30.
2 At p 33.

5.60 Thus, the Divisional Court, in its discretion, having regard to *R v Hartley*,[1] granted the application for prohibition and discharged the applicant. The factors that principally affected this finding were:[2]

(a) the finding of the Rhodesian court to that effect;

(b) the fact that it was to be inferred that the Metropolitan police were clearly in communication with the South African authorities at the material time;

(c) the fact that the Metropolitan police were well aware that extradition was not lawfully possible. Whilst the Metropolitan police did not initiate the proceedings, they adopted the procedure willingly and quickly;

(d) no attempt was made to extradite the applicant after Zimbabwe-Rhodesia had returned to direct rule under the Crown in December 1979;

(e) the act of returning the applicant's passport to the Metropolitan police was one which was indicative of the UK authorities having positively requested the applicant's return to the UK, notwithstanding their denial that they had; and

(f) the circumstances of the applicant's flight to the UK. At Gatwick, when the purpose of the Rhodesian authorities had been accomplished, they maintained their arrest of the applicant until the arrival of the Metropolitan police; if it had genuinely been deportation '... it would have been sufficient, if deportation was the principal object of the exercise, simply to ask him to walk down the steps'.

1 Above para **5.57**.
2 At pp 29–30.

Ex parte Healy

5.61 On the other side of 'the line' is *R v Guildford Magistrates Court, ex p Healy*.[1] Mr Healy was arrested in the UK on a number of serious charges.

He was released on bail on condition that he surrender his passport. He subsequently fled the UK and unlawfully entered the US on a false passport. Two British police officers went to New York to pursue their inquiries in respect of the applicant. The applicant flew from New York to Los Angeles and was arrested in Los Angeles by the US authorities and charged with being an illegal immigrant. At a bail hearing, which took place before the Immigration Tribunal in Los Angeles, the two British officers gave evidence and told the judge the nature of the crimes with which the applicant had been charged in the UK. They also gave him an estimate of the likely sentence if the applicant were to be convicted. The applicant told the immigration judge 'a pack of lies' at that hearing. The two police officers then returned to the UK. There were a number of further hearings of the tribunal in Los Angeles after which the judge made a deportation order against the applicant. The applicant was deported to the UK and arrested on his arrival.

1 [1983] 1 WLR 108, DC

5.62 The defence raised before the Magistrates' Court, as a preliminary point, the question whether the method by which the applicant had been brought from the US to the UK had involved improper co-operation between the authorities of those two countries in order to circumvent the need for extradition proceedings. After hearing the evidence of a number of witnesses, the magistrate found that the British police had not attempted to interfere or collude in any improper manner to secure the deportation of the applicant. That ruling was upheld by the Divisional Court, Griffiths LJ (who, ten years later, was to give the leading judgment in the House of Lords in *Bennett*[1]) holding that the facts did not disclose an abuse of process. There was:

> '… no ground whatever for supposing the police have tried to persuade the United States' authorities to deport this applicant so that they could arrest him in this country and thus circumvent the provisions of the extradition treaty between the two countries. The facts of the matter are that this man entered the United States on a false passport having allegedly left a trail of crime behind in this country. In those circumstances it was perfectly reasonable that the police should leave this country to try to trace him in America. So far as the United States were concerned, it was perfectly proper for the British police, if they did, to inform the United States of their fears that this man had entered their territory on a false passport. We do not know if his arrest in Los Angeles was as a result of any information given by the British police that they knew he was leaving from New York for Los Angeles, but even if they did give that information to the United States' authorities, we can see nothing improper in that at all. Thereafter, once the man was arrested by the United States' authorities… [n]aturally enough, the court inquiring into the status of an alleged illegal immigrant would want as much information about the man as they could get. The British police were there in the United States, they apparently knew a great deal about this man and what more natural than that the immigration authorities there should call them before the judge to tell the judge what they knew of him. That is what was done and it would have been improper for them to have refused to give the evidence they did. Thereafter there were prolonged

inquiries by the judge into the status of the applicant in America and there is nothing whatever to show that the British police in any way influenced the course of those inquiries. Indeed, they were not in the country during the time that many of the hearings took place …It is quite clear to this court that the decision of the United States' authorities to deport this man was not prompted by the British police, although no doubt the information given at the request of the United States' authorities must have played a part in Judge Indelicato's final decision.'[2]

1 Above para **5.31**.
2 At p 112.

5.63 Griffiths LJ further observed that the evidence did not warrant the inference that the British Government paid for the flight, and that, in the absence of such evidence, the court was unable to draw the 'inference that this was truly a concealed extradition'. Finally, as to the submission that, because the applicant was brought back under escort and under restraint, that provided further material from which the inference should be drawn that he was being deported at the request of the British police to avoid extradition proceedings, Griffiths LJ held that:

> 'The reason he was in handcuffs [was because he had escaped on a number of occasions and his guard was expressly requested by the captain of the aircraft]… and if a criminal wanted in this country is being deported by the United States' authorities of their own motion and for their own purposes, there is no reason whatever why the authorities in the United States should not report to the authorities in this country that they are deporting him and inform this country of the aircraft upon which he will be arriving so that he can be arrested as soon as he arrives here and brought to justice in this country. It is in the interest of the law abiding community that there should be international co-operation to bring wanted criminals to justice: there is no reason whatever to assume because that is done that there is a collusive agreement between the two countries to use the deportation process as a short cut to extradition.'[1]

1 At p 113.

Ex parte Driver

5.64 In *R v Plymouth Justices, ex p Driver*,[1] as noted above,[2] the Divisional Court held there to be no power to inquire into the circumstances in which a person, lawfully before the court, had come to be within the jurisdiction. But, for present purposes, the judgment remains of interest because the Divisional Court also determined how such a power would have been exercised on the facts of the case before it, had it existed.

1 [1986] QB 95, DC.
2 At para **5.38**.

5.65 Mr. Driver, an Australian citizen, came to England on holiday. During his stay, an elderly woman was killed, and on the following day, before her body was discovered, he left England for France, having made arrangements for the journey some time previously. The police, suspecting him of the woman's murder, made inquiries as to his whereabouts through Interpol. Independently of this, the Turkish authorities subsequently arrested Driver in Turkey on the strength of a newspaper report relating to the murder. The English police were informed and, while not requesting his detention or continued detention, sought, and received, the co-operation of the Turkish authorities by confirming the applicant's identity and assisting in establishing his connection with the killing. There was no extradition treaty between the UK and Turkey and the police told the Turkish authorities that they had no authority to request the applicant's extradition or deportation from Turkey, but that *if it was within their power* to deport him to the UK it would assist the police to interview him. The Turkish authorities replied that they would expel the applicant in the 'United Kingdom direction' but that he would not be accompanied by a police officer on the journey and his arrival could not be guaranteed. They also asked the English police to pay for his fare, which they did. The Turkish authorities told the applicant, untruthfully, that the English police were no longer interested in him and that he was to be released, but they required him to leave Turkey and put him, unaccompanied, on a non-stop flight to London (purportedly the first available flight out of Turkey). The action of the Turkish authorities in returning the applicant to England was unlawful in Turkish law (amounting to an offence of 'a public official using the powers of his office in bad faith'). Upon his arrival in London, the applicant was arrested and charged with murder.

5.66 Stephen Brown LJ held[1] that, even if the court had a discretion to prohibit committal proceedings against a person where there had been an abuse of process within the jurisdiction which had procured his presence there:

> 'The evidence before this court does not establish any impropriety, illegality or collusion on the part of the Devon and Cornwall police in relation to any unlawful act which the Turkish authorities may have committed in requiring the applicant to leave Turkey … the only action taken … was to notify the Turkish police that the applicant was suspected of a crime committed in this country and that they desired to interview him. They agreed to pay his fare. However, they did not at any time seek his detention or continued detention in Turkey. They sought and received the co-operation of the Turkish police to establish the applicant's identity. They told the Turkish authorities that the police in this country had no authority to request the applicant's extradition or deportation from Turkey. It is true that they notified the Turkish authorities that the applicant was wanted in the United Kingdom on suspicion of having committed the murder of Mrs. Hopkins and said that if it was within their power to deport him to the United Kingdom it would assist the police to interview him. I stress that both the affidavits make it clear that this request was subject to the important condition that any action taken should be within their power. There was no request by the British police to encourage the Turkish authorities to act illegally in any way, although they agreed to pay his fare. In these circumstances, it is not established that the authorities in this country were guilty of any improper dealing.'

1 At p 114.

State v Ebrahim

5.67 Finally, abuse of process was found by the Supreme Court of South Africa in *State v Ebrahim*.[1] The appellant, a South African citizen, was a member of the military wing of the African National Congress (ANC) and had fled South Africa to Swaziland whilst under a restriction order (imposed following conviction for offences of sabotage). He had been forcibly abducted from his home in Swaziland by persons claiming to be members of the South African State. Although the State denied involvement, the Supreme Court found that the abduction was carried out by agents of the State (other than the South African police). He had been bound, blindfolded, gagged and taken back across the border into Pretoria, South Africa, where he had been handed over first to the security services, and then to the police, and detained under the terms of security legislation. He was subsequently charged with treason in a Circuit Local Division. The appellant applied for an order to the effect that the court lacked jurisdiction to try the case as a result of his abduction in breach of international law. The application was dismissed and the trial continued. He was convicted and sentenced to 20 years' imprisonment. There was no evidence that the government of Swaziland protested over the abduction.

1 1991 (2) SA 553.

5.68 On appeal against the dismissal of the above application, Steyn JA, on behalf of the Supreme Court, held that the removal of a person from an area of jurisdiction in which he had been illegally arrested to another area was tantamount to abduction and thus constituted a serious injustice. A court before which such a person was brought lacked jurisdiction to try him, even where such a person had been abducted by agents of the authority governing the area of jurisdiction of the said court.

> 'The individual must be protected against unlawful detention and abduction, the bounds of jurisdiction must not be exceeded, sovereignty must be respected, the legal process must be fair to those affected and abuse of law must be avoided in order to protect and promote the integrity of the administration of justice. This applies equally to the State. When the State is a party to a dispute, as for example in criminal cases, it must come to court with 'clean hands'. When the State itself is involved in an abduction across international borders, as in the present case, its hands are not clean. Principles of this kind testify to a healthy legal system of a high standard.'

Ex parte Bennett

5.69 Having decided the issue of principle in *ex parte Bennett*,[1] the House of Lords remitted the matter to the Divisional Court to determine the facts; *R v Horseferry Road Magistrates' Court, ex p Bennett (No 3)*.[2] Based upon the facts outlined above,[3] Bennett argued that his case disclosed that, having taken the decision not to employ the extradition process, the English police colluded with the South African police to have him arrested in South Africa and forcibly deported against his will. Mann LJ observed that:

> '... the inquiry involved the liberty of a subject and we have to be satisfied on a high balance of probabilities that the applicant was properly available for arrest at Heathrow.'[4]

1 Above para **5.34**.
2 [1995] 1 Cr App R.147, DC.
3 At paras **5.39–5.40**.
4 At p 149.

5.70 The English police gave evidence that they did not know that Bennett was being dispatched via England until the night before. However, against this 'well intentioned' evidence there existed an internal CPS memo showing that they had known about the deportation more than two weeks earlier. Mann LJ concluded that:

> '...the desire to bring him to trial is understandable but a propriety of procedure in regard to the liberty of any who are brought within our jurisdiction is transcendent.'[1]

1 At p 149.

5.71 The termination of the English proceedings was, however, not the end of Bennett's problems. Bennett also faced a warrant for his arrest issued by the Sheriff of Grampian, Highland and Islands, at Aberdeen in respect of offences of dishonesty relating to his purchase of a different helicopter and a Lamborghini motor car. Upon his release, he was brought before the Scottish courts. He argued that the factual findings in *R v Horseferry Road Magistrates' Court, ex p Bennett (No 3)*,[1] namely that his presence within the UK had been procured by abuse, applied to render the Scottish proceedings also abusive, the Lord Advocate not being entitled to take advantage of that impropriety.

1 Above para **5.69**.

5.72 The matter came before the High Court of Justiciary in *Bennett v HM Advocate*.[1] It was accepted that the Scottish authorities had played no part in the affair. It was also ultimately accepted by the Court that the Scottish authorities would not be permitted to turn a blind eye to, and take advantage of, English illegality or impropriety.

1 (1995) SLT 510.

5.73 But the Scottish authorities had conducted further factual enquiries and, as a result, argued that there had not, in fact, been any illegality or collusion on the part of the English authorities. That new evidence indicated that the English authorities understood the South African intention to be repatriation to New Zealand via Australia and the English intention was to seek extradition from either New Zealand or Australia. The English police then fortuitously learned that the South African plan involved transit via London (a route dictated by international travel difficulties in respect of South Africa in 1991 owing to international sanctions in operation against that country) and determined to take advantage of that fortuity, hence the CPS memo. But, because of the cost, the South African plan changed and Bennett was instead flown to Taiwan for transfer (via Hong Kong) to New Zealand. Of itself, as the Lord Justice General (Lord Hope) observed, this confirmed that the English authorities could not have been 'in collusion' in respect of the initial transit route.[1] But, en route to Taiwan, Bennett had destroyed his passport, with the result that the Taiwanese authorities refused him permission to disembark and returned him to South Africa. It was only then that the South African authorities reverted to their initial proposed route via London, and advised the English authorities – hence the evidence given to the High court in *R v Horseferry Road Magistrates' Court, ex p Bennett (No 3)*[2] by the English police that they did not know that Bennett was being dispatched via England until the night before. On the evidence now available, Lord Hope concluded that:

> '... the Lord Advocate was entitled to conclude that what occurred in this case is different from what had been assumed in the decision taken in England by the House of Lords and by the Divisional Court... there was, so far as the English authorities were concerned, no illegality... In our opinion it would be unreasonable, where there has been no collusion, to insist that the police must refrain from arresting a person who is wanted for offences committed in this country when he arrives here simply because he is in transit to another country.'[3]

1 At p 518 '... if there was already a collusive agreement for him to be sent to London in order that he might be arrested there, it would have been a breach of it to send him instead to Taipei as by that route he would never reach London. Read in its context, the memorandum appears to us to do no more than report on a decision which had been taken by the South African police and which the English police saw as being to their advantage. It does not, in any way, reveal that the English authorities were in collusion with the South African police on this matter. All the information ... indicates that the South African authorities were taking their own decisions about the method of deportation.'
2 Above para **5.69**.
3 At p 518.

Post-Bennett authorities

Ex parte Westfallen

5.74 In *R v Staines Magistrates' Court, ex p Westfallen & others,*[1] the applicants Westfallen and Soper were wanted for offences in England. Both flew to Norway on forged passports where they were immediately detained by Norwegian immigration. Their identities and criminal records were confirmed by Interpol, but not the fact that they were wanted. The Norwegian authorities determined to deport them (on the ground that they were believed to be going to commit offences in Norway) to the UK from where they had come. Upon arrival in England they were arrested.

1 [1998] 1 WLR 652, DC.

5.75 The applicant Nangle appeared before Swindon Crown Court on charges of burglary and escape from lawful custody. Sentence was deferred. Prior to the deferred date, he fled to Canada where he was convicted of 48 other offences, received a term of six years' imprisonment, and was recommended for deportation. During his imprisonment, a deportation order was duly made and served on him. During his imprisonment, the London Police, via Interpol, made their Canadian counterparts aware of the fact that Nangle was wanted in the UK and stated that '... should the subject be deported to the UK please inform us prior to any deportation in order that we can arrange for him to be met.' At the end of his sentence, Nangle was informed that he was to be deported to Ireland where he had been granted citizenship. There were no direct flights to Dublin and so he was flown via Glasgow, this being, on the evidence, the most expedient route. When the flight arrived in Glasgow, Nangle was arrested.

5.76 All three applicants contended that the UK authorities had improperly procured their presence in the UK by means other than extradition which, in their submission, was the only way of properly procuring their presence in the UK. They contended that what had happened was disguised extradition, which the House of Lords in *ex parte Bennett*[1] had condemned as an abuse. For their part, the authorities denied this; there was no taint of impropriety and what had happened was not disguised extradition but simply undisguised deportation. In all three cases, the UK police and CPS denied having attempted to influence the foreign authorities in any way. Bingham CJ perceived the test for the court to be as follows:

> 'The question in each of these cases is whether it appears that the police or the prosecuting authorities have acted illegally or procured or connived at unlawful procedures or violated international law or the domestic law of foreign States or abused their powers in a way that should lead this court to stay the proceedings against the applicants.'[2]

1 Above para **5.34**.
2 At pp 665B–665C.

5.77 In respect of Westfallen and Soper, Lord Bingham CJ held that;

> '... the answer to that question is in my judgment plainly in the negative. The Norwegians were entitled under their own law to deport these applicants. The propriety of the deportations is acknowledged and indeed could not be challenged. It is difficult to see why the Kingdom of Norway should be obliged to keep the applicants whilst the British applied for extradition if they wished to deport them. It was indeed a natural step for Norway to send the applicants back to where they had come from. There is in the material before us nothing to suggest that the British authorities procured or influenced that decision. It is true that they did not in any way resist it, and there is no reason why they should have resisted it. It is very probable that they welcomed the decision, but in my judgment they would have been failing in their duty as law enforcement agencies if they had not welcomed it. In my judgment there is nothing to suggest any impropriety'[1]

1 At pp 665C–665E.

5.78 In respect of Nangle, Lord Bingham CJ held that:

> 'The decision was taken to deport him to Ireland, which is where the applicant wished to go, and the Canadian authorities bought him a ticket to that destination. They chose an obvious route in the absence of a direct flight from Canada to Ireland ... [I]t is not suggested ... that the flight via Glasgow was in any way contrived or sinister or other than an ordinary route to choose in order to reach that destination. There is nothing whatever

to suggest that the British authorities influenced the Canadian authorities to deport or procured the choice of route. Again, they did not resist it and probably welcomed the outcome. But again, there is no reason why they should have resisted that decision and no reason why they should not have welcomed it. There was in my judgment no illegality, no violation of international law, no violation of the domestic law of Canada, and no abuse of power.'[1]

1 At pp 665F–665H.

R v Mullen

5.79 In *R v Mullen,*[1] in contrast to *ex parte Westfallen*, the court found that there had been collusion and illegal behaviour on the part of the UK authorities. Shortly before his proposed arrest for terrorist offences in England, Mullen fled to Zimbabwe. Whilst there, during early 1989, the British and Zimbabwean intelligence agencies secretly agreed a process whereby Mullen would be arrested and deported to England from Zimbabwe in a manner which would prevent him from exercising legal rights available to him under Zimbabwean law which could have frustrated this plan. From MI6 files disclosed at the appeal, it was clear that MI6 had informed their Zimbabwean counterparts that Mullen should not be permitted to become involved in protracted extradition proceedings. In the event, Mullen was swiftly deported in breach of Zimbabwean law.

1 [2000] QB 520.

5.80 Before considering the judgment of the Court of Appeal, it is important to appreciate that Mullen accepted that he had received a fair trial and was properly convicted of extremely serious offences. Furthermore, with the law on abuse as it stood in 1990,[1] the year of his trial, it is unlikely that, had the circumstances concerning his deportation from Zimbabwe been disclosed by the prosecution, a stay would then have been granted, or that the Court of Appeal would have intervened. At the hearing of Mullen's appeal 10 years later, when the circumstances in which he was deported to England came to light, the Crown's argument, having conceded the fact of improper collusion between the two authorities, was that the grounds for his deportation under Zimbabwean law were so convincing that, even if the proper extradition procedures had been followed, his removal back to England would inevitably have been the same. Discretion should not, therefore, be exercised in the appellant's favour despite the abuse.

1 Above para **5.38**.

5.81 In deciding whether or not to hold that there had been an abuse, Rose LJ set out the factors considered by the Court of Appeal to be of significance in reaching its decision. The first[1] was the seriousness of the offence: 'As a primary consideration, it is necessary for the courts to take into account the gravity of the offence in question'. Mullen was a member of the IRA and had ultimately been sentenced in England to 30 years' imprisonment for conspiracy to cause explosions. Secondly,[2] whether Mullen constituted a threat to peace and security in Zimbabwe: it was held that he did not. Thirdly:[3] 'It is necessary to consider the nature of the conduct of those involved in the deportation on behalf of the British government'. Having assessed the evidence, Rose LJ concluded that the British authorities had:

> '… initiated and subsequently assisted in and procured the deportation of the appellant by unlawful means, in circumstances in which there were specific extradition facilities between this country and Zimbabwe. In so acting they were not only encouraging unlawful conduct in Zimbabwe but they were also acting in breach of public international law.'[4]

1 At pp 534C–534D.
2 At p 534E.
3 At p 534F.
4 At p 534F–535E.

5.82 Having reached this conclusion of bad faith, Rose LJ then considered the various and competing public interests involved – the serious nature of the offences committed by Mullen versus the need to discourage wrongful official conduct on the part of those who are responsible for criminal prosecution. Rose LJ concluded that, in Mullen's case: 'The discretionary balance comes down decisively against the prosecution of this offence'. In arriving at this conclusion, Rose LJ purported to apply the balancing exercise described by Lord Steyn in *R v Latif*.[1] Rose LJ observed that:

> 'In arriving at this conclusion we strongly emphasise that nothing in this judgment should be taken to suggest that there may not be cases, such as *Latif*, in which the seriousness of the crime is so great relative to the nature of the abuse of process that it would be a proper exercise of judicial discretion to permit a prosecution to proceed … notwithstanding an abuse of process in relation to the defendant's presence within the jurisdiction. In each case it is a matter of discretionary balance, to be approached with regard to a particular conduct complained of and a particular offence charged.'[2]

1 Above para **5.53**.
2 At pp 536G–537A.

5.83 Interestingly, in his judgment Rose LJ sought to distinguish the abuse jurisdiction from all other cases where an exercise of judicial discretion is called for:

> 'It arises not from the relationship between the prosecution and the defendant but from the relationship between the prosecution and the court. It arises from the court's need to exercise control over executive involvement in the whole prosecution process, not limited to the trial itself.'[1]

1 At pp 537D–537G.

5.84 Accordingly, despite the absence of any assertion of innocence from Mullen, Rose LJ held[1] that the abuse was sufficient to merit the quashing of his conviction:

> 'Having regard to the fact that the defendant, as he now concedes, was properly convicted, this court must approach the exercise of its discretion on a rather different basis from that which would have been appropriate if

> an application had been made to the trial judge. In particular, there is before this court no question of consideration of the strength of the evidence of the defendant's guilt of the offence charged. However, as appears from the passage already cited from the speech of Lord Lowry in *Reg. v. Horseferry Road Magistrates' Court, Ex parte Bennett* [1994] 1 A.C. 42, 76, certainty of guilt cannot displace the essential feature of this kind of abuse of process, namely the degradation of the lawful administration of justice.'

1 At pp 534B–534C.

Mohamed & Dalvie v The President

5.85 In *Mohamed & Dalvie v The President of the Republic of South Africa & others*,[1] the applicant Mohamed was wanted by the American authorities in respect of the bombing of the US embassies in Nairobi and Dar es Salaam. He entered South Africa under an assumed name and a false passport. The FBI identified Mohamed while searching through asylum-seekers' records in Cape Town. Extradition proceedings between South Africa and America were possible, but, at the invitation of the FBI, the South African immigration authorities arrested Mohamed as a prohibited person. He was questioned and allegedly confessed in circumstances that violated his right not to incriminate himself, and his right to legal representation. He was then handed over to the FBI, whereupon he was questioned again (allegedly repeating his confession). During a subsequent search of Mohamed's address, both the FBI and South African officials untruthfully advised Mohamed's employer that Mohamed was being deported to Tanzania and told him that it would be a waste of money to employ a lawyer for him as he had admitted entering the country on a false passport. They also informed the employer 'disingenuously' that he was not permitted to visit Mohamed. The employer was '… fobbed off to ensure that Mohamed would continue to be denied access to a lawyer and would remain incommunicado … to facilitate his removal by the FBI agents', which was promptly carried out. Mohamed was flown out of South Africa by the FBI, in the company of the US Prosecuting Attorney. Mohamed was questioned by the FBI and Prosecuting Attorney during the flight. On arrival in New York, the trial judge formally notified Mohamed that he faced the death penalty.

1 2001 (3) SA 893 (CC). For further discussion see Watney, M, 'A South African perspective on mutual legal assistance and extradition in a globalized world' [2012] PER 24.

5.86 After Mohamed's arrival in New York, proceedings were brought on his behalf before a nine-judge South African Constitutional Court, challenging the propriety of the removal, alleging that it constituted disguised extradition, which deprived him of, amongst other rights, protection against the imposition of the death penalty. The Supreme Court of South Africa observed that, whilst the facts of the case could have justified the South African authorities in deporting him:

> 'That, however, is only part of the story, for the crucial events are those that happened after Mohamed had secured his temporary visa. Having been identified by the FBI as a suspect for whom an international arrest warrant had been issued in connection with the bombing of the United

States embassy in Tanzania, he was apprehended by the South African immigration authorities in a joint operation undertaken in cooperation with the FBI. Within two days of his arrest and contrary to the provisions of the Act he was handed over to the FBI by the South African authorities for the purpose of being taken to the United States to be put on trial there for the bombing of the embassy. On his arrival in the United States he was immediately charged with various offences relating to that bombing and was informed by the court that the death sentence could be imposed on him if he were convicted. That this was likely to happen must have been apparent to the South African authorities as well as to the FBI when the arrangements were made for Mohamed to be removed from South Africa to the United States …'[1]

1 At para 44.

5.87 Whilst unable to provide tangible relief to Mohamed, the Constitutional Court ruled that it should nonetheless make its following views known to the American trial court:

> 'For the South African government to cooperate with a foreign government to secure the removal of a fugitive from South Africa to a country of which the fugitive is not a national and with which he has no connection other than that he is to be put on trial for his life there, is contrary to the underlying values of our Constitution. It is inconsistent with the government's obligation to protect the right to life of everyone in South Africa, and it ignores the commitment implicit in the Constitution that South Africa will not be party to the imposition of cruel, inhuman or degrading punishment … The fact that the government claims to have deported and not to have extradited Mohamed is of no relevance. European courts draw no distinction between deportation and extradition in the application of Article 3 of the European Convention on Human Rights … The removal of Mohamed to the United States could not have been effected without the cooperation of the South African immigration authorities. They cooperated well knowing that he would be put on trial in the United States to face capital charges. That he should be arrested and put on trial was clearly a significant and possibly the predominant motive that determined the course that was followed. Otherwise, why instruct the officials at the border to prevent him from leaving South Africa? And why cooperate in the process of sending him to the United States, a country with which he had no connection? They must also have known that there was a real risk that he would be convicted, and that unless an assurance to the contrary were obtained, he would be sentenced to death. In doing so, they infringed Mohamed's rights under the Constitution and acted contrary to their obligations to uphold and promote the rights entrenched in the Bill of Rights.'[1]

1 At paras 59–61.

R v Burns

5.88 In *R v Burns*,[1] the appellant had been arrested in respect of substantial drugs offences and remanded in custody. He escaped and made his way to

Venezuela (entering Venezuela unlawfully under a false name, and using a false passport). An arrest warrant was issued and an Interpol Notice asserted that extradition would be requested from any country with which the UK had an extradition treaty or similar arrangement. The appellant was later arrested in Venezuela for an unrelated drugs offence committed there. The arrest was a purely domestic matter within Venezuela, and the British authorities were neither involved in nor connected with it. The UK authorities were advised of the appellant's presence in Venezuela. There existed no bilateral extradition treaty between the UK and Venezuela, and accordingly, any extradition request would have to have been ad hoc (pursuant to s 15 of the Extradition Act 1989).

1 [2002] EWCA Crim 1324.

5.89 The UK authorities were further advised that the appellant would probably be deported. The UK authorities were then asked to, and did, provide the Venezuelan investigatory judge with the appellant's details, including the fact that he was wanted in England. The Judge ordered the appellant's deportation to England since this was his country of origin. The UK authorities paid for the flight and accompanied him back to London where he was arrested. The trial judge rejected the contention that the British authorities had connived at, or colluded with, any impropriety by the Venezuelan authorities. That conclusion was upheld on its facts by the Court of Appeal, Judge LJ observing that the UK authorities:

> '… were not involved in the initial arrest. They provided the Judge, or investigating magistrate, with facts with which she wished to be provided. They did not exaggerate or falsify. They understood that the process in Venezuela, if not subject to judicial supervision, certainly involved a judicial element. They understood that, on the known facts, the appellant would be likely to be deported to this country. It is of course true that the British authorities did not try and discourage the authorities in Venezuela from the process, on which they seemed determined, nor question or challenge its legality. It was not incumbent on them to do so. And given their understanding of the view likely to be taken by the Venezuelan authorities, they sought to co-operate in the process, no doubt in the hope of achieving the appellant's return to the United Kingdom where he could be arrested. In our judgement, the process of this court was not subverted.'[1]

1 At paras 29–30.

5.90 What is perhaps more interesting from the Court of Appeal's ruling, is its treatment of a somewhat ambitious submission mounted on behalf of the appellant that, *whatever the merits, or the circumstances, of his expulsion*, if his client should have been extradited from Venezuela, and the British authorities participated in the process by which extradition proceedings were bypassed, an abuse of process was established. Rejecting that submission of principle, Judge LJ observed[1] that:

> '… while [*ex parte Bennett* and *R v Mullen*] and other, cases identify clear principles, and are thus helpful if they might be in any doubt, the decisions on the individual facts are not decisive of subsequent cases, where similar, but not identical issues are raised. While preventing, or more accurately,

acting to prevent the prosecution from benefiting from abuses of the process amounting to what Lord Steyn in *R v Latif* (1996) 1 WLR 104 at 112, graphically described as conduct "so unworthy or shameful that it was an affront to the public conscience to allow the prosecution to proceed," the principles are not apt to require that the conduct of the prosecution at every stage of the process should be unblemished and immaculate. Errors will be made and oversights will occur, and combinations of errors and oversights will take place, which do not justify the conclusion that the process has been abused

… As Lord Lane CJ, pointed out in … *ex parte Mackeson* … the decision in an individual case is "very largely a question of fact and the inference which one draws from the available facts on affidavits and on documentary evidence which are before us." An indicative, but not determinative line, may be drawn between cases where the prosecuting authorities have acted in bad faith, or with an excess of misguided enthusiasm for what is perceived to be a proper objective, deliberately subverting the defendant's rights not to be forcibly abducted to this country without proper process, and those cases where the prosecuting authorities, acting in good faith, have undermined or contributed to the undermining of the rights of the defendant. In *R v Mullen* … Rose LJ pointed out further considerations: "In each case it is a matter of discretionary balance, to be approached with regard to the particular conduct complained of and the particular offence charged." In short, when deciding whether to exercise its undoubted powers to prevent an abuse of its process, the exercise of the court's discretion is fact specific.

… We therefore reject the submission that unless the extradition process, or its equivalent, has taken place, the court here is obliged to stop the prosecution. That is not what the House of Lords decided in *Bennett*. The existence of and the need to, exercise a discretion in each case where the issue is raised clearly contradicts the proposition that failures or breaches in the extradition process lead ineluctably to the termination of the trial. Moreover, if the contention were correct, it would apply to cases where the only interference with the extradition process would have been misconduct by the authorities in the foreign country (over which this court has no supervisory control) without any significant contribution by the British authorities (over which it has).'

1 At paras 26–28.

Tague v Governor of Full Sutton Prison

5.91 In *Tague*[1] the applicant had faced trial at the Crown Court for various drugs and firearms offences. The applicant had appeared at trial during the presentation of evidence but absconded prior to the conclusion of the trial. A bench warrant for the applicant's arrest was issued by the trial judge for failure to answer bail. As the applicant's absconsion occurred late in proceedings the trial judge considered that the applicant would not suffer any prejudice if the permitted to proceed to its conclusion. In the course of his summing-up, the trial judge informed the jury that they should not make any negative inferences from the applicant's absence. On 14 and 17 April 2000, the jury found the applicant guilty of six drug dealing offences and one firearms offence. The applicant was then sentenced to 23 years imprisonment.

In 2006, a European Arrest Warrant ('EAW') was issued pursuant to the Extradition Act 2003. Under the arrangements for EAWs, the Serious Organised Crime Agency ('SOCA') was responsible for transmitting EAWs to foreign states and co-ordinating arrangements for the return of those subject to EAWs.

Seven years later the applicant was arrested in Spain conducted as a joint operation between SOCA and Spanish police. The applicant did not consent to his extradition 2013 the case was heard in front of the Spanish High Court. SOCA were not represented at this hearing. On 17 July 2013, the Spanish High Court ordered the applicant's extradition. However, a condition of the order was that the applicant was to be given a retrial, if he requested it. This condition was included as the Spanish High Court held that Spanish law did not permit trials in absentia where the sentence was greater than two years imprisonment. The Spanish High Court was seemingly unaware that the UK was not in a position to grant such a retrial under domestic law.

At the hearing before the High Court, expert evidence regarding the lawfulness of the Spanish High Court's order requiring a retrial was heard. Expert testimony was uncertain whether the Spanish High Court was required under Spanish domestic law to order that extradition to the UK be made condition upon a retrial being granted or whether this power was discretionary. Further, experts could not say whether, if the power were discretionary, the court would have varied the order had they known the UK was not able to grant a retrial.

A copy of order of 17 July in its original Spanish was then sent to SOCA in the UK via Interpol. An email from Interpol included brief text in English which confirmed the applicant was to be surrendered to the UK but did not mention the retrial condition. Crucially the order was not translated from the original Spanish by SOCA. SOCA officials proceeded with the applicant's extradition without ever having the full text of the order and were therefore unaware of the condition to grant the applicant a retrial.

The applicant was extradited to the UK on 5 August 2013 and transferred to Full Sutton prison to serve out his 23-year sentence. In October 2013 the CPS sought to prosecute the applicant for the breach of bail. To bring fresh proceedings, it was necessary to demonstrate the charges relating to the breach of bail had been included in the EAW and the order of 17 July was finally translated in full. It transpired that the bail proceedings could not be pursued but the applicant then brought proceedings alleging an abuse of process by SOCA for its role in the extradition proceedings.

Leveson, P observed that the role of the court when considering whether to grant a stay in such a case depended on balancing the public interest in bringing those charged with serious crimes to trial against the competing public interest that the misconduct of the executive should not convey the impression that such misconduct justified the means. When discussing striking that balance Leveson, P held:

'48. Exercising that balance is far from straightforward. Lord Steyn's words of caution (the ends must not be seen to justify the means) have to be read alongside Lord Lowry's observation that abuse of process is not a disciplinary jurisdiction…

49. This problem arises because maintaining confidence in the criminal justice system (or, as it has been put, avoiding "an affront to the public conscience") is an aim or aspiration which has to be perceived from different directions. On the one hand, there is gross misconduct which the criminal justice system cannot approbate (as in cases such as *Bennett* and *Mullen*). On the other hand, however, it is important that conduct or results that may merely be the result of state incompetence or negligence should not necessarily justify what might be colloquially described as a "Get Out of Jail Free" card: in those cases, the public might conclude that the justice system was little more than a game. There is no bright line and a broad brush approach is likely to be necessary.'

Considering the misconduct of SOCA in procuring the applicant's extradition Leveson, P stated:

'54. …on the face of the evidence presented, the present case reveals no more than a lack of care and precision. I do not accept Mr Summers' argument that SOCA's conduct taken together amounts to a deliberate bad faith policy to ignore or exercise wilful blindness to conditions placed on EAW extraditions by executing Member States. This is not least for the reason that SOCA would assume that the applicant's own lawyer in Spain would have made the retrial condition abundantly clear to him, if the prospect of such a condition had been ventilated during the EAW execution proceedings. If SOCA had appreciated the condition, I have no doubt that advice would have been sought as to the extent to which it could be removed and what steps could be taken to safeguard the position in relation to this most wanted fugitive.

…

56. Mr Summers further argues that the present case should be compared to abduction cases such as *Bennett* and *Mullen*, entrapment cases where an individual is lured into the UK's jurisdiction such as Latif, or other instances where "but for" the executive conduct at issue an individual would not be in the jurisdiction. I do not accept that it can be said with any certainty that such causation existed in the present case… [I]t is unclear whether the [Spanish High Court] would have still ordered execution of the EAW even if it had known the UK could not have complied with its right to request a new trial condition.

…

61. …I accept that the failure by the authorities to ensure that the Spanish court and all affected were aware of the restriction on right to retrial is and was highly regrettable as was the failure to appreciate the condition in the order at a time when it may well be that Spanish law… could be investigated and representations made. I reject the characterisation of these failures as

deliberately deceitful or a manifestation of wilful blindness. There was negligence but no more.'

The applicant's appeal was therefore dismissed as the conduct of SOCA was not so serious that the continued imprisonment of the applicant was an affront to justice.

1 [2015] EWHC 3576 (Admin).

Article 5 ECHR

5.92 Unlike abuse of process generally, issues of disguised extradition do engage Article 5(1)(f) ECHR. In *Bozano v France*,[1] Mr Bozano had been convicted in his absence in Italy and sentenced to life imprisonment in respect of offences relating to a Swiss national. He had taken refuge in France. He was arrested in France on other matters and kept in custody for the purposes of extradition. The French Court of Appeal ruled against extradition (holding that the Italian procedure relating to trial in absence and the absence of recourse to retrial was contrary to French public policy). Under French law, that ruling was final and binding upon the French government. Upon release from custody, Mr Bozano was forced into a car by three armed plainclothes policemen. He was handcuffed and taken to police headquarters and served with a deportation order (which was later quashed by the French courts as an abuse of power). He was denied access to the courts or to legal representation, or in fact to anybody. Rather than take him to the nearest (Spanish) border, or to a border of his choice, he was driven hundreds of miles to the Swiss border. He was there met by Swiss police officials, handcuffed, and conveyed into Swiss custody. From Switzerland, Mr Bozano's extradition to Italy was readily granted under the terms of the European Convention on Extradition 1957. The European Court of Human Rights unanimously found a violation of Art 5, ruling[2] that:

> 'Viewing the circumstances of the case as a whole … the applicant's deprivation of liberty was neither lawful within the meaning of Article 5(1)(f) nor compatible with the right to security of person. Depriving Mr Bozano of his liberty in this way amounted in fact to a disguised form of extradition designed to circumvent the negative ruling … of the Court of Appeal and not detention necessary in the ordinary course of action taken with a view to deportation …the deportation procedure was abused in the instant case for objects and purposes other than its normal ones.'

1 (1986) 9 EHRR 297.
2 At paras 60–61.

5.93 In *Stocké v Germany*, the applicant, a German national, was subject to criminal proceedings before the German courts in respect of tax offences. He failed to comply with the provisions of his bail and was ordered to be re-detained. However, he had fled to France (via Switzerland) to avoid arrest. The Court again considered the issues surrounding 'disguised extradition'. The German authorities first unsuccessfully sought to persuade the government of Luxembourg to receive and expel him on 'trumped up charges'. A plan was then devised by a police informer to lure Mr Stocké either directly into Germany or into a country from which he could be extradited, by means of attending a 'meeting' in respect of a fictitious building project. Mr Stocké was thus enticed onto a private charter plane ostensibly headed for Luxembourg but which proceeded to make an unscheduled stop in Germany, whereupon Mr Stocké was arrested. The police informant was later reimbursed for the cost of the charter hire, and provided with a reward by the German prosecutor.

5.94 Before the European Court of Human Rights,[1] Mr Stocké claimed to be the victim of collusion between the German authorities and the police informer for the purpose of kidnapping him and bringing him back to the Federal Republic of Germany against his will with a view to arresting him in violation of Art 5(1). It was argued that the prosecuting authorities 'considered that it was too uncertain whether an extradition request to France would succeed and had preferred to make use of a police informer to do "the dirty work abroad".' The Court noted[2] that the applicant was induced by a trick to board a plane chartered by the informant, although he had been warned that they were going to fly over a small part of German territory. French inquiries that had been made had shown that the applicant had boarded the plane of his own free will and not under duress. The Commission examined witnesses; all denied having known about the informant's plan to bring Mr Stocké back to Germany against his will or having agreed to such a plan being carried out; the Commission did not consider their evidence to be inconsistent or unreliable. The Court considered, like the Commission, that it had not been established that the cooperation between the German authorities and the informant extended to unlawful activities abroad.[3] The clear implication of this judgment is that, as in *Bozano v France*,[4] had illegitimate cooperation, in fact, been found to have occurred, Art 5 issues would have been engaged.

1 (1991) App No 11755/85, 19 March.
2 At paras 49–50.
3 At paras 51 and 54.
4 Above para **5.92**.

5.95 Although neither *Bozano v France*[1] nor Art 5(1) contributed heavily, if indeed at all, to the formation of the *R v Hartley*[2] / *State v Ebrahim*[3] / *ex parte Bennett*[4] common law abuse of process principles, it appeared that the principles governing each would largely reflect and complement the other. However, there then followed a series of Strasbourg judgments which appeared to herald a significant division between the two lines of principle, such that Art 5 was likely to be of little assistance to the further development of the common law.

1 Above para **5.92**.
2 Above para **5.57**.
3 Above para **5.67**.
4 Above para **5.38**.

5.96 In *Sanchez Ramirez v France*,[1] the applicant, a Venezuelan citizen, was wanted by the French authorities in respect of a fatal car bomb explosion in Paris, for which he had been convicted *in absentia* and sentenced to life imprisonment. Mr Sanchez Ramirez was living in Khartoum, Sudan, under the protection of the Sudanese national security forces. There existed no extradition treaty between France and the Sudan. Mr Sanchez Ramirez alleged that he had been forcibly expelled from the Sudan at the request of the French Interior Ministry. He alleged that he had been attacked by 12 or so men, including members of his own guard, handcuffed, fettered, tranquilised, and hooded. He was transported to the airport where Frenchmen were waiting. Once on the airplane, he alleged that he was placed in a bag and strapped around his feet, knees, and shoulders and flown to a military airbase in France. The French Court of Cassation ruled that French national courts have no jurisdiction to examine the circumstances in which a person is arrested abroad by local authorities acting alone and in the exercise of their sovereign powers. On an application to the European Commission on Human Rights, Mr Sanchez Ramirez argued that his arrest amounted to disguised extradition in violation of Art 5(1).

1 (1996) 86-B DR 155.

5.97 The Commission ruled[1] that the circumstances in which the applicant was deprived of his liberty in Sudan were outwith the jurisdiction of the Convention.[2] The Commission further observed, without reference to *Bozano v France*,[3] that:

> 'It does not appear to the Commission that any cooperation which occurred in this case between the Sudanese and French authorities involved any factor which could raise problems from the point of view of Article 5 of the Convention particularly in the field of the fight against terrorism, which frequently necessitates cooperation between States ... The Convention contains no provisions either concerning the circumstances in which extradition may be granted, or the procedure to be followed before extradition may be granted. It follows that even assuming that the circumstances in which the applicant arrived in France could be described as a disguised extradition, this could not, as such, constitute a breach of the Convention.'

1 At pp160–161.
2 See, to similar effect, *Freda v Italy* (1980) 21 DR 250; *Altmann v France* (1984) 37 DR 225 and *Reinette v France* (1989) 63 DR 189.
3 Above para **5.92**.

5.98 In *Conka v Belgium*[1] the Bozano approach appeared to have been restored when it found Art 5 violations in a 'disguised expulsion' case involving the tricking of Slovakian Romany asylum seekers by the Belgian authorities into a police station under the false pretence that their attendance was required to enable asylum forms to be completed. When they attended, the applicants were served with orders to leave Belgium and were informed that the orders were final. They were taken to a closed transit centre and thus removed from Belgium to Slovakia by deceit (a 'little ruse'). The European Court of Human Rights found[2] a violation of Art 5(1) by reason of deliberate abuse of power and thus arbitrariness, citing *Bozano v France*.[3]

1 (2002) 34 EHRR 54.
2 At paras 38–42.
3 Above para **5.92**.

5.99 In May 2005, however, the Grand Chamber gave judgment in *Ocalan v Turkey*.[1] Mr Öcalan was the leader of the Workers' Party of Kurdistan (PKK). The Turkish courts had issued seven warrants for Mr Öcalan's arrest and a wanted notice (Red Notice) had been circulated by Interpol. In each of those documents, the applicant was accused of founding an armed gang in order to destroy the territorial integrity of the Turkish State and of instigating various terrorist acts that had resulted in loss of life. The offences alleged were punishable with death. Mr Öcalan had been living in Syria for many years, but was expelled from there. He travelled to Greece and claimed political asylum which was refused. He was taken by the Greek authorities to Kenya and accommodated at the Ambassador's residence, the Greek authorities ensuring that he was able to enter without declaring his identity or going through passport control. When they learned of his presence, the Kenyan Ministry for Foreign Affairs announced that Kenyan diplomatic missions abroad had been the target of terrorist attacks and that the applicant's presence in Kenya constituted a major security risk.

1 (2005) 41 EHRR 45, paras 83–99.

5.100 Mr Öcalan was informed by the Greek Ambassador, after the latter had returned from a meeting with the Kenyan Minister for Foreign Affairs, that he was free to leave for the destination of his choice and that the Netherlands were prepared to accept him. Kenyan officials went to the Greek embassy to take Mr Öcalan to the airport. The Greek Ambassador said that he wished to accompany the applicant to the airport in person and a discussion between the Ambassador and the Kenyan officials ensued. In the end, the applicant got into a car driven by a Kenyan official. On the way to the airport, this car left the convoy and, taking a route reserved for security personnel in the international transit area of Nairobi Airport, took him to an aircraft in which Turkish officials were waiting for him. The applicant was then arrested after boarding the aircraft. No proceedings had been brought to extradite him from Kenya and the Kenyan authorities had denied all responsibility for his transfer to Turkey. Mr Öcalan was kept blindfolded throughout the flight except when the Turkish officials wore masks. He also alleged that he had been given tranquillisers, probably at the Greek embassy in Nairobi. He was found guilty by the National Security Court and sentenced to death. That conviction was upheld by the Turkish Court of Cassation, but his death sentence was later commuted to one of life imprisonment.

5.101 Mr Öcalan brought proceedings before the European Court of Human Rights alleging, inter alia, that he had been deprived of his liberty unlawfully, without the applicable extradition procedure being followed, in violation of Art 5(1). He maintained that his interception by Kenyan officials and transfer to the Turkish aircraft where Turkish officials were waiting for him was prima facie evidence that he had been abducted by the Turkish authorities operating abroad beyond their jurisdiction. The Grand Chamber found no violation of Art 5. As regards issues of principle, the Grand Chamber observed that an arrest made by the authorities of one State on the territory of another State, without the consent of the latter, affects the person's individual rights to security under Art 5.[1] The Convention does not prevent cooperation between States, within the framework of extradition treaties or in matters of deportation, for the purpose of bringing fugitive offenders to justice, provided that it does not interfere with any specific rights recognised in the Convention.[2] The fact that a fugitive has been handed over as a result of cooperation between States does not in itself make the arrest unlawful and does not therefore give rise to any problem under Art 5.[3] The Convention contains no provisions concerning the circumstances in which extradition may be granted, or the procedure to be followed before extradition may be granted. Subject to it being the result of cooperation between the States concerned, and provided that the legal basis for the order for the fugitive's arrest is an arrest warrant issued by the authorities of the fugitive's State of origin, *even an atypical extradition cannot as such be regarded as being contrary to the Convention*.[4] Irrespective of whether the arrest amounts to a violation of the law of the State in which the fugitive has taken refuge – a question that only falls to be examined by the Court if the host State is a party to the Convention – the Court requires proof in the form of concordant inferences that the authorities of the State to which the applicant has been transferred have acted extra-territorially in a manner that is inconsistent with the sovereignty of the host State and therefore contrary to international law. Only then will the burden of proving that the sovereignty of the host State and international law have been complied with shift to the respondent Government.[5]

1 At para 85.
2 At para 86. For similar reasoning, see *Adamov v Switzerland*, App. No.3052/06, 21.06.2011 at paras 58–59.
3 At paras 87.
4 At para 89.
5 At para 90.

5.102 Applying those principles to the facts before it, the Grand Chamber noted that the applicant was arrested by members of the Turkish security forces inside an aircraft registered in Turkey in the international zone of Nairobi Airport. After being handed over to the Turkish officials by the Kenyan officials, the applicant was effectively under Turkish authority and therefore within the 'jurisdiction' of that State. Insofar as the applicant's interception in Kenya immediately before he was handed over to Turkish officials on board the aircraft at Nairobi Airport was concerned, the Court sought to determine whether it was 'the result of [illegitimate] acts by Turkish officials that violated Kenyan sovereignty and international law …, or of [legitimate] cooperation between the Turkish and Kenyan authorities in the absence of any extradition treaty between Turkey and Kenya laying down a formal procedure'.[1] Having regard to the facts that: (a) the applicant entered Kenya without declaring his identity to the immigration officers, (b) the Kenyan authorities invited the Greek Ambassador to arrange for the applicant to leave Kenyan territory, (c) as he was being transferred from the Greek embassy to the airport, Kenyan officials intervened and separated the applicant from the Greek Ambassador, (d) the car in which the applicant was travelling was driven by a Kenyan official who took him to the aircraft in which Turkish officials were waiting to arrest him, (e) the Kenyan authorities did not perceive the applicant's arrest by the Turkish officials on board an aircraft at Nairobi Airport as being in any way a violation of Kenyan sovereignty, and (f) the Kenyan authorities did, however, issue a formal protest to the Greek government, the Court concluded[2] that, contrary to the statement by the Kenyan Minister for Foreign Affairs, the Kenyan authorities were involved in the applicant's transfer:

'… at the material time the Kenyan authorities had decided either to hand the applicant over to the Turkish authorities or to facilitate such a handover. The applicant has not adduced evidence enabling concordant inferences … to be drawn that Turkey failed to respect Kenyan sovereignty or to comply with international law in the present case.'

1 At para 93.
2 At paras 97–98.

5.103 More recently, the European Court has firmly set its face against executive misconduct of this sort. In extradition cases, the First section of the ECtHR has repeatedly found violations of Art 3 in cases of forced expulsion (ie State kidnapping) in contravention of extradition laws from a Convention State; see *Kasymakhunov v Russia,*[1] *Dzhurayev v Russia,*[2] *Abdulkhakov v Russia,*[3] *Iskandarov v Russia.*[4]

The Grand Chamber had opportunity to reconsider Arts 3 and 5 issues surrounding unlawful extradition in *El-Masri v FYROM.*[5] Mr El-Masri was a German citizen travelling to Macedonia on holiday. At the Serbia-Macedonia border Mr El-Masri was interrogated for several hours before being confined in a hotel in Macedonia for the next 23 days. The next day Mr El-Masri was taken to Skopje airport and handed over to a CIA 'rendition team'. Following this Mr El-Masri was severely beaten in a room at the airport and transported by plane to Afghanistan and held in a detention facility for the next four months. Over this time, he was repeatedly beaten and interrogated. El-Masri was eventually sent back to Germany. Subsequent investigations revealed that the CIA had requested that Macedonian security services detain and secure Mr El-Masri until he could be handed over to the CIA. In the subsequent proceedings Macedonian officials did not produce a warrant for Mr El-Masri's detention or transfer.

Mr El-Masri brought proceedings in the European Court of Human Rights alleging, *inter alia*, that during his detention he had been subject to torture or treatment amounting to inhuman or degrading treatment in breach of Art 3 and, further, that he had detained unlawfully in breach of Art 5. The applicant alleged that Macedonia was responsible for both the initial breaches by the Macedonian security services and the subsequent breaches by the CIA. Third party interveners submitted that the secret abduction, rendition and detention amounted to an enforced disappearance. The Court held that Macedonia was in breach of Arts 3 and 5 for the entire duration of Mr El-Masri's detention.

The court found Art 3 breaches relating to the applicant's initial detention in the hotel by Macedonian security services. The Court also found that beatings carried out by the CIA rendition team at the airport were a breach of Art 3 and were attributable to Macedonia as its agents 'actively facilitated the treatment and then failed to take any measures that might have been necessary in the circumstances of the case to prevent it from occurring'.[6] The Court further held that the transfer of the applicant to the CIA was a breach of Art 3 as Macedonia was aware of the destination the applicant was being transferred to and had knowledge of the treatment the applicant may have been subject to at that destination.[7] On this basis the Court found that the applicant was 'subjected to "extraordinary rendition", that is, an "extrajudicial transfer of persons from one jurisdiction or State to another, for the purposes of detention and interrogation outside the normal legal system, where there was a real risk of torture or cruel, inhuman or degrading treatment"'.[8]

In contrast to *Öcalan* the initial arrest and detention of the applicant occurred in a convention state. The lack of legal authority for the applicant's detention was therefore a breach of Art 5.[9] The Court reiterated that contracting states were under an obligation take appropriate steps to provide protection against an unlawful interference with those rights to everyone within its jurisdiction. The Court went on to hold that the CIA detention programme amounted to arbitrary detention and that, by handing the applicant over to the CIA, Macedonia had exposing the applicant to 'a real risk of a flagrant violation of his rights under Article 5'.[10]

1 (2013) App. 29604/12, 14 November 2013.
2 (2013) 57 EHRR 22.
3 (2012) App. No. 14743/11, 2 October 2012.
4 (2010) App. No. 17185/05), 23 September.
5 *El-Masri v The Former Yugoslav Republic of Macedonia* (Application no. 39630/09) 13 December 2012.
6 At para 211.
7 At paras 217–218.
8 At para 221.
9 At para 236.
10 At para 239.

5.104 The state of Strasbourg case law is therefore unclear. The obvious difference between *Sanchez Ramirez* and *Öcalan* on the one hand, and *Conka*, *Kasymakhunov, Dzhurayev, Abdulkhakov, Iskandarov* and *El-Masri* on the other hand, is that the former concern receipt of a defendant by a Convention State from outside the Council of Europe and the latter concern the obverse situation (expulsion by a Convention State to a country outside the Council of Europe). But *Bozano* and *Stocké* cannot be so distinguished and, in any event, it is difficult to discern any logical or principled basis to apply different standards to the same executive lawlessness in these situations. Executive lawlessness in conspiring with a foreign state to obtain jurisdiction over a criminal suspect is no different to conspiring with a foreign state to enable that foreign state to obtain jurisdiction over a criminal suspect. Both circumvent the rule of law generally and extradition laws in particular and both disregard entirely the liberty of the individual. But if *Sanchez Ramirez* and *Öcalan* remain good law, they undoubtedly run counter to significant statements of high principle contained in other Strasbourg case law and flatly conflict with the principles espoused by the House of Lords in *ex parte Bennett*,[1] the South African Supreme Court in *State v Ebrahim*,[2] the South African Constitutional Court in *Mohamed v The President*,[3] and the New Zealand Court of Appeal in *R v Hartley*.[4] Constituting, at their core, instances of state cooperation, cases such as *ex parte Mackeson*[5] and *R v Mullen*[6] would likely suffer a different fate if decided under the principles articulated by the Grand Chamber. Conversely, the facts of *Sanchez Ramirez* and *Öcalan* would almost certainly suffer a different fate if decided under the common law abuse of process principles. It is surely inconceivable that *ex parte Bennett* would be reconsidered along the same lines. It is, therefore, likely that, at least whilst *Sanchez Ramirez* and *Öcalan* have life, Art 5 and the common law doctrine of abuse of principle will remain but distant cousins, each effectively offering little to the jurisprudential development of the latter.

1 Above para **5.38**.
2 Above para **5.67**.
3 Above para **5.85**.
4 Above para **5.57**.
5 Above para **5.58**.
6 Above para **5.79**.

UNLAWFUL ACTS COMMITTED BY UK STATE AGENTS OVERSEAS

5.105 The decision of the House of Lords in *ex parte Bennett* establishes that, where a complaint is made of unlawfulness of State agents in foreign jurisdictions and/or breaches of foreign law by State agents resulting in the arrival of the accused into this jurisdiction, then an English court is competent to hear this complaint pursuant to its abuse jurisdiction.

5.106 The issue next to be considered is whether similar principles apply where similar complaints of illegality are made outside the context of an alleged illegal extradition:

(a) where it is alleged that the way in which evidence was obtained against the accused by UK agents operating overseas was unlawful under the law of the jurisdiction in which they operated; and

(b) whether those agents in the course of their investigation assisted or procured breaches of foreign law committed by agents or officials of that foreign jurisdiction.

5.107 Crime, as it is always said in the context of mutual assistance, is increasingly international. From terrorism to organised crime, from paedophiles to fraudsters, and especially via the internet, the notion of national frontiers demarcating one crime from another is regarded as increasingly anachronistic. Hence the convergence of law enforcement agencies within the EU and beyond where international operations, previously largely reserved for anti-drug trafficking, have become almost routine. Heightened fears concerning international terrorism have galvanised this acceptance of international co-operation to combat organised crime.

5.108 The nature of international law enforcement has changed. However, the traditional legal framework concerning mutual assistance remains rooted in two concepts which have been seen as antipathetic to the developments outlined in para **5.107**: first, that of the integrity of the sovereign nation-State, and secondly, an emphasis on mutual assistance being connected to extant or antecedent court proceedings. Traditional use of mutual assistance relates to the obtaining of evidence by one State on behalf of another for use in proceedings. 'Proceedings' here mean court or judicial proceedings. This approach underlies the Council of Europe's European Convention on Mutual Assistance 1959.

Essentially the Convention is concerned with the foreign State gathering or obtaining evidence on behalf of the Requesting State. Following Brexit, the UK/EU relationship has been modified by Part 3, Title VIII of the Withdrawal Agreement.

5.109 The scenario to be considered in this section is, however, not addressed or contemplated by the formal mutual assistance arrangements in the Convention. It relates to situations where there are no court proceedings in existence and UK State agents are operating on foreign soil in a law enforcement capacity.[1] In this scenario, the agents are investigating crimes which are in the course of being committed in the foreign State. This was the situation in *R v McDonald*.[2]

1 This in contradistinction to an intelligence-gathering capacity, the traditional function of MI6.

2 (April 2002, unreported), Woolwich Crown Court.

R v McDonald

5.110 The accused were all alleged to be participating members of 'The Real IRA', a proscribed terrorist organisation. Further, pursuant to offences under the Terrorism Act 2000, they were alleged to have solicited funds and weapons and conspired to cause explosions. The significance of these offences was that the UK courts had jurisdiction to try such offences irrespective of where they were alleged to have been committed. The evidence adduced by the prosecution related to two recorded conversations between the accused and undercover MI5 agents which had occurred in Slovakia. This evidence was the culmination of contacts between the accused and MI5 agents over several months, which had taken place in several other countries including Ireland, Austria and Hungary. Two novel features of the investigation were apparent. First that 'Operation Samnite' was an investigation conducted and led by MI5 almost entirely overseas. Secondly, and in consequence, the police were only brought in at a very late stage when MI5 was minded to curtail its operation, their role being to advise on evidence and apply for an international arrest warrant.

5.111 In relation to their abuse applications, the accused alleged abuse and bad faith as follows:

(a) the extradition of the accused from Slovakia at the request of the British authorities was unlawful in that due process requirements under Slovakian law were not observed by the Slovakian authorities, and Art 8 of the European Convention on Human Rights was, in any event, violated;

(b) Slovakia was chosen by MI5 as the preferred country of arrest and extradition and thus the accused were lured into this jurisdiction from another (Ireland), where their extradition would have been more difficult; and

(c) the surveillance methods used by MI5 were unlawful in several of the countries in which that activity occurred.

Accordingly in relation to such complaints, full disclosure of all relevant material was sought.

5.112 It is interesting to note that, at least during its lifetime of Operation Samnite, no treaty existed between the UK and another State in relation to the conduct of UK agents working abroad. It must therefore inevitably follow that it was either conducted without the consent of the host-State and was thus a flagrant violation of its sovereignty or, and much more likely, there were secret diplomatic agreements or protocols between the UK and the relevant countries permitting MI5 activity in those countries. In fact, in *McDonald*, the prosecution admitted that agreements had been reached concerning the permitting of MI5 activity. It was, however, anxious that there should be no disclosure of these.

5.113 Parliament has already contemplated the overseas use of UK agents. The Regulation of Investigatory Powers Act 2000, s 27(3) and the Intelligence Services Act 1994, s 5 are both concerned with the authorisation within the UK of covert operations conducted on foreign soil. In *McDonald,* the prosecution contended that Operation Samnite was validly authorised pursuant to those sections.

The issues raised

5.114 Put at its simplest, the issue raised by this subject is whether, as in the instance of illegal extradition as in *ex parte Bennett*, the courts here are willing to supervise, via their abuse jurisdiction, executive conduct in relation to the overseas gathering of evidence and deployment of agents during a criminal investigation. As a matter of policy, should the courts eschew any willingness to supervise such conduct or should they hold that their constitutional duty to ensure the fairness of criminal trials requires that no area of executive conduct is beyond their jurisdiction?

5.115 Clearly, there are valid arguments against the courts assuming jurisdiction. International relations or 'international comity' suggest that a court in one jurisdiction should not determine whether a foreign government agency has acted in breach of its own domestic law in another jurisdiction. There is plenty of authority to the effect that territorial sovereignty requires that an English court should not pronounce upon the validity of a law of a foreign State within its own territory.[1] In addition to reasons of comity, the courts have also imposed self-restraint in relation to sensitive areas of diplomacy between States.[2] This, however, is to be distinguished from the courts' power to comment on and address the misconduct of its own state agents in a foreign state.

1 See for example *Buck v A-G* [1965] Ch 745; *British Airways v Laker* [1985] AC 58 and *Kuwait Airways v Iraqi Airways* [2002] 2 AC 883, HL.

2 See for example the judgment of the Court of Appeal *R (Abbassi) v Secretary of State for Foreign Affairs* [2002] EWCA Civ 1598, where, although the Court regarded as objectionable the fact that the British citizen was subject to indefinite detention in territory over which the US had exclusive control with no opportunity to challenge the legitimacy of his detention before any court or tribunal, it was held that there was no direct remedy in the English court.

5.116 In respect of a foreign state, however, from a pragmatic perspective, the courts here may rightly be reluctant to consider themselves competent to decide whether, for example, the criminal law of another EU State complies with the European Convention on Human Rights or whether the UK agent active in that State acted in breach of relevant domestic law. Such considerations may quickly embroil an English court in a clash of experts concerning foreign law with the attendant risk of that court interpreting such law in a way inconsistent with its interpretation by the national State courts.

5.117 There are, however, strong countervailing arguments. The principle firmly established in *ex parte Bennett* is that the rule of law requires any area of executive misconduct to fall within the purview of the courts. An assertion that there are some activities of State affecting the fairness of a criminal trial, which, as a class, should not be subject to judicial accountability, is one which no longer finds any support in English law (see for example, the facts of the *Warren* case (above paras **5.14–5.28**).

5.118 Furthermore, if Parliament is to assume extraterritorial criminal jurisdiction in relation, for example, to terrorism under the Terrorism Act 2000, such that an individual can be tried for offences under that statute wherever they occurred, then questions of comity lose much of their attraction. Moreover, Parliament has also created a legislative framework in relation to overseas actions of executive agents as outlined above. It should also be noted that the ECtHR has concluded that state agents are capable of committing violations of the ECHR in other jurisdictions if they exercise 'physical power and control over the person'.[1] Against this backdrop, it is difficult to comprehend why the safeguard of judicial accountability should be excluded.

1 *Al-Skeini v the United Kingdom* (2011) 53 EHRR 18 at paras 136–7.

5.119 For themselves, the courts have expressed a willingness to consider whether the obtaining of evidence for admission into a trial here was in breach of foreign law. Three authorities[1] can briefly be considered:

(a) In *R v Khan*,[2] Lord Nolan said: 'I am prepared to accept that if evidence has been obtained in circumstances which involve a breach of Article 8, or for that matter an apparent breach of the law of a foreign country, that is a matter which may be relevant to the exercise of the section 78 power'.[3]

(b) In *R v P, C and S*,[4] Potter LJ accepted that an English court could hear evidence relating to the legality of obtaining foreign intercepts under foreign law.

(c) *HM Advocate v Al Megrahi (No 3)*:[5] in the Lockerbie trial, the Scottish court considered whether Maltese officials had breached Maltese law in their dealings with Scottish police officers.

1 For a Commonwealth authority on this point, the decision of the Supreme Court of Canada in *R v Cook* [1998] 2 SCR 597 is instructive.
2 [1997] AC 558, HL.
3 [1997] AC 558, HL at 582.
4 (Unreported, 16 May 2000).
5 2000 SLT 1401.

5.120 In *R v Hardy (Donovan Anthony),*[1] the four appellants were convicted of conspiracy to evade the prohibition on the importation of cocaine. At trial, the appellant Hardy had objected to the admission of evidence of the finding of cocaine in his Dutch hotel room. The British authorities had acted wholly appropriately in making a formal application for assistance from the Dutch, who had taken up the investigation from there. On appeal, Hardy and his co-accused Annal argued that the trial judge was wrong to allow that evidence to go before the jury on the basis that it was inadmissible and/or because the judge should have exercised his powers to exclude that evidence under PACE, s 78, on the basis that there had been breaches of the Dutch Criminal Code during the search of the hotel. The appellants complained that the Dutch Criminal Code had been violated in that, firstly, rules relating to the search were not complied with and, secondly, there had been no application to a court for permission to hand over the drugs to the English authorities. On the latter point, the Court of Appeal concluded that, 'no doubt … there was a breach of the code'.[2]

1 [2003] EWCA Crim 3092.
2 At para 28.

5.121 The Court has thereby once again shown a willingness to consider whether the law of a foreign country has been breached (albeit here not by UK agents), finding that it had been so in Hardy's case,[1] and then going on to consider whether the search of the hotel room amounted to a violation of ECHR, Art 8. Ultimately, the Court found that Art 8 was not engaged and noted that, according to *R v Khan,*[2] an apparent breach of the law of a foreign country was only a matter that 'may' be relevant to the exercise of a judge's power under s 78. The Court of Appeal concluded that any breach did not affect the fairness of the appellants' trial in England, nor did it deprive Hardy of his ability to deal properly with the evidence in his case.

1 At para 43.
2 Above para **5.119**.

5.122 In addition, in *CC v Secretary of State for the Home Department*, the Court was prepared to investigate the conduct of state agents overseas, demonstrating that it considered alleged executive lawlessness to be within its own jurisdiction.[1] Similarly, in *Warren*, the courts considered the illegality of the evidence-gathering overseas in relation to the question of whether a stay should be granted.[2]

1 See above at paras **5.29–5.31**.
2 See above paras **5.14–5.28**

UNLAWFULLY OBTAINED EVIDENCE

5.123 Both the ECtHR and the common law have held that the fact that evidence has been unlawfully obtained does not lead to automatic exclusion. In *Khan v United Kingdom,*[1] the European Court held that the fact that the sole evidence obtained against the accused had been obtained unlawfully in breach of Art 8, did not necessarily require its exclusion pursuant to Art 6. This approach was then adopted and followed by the House of Lords in *Attorney-General's Reference (No 3 of 1999)*,[2] in *R v P*,[3] in *Public Prosecution Service v McKee*,[4] and has since been applied at the European level in *Chalkley v United Kingdom*[5] *and Hewitson v United Kingdom*[6] (both cases relating to the use of evidence obtained from covert listening devices installed in violation of Art 8).

1 (2000) 8 BHRC 310.
2 [2001] 2 AC 91, HL.
3 [2002] 1 AC 146, HL.
4 [2011] NICA 61.
5 (2003) 37 EHRR 30.
6 (2003) 37 EHRR 31.

5.124 The exception to the principle that evidence obtained unlawfully will not be automatically excluded concerns evidence obtained by torture.[1] In *A & Others v Secretary of State for the Home Department (No. 2)*,[2] the House of Lords made clear that the common law of England, European Convention on Human Rights, and international law (as embodied in the International Convention against Torture and other Cruel, Inhuman or Degrading Treatment 1984 and as a principle of *jus cogens*) prohibited in absolute terms the admissibility of evidence (confessions) obtained by torture. Where a court is persuaded that there is a real risk[3] that evidence was obtained by torture, it will refuse to admit that evidence.

1 *Jalloh v Germany* (2007) 44 EHRR 32 at para 105.
2 [2006] 2 AC 221, HL. See also *R (on the application of Mohamed) v Secretary of State for Foreign and Commonwealth Affairs* [2009] EWHC 152 (Admin).
3 Whilst their Lordships were unanimous on the principle that evidence obtained by torture will be excluded, they were divided on the test by which that principle should be applied. Lord Bingham criticised the conclusion of the majority, that it must be established on the balance of probabilities that evidence was obtained by torture before it will be excluded, taking the view that such a test could never be satisfied in the real world, as the torturer (a foreign party in that case) 'does not boast of his trade' and 'the [domestic] security services…do not wish to imperil their relations with regimes where torture is practised' by disclosing such information'. The detainee, Lord Bingham reasoned, was 'in the dark' and 'it is inconsistent with the most rudimentary notions of fairness to blindfold a man and then impose a standard which only the sighted could hope to meet'. The ECtHR has agreed. In *Othman (Abu Qatada) v United Kingdom* (2012) 55 EHRR 1, the European Court held that the use of evidence obtained by torture during a criminal trial would necessarily amount to a flagrant denial of justice. Torture and the use of torture evidence were banned under international law. Allowing a criminal court to rely on torture evidence would legitimise the torture of witnesses and suspects pre-trial. It would render the whole trial immoral and illegal. Moreover, torture evidence was unreliable, because a person being tortured would say anything to make it stop. The balance of probabilities test applied in *A v Secretary of State for the Home Department (No.2)* was not appropriate in this context and it was not an authority for the general proposition that, subject to a balance of probabilities test, evidence alleged to have been obtained by torture would be admissible in criminal proceedings in the United Kingdom. Due regard must be had to the difficulties of proving allegations of torture. In a criminal justice system where the courts were independent of the executive, cases were prosecuted impartially, and where allegations of torture were conscientiously investigated, a defendant might be required to prove to a high standard that the evidence against him had been obtained by torture. However, in a criminal justice system which was complicit in the very practices which it existed to prevent, such a standard of proof was wholly inappropriate. Therefore, it is for the applicant to adduce evidence capable of proving that there are substantial grounds for believing that there is a real risk that evidence was obtained by torture. Where such evidence is adduced, it is for the Government to dispel any doubts about it.

5.125 Short of torture, the subject of evidence obtained unlawfully raises important questions of ends justifying means and the extent to which courts should uphold the principle of legality. Superficially at least, it might seem surprising that a court would agree to receive such evidence, since a court, above all else, is responsible for upholding the rule of law, and evidence obtained in violation of legal safeguard must tend to undermine that value. In *R v Sang,*[1] Lord Diplock regarded a complaint of evidence obtained unlawfully as not one to be properly considered by a criminal court at all. In his view any disciplining of the police or violation of a legal remedy was the exclusive province of a civil court to which an unhappy defendant should direct his complaint.

1 [1980] AC 402, HL, above para **5.41**.

5.126 Since the landmark decision in *ex parte Bennett* and the acceptance by the courts of a responsibility to oversee executive conduct, the view of Lord Diplock now appears antique. Moreover, his view has been overtaken by the PACE, s 78 power which vested in every trial judge a power to exclude evidence in order to preserve the fairness of a trial. This combination of the common law abuse power in relation to executive misconduct and s 78 in relation to trial fairness must mean that the legal position concerning unlawfully-obtained evidence has become more complicated. However, the decisions in *Maxwell* and *Warren* confirm that, in assessing whether to stay proceedings because of illegal misconduct in the gathering of evidence, the judge will balance the public interest in preserving the integrity of the criminal justice system against the public interest in the prosecution of criminals. In both decisions, the courts confirmed that it was not the role of the courts to 'punish' wrong-doing and that it was unlikely that the appellate courts would intervene in a judge's decision without evidence that s/he had erred in the law.[1] But before the common law and statutory position are considered, the jurisprudence of the European Court will be reviewed.

1 See discussion of *R v Maxwell* above at paras **5.07–5.13** and *Warren v Attorney General of Jersey* at paras **5.14–5.28.**

The ECtHR jurisprudence

5.127 Perhaps the best explanation for the decision of the court in *Khan v United Kingdom*[1] lies in its established principle that the matter of legal conditions governing the admission of evidence is best left to national courts to determine.[2] In other words, in the field of exclusion of evidence obtained in breach of Art 8, the European court affords a substantial margin of appreciation to Member States. This policy in relation to this subject was first applied in *Schenk v Switzerland*.[3] However, in determining whether the right to a fair trial has been breached, the ECtHR has also consistently reiterated that it will look at the fairness of proceedings as a whole.[4] In *Khan,* the UK respondent did not dispute that the evidence presented at the applicant's trial had all been obtained in breach of his Art 8 right and that accordingly his conviction rested entirely upon such tainted evidence. The applicant submitted that the admission of such evidence vitiated the fairness of his trial as a whole in breach of Art 6.

1 Above para **5.123**.

2 This self-denying principle however is disregarded in certain cases. For example, the court interfered in *Saunders v United Kingdom* (1996) 23 EHRR 313 to hold that evidence obtained by compulsive questioning violated Art 6. In *Teixeira v Portugal* (1998) 28 EHRR 101, the same view was taken as regards evidence obtained through police incitement.

3 (1988) 13 EHRR 242.

4 See, for example, *Teixeira de Castro v Portugal* (1999) 28 EHRR 101, *Campbell and Fell v the United Kingdom* (1985) 7 E.H.R.R. 165 and many others.

5.128 In its judgment, the European Court held[1] that:

> 'The central question in the present case is whether the proceedings as a whole were fair. With specific reference to the admission of the contested tape recording, the court notes that, as in the *Schenk* case, the applicant had ample opportunity to challenge both the authenticity and the use of the recording. He did not challenge its authenticity, but challenged its use at the 'voir dire' and again before the Court of Appeal and the House of Lords. The court notes that at each level of jurisdiction the domestic courts assessed the effect of admission of the evidence on the fairness of the trial by reference to s 78 of PACE, and the courts discussed, amongst other matters, the non-statutory basis for the surveillance. The fact that the applicant was at each step unsuccessful makes no difference (see the above-mentioned *Schenk* judgment, paragraph 47).
>
> The court would add that it is clear that, had the domestic courts been of the view that the admission of the evidence would have given rise to substantive unfairness, they would have had a discretion to exclude it under s 78 of PACE.
>
> In these circumstances, the court finds that the use at the applicant's trial of the secretly taped material did not conflict with the requirements of fairness guaranteed by article 6(1) of the Convention.'

1 At paras 38–40.

5.129 Commenting upon the ratio in this case, Lord Hobhouse, in *R v P*,[1] later said:

> 'It should be noted that the ECtHR again emphasised that the defendant is not entitled to have the unlawfully obtained evidence excluded simply because it has been so obtained. What he is entitled to is an opportunity to challenge its use and admission in evidence and a judicial assessment of the effect of its admission upon the fairness of the trial as is provided for by s 78.'

1 [2002] 1 AC 146, HL, above para **5.123**.

5.130 In essence, therefore, the Court held that the applicant's ability to test and object to the admission of evidence obtained unlawfully via a s 78 application was a sufficient measure of legal protection in domestic law against arbitrary interferences by public authorities with the rights safeguarded by the Convention. The ECtHR has thus consistently emphasised that a defendant is not entitled to have evidence excluded simply because it has been unlawfully obtained. Rather, s/he is entitled under the Convention to an opportunity to challenge its use and admissibility and that there must be a judicial assessment of the effect of its admission upon the fairness of the trial as is provided for by s 78. The guarantee is thus one of procedure, not outcome. *Khan* was followed in *PG and JH v United Kingdom*[1] and has been considered in a host of other cases at the European level.[2]

1 [2002] Crim LR 308.
2 See for example *Taylor-Sabori v United Kingdom* (2003) 36 EHRR 17; *Allan v United Kingdom* (2003) 36 EHRR 12; *Armstrong v United Kingdom* (2003) 36 EHRR 30; and *Lewis v United Kingdom* (2004) 39 EHRR 9.

5.131 Interestingly, by way of contrast, in *Jalloh v Germany*,[1] the Strasbourg court determined that, whilst dependent upon the facts of the particular case, the admission of evidence obtained in breach of Art 3 violated the defendant's Art 6 rights (there, the forcible administration of drugs to expel drugs previously swallowed). The distinction here doubtless lies in the fact that the actions of the authorities constituted inhuman and degrading treatment, and the evidence had, therefore, been obtained by a violation of one of the Convention's core rights. The public interest in securing the applicant's conviction could not justify recourse to such a grave interference with his physical and mental integrity. This is consistent with the ECtHR's absolute prohibition on the admissibility of evidence obtained via torture. As discussed above, the Court has ruled consistently in that context that 'the admission of torture evidence is manifestly contrary, not just to the provisions of Article 6, but to the most basic international standards of a fair trial'.[2]

1 (2007) 44 EHRR 32.
2 *Othman (Abu Qatada) v United Kingdom* (2012) 55 EHRR 1 at 267.

The common law

The vital role accorded to PACE, s 78

5.132 As the Strasbourg authorities considered above emphasise, evidence obtained unlawfully may be capable of exclusion from proceedings, enabling a defendant to obtain a fair trial without the need for a stay. In *Warren v Attorney General for Jersey*, the Judicial Committee of the Privy Council noted that, '[t]he admission of unlawfully obtained evidence raises, of course, distinct, albeit to some extent related, considerations to those arising on abuse of process applications'.[1] The crossover between s 78 and Art 8 was also considered. The cases below consider the application of s 78 in such cases.

1 [2012] 1 AC 22 at para 77.

5.133 In *Attorney-General's Reference (No 3 of 1999)*,[1] the House of Lords considered the decision of the trial judge, subsequently supported by the Court of Appeal, that evidence against an accused should be excluded pursuant to s 78 on the ground that it had been obtained in express breach of a statutory provision of PACE.[2] The House of Lords took the view, however, that the courts below had been unnecessarily restrictive about the admissibility of evidence. Whilst Lord Steyn held, as a matter of statutory construction, that the provisions of the section had been misconstrued and thus the evidence had not been unlawfully obtained, he added that in any event the courts should be prepared to accept such evidence. There were, in his view,[3] a triangulation of interests to be considered and given equal respect:

'The purpose of the criminal law is to permit everyone to go about their daily lives without fear of harm to person or property. And it is in the interests of everyone that serious crime should be effectively investigated and prosecuted. There must be fairness to all sides. In a criminal case this requires the court to consider a triangulation of interests. It involves taking into account the position of the accused, the victim and his or her family, and the public. In my view the austere interpretation which the Court of Appeal adopted is not only in conflict with the plain words of the statute but also produces results which are contrary to good sense. A consideration of the public interest reinforces the interpretation which I have adopted.'

1 [2001] 2 AC 91, HL, above para **5.123**.
2 A DNA sample which proved crucial evidence against the accused which, because of his previous acquittal on another charge, ought, pursuant to s 63 PACE, to have then been destroyed.
3 At p 118.

5.134 Applying this framework, Lord Steyn held that an inflexible rule, which required the exclusion of evidence obtained unlawfully, would give the accused an unfair preference or trump over the public interest and was thus unjustifiable.

5.135 In *R v P*,[1] the House of Lords delivered a similar view. Here, as in *R v Khan*,[2] evidence against the accused had been obtained in breach of their Art 8 rights. The issue was to what extent should a proven breach of this right affect or impair the fairness of a trial? Lord Hobhouse commenting upon *Khan v United Kingdom* said:[3]

'The importance of the ECtHR decision is that it confirms that the direct operation of articles 8 and 6 does not invalidate their Lordships' conclusion or alter the vital role of s 78 as the means by which questions of the use of evidence obtained in breach of article 8 are to be resolved at a criminal trial. The criterion to be applied is the criterion of fairness in article 6 which is likewise the criterion to be applied by the judge under s 78. Similarly, the ECtHR decision that any remedy for a breach of article 8 lies outside the scope of the criminal trial and that article 13 does not require a remedy for a breach of article 8 to be given within that trial shows that their Lordships were right to say that a breach of article 8 did not require the exclusion of evidence. Such an exclusion, if any, would have to come about because of the application of article 6 and s 78.'

1 [2002] 1 AC 146, HL, above para **5.123**.
2 [1997] AC 558, HL, above para **5.119**.
3 At pp 161–162.

5.136 The effect of Lord Hobhouse's speech is to emphasise the primary role of s 78 as a remedy to ensure the fairness of the trial and to marginalise the significance in a criminal case of any breach of Art 8. What really matters in this context is a procedural consideration centred on s 78 – did the accused have a fair hearing of his/her application to apply for exclusion under s 78?[1] This mirrors the approach taken by the ECtHR (set out above) in relation to the overall fairness of proceedings. Accordingly, the only important article to consider in this context is Art 6, which contains the same test of fairness as s 78. Lord Hobhouse was not suggesting that Art 8 rights are unimportant, rather that, if a judge is satisfied that the consequence of such a breach has no impact upon the accused's right to a fair trial under Art 6 or s 78, then the evidence so obtained from the breach ought to be admitted. In a view reminiscent of that of Lord Diplock in *R v Sang*[2] mentioned above, Lord Hobhouse's view is that, absent trial unfairness, breaches of Art 8 are best left to the civil courts. Contrast the situation under Art 3 discussed above.

1 This issue in relation to disclosure is considered in **Chapter 4**.
2 [1980] AC 402, HL, above para **5.41**.

5.137 Similar views as to the vital role of s 78 were expressed by Lord Hope in the subsequent case of *R v Sargent*:[1]

> '... the scope of this discretionary power [s 78] is plainly wide enough to enable the trial judge to take into account any disadvantage that may result from the rules about the non-disclosure of intercepts.'

1 [2003] 1 AC 347, HL, at para 17.

5.138 The application of this approach established by the House of Lords can be contrasted with the decision of the trial judge in *R v Veneroso*.[1] Here, the trial judge found that the evidence adduced by the prosecution had been obtained by an unlawful search. Consequently, the accused's Art 8 rights had also been violated. The judge ruled that, in this circumstance, the evidence ought to be excluded under s 78, holding that there was no justification, before it commenced, for the police conducting their search and only a small quantity of drugs had been found. It is submitted that on the strength of *R v P*, this case may have been wrongly decided. Assuming that the evidence was probative of the offence charged and that the accused had an opportunity to challenge it at trial, Lord Hobhouse would have admitted it. However, it is also possible to argue that this case is distinguishable because the public interest in bringing the defendant to trial for such a small amount of drugs did not outweigh the need to protect his individual rights.

1 [2002] Crim LR 306.

5.139 Overall, the unstructured and open-ended discretionary exclusionary approach engendered by the wording of s 78 has been unaltered by the Human Rights Act 1998 challenges, even when there have been blatant violations of Art 8.[1] In *R v Button*,[2] the Court of Appeal dismissed submissions that the admission of evidence obtained in breach of Art 8 constituted a continuing or repeating violation of that article in a way that was incompatible with the Convention. In applying the principle established in the *Attorney-General's Reference (No 3 of 1999)*,[3] the Court recalled that relevant evidence obtained unlawfully was admissible, subject to the discretion to exclude that evidence provided by s 78 of PACE.

1 See, for example, *R v Mason* [2002] Crim LR 891. Here the court accepted that, despite their violations, the police had acted in good faith.
2 [2005] EWCA Crim 516.
3 Above para **5.133**.

COMMISSION OF CRIMINAL OFFENCES OR UNLAWFUL CONDUCT BY INVESTIGATORS

5.140 The cases of *Maxwell* and *Warren* suggest that unlawful executive conduct is but one factor to take into account when balancing the competing public interests engaged by the question of whether to stay proceedings. Such misconduct will not lead automatically to a stay of proceedings. So, to what extent is it permissible for law enforcement agents to break the law in order that evidence may thereby be obtained against the accused? Is the law, especially the criminal law, to be obeyed by all no matter how noble their objective, or rather is the commission of criminal offences by State agents sometimes acceptable in the pursuit of those guilty of serious crime? In *R v Looseley,*[1] Lord Hoffmann put the issue as follows:

> 'Drug dealers can be expected to show some wariness about dealing with a stranger who might be a policeman or informer and therefore some protective colour in dress or manner as well as a certain degree of persistence may be necessary to achieve the objective. And it has been said that undercover officers who infiltrate conspiracies to murder, rob or commit terrorist offences could hardly remain concealed unless they showed some enthusiasm for the enterprise. A good deal of active behaviour in the course of an authorised operation may therefore be acceptable.'[2]

1 [2001] 1 WLR 2060, HL (discussed in detail in **Chapter 6**).
2 At para 69.

5.141 He continued:

> 'No doubt a test purchaser who asks someone to sell him a drug is counselling and procuring, perhaps inciting, the commission of an offence. Furthermore, he has no statutory defence to a prosecution. But the fact that his actions are technically unlawful is not regarded in English law as a ground for treating them as an abuse of power.'[1]

1 At para 70.

5.142 As Lord Hoffmann reasons in the above passages, police undercover operations, especially into organised crime, cannot in reality be conducted on the basis that the officers involved must never contravene the criminal law. The committing of illegal acts may be essential for those officers to gain the necessary credibility and win the trust of those they are seeking to apprehend. To take another case as an example, the facts in *R v Latif*[1] can be considered. Here, Customs officers wanted to apprehend L, a suspected organiser of large importations of heroin into the UK from Pakistan. Based in Pakistan, a country with no extradition treaty with the UK, L could act with impunity insofar as UK law was concerned. Accordingly, an agent H was recruited to approach L on the basis that H had a network of heroin distributors set up in England which could be placed at L's disposal. So that L could be beguiled by H, Customs arranged for an actual shipment of heroin to be imported from Pakistan via Heathrow. In so doing, the officers breached s 3 of the Misuse of Drugs Act 1971 prohibiting drug importations in any circumstances. Clearly, therefore, the importation amounted to a serious offence committed by Customs. Ultimately, the ruse worked, as L was then lured into the UK to meet H whereupon he was arrested and charged with conspiracy to import heroin. The question for the courts in *Latif* was thus whether the means adopted by Customs justified the end of capturing L.

1 [1996] 1 WLR 104, HL.

5.143 To demonstrate the difficult issues of public policy involved, another case can be briefly considered. In *R (Pretty) v DPP (Secretary of State for the Home Department intervening)*[1] the dying applicant wished her partner to assist her in committing suicide. However, if the partner did so, an offence would be committed under the Suicide Act 1961. The applicant sought a declaration from the Director of Public Prosecutions that, in her extreme circumstances, the partner would not run the risk of prosecution if he so assisted. The DPP refused to oblige and the applicant sought judicial review. In his letter to the applicant, the DPP wrote:

> 'Successive Directors—and Attorneys General—have explained that they will not grant immunities that condone, require, or purport to authorise or permit the future commission of any criminal offence, no matter how exceptional the circumstances. I must therefore advise you that the Director cannot provide the undertaking that you seek.'

1 [2002] 1 AC 800, HL at para 115.

5.144 The House of Lords endorsed this letter as a correct statement of the DPP's position. Expressing the role of the DPP in constitutional terms, Lord Hobhouse said:

> 'The power to dispense with and suspend laws and the execution of laws without the consent of Parliament was denied to the Crown and its servants by the Bill of Rights 1688.'[1]

1 At para 117.

5.145 Whilst *Pretty* was concerned with the power of the DPP in advance to immunise a proposed breach of the criminal law, in undercover operations there is an obvious, albeit unspoken, presumption that agents who commit offences in the course of such operations will not subsequently face prosecution by, for example, the CPS. In *R v Latif*[1] no Customs officer ever faced prosecution despite their having committed the *actus reus* of the offence for which L was prosecuted. De facto, therefore, the DPP does grant immunities despite the impression conveyed in the speeches in *Pretty*.

1 Above para **5.142**.

5.146 State illegality is an obvious subject for the abuse doctrine in determining the extent to which the courts will uphold the principle of the rule of law. As Dr Johnson put it:

> 'Laws are not made for particular cases but for men in general… To permit a law to be modified at discretion is to leave the community without law. It is to withdraw the direction of that public wisdom by which the deficiencies of private understanding are to be supplied.'[1]

1 Boswell *Life of Johnson* (3rd Edn, 1970) at pp 735, 496.

Pre-Latif cases

5.147 The scathing judgment of Goddard CJ in *Brannan v Peek*[1] is often recited:

> 'The court observes with concern and with strong disapproval that the police authority … apparently thought it right in this case to send a police officer into a public house for the purpose of committing an offence … I hope that the day is far distant when it will become common practice in this country for police officers, who are sent into premises for the purpose of detecting crime, to be told to commit an offence themselves for the purpose of getting evidence against another person … I think, this conviction must be set aside.'[2]

1 [1948] 1 KB 68, DC.
2 At p 72.

5.148 In *Yip Chiu-Cheung v R*,[1] the Privy Council considered a case where, on the facts, the undercover officer had committed an offence under Hong Kong anti-drugs trafficking law. Giving judgment on behalf of the Board, Lord Griffiths clearly regarded with distaste a submission that the undercover officer had not committed a criminal offence. He said:

> 'Neither the police, nor customs, nor any other member of the executive have any power to alter the terms of the Ordinance frustrating the export of heroin and the fact that they may turn a blind eye when the heroin is exported does not prevent it from being a criminal offence.'

1 [1995] 1 AC 111, PC.

5.149 Lord Griffiths quoted with approval the ruling of the High Court of Australia in *A v Hayden (No 2)*.[1] There it declared emphatically that there was no place in Australian criminal law for a general defence of superior orders or of Crown or executive authority. Gibbs CJ said:

> 'It is fundamental to our legal system that the executive has no power to authorise a breach of the law and that it is no excuse for an offender to say that he acted under the orders of a superior officer.'[2]

Having quoted this passage, Lord Griffiths observed:

> 'This statement of the law applies with the same force in England and Hong Kong as it does in Australia.'[3]

1 (1984) 156 CLR 532.
2 (1984) 156 CLR 532 at p 540.
3 Above para **5.148** at p 118.

5.150 *R v Schlesinger*[1] is an example of investigative impropriety and *mala fides*, which the Court of Appeal described as 'disgraceful'. In 1985, the appellants were convicted of illegally exporting arms to Iraq. Before their trial, the defence became aware of various embassy officials in London who were prepared to state that the arms had not in fact gone to Iraq. However, before witness statements could be taken, the officials announced they could no longer assist, their permission to do so from their embassies having been withdrawn. In the event the defendants pleaded guilty.

1 [1995] Crim LR 137, CA.

5.151 In 1993, the Scott Inquiry discovered why this *volte-face* had occurred. The Foreign Office, at the behest of Customs (the prosecutorial agency), had urged the embassies not to allow their officials to assist the defence. When this information was published, the defendants appealed against their convictions. The Court of Appeal readily quashed the convictions. It held that the prosecution had, in the first instance, improperly interfered with the course of justice and, secondly, had concealed this from the defence and trial judge. In holding the proceedings to be an abuse, the Court held that a defendant does not receive a fair trial if he is prevented by the prosecution from calling witnesses who are believed will be helpful to the defence.

R v Latif

5.152 *R v Latif,*[1] the facts of which are recounted above,[2] provided the House of Lords with an opportunity two years on to survey the effects of its momentous decision in *ex parte Bennett.* In the case before it, one of alleged entrapment, the House had to consider whether the principles in *ex parte Bennett,* formulated in response to illegal extradition, be applied to this linked but conceptually separate subject. Clearly, the House of Lords in *R v Latif* could have chosen to withdraw from the sentiments expressed in *ex parte Bennett* and so confine the wider abuse jurisdiction to the rare situation of alleged unlawful extradition. Instead, however, the House opted to confirm its *ex parte Bennett* stance. Giving the only speech, Lord Steyn held that the court had jurisdiction in a case of entrapment to stay the prosecution on the ground that the integrity of the criminal justice system would be compromised by allowing the State to punish someone whom the State itself had caused to transgress.

1 [1996] 1 WLR 104, HL.
2 Above para **5.142**.

5.153 Lord Steyn first confirmed the earlier decision of the House in *R v Sang*[1] that entrapment did not afford a substantive defence. But he then held that entrapment raised important public policy issues concerned with abuse of power. There was a dilemma, which he described as follows:

> 'If the court always refuses to stay such proceedings, the perception will be that the court condones criminal conduct and malpractice by law enforcement agencies. That would undermine public confidence in the criminal justice system and bring it into disrepute. On the other hand, if the court were always to stay proceedings in such cases, it would incur the reproach that it is failing to protect the public from serious crime'[2]

1 Above para **5.41.**
2 At p 112.

5.154 Lord Steyn then held that this dilemma could only be resolved as follows:

> 'The weakness of both extreme positions leaves only one principled solution. The court has a discretion; it has to perform a balancing exercise ... the judge must weigh in the balance the public interest in ensuring those that are charged with grave crimes should be tried and the competing public interest

in not conveying the impression that the court will adopt the approach that the end justifies any means.[1]

… In this case the issue is whether, despite the fact that a fair trial was possible, the judge ought to have stayed the criminal proceedings on broader considerations of the integrity of the criminal justice system. The law is settled. Weighing countervailing considerations of policy and justice, it is for the judge in the exercise of his discretion to decide whether there has been an abuse of process, which amounts to an affront to the public conscience and requires the criminal proceedings to be stayed.'[2]

1 At pp 112–113.
2 At p 113.

5.155 On the facts of this case, including the illegal acts committed by the Customs officers, Lord Steyn said:

'The conduct of the customs officer was not so unworthy or shameful that it was an affront to the public conscience to allow the prosecution to proceed. Realistically, any criminal behaviour of the customs officer was venial compared to that of Shahzad. In these circumstances I would reject the submission that the judge erred in refusing to stay the proceedings.'[1]

1 At p 113.

5.156 What is perhaps most notable about Lord Steyn's speech is that he paid no particular regard to the fact that the prosecution of the accused was in part founded upon deliberate breaches of the criminal law by the officers. The conceptual emphasis was placed elsewhere – did the acts of the officers amount to an affront to the public conscience or were they instead merely venial? This apparent lack of emphasis by Lord Steyn on the issue of whether the executive flouted the law is echoed later by Lord Hoffmann in *R v Looseley*[1] in a passage quoted above:[2]

'But the fact that his actions are *technically* unlawful is not regarded in English law as a ground for treating them as an abuse of power.' [Emphasis added]

1 [2001] 1 WLR 2060, HL.
2 At para 70; discussed above at paras **5.140–5.142**.

5.157 Moreover, Lord Steyn decided, having set out his two parameters, not to offer any further guidance to judges as to whether unlawful conduct was either an affront or venial, saying: 'general guidance as to how the discretion should be exercised in particular circumstances would rarely be useful.'

5.158 A trial judge following *R v Latif* has to conduct a balancing exercise between competing public interests. First, the imperative for the courts, as part of a criminal justice system based fundamentally on the rule of law, to preserve their moral integrity by disassociating themselves from investigative impropriety. The fair administration of justice cannot be sacrificed for the sake of expedience. Secondly, those who are charged and convicted of the serious crimes should not escape justice because such a situation would undermine public confidence in the criminal justice system.

5.159 It is submitted that an analysis of Lord Steyn's reasoning reveals the following key principles that influenced the court:

(1) *That the crime was already in existence.* The appellants had already planned to be involved in the importation of the heroin into England before the customs officer became involved and were therefore already guilty of conspiracy to import heroin into England. Lord Steyn rejected the appellants' assertion that they had been incited.

(2) *Motive.* Lord Steyn accepted that the officer was acting under the authority of his superiors and was motivated by a courageous desire in his attempt to break a drugs ring and ensure the punishment of those involved.

(3) *Comparative involvement in the crime.* Lord Steyn compared the degree of criminality of the customs officer ('venial') and that of the appellants who were major drug smugglers.

Post-Latif cases

5.160 Following *R v Latif*, an example of 'venial', but nonetheless unlawful, conduct by investigators is *R v Khan.*[1] In this case, a former Thai diplomat brought with him to Heathrow from Thailand a quantity of heroin in his diplomatic bag. On arrival, the bag was searched and the drugs discovered. At his trial an abuse submission was made on the ground that this search was unlawful as, it was claimed, it was in breach of the Vienna Convention. At the time of the search the defendant was entitled to diplomatic immunity and there was no lawful authority, until this was waived, to search his bag. The trial judge was not impressed by this argument and dismissed the application.

1 (1998, unreported) Crown Court.

R v Carrington[1]

5.161 In this instance, the defendants were charged with drug trafficking. The prosecution's case rested on the discovery of a cargo of cannabis resin in a boat which was bound for the UK. At the time of the seizure of the boat and discovery of the cannabis, the boat was in international waters off the coast of Portugal. By reason of international maritime law, before the boat could be lawfully intercepted and boarded by agents of HM Customs (in this case British Special Forces), the consent was required of the Attorney-General of Malta. This was because the boat had begun its voyage from there and such consent was required in order to make the interception lawful. This would remain the legal position until the boat entered the territorial waters of another State. However, for some reason, Customs did not wish to track the boat until it entered the territorial waters of the UK and then board it, but instead wished to do so on the High Seas.

1 (February 1999, unreported), Foley HHJ.

5.162 When the consent of the Maltese Attorney-General was sought, it transpired that he was informed by Customs that the location of the boat was 'off the coast of the United Kingdom.'[1] Having made this false representation, consent from the Maltese was forthcoming. At the trial the defence submitted that the prosecution intended to mislead the Maltese and this constituted *mala fides*, which in turn constituted an abuse. At the *voir dire* to investigate the matter, Maltese witnesses confirmed that they would not have given consent if they were aware of the true position of the boat. The trial judge held that the behaviour of customs was shameful:

> '… this case has revealed a culture, a climate, of carelessness and recklessness for disregard for the rules of procedures, convention of Maltese law, British law and International law … this court cannot abdicate its judicial responsibility. It gives me no pleasure, the case for a stay is overwhelming, there was mala fides here.'[2]

1 It appears that when the request was made, the boat was in fact 900 miles from Britain off the coast of Portugal.

2 Page 1051 of the transcript.

R v Doran[1]

5.163 The facts of this case are complex and therefore difficult to summarise. There is also a history of trial, appeal, and retrial. It transpired at the retrial that both the judge in the first trial and the defence had been deliberately misled by Customs concerning two factual issues. Firstly, had consent been obtained from the management of various hotels to the bugging of hotel rooms by Customs officers? Contrary to what was claimed, it was established that such consent had not been obtained. Secondly, it transpired that Customs' own internal authorisation procedures, which the investigating officers should have obeyed before placing the defendants under surveillance, had in fact been ignored. Moreover, to conceal this fact, the officers had allegedly created a trail of false paperwork. The trial judge, Turner J held:

> 'By abuse of executive authority, the prosecution, viewed as a single entity, have, by means which are at least arguably unlawful, deprived the defence of its strategic ability to mount the challenge to the integrity of the prosecution case.'

1 (6 July 1999, unreported) Turner J.

5.164 In assessing the seriousness of the officers' conduct, Turner J held that:

> '… the conduct which I have already discussed in some detail cannot fairly be dismissed as 'venial' or as mere 'regrettable error' as the prosecution have invited me to accept … it is wholly inaccurate to describe what has happened as 'regrettable error.' What has happened has had a significant impact on the ability of the defendants properly to defend themselves and to that extent, as a matter of probability, they have been seriously prejudiced in the conduct of their defence'

In those circumstances, Turner J held that the prosecution were guilty of abuse and that the conduct of the officers struck at the rule of law.

R v Sutherland[1]

5.165 Here, remarkably, members of Lincolnshire Constabulary investigating a murder decided that privileged conversations between the suspects and their solicitors whilst the suspects were detained at police stations ought to be recorded. Following the prosecution of those suspects for murder, the prosecution unsuccessfully applied to have the fact of the eavesdropping and its product withheld from the defence on public interest immunity grounds. That application having been refused, applications for abuse were made. The trial judge, Newman J, found the police conduct reprehensible and unlawful. He regarded the eavesdropping as amounting to a violation of a fundamental principle of law and human rights, a violation so serious that considerations relating to whether or not any of the accused had been prejudiced were immaterial. The fact that there had been deliberate interference with an accused's right to private legal advice was sufficient, in and of itself, to prevent a fair trial from taking place. Accordingly, the prosecution of all five accused was stayed.

1 (29 January 2002, unreported) Newman J.

R v Grant[1]

5.166 The immateriality of prejudice to the accused in such circumstances was purportedly confirmed by the Court of Appeal in *R v Grant*, a case stemming out of the same activities on the part of Lincolnshire police as had led to the stay of proceedings in *Sutherland.*[2] In this case, the police tape-recorded conversations between the defendant and his solicitor in the police station yard following his arrest (also for conspiracy to murder) and whilst the interview process was in motion. None of the material obtained by the police was used for the purposes of the prosecution and, on that basis, the conduct of the police did not impact unfairly upon the accused's trial. In considering that the trial judge ought to have stayed proceedings, Laws LJ said that:

> 'Acts done by the police, in the course of an investigation which leads in due course to the institution of criminal proceedings, with a view to eavesdropping upon communications of suspected persons which are subject to legal professional privilege are categorically unlawful and at the very least capable of infecting the proceedings as abusive of the court's process. So much seems to us to be plain and obvious and no authority is needed to make it good. The only question that requires examination is whether such proceedings ought to be characterised as an abuse of the process, and the prosecution stopped, if the defendant or defendants have suffered no prejudice in consequence of the relevant unlawful acts.'[3]

> 'We are in no doubt but that, in general, unlawful acts of the kind done in this case, amounting to a deliberate violation of a suspected person's right to legal professional privilege, are so great an affront to the integrity of the justice system, and therefore the rule of law, that the associated prosecution is rendered abusive and ought not to be countenanced by the court.'[4]

1 [2006] QB 60, CA.

2 The third case, other than *Sutherland* and *Grant*, to come of the eavesdropping technique employed by Lincolnshire police between November 2000–November 2001 was *R v Sentence* (unreported, Lincoln Crown Court), in which the trial judge, HHJ Heath, also stayed proceedings as an abuse of process.
3 At para 52.
4 At para 54.

5.167 Laws LJ concluded:

> 'Where the court is faced with illegal conduct by police or State prosecutors which is so grave as to threaten or undermine the rule of law itself, the court may readily conclude that it will not tolerate, far less endorse, such a state of affairs and so hold that its duty is to stop the case... We are quite clear that the deliberate interference with a detained suspect's right to the confidence of privileged communications with his solicitor, such as we have found was done here, seriously undermines the rule of law and justifies a stay on grounds of abuse of process, notwithstanding the absence of prejudice consisting in evidence gathered by the Crown as the fruit of police officers' unlawful conduct.'[1]

1 At paras 56–57.

5.168 However, Laws L.J observed that it 'is not in general the function of criminal courts to discipline the police.'[1] That approach concurred with the later judgment of the Court of Appeal in *R v Woolley*,[2] where, in refusing an appeal on the ground of abuse of process (the police being said to have failed to obtain potentially exculpatory CCTV evidence), Hallett LJ observed that:

> '... there is a public interest in having allegations of serious offences such as the present tried and applications to stay on the grounds of abuse of the process of the court should not be granted simply as a way of punishing investigating police officers, even if that is merited [which the Court of Appeal doubted it was in this case in any event].'[3]

1 At para 55.
2 [2006] EWCA Crim 2138.
3 At para 20.

5.169 However, the Judicial Committee of the Privy Council in *Warren* directly disapproved of *R v Grant*.[1] The Committee emphasised that it was not the role of the court to supervise the conduct of the executive and to stay proceedings to express its disapproval of the methods by which evidence was obtained. Therefore, the fact that there would have been no proceedings but for the executive's misuse of their powers was nothing more than one of the relevant factors. In this light, *Grant*, where those two factors were determinative parts of the reasoning, was wrongly decided. Lord Dyson confirmed:

> "[I]t may not always be easy to distinguish between (impermissibly) granting a stay in order to express the court's disapproval of official conduct "pour encourager les autres" and (permissibly) granting a stay because it offends the court's sense of justice and propriety. But it is difficult to avoid the conclusion that in Grant the proceedings were stayed in order to express the court's disapproval of the police misconduct and to discipline the police".[2]

1 *Warren* [2012] 1 AC 22 at paras 35–37. See above paras **5.14–5.28**.
2 At para 37.

5.170 The Court's reasoning on this point has been sharply criticised.[1] However, it may perhaps be of note that the Board, in *Warren*, seemed to have attached some importance to the fact that the misconduct of the police had been guided by the Crown Advocate, who had advised that these were 'operational decisions' for the police to take and that a court was unlikely to exclude the evidence so obtained. This was not to be considered as any form of protection as Lord Hope warned:

> 'But the range of operational decisions that the police may take does not include deliberate law-breaking, either at home or abroad. The police cannot take the law into their own hands. If conduct of that kind were to be permitted it would undermine the rule of law itself. That is why any abuse of state, or police, power must always be taken very seriously. It may lead the court to conclude that, however strong the evidence may appear to be against him, the defendant cannot have a fair trial or that, even if he can, it would be an affront to the public conscience to allow the proceedings to continue.'[2]

1 O'Connor, '"Abuse of Process" after Warren and Mitchell', *Criminal Law Review* (2012) 672.
2 *Warren* [2012] 1 AC 22 at para 62.

5.171 With that in mind we turn finally to consider unlawful acts committed by the police in the context of entrapment. In *R v Harmes & Crane,*[1] the police engaged in criminal acts as part of undercover drugs operations. The Court of Appeal concluded that 'the officers' conduct [within a drugs conspiracy] was criminal'.[2] However, the Court of Appeal decided that the officers' criminal conduct was 'not to be regarded as so seriously improper as to require the court to intervene to prevent the prosecution for conspiracy.' In coming to this conclusion, the Court noted that officers must show a degree of enthusiasm and persistence to provide protection for their undercover activities and that a good deal of active behaviour – albeit in the context of an entrapment case – may be acceptable.[3] The Court of Appeal's conclusion that the officers' conduct 'did not stray beyond that which was permissible to investigate and prosecute crime'[4] demonstrates the presumption[5] that agents who commit offences in the course of such operations, whether authorised or not, will not subsequently face sanction for their criminal acts.

1 [2006] EWCA Crim 928. Discussed in detail in Chapter 6.
2 At para 51.
3 At para 51.
4 At para 54.
5 Referred to above at para **5.145**.

Illegitimate funding of the prosecution

5.172 *R v Hounsham & others*[1] concerned allegations against car dealers of working in consort to defraud motor insurers by making false insurance claims in respect of 'staged' traffic accidents. Towards the end of the proceedings, it was disclosed to the defendants that the insurance companies in question had funded the police investigations that had resulted in their arrest. The defendants applied for the proceedings to be stayed as they were an abuse of the process of the court. On appeal, the prosecution conceded that, in seeking and accepting payments from the insurance companies, the police were acting *ultra vires* their statutory powers. Whilst the Court of Appeal rejected bad faith on the part of the police, it was argued that the conduct of the police was unlawful and so contrary to public policy that the court should not allow the prosecution to proceed, whether or not the police had acted in good faith.

1 [2005] EWCA Crim 1366.

5.173 Gage LJ rejected that contention, ruling[1] that:

> '...soliciting by the police of funds from potential victims of fraud, or any other crime, quite apart from being *ultra vires* police powers, is a practice which is fraught with danger. It may compromise the essential independence and objectivity of the police when carrying out a criminal investigation. It might lead to police officers being selective as to which crimes to investigate and which not to investigate. It might lead to victims persuading a police investigating team to act partially. It might also lead to investigating officers carrying out a more thorough preparation of the evidence in a case of a 'paying' victim; or a less careful preparation of the evidence in the case of a non-contributing victim. In short, it is a practice which, in our judgment, would soon lead to a loss of confidence in a police force's ability to investigate crime objectively and impartially... However, in this case, the judge found that PS Wade acted in good faith. He consulted his superior officer, who in turn sought advice. Apart from the issue of disclosure, to which we turn next, none of the appellants' counsel has been able to point to any prejudice caused by the acceptance of the total sum of £4,500 from three insurance companies. The conduct of the police complained of in this case, falls far short of the conduct which led the proceedings in *ex parte Bennett* to be stayed; and the court in *Mullen* to quash the conviction. On its own we are not persuaded that this conduct was such that the judge was wrong to refuse a stay.'

1 At paras 31–33. See also *R (Virgin Media Ltd) v Munaf Ahmed Zinga* [2014] EWCA Crim 52 at paras 44–45 and 53–54.

DEPRIVATION OF FOREIGN RIGHTS

5.174 One situation, not considered by Lord Steyn in *R v Latif*,[1] is where a defendant is lured by investigators into this country for the purposes of arrest, the consequence of this being that he is thereby denied legal rights and privileges which would have been available to him in the foreign jurisdiction had the investigators instead sought his extradition.

1 Above para **5.152**.

5.175 A defendant so lured has been deprived of the right to resist extradition, to insist upon compliance with extradition time limits, to test a prima facie case, to obtain bail based upon local community ties, and to be present during searching of premises in the state from which he was lured. The legal rights and privileges denied to the defendant may be significant and are discussed in detail in **Chapter 8**. In some cases, notably those involving the US, the extradition process will also immunise a defendant against the possibility of the imposition of the death penalty. In any extradition case, the extradition process will clothe a defendant with the principle of 'specialty' discussed at para **8.97**. Following extradition, a Requesting State may only prosecute for the conduct in respect of which extradition has been granted; the rule of 'specialty'. The rule, and the various exceptions to it, is reflected in every international extradition treaty. A defendant lured or tricked into the jurisdiction of the Requesting State is deprived of this fundamental protection. Therefore, to the State that wants a particular individual returned, deportation is more advantageous. There are no restrictions in terms of what the person, once lured into that State, can be prosecuted for.

5.176 High authority exists in respect of defendants lured into one country for the purpose of onward extradition to another: see *Somchai Liangsiriprasert v Government of the United States of America*[1] and *In re: Schmidt*;[2] both of which were applied in *R v Gokal.*[3] In the latter case, Mr Gokal was sought by the Serious Fraud Office in respect of the collapse of BCCI. He was resident in Pakistan, with whom the UK had no extradition treaty. The US authorities wished to interview him (on the understanding that he would not be arrested by them). The US authorities assured Mr Gokal that they had been assured by the SFO that he was free to travel to New York and return home without fear of arrest or detention. He was thus encouraged to leave the sanctuary of Pakistan and travel (via Frankfurt) to New York. Upon arrival in Frankfurt, he was arrested and extradited to the UK. Mr Gokal appealed against his subsequent conviction for fraud on the basis, amongst others, that the circumstances of his arrest constituted an abuse of process, that the facts gave rise to an inference of collusion between the SFO and the US authorities, whereby the appellant was tricked into believing he had a free passage or that, alternatively, the prosecution had deceived the US authorities, giving rise to executive lawlessness requiring a stay.

1 [1991] 1 AC 225, PC; discussed in detail at Chapter 8 para **8.114**.
2 [1995] 1 AC 339, HL; discussed in detail at Chapter 8 para **8.42**.
3 (11 March 1999, unreported), CA.

5.177 The Court of Appeal found, on the facts, that the SFO had neither colluded with, nor deceived, the US authorities into tricking the appellant into believing he had a free passage. They had, in fact, made it clear to the US authorities and the appellant that he would be arrested. The UK had taken advantage of the US authorities 'letting slip' the existence of the meeting in New York. But even if the position were otherwise, Rose LJ upheld[1] the trial judge's ruling that no abuse would arise:

> '… if correct, this amounted to tricking the appellant into leaving Pakistan. But, in the light of *Schmidt* and *Liangsiriprasert*, there was no abuse of power by the SFO because they had none in Pakistan, the defendant left voluntarily, and there was no threat to basic rights or the rule of law. The circumstances were akin to the enticement in *Liangsiriprasert*, not the forcible abduction in *Bennett* … Although *Liangsiriprasert* was an extradition case, the principles enunciated applied to abuse. The judge went on, in a balancing exercise by reference to *Latif*, to say he had no doubt that it was of the first importance that conspiracy to undermine the international

banking system should be tried. The conduct of the prosecution, even if a trick were proved, was not an affront to the public conscience; on the contrary, it would be an affront if the proceedings were stayed … there was no unlawful or criminal behaviour by the prosecution; on the authorities, luring was permissible.'

1 At transcript 13–15.

5.178 The Courts have, thus far, treated such conduct as far-enough removed from *Bennett*-type abduction scenarios so as not to be abusive but have recently shown indications that it may be prepared to do so. In *Bat v Germany*,[1] whilst the appellant ultimately did not establish that he had been lured into the jurisdiction for the purpose of arresting him, the court nonetheless entertained the factual inquiry as to the circumstances of his arrival. Moses LJ commented that:

> 'It must show that the appellant was lured to this country on the pretext that he would be welcome as an official to discuss security matters of mutual interest. It may be, if that were established, that it would amount to conduct which would bring the United Kingdom criminal justice system into disrepute. The most recent account of the approach of the court to such an allegation is contained within the opinion of the Privy Council given by Sir John Dyson SCJ in *Warren v AG of Jersey* [2011] UKPC 10 at paragraph 22. The Board was at pains not to impose rigid classifications (see paragraph 26). The court must balance the public interest in ensuring that those who are accused of serious crimes should be tried and the competing public interest in ensuring that executive conduct does not undermine public confidence in the Criminal Justice System. I am, therefore, reaching no conclusion as to whether, if the appellant could establish that he had been lured into this country, such conduct would amount to an abuse of process.'[2]

1 [2011] EWHC 2029 (Admin).
2 At para 51.

Chapter 6

Entrapment

INTRODUCTION

6.01 Entrapment is a legal term which carries a strong connotation of impropriety, but whose definition has proved problematic and often elusive. In the watershed case of *R v Looseley*,[1] Lord Hoffmann offered this definition:

> 'Entrapment occurs when an agent of the State – usually a law enforcement officer or a controlled informer – causes someone to commit an offence in order that he should be prosecuted.'

But then promptly added, 'I shall in due course have to refine this description but for the moment it will do.'

1 [2001] 1 WLR 2060, HL, at para 36. This appeal was joined with that of *Attorney-General's Reference (No 3 of 2000)* but for convenience, this case will simply be referred to as *Looseley*.

6.02 Writing about entrapment, Professor Ashworth defined it as 'the use of deceptive techniques to test whether a person is willing to commit an offence.'[1] Historically, when dealing with this subject, the courts eschewed attempts at comprehensive definitions and showed a marked unwillingness even to articulate general principles. The favoured approach has been a pragmatic one, always emphasising that, in cases of encouraged or induced crime, whether this constitutes the label of entrapment or not, is highly fact-dependent. Each case, it has been repeatedly said, turns on its own facts.

1 'Re-drawing the boundaries of entrapment' [2002] Crim LR 161.

6.03 However, the growth of intelligence-led policing, particularly in relation to drugs and terrorism offences, including the use of undercover techniques has meant that complaints of entrapment by the accused in relation to their pre-arrest dealings with undercover officers have been made with ever growing frequency.

The fundamental tensions remain, as recently articulated by Lord Justice Gross:

> 'In the criminal justice system, covert operations give rise to the need to balance competing interests. There is an obvious public interest in protecting society by combating serious crime, such as terrorism, drug trafficking and sexual grooming on the internet – and covert operations are of the first importance in doing so. Realism is essential as to what is entailed in such operations, including a recognition of the means necessary for success. On the other hand, the right to a fair trial, whether under the common law or the European Convention on Human Rights ("ECHR") is of fundamental

importance, so that the need for limits on covert operations to protect the rule of law and the integrity of the justice system is equally well-recognised. Ends do not always justify means. Sometimes, the line between legitimate law enforcement operations and abusive conduct is not as easy to draw in practice as it can be articulated in theory. On other occasions, it can readily be seen on which side of the line a particular covert operation falls.'[1]

1 *Syed (Haroon)* [2018] EWCA Crim 2809, [2019] 1 WLR 2459 at para 3.

6.04 *R v Looseley* remains the seminal case in relation to entrapment. The principles established in this case were later distilled by Professor David Ormerod into five key factors:

(i) reasonable suspicion of criminal activity as a legitimate trigger for the police operation;

(ii) authorisation and supervision of the operation as a legitimate control mechanism;

(iii) necessity and proportionality of the means employed to police particular types of offence;

(iv) the concepts of the 'unexceptional opportunity' and causation; and

(iv) authentication of the evidence.[1]

More recent decisions have not changed the approach applied in *Looseley*. Indeed, the factors set out by Ormerod were considered and applied by the Court of Appeal in *Syed (Haroon)*[2] (see para **6.109** below), where the Court of Appeal held that the *Looseley* principles continue to be compliant with Art 6 of the ECtHR.

Not all issues of ambiguity have been clarified. However, the continued application of those principles in predominantly unsuccessful appeals, has helped to crystallise the parameters within which a defendant will have a meritorious claim to have been entrapped. Whilst the notoriously fact-specific nature of the issues raised in cases of alleged entrapment contributes to a continuing lack of ease in providing an exhaustive statement of the law in this area, the case law demonstrates, from a defendant's or appellant's point of view, a restrictive approach in the courts' application of the *Looseley* principles.

1 *Recent Developments in Entrapment* [2006] Covert Policing Review 65.
2 [2018] EWCA Crim 2809, [2019] 1 WLR 2459.

6.05 For a rare example of a successful appeal against conviction on the ground of entrapment since the successful defendant in *Attorney-General's Reference (No 3 of 2000)* (decided at the same time as *Looseley*), see *R v Moon*.[1]

The case law since *Looseley*, and the developments in the law relating to the difficulty of private or commercial entrapment in the context of criminal proceedings, serve firmly to illustrate the difficulties that face the defendant who aims to have proceedings stayed as an abuse of process on the ground of entrapment.

1 [2004] EWCA Crim 2872, discussed below at para **6.82**.

6.06 As *R v Looseley* remains the authoritative ruling, an understanding of that case still requires a grasp of preceding judicial attempts to inject consistency and fairness into this subject.

THE RIGHT REMEDY: S 78 OR ABUSE OF PROCESS?

Entrapment is not a substantive defence

6.07 Traditionally, the courts have disapproved of the use of entrapment by the police. See, for example, the terse comments of Lord Goddard in *Brannan v Peek*,[1] in a case involving undercover officers attempting to buy alcohol in pubs shortly after closing time.

1 [1948] 1 KB 68, DC.

6.08 This admonition, however, was uttered in the context of a civil case and consequently the issue of whether, like the defences of insanity or duress or automatism, entrapment in a criminal case was to be afforded such a status remained unresolved. In some jurisdictions, including the US, entrapment is a substantive defence[1] where it is held that, when entrapped, the accused lacks the necessary guilty intent or *mens rea*.

1 *Sherman v United States* 356 US 369 (1957).

6.09 The House of Lords in *R v Sang*,[1] rejected any suggestion that entrapment should be added to the list of substantive defences. Essentially, the House of Lords rejected the notion that where the accused has been induced to commit the *actus reus* of the offence, he thereby lacks the *mens rea*. In the view of the House of Lords, an entrapped accused was as guilty as any other who would have committed the offence without the entrapment. Accordingly in *R v Sang*, it was held that the only appropriate judicial reactions to a proven case of entrapment were either reduction in sentence or public criticism of police conduct.

1 [1980] AC 402, HL.

6.10 The speeches in *Sang*, however, travelled wider than simply being concerned with the legal status of entrapment. This case can be regarded as the high watermark of judgments which sought to disclaim any responsibility for trying and convicting an accused whose presence before the court was only a consequence of state misconduct or abuse of power[1] and that the criminal courts should not be concerned as to how evidence was obtained. In this way, *R v Sang* was a profound move away from what Lord Devlin had famously said earlier in *Connelly v DPP* about the courts' 'inescapable responsibility'.[2]

1 See for example Lord Scarman at pp 451 and 455.
2 See para **7.81**.

6.11 Parliament in part reversed *R v Sang* in PACE, s 78. Section 78 gives the judge the discretion to exclude prosecution evidence to safeguard the fairness of proceedings, including evidence obtained by entrapment. The common law also moved away notably in the landmark decision of the House of Lords in *R v Horseferry Road Magistrates' Court, ex p Bennett*.[1]

1 [1994] 1 AC 42, HL.

ABUSE OF EXECUTIVE POWER

6.12 The decision in *Bennett* is considered in detail in Chapter 5. For present purposes, it is sufficient to recall the leading speech of Lord Griffiths, who held that the courts possessed a discretionary power to stay proceedings where anterior executive action amounted to a threat to human rights or the rule of law. In essence, Lord Griffiths described this jurisdiction as one to prevent abuse of executive power which would be considered an affront to the integrity of the criminal justice system. This approach has been confirmed in cases such as *R v Maxwell*[1] and *Warren v Attorney General of Jersey*.[2]

1 [2011] 1 WLR 1837.
2 [2012] 1 AC 22.

6.13 Whilst *Bennett* was not concerned with entrapment, the House of Lords in *R v Latif*[1] was later to hold on the same underlying principles that a stay could be granted on the ground of entrapment if (and only if) the prosecution founded on this amounted to 'an affront to the public conscience'.[2] This was not about fairness: it was 'to protect the integrity of the criminal justice system'.[3]

1 [1996] 2 Cr App R 92.
2 For further discussion of this case see paras **5.152–5.159**.
3 At para 101, per Lord Steyn.

6.14 In *R v Looseley,* similar language was used. Lord Nicholls described the abuse jurisdiction as follows:

> 'My Lords, every court has an inherent power and duty to prevent abuse of its process. This is a fundamental principle of the rule of law. By recourse to this principle courts ensure that executive agents of the State do not misuse the coercive, law enforcement functions of the courts and thereby oppress citizens of the State. Entrapment, with which these two appeals are concerned, is an instance where such misuse may occur. It is simply not acceptable that the State through its agents should lure its citizens into committing acts forbidden by the law and then seek to prosecute them for doing so. That would be entrapment. That would be a misuse of State power, and an abuse of the process of the courts. The unattractive consequences, frightening and sinister in extreme cases, which State conduct of this nature could have are obvious. The role of the courts is to stand between the State and its citizens and make sure this does not happen.'[1]

1 Above para **6.01**, at para 1.

6.15 Turning his particular attention to issues of unfairness thrown up by entrapment, Lord Nicholls considered what he termed 'state-created crime' as a type of state conduct which ought to result in a stay:

> 'Entrapment goes to the propriety of there being a prosecution at all for the relevant offence, having regard to the state's involvement in the circumstance in which it was committed'.[1]
>
> Further:
>
> 'Police conduct which brings about, to use the catch-phrase, state-created crime is unacceptable and improper. To prosecute in such circumstances

would be an affront to the public conscience, to borrow the language of Lord Steyn in *R v Latif* [1996] 1 WLR 104, 112. In a very broad sense of the word, such a prosecution would not be fair.'[2]

1 At para 17.
2 At para 19.

6.16 Lords Nicholls and Hoffmann in *R v Looseley* both considered whether this jurisdiction to stay was best understood as emanating from the statutory jurisdiction created by PACE, s 78 or alternatively from the common law abuse of process doctrine. In both speeches, their Lordships preferred the latter, holding that when a complaint of entrapment is made by an accused, almost invariably it is directed at a stay of the entire proceedings rather than the exclusion of evidence. Lord Hoffmann said:

> 'The section 78 discretion enables the judge to safeguard the fairness of the trial. But the entrapped defendant is not ordinarily complaining that the admission of certain evidence would prejudice the fairness of his trial. He is saying that whatever the evidence, he should not be tried at all. The appropriate remedy, if any, is therefore not the exclusion of evidence but a stay of the proceedings.'[1]

1 At para 42.

6.17 Where the principle underlying the rationale for a stay is to preserve the integrity of the criminal justice system, then the abuse doctrine will be preferred over s 78. This is so when the accused's complaint is not particularly concerned with the reliability of evidence to be adduced by an undercover officer or their credibility. Essentially, the accused is not disputing that their trial will be fair but that, for a matter of policy or law, they have been treated unfairly and thus ought not be tried at all. In *R v Latif*, Lord Steyn analysed this issue as follows:

> 'If the court concludes that a fair trial is not possible, it will stay the proceedings. That is not what the present case is concerned with. It is plain that a fair trial was possible and that such a trial took place. In this case the issue is whether, despite the fact that a fair trial was possible, the judge ought to have stayed the criminal proceedings on broader considerations of the integrity of the criminal justice system.'[1]

1 Above para **6.13**, at p 112.

6.18 In *Looseley*, in relation to the complaint of having been treated unfairly, the test was succinctly described by Lord Mackay as being whether:

> '…the state through its agents had lured the accused into committing an act or acts forbidden by law for which the state is now seeking to prosecute.'[1]

1 At para 34.

ECtHR Jurisprudence

6.19 Finally, the jurisprudence of the ECtHR on this point should be considered. It demonstrates two important issues: 1) how the ECtHR has approached the domestic states' use of evidence obtained by entrapment, and 2) how the ECtHR has attempted to define the substantive test of entrapment. The principal case on entrapment is *Teixeira de Castro v Portugal.*[1] In *Teixeira,* the applicant complained that he had not had a fair trial, in violation of Art 6(1), because he had been incited to commit the offence by the police. Having considered the facts of the complaint and upheld it, the court stated:[2]

> 'In the light of all these considerations, the Court concludes that the two police officers' actions went beyond those of undercover agents because they instigated the offence and there is nothing to suggest that without their intervention it would have been committed. *That intervention and its use in the impugned criminal proceedings meant that, right from the outset, the applicant was definitively deprived of a fair trial.* Consequently, there has been a violation of article 6(1).' (Emphasis added)

This passage from *Teixeira* establishes that our domestic courts' preference for conceptualising entrapment as an abuse, rather than an admissibility issue, is mirrored by the approach adopted by the ECtHR.

1 (1998) 28 EHRR 101, above para **6.03**.
2 At para 39.

6.20 The ECtHR has since affirmed its approach in *Teixeira* in *Vanyan v Russia.*[1] In *Vanyan*, the police had instructed 'OZ' to affect a test purchase of drugs from the applicant by asking him to obtain drugs for her. As in *Teixeira*, the police had no reason to suspect Vanyan of being a drug dealer before their involvement and there was 'nothing to suggest that the offence would have been committed had it not been for the … intervention of OZ'.[2] In holding that the police had incited the offence, such that the use of the evidence obtained as a result of their intervention against the applicant 'irremediably undermined the fairness of his trial', the Court said that:

> 'Where the activity of undercover agents appears to have instigated the offence and there is nothing to suggest that it would have been committed without their intervention, it goes beyond that of an undercover agent and may be described as incitement. Such intervention and its use in criminal proceedings may result in the fairness of the trial being irremediably undermined.'[3]

1 Application No 53203/99, First Section (15 December 2005). See also *Khudobin v Russia* (2009) 48 EHRR 22.
2 At para 49.
3 At para 47.

6.21 In attempting to define what constitutes entrapment, the ECtHR has considered whether there was evidence of prior involvement in the activity being investigated,[1] the active or passive behaviour of the authorities and the level of infiltration, particularly to assess if the state was improperly enlarging the scope or scale of the crime.[2]

1 Application No 58753/00, Second Section (7 September 2004).
2 *Grb. v Croatia* Application no. 47074/12 (23 February 2018).

6.22 In *Edwards and Lewis v UK* (2005),[1] the applicants contended that they had been the victims of entrapment. Crucially, the trial judge – who decided the issue of entrapment – had seen evidence, withheld from the defence but on which the prosecution relied in the course of a public interest immunity hearing. The ECtHR found a violation of Art 6(1) on the basis that the procedure adopted by the trial judge to determine the issue of entrapment had paid insufficient attention to the requirements to provide adversarial hearings and equality of arms. The ECtHR accepted that the right to disclosure is not absolute, but stated that the rights of the defence must only be restricted to the extent that this is strictly necessary. *Edwards and Lewis* was a case decided prior to the House of Lords establishing the governing principles and safeguards which apply to public interest immunity hearings in *H.*[2] As such, it is submitted that the ECtHR may take a different approach if a similar case were examined today, in light of these safeguards.

1 (2010) 40 EHRR 24.
2 [2004] UKHL 3.

6.23 In *Ramanauskas v Lithuania,*[1] the applicant argued that he had committed the offence of accepting a bribe because he had been incited by police officers to commit it. The ECtHR found that the actions of the police went beyond 'investigating criminal activity in an essentially passive manner', considering that:

> 'Firstly, there is no evidence that the applicant had committed any offences beforehand, in particular corruption-related offences. Secondly …all the meetings between the applicant and [the police agent] took place on the latter's initiative, a fact that appears to contradict the [Lithuanian] Government's argument that the authorities did not subject the applicant to any pressure or threats. On the contrary, through the contact established on the initiative of [the police], the applicant seems to have been subject to blatant prompting on their part to perform criminal acts, although there was no objective evidence – other than rumours – to suggest that he had been intending to engage in any such activity.'[2]

1 (2010) 51 EHRR 11.
2 At para 67.

6.24 In *Ramanauskas,* the Lithuanian government argued that the police officers concerned had, prior to their authorisation, acted on their 'private initiative without having first informed the authorities.'[1] The Court dismissed this argument, ruling that national authorities cannot abrogate their responsibility for the actions of police officers simply by arguing that the officers had acted in a 'private capacity', whilst still carrying out police duties.[2] The Court also noted that 'there is no indication that the offence would have been committed without their intervention.'[3] Consequently, these actions violated Art 6(1).

1 At para 62.
2 At para 63.
3 At para 73.

6.25 A more recent consideration in the ECtHR on the definition of entrapment came in *Furcht v Germany.*[1] The complaint of entrapment was upheld and the court found that there was a breach of Art 6(1) in circumstances where there was nothing to suggest that the complainant had any predisposition towards criminal activity until approach by an undercover officer. The Court held that the officer had not acted in a passive manner, but exerted influence such as to incite the commission of an offence that would not have otherwise been committed. The factors in deciding whether an investigation was passive include examining the conduct of the officer, the basis for the suspicions (or whether there was in fact a lack of predisposition), and the extent of any pressure applied. The Court held that a substantial mitigation in sentence was not a sufficient remedy for a breach of Art 6(1), again aligning itself with the approach of the courts in England and Wales in preferring the abuse doctrine in these circumstances.

1 (2015) 61 EHRR 25, ECtHR.

WHAT COUNTS AS ENTRAPMENT?

The difficulties of definition

6.26 Where there has been an abuse of executive power amounting to an affront to the public conscience, then a stay will be granted. Like almost all abuse of process arguments, this determination will follow a balancing test of the relevant public interests: the public interest in prosecuting serious crime and the public interest in protecting the integrity of the criminal justice system (see *Warren v Attorney General of Jersey* discussed in Chapter 5 at paras **5.14–5.28**). But, of course, this broader proposition begs an enormous practical question – what constitutes, in relation to entrapment, such an abuse? Alternatively, if the law is to state that undercover officers should not act as *agents provocateurs* or entice people to commit offences, what do these expressions mean? How are the unacceptable actions of such an agent to be distinguished from acceptable or fair state participation in criminal conduct? What are the standards or thresholds to be employed here allowing a court, seized of a particular case to determine on a principled basis, what is fair and unfair?

6.27 The inherent problem with any definition of entrapment was neatly encapsulated by Lord Diplock in *R v Sang*:

> '… [w]hat is unfair, what is trickery in the context of the detection and prevention of crime, are questions which are liable to attract highly subjective answers.'[1]

1 Above para **6.09**, at p 431.

6.28 Appreciating this difficulty, one has to look at how the courts have attempted to discern principles and identify the factors where emphasis has been placed. The speeches in *R v Looseley* were not, and did not purport to be, a redefinition of entrapment or the imposition of a new set of principles. Instead they were an attempt to make more explicit the core of the entrapment doctrine and to formulate some fresh and more helpful guidelines.

REJECTED RATIONALES FOR ENTRAPMENT

6.29 In considering complaints of entrapment made by the accused, what doctrine of entrapment have the courts preferred? What has been their approach?

The active/passive distinction

6.30 In *R v Smurthwaite and Gill*,[1] Lord Taylor CJ sought to provide some guidelines to assist the courts in determining whether or not on the facts before them a finding of entrapment against undercover officers should be made. One of these directed attention to whether the officer's conduct had been active or passive:

> 'Was the officer acting as an agent provocateur in the sense that he was enticing the defendant to commit an offence he would not otherwise have committed? How passive or active was the officer's role in obtaining the evidence?'[2]

If the latter then this would, in Lord Taylor CJ's view, point towards entrapment; only passive conduct being permissible.

1 (1994) 98 Cr App R 437, CA.
2 At p 440.

6.31 The coherence of this dichotomy of active and passive rests upon a presupposition concerning causality: that an active undercover officer is likely to have enticed the accused into committing the offence whereas a passive one would not. Accordingly, but for this enticement or encouragement, the offender would not have committed the crime. Thus, once this causality is established as viewed through the lens of whether the officer was active or not, a finding of entrapment is likely to follow.

6.32 Unfortunately, the presupposition upon which this analysis is founded is perhaps over-simplified. First, in practice how is one to distinguish passivity from activity? Is an officer's acquiescence with another's criminal enterprise always to be deemed a passive act even if this may in fact serve to encourage the other? Passivity and activity may not always correspond with omission and commission respectively. In the context of a retail test-purchase case, is the officer being active in attempting to buy? Surely so, but does this attempt amount to entrapment with the consequence that, to avoid this allegation, the officer must somehow linger in the store waiting for a member of staff to approach and offer to sell? Is an officer being 'active' where, in an operation to deter kerb-crawling by means of identifying male offenders, she disguises herself as a sex worker? At the other extreme of criminality, how can a passive officer expect to ingratiate him/herself into a criminal gang without some cover story and sign of credibility?

6.33 In practice, it is submitted, this supposed dichotomy quickly breaks down. Accordingly, it is of little use in helping to find an answer to the underlying or basic issue of whether the officer's conduct was unacceptable or unfair. Nonetheless, the supposed distinction has attracted support. In *Teixeira*, the ECtHR seemed to have relied upon it in part when determining a violation of Art 6 on the ground of entrapment:

> 'The two police officers did not confine themselves to investigating Mr Teixeira de Castro's criminal activity in an essentially passive manner, but exercised an influence such as to incite the commission of the offence.'[1]

1 Above para **6.19**. See also *Furcht v Germany* above at para **6.25** and *Ramanauskas v Lithuania*, above at para **6.23**.

6.34 In *Nottingham City Council v Amin*,[1] this extract was relied upon in argument to the effect that, in flagging down the unlicensed taxi, the officers had entrapped Amin into committing the relevant offence. This interpretation was rejected by Lord Bingham CJ.[2] In *R v Looseley* this concept was abandoned altogether. Lord Hutton[3] endorsed the view of Lord Bingham in *Amin* and Lord Hoffmann expressed no enthusiasm for the concept confirming:

'A good deal of active behaviour in the course of an authorised operation may therefore be acceptable without crossing the boundary between causing the offence to be committed and providing an opportunity for the defendant to commit it.'[4]

1 [2000] 1 WLR 1071, DC.
2 At p 1080.
3 Above para **6.01**, at para 110.
4 At para 69.

6.35 Taken literally, the active/passive distinction would treat as entrapment any offer to buy controlled drugs. It is submitted that this cannot be correct and the later domestic authorities have not found it to be so. Indeed, in *Syed*[1] (see para **6.109** below), the court recognised that the ECtHR could not have meant the distinction to have been taken literally, as this '…would render empty that Court's recognition of the importance and need for undercover techniques, especially when combatting egregious and organised crime.'

1 *Syed (Haroon)* [2018] EWCA Crim 2809, [2019] 1 WLR 2459, para 110 (ii).

Providing an opportunity

Strict causation, the test in *Amin*

6.37 In *Nottingham City Council v Amin*,[1] the officers were testing whether taxi drivers were complying with the restrictions imposed on their permits concerning where in Nottingham they could not ply for hire. Amin was duly hailed in an area where he should not stop and accept a fare. He did and was consequently prosecuted. The question was whether Amin had been entrapped. Lord Bingham CJ formulated the following test:

> 'On the one hand it has been recognised as deeply offensive to ordinary notions of fairness if a defendant were to be convicted and punished for committing a crime which he only committed because he had been incited, instigated, persuaded, pressurised or wheedled into committing it by a law enforcement officer. On the other hand it has been recognised that law

enforcement agencies have a general duty to the public to enforce the law and it has been regarded as unobjectionable if a law enforcement officer gives a defendant an opportunity to break the law, of which the defendant freely takes advantage, in circumstances where it appears that the defendant would have behaved in the same way if the opportunity had been offered by anyone else.'[2]

1 Above para **6.34**.
2 At p 1076.

6.38 In effect, if the officers incited, then they can be taken to have caused or created the crime, whereas if they only acted like ordinary members of the public and thus merely provided an opportunity, they are deemed not to have caused it. However, *Amin* creates a highly strict test of causality in relation to entrapment; a finding of incitement should only be made if the accused *only* committed the crime because of it.

6.39 There is, it is submitted, a fundamental difficulty with this test: its notion of causality. In *Amin,* Lord Bingham CJ was seeking to restrict causality to those situations where the offence is committed only as a consequence of the incitement. By so restricting it, Lord Bingham CJ could then distinguish such incitement, which in effect he defined as entrapment, from the supposedly non-causal situation of providing an opportunity. But causality may play an equal role in both instances. But for the hailing of the taxi in *Amin* in a planned operation by the officers, the offence charged would not have been committed.

6.40 An attempt to distinguish incitement from providing an opportunity on the basis that only the former causes the commission of the offence is, it is submitted, unsustainable. In both paradigms, it could fairly be argued that officers are acting as *agents provocateurs*. The means by which acceptable law enforcement stratagems for apprehending offenders can be distinguished from unacceptable is unlikely to be a reliance on a simply causal analysis as suggested by Lord Bingham CJ in *Amin*.

6.41 Moreover, what can be inferred from Lord Bingham CJ's emphasis on entrapment only being held if the sole cause or reason for the accused committing the offence was the instigation? Criminal cases are rarely so straightforward. On the facts of *Amin*, was the only cause of the offence the driver being hailed in the prohibited area? Or was it also that he chose to be there in the first place? Alternatively, in a drugs case where a suspected dealer is approached in a nightclub by undercover officers and agrees to their request to sell drugs, can it be said that the only cause of his prosecution was this approach? Or is the simple fact that the accused had already situated himself in the club also relevant to causation?[1] An endless debate can open up on what facts should count as causes. To resolve this, one would first have to propound a defensible concept of what counted as a cause and what did not, but such an exercise is unlikely to be fruitful. In consequence, it is probably unhelpful and unduly simplistic to speak in terms of single or 'only' causes. If causation is to be the key criterion, it would perhaps be more realistic to speak of predominant rather than 'only' causes.

1 See *R v Mayeri* [1999] 1 Cr App R (S) 304, CA.

6.42 In *R v Looseley,* the House of Lords preferred a more holistic approach. The view of Lord Hoffmann, for instance, was that whilst causation is certainly relevant, it is unlikely to be an adequate test of entrapment in itself:

> 'Many cases place emphasis upon the question of whether the policeman can be said to have caused the commission of the offence, rather than merely providing an opportunity for the accused to commit it with a policeman rather than in secrecy with someone else. There is no doubt that this will usually be a most important factor deciding whether or not the police have overstepped the line between legitimate crime detection and unacceptable crime creation. But a note of caution must be sounded. First, as Lord Steyn said in *R v Latif* [1996] 1 WLR 104, 111, it is important but not necessarily decisive. Other factors, some of which I shall mention in a moment, may have to be taken into account as well. Secondly, a good deal will depend upon what is accepted as evidence that the accused would have committed the offence with someone else.'[1]

1 Above para **6.01**, at para 50.

6.43 Further, Lord Hoffmann considered the nature of the conduct in providing the opportunity to be important. The officers had created this 'opportunity' by pretending to be ordinary members of the public. Lord Hoffmann explained the *Amin* decision in this way:

> 'In referring to whether the defendant would have behaved in the same way if the opportunity had been offered by anyone else, Lord Bingham CJ obviously did not mean only that the defendant would have responded in the same way to someone who was not a policeman. Since the defendant in such cases ex hypothesi does not know that he is dealing with a policeman, such a condition would invariably be satisfied. What he meant was that the policemen behaved like ordinary members of the public in flagging the taxi down. They did not wave £50 notes or pretend to be in distress.'[1]

1 At para 54.

Test purchases

6.44 Whilst this test models the 'ordinary member of the public' concept, asking the same question of whether the officer merely provided an opportunity, it does not rely upon strict causation. It omits it by simply posing the issue of whether or not the officer's conduct was consistent with an everyday purchase made by an ordinary person. If this condition is satisfied, then causation and even enticement become peripheral. The emphasis is on whether the accused freely took advantage of an opportunity presented to him by the officer, this opportunity being the same as that as would have been presented by a normal customer.

6.45 In many senses, the test disregards concerns connected with causation and incitement, considering that a simple test purchase is in a special category because it is unobjectionable, almost a sort of occupational hazard that is foreseeable and ought to be expected by regulated sellers, and therefore legitimate.

6.46 Some support for this test was evident in the speeches in *R v Looseley*. Lord Hutton said:

> 'In my opinion if a person freely takes advantage of an opportunity to break the law given to him by a police officer, the police officer is not to be regarded as inciting or instigating the crime in the context of the prohibition of entrapment. The conduct of the police officer should not be viewed as constituting incitement or instigation where, as McHugh J states in *Ridgeway v Queen* (1995) 184 CLR 19, 92, that conduct is "consistent with the ordinary temptations and stratagems that are likely to be encountered in the course of criminal activity"....'.[1]

1 Above para **6.01**, at para 112.

6.47 Lord Hoffmann said:

> 'The test of whether the law enforcement officer behaved like an ordinary member of the public works well and is likely be decisive in many cases of regulatory offences committed with ordinary members of the public, such as selling liquor in unlicensed quantities (*DPP v Marshall* [1988] 3 All ER 683), selling videos to children under age (*Ealing London Borough Council v Woolworths plc* [1998] Crim LR 58, DC), and operating a private hire vehicle without a licence (*Taunton Deane Borough Council v Brice* (1997) 31 Licensing Review 24).'[1]

1 Above para **6.01**, at para 55.

6.48 It is submitted that underlying the acceptability of test purchases is the view that, unless they were a permissible method of law enforcement, the types of offences concerned might never be detected. There are practical difficulties for example in local authority trading standards officers mounting surveillance operations, these difficulties lead them to require the use of test purchase situations. Accordingly, subject to the limitation of the ordinary-person paradigm, overlooking concerns about enticement is fair *quid pro quo* for the offence under investigation being relatively low level.

6.49 Furthermore, because it is well known what ordinary purchasers do in these situations, it can be safely assumed, how an ordinary person would behave. Such an assumption can then easily be compared to how the officers behaved to see if their conduct roughly corresponded. Generally, this comparison will not be controversial.

6.50 Lord Hoffmann however identified the severe limitations of this test that become apparent when serious crime is involved:

> 'But ordinary members of the public do not become involved in large scale drug dealing, conspiracy to rob (*R v Mealey and Sheridan* (1974) 60 Cr App Rep 59) or hiring assassins (*R v Gill* [1989] Crim LR 358; *R v Smurthwaite* [1994] 1 All ER 898). The appropriate standards of behaviour are in such cases rather more problematic.'[1]

1 Above para **6.01**, at para 55.

6.51 In such cases, reliance upon supposed norms of behaviour becomes far less credible and, accordingly, concerns about enticement and acceptable state behaviour return to the fore. In other words, in relation, for example, to drug trafficking or terrorism, the question of 'whether the defendant was given an opportunity to commit the offence of which he freely availed himself' or whether he/she was entrapped cannot be answered by a simplistic appeal to how an ordinary person would have behaved. In reality, these 'serious crime' cases can only be addressed by a different approach based on enticement. Was there any inducement, encouragement etc by the officers?

Random virtue-testing

6.52 This is another variant of the 'providing an opportunity' test. Whereas test purchases are aimed at regulated traders, this form of deceptive crime-detection is aimed at the public at large. In conducting an operation of this kind, law-abiding as well as dishonest citizens are equally targeted. The public are subject to some extraordinary temptation as in *Williams and O'Hare v DPP*.[1] Here Essex Police devised an operation to apprehend people who were stealing from cars. A white van was parked up and left with its rear doors open with cartons of cigarettes on view. Eventually, two passing men were successfully baited and arrested red-handed. At their trial and appeal they argued entrapment, but this was rejected on the ground that there had not been any police persuasion or encouragement.

1 (1994) 98 Cr App R 209, CA.

6.53 In *R v Looseley*, Lord Hoffmann held that this police operation was legitimate, not because virtue-testing provided a workable test, but because it was validly authorised:

> 'It was justified because it was an authorised investigation into actual crime and the fact that the defendants may not have previously been suspected or even thought of offending was their hard luck.'[1]

1 Above para **6.01**, at para 65.

6.54 The difficulty with virtue-test cases, like *Williams,* is that whilst it is fair to say that the accused freely took advantage of an opportunity offered to him/her, it would be wrong to hold that the opportunity was unexceptional. Deserted van doors open with cigarettes on view or open wallets left full of money are not ordinary events or temptations. This is precisely why such temptations are laid.

6.55 Furthermore, on the facts of *Williams,* it is clear that neither defendant already had the intent to commit the crime prior to being tempted. The police did far more than merely provide an opportunity: it could be said that they implanted the necessary intent.

6.56 In *Looseley*, Lord Hoffmann stated:

> '… normally it is not considered a legitimate use of police power to provide people not suspected of being engaged in any criminal activity with the opportunity to commit crimes. The only proper purpose of police

participation is to obtain evidence of criminal acts which they suspect someone is about to commit or in which he is already engaged. It is not to tempt people to commit crimes in order to expose their bad characters and punish them.'[1]

1 Above para **6.01**, at para 56.

6.57 It is submitted that Lord Hoffmann's analysis is entirely correct. His observation[1] that the operation was licit merely because it was validly authorised and accordingly the accused cannot complain as to their misfortune, is inconsistent with this observation. Clearly, Lord Hoffmann did not intend to make authorisation the sole criterion of police conduct, otherwise the bulk of his speech in *R v Looseley* would be otiose. He was in the above passage, it is submitted, making a narrower point concerning what can constitute reasonable suspicion, of which more below.

1 Above para **6.53**.

6.58 As Lord Nicholls stated:

> 'If the defendant was already presently disposed to commit such a crime, should opportunity arise, that is not entrapment. That is not state-created crime. The matter stands differently if the defendant lacked such a predisposition, and the police were responsible for implanting the necessary intent.'[1]

1 Above para **6.01**, at para 21.

Predisposition

6.59 As the previous section has demonstrated, the courts attach great importance, when considering a claim of entrapment, to whether the undercover officer simply gave the accused an opportunity to break the law. If so, then the courts feel entitled to presume that the accused would have behaved in the same way if someone else had offered the same opportunity. Accordingly, having taken such free advantage, the courts reject the complaint.

6.60 But, how to differentiate safely the objectionable luring or tempting from the acceptable taking free advantage? How to distinguish, for example, a *bona fide* police operation into ongoing crime from a vendetta against an individual? As the House of Lords observed in *R v Looseley*, in finding a violation in *Teixeira*, the ECtHR attached importance to the lack of good reason to suspect that the applicant was engaged in crime and quoted from the *Teixeira* case:

> 'It does not appear either that the competent authorities had good reason to suspect that Mr Teixeira de Castro was a drug-trafficker; on the contrary, he had no criminal record and no preliminary investigation concerning him had been opened. Indeed, he was not known to the police officers, who only came into contact with him through the intermediaries[1] ... the two police officers' actions went beyond those of undercover agents because they instigated the offence *and there was nothing to suggest that without their intervention it would have been committed.* That intervention and its

use in the impugned criminal proceedings meant that, right from the outset, the applicant was definitively deprived of a fair trial.'[2] (Emphasis added)

1 At para 38 of the *Teixeira* case. At para 107 of the *Looseley* decision.
2 At para 39 of the *Teixeira* case. At para 107 of the *Looseley* decision.

6.61 An obvious method of determining whether the approach made to the accused was acceptable is to consider how predisposed they were to have committed the offence in any event. In *R v Edwards*[1] the Court held that 'from the way in which E behaved, including his reaction to the request for drugs, his familiarity with the drugs scene … and his agreement to discount future supplies, it is manifestly plain that, at the time of the approach [by the officer], he was already an established drugs dealer…'. Similarly, in *R v Shannon,*[2] Potter LJ said:

> 'As the judge also found, by reason of the defendant's obvious familiarity with the current price of cocaine and his ready advice as to obtaining it … he displayed a familiarity with the dealing scene which itself suggested a predisposition to be part of it.'[3]

1 [1991] Crim LR 45, CA.
2 [2001] 1 WLR 51, CA.
3 At para 49.

6.62 It can be observed that, in both the cases, the courts were justifying the operation with the benefit of hindsight. However, to avoid arbitrariness and for there to be some objective criterion, there must be a basis for suspicion beforehand.

6.63 The need to adduce prior grounds of predisposition has normally led to a reliance upon a target's previous convictions or current lifestyle.[1] However, the difficulty with this approach is that, first, it inevitably exposes some individuals to police attention on inherently speculative grounds; the fact that an individual has previous drugs convictions or is an addict does not provide a sound basis for inferring that they are currently engaged in crime. Secondly, such a view is objectionable as it can be based upon conscious or unconscious racist, classist, xenophobic, or misogynist views. It condones wholesale police intrusions against people who become fair game simply because of their background. In turn, this must raise considerable concerns in connection with the Art 8 right to private and family life and the need for proportionality.

1 For example, that they are a drug addict.

6.64 It is submitted that, in common with virtue-testing, predisposition fails altogether to address the required justification for mounting an undercover operation; that there are adequate grounds to suggest that the target is either presently engaged in, or at least presently disposed to commit, the crime under investigation. His/her personal history and current lifestyle may be relevant to this issue but they can be neither sufficient nor necessary factors in establishing a current predisposition. Both Lords Nicholls and Hoffmann in *R v Looseley* enunciated disdain for this test. For example, in relation to why previous convictions are an insufficient guide to predisposition, Lord Hoffmann said:

> 'Suspicion may attach to a person who has previously escaped conviction and, contrariwise, the fact that a person has been previously convicted may provide no ground for suspecting a current course of criminality which would justify the use of covert operations.'[1]

1 Above para **6.01**, at para 68.

6.65 More generally, Lord Nicholls expressed disquiet about whether, even if the accused had been predisposed, this would be acceptable police conduct. He observed that:

> 'Predisposition does not make acceptable what would otherwise be unacceptable conduct on the part of the police or other law enforcement agencies. Predisposition does not negative misuse of state power.'[1]

1 Above para **6.01**, at para 22.

THE ACCEPTED RATIONALE; REASONABLE SUSPICION

6.66 In essence, this is a test of police good faith that there were reasonable grounds for suspecting an individual, or a group, of ongoing involvement in a particular crime. The need to satisfy this requirement is an adequate guard against ill thought-out and unjustified intrusive police operations. Arbitrary investigations of citizens selected at random would thus be regarded as unacceptable police conduct amounting to entrapment.

6.67 Unfortunately, confusion and disagreement will inevitably arise when identifying what counts as reasonable suspicion. How in practice does this requirement operate to prevent arbitrary or unjustified investigations? This issue is demonstrated by the approach of Lord Hoffmann in *R v Looseley*, who held that:

> 'The requirement of reasonable suspicion does not necessarily mean that there must have been suspicion of the particular person who happens to have committed the offence.'[1]

On the example of the facts in *Williams v DPP*,[2] Lord Hoffmann opined that such an operation could satisfy the requirement of reasonable suspicion if the operation had been conducted in an area where the crime in question was prevalent. Accordingly, the requirement may be satisfied not in relation to an individual at all; reasonable suspicion may be directed at an area and by implication, to premises, or an organisation. Lord Nicholls adopted a similar approach: '… having grounds for suspicion of a particular individual is not always essential. Sometimes suspicion may be centred on a particular place, such as a particular public house.'[3]

1 Above para **6.01**, at para 65.
2 Above para **6.52**.
3 Above para **6.01**, at para 27.

6.68 The difficulty with this diluted concept of reasonable suspicion, which need not be individual-related, is that it justifies, as in *Williams*, the tempting of individuals merely because they happen to be in the wrong place at the wrong moment. Subject only to an undefined requirement of the relevant crime being prevalent in the area, random virtue-testing becomes acceptable. In the context of a nightclub where drug dealing is suspected, this means that it is acceptable for anyone inside it to be approached by undercover officers and asked to supply them with drugs; there, in this example, being no need, beforehand, to identify likely dealers on the basis of prior surveillance.

6.69 It is submitted that this requirement in its diluted form is difficult to reconcile with *R v Looseley*, that arbitrary investigation is an unworthy form of state conduct.[1] Nonetheless, in the conjoined appeal with *Looseley*, *Attorney-General's Reference (No 3 of 2000)*, a lack of reasonable suspicion proved determinative to a finding by the House that the accused had been entrapped. Here, it was held that there were not any grounds to suspect that the accused, who was dealing in contraband cigarettes, also dealt in heroin. Accordingly, the offer to buy heroin from him by the undercover officers, was held as an example of state-created crime.

1 See, for example, per Lord Hoffmann at para 56.

THE LOOSELEY FACTORS FOR ENTRAPMENT

6.70 Lords Hoffmann and Nicholls emphasised that the boundary between acceptable and unacceptable state participation in criminal conduct depends upon a comprehensive review of the operation as a whole. The following extract from Lord Hoffmann's speech fairly describes this approach:

> '... the principles of English law on which a stay of proceedings may be granted on grounds of entrapment involve the consideration of a number of aspects of the behaviour of the law enforcement authorities, some of which I have examined in detail, and deciding whether the involvement of the court in the conviction of a defendant who had been subjected to such behaviour would compromise the integrity of the judicial system.'[1]

The relevant factors identified were as follows.

1 Above para **6.01**, at para 71.

Reasonable suspicion

6.71 Arbitrary investigations into citizens selected at random is considered an unworthy form of state abuse. Lord Hoffmann said:

> '... normally it is not considered a legitimate use of police power to provide people not suspected of being engaged in any criminal activity with the opportunity to commit crimes. The only proper purpose of police participation is to obtain evidence of criminal acts which they suspect someone is about to commit or in which he is already engaged. It is not to tempt people to commit crimes in order to expose their bad characters and punish them.'[1]

1 Above para **6.01**, at para 56.

6.72 Lord Nicholls confirmed that demonstrating reasonable suspicion was a way of confirming *bona fide* action:

> '[T]he police must act in good faith and not, for example, as part of a malicious vendetta against an individual or group of individuals. Having reasonable grounds for suspicion is one way good faith may be established, but having grounds for suspicion of a particular individual is not always essential.'[1]

1 At para 27.

6.73 The preference in *R v Looseley* for this factor is considered in detail above.[1] It is evident that the House of Lords did not require that suspicion has to be directed at a particular individual; it was sufficient that it attached to an area or an organisation. So, in the example of an alleged terrorist organisation, it is sufficient justification to target any member or representative. Lord Nicholls confirmed that:

'The defendant's criminal record is unlikely to be relevant unless it can be linked to other factors grounding reasonable suspicion that the defendant is currently engaged in criminal activity … [P]ast crimes do not forever outlaw the criminal and open him to police practices, aimed at securing repeated convictions, from which the ordinary citizen is protected…'[2]

1 Above para **6.67**.
2 At para 29.

Supervision

6.74 This was considered a critical factor, one necessary for the operation to be considered acceptable at all. Lord Hoffmann said:

> 'Although the United Kingdom technique for authorising and supervising such operations (as described in the Code of Practice) is very different from the judicial supervision in continental countries, the purpose is the same, namely to remove the risk of extortion, corruption or abuse of power by policemen operating without proper supervision.'[1]

1 Above para **6.01**, at para 72.

6.75 The necessary elements of proper supervision are as follows:

(i) Were the appropriate authorities obtained under the relevant statutory framework?[1] Seriousness of the alleged offence will not justify such provisions being ignored.

(ii) Was the conduct of the undercover officers monitored during the currency of the operation? For example, were the meetings between the officers and the target(s) recorded?

1 For example, the various codes of practice concerned with undercover operations and the authorisation requirements under RIPA 2000.

6.76 The ECtHR certainly regards proper authorisation as fundamental. In *Teixeira*, it was said that:

'The use of undercover agents must be restricted and safeguards put in place even in cases concerning the fight against drug-trafficking. While the rise in organised crime undoubtedly requires that appropriate measures be taken, the right to a fair administration of justice nevertheless holds such a prominent place that it cannot be sacrificed for the sake of expedience.'[1]

1 Above para **6.19**, at para 36. Similar sentiments were expressed in *Kopp v Switzerland* (1998) 27 EHRR 91, see especially para 64, where the court held that 'because of the lack of public scrutiny and the risk of misuse of power, the domestic law must provide some protection to the individual against arbitrary interference with Article 8 rights'.

The nature and extent of state participation in the crime: necessity, proportionality and 'unexceptional opportunity'

6.77 The following were considered as relevant factors:

(i) Necessity: Proactive conduct by officers may be acceptable in relation to consensual crimes which would otherwise be difficult to prosecute. Trafficking in drugs would be an example here where victims rarely report the crime and there are unlikely to be available witnesses.[1] In other words, such is the nature of the offence that evidence will only be obtained if undercover methods are used.

(ii) Proportionality: The greater the degree of intrusiveness, the more demanding will be the justification for resorting to this method. The test of proportionality applies here.[2] Essentially this factor is based on the seriousness of the suspected offence under investigation. Does it present a danger to society, such that the state has a duty to seek to thwart it? In relation to an alleged terrorist organisation or criminal gang, intrusiveness may be justified at least partly on the basis of past crimes and the overall threat posed to the public.

(iii) Unexceptional opportunity: Did the state do no more than give the accused an unexceptional opportunity to break the law of which he/she freely took advantage in circumstances in which it appears that, if the opportunity had been presented by someone who was not an agent, the accused would have acted similarly?[3] If so, then such conduct is unlikely to be regarded as inciting or instigating crime. Lord Nicholls quoted with approval McHugh J in *Ridgway v R*:[4]

> 'The state can justify the use of entrapment techniques to induce the commission of an offence only when the inducement is consistent with the ordinary temptations and stratagems that are likely to be encountered in the course of criminal activity. That may mean that some degree of deception, importunity and even threats on the part of the authorities may be acceptable. But once the State goes beyond the ordinary, it is likely to increase the incidence of crime by artificial means.'

Consequently, Lord Nicholls concluded that:

> 'The greater the inducement held out by the police, and the more forceful or persistent the police overtures, the more readily may a court conclude that the police overstepped the boundary … In assessing the weight to be attached to the police inducement, regard is to be had to the defendant's circumstances, including his vulnerability.'[5]

1 At paras 2 and 4.
2 At para 24.
3 At paras 53 to 55.
4 At para 23.
5 At para 28.

6.78 In relation to persuasion, if the accused was approached several times before agreeing to commit the offence, the state will need to justify why such persistence or persuasion was necessary and was not tantamount to incitement. On this point, Lord Hoffmann observed:

> 'Drug dealers can be expected to show some wariness about dealing with a stranger who might be a policeman or informer and therefore some protective colour in dress or manner as well as a certain degree of persistence may be necessary to achieve the objective. And it has been said that undercover officers who infiltrate conspiracies to murder, rob or commit terrorist offences could hardly remain concealed unless they showed some enthusiasm for the enterprise. A good deal of active behaviour in the course of an authorised operation may therefore be acceptable without crossing the boundary between causing the offence to be committed and providing an opportunity for the defendant to commit it.'[1]

1 Above para **6.01**, at paras 69 and 102.

6.79 On the basis of these factors, the House of Lords in *R v Looseley* recommended the approach for assessing complaints of entrapment, in other words, in determining whether the conduct of the state was so unworthy or shameful such that a prosecution based upon it would be an affront to the public conscience. It has been acknowledged that:

> 'While this may appear superficially attractive, its application is dependent on individual trial judges' perceptions of what might "ordinarily" be expected in particular situations involving criminality.'

Post-Looseley case law

6.80 The post-*Looseley* case law is notable for the restrictive manner in which the courts have applied the principles laid down by the House of Lords. What follows is a practical summary of cases that have been decided since *Looseley* to guide the practitioner.

6.81 The principle clearly still stands that 'entrapment of itself does not necessarily give rise to such an abuse of process as would require a stay of proceedings'.[1] The mere fact that an offence would not have been committed *but for* the actions of the police will not warrant a stay of proceedings. This is consistent with the views expressed in *Warren v Attorney General of Jersey* which confirmed that the 'but for' test is but one relevant factor to be taken into consideration when deciding on a stay for abuse of process.[2] It is not determinative.

1 *R v Lewis* [2005] EWCA Crim 859 at para 22.
2 [2012] 1 AC 22 at para 30. See further discussion in Chapter 5, para **5.14**.

6.82 An example of a successful appeal to the Court of Appeal on the ground of entrapment since *Looseley* can be found in *R v Moon.*[1] Moon was a vulnerable drug addict, with no predisposition to dealing, who was targeted and approached by police and asked (persistently) to supply an undercover officer with a small quantity of heroin, which she was to obtain from her dealer. Upon so doing, she told the undercover officer that she [the officer] was never to approach her again and that she would never help her again. Moon was charged and successfully prosecuted for possession with intent to supply the drug, the judge at first instance having refused to stay proceedings as an abuse of process on the ground of entrapment following a *voir dire*. The Court of Appeal held that Moon had been entrapped, taking into account the fact that she had only ever held the status of a drug addict, against whom there was no evidence of any previous dealing in or supply of heroin,[2] and that she had taken some persuading to commit the offence after taking sympathy on the undercover officer – who pretended to be an addict displaying the unhappy physical consequences of drug withdrawal[3] – such that she had been lured[4] into committing the offence.

1 [2004] EWCA Crim 2872, above para **6.05**.
2 At para 44.
3 See para 9.
4 At para 51.

6.83 Whilst *Looseley* established that a defendant's predisposition to commit an offence of the type concerned would not negate or preclude any claim made by him to have been entrapped ('predisposition does not negative misuse of state power'), the Court in *R v Moon* confirmed that:

> 'Nothing said there [in *Looseley*] by Lord Nicholls, however, would support a view that the *absence* of predisposition of a defendant to commit the crime in question is not relevant to the judge's consideration…'[1]

Whilst that observation is of benefit to the defendant of good character (or at least no previous convictions for offences of the same type as those for which he is to be tried) who makes claim to an entrapment, *R v Moon* displays the gravity of circumstances that must otherwise fall in a defendant's favour before a claim of entrapment is likely to succeed.

1 At para 29.

6.84 In *R v Holt,*[1] an extensive undercover police operation resulted in officers infiltrating a loose organisation which imported large quantities of cannabis into the UK. Holt was not initially in contact with the officers but, during their efforts to obtain evidence against the head of the organisation, he was introduced to them as being part of the operation, and evidence was consequently obtained against him as well. The Court of Appeal found that there was no reason for going behind the trial judge's conclusion – that Holt had not been entrapped – on that ground[2] and, more notably, affirmed that the Court '…is and should be slow to interfere with the judge who has clearly had regard to the correct principles of law and formed his own judgment as to what is and what is not fair in the trial of which he has the conduct.'[3]

1 [2003] EWCA Crim 1891.
2 At para 19.
3 At para 15.

6.85 In *R v Winter*,[1] the appellant told his friend (M) of his intention to kill his wife and M informed the police. The police authorised M covertly to record conversations between himself and the appellant in order to gather evidence in relation to the intended murder. The appellant was eventually convicted of two offences of soliciting murder and a third of attempting to pervert the course of justice. As well as recording conversations, the police had M introduce an undercover police officer (T) to the appellant on the pretence that T was an acquaintance of M's and would drive the appellant's car in the view of CCTV cameras on the day of the murder so as to provide the appellant with an alibi. The Court of Appeal held that there had been no entrapment. It is submitted that the claim of entrapment in that case was inherently weak in any event, as the offences for which the appellant had been convicted were by no means 'state-created crime'; the appellant's plan to murder his wife had been in place and was discussed with M before the police were contacted[2] (just as the appellant in *R v Holt* had been introduced to the undercover police officer through pre-existing drugs deals relating to intended drugs supply, seemingly with criminal intent in mind, rather than having been sought out or targeted by the police). The police in *Winter*'s case merely allowed the plan to continue (albeit facilitating the plan by the offer of an alibi) giving him only the opportunity that he had wished for to commit the offence of his own volition,[3] in such a way that it could be evidenced for the purposes of prosecution. The Court so held in dismissing the appeal: 'It is quite clear from the transcript that, whether or not the appellant had a driver to provide an alibi, he was going to commit the offence.'[4]

1 [2007] EWCA Crim 3493.
2 Note, at para 15, that even the appellant accepted that he could have been arrested and the plan stopped when M first contacted the police, suggesting that his real complaint was about the fact that the police had allowed the plan to continue and thus strengthened the case against him by the gathering of covert evidence.
3 At paras 28 and 33.
4 At para 30.

6.86 Interestingly, in *Jenkins v Government of the United States of America*,[1] the Administrative Court displayed its pre-*Looseley* willingness[2] to allow the courts to gauge whether the police had behaved as would an ordinary customer of trade being carried on by the defendant, even in cases concerning the highest level of criminal enterprise.[3] It might have been thought that only those involved in the sale of decommissioned radioactive metals could know how an ordinary customer of the trade would behave, the type of offending concerned being far removed from 'common place' crimes in which the typical actions of the perpetrators could easily be envisaged by the courts.

1 [2005] EWHC 1051 (Admin).
2 See above paras **6.43–6.51**.
3 See Sedley LJ para 20. This was an extradition case involving undercover police officers offering to supply the requested persons with drugs as payment for approximately £220m worth of radioactive material.

6.87 In *R v Jones (James)*,[1] the Court of Appeal considered the conduct of a person willing to offend. It held that a defendant had not been trapped into committing an offence of incitement to produce cannabis. The defendant was a shop owner selling smoking paraphernalia and hydroponics equipment, which could be used for the production of cannabis. He was approached by a police officer on four occasions who had asked for advice on growing cannabis. The defendant told the officer that it was illegal to grow cannabis and that he could only talk about tomato plants. He then gave the officer advice about growing 'tomatoes'. He was charged with incitement to produce.

1 [2010] EWCA Crim 925.

6.88 Lord Leveson confirmed that:

> '…the context within which this discussion [between the defendant and the undercover officer] took place is of very real significance'.[1]

The officer had been persistent, but the context of the officer's behaviour was that his enquiries would only have been made by a lay person who was prepared to break the law:

> '…the appropriate test would involve a member of the public interested in growing cannabis, that is to say, one who was prepared to break the law. Once that concession is made, it is simply not tenable to suggest that such a member of the public would have desisted: had the prospective purchaser not been prepared to consider breaking the law, there would have been no purpose (save only for the intellectually curious) in going into the shop.'[2]

1 At para 13.
2 At para 12.

6.89 The approach in *Looseley* had been correctly followed and it had to be borne in mind that 'a dealer in drugs will not voluntarily offer drugs to a stranger unless first approached, and that this approach may need to be and can be persistent without crossing the line'.[1]

1 At para 15.

6.90 The application of *Looseley* was considered again in *R v M*[1] in respect of the nature of appropriate police conduct during undercover operations. M was a drug addict with no convictions for supplying. He had been targeted by police as part of an undercover drugs operation. An undercover officer had befriended M and gained his confidence. He had then asked 'where can I get some white?' M had arranged for drugs to be delivered to the alleyway outside a public house. M and the officer had gone to the alleyway together. The drugs (diamorphine) were delivered by car and M had completed the deal for the officer as the latter was known to the dealers. He contended at his trial that he had been entrapped.

1 [2011] EWCA Crim 648.

6.91 The Court of Appeal acknowledged that the officer had cultivated a 'bond of trust and friendship' and that M was essentially helping out what he believed to be a fellow addict.[1] Stanley Burnton LJ, giving judgment noted that *Looseley* emphasised that, whether a prosecution is an abuse of the process by reason of the entrapment of the defendant, depends on the facts of each case.

In this case, the court noted that the officer had not asked M to supply him with drugs but asked where he could get them. It was also 'particularly significant' that there was:

> 'No pressure or persuasion was used by [the officer], who offered no inducement to M to commit the offence.'[2]

1 At para 9.
2 At para 14.

6.92 The Court of Appeal noted that:

> 'There may be a difficult line to draw between legitimate police conduct and improper entrapment. In general, however, conduct that is open to a finding of such entrapment as to render a prosecution improper involves some pressure or persuasion on the defendant to commit the crime. Providing the opportunity for the commission of the crime will not of itself lead to a finding of entrapment.'[1]

It was 'an inherent aspect of any undercover police operation' that the undercover police officer insinuated himself into the confidence of those involved in the criminal conduct at which the operation is directed. This was not entrapment. The judgment confirms that something more than an opportunity is required: there must be pressure or persuasion from state agents.

1 At para 15.

6.93 The Court of Appeal took a similarly broad approach in *R v Moore (Mia)*.[1] Here, the appellant claimed that undercover police officers had entrapped her into supplying cocaine after they had 'lured' her by supplying her with cheap goods which she could sell on for profit. The police were undertaking a surveillance operation. Moore was not an authorised target nor was she suspected of dealing in drugs, although her father and step-father were. She was asked whether she knew if 'anyone round here' had any cocaine, responding that she could obtain some and then doing so. The Court held that the assessment to be applied on the basis of the 'principles laid down in [*Looseley*] is very much a fact-sensitive matter' and the court would not interfere with the trial judge's assessment of the facts unless there was a serious error.[2]

1 [2013] EWCA Crim 85. See case comment A Robert, 'R v Moore (Mia): abuse of process' (2014) Crim. L.R. 364.
2 At para 49. This mirrors the approach taken in relation to abuse of process in *Warren v Attorney General of Jersey* [2012] 1 AC 22 at para 22, *R v Maxwell* [2011] 1 WLR 1837 at para 13.

6.94 In *Moore*, Lord Justice Rix noted that the 'the key question, if it is possible to isolate any such question' was, (referencing Lord Nicholls at para 25 in *Looseley*) whether the conduct of the police or other law enforcement agency was so seriously improper as to bring the administration of justice into disrepute.[1] In considering this key issue, the court approved of an article by Professor Ormerod[2] which identified five factors as of particular relevance:

(i) reasonable suspicion of criminal activity as a legitimate trigger for the police operation;

(ii) authorisation and supervision of the operation as a legitimate control mechanism;

(iii) necessity and proportionality of the means employed to police particular types of offence;

(iv) the concepts of the 'unexceptional opportunity' and causation; and

(iv) authentication of the evidence.[3]

1 At para 50.
2 *Recent Developments in Entrapment* [2006] Covert Policing Review 65.
3 Cited in *R v Moore* [2013] EWCA Crim 85 at [52].

6.95 Applying these criteria to the facts, the Court held that this was not 'random virtue testing' but that, following *Looseley*:

> 'there was plainly reasonable suspicion of drug dealing (and other criminality) in the Abbeywood area which justified the taking of covert policing operations. The fact that [the appellant] was, herself, not personally suspected in this context, nor a named target, is no doubt something to be taken into account: but as Lord Nicholls observed, having grounds for suspicion of a particular person is not always essential.'[1]

1 At para 68.

6.96 Additionally, Lord Rix held that:

> 'The conduct of the undercover officers was not so seriously improper as to bring the administration of justice into disrepute and there is no affront to the public conscience in these prosecutions. Although this case does not fit precisely into any particular mould, as reflected in decided cases, in our judgment the essence of it is similar to M and not to the Attorney General's Reference (No 3 of 2000). The undercover officers here did no more than provide Ms Moore with an opportunity, which she seized immediately and resolutely, to volunteer herself as a participant in substantial offending. They did not create her offending, indeed they even sought to distance her from it, but she persisted. This remains the case even if, as we assume, Ms Moore had never supplied drugs before and even if it could be said that, but for the opportunity created, she would not have done so on these occasions.'[1]

In *Moore*, 'reasonable suspicion' applied to a wide geographical area: this was not the 'public house' referenced by Lord Nicholls in *Looseley*. The defendant was hardly to be distinguished from many others within that area. The possibility of establishing entrapment was further curtailed by the high threshold established for police misconduct. The court confirmed that the conduct from state agents needs to be 'seriously improper' before a successful entrapment argument will be made out.

1 At para 76.

Non-compliance with procedural requirements

6.97 Improper conduct may, of course, arise from non-compliance with the procedural requirements of undercover work. The facts in *R v Chandler*[1] were similar to those in *R v Moon*[2] – an undercover police officer posed as a drug addict suffering a state of withdrawal and purchased class A drugs from the appellant, who was convicted of four counts of supplying the drugs. Unlike *R v Moon* however, the appellant in *Chandler* had displayed signs of being a drug dealer and was seemingly not lured into committing the offence. Applying the *Looseley* principles, the Court of Appeal found that there had been no entrapment and, on the facts of the case, there was nothing notable about the ruling to that extent.

1 [2002] EWCA Crim 3167.
2 Above para **6.82**.

6.98 However, in *R v Chandler* there was an absence of an unassailable record of the undercover officer's conversations with the appellant. The relevance of the absence of an unassailable record was not addressed in *Looseley* and the position therefore stood since it was decided in *R v Smurthwaite and Gill*,[1] that a record was desirable rather than an absolute requirement. It was argued that recordings enable the Court to assess the degree of pressure imposed on the suspect and his willingness to offend. It was submitted that the Courts should be loathe to admit evidence without recordings, even if the absence is explained as being to prevent an officer's cover being blown. However, the Court of Appeal concluded that:

> 'It seems to us that the position with regard to the absence of an unassailable record is and should continue to be regarded as it was stated in *Smurthwaite*; that is to say that the absence of an unassailable record is but one relevant factor to be taken into account in deciding whether or not to admit evidence from officers of what was said by defendants in the course of crimes committed in the context of undercover activity…The weight to be given to the absence of an unassailable record will vary from case to case. Where the conversation of which there is no unassailable record is substantially the whole of the evidence against a defendant, then the absence of an unassailable record will be a matter of greater importance than in a case where the conversation does not lie at the heart of the prosecution case and where there is substantial other evidence of what took place between the defendant and the officers…Another factor which is highly material to the question of what weight should be given to the absence of an unassailable record is the extent to which the oral evidence given by the officer of what took place during the conversation is contested. In a case where there is a stark and fundamental conflict of evidence between the police officer or officers on the one hand and the defendant on the other as to what was said, then the absence of an unassailable record will plainly be a more important factor than in a case where there is little or no such dispute.'[2]

1 Above para **6.30**.
2 At paras 44–46.

Non-authorisation

6.99 It will be recalled that the House of Lords, in *R v Looseley*, regarded proper authorisation as a condition precedent, a critical factor.[1] One of the factors that caused the Court of Appeal to allow the appeal against conviction in *R v Moon*[2] was that the police operation had not been authorised.[3]

1 Above paras **6.74–6.76**.
2 Above para **6.82**.
3 See paras 50–51: 'Thus whether the matter is looked through the lens of the proper safeguards of authorisation, or through the lens of the appellant's absence of predisposition or antecedents, or through the lens of the actual nature of the police activities in relation to this appellant, the conclusion to which we are driven is that this appellant was lured into crime or was entrapped, and that it was a case of causing crime rather than merely providing an opportunity for it, and ultimately that it would be unfair for the state to prosecute her for this offending.'

6.100 *R v Harmes and Crane*[1] concerned procedural non-compliance of the police in conducting proactive investigatory techniques. The appellant relied heavily on this in arguing that his prosecution should have been stayed as an abuse of process on the basis of entrapment.[2] The police actions had breached the provisions of the Regulation of Investigatory Powers Act 2000 ('RIPA') and the Covert Human Intelligence Sources Codes of Practice ('the Codes of Practice'), made under RIPA, s 71. In respect of the extent of the violations of those provisions, the Court observed that:

> 'In our judgment there were serious breaches of the Act and the Code in the process of authorisation [of the undercover operation]. The importance of compliance with the Act and Code in the procedure to be adopted for authorisation should not be underestimated. Absent careful compliance with the requirements of the Act and of the Code, the purpose of the Act is frustrated. Without a careful record of that which is proposed and approved, a court is deprived of the opportunity of assessing whether the undercover actions of officers are necessary and proportionate…The suggestion, which admittedly came from the officers, that they should be supplied with cocaine in exchange for the soft drinks, was a crime. It was not authorised. That it was merely a small part in infiltrating what was suspected to be a gang of drug smugglers may be relevant to the question of the proportionality of the operation viewed as a whole. But the judge misdirected herself as to the criminal nature of the officers' activities at this point in her ruling…We conclude that, for the reasons we have given, there were substantial defects in the process of authorisation in the instant case. There is no evidence that it was impracticable to obtain authorisation for what was done in advance. Such authorisation was not obtained.'[3]

1 [2006] EWCA Crim 928.
2 The police had infiltrated a criminal conspiracy in the importation of drugs. The appellant Harmes had himself revealed to the undercover officers a system of drugs importation by which the major importation of cocaine (200 kilos) was to take place; although the police had played a role in the initial deal that instigated trade between themselves and the appellants (Harmes had been supplied with soft drinks, which he needed to facilitate his criminal enterprise, in exchange for a small amount of drugs). Counsel for Harmes contended that he had been entrapped because, even though the initial deal with the soft drinks did not trap the appellants into the major conspiracy, it had been the trigger for the revelation of the system by which the major drugs importation would take place.
3 At paras 42 and 45–46.

6.101 In determining what the Court of Appeal regarded as the 'essential issue in [the] case…[of] whether the undercover officers' declared willingness to deal in drugs and the officers' own criminal conduct was such that the prosecution for conspiracy should have been stayed', the Court of Appeal ruled that: 'The breach of the Code is an important factor but not dispositive.'[1] Ultimately, the Court of Appeal ruled that the trial judge had correctly concluded that it was the 'hope of big returns for himself' that caused Harmes to partake in the offences for which he was convicted and, for that reason, there was no entrapment to which non-authorisation could attach as a factor militating in favour of a stay. In dismissing the appeal, the Court held that:

> 'We have already concluded that the officers' conduct was criminal and it was not properly authorised. Nonetheless, we take the view that it should not be regarded as so seriously improper as to require the court to intervene to prevent the prosecution for conspiracy. It was conduct which merely exposed, for the purposes of the undercover operation, the undercover officers' interest in drugs and eagerness to receive a small quantity. That was, in our judgment, no more than might be expected of any criminal willing to engage in illicit dealing in drugs…Undercover officers, seeking to expose drug dealers, must show enthusiasm and a degree of persistence to provide protection for their undercover activities. As Lord Hoffmann accepts [in *R v Looseley*], a good deal of active behaviour may be acceptable (see paragraph 69).
>
> In our judgment the conduct of the police officers was not exceptional and did not go beyond that which was necessary to show their willingness to deal in drugs. An exchange of a small amount of cocaine triggered the revelation that these defendants were not only happy to import very substantial quantities of cocaine but had the ability to do so. The officers' activities pale into insignificance in comparison to the offers made by Harmes to import, on their behalf, large amounts of cocaine of a high value.
>
> … But in our judgment, the trial judge, whilst underestimating the breaches of the Code, correctly concluded that the prosecution for conspiracy should not be stayed. The officers' conduct, viewed as a whole, did not stray beyond that which was permissible to investigate and prosecute crime. In the instant case, that which had originally been suspected, namely, that the appellants were members of a gang engaged in the distribution of large amounts of cocaine, proved to be only too true.'[2]

1 At para 47.
2 At paras 51–52 and 54.

6.102 Whilst the Court's approach to the issues in *R v Chandler* and *R v Harmes* is in keeping with the fact-dependent nature of almost all issues that arise in entrapment cases, the intrusive nature of the policing technique employed in such cases might engender an intuitive desire to ensure that unassailable records are kept and the Codes of Practice are complied with in all such cases. It is difficult to envisage an undercover operation in which the Codes might be violated to a greater extent than they were in *Harmes*.

6.103 Nevertheless, in *R v Brett*[1] the Court of Appeal reiterated the significance of adherence to RIPA and the Codes of Practice, saying, at para 14, that:

'… if the requirements of section 29 [of RIPA] and indeed the [Code of Practice] were shown to have been flouted or ignored by the police, that circumstance might very well give rise to an inference that the conduct of the police or prosecution was indeed seriously improper within the approach given by [*R v Looseley*]'.

In that case, the Court found that it was not seriously improper, unnecessary, or disproportionate for the police to have directed their undercover operation against the appellant, whose conviction was upheld.

1 [2005] EWCA Crim 983.

6.104 The Court of Appeal has, therefore, refused to erect a strict hurdle over which the prosecuting authorities must jump (by compliance with the Codes of Practice, for example) to ensure that a case is not automatically stayed as an abuse on the ground of entrapment, even where the statutory safeguards in place for the benefit of a defendant have been flagrantly ignored and violated. Non-authorisation and procedural non-compliance remain but two of the myriad factors that feed into entrapment abuse judgments, none being determinative at the absolute discretion of the trial court.

6.105 In *R v Jones*[1] the appellant had left graffiti messages on toilets and trains asking girls of eight to thirteen years of age for sex, offering payment in return and leaving his contact number. A journalist instigated contact with the appellant before informing the police, who struck up a 'relationship' with the appellant through an officer posing as a girl of 12 years of age and arrested him at an arranged meeting place. Much of the case regarded the interpretation of s 8 of the Sexual Offences Act 2003, the appellant arguing (unsuccessfully) that the offence was not made out because he was in fact not in contact with a 12-year-old girl, and only believed that he was because the police had, arbitrarily by his contention, chosen that age when in contact with the appellant so as to make out a charge under s 8 of the Act. The appellant argued that he had been entrapped by the conduct of the police generally and that the offence amounted to state-created crime because no offence under s 8 would have been committed had the police not pretended to be a girl of 12 years of age.

1 [2008] 1 QB 460, CA.

6.106 With regard to the choice of the fictitious girl's age, the court found that, as 'the essence of the criminality is in the incitement … the crime does not need an identifiable person as the object of the incitement.'[1] The offence could not, therefore, amount to state-created crime by virtue of the police choosing the age of 12 when making contact with the appellant, not least because he had offered sex to girls between eight and thirteen in his graffiti.

1 At paras 16 and 22.

6.107 Of significance in more general terms was the Court's finding that the actions of the police on the whole did not amount to entrapment, notwithstanding the protracted contact they had engaged in with the defendant. In finding that the police did no more than offer the appellant an opportunity to commit the offence, and that given the nature of the offence,[1] the investigative technique used was necessary to gather evidence to bring the prosecution at all,[2] the Court placed weight on the fact that the police officer's conduct in relation to the appellant followed on from the actions as between the appellant and the journalist who instigated the contact:

> '…It is also relevant to take into account the actions of the journalist in answering the [graffiti] message as a further measure by which the acceptability of the conduct of the police can be judged…'[3]

1 At para 21.
2 At para 28.
3 At para 32.

6.108 Whilst the court, in making that observation, was clearly using the journalist's conduct as a yardstick by which to judge whether the police officer's actions were no more than might have been expected of any ordinary member of the public, this consideration suggests that where, as with *R v Winter*,[1] the police simply facilitate the continuance of a course of conduct in which the defendant is already engaged so as to found a prosecution, that is a factor that will weigh strongly against a finding that there has been an entrapment. Such a conclusion also appears to legitimise the actions of the journalist in the first place, as something of a private entrapper (or at least suggests that the defendant could not have proper complaint at having been entrapped by the journalist to begin with). This raises the question of the extent to which a defendant might claim to have been the victim of entrapment committed by a private party. Does the defendant have any recourse in such circumstances? If so, to what extent do the courts offer protection against 'private entrapment'? These questions are considered further below at para **6.109**.

1 Discussed above at para **6.85**.

6.109 Finally, in *Syed (Haroon)*,[1] the Court of Appeal reviewed the European jurisprudence since *Looseley*, and held that the approach in *Looseley* remained compliant with Art 6 of the ECHR.

In this case, the Applicant pleaded guilty to the preparation of terrorist acts contrary to the Terrorism Act 2006, s 51. Between 13 April 2016 and the applicant's arrest on 8 September 2016, Security Service officers posing as 'Abu Yusuf' communicated with the applicant via social media. The Crown's case was that during these online conversations, the applicant engaged in what he believed to be the purchase of weapons, a bomb, and target research for an attack in the UK. The defence case was that the applicant had been targeted and groomed, and therefore he had been subject to state entrapment.

The trial court refused the defence application to stay the proceedings. The Court of Appeal similarly dismissed the application to appeal and treated the burden of proof to be upon the Applicant to demonstrate that he had been lured into committing the offence by a state agent. In doing so, the Court of Appeal quoted extensively from *Looseley*, specifically quoting the test of 'unexceptional opportunity'. The judgment demonstrates the contextually sensitive approach required to examine the issue of 'unexceptional opportunity'. The Court examined the content of the online chat material and concluded that the Applicant was in the 'driving seat' and already planning the actions when he first made contact with Abu Yusuf.[2]

The Court also addressed the ECtHR jurisprudence and the Applicant's submission that the domestic jurisprudence was taking a different approach to police incitement, such that it was incompatible with Art 6(1). The Court found there was no material difference between English law and the Strasbourg jurisprudence and that the underlying rationale in both systems was to protect the integrity of the justice system. As such, the Court clarified the approach taken by the House of Lords in *Looseley*, in which focus was placed upon whether the defendant was presented with an 'unexceptional opportunity' to commit an offence, remained compliant with Art 6(1).

The Court again applied the five factors as set out by Ormerod and considered in *Moore*[3] to conclude that on the facts of this case there was reasonable suspicion, authorisation and supervision were not in issue, the necessity and proportionality of the means could not be questioned and the players did not go beyond giving the Applicant an 'unexceptional opportunity of committing the offence'.[4] It is submitted therefore that these factors can be deemed to be the principles that practitioners should focus on when considering entrapment.

In respect of whether the Strasbourg jurisprudence places the burden of proof upon the prosecution, the Court of Appeal stated that it was not clear from the relevant cases the extent to which this is in fact the position. The Court stated that, since there was no entrapment on these facts, further exploration of this issue would have to await a case where it was necessary for the decision. Such a case is still awaited.

1 [2018] EWCA Crim 2809, [2019] 1 WLR 2459.
2 See para 124.
3 See para **6.94** above.
4 [2018] EWCA Crim 2809, [2019] 1 WLR 2459 at para 129.

PRIVATE OR NON-STATE ENTRAPMENT

6.110 Although the *Looseley* principles apply to state actors, there are now authorities addressing the application of these principles in cases of private or non-state entrapment.

Before examining these authorities, it is important to note that private prosecutions may be stayed as an abuse of process. In *R (on the application of Dacre) v Westminster Magistrates' Court*,[1] the court held that the District Judge should have stayed a private prosecution brought against a newspaper. In this case the grounds for the abuse were not entrapment, but were based upon the motive of the prosecutor.[2] However, this demonstrates that a private prosecution is capable of amounting to an abuse.

1 [2008] EWHC 1667 (Admin).
2 See para **4.17**.

6.111 But what of the cases of private individuals, acting in a manner that may constitute entrapment? For example, journalism based on the deception and entrapment of celebrities or those in the public eye by undercover newspaper reporters. There has also been a rise in citizen groups aiming to expose adults seeking to have sex with children, using undercover methods such as posing as children in online chatrooms to do so.

6.112 Private forms of entrapment are, by their nature, not carried out by state agents and may not even be conducted for law enforcement purposes.[1] Seeing the celebrity ultimately prosecuted based on evidence obtained by undercover journalists may constitute a public interest purpose but the rationale for the 'sting' is to increase circulation and to entertain the readership. In *Morley and Hutton*[2] in 1994, the Court of Appeal observed that:

> 'Although one might dislike the activities of certain informants or journalists, the criterion for admissibility did not depend on this or the motive of a newspaper to sell a story or make money. It was clear that there was no defence in English law of entrapment, and it made no difference whether an undercover officer or a journalist was involved… [The appellants] were not making admissions which might be unreliable but actually committing offences in front of the camera. They were not enticed or provoked by the reporter to commit offences.'

1 For further discussion, see Hofmeyr, 'The problem of private entrapment', (2006) Crim. L.R. 319.

2 [1994] Crim LR 919, CA. That the identity and motives of the entrapper were not primarily concerned with law enforcement, but for a private commercial purpose, was also held to be immaterial in *R v Tonnessen* [1998] 2 Cr App R (S) 328, CA.

6.113 The leading case of *Looseley* was focused on state agents. There is an inherent difficulty in applying these principles to non-state actors. *R v TL*[1] is the most recent and perhaps leading case on private entrapment. It leaves the door open for proceedings that follow a situation of private entrapment to be stayed. However, it is submitted that the case sets such stringent tests for a stay in these circumstances, that the possibility of a successful application will be a rarity.

1 [2018] EWCA Crim 1821.

Early authorities

6.114 In *R v Shannon*[1] an actor from the then popular television show *London's Burning* was steered into supplying drugs for a party by a *News of the World* journalist. Shortly afterwards, the newspaper published a front-page article under the headline 'London's Burning Star is Cocaine Dealer', based on the evidence of drug offences procured by the sting. The actor was later prosecuted for offences involving drugs supply, and the Crown relied primarily upon evidence collected by the newspaper. Shannon was subsequently convicted, having failed in his attempt to have the evidence excluded under s 78 of PACE on the basis of entrapment, and appealed against the decision to admit that evidence.

1 Above para **6.61**.

6.115 In dismissing the appeal, Potter LJ rejected an argument that commercial entrapment was unworthy and that, in such cases, the incitement or encouragement of journalists to commit the offence should found a stay. In Potter LJ's view, the principles to be considered were the same as those in proactive policing cases. Citizens do not enjoy any right not to be tempted by either law enforcement or private agents. Potter LJ endorsed the trial judge's observations that:

> 'In so far as abuse of process considerations might be relevant, there was no suggestion of criticism of the part played by the police or Crown Prosecution Service, the organs of the state responsible for gathering and presenting the evidence and of instituting proceedings …, [If the unfairness complained of by the defendant was no more than] … a visceral reaction that it is in principle unfair as a matter of policy, or wrong as a matter of law, for a person to be prosecuted for a crime which he would not have committed without the incitement or encouragement of others, then it is not itself sufficient, unless the behaviour of the police (or someone acting on behalf of or in league with the police) and/or the prosecuting authority has been such as to justify a stay on the grounds of abuse of process.'

6.116 These passages suggest that the subsequent conduct of the police and/or the prosecuting authority is a determinative factor of an application for a stay of proceedings on the grounds of abuse of process in cases involving private entrapment.

6.117 This was further demonstrated in the case of *R v Hardwicke and Thwaites.*[1] In this case the Earl of Hardwicke and his co-defendant had been plied with alcohol at the Savoy Hotel by undercover journalists, including the same journalist who had conducted the sting in *Shannon*. They posed as business people interested in the sale of motor scooters for export to the Middle East. The journalists steered the alcohol-induced conversations towards drug use and the appellants eventually arranged for the group to be supplied with heroin. They were subsequently prosecuted and convicted for that supply on the evidence obtained by the undercover journalists.

1 (2000) Times, November 16, CA.

6.118 When returning their guilty verdicts the jury added this rider:

> 'The jury would like to say that the circumstances surrounding this case have made it very difficult for us to reach a decision. Had we been allowed to take the extreme provocation into account we would undoubtedly have reached a different verdict.'[1]

1 At para 10.

6.119 The rider plainly demonstrated the sense of discomfort that the jury held at the thought of a criminal prosecution being founded upon private entrapment. The appellant Hardwicke understandably took the point, on the strength of the rider, that his conviction amounted to an affront to the public conscience.[1] The Court of Appeal nevertheless stressed the difference between the extent to which an appellant might rely upon their prosecution bringing the system into disrepute when there has been malpractice by the state as compared with the extent to which it can be relied upon in cases of private entrapment;

> 'It is of some importance to note that what [*R v Latif*[2]] seeks not to condone is "malpractice by law enforcement agencies" which "would undermine

public confidence in the criminal justice system and bring it into disrepute". Obviously that is not a consideration which applies with anything like the same force when the investigator allegedly guilty of malpractice is outside the criminal justice system altogether.'[3]

1 At para 34.
2 Above para **6.13**.
3 At para 22.

Recent case law

6.120 The apparent need for a defendant to be entrapped at the hands of *the state* in order for a stay to be granted was demonstrated upon Shannon's application for leave to appeal to the ECtHR,[1] which rejected the application as 'manifestly ill-founded'. It should be recalled that the appeal was based upon the refusal of the trial judge to exclude the evidence obtained by the *News of the World* under s 78 of PACE,[2] rather than to have the proceedings stayed as an abuse of process. Nonetheless, considering its earlier ruling in *Teixeira de Castro*[3] on entrapment, the ECtHR observed that:

> '… [I]n the first place that, in concluding that the applicant was from the outset deprived of a fair trial, the Court in its *Teixeira* judgment was addressing the facts and circumstances of the case before it. The Court recalls that, as emphasised by the national courts, the *Teixeira* case was concerned with an entrapment operation undertaken by police officers and that the Court's judgment did not address the question of entrapment by individuals other than agents of the State. The operation which was there being examined constituted a misuse of State power, the police officers having gone beyond their legitimate role as undercover agents obtaining evidence against a suspected offender to incite the commission of the offence itself. The Court considers that the principles set out in the *Teixeira* judgment are to be viewed in this context and to be seen as principally directed to the use in a criminal trial of evidence gained by means of an entrapment operation carried out by or on behalf of the State or its agents.'

1 *Shannon v the United Kingdom* (Application No 67537/01, Fourth Section, 6 April 2004).
2 The ECtHR found that there was no reason to question the assessment of the domestic courts in deciding to admit the evidence concerned, and that it could not reach a different conclusion as to the admission of that evidence on its own examination of the material before it.
3 Above para **6.19**.

6.121 Whilst the ECtHR held against Shannon, it must be observed that neither *Teixeira* nor *R v Looseley* involved any consideration of the extent to which the principles laid down in respect of police entrapment would apply to cases of private entrapment. This simply was not an issue in the matters before them.

6.122 In *R v Marriner*,[1] the defendants were members of a group of organised football fans convicted of committing a series of violent offences as part of that group. The evidence was obtained by undercover journalists reporting for the programme *MacIntyre Undercover*. The journalists themselves committed illegal acts and employed 'undoubted flattery, wheedling, falsehoods and the making of apparent offers of legitimate and illegitimate business' as part of a 'journalistic operation'[2] through which the evidence was procured.

1 [2002] EWCA Crim 2855.
2 At para 39.

6.123 Despite the 'elaborate trick' that had been played by the journalists, the Court of Appeal held that the trial judge properly left the evidence obtained by them to the jury and dismissed the appeal brought on the ground that the prosecution should have been stayed as an abuse of process,[1] noting that:

> 'The present case is not concerned with conduct of the police or prosecuting authorities. The inducements to talk were applied in quite different circumstances and were of a quite different order. The judge was in the best position to evaluate whether it was fair to allow the proceedings to go before the jury on their basis, and we consider that his decision to do so cannot be faulted.'[2]

1 Considered in the context of the appellants' submission that their privacy had been infringed, as the ECtHR had held in *Allan v United Kingdom* (2003) 36 EHRR 12.
2 At para 39.

6.124 In *R v Paulssen,*[1] the defendant was held in custody on remand awaiting trial for conspiracy to defraud. He had sought the help of a fellow inmate (MG) to murder a co-defendant in the conspiracy case. MG informed the police and, via a plan devised by the police, introduced an undercover police officer (David) to the defendant on the pretence that David would offer his services as a hit-man to carry out the killing. The defendant applied for permission to appeal against his convictions for soliciting both MG and the undercover officer to murder on the ground of entrapment. Much of the Court of Appeal's ruling deals with the issue of whether a conviction stemming out of a guilty plea might be 'unsafe',[2] with the result that the submissions focused on the concept of convictions in such circumstances being an 'affront to justice' rather than considering the wider definition and remedies available in cases of private entrapment.

1 [2003] EWCA Crim 3109.
2 For specific consideration of this issue see *R v Togher* [2001] 3 All ER 463, CA and *R v Rajcoomar* [1999] Crim LR 728, CA.

6.125 Nonetheless, in dismissing the application the Court of Appeal noted that any entrapment that might have occurred, in so far as the defendant might have been entrapped to solicit MG to murder, took place without the authorisation of the police (ie before they were informed of the plan by MG), who duly authorised the continuance of the operation when they became involved.[1] This highlights the role of the state as being a fundamental factor in deciding whether proceedings should be stayed as an abuse of process, although it is difficult to see how there could have been entrapment at any point in this case when its similarity with the facts[2] in the (albeit later) case of *Winter*[3] is considered.

1 At para 48.
2 In particular, see paras 9, 10, 11 and 18, relating to the trial judge's ruling that the offence of soliciting MG to murder was complete before MG left the prison, again noting that anything that MG did to 'entrap' the appellant was done without the authority of the State and therefore did not amount to a basis upon which to stay proceedings.
3 Above para **6.85**.

Re Saluja

6.126 *Council for the Regulation of Healthcare Professionals v General Medical Council (Re Saluja)*[1] was a quasi-criminal case in which a doctor (S) was charged before the GMC with serious professional misconduct for providing a sickness certificate to an undercover journalist posing as a patient. The patient had asked for the certificate to enable her to take time off work and have a holiday, S knowing that she was not sick at all. The tribunal at first instance, the Fitness to Practice Panel of the GMC, found that S had been entrapped and the proceedings against him were stayed. The Council for the Regulation of Healthcare Professionals appealed to the Administrative Court.

1 [2007] 1 WLR 3094, DC.

6.127 The Council argued that, on a proper analysis, abuse of process was essentially about deliberate misuse of executive power, but accepted that there might be exceptional cases where conduct by non-state agents might found a basis for a stay of proceedings. The Council submitted that the panel had therefore fallen into error[1] in failing to draw the distinction between journalists and agents of the state in merely substituting journalists for police in the test set out in *Looseley*.

1 Paras 97–98.

6.128 Goldring J reviewed the earlier authorities and derived from them the following nine points of law to be applied to a private entrapment case:[1]

> '[79]. First, to impose a stay is exceptional.
>
> [80]. Second, the principle behind it is the court's repugnance in permitting its process to be used in the face of the executive's misuse of state power by its agents. To involve the court in convicting a defendant who has been the victim of such misuse of state power would compromise the integrity of the judicial system.
>
> [81]. Third, as both domestic and European authority make plain, the position as far as misconduct of non-state agents is concerned, is wholly different. By definition no question arises in such a case of the state seeking to rely upon evidence which by its own misuse of power it has effectively created. The rationale of the doctrine of abuse of process is therefore absent. *However, the authorities leave open the possibility of a successful application of a stay on the basis of entrapment by non-state agents. The reasoning I take to be this: given sufficiently gross misconduct by the non-state agent, it would be an abuse of the court's process (and a breach of article 6) for the state to seek to rely on the resulting evidence. In other words, so serious would the conduct of the non-state agent have to be that reliance upon it in the court's proceedings would compromise the court's integrity.* There has been no reported case of the higher courts, domestic or European, in which such 'commercial lawlessness' has founded a successful application for a stay. That is not surprising. The situations in which that might arise must be very rare indeed. [emphasis added]

[82]. As will become apparent, I do not accept that for a journalist to go into a doctor's surgery and pretend to be a patient in circumstances such as the present is similar to abuse of power by an agent of the state.

[83]. Fourth, in the present disciplinary hearing there is no state involvement in the proceedings being brought. These are proceedings brought against a doctor by his regulator in order to protect the public, uphold professional standards and maintain confidence in the profession. These are to a significant degree different considerations from those that apply to a criminal prosecution and misuse of executive powers by the state's agents.

[84]. Fifth, it would be an error of law in considering any application for abuse of process for the tribunal not to have well in mind the differences to which I have referred. It would not be appropriate for an FPP to approach the conduct of journalists as though they were agents of the state.

[85]. Sixth, "commercial lawlessness" can be a factor in an application to exclude evidence under section 78, although again different considerations apply as between state and non-state agents.

[86]. Seventh, when deciding in any given case whether there has been an abuse of process, the tribunal, here the FPP, is exercising a discretion. In doing so, it must consider all the facts of the case as well as the factors to which I have already referred. While guidance can be obtained from such aspects as were referred to in *R v Looseley* [2001] 1 WLR 2060, no one aspect is determinative and the aspects there set out are not exhaustive.

[87]. Eighth, if the defendant's article 8 rights have been infringed that is merely a matter to be taken into account when deciding whether there has been an abuse of process or, (and it amounts to the same thing), his article 6 rights have been infringed: see for example *R v P* [2002] 1 AC 146 and *Jones v University of Warwick* [2003] 1 WLR 954.

[88]. Ninth, section 78 is concerned with the admissibility of evidence. As Lord Nicholls said in *R v Looseley* [2001] 1 WLR 2060, para 12, it is directed primarily at matters going to the fairness of the conduct of the trial; the reliability of the evidence, how the defendant might test it and so on. Entrapment does not mean the evidence must be excluded. It is a factor to take into account. In considering broader matters going to fairness it is necessary to bear in mind the features referred to above (among others)'.

1 At paras 79–88.

6.129 In ruling for the Council, Goldring J thus made clear that the position as far as misconduct of non-state agents was concerned was wholly different from misconduct of state agents.[1] He left open the possibility of a successful application for a stay on the basis of entrapment by non-state agents in exceptional cases. He found that, had the panel applied the law properly in that regard, it would not have stayed proceedings as an abuse of process. For a journalist to go into a doctor's surgery and pretend to be a patient in circumstances similar to those in this case would seemingly be no more than to offer the doctor an unexceptional opportunity to commit the offence in any event, such that it is unlikely that the facts of this case, if undertaken with state authority, would ever have amounted to an entrapment, even on the *Looseley* guidelines.[2]

1 At para 125.
2 See paras 3, 10, 129 and, by way of comparison, para 73 of the judgment.

6.130 *Re Saluja* at its highest, in relation to alleged misconduct by non-state agents such as journalists, can be said to leave open the possibility of a stay on the basis that, in the case of sufficiently gross misconduct it might be an abuse for the state to rely on the resulting evidence.[1]

1 *Besnik Qema v News Group Newspapers Limited* [2012] EWHC 1146 (QB) at para 60.

R v TL

6.131 Most recently, in *TL*,[1] the prosecution appealed against the trial Judge's decision to stay proceedings as an abuse of process. This was a case concerning a group calling themselves 'Predator Hunters', set up to try and expose adults seeking to have sex with children. One of their members, Mr U, posed as a 14-year-old girl in an online chatroom. The Defendant was accused of communicating online with this person, a girl whom he believed to be 14 years old and arranging for this girl to go his flat to take part in a threesome with his girlfriend. Mr U tipped off the police and when he and others attended the Defendant's flat, the Defendant was arrested. The trial judge stayed the prosecution as an abuse of process. The prosecution then successfully appealed this determination. The Court of Appeal held that the trial judge had wrongly failed to distinguish between the behaviour of the state, as envisaged in the decision in *Looseley*, and that of a private citizen, in considering whether to stay a prosecution. After setting out the relevant principles in *Looseley,* the court then considered those in *Saluja*, making reference to Golding J's conclusion that a stay in cases of alleged entrapment by a non-state actor was exceptional.[2]

The court set out the following:

> 'Consideration of the speeches in the *Looseley* case demonstrates that the principles there explained apply to the conduct of agents of the state. Involvement of agents of the state in unacceptable behaviour is at the heart of the reasoning. It is the court's unwillingness to approbate seriously wrongful conduct by the state, by entertaining a prosecution, that is the foundation of this aspect of the abuse jurisdiction. So much is clear from *Looseley* itself and was recognised in *Shannon* in both the domestic proceedings and in Strasbourg and also in *Marriner*. The judge's approach allowed no distinction between the conduct of Mr U, as a private citizen, and agents of the state, when considering whether to stay the prosecution as an abuse of process. In our judgment he erred in that respect. For that reason, the judge's conclusion cannot be supported.
>
> In both domestic jurisprudence [*Saluja*] and in Strasbourg when looking at conduct for the purposes of article 6 [*Shannon*] there is a recognition that the conduct of a private citizen may in theory found a stay of proceedings as an abuse of process. As Goldring J recognised in the

former case, no question of the state seeking to rely upon evidence which flows from its own misuse of power arises. The underlying purpose of the doctrine of abuse of process is not present. Nonetheless, a prosecution needs evidence; and it is not inconceivable that given sufficiently gross misconduct by a private citizen, it would be an abuse of the court's process (and a breach of article 6) for the state to seek to rely on the product of that misconduct. The issue would be the same: would the prosecution be "deeply offensive to ordinary notions of fairness" or "an affront to the public conscience" or "so seriously improper as to bring the administration of justice into disrepute". In other words, as Goldring J put it: "so serious would the conduct of the non-state actor have to be that reliance upon it in the court's proceedings would compromise the court's integrity". He observed that there had been no reported case in which such activity has founded a successful application for a stay. Like him, we do not find that surprising. Given the absence of state impropriety, the situations in which that might occur would be rare.'

The court then sought to examine the behaviour of Mr U. concluding that he had committed no offences in the course of his conduct and at no time did he take the lead. As such, 'A starting point in considering whether the conduct of a private citizen should result in a stay of proceedings is to ask whether the same, or similar, conduct by a police officer would do so. A precise comparison may be difficult because when the police or other state investigators or prosecutors act in this way, they do so subject to codes of conduct and strict hierarchical oversight.'[3] The court concluded that 'If police officers had engaged in broadly similar conduct an application to stay the proceedings as an abuse of process should have failed'.[4]

1 [2018] EWCA Crim 1821.
2 [2018] EWCA Crim 1821 at para 28.
3 [2018] EWCA Crim 1821 at para 35.
4 [2018] EWCA Crim 1821 at para 37.

Conclusions on private entrapment

6.132 *TL* clearly allows the possibility for an abuse of process doctrine in cases of private entrapment. However, it is submitted that the circumstances where such an abuse will be founded will be very rare. Such circumstances are yet to be defined clearly and the authority does not provide a practical benchmark to measure such egregious behaviour, beyond stating that the starting point is to consider the same conduct as carried out by the police/state. It is submitted that a defendant who has been the victim of a private entrapment is, in reality, likely to have better potential recourse by way of an application to exclude the evidence under s 78 of PACE rather than an application to stay as an abuse.

6.133 Both *Saluja* and *TL* invite the question of what amounts to 'gross misconduct', or conduct of a non-state agent 'so serious' as to merit a stay of proceedings for these purposes. Bearing in mind the preceding authorities, both in relation to commercial and state entrapment,[1] it might be suggested that 'gross misconduct' and conduct 'so serious' as to warrant a stay might mean conduct which (i) preys upon the vulnerability of a defendant whose capacity to resist the course of action being encouraged by the entrapper is seriously impaired,[2] (ii) amounts to a violation of the defendant's human rights by the non-state agent or (iii) is driven by a real degree of bad faith on their part – with malicious intent towards the victim of the entrapment in mind. Although this list is by no means intended to be exhaustive, it seems that, in reality, only considerations such as these would be likely to render the state's subsequent reliance on evidence obtained by non-state agents an abuse of process in and of itself.

1 Recalling the case of *R v Moon* (discussed above para **6.82**), Goldring J's ruling in *Re Saluja*, that a different threshold needs to be met for a stay to be granted in cases of private entrapment as compared with cases of entrapment by state agents, one wonders whether the proceedings against the defendant in *Moon* would have been stayed as an entrapment had she been persuaded to sell drugs to an undercover journalist reporting, say, on the prevalence of street drug dealing in the UK or in a particular area of the country, rather than by a police officer. In those circumstances, *Moon* would surely still have been on strong ground in arguing that her conviction would affront the public conscience, given that the basis upon which the Court of Appeal ruled that she had been entrapped related in the main part to her state of mind as a drug addict, who supplied drugs out of sympathy to another 'addict' who was displaying the symptoms of withdrawal, ie even if the police did not positively act in bad faith in persuading *Moon* to supply drugs, the effect of that persuasion on a person in her vulnerable position rendered a stay of proceedings appropriate.

2 See the discussion of *R v Moon* at para **6.82** above.

Entrapment as mitigation

6.134 As most defendants who lay claim to having been entrapped will have little remedy other than recourse to this point in mitigation, this chapter will briefly mention of the effect of entrapment on sentence.

6.135 The general position, set out in *R v Underhill*,[1] is that a court may, in principle, mitigate the penalty imposed upon an offender if it takes the view that he would not have committed the offence of which he has been convicted but for the actions of the entrapper.

1 1 Cr App R (S) 270. The defendant's sentence was not reduced in this case, on account of the Court of Appeal's conclusion that, on the evidence, the appellant had regularly been engaged in drug trafficking in any event so that there was no justification for reducing his sentence. See also *R v M* [2011] EWCA Crim 648.

6.136 In *R v Beaumont*,[1] entrapment was held to be a substantial mitigating factor (*Underhill* was not cited in that ruling). That approach was applied in *R v Chapman and Denton*[2] and *R v Mackey and Shaw*,[3] where the appellant's sentences were reduced on account of 'entrapment'. However, the Court of Appeal in *R v Springer*[4] held that where undercover police officers purchased drugs from established dealers, that would not afford mitigation in sentence, following the approach actually applied to the facts in *R v Underhill* itself. Each case must be considered on its facts.[5]

1 9 Cr App R (S) 342, CA.
2 11 Cr App R (S) 222, CA.
3 14 Cr App R (S) 53, CA.
4 [1999] 1 Cr App R (S) 217, CA.
5 *R v Pittman* [2003] EWCA Crim 460 at para 20.

6.137 However, it is notable the sentencing guidelines in relation to drugs offences do not list entrapment or the involvement of test purchase officers as mitigating factors in drugs offences. Though in *R v Omar*,[1] the defendant pleaded to 6 counts of supplying a class A drug and one of offering to supply a class A drug. The supply offences arose out of six occasions when the Defendant met an undercover police officer and sold him cocaine. The Court of Appeal reduced the sentence originally given by the trial judge, having regard to totality. The Court specifically made reference to the fact that there was no actual supply and that the counts were in relation to a continuing relationship with an officer, rather than wholly independent transactions.

1 [2020] EWCA Crim 684.

Chapter 7

Double Jeopardy

7.01 In criminal proceedings, the principle relating to 'double jeopardy' is as follows: a defendant should not be tried or convicted twice in respect of the same general allegation. In other words, a defendant should not be tried or convicted more than once for the same offence. Closely associated with the concept of *res judicata*, the prohibition seeks to prevent re-litigation of similar factual and legal issues. It also serves the function of stopping prosecutors from re-trying a defendant against whom an earlier prosecution has failed in court proceedings. Importantly, it operates to prevent further prosecution for more serious offences when court proceedings have already resulted in a conviction in respect of that offending behaviour.

There are some significant exceptions to the principle, most notably the provisions of the Criminal Justice Act 2003, which allow the prosecution to apply to the Court of Appeal for the quashing of an acquittal and retrial of certain qualifying offences where there is 'new and compelling' evidence and where it is in the interests of justice for such a retrial (see **7.65** below).[1]

1 Criminal Justice Act 2003, ss 75–84.

7.02 The celebrated jurist Sir William Blackstone in his Commentaries, Book IV (1759 ed.), stated that 'the plea of auterfoits acquit, or a former acquittal, is grounded on this universal maxim of the common law of England, that no man is to be brought into jeopardy of his life, more than once, for the same offence'.

In the 8th edition of Hawkins's Pleas of the Crown, printed in 1824, is the commentary on the principle that 'from whence it is generally taken, by all the books, as an undoubted consequence, that where a man is once found 'not guilty' on an indictment or appeal free from error, and well commenced before any court which heath jurisdiction of the cause, he may, by the common law, in all cases whatsoever plead such acquittal in bar of any subsequent indictment or appeal for the same crime'.

In *Green v United* States,[1] Black J explained the principle in the following terms:

> 'The underlying idea, one that is deeply ingrained in at least the Anglo-American system of jurisprudence, is that the State with all its resources and power should not be allowed to make repeated attempts to convict an individual for an alleged offence, thereby subjecting him to embarrassment, expense and ordeal and compelling him to live in a continuing state of

> anxiety and insecurity, as well as enhancing the possibility that even though innocent he may be found guilty.'

More recently, writing in the *Criminal Law Review*, Professor Choo has put forward one rationale for why double jeopardy should be regarded as repugnant to justice:

> 'to put a person in double jeopardy may increase the chances of his or her being convicted even though innocent, and will also undermine the moral integrity of the criminal process. The accused may, as a result of having revealed his complete defence at the first trial, be at a greater disadvantage at the second trial and thus less able to defend him or herself effectively. Irrespective of this, it is in any event morally objectionable to subject someone to the embarrassment, expense and anxiety of a second prosecution, with the possibility that a verdict might be returned which is inconsistent with that reached the first time. Considerations such as these ought to be borne in mind when considering stays of proceedings in the double jeopardy context'.[2]

1 (1961) 356 US 165.
2 A L-T Choo 'Halting Criminal Prosecutions' [1995] Crim LR at 866.

7.03 So, the origin of the rule against double jeopardy lies in the ancient remedies of *autrefois acquit* and *autrefois convict*. These remedies are known as 'pleas in bar'. They constitute an alternative plea to guilty or not guilty. A defendant who pleads either *autrefois acquit* or *autrefois convict* challenges the validity of the indictment, whereas a plea of guilty or not guilty presupposes its validity. Regarding *autrefois convict*, Blackburn J in *Wemyss v Hopkins*[1] reasoned that it is:

> 'a well established common law principle that where a person has been convicted and punished for an offence by a court of competent jurisdiction … the conviction shall be a bar to all further proceedings for the same offence, and he shall not be punished again for the same matter'.

1 (1875) LR 10 QB 378 at 381.

7.04 The scope *of autrefois acquit and autrefois convict* and their relationship with the rule against double jeopardy was considered at length by the House of Lords in *Connelly v DPP.*[1]

1 [1964] AC 1254.

7.05 In *Connelly*, the speeches of all five Law Lords included discussion as to whether the principle against double jeopardy should be understood only as a modern reformulation *of autrefois acquit* and *autrefois convict*, thus being co-terminous with their scope, or as a principle founded in the court's wider, discretionary power to halt a prosecution because it was, for some reason, unfair.

7.06 In *Connelly*, the court reasoned in favour of the latter and since *Connelly*, the leading authorities on double jeopardy have adopted the same approach. In *Humphrys*,[1] Lord Salmon recognised the existence of judicial power to intervene: 'if the prosecution amounts to an abuse of the process of the court and is oppressive and vexatious'. Lord Edmund-Davies took a similar view: '... in my judgment, *Connelly* ... established that [judges] are vested with the power to do what the justice of the case clearly demands'.[2] More recently, in *R v Beedie*,[3] the Court of Appeal confirmed that the rule in relation to double jeopardy should not be regarded as being within the doctrine of *autrefois acquit* or *autrefois convict*, but should, instead, be conceived as part of the court's wider discretionary power to stay proceedings that constitute an abuse of process. In *Beedie*, Lord Rose held that, in *Connelly*, the court had 'identified a narrow principle of *autrefois*, applicable only where the same offence was alleged in the second indictment'.[4]

1 [1977] AC 1 at 46.
2 [1977] AC 1 at 55.
3 [1998] QB 356.
4 [1998] QB 356 at 360.

7.07 Whilst *Connelly* did not go so far as to hold *that autrefois acquit* and *autrefois convict* were otiose, the court seemed to have intended to relegate them and the concept of pleas in bar to a subsidiary role. The effect was as follows: where a situation of double jeopardy was alleged, unless the situation came clearly within *autrefois acquit* and *autrefois convict*, the discretionary jurisdiction of abuse of process was to be preferred.

7.08 This chapter separates into two parts: the first relates to the scope and availability of the pleas in bar, *autrefois acquit* and *autrefois convict*; and the second to the scope and availability of the abuse of process jurisdiction relating to double jeopardy.

AUTREFOIS ACQUIT AND *AUTREFOIS CONVICT*

The scope of the pleas as determined in Connelly

The factual situation

7.09 The facts in *Connelly*[1] were as follows. An armed robbery took place at a dairy in south London, during which the robbers shot and killed an employee of the dairy. Subsequently, Connelly was arrested and charged with the murder. The prosecution did not allege that he was the person who had carried out the physical act of killing, but alleged that he was part of the gang that had committed the murder. Therefore, the prosecution case was that he had the requisite criminal intent of murder. At his trial before Roskill J, Connelly's defence was essentially two-fold. First, he claimed alibi: he had not been present at the scene of the crime and had not been involved in any way with the robbery; and, secondly, in any event, the prosecution had not proved that he had the requisite intent, even if he had been a member of the gang and had been present.

1 [1918] 1 KB 416.

7.10 When it retired to consider its verdict, the jury at Connelly's trial had numerous options available to it: to find him guilty of murder, to find him not guilty of murder, or (if not guilty of murder) then to find him guilty or not guilty of manslaughter. In the event, the jury convicted Connelly of murder. His subsequent appeal to the Court of Appeal was grounded on important misdirections by Roskill J during his summing up. Although expressing reluctance, the Court of Appeal agreed and, accordingly, quashed Connelly's conviction for murder. In law, therefore, Connelly had been acquitted of murder.

7.11 However, after this appeal hearing, the prosecution proceeded, with the leave of the Court of Appeal, to lay a second indictment against Connelly, alleging now that he had committed a robbery at the dairy. Due to practice at the time of the first trial, there had been no alternative count of robbery on the original indictment.

7.12 At the opening of his second trial, Connelly pleaded *autrefois acquit*, a plea that the trial judge rejected on the basis that *autrefois acquit* could not apply as Connelly was not being retried for murder, the offence for which he had been acquitted. However, while the trial judge rejected Connelly's plea of *autrefois acquit*, he declared that the prosecution ought not to proceed against Connelly for the count of robbery. In the judge's considered view, that course of action was unjust: the factual issue of whether Connelly had taken part in the robbery had already been decided in the previous proceedings in Connelly's favour. The trial judge reasoned that the Court of Appeal's quashing of the conviction of murder meant that the Court had been determined that he was not present at the crime. The prosecution, however, disagreed and sought to proceed to trial. In this circumstance, the judge ruled that, *as autrefois acquit* was not engaged, he had no power to prevent the prosecution from proceeding, despite his disapproval. Subsequently, the second jury convicted Connelly of robbery; and he was sentenced to imprisonment. He appealed the conviction on the basis that the ruling of the trial judge was erroneous.

7.13 The appeal eventually came before the Appellate Committee of the House of Lords. The Court was unanimous in concluding that the plea *of autrefois acquit* had properly been rejected by the trial judge and it upheld Connelly's conviction. He appellant had not been acquitted of robbery and the plea of *autrefois acquit* related in that case only to the offence of murder. There was no factual issue estoppel. The Court also held that the situation that had occurred in *Connelly* should not recur, i.e., that in future an indictment could be framed containing counts of murder and other, offences properly joined under the Indictments Act 1915, for example, robbery. The debate that divided the Lords was however the scope and availability of the pleas in bar. The majority of the court preferred a new approach, namely that the court had an inherent power to protect its process from abuse and that the principles of *autrfois acquit* and *autrefois convict* had evolved from that power but remain an available plea.

The governing principles underlying the availability *of autrefois acquit* or *autrefois convict*

7.14 In a comprehensive judgment, Lord Morris considered all the authorities concerning pleas in bar in order to formulate a set of 'governing principles', which ought to determine in future the availability of *either autrefois acquit* or *autrefois convict*. These principles remain good law.

Same offence

7.15 The first and basic norm underlying both pleas in bar is that a person cannot be tried for an offence in respect of which they have previously been acquitted or convicted. As Lord Devlin reasoned in *Connelly*, 'it must be the same offence both in fact and in law'.[1] The narrowness of this test means that a person can be tried a second time for the same conduct where the offence charged is different from that charged at the earlier trial.[2] This was the situation in *Connelly*. The effect of this rule is now circumscribed both by the Criminal Procedure and Investigations Act 1996, ss 54–56, which deal with tainted acquittals, as well as Pts 9 and 10 of the Criminal Justice Act 2003, dealing with prosecution appeals and retrial for serious offences: see paras **7.75–7.76** and **7.65–7.71**.

1 [1998] QB 356 at 449.
2 See also Reid LJ's speech at 419.

7.16 As the test for *either autrefois acquit* or autrefois convict focuses on the offence(s) alleged, it is not fatal that the facts under examination or the witnesses being called in the subsequent proceedings are the same as those in the earlier proceedings. Instead, the primary question is whether the offence charged in the later indictment is the same as that offence charged in the earlier indictment.

7.17 The effect of this test can be illustrated by the facts in *Connelly* and *DPP v Humphrys*.[1] In *Connelly*, the facts of which have already been outlined in paras **7.9** and **7.13**, the evidence called and the facts relied on by the prosecution during the trial for robbery were the same as the prosecution had relied on during the earlier trial for murder, an offence for which the defendant had been acquitted. However, the Law Lords were unanimous in holding that the coincidence of factual evidence at the two trials did not form the basis of a successful plea for *autrefois acquit*.[2]

1 [1977] AC 1.
2 See also *Thomas* [1950] 1 KB 26, where a plea *of autrefois convict* failed in circumstances where the defendant had been convicted of wounding and was subsequently following the death of the victim charged with murder.

7.18 In *Humphrys* (the first occasion after *Connelly* when the House of Lords considered issues relating to double jeopardy), the court similarly rejected a plea of *autrefois acquit*. In that case, the defendant had been charged with driving a motor vehicle while disqualified. He had pleaded not guilty and, in his defence, he had given evidence asserting that not only had he not driven on the date in question, but that he had also not driven for a period of one year prior to that date. The jury acquitted Humphrys, obviously believing his testimony. Subsequently, fresh information concerning the veracity of Humphrys' evidence came to light, suggesting that he had driven at times during that preceding year. Using that new information, he was charged with perjury in relation to his evidence given at the first trial. He *pleaded autrefois acquit* partly on the basis that the main witness against him, a police officer at the first trial who claimed to have observed Humphrys driving, would be giving the same evidence at the proposed second trial – evidence that the jury at the first trial must have rejected. The House of Lords rejected the plea of *autrefois acquit*, holding that the offence of driving while disqualified and of perjury were different and separable. What mattered was not that similar facts would be under scrutiny in both trials, but whether similar alleged offences would be under scrutiny. The plea *of autrefois acquit* related only to offences, not also to facts in this manner, and it was, therefore, unavailable.[1]

1 It should not be overlooked that H had pleaded guilty to forging an MOT certificate in relation to the car he had denied driving. This admission may have jaundiced the view of H's protestation of innocence.

7.19 In *Humphrys*, the House of Lords also approved the Scottish case of *HM Advocate v Cairns*.[1] In that case, the defendant had been acquitted of murder and then subsequently confessed to a newspaper that he was guilty. On the strength of this confession, he was subsequently tried for perjury, despite the fact that the evidence would in effect be that he had committed the murder for which he had been acquitted. Lord Grant held that this did not bar a second trial: the 'identity of the charges and not of the evidence is the crucial factor'.

1 1967 JC 37.

Prosecution of an alternative offence

7.20 The second principle that Lord Morris described in *Connelly* is that a person cannot be tried for an offence in respect of which they could in previous proceedings have been lawfully convicted. It applies where the offence tried in the earlier proceedings, in which the defendant was either convicted or acquitted, constituted an alternative to the offence now proposed to be tried.

7.21 This principle is not concerned with the similarity of the evidence within the two sets of proceedings. It is purely a legal question of whether the person's acquittal in the first proceedings necessarily in law involves an acquittal in the second. An 'implied' acquittal would be a case in which the jury could lawfully have convicted the defendant on an alternative charge to the one being tried, but returned no verdict on it. An 'express' acquittal arises when there are alternative charges. For example, such a case could involve theft and handling, which are expressly averred in the indictment, but are indicted as alternatives to each other. Where a jury returned a verdict on one count and not another forming an alternative, this would allow a defendant to plead autrefois to the other in any subsequent proceedings alleging the substance of that other, alternative count.

7.22 Two examples may assist to illustrate the point. First, there is the issue of an implied acquittal. In *Connelly*, the jury could, in the first trial, have convicted the defendant of murder or manslaughter. Accordingly, once the Court of Appeal had acquitted the defendant of murder, this also constituted in law an acquittal of manslaughter. This shows the operation of the principle of an implied acquittal. The defence argument in *Connelly* was that there was also an implied acquittal in relation to a charge of robbery. It was with this that the House of Lords disagreed. The court held that the prosecution evidence relied on to charge robbery would have been insufficient to procure a conviction for manslaughter. His acquittal of murder and implied acquittal of manslaughter did not bar the subsequent trial for robbery.

7.23 Second, there is an express acquittal. In the more recent case of *R v Velasquez*,[1] the defendant was tried for two offences, rape and attempted rape, in relation to the same victim. In returning its verdicts, the jury acquitted Velasquez of attempted rape, but then went on to convict him of rape. The defendant then appealed his conviction for rape, arguing that he was entitled to a plea *of autrefois acquit* and his conviction for rape should be quashed. As he was acquitted of the attempt, the prosecution should then have been barred from seeking his conviction for the substantive offence. The Court of Appeal rejected this argument, holding that the defendant had not in law been acquitted of the substantive offence in relation to the attempt. The court held that it did not offend the autrefois principles where the facts were exactly the same for a defendant to be found not guilty of the attempt, but guilty of the substantive offence. The charges were logical alternatives.

1 [1996] 1 Cr App Rep 155.

Substantially the same offence

7.24 The third principle is concerns cases in which the offence(s) alleged are the same or substantially the same as the offence(s) in respect of which the defendant has previously been acquitted or convicted (or could have been convicted by way of alternative verdict). This rule is subject to one proviso: the offence charged in the second indictment must have been committed at the same time as the first alleged offence.

7.25 In Lord Morris' view in *Connelly*, the most appropriate test of whether the second charge is the same or substantially the same as the earlier is whether the evidence which is necessary to support the second charge would have been sufficient to prove a legal conviction in relation to the first.[1] An example of this would be where it is shown that the offence of which the accused was convicted is a necessary step towards proving the offence now charged. As Lord Hodson put it in *Connelly*, the question concerns whether the acquittal of the first charge necessarily involved an acquittal of the second'.[2] This principle can be illustrated by the following three cases:

(1) In *R v Dabhade*,[3] the defendant was first charged with obtaining property by deception contrary to the Theft Act 1978, s 15(1). He pleaded not guilty and the prosecution decided to offer no evidence, leading to the charge being dismissed. A new charge based on the same facts, theft contrary to s 1 of the Theft Act 1968, was then preferred. Dabhade *pleaded autrefois acquit* in relation to the new charge, submitting that the two charges were, in the circumstances of his case, the same or substantially the same (even though theft is not an alternative verdict on a charge of obtaining by deception). The Court of Appeal rejected the plea of AA, holding that it did not come within the requirement that the evidence supporting the theft charge would have sufficed to secure a conviction of the obtaining by deception charge. It held that, though based on the evidence in some cases theft is an alternative verdict to obtaining by

deception, the evidence in this case to support a charge of theft would not suffice alone to support a charge of obtaining by deception.

(2) In *R v Valasquez*,[4] the Court of Appeal applied Lord Hodson's proposition (quoted above) and held that an acquittal of an attempt should bar a conviction for the full offence on a later indictment. The two crimes charged, rape and attempted rape, were arguably substantially the same. However, it held on the facts before it that there was no necessary inconsistency between the verdicts delivered in that case. In its discretion, therefore, the court seems to have declined to follow this principle. In *Velasquez*, the court appears to have been applying its discretion to refuse relief, reasoning that the verdicts had caused no injustice to the defendant.

(3) In *Salvi*,[5] the defendant, having been acquitted of a charge of wounding with intent to murder was, after the victim's death, indicted for murder and convicted. His plea *of autrefois acquit* failed in the Court of Appeal. The court held that a person can be convicted in law for murder without an intention to murder being proven. Therefore, the evidence supporting the indictment for murder would not necessarily have supported a conviction in relation to the first, namely wounding with intent to murder.

1 [1964] AC 1254 at 1310–1311.
2 [1964] AC 1254 at 1332.
3 (1992) 96 Cr App Rep 146.
4 See para **7.23**.
5 (1857) 10 Cox CC 481n.

7.26 The judgment of the Court of Appeal in *Valasquez* appears to be an endorsement of Lord Devlin's reasoning in *Connelly*. Lord Devlin disagreed with Lord Morris that this third principle should properly form part of the autrefois doctrine. Lord Devlin's reasoning was that this principle belonged more to courts' inherent discretionary power, pursuant to an abuse of process, rather than to autrefois:

> 'I have no difficulty about the idea that one set of facts may be substantially, but not exactly the same as another. I have more difficulty with the idea that an offence may be substantially the same as another in its legal characteristics; legal characteristics are precise things and are either the same or not. If I had felt that the doctrine of autrefois was the only form of relief available to the defendant I should be tempted to stretch the doctrine as far as it would go. But as that is not my view I am inclined to favour keeping it within limits that are precise'.[1]

1 [1964] AC 1254 at 1340.

7.27 In *R v Beedie*,[1] the Court of Appeal reasoned that this principle should not be viewed as part of the doctrine of autrefois at all. Instead, in the absence of special circumstances, it should be considered to lead to the exercise of the wider discretionary power to stay proceedings on the ground of abuse of the process. In the light of *Beedie*, it may be that the decision in *Dabhade* should be understood as falling under the jurisdiction of abuse of process, not that of *autrefois*.

More recently, in *R v Wangige*,[2] the Court of Appeal followed *Beedie* and *Phipps*. It held that a second prosecution in relation to substantially the same facts was unfair and oppressive. The magistrates' court had convicted the defendant of charges relating to a hit-and-run incident; two years afterward, there was a further prosecution in the Crown Court. The basis for the new prosecution was solely an expert report concerning the car's speed. That report had not been produced until a time after the defendant's conviction in the magistrates' court. Considering the earlier decisions of *R v Dwyer* and *R v Antoine*,[3] the Court of Appeal reasoned that this report was not a special circumstance sufficient to justify the second prosecution.[4] Beginning the judgment of the court, Davis LJ reasoned that the doctrine of *autrefois convict* is 'narrowly circumscribed', but that it connects closely with the abuse jurisdiction. Davis LJ framed the issue as 'whether such principle … should have required the Crown Court judge to stay, as an abuse, an indictment alleging causing death by dangerous driving'.[5] Such an approach further supports the view *that autrefois convict* is best understood as a distinctive—but constituent—part of the abuse jurisdiction,

1 See para **7.99**.
2 [2020] EWCA Crim 1319.
3 [2012] EWCA Crim 10; [2014] EWCA Crim 1971.
4 [2020] EWCA Crim 1319, [60]–[82]; [2021] 4 WLR 23.
5 [2020] EWCA Crim 1319, [1].

'In peril' of conviction

7.28 Lord Morris' fourth principle is that, for the previous set of criminal proceedings to be able to form the basis for a plea *of autrefois acquit* or *autrefois convict*, they must have had the following two features:

(a) that the defendant's guilt must have been decided upon; and

(b) the proceedings must have been 'adjudicated', i.e. by a court of competent jurisdiction.

7.29 The court in *DPP v Nasralla*[1] interpreted the meaning of 'adjudication' in strict way, namely the occurrence of any of the following events: a jury's express verdict, a plea of guilty being entered and accepted, or a verdict of not guilty having been directed pursuant to the Criminal Justice Act 1967, s 17.[2]

1 [1967] 2 AC 238.
2 In reciting this list, the court perhaps should have included Magistrates' Court Act 1980, s 27; a magistrates' dismissal of a prosecutor's information under s 15 constitutes an acquittal.

7.30 There are three broad requirements for a person to be deemed to be 'in peril'. First, the court must be competent to try the person for the offence. Second, the trial must be on a good indictment on which a conviction could be entered. Third, any acquittal must be on the merits. A defendant is 'in peril' in the Crown Court when they are put in the charge of a jury. In a magistrates' court, a defendant is only 'in peril' when the magistrates (or the judge) conduct a hearing for the purpose of determining whether the defendant was guilty; that may be the first hearing when a charge is put to the defendant, but it is most likely to be at the date of the summary trial.[1]

1 See *R v JFJ* [2013] EWCA Crim 569.

7.31 An example of the narrow interpretation of adjudication is where a court has acted *ultra vires* and the defendant could never have been legally convicted. It has been held that the accused was never, therefore, technically in peril or in jeopardy. See, for example, *R v West*,[1] a case in which the magistrates purported to acquit the defendant of the offence that was triable only on indictment. Having realised this error, the prosecution then recharged the accused, who then *pleaded autrefois acquit* in order to resist his sending to the Crown Court for trial. This was rejected: as the summary proceedings were a nullity, the sending and trial on indictment were unobjectionable.

1 [1964] 1 QB 15.

Situations that do not form a basis for a plea of autrefois acquit or autrefois convict

7.32 The cases considered below are mostly concerned with proceedings in a magistrates' court. As a matter of legal form, the pleas of *autrefois acquit* and *autrefois convict* are unavailable in those proceedings as they are pleas in bar to an indictment. However, in practice, they tend to be recognised as valid defences in the lower courts on the basis that they are bound by the rule against double jeopardy. For further detail, see *Williams v DPP*.[1]

1 [1991] 3 All ER 651 at 654.

Discharge of an accused at committal proceedings following a ruling of no case to answer

7.33 In *R v Manchester City Stipendiary Magistrate, ex p Snelson*,[1] the defendant was acquitted, following the offering of no evidence by the prosecution. Subsequently, the prosecution initiated fresh proceedings in relation to which the defendant asserted *autrefois acquit*. His plea was that, as the magistrates had already discharged him for the offence in question, they were unable to reconsider it. The magistrates disagreed and convicted the defendant at trial. The defendant sought judicial review of this finding. Lord Widgery CJ upheld the magistrates' decision, holding that a plea of *autrefois acquit* was unavailable to a defendant by reason of his earlier discharge in the committal proceedings.[2]

1 [1978] 2 All ER 62.
2 But see also limits imposed as a matter of discretion on the prosecution's right to pursue charges basically the same as those already dismissed, *R v Horsham Justices, ex p Reeves* (1980) 75 Cr App R 236n considered at para **7.84** below.

Withdrawal of a summons by the prosecution in the magistrates' court prior to the accused having pleaded to it

7.34 In *R v Grays Justices, ex p Low*,[1] the prosecution issued a summons for a charge of assault occasioning actual bodily harm against the defendant, which was subsequently withdrawn once the defendant accepted a bind over. Subsequently, the complainant in relation to the alleged assault (who was aggrieved by the prosecution's decision to accept the bind over) launched a private prosecution. A second summons was issued. The defendant *pleaded autrefois acquit* in relation to this second summons. The magistrates disagreed; the defendant sought judicial review. The higher court upheld the magistrates' refusal to recognise a plea of *autrefois acquit*. The court held that the withdrawal of a summons did not operate as a bar to the issuance of a further summons for the same charge because there had been no adjudication by the court on the merits of the allegation contained in the first summons. As a result, the defendant had not been put in peril of conviction.[2]

1 [1990] 1 QB 54.
2 However, on the ground of abuse of process, the court set aside the summons—the complainant had not informed the court, as he should have done, when he applied for the issuance of the second summons about there having been an earlier set of proceedings and what had happened in those proceedings.

7.35 The same point was also made in *R v Liverpool Magistrates' Court, ex p Slade.*[1] If a summons is withdrawn before a trial and, therefore, the case is dismissed, a plea *of autrefois acquit* cannot be made in relation to a subsequent summons for the same offence because there has been no earlier trial on the merits. See also *Brookes,*[2] where acceptance by the prosecution of a plea of not guilty to unlawfully and maliciously inflicting grievous bodily harm (Offences Against the Person Act 1861, s 20) did not establish a plea *of autrefois acquit* to bar a subsequent charge of causing GBH with intent to cause GBH (s 18).

1 [1998] 1 All ER 60.
2 [1995] Crim LR 630.

Notices of discontinuance

7.36 In the same vein, a plea *of autrefois acquit* cannot arise in relation to proceedings commenced in relation to the same offence charged in earlier proceedings, but which are terminated by the prosecution pursuant to it serving a notice of discontinuance under the Prosecution of Offences Act 1985, s 23. A plea in bar will not prevent a prosecution proceeding against the same defendant in respect of whom they were earlier discontinued.

Where 'the accused was, as a matter of fact, never in peril or in jeopardy because the earlier proceedings against him were irregular and/or without jurisdiction'

7.37 This rule can be broken down into three sub-categories as follows:

(1) *Where the summons or charge against the accused has been dismissed before he has pleaded to it.* This concerns what Roujier J, in *Williams v DPP,*[1] conceived as a 'temporal question'. In *Williams*, a motorist was charged with driving with excess alcohol in his breath. When he was called on to plead at court, but before he did so, his advocate made a legal objection to the charge, which, because of an error in procedure committed by the police, was bound to succeed. The prosecution, realising its mistake applied for an adjournment to enable the bringing of an amended summons, but the court refused the application and

then dismissed the summons. However, subsequently, the prosecution corrected the legal error and brought a fresh summons. The defendant *pleaded autrefois acquit* contending that, because the earlier summons had been dismissed, he could not be tried again on a charge based on the same facts. The prosecution conceded that the offence charged in the second proceedings was the same or substantially the same offence as that charged in the first, i.e. driving on a road after having consumed an amount of alcohol exceeding the prescribed limit. The issue, however, was whether the defendant had been in jeopardy at the time when the justices dismissed the original charge. Roujier J concluded, pursuant to his 'temporal question', that the first set of proceedings had not reached such a stage that the defendant had been in danger of conviction. Roujier J held that this would only have arisen once the defendant had actually pleaded; only then would he have been in jeopardy or in peril. To support this view, Roujier J quoted with approval the remarks of Lush J in *Haynes v Davis*,[2] who held in relation to the expression 'acquittal on the merits' that 'the expression is used by way of antithesis to a dismissal of the charge upon some technical ground which had been a bar to the adjudicating upon it'.

(2) *Dismissal of proceedings against an accused, following the withdrawal of a charge by the prosecution on the grounds of its legal defectiveness.* The case of *Dabhade* has already been considered in para **7.25**. The defendant was originally charged with obtaining property by deception, but the prosecution offered no evidence and the charge was dismissed. A new charge of theft was subsequently preferred. The defendant *pleaded autrefois acquit* and sought judicial review. The court held that, because of the manifest defects in the original charge, the defendant had in fact never been in danger of conviction in relation to it. The court held that there was a principle in law that, if the summary dismissal of a charge is because it is defective for any reason, then the defendant has never been in danger of conviction and so cannot claim *autrefois acquit*. There was '*no real sense'* in which it could be said that the defendant was in jeopardy on the first charge. To support this view, the court stated that it would be absurd to prescribe a situation whereby the prosecution kept alive a charge it had no intention of pursuing, merely to defeat a feared attempt of a plea *of autrefois acquit* '*in circumstances which are both technical and without merit.*' If a new charge, which was more appropriate to the facts, was substituted, then a consensual dismissal of the original charge and the substitution of a new one does not give rise to *autrefois acquit.*

(3) Where the proceedings are a legal nullity, a plea *of autrefois acquit or autrefois convict* arising from them cannot be entered in relation to subsequent proceedings. Thus, in *R v Kent Justices, ex p Machin*,[3] the court reasoned that the prosecution would be entitled to bring fresh proceedings where the magistrates had acted ultra vires in convicting the defendant and then committing the defendant for sentence, without having followed the correct procedure for determining the mode of trial. In *R v West*,[4] the defendant was not entitled to rely *on autrefois*

acquit where the magistrates had acted ultra vires in acquitting him of an indictable only offence.

1 [1991] 1 WLR 1160.
2 [1915] 1 KB 332 at 340.
3 [1952] 2 QB 355.
4 (1964) 1 QB 15.

7.38 In less clear-cut cases, the application of this rule may appear to have a harsh effect on the defendant. In both *R v Pressick*[1] and *R v Dorking Justices, ex p Harrington*,[2] the prosecution, at a hearing listed for a trial, sought an adjournment of it, but this application was refused by the magistrates who also dismissed the charges. Subsequently, the prosecution initiated fresh proceedings in respect of which the accused pleaded *autrefois acquit*. In *Pressick*, the Divisional Court held that the magistrates had acted within their jurisdiction to refuse the adjournment and to dismiss the charge and, therefore, a plea *of autrefois acquit* was properly founded. However, in *ex p Harrington*, Lord Roskill reasoned that the magistrates had acted in a grossly unfair way towards the prosecution, so that the dismissal of the prosecution's summonses was without jurisdiction and was a legal nullity. A remedy of mandamus was granted to the prosecution, with the effect that the case was remitted to the magistrates' court for re-hearing. *Holmes v Campbell*[3] illustrates a third aspect. The prosecutor did not appear at the trial following a mistake over dates and the summonses were dismissed. The Divisional Court held that, though the magistrates had been entitled to dismiss the charges against the defendant, the first hearing was not a nullity, following *Harrington*. Nonetheless, because for legal reasons he could not have been convicted, there had been no acquittal on the merits.

1 [1978] Crim LR 377.
2 [1994] 2 All ER 474.
3 (1998) 162 JP 655, QBD.

7.39 For a defendant who could not be held responsible for the magistrates' decision to dismiss and who, presumably, had arrived in court in the expectation (and possibly apprehension) of a trial then to face a complete retrial because of magistrates' misbehaviour, there remains the possibility that the principles *of autrefois acquit and autrefois convict* operate to prevent further proceedings. In a sense, these principles are defendant-oriented. Furthermore, in *Harrington*, the court severed the link between a defendant's sense of ordeal of being subject to trial and successive legal proceedings against the defendant, the former appearing to have little relevance to the latter.

Where charges are dismissed as part of the reorganisation of the prosecution case

7.40 Where a defendant is charged and enters a plea to an offence, and the prosecution subsequently indicates that it intends to prefer a more serious charge, the dismissal of the earlier charge does not act as a bar to the continuance of the more serious proceedings. In *JFJ*,[1] the prosecution offered no evidence to a common assault charge, having informed the court and the defendant that it intended to charge the defendant with assault occasioning actual bodily harm. The court record stated that the assault was 'dismissed (no evidence offered)'. The Court of Appeal did not accept that the dismissal gave rise to a plea of *autrefois acquit*, as the defendant could not be said to be 'in peril', since the dismissal had only formed part of the prosecution's reorganisation of its case.

1 *R v JFJ* [2013] EWCA Crim 569.

Where charges are dismissed for want of prosecution

7.41 In *DPP v Jarman*,[1] the administrative court made clear that a defendant has not been 'in peril' where a magistrates' court has dismissed a charge for want of prosecution. In that case, though there was a valid charge for which the defendant could be tried, and the court was competent to try him, the fact that the prosecutor did not arrive at court and the magistrates had heard no evidence meant that the defendant had never been 'in peril' sufficient to found a plea of autrefois convict.

1 [2013] All ER (D) 116.

A finding of contempt of court in relation to similar facts in respect of which the accused was subsequently convicted

7.42 In *R v Sherry*,[1] the defendant was convicted of conspiracy to abduct a child. However, prior to his trial, he had been sent to prison for contempt, due to a violation of a civil court injunction that banned him from removing the child from their mother. The defendant claimed that the finding that he was in contempt constituted a valid plea *of autrefois convict* in relation to his subsequent trial for conspiracy. However, for two reasons, the Court of Appeal disagreed:

(a) *Autrefois convict* did not arise because the defendant had never before been charged with the offence of conspiracy and there had been no proceedings in which he could possibly have been convicted of this offence; and

(b) in any event, the proceedings for contempt were civil and not criminal proceedings, meaning *that autrefois convict* could not arise. In *R v Green*,[2] it was held that, though a plea of double jeopardy is available in civil as in criminal proceedings, such a plea cannot jump the boundary between the two different types of proceedings.

1 [1993] Crim LR 536.
2 [1993] Crim LR 46.

7.43 The court in *DPP v Tweddle*[1] came to the same conclusion. The applicant had breached a non-molestation injunction and received a sentence of ten weeks' imprisonment for contempt. Later, he was prosecuted for an allegation of assault arising from the same incident. The applicant raised the issue of a plea of *autrefois convict,* which the court rejected on the ground that the contempt jurisdiction was civil and not to criminal and, in any event, his criminal prosecution was not vexatious. Section 1 of the Domestic Violence,

Crime and Victims Act 2004, which came into force on 1 July 2007, provides that breach of a non-molestation order will be punishable as a criminal offence. It is specifically provided that a person convicted of this offence cannot also be punished for contempt in relation to the same conduct.

1 (1 March 2001, unreported).

A finding of a foreign court of competent jurisdiction that the defendant is guilty of the same offence for which they have been tried by an English court but where there is no prospect of the defendant being punished by the foreign court in relation to the conviction awarded

7.44 In *Treacy v DPP*,[1] Lord Diplock held that *autrefois acquit and autrefois convict* was 'a doctrine which has always applied whether the previous conviction or acquittal based on the same facts was by an English court or by a foreign court'. This view was, however, expressed as obiter. As a result, there seems to be little authority directly on this issue. In its 2001 report on double jeopardy, the Law Commission[2] was unable to unearth any case. The only case is *R v Aughet*,[3] a First World War case in which the English court upheld a claim *of autrefois convict* on the basis that the accused had already been convicted of the same offence by a court-martial in Belgium. Yet *R v Thomas* did not follow *Treacy*.[4] Thomas was tried in England for the same conduct of which an Italian court had convicted him in his absence. He *pleaded autrefois convict* in relation to the English trial. The court rejected this plea holding that the mere fact of a foreign conviction is not, of itself, sufficient to found a plea of *autrefois convict*, unless the accused had genuinely been in jeopardy. In this case, that meant being in jeopardy of punishment post-conviction. On the facts, Thomas had fled to England and could not be extradited to Italy. In the light of this, the Court of Appeal held that he was in no real risk of danger of punishment in Italy and, therefore, had never been in peril or in jeopardy in relation to the Italian proceedings. The court also took into account the fact that the defendant had been convicted in Italy in his absence and had taken no part in his trial there.

1 [1971] AC 537 at 562.
2 Cmnd 5048, March 2001.
3 (1918) 13 Cr App R 101.
4 [1985] QB 604.

7.45 In *Richards v R*, the Privy Council followed the principle enunciated in *Thomas* concerning the necessary connection between jeopardy or peril and punishment.[1] The Board held that a finding of guilt alone is not a sufficient condition for a plea of *autrefois convict*; that finding must be accompanied by the imposition of a penalty in order for the plea to succeed. Lord Bridge held that the underlying rationale *of autrefois convict* was to prevent double punishment and, accordingly, it could only rest on a complete adjudication against the defendant which, as a matter of definition, must include the final disposal of the case by way of a sentence.

1 [1993] AC 217.

The taking of an offence into consideration when passing sentence for other offences of which the offender has been convicted

7.46 In *R v Nicholson*,[1] the defendant was convicted and, at his sentence hearing, asked for the other offences to be taken into consideration. This occurred. Subsequently, his conviction was quashed and the prosecution decided to proceed in relation those offences taken into consideration. The defendant pleaded *autrefois convict*, but this plea was rejected on the ground that he had not been 'convicted' in respect of them. The Court of Appeal, however, reasoned that the practice of trying a person for offences previously only taken into consideration was generally undesirable.

1 (1947) 32 Cr App R 98.

The issuing of a police caution

7.47 In *Jones v Whalley*,[1] a police caution was issued for an offence of assault occasioning actual bodily harm. The complainant in relation to the offence then began a private prosecution. The Administrative Court held that a police caution could not found the basis for a plea of *autrefois convict*, as it did not have the status of a conviction. On appeal to the House of Lords,[2] the court overturned that decision on the narrow ground that the defendant was assured in taking the caution that he would not subsequently be prosecuted and, therefore, had a legitimate expectation to that effect.[3]

1 [2005] EWHC 931 (Admin).
2 [2006] UKHL 41, [2007] 1 AC 63.
3 The broader question as to whether it would ever be other than an abuse of process to bring a private prosecution following the issuing of a caution was, unfortunately, not decided. As a result, it seems that the issue will depend upon the wording of the caution issued.

7.48 Lord Justice Stanley Burton clarified the position regarding the status of a caution in relation to pleas *of autrefois convict* in the case of *DPP v Alexander*:[1]

> 'It is clear and common ground that a caution is not a conviction for the purposes of the defence of autrefois convict, or for that matter autrefois acquit. Where, however, criminal conduct has been the subject of an agreed caution, in the absence of good reason for it to the subject of a subsequent prosecution, such a prosecution will generally constitute an abuse of the process of the court. Information or evidence obtained subsequent to a caution, such as details of injury to a victim significantly exceeding what had previously been known would generally constitute a good reason'.

1 [2011] 1 WLR 653.

7.49 In *R v G*,[1] the Court of Appeal held that a person who has been cautioned by the police for one form of offence arising from a particular incident may thereafter be prosecuted for a more serious offence in respect of the same incident in the light of medical evidence subsequently obtained. The court considered that the wording of the caution had not given G an unequivocal assurance that he would not be prosecuted. Furthermore, the facts were not the same in respect of the caution and the subsequent prosecution, given that more medical evidence had come to light.

1 [2013] EWCA Crim 1492.

7.50 The position is the same in relation to fixed penalty notices. In *Gore and Mather*,[1] the police had issued fixed penalty notices against individuals for assault. The injuries to the victim were subsequently discovered to be more serious and charges were brought against the same individuals. The Court of Appeal held that there was nothing in the nature or form of a penalty notice that prohibited subsequent criminal proceedings taking place.

1 [2009] EWCA Crim 1424.

A finding of guilt in disciplinary proceedings, even where that finding is followed by the imposition of a penalty

7.51 In *R v Hogan*,[1] prison escapees were punished by justices with loss of remission pursuant to the Prison Rules. Subsequently, they stood trial for an offence of escaping by force and pleaded *autrefois convict*. This was rejected.

However, in the much more recent case of *R v Robinson*, the Court of Appeal quashed a decision of an independent adjudicator in a prison adjudication. The adjudication was void because it had proceeded when the police had arrested and charged the defendant in connection with the same incident. The adjudicator had been unaware of this fact at the time. The Court of Appeal did not need to decide the issue of *R v Hogan* and the meaning of a body or court of competent jurisdiction. However, *obiter*, it reasoned that the case law of the European Court of Human Rights meant that *Hogan* was likely no longer good law. It considered that, if a (valid) prison adjudication involves punishment by loss of liberty, it can amount to 'criminal proceedings' by a body of competent jurisdiction and the rule against double jeopardy applies'.[2]

1 [1960] 2 QB 513.
2 [2017] EWCA Crim 936, [24].

7.52 This issue also arose in *Secretary of State for Trade and Industry v Baker*.[1] Baker was a director of a bank, which later became insolvent. The Secretary of State decided to seek his disqualification as a director, pursuant to the Company Directors Disqualification Act 1986. Baker *pleaded autrefois convict* because he had already faced disciplinary proceedings, brought against him by his regulator, the Securities and Futures Authority (SFA). Those proceedings had been based substantially on the same conduct as that on which the disqualification proceedings were founded. This claim was rejected. The Court of Appeal held that the SFA proceedings were concerned with whether Baker had professional competence (and was therefore a fit and proper person to run a bank), whereas the CDDA action was concerned with whether, acting as a director of a company, he was unfit to be concerned with its management.

1 (1998) *Times*, 6 July.

7.53 In *R (Redgrave) v Metropolitan Police Comr*,[1] a police officer faced a disciplinary charge arising from conduct that had led to a criminal charge.

In respect of the criminal charge, he had been discharged at committal. He submitted *autrefois acquit*, as the factual allegation was the same in both sets of proceedings. The Administrative Court disagreed: a discharge at committal is not equivalent to an acquittal. In addition to that, the court held that, as a matter of principle, *autrefois convict* applied only to courts of competent jurisdiction and not a disciplinary tribunal.

1 [2003] EWCA Civ 4, (2003) 1 WLR 1136. See, too, *R (Mandic-Bozic) v British Association for Counselling and Psychotherapy* [2016] EWHC 3134 (Admin).

A finding of fact in care proceedings

7.54 In *R v L*,[1] the defendant's three-month-old son, E, had died. In the course of care proceedings concerning the other son of the defendant's partner, the Family Court concluded that E had died of non-accidental injuries, but that it could not be ascertained whether the defendant or E's mother had caused the injuries. In the defendant's subsequent trial for the murder of E, an application to stay proceedings was rejected. The Court of Appeal later upheld the refusal. The family proceedings had been concerned with different issues; the defendant had never been at risk of conviction.

1 [2007] 1 Cr App R 1.

Proceedings before the Special Immigration Appeals Commission ('SIAC')

7.55 In *R v IK, R v AB, R v KA*[1] a certificate was issued by the Secretary of State for the Home Department against IK under s 21(1) of the Anti-Terrorism, Crime and Security Act 2001 on the basis that IK was believed to have links with Al-Qaeda. As a result, IK was detained for sixteen months. The decision was appealed to the SIAC and the certificate was cancelled. Criminal proceedings were then commenced under the Terrorism Act 2000. The proceedings were stayed as an abuse of process on the basis that, though the SIAC was not a criminal court, the consequences for the defendant were so similar that the proceedings should be stayed. The Court of Appeal allowed the prosecutor's appeal, following *R v L* (above) and maintaining the strict principle that, whatever the practical consequences, the SIAC proceedings were not in a criminal court. As such, IK had never been at risk of conviction and the proceedings could not preclude a subsequent criminal prosecution. In addition to that, the criminal proceedings involved both issues and evidence different from the SIAC proceedings.

1 [2007] 2 Cr App R 15.

Civil proceedings following acquittal in criminal proceedings

7.56 In *Raja v Van Hoogstraaten*,[1] an acquittal in criminal proceedings for murder and manslaughter was held not to be a bar to civil proceedings pursued by the estate of the alleged murder victim. In particular, the High Court had regard to the lower standard of proof in civil proceedings and the different rules relating to the admissibility of evidence.[2] In *Y v Norway*,[3] the European Court of Human Rights supported such an approach, so long as the decision about compensation did not contain a statement imputing the criminal liability of the defendant. The issue is likely to be relevant to criminal practitioners in the context of criminal behaviour orders ('CBOs', previously formulated as anti-social behaviour orders). Although classified as civil proceedings and without the criminal rules of evidence, the applicable standard of proof is the criminal standard. Two main questions have arisen in relation to CBOs (or, their predecessor, ASBOs). Unfortunately, the courts have given no definite answer to either of them.

1 [2005] All ER (D) 264 (Dec).

2 *Raja v Van Hoogstraten* was followed in *Ashley and another v Ch Const Sussex Police* [2008] 3 All ER 573, HL.

3 (2005) 41 EHRR 7.

7.57 In *Daar v Ch Const of Merseyside Police*,[1] the appellant brought civil proceedings against the police for false imprisonment, assault and malicious prosecution, stemming from matters for which he had been charged and acquitted. The local authority, at the police's request, then brought proceedings for an ASBO relying, in part, on the incidents of which the defendant had been acquitted. The ASBO was granted. The District Judge found that the allegations for which the defendant had been acquitted were proved. All three proceedings were based on essentially the same evidence. The question the court decided was that, on the facts of that case, the civil proceedings were not an abuse of process by calling into question the determination made against the appellant in the ASBO proceedings.

1 [2005] EWCA Civ 1774.

7.58 In relation to the ambit of the case, it was deemed 'not fruitful to consider' whether the ASBO application may have been stayed as an abuse of process. In the light of this approach, it seems that each ASBO application will turn on its own facts. If the evidence submitted is the same as that used in the proceedings leading to an acquittal, then it would be an abuse of process for those matters to be re-litigated. However, in many cases, there will be hearsay evidence, inadmissible in the criminal proceedings, which may justify the court coming to the conclusion that it can satisfied to the criminal standard of proof.

7.59 In *R(W) v DPP*,[1] one of the questions before the court was whether, where an ASBO specifically prohibited conduct that would be an offence in any event, a defendant would be entitled to plead *autrefois convict* to an alleged breach of the order where that defendant has already been convicted of the specific offence in criminal proceedings. Due to the judgment on a preceding question, it was unnecessary to give an answer to this question. However, in such circumstances, the most compelling view is that the offence of which the accused has already been convicted or acquitted is a necessary step towards proving the offence now charged and a defendant should be entitled to *plead autrefois acquit* or *convict* in such a case. Alternatively, it may be that such proceedings would be considered a clear abuse of process, involving sequential prosecutions arising out of the same activity.

When considering the case law relating to ASBOs, however, practitioners should exercise care. The introduction of criminal behaviour orders means that, though there is likely to be some degree of analogy with the existing case law, the new regime may require a different approach to double jeopardy. A precise answer is not yet confirmed.

1 [2005] EWCA Civ 1333, (2005) *Times*, 20 June.

Procedure on autrefois pleas

7.60

Timing and form of plea

The most obvious moment for pleading *autrefois* is at the point of arraignment, but before the indictment is put to the defendant. If the accused is legally represented, the conventional procedure is for the plea to be entered in writing and signed by counsel using the following form of words:

> '[*Name of accused*] says that the Queen ought not further to prosecute the indictment against [the defendant] because [the defendant] has been lawfully [acquitted or convicted] of the offence charged therein.'

In the rare case of an indictment relating to a charge of treason, the following wording should be added:

> 'and as to the charge in the said indictment [the defendant] says that [the defendant] is not guilty.'[1]

Having made the plea, the prosecution must either admit it is good or take issue with it. Pursuant to s 122 of the Criminal Justice Act 1988, it is then the role of the trial judge, sitting without a jury, to determine whether or not the plea is correct.

1 For examples of the custom, see *R v Walker* (1843) 174 ER 345 and *Flatman v Light* [1946] KB 414.

7.61

Burden of proof

In *Coughlan*,[1] the Court of Appeal held that, if a person enters a plea of *autrefois acquit* or *convict*, they must establish their plea on a balance of probabilities. Evidence can be called in support of contentions made by either side as if the hearing were a voir dire. The court can also consider the validity of the earlier court's jurisdiction: see *West*.[2] If the plea succeeds, it bars any further proceedings in relation to the indictment. If it fails, the indictment must then be put to the defendant and the defendant can then plead guilty or not guilty in the usual way.[3]

1 (1976) 63 Cr App R 33.
2 See para **7.37**.
3 For examples of the custom, see *R v Walker* (1843) 174 ER 345 and *Flatman v Light* [1946] KB 414.

7.62 In seeking to prove the validity of either *autrefois acquit* or *convict*, a defendant is not confined to a comparison between the latter and the earlier indictment or to the records of the court. Evidence can be called from other sources in relation to the identity of the persons, dates and facts as is required. In other words, the test is one of substance and not of form. In *West*, the court interpreted this principle as entitling a later court to inquire into the validity of an earlier court's jurisdiction and hold that the initial proceedings were a nullity.

7.63 A plea can be made at any time during the currency of the criminal proceedings, even after the defendant has pleaded guilty. In *Cooper v New Forest District Council*,[1] the defendant pleaded guilty to various breaches of planning enforcement notices and was sentenced by the magistrates. Subsequently, the defendant was advised that a plea of *autrefois* was available; therefore, he appealed to the Crown Court in its appellate capacity. The Crown Court refused the appeal because of the previous unequivocal plea of guilty before the magistrates. The defendant sought judicial review of this refusal. The Divisional Court held that, despite the plea of guilty, a plea in bar was so fundamental to the fairness of the proceedings that it was a special plea. Accordingly, the court reasoned that the Crown Court should have accepted the plea and considered it.

1 [1992] Crim LR 877.

Statutory exceptions to the autrefois rule: Criminal Justice Act 2003

7.64 Part 9 of the Criminal Justice Act 2003 (CJA) is entitled 'Prosecution Appeals'. First, since 4 April 2005, the prosecution has been able to apply for leave to appeal against any terminatory ruling other than a ruling discharging the jury, or a ruling that may be challenged under another procedure. Second, when brought into force, the prosecution will be allowed to apply for leave to appeal against any ruling or rulings as to the admissibility or inadmissibility of prosecution evidence in relation to cases involving certain sexual, violent or drug offences, made prior to the opening of the defence case. Leave will only be given if the ruling or rulings significantly weaken the prosecution case. The Court of Appeal can only reverse the ruling if it was wrong in law, involved an error of law or principle, or was unreasonable.

Retrial post acquittal for Serious Offences

7.65 Part 10 of the Criminal Justice Act 2003 is entitled 'Retrial for Serious Offences' and was brought into force on 4 April 2005. Pursuant to s 76(1), the DPP may apply to the Court of Appeal for an order quashing a person's acquittal in proceedings within s 75(1) and ordering that the person be retried. The court may only grant such orders if it is satisfied that, first, there is new and compelling evidence, and, second, a retrial is in the interests of justice (ss 78 and 79).

7.66 'New' evidence is defined in s 78(2) of the CJA as evidence not adduced in the proceedings in which the person was acquitted. This contrasts with an early draft of the Criminal Justice Bill, which defined new evidence as evidence 'not available to or known to an officer or prosecutor at the time of the acquittal'. The s 78(2) definition may conflict with the UK's obligations under the International Covenant on Civil and Political Rights, art 14.7[1] as it may allow a retrial on the basis of evidence which was known, but not used at the time of the original trial for example, for tactical reasons.[2] Some illustration is provided of the intent behind the wording of s 78(2) by the case of *R v Baker*,[3] who had been acquitted in 1999 of the rape of an elderly woman after the trial judge excluded DNA evidence on the ground that it was inadmissible following a breach of ss 61–65 of the Police and Criminal Evidence Act 1984. The House of Lords subsequently held that the evidence was in fact properly admissible;[4] the Court of Appeal later quashed the acquittal and ordered a retrial, holding that the evidence was 'new' for the purposes of s 78(2) because it was not adduced in the original trial. It is apparent that s 78(2) goes to evidence that has been adduced before a jury, not simply evidence put before a judge before being the subject of a pre-trial ruling on admissibility.

1 See para **7.133** below.
2 See Joint Committee on Human Rights 'Criminal Justice Bill: Further Report' HL Paper 118, HC 724.
3 *Sub nom Baker* [2012] EWCA Crim 414.
4 *Attorney General's Reference (No 3 of 1999)* [2001] 2 AC 91.

7.67 At the time of writing, there remains only a small number of successful applications to the Court of Appeal under Part 10, which indicates that only rarely are prosecutors able to avail themselves of the 'new and compelling evidence' exemption to double jeopardy. This is in line with the rule against double jeopardy being of fundamental importance. Lord Judge CJ reasoned, in this respect in a Part 10 case that, 'Inroads into the principle against double jeopardy must be examined closely on a case-by-case basis. The jurisdiction should be exercised with due caution and with the statutory criteria well in mind'.[1]

1 *Celaire* [2009] EWCA Crim 633 at [23]2, [2009] EWCA Crim 1077.

7.68 Section 78(3) requires that the new evidence be 'highly probative of the case against the acquitted person'. This refers to the probative value of the evidence itself: would the evidence in itself be strong enough to justify ordering a retrial? In *R v G (G)*, Hughes LJ reasoned that 'it is only where there is compelling new evidence of guilt, of the kind which cannot realistically be disputed, that the exceptional step of quashing an acquittal will be justified'. However, this does not mean that absolute proof of guilt is required.[1] The Court of Appeal determines whether the evidence is new, compelling and reliable in its opinion—not whether it would be deemed reliable by a jury. This means that the court will subject the evidence deemed to be 'new and compelling' to detailed examination when considering a Part 10 application.

1 Per Lord Judge CJ in *R v Dobson* [2011] EWCA Crim 1255 at [20].

7.69 The Court of Appeal decisions on Part 10 can be divided into four broad categories based on the type of 'new and compelling' evidence said to have arisen:

(i) The first of these categories concerns cases in which 'similar fact' evidence has arisen subsequent to the acquittal. In *Andrews*,[1] the defendant was acquitted of the rape of a minor following a full jury trial in 2004. After the acquittal, the police conducted further inquiries, which led to allegations by seven other minors. The Court of Appeal ordered a re-trial on the basis that the new complaints showed substantial similarities with the original complaints and went to the propensity of the defendant to commit such offences. Similarly, in *Khatkar*,[2] the defendant had been acquitted in 2012 of the rape of a woman in her home, but he was arrested only weeks later in relation to a series of further attacks with similarities to the offence of which he had been acquitted. The Court of Appeal quashed the acquittal because of the 'similar fact' evidence and the prosecution tried Khatkar on an indictment including both the original rape charge and the subsequent offences, of which he was convicted. Finally, in the case of *Celaire*,[3] the Court of Appeal quashed the acquittal of the defendant for the murder of his ex-girlfriend after he subsequently attacked another ex-girlfriend. A retrial was ordered of the original murder offence based on the circumstantial similarities between the attacks.

(ii) In cases in which the 'new and compelling evidence' is by way of a confession, the Court of Appeal has reached contrasting decisions. In *R v Dunlop,*[4] the first such application to come before the Court of Appeal under these provisions, the defendant had subsequently confessed to a murder of which he had been acquitted and had pleaded guilty to perjury for lying at the original murder trial. Arguments were raised before the court that it would be unjust to try the defendant because he had only confessed to the murder on the basis that he could not be re-tried for it. This was held to be an insufficient reason to prevent a retrial taking place. The decision in *Dunlop* contrasts with subsequent decisions in the cases of *R v Miell*[5] and *R v Whittle.*[6] Similar facts arose in these cases, except that the defendants had retracted their confessions and, in the course of argument before the Court of Appeal, significant doubts were raised as to the reliability of those confessions. In the circumstances, the applications for re-trial was refused, distinguishing *Dunlop*. Furthermore, Dunlop had admitted perjury at his trial for murder, a point of which Judge CJ took account in *Whittle.*[7]

(iii) The Court of Appeal has twice refused to order a re-trial where the 'new and compelling evidence' was an account of the incident by a co-defendant, who in both cases had provided the evidence pursuant to a s 74 SOCPA agreement with the prosecution.[8] The Court held that the evidence was not 'compelling', as it was not reliable due to the co-accused's lack of credibility.

(iv) The final category of 'new and compelling' evidence that has come before the court in Part 10 applications is forensic evidence. The Court of Appeal has ordered a re-trial in two rape cases[9] and two murder cases in which new DNA evidence later became available.[10] The case of Gary Dobson is undoubtedly the most high-profile Part 10 case. Dobson was one of three defendants acquitted in 1996 in a private prosecution of the much publicised, racist murder of fifteen-year-old Stephen Lawrence in 1993. New forensic evidence was uncovered, the most significant of which was a bloodstain on the collar of Dobson's jacket, a match that had the probability of a billion to one that it came from someone other than Stephen Lawrence. The Court of Appeal quashed his acquittal; Dobson was convicted of the murder at a re-trial in 2012. A more recent example comes from *R v Bishop*. The defendant had been acquitted of the murder of two nine-year-old girls in 1987. Despite the similarities between this allegation and the later attack, the principle preventing double jeopardy had originally stopped a re-trial. However, new and compelling evidence emerged from the original exhibits, including DNA, clothing fibres and paint. Following *Dobson*, the Court of Appeal, therefore, quashed the acquittals and ordered a re-trial in the interests of justice.[11]

1 [2008] EWCA Crim 2908.
2 *Guardian*, 7 December 2013.
3 [2009] EWCA Crim 663.
4 [2007] 1 WLR 1657.
5 [2008] 1 Cr App R 23.
6 [2010] EWCA Crim 2954.
7 At [24].
8 *R v B (J)* [2009] EWCA Crim 1036; *R v G (G)* [2009] EWCA Crim 1077.
9 *R v D* [2012] EWCA Crim 2370; *McGuire*, unreported.
10 *R v Weston* [2010] EWCA Crim 1576; *R v Dobson* [2011] EWCA Crim 1255.
11 *R v Bishop* [2018] EWCA Crim 27, [130]–[133].

7.70 Once the Court of Appeal has determined that there is 'new and compelling evidence', it must then determine whether it is in the interests of justice to quash the acquittal and order a re-trial. Section 79 of the CJA contains a non-exhaustive list of factors which the court should take into account when determining this question; however, in reality, if the evidence is held to be new and compelling, a re-trial will almost always be in the interests of justice. Where there is new and compelling evidence, the court has always found that it would be in the interests of justice for there to be a re-trial.

7.71 The DPP must be satisfied, when applying for such an order, that it would be consistent with the UK's obligations under Arts 31 or 34 of the European Union Treaty relating to the principle of '*ne bis in idem*'. However, in the light of the UK's departure from the European Union, there is argument about the position going forward. According to the existing authorities, the Court of Appeal does not have to be satisfied that these specific obligations are not interfered with; however, it may be able this factor in deciding whether a re-trial is in the interests of justice.

Case stated

7.72 Pursuant to s 111 of the Magistrates' Courts Act 1980, the prosecution may appeal to the Divisional Court in the case of a summary acquittal on the ground that the acquittal 'is wrong in law or is an excess of jurisdiction'. If the prosecution appeal succeeds, the Divisional Court can substitute its own finding or order a re-hearing.

Appeal to the Supreme Court

7.73 Pursuant to ss 1 and 2 of the Administration of Justice Act 1960, when the Court of Appeal quashes a conviction, the prosecution can appeal to the Supreme Court.

Retrial following successful appeal against conviction

7.74 Pursuant to s 1 of the Criminal Appeal Act 1968, the Court of Appeal has the power to order re-trial whenever it allows an appeal against conviction if it considers that this would be in the interests of justice.

Tainted acquittals

7.75 Pursuant to ss 54–56 of the Criminal Procedure and Investigations Act 1996, a procedure has been created whereby a person can be re-tried for an offence for which they have already been acquitted, so long as that acquittal is judged to be 'tainted'.

7.76 These sections were inserted into the CPIA 1996 as a result of fears concerning the practice of 'jury nobbling'. Such was the concern that major offenders were evading justice by corrupting or intimidating jurors that Parliament created an unprecedented procedure whereby a valid acquittal could be quashed by the High Court if it were satisfied that the four conditions set out in s 55 CPIA were satisfied. The first condition, the most significant for present purposes, is as follows: 'that it appears to the High Court likely that, but for the interference or intimidation [of a juror or witness], the acquitted person would not have been acquitted'. The relevant procedure to be followed is set out in Pts 36 and 39 of the Criminal Procedure Rules.

Army Act 1955, s 33

7.77 A person tried by a court-martial shall not subsequently retried by a civil court.

Magistrates' Courts Act 1980, s 27

7.78 'Where on the summary trial of an information for an offence triable either way the court dismissed the information, the dismissal shall have the same effect as an acquittal on an indictment.'

Extradition

7.79 See Chapter 8 of this work for consideration of this topic.

Issue estoppel

7.80 One of the issues considered by the House of Lords in *Humphrys* was whether the doctrine of issue estoppel applied to criminal cases and whether it was available as a plea in bar to an indictment. The doctrine may be defined as follows: if in the course of deciding a cause of action one specific issue is determined, then, should that issue arise as an essential ingredient in subsequent proceedings between the prosecution and defence, it cannot be re-litigated.

7.81 In *Connelly*, the appellant contended that the doctrine did apply and operated in favour of the accused, which should have prevented his second trial for robbery. On the facts (see para **7.9**), the appellant contended that the quashing of the murder conviction must constitute a finding in favour of the defendant on the essential issue of alibi, i.e. the court must have held that his alibi was correct and therefore, as it concerned the second trial, the prosecution could not seek to argue that he was present during the robbery. While this submission was rejected after discussion of the principle of issue estoppel, the availability of the doctrine was not decided by the House in *Connelly*. The matter was left to the consideration of the House of Lords in *Humphrys*.[1] The court held that the doctrine had no place in English criminal proceedings. The House held that it cannot be known how juries arrive at their verdicts, with reasons never being given. As a result, it would be an exercise fraught with both speculation and uncertainty in a particular case to speculate about which issues a jury had determined in favour of the defence or the prosecution.

1 [1977] AC 1.

7.82 That said, the doctrine may have survived, albeit in a rudimentary form. In *R v Hay*,[1] the defendant was alleged to have made a statement to the police admitting two offences, burglary and arson. He was tried, first, on the arson charge, the prosecution asserting that he had made a true confession. The defendant said that he had never made the confession; it was a police fabrication. He was acquitted. The prosecution then decided to proceed with a second trial for burglary, again relying on the disputed confession. The defendant asserted that this was fabricated and, in support of that claim, sought to rely on his previous acquittal. The trial judge refused to admit evidence of the acquittal in the first trial. The Court of Appeal disagreed with this refusal, holding that the jury's acquittal was conclusive evidence that the defendant was not guilty of arson and that his confession to that offence was untrue. The jury should, therefore, have been made aware of this and directed that, in deciding the issue in relation to the burglary, it should bear in mind that the admission in relation to the arson made at the same time as that relating to the burglary had to be regarded as untrue.

1 (1983) 77 Cr App R 70. See also *R v B* (3 December 1999, unreported).

7.83 However, the distinction between this principle and the possibility of issue estoppel somewhat exploded in Lane LCJ's reasoning in *H*,[1] where he considered that fairness, rather than any abstruse legal principle, was the basis on which a judge's reasoning should be based. Lord Lane clearly considered that issue estoppel was unnecessary, given the availability of the abuse of process discretion in a double jeopardy context.

1 (1989) 90 Cr App R 440.

7.84 The effect of this rejection of issue estoppel in the jurisprudence of the courts of England and Wales on abuse of process also appears in *R v Horsham Justices, ex p Reeves*.[1] In that case, the accused's submission of no case to answer in respect of various charges against him was upheld by the magistrates at the committal and he was discharged in respect of them. Subsequently, the prosecution restarted its case and recharged the same offences. The accused pleaded *both autrefois acquit* and issue estoppel; the case went to the Divisional Court. Ackner LJ dismissed both pleas. *Autrefois acquit* did not arise because, as the court held in *Snelson*,[2] *autrefois acquit* does not lie in respect of a discharge at committal proceedings. In relation to issue estoppel, despite the fact that the magistrates had already explicitly and directly considered and dismissed the charges against him, estoppel could not be asserted because of the decision in *Humphrys*, which rejected the applicability of the doctrine. Ackner LJ, however, reasoned that the court was not powerless to prevent repeated attempts by the prosecution to have the accused committed for trial. If, following scrutiny of all the circumstances, such attempts were vexatious and/or oppressive and constituted an abuse of process, the case could be stayed.

1 See para **7.103**.
2 See para **7.103**.

7.85 Bearing in mind this wholesale rejection of issue estoppel, a doctrine regarded as a fundamental part of the US jurisprudence concerned with double jeopardy, three observations can be made:

(1) In accepting that abuse of process should be the principal remedy against situations of double jeopardy, the Court in *Humphrys*, in effect, decided that a court's approach would be based on discretion and fairness, not on more rigid legal concepts such as estoppel.

(2) In determining whether proceedings were fair or unfair, a court of review should avoid being drawn into an assessment of how, for example, a jury arrived at its verdict. This is important in order to avoid any temptation of creating a notional and rational jury that is, ultimately, a product of judicial fiction.

(3) In considering its abuse jurisdiction as to whether a second trial for the defendant would be vexatious or oppressive, a court can certainly consider what issues the first trial raised and whether they were resolved in favour of the defence. If so, this consideration is highly relevant to the question of whether a defendant should be in danger of being tried twice. See para **7.109** for consideration of the ruling of Buckley J in *R v Maxwell*.[1]

1 (September 1996, unreported).

Authorities post-Connelly

7.86 In *Connelly*, the Court held that there was an inherent jurisdiction to stay prosecutions on the grounds of unfairness created by double jeopardy. It was then left to the courts to apply it to the facts of different cases. The first post-

Connelly authority on this issue was *Riebold.*[1] In *Riebold*, the two defendants were indicted on twenty-nine counts, the first two being counts of conspiracy. The remaining twenty-seven related to overt acts relied on by the prosecution as acts in furtherance of the conspiracy and, therefore, probative of the conspiracy counts. At the first trial, the prosecution proceeded only on the second count of conspiracy. The defendants were acquitted. The prosecution then sought leave to proceed on all the remaining counts. Barry J refused leave on the ground that the prosecution was effectively seeking to secure a re-trial of the whole case. Barry J held that the subject matter of counts three to twenty-nine:

> '… did in fact constitute the whole of the overt acts of conspiracy on which the prosecution relied, and there were no additional facts or evidence on which the prosecution relied in order to secure a conviction on the conspiracy charge'.[2]

1 [1965] 1 All ER 653.
2 At 656.

7.87 *Riebold*[1] is an important authority, establishing that it is impermissible for prosecutors to enjoy a free licence to have, as it were, a 'second bite of the cherry'. In *Riebold*, the defendants had been been acquitted in circumstances in which the prosecution had carefully chosen the count on to proceed in the first trial. Those defendants were entitled to expect that a second trial would not commence against them based on the same evidence given in the first trial. The prosecution's desire to maximise the chances of a conviction had to be constrained by the values of both fairness and the avoidance of oppression.

1 [1965] 1 All ER 653.

7.88 The issue of double jeopardy in the context of complex conspiracy cases must be examined carefully, however. In *Ali and Others*,[1] the police uncovered a plot alleged to involve the detonation of improvised explosive devices (IEDs) on a number of transatlantic airliners by suicide bombers, with the intention of causing loss of life. Eleven defendants were indicted and sent for trial on an indictment. At the first trial of some of the defendants, the first count on the indictment alleged that the defendants had 'conspired together and with others to murder person unknown'. Following representations from counsel, Count 1 became Count 1A and a new Count 1 was inserted, which alleged that the defendants 'conspired together to murder persons unknown by the detonation of [IEDs] on board transatlantic passenger aircraft'. Three of the appellants had been convicted of count 1A, but the jury had been unable to agree about count 1 in relation to any of the appellants. The jury had also been unable to agree about count 1A in relation to four of the appellants. The prosecution sought a re-trial for those not convicted of count 1A and for all in relation to count 1. With a further mixture of verdicts at the second trial, there was then a third trial, which eventually led to the last appellants being convicted of count 1A. The primary ground of appeal was abuse of process, relying on the principle of *autrefois convict.*

Dismissing the appeals, the Court of Appeal held that the two different conspiracy counts reflected different offences: one a general conspiracy to murder and the other a conspiracy to murder in a specific way. There was the possibility of two distinct agreements on the evidence advanced by the prosecution. Although the object was to commit the same underlying offence of murder, they were distinct and different agreements, as the latter involved a more complex and sophisticated agreement to do so by detonating explosives on aircraft. The two conspiracy counts were, therefore, not the same in fact and in law for the purposes of autrefois convict. The appeals were dismissed.

1 [2011] EWCA Crim 1260.

7.89 Similarly, in the case of *R v Coughlan and Young*, the defendant was convicted at the Crown Court sitting at Manchester of conspiracy to cause explosions in the United Kingdom between 1973 and 1974. He was subsequently indicted in the Crown Court sitting at Birmingham with conspiring to cause explosions in the same time period and pleaded *autrefois convict*. The Court of Appeal held that there was no difficulty in law about alleging a separate conspiracy to cause explosions in Manchester and another to cause explosions in Birmingham, even though the acts were part of a wider conspiracy to cause explosions in the United Kingdom. The principle was stated as follows:

> 'The wider agreement or conspiracy would not preclude the existence of sub-agreements or sub-conspiracies to cause explosions in particular places, and as a matter of law these sub-conspiracies or agreements could properly be charged as separate offences. Acquittal or conviction on a charge of one such offence would be no bar to the trial of the same accused on another'.[1]

1 [1976] 63 Cr App Rep 33 at [35].

7.90 Post-*Riebold,* double jeopardy was reconsidered by the House of Lords in *Humphrys* (as noted above). It is apparent from the Law Lords' speeches that case that the Lords were concerned that the decision in *Connelly* would be interpreted by lower courts as tantamount to a near unbridled discretion to stop a prosecution if the tribunal considered it to be unfair or oppressive. The Lords sought to correct this perceived error and make plain that a judge should only intervene where there is, on the clearest grounds, an abuse. For example, Lord Salmon said:

> '… a judge [has no] power to refuse to allow a prosecution to proceed merely because he considers that, as a matter of policy, it ought not to have been brought. It is only if the prosecution amounts to an abuse of process of the court and is oppressive and vexatious that the judge has the power to intervene'.[1]

1 [1977] AC 1 at 46.

7.91 Viscount Dilhorne echoed similar sentiments, warning that the power to stop a prosecution should only be used 'in the most exceptional circumstances'. Viscount Dilhorne continued that 'a judge has no power to quash a properly preferred indictment because he thinks that the prosecution of the defendant for the defence should not have been instituted'.[1] Further, 'the judge must not appear to have any responsibility for the institution of a prosecution'.[2]

1 At 509.
2 At 511.

7.92 Since *Humphrys*, courts intermittently deemed it necessary to restate similar principles, perhaps perceiving that various tribunals have shown an undue willingness to stay prosecutions. An example is the judgment of Bingham LCJ in *Environment Agency v Stanford*.[1] Lord Bingham considered that a magistrate had improperly refused to commit a defendant for trial in view of a perceived abuse. Lord Bingham reasoned that, even if on reasonable grounds a court considers that a prosecution should never have been brought, such views are only to be reflected by mitigating the sentence imposed. Furthermore, it was of no benefit to the defendant if a stay were granted by the magistrates' court only to be reversed on appeal. Post-*Humphrys*, then, the main authorities concerning double jeopardy can be considered.

1 [1998] COD 373.

'Same activity' cases

7.93 Cases falling within this category are largely road traffic cases. In *R v Moxon-Tritsch*,[1] the defendant was convicted of driving without due care and attention and driving when having drunk an amount of alcohol exceeding the prescribed limit. A private prosecution was later instituted for causing death by reckless driving. The defendant applied for a stay, which was successful. It was clear that the proposed prosecution arose from the same facts as those on which the defendant had already been convicted. In essence, the case concerned whether the court should countenance a situation in which a conviction is followed by a prosecution for a greater and encompassing offence. The defendant's careless driving was necessarily subsumed into the question of whether such driving was also reckless. Faulks J was satisfied that it would be an abuse to allow the private prosecution to continue. It was oppressive for the defendant to be tried twice and, this time, for a more aggravated form of the same offence to which the defendant had already pleaded guilty.

1 [1988] Crim LR 46.

7.94 A similar situation arose in *R v Forest of Dean Justices, ex p Farley*.[1] There was a clear overlap of fact between two charges of driving having drunk an amount of alcohol exceeding the prescribed limit and causing death by reckless driving. The defendant was charged with both offences, but he was first brought before the magistrates only for the first charge. The prosecution opposed the defence's application for an adjournment of this charge until the determination of the graver charge, causing death by reckless driving. The prosecution submitted that the trial relating to the summary offence should proceed, as it was important to ascertain in relation to both charges whether the defendant had driven having drunk too much alcohol. Furthermore, so the prosecution argued, a conviction in respect of this offence would then mean that, at the trial of the graver offence, the prosecution could seek to rely on the fact and circumstances of the conviction, giving rise to the presumption in s 74(2) of the PACE. In other words, the prosecution made plain its wish to have a trial in the magistrates' court for the purpose of obtaining evidence to use against the defendant at a later trial in the Crown Court for a more serious offence.

1 [1990] RTR 228.

7.95 The defence argued that this was unfair and was an abuse, particularly because the only foundation for the allegation of reckless driving was the alleged excess alcohol. In addition to that, the defendant would be forced to give evidence at two separate trials and would be open to cross-examination at the second trial on any discrepancy between these two sets of evidence. The prosecution response to this submission was that the prosecution enjoyed a discretion of how to proceed with cases and, in any event, the unfairness could be dealt with by the trial judge under s 78 of the PACE. The Divisional Court held that the prosecution's attempt to reverse the burden of proof, using s 74(2), constituted an abuse. Neil J relied on the general 'rule' that, after trial on a lesser charge, a person should not be tried again on the same facts for a more serious offence. There are, however, two special features of *Farley* that should not be overlooked. First, it related to subsequent trials and not two charges brought on the same occasion to be tried together. Second, in *Farley*, the only basis for alleging reckless driving was the evidence of excess alcohol. Where there is additional evidence of a dangerous manoeuvre, for example, the outcome may be different. *Farley* was distinguished in *R v LSA*[1], *R v Prigmore*[2] and *R v Hartnett*[3] on the basis of these special features. It was, however, followed in *R v Phipps*,[4] a case in which a prosecution for dangerous driving was stayed as an abuse as it appeared to have arisen from an injured party's dissatisfaction with the sentence for the original offence relating to excess alcohol.

1 [2008] RTR 25.
2 [2005] EWCA Crim 2476.
3 [2003] EWCA Crim 345.
4 [2005] EWCA Crim 33.

7.96 In *R v K, B and A*,[1] an application to stay the prosecution was made on the grounds that material available to the prosecution in the course of prior forgery proceedings should have been sufficient to alert the prosecution to the defendants' alleged terrorist activities. It was argued successfully in the Crown Court that the prosecution's failure to charge the defendants at that earlier stage should bar subsequent proceedings under the Terrorism Act 2000. The Court of Appeal, however, overturned stay. The mere existence of evidence was insufficient to put the defendants in jeopardy of conviction and, in any event, the facts of the two offences were held to be too different.

1 See para **7.55** above.

7.97 These cases contrast with the situation in *R v Thomson Holidays Ltd.*[1] In that case, the defendants pleaded guilty to an offence under the Trade Descriptions Act 1968 in relation to the making of false statements in a travel brochure. The statements related to a particular hotel in Greece and its amenities. One year later, they were charged under the same provision in relation to the same statement. Both prosecutions had arisen from separate complaints made by people who had booked separate holidays at the hotel. The defendants submitted that the second proceedings constituted an abuse. The Court of Appeal, however, disagreed. It held that the Trade Descriptions Act contemplated that more than one prosecution could be brought in respect of the same course of conduct. The Act was designed to protect members of the public as individuals.

1 [1974] QB 592.

7.98 *Thomson Holidays* was followed in *North Yorkshire Trading Standards v Coleman*.[1] The defendant was prosecuted for the same offences under the Trade Descriptions Act, as it had been previously before a different court. However, it had been acquitted in that earlier trial and so argued abuse in relation to the second trial, bearing in mind that the facts in both were closely similar. This argument was rejected.

1 [2001] EWHC 818, (2001) 166 JP 76.

Separate prosecutions by different prosecution agencies: Sequential trials and special circumstances

7.99 The diversity of statutes creating criminal offences has led to a diversity of separate and independent prosecutors. An important example of lack of co-ordination leading to the finding of an abuse was *R v Beedie*.[1] In *Beedie*, a tenant died of carbon monoxide poisoning caused by defects in a gas fire in premises owned by the defendant landlord. The death was investigated by a variety of agencies, including the Health and Safety Executive ('HSE') and the police. Before the police reported to the Crown Prosecution Service concerning a prosecution by it, the landlord had already been charged and convicted at the behest of the HSE in relation to offences against the Health and Safety at Work etc Act 1974. Furthermore, the local authority had also prosecuted him in relation to dangerous gas fires. Only after these two convictions and an inquest was the landlord charged with manslaughter by the CPS.

1 [1998] QB 356.

7.100 At trial, the landlord both pleaded *autrefois convict* and argued for a stay. The judge rejected this argument. The defendant's appeal was principally based on whether the judge should have stayed the prosecution because of the rule established in *Connelly* that, apart from special circumstances, there should be no sequential trials on an ascending scale of gravity. In recognising this rule and applying it in this case, the Court of Appeal held that the rule is not part of the doctrine of *autrefois* but should, absent exceptional circumstances, give rise to the exercise of the wider discretionary power to stay proceedings as an abuse. Here, the charge of manslaughter should have been stayed because of the previous sets of proceedings. In the court's view, there were no special circumstances that should have persuaded the judge otherwise. Rose LJ reasoned that, for example, the principle might not apply where a charge of murder or manslaughter was brought where the alleged victim has died after proceedings for assault. The additional fact of the death means that exceptional circumstances would exist. This was indeed the decision of the Court of Appeal in *R v Young*.[1]

1 (2005) EWCA Crim 2963.

7.101 Another illustration of 'special circumstances' is the decision of the Court of Appeal for Gibraltar in *A-G for Gibraltar v Leoni*.[1] In that case, the court held that the discovery of new evidence may amount to a special circumstance. It should also be noted that, in both *Beedie* and *Phipps*,[2] it was held that, unlike other cases of abuse of process, the burden is not on the defence to show that there cannot be a fair trial. Instead, the burden is on the prosecution to show that there are special circumstances justifying a second trial.

1 Criminal Appeal No 4 (1998).
2 See para **7.95** above.

7.102 An instance of the principle against sequential trials not being applied was in *R v South Hampshire Magistrates' Court, ex p Crown Prosecution Service*.[1] The defendant was tried in December 1995 and acquitted. In January 1996, along with others, he was re-arrested and charged with a series of connected but different offences. He argued that the failure of the prosecution to consolidate all their charges against him in one indictment and in one trial was an abuse. At committal, the magistrates agreed, but the Divisional Court, on a judicial review application brought by the DPP, disagreed. A second trial on the same or similar facts was, in the view of the court, not necessarily oppressive. In this case, there were special circumstances that made it just and convenient for there to be two trials. For example, there was the lack of a significant evidential overlap between the two proceedings and the delay to the first trial, which would have occurred had it not proceeded but been consolidated with the second.

1 [1998] Crim LR 422.

Repeated committal proceedings cases

7.103 In *R v Manchester City Stipendiary Magistrate, ex p Snelson*,[1] it was held that a discharge at committal proceedings did not prohibit fresh committal proceedings for the same offence. The doctrine *of autrefois acquit* did not apply, neither was it an abuse. However, in *R v Horsham Justices, ex p Reeves*,[2] it was held that the second set of committal proceedings should be stayed as an abuse. The court held that the prosecution had treated the first set of proceedings as a 'dummy run' and, having learnt lessons, had brought the same proceedings, albeit then in a simplified form. Ackner LJ began his judgment reasoning that the case provided a cautionary tale, 'the moral of which is do not overload a prosecution with unnecessary charges'.[3] He held that to allow the prosecution to proceed would be wrong:

> 'to grant such an indulgence would in my judgment, encourage poor preparation with a resultant waste of time and money … the prosecution must direct its energies to the simplification of cases they desire to proceed'.[4]

In a call for such simplification, Ackner LJ considered that:

> 'All too often juries, and to a lesser extent magistrates, are treated like computers into whom superfluous and ill-digested material is fed in the over-optimistic hope that somehow or another they will produce the right result'.

1 (1977) 66 Cr App R 44.
2 (1980) 75 Cr App R 236n.
3 (1980) 75 Cr App R 236n.
4 (1980) 75 Cr App R 236n at 240.

7.104 *Reeves* was, however, distinguished in *R v Willesden Justices, ex p Clemmings*.[1] In this case, the first set of committal proceedings had been dismissed by the magistrates for failure to serve the advance information on time. A fortnight later, the defendant had been re-charged and the advance information properly served. The defendant, relying on *Reeves*, argued that this was an abuse. Lord Justice Bingham disagreed. In refusing a stay, Bingham LJ reasoned that:

> 'The ultimate objective of this discretionary power is to ensure that there shall be a fair trial according to law which involves fairness both to the defendant and the prosecution, for as Lord Diplock said in *Sang* "The fairness of the trial ... is not all one sided".'

In the reasoning of Bingham LJ, the decision to re-charge the defendant was not manifestly unreasonable, there was no evidence that the second proceedings would unfairly prejudice the defendant and there was no evidence of the prosecution's desire to deprive the defendant of any lawful protection.

1 (1987) 87 Cr App R 280.

Sequential trials in complex trials arising out of severance of the indictment

7.105 Particularly in the area of serious or complex fraud, the courts have repeatedly emphasised the need for severance of an indictment so as to ensure manageable and not unduly long trials.[1] The best example of a prosecutor's failure to heed this exhortation was the *Blue Arrow* case, the Serious Fraud Office's ('SFO') prosecution of *R v Cohen*[2] in which the Court of Appeal criticised both the trial judge and the SFO for failing to exercise the power of severance to ensure a fair and manageable trial. The consequence of severance, however, must be more than one trial.

1 See for example *R v Novac* (1977) 65 Cr App Rep 107 and *R v Kellard* [1995] 2 Cr App Rep 134.

2 [1992] NLJR 1267, CA.

7.106 In the context of double jeopardy, the interplay between severance and abuse arose in the proposed second trial of Kevin Maxwell, following his acquittal in the first. Prior to the first trial, with the consent of all concerned, the SFO had severed the indictment, accepting that not all counts could be tried together. At the first trial, Kevin Maxwell and the other defendants were tried on only two counts (counts 4 and 10) of the original ten-count indictment on which they were arraigned. Following the acquittal on these counts, the prosecution proposed a second trial of counts 1, 2 and 9. The prosecution contended that these counts were in a separate category from 4 and 10, and factual issues in the first trial would not need to be re-litigated in the second.

7.107 In answer to the defence contention that it would be oppressive for Kevin Maxwell to be tried again, the prosecution contended that the second trial was a result of the earlier severance of the indictment, to which the defence had agreed. Furthermore, the prosecution had agreed to this, respecting the courts' entreaties to avoid long trials. Were a second trial to be stayed, it would mean that mere complexity of the issues would result in the prosecution being unfairly and permanently deprived of presenting a significant part of its case to a jury. How, then, could it be unfair and an abuse of process to proceed with the second trial?

7.108 The defence fundamentally disagreed, arguing that all along the prosecution's case had been presented as one continuing offence of fraud and that, in any event, it would be impossible to separate the factual issues raised in the first trial from those to be raised in the second. For example, Kevin Maxwell's honesty or dishonesty was a central feature in the first trial; it would again be in the second trial.

7.109 Buckley J ruled that a second trial would constitute an abuse. He held that a central theme in the first trial was Kevin Maxwell's alleged dishonesty, and that there would be a significant overlap of factual issues between the first and the proposed second trial. Furthermore, Buckley J held that the counts, 4 and 10, tried at the first trial:

> 'constituted a fair presentation of the real dishonesty or fraud alleged by the prosecution … I have no doubt that those were clearly the most serious examples the prosecution had of the fraudulent course of conduct alleged doubtless that is why they were put forward as a basis for the first trial'.[1]

1 At p 22.

7.110 Buckley J also noted the fact that he had:

> 'not been referred to any long fraud case in which after an acquittal a further trial has proceeded. Mr Lissack drew my attention to several instances of retrials following abortive first trials or appeals. I do not consider those analogous. In such cases there have been either no acquittal on the merits or determination at all'.[1]

1 At p 23.

7.111 In the most significant passage of his judgment dealing with both the prosecution and the defence submissions, Buckley J reasoned that:

> 'I wish to make it plain, I am not suggesting that an acquittal even after a long trial necessarily means that severed counts cannot be tried. Each case will turn on its own particular circumstances; there are many factors to be considered as I have already observed. I am suggesting that if all parties have played their part and the essential criminality alleged has been placed before a jury who have acquitted, it should be unusual for a second trial to take place. The reason is that it would be very likely to appear to the public that the authorities were not prepared to accept the verdict of a jury and were determined to pursue the defendant at whatever cost to the public purse, or time, or disruption of the defendant's personal life, business or professional career. But that must not happen'.[1]

1 At p 23.

SIMILAR FACT

7.112 Now replaced by the Criminal Justice Act 2003, the 'similar fact' principle at common law was considered in the decision of *R v Z*.[1] In that case, the defendant was tried for rape and his defence was consent. To rebut this defence, the prosecution sought and obtained the leave of the trial judge to admit evidence of three previous allegations of rape against the defendant, which he had similarly denied this on the basis of purported consent. In particular, the prosecution sought to call the complainants in relation to those allegations. By admitting such evidence, the relevance of which was accepted by all as sufficient to fall within the 'similar fact' principle, the prosecution aimed to undermine the defence of consent. The issue of double jeopardy arose because the defendant had previously been tried and acquitted of each of these rape allegations.

1 [2000] 2 AC 483.

7.113 In *Sambasivam*, the defendant was charged with possession of a firearm and possession of ammunition (some of which was loaded in the firearm). The defendant was acquitted of possession of the ammunition and a re-trial ordered on possession of the firearm. On the re-trial the prosecution relied on a statement, which the defendant denied making, in which he allegedly stated that he had been in possession of a firearm and ammunition. The defendant was convicted of possession of a firearm.

Prior to Z, the rule in *Sambasivam* had been used to prevent the prosecution bringing any proceedings or calling any evidence, which suggested that the previous acquittal was wrong. However, in Z, the House of Lords restricted the rule while confirming the correctness of the original decision. The defendant in *Sambasivam* should not have been tried again on the basis that a defendant should not be prosecuted again where two offences arose out of one incident and a conviction in respect of one count would be inconsistent with acquittal in respect of the other.

Viewed in this way, *Sambasivam* was a simple case of double jeopardy and was in fact one of the cases considered and approved in *Connelly*. However, as a rule of evidence in proceedings for a separate offence, the House of Lords held that the principle of double jeopardy was not breached by suggesting that the accused was guilty of that offence based on his alleged commission of similar offences, for which he had been tried and acquitted.

7.114 In *R v Terry*,[1] the Court of Appeal held that the principles in Z were not simply limited to 'similar fact' evidence. In *R v Nguyen*,[2] the court also affirmed that Z applied not only to previous allegations of which a defendant had been acquitted, but also to allegations that the prosecution had chosen not to pursue.

1 (2005) 2 Cr App R 7.
2 [2008] EWCA Crim 585, (2008) *The Times*, 16 May.

DOUBLE JEOPARDY UNDER EUROPEAN HUMAN RIGHTS LAW

7.115 Bearing in mind that the prohibition of double jeopardy has been an elemental principle of the English common law for a long period, and that English jurists played a major role in the drafting of the European Convention on Human Rights ('ECHR'), it is surprising that the ECHR itself does not contain any explicit prohibition on double jeopardy. Recognising this omission in the case of *X v Austria*,[1] the Commission held that such a prohibition may be implicit within the terms of Art 6.[2] However, in *S v Germany*,[3] the Commission took a contrary view, holding that the prohibition was 'neither expressly nor by way of implication' included within Art 6 guarantees.

1 (1970) 35 CD 151.
2 On occasions the court has been willing to imply into Art 6, guarantees which are not mentioned within its text, eg *Funke v France* (1993) 16 EHRR 297 (protection against self-incrimination).
3 (1983) 39 DR 43.

7.116 The Seventh Protocol to the Convention is generally concerned with additional fair trial guarantees in criminal cases. Article 2 of the Protocol, for example, is concerned with the granting of a right to a review of a criminal conviction or sentence. Article 4 is directly concerned with double jeopardy. Before reciting this article, however, it is important to bear in mind that the Protocol has not yet been formally ratified by the UK and, therefore, does not form part of the Convention implemented in our domestic law by way of the Human Rights Act 1998. The then-government indicated an intention to ratify this Protocol, in its White Paper, 'Rights Brought Home'.[1] The paper states that, 'in general, the provisions of Protocol 7 reflect principles already inherent in our law'. Pursuant to the 1998 Act, the Protocol can be made enforceable via an order under s 1(4). Since 2001, successive governments have indicated that the Protocol would be ratified once legislation has been implemented to amend certain family law provisions. However, the family law provisions remain unamended and the Protocol unratified.

1 Cm 3782, p 18.

7.117 Article 4 of Protocol 7 provides:

'(1) No one shall be liable to be tried or punished again in criminal proceedings under the jurisdiction of the same state for an offence for which he has already been finally acquitted or convicted in accordance with the law and penal procedure of that state;

(2) The provisions of the preceding paragraph shall not prevent the re-opening of the case in accordance with the law and penal procedure of the state concerned, if there is evidence or new or newly discovered facts, or if there has been a fundamental defect in the previous proceedings, which could affect the outcome of the case;

(3) No derogation from the Article shall be made under article 15 of the Convention'.

7.118 Article 4(1) speaks of 'final acquittal or conviction' and this being 'in accordance with the law and penal procedure of that State'. The Explanatory Report to Protocol 7 states that an acquittal or conviction is only to be regarded as final:

> 'if, according to the traditional expression, it has acquired the force of res judicata. This is the case where it is irrevocable, that is to say when no further ordinary remedies are available or when the parties have exhausted such remedies or have permitted the time limit to expire without availing themselves of them.'

This, in other words, means that there is no prohibition of an appeal against acquittal per se, so long as the appeal does not constitute fresh proceedings.

European Court of Human Rights ('ECtHR') authorities

7.119 In *Gradinger v Austria*,[1] the applicant was convicted of causing death by negligent driving. Subsequently, an administrative penalty was imposed on the applicant for driving with excess alcohol, evidence of alcohol presumably not being available at the original trial. The applicant submitted that the subsequent penalty was a breach of art 4(1). The ECtHR agreed, both charges having rested on the same conduct, although the offences were different. The ECtHR was also persuaded that the administrative authorities that had imposed the penalty were 'criminal' for the purposes of this article. (Had the ECtHR been persuaded that the authorities were in fact 'civil', it would not have found a violation.)

1 (1995) Series A/328-C.

7.120 In *Oliveira v Switzerland*,[1] the ECtHR held that successive prosecutions were not necessarily in violation of art 4 if they related to separate offences arising from the same act. The applicant was originally convicted of a lesser offence of failure to control a motor vehicle and, subsequently, for a more serious offence of negligently inflicting personal injury. The applicant complained that she had been prosecuted twice in respect of the same offence, but this was rejected. The ECtHR held that art 4:

> 'does not preclude separate offences, even if they are all part of single criminal act, being tried by different courts especially where, as in the present case, the penalties were not cumulative, the lesser being absorbed by the greater'.[2]

1 [1998] V 1990.
2 At para 27.

7.121 *Oliveira*, therefore, suggests that a breach of art 4(1) occurs only when the offence with which the applicant is charged is, in law, the same offence as that of which the applicant was previously acquitted or convicted. In other words, the ambit of art 4(1) is no further than the autrefois rule considered above.

7.122 There appears to be a conflict between *Gradinger* and *Oliveira*, the former preferring a substantive approach to a formalistic one to the principle of double jeopardy. The latter seems to have preferred the reverse.[1] In a line of subsequent cases, the court has followed the approach in *Gradinger*, with it reasoning in *Franz Fischer v Austria*[2] that:

> '... whilst it is true that the mere fact that a single act constitutes more than one offence is not contrary to [art 4], the Court must not limit itself to finding that an applicant was, on the basis of one act, tried or punished for nominally different offences.'

1 See the dissenting judgment in *Oliveira* of Repik J.
2 37950/97. [2001] ECHR 352, 29 May 2001.

7.123 Article 4(2) allows for the re-opening of a case after a final decision has been made, when a decision is res judicata. Re-opening in this sense contrasts with a fresh prosecution; what is envisaged by art 4(2) is a way of challenging an acquittal by persuading a higher court to re-open it. Article 4(2) allows for this to occur only on two specified grounds: discovery of new evidence; or acceptance that there was a fundamental defect in the original proceedings.

7.124 The European Court has recently considered art 4(2) in the case of *Margus v Croatia*.[1] The applicant was charged in 1993 with various crimes, including murder, committed in 1991 during the war against the Republic of Croatia. On 24 September 1996, the General Amnesty Act was enacted, which provided that a general amnesty was to be applied in respect of all criminal offences committed in connection with the war in Croatia between 1990 and 1996, save in respect of those acts that amounted to war crimes or grave breaches of humanitarian law. In 1997, pursuant to the General Amnesty Act, the criminal proceedings against Margus were terminated by the Osijek County Court. In 2007, the Supreme Court of Croatia held that the decision of the Osijek County Court violated the General Amnesty Act, as there did not exist a direct and significant connection between the criminal offence allegedly committed by Margus and the armed conflict. Margus was then tried and found guilty of war crimes against the civilian population. He appealed to the European Court alleging a breach of art 4(1) to Protocol 7.

The European Court left open the question whether the decision of the Osijek County Court under the General Amnesty Act could be regarded as a 'final acquittal' within the meaning of art 4, noting that that decision did not presuppose any investigation into the charges brought against the applicant and did not amount to an assessment of the applicant's guilt. The court instead considered the case under paragraph 2 of art 4. It held that the granting of amnesty to the applicant in respect of acts characterised as war crimes amounted to a fundamental defect in the proceedings, such that there had been no violation of art 4.

1 Application No 4455/10.

7.125 In relation to tainted acquittals that the High Court can now quash pursuant ss 54 and 56 to the Criminal Procedure and Investigations Act 1996, this appears to be consistent with art 4(2). On that basis, it seems to be the case that, if jurors or witnesses have been intimidated or interfered with, this must amount to a 'fundamental defect' in the proceedings.

7.126 In relation to prosecution right of appeal under Pt 9 of the Criminal Justice Act 2003, a similar system was considered in *State of Trinidad and Tobago v Boyce*.[1] The court considered article 4(2) and held that the ability of an appellate court to correct an error of law, which had led to an acquittal, was not incompatible with the general principles of fairness. It is, therefore, submitted that the new provisions are compatible with art 4(2), as the matter will not constitute *res judicata* until the appellate court has had the opportunity to consider whether there has been a 'fundamental defect'.

1 [2006] 2 WLR 284, PC.

7.127 Based on this overview of European authorities, the English law on double jeopardy seems consistent with ECtHR law.

OTHER RELEVANT INTERNATIONAL OBLIGATIONS

7.128 Following *Criminal Proceedings against Pupino*,[1] courts in the UK are obliged to interpret national law in conformity with European Union law, so far as possible. This, of course, no longer applies, following the UK's departure from the European Union. Prior to the departure, the obligation included giving effect to preliminary rulings by the European Court of Justice on the interpretation of framework decisions. Furthermore, as noted above, under the Criminal Justice Act 2003 provisions for re-trial for serious offences, the DPP is required to consider the UK's obligations under the principle of *'ne bis in idem'* before applying for such a retrial. The concept of *'ne bis in idem'* in civil jurisdictions corresponds approximately with the common law concept of double jeopardy and appears in a number of the UK's international obligations. Article 50 of the European Charter of Fundamental Rights provides that:

> 'No one shall be liable to be tried or punished again in criminal proceedings for an offence for which he or she has already been finally acquitted or convicted within the Union in accordance with the law.'

1 C105/03 (16 June 2005) ECJ.

7.129 The Charter only applies to Member States insofar as they apply European Union law. The principle was enshrined in European jurisprudence by the Convention implementing the Schengen Agreement, art 54 of which reads:

> 'A person whose trial has been finally disposed of in one Contracting Party may not be prosecuted in another Contracting Party for the same acts provided that, if a penalty has been imposed, it has been enforced, is actually in the process of being enforced or can no longer be enforced under the laws of the sentencing Contracting Party.'

7.130 In *Criminal Proceedings concerning van Esbroeck*,[1] the European Court of Justice decided that the reference to 'the same acts' meant that the legal classification of the offence was irrelevant in deciding whether a person could be prosecuted in two different Member States. The criterion was whether the two proceedings involved inextricably linked facts. In that case, it was decided that proceedings in one Member State for exporting narcotic drugs, after the defendant had been prosecuted and convicted in another Member State for importing the same drugs, were in principle contrary to art 54.

1 C-436/04 (9 March 2006), ECJ.

7.131 In *Criminal Proceedings against Hüseyin Gözütok and Klaus Brügge*,[1] proceedings in the Netherlands were discontinued after the defendants agreed to pay a sum of money determined by the prosecution. The ECJ held that subsequent proceedings brought by the German authorities were barred. It was relevant to this decision that the payment of the money constituted a definitive bar to further proceedings under Dutch law.

1 C-187/01 and C-385/01 (11 February 2003), ECJ. See, for a more recent example of consideration of the principle of *ne bis in idem*, *Nichicon Corp v European Commission* (T-342/18) (29 September 2021), paragraphs 512–517.

7.132 The European Commission produced a Green Paper[1] dealing with the problems of allocation of jurisdiction and ne bis in idem, as well as the specific problem of what constitutes 'the same facts'. No legislative proposal has been produced as a result.

At present, the status of these decisions remains uncertain. Practitioners may draw on the existing case law, but they should exercise caution in the absence of guidance from the domestic courts on this issue.

1 COM (2005) 696 Final.

7.133 The International Covenant on Civil and Political Rights, art 14.7, is also binding on the UK and provides that:

> 'No one shall be liable to be tried or punished again for an offence for which he has already been finally convicted or acquitted in accordance with the law and penal procedure of each country.'

SENTENCING

7.134 When it comes to references made by the Attorney General to the Court of Appeal in respect of unduly lenient sentences, pursuant to ss 35 and 36 of the Criminal Justice Act 1988, the Court of Appeal has often allowed some reduction to the revised sentence passed, should the original sentence be considered unduly lenient. In turn, this has led to many defendants expecting such a reduction when awaiting the outcome of appeal proceedings. This appears to constitute what has been known—perhaps erroneously—as a reduction to acknowledge 'double jeopardy'.

However, such reductions have become increasingly difficult to secure. In a line of decisions beginning with *AG's Reference (Nos. 14 and 15 of 2006)*, and including both *AG's Reference (No. 38 of 2013)* and *AG's Reference (No. 45 of 2014)*, the Court of Appeal has emphasised how dependent any reduction will be on the circumstances of the particular case. An extremely long determinate sentence will usually remove the possibility of any reduction. By contrast, the principle may have an effect in other circumstances, such as when the sentence is relatively short or the defendant has already been released.[1]

That said, there remains some possibility, in certain circumstances, for a reduction to be applied based on this principle. For example, in *R v Roberts*, the Court of Appeal reasoned that 'double jeopardy' could be relevant consideration when evaluating the possibility of an offender returning to custody (given the associated distress, anxiety and pain to the offender). Yet, in *Roberts*, the Court of Appeal noted the absence of applicable guidelines for the offence, an aspect that may distinguish the case from others.[2]

1 [2006] EWCA Crim 1335; [2013] EWCA Crim 1450; [2014] EWCA Crim 1566.

2 [2019] EWCA Crim 1931, [4]. For another example of a reduction being applied, see *R v Ferizi (AG's Reference)* [2016] EWCA Crim 2022.

Chapter 8

Abuse in extradition proceedings

8.01 Requests to the UK for extradition can give rise to bad faith, the manipulation of domestic proceedings or other acts of abuse on the part of the requesting state, particularly in high profile, politically-sensitive or urgent cases. Together with the statutory 'extraneous considerations' bar, and the wider human rights protections, provided for by the Extradition Act 2003, the common law abuse of process jurisdiction provides for an important protection against executive abuse. Although now relatively strictly regulated, the abuse jurisdiction has a powerful heritage and continues to have potential application to a wide range of factual scenarios.

8.02 It is crucial at the outset to appreciate that extradition proceedings cannot be equated to domestic criminal proceedings. Not only are they governed by different rules and procedures, but they are also fashioned from different public interests.

8.03 The Supreme Court of Canada put it thus in 1991:

> 'Extradition occupies a unique and important position in the structure of law enforcement … the investigation, prosecution, and suppression of crime for the protection of the citizen and the maintenance of peace and public order is an important goal of all organized societies. The pursuit of that goal cannot realistically be confined within national boundaries. That has long been the case, but it is increasingly evident today. Extradition is a practice which has deep historical roots in this country … While the extradition process is an important part of our system of criminal justice, *it would be wrong to equate it to the criminal trial process. It differs from the criminal process in purpose and procedure and, most importantly, in the factors which render it fair. Extradition procedure, unlike the criminal procedure, is founded on the concepts of reciprocity, comity and respect for differences in other jurisdictions.* This unique foundation means that the law of extradition must accommodate many factors foreign to our internal criminal law. While our conceptions of what constitutes a fair criminal law are important to the process of extradition, they are necessarily tempered by other considerations. Most importantly, our extradition process, while premised on our conceptions of what is fundamentally just, must accommodate differences between our system of criminal justice and the systems in place in reciprocating states. The simple fact is that if we were to insist on strict conformity with our own system, there would be virtually no state in the world with which we could reciprocate. Canada, unable to obtain extradition of persons who commit crimes here and flee elsewhere, would

be the loser. For this reason, we require a limited but not absolute degree of similarity between our laws and those of the reciprocating state. We will not extradite for acts which are not offences in this country. We sign treaties only with states which can assure us that their systems of criminal justice are fair and offer sufficient procedural protections to accused persons. We permit our Minister to demand assurances relating to penalties where the Minister considers such a demand appropriate. But beyond these basic conditions precedent of reciprocity, much diversity is, of necessity, tolerated.'[1] (emphasis added)

1 *Kindler v Canada (Minister of Justice)* [1991] 2 SCR 779 per McLachlin J at 843–845.

STATUTORY PROTECTIONS AGAINST ABUSE

8.04 In *Knowles v Government of the United States of America & another,*[1] Lord Bingham of Cornhill observed that:

> 'Laws governing extradition seek to reconcile two objectives, both of concern to states recognising the rule of law. One objective is to give effect to the principle that, in the ordinary way, persons in one state who are credibly accused of committing serious crimes triable in another should be surrendered to that other to answer for their alleged misdeeds. This is a principle which national authorities, including courts, will seek to honour. The second objective is to protect those whose surrender is sought against such surrender in circumstances where they would, putting it very generally, suffer injustice or oppression. States ordinarily seek to provide some safeguards against the surrender of those within their borders in such circumstances.'

1 [2007] 1 WLR 47, PC at para 12.

8.05 Traditionally, extradition legislation has sought to meet this 'second objective', not by providing the courts with an overriding abuse of process jurisdiction, but by providing specific statutory redress for specific injustice or oppression. Thus the Extradition Act 2003 (the '2003 Act') itself provides many significant inherent safeguards, over and above those which exist in domestic criminal proceedings, that indirectly militate against abuse. In respect of all countries except Part 1 territories[1] and specifically designated Part 2 territories,[2] the requesting government must adduce evidence before a district judge, which constitutes a prima facie case in respect of the charges. Additionally, the many technical prohibitions upon extradition, authentication requirements,[3] and strict time limits[4] of the Extradition Act 2003 provide some general safeguards to a defendant against abuse. As will be seen, the abuse jurisdiction is therefore 'residual in nature' and 'applies only where the issues raised cannot be addressed by the statutory provisions'.[5]

1 Presently Austria, Belgium, Bulgaria, Croatia Cyprus, Czech Republic, Denmark, Estonia, Finland, France, Germany, Gibraltar, Greece, Hungary, Ireland, Italy, Latvia, Lithuania, Luxembourg, Malta, The Netherlands, Poland, Portugal, Romania, Slovakia, Slovenia, Spain, Sweden.

2 Presently Albania, Andorra, Armenia, Australia, Azerbaijan, Bosnia and Herzegovina, Canada, Georgia, Iceland, Israel, Liechtenstein, Macedonia FYR, Moldova, Montenegro,

New Zealand, Norway, Russian Federation, Serbia, South Africa, South Korea, Switzerland, Turkey, Ukraine, United States of America.

3 Section 202.

4 See *Nikonovs v Governor of Brixton Prison & another* [2006] 1 WLR 1518, DC in which discharge was ordered in a case where the defendant was not brought to court for his first appearance 'as soon as practicable', contrary to s 4(2) of the Extradition Act 2003. See also *Huczko v Governor of Wandsworth Prison* [2012] EWHC 4134. In respect of the bringing of appeals, the courts have applied the statutory time limits strictly: *District Court of Vilnius v Barcys* [2007] 1 WLR 3249; *R (on the application of Mendy) v Crown Prosecution Service* [2007] EWHC 1765; *Mucelli v Government of the Republic of Albania* [2007] EWHC 2632 (Admin); *Gercans v The Government of Latvia* [2008] EWHC 884 (Admin) and *Moulai v Deputy Public Prosecutor in Creteil France* [2008] EWHC 1024 (Admin). For example, in *Barcys*, a Requesting State's appeal against discharge was held to be out of time where the Requesting State had been prevented from filing its Notice of Appeal within the applicable seven-day period owing to an electrical blackout in London which had closed the High Court. However, in *Lukaszewski and others, R (on the application of Halligen) v Secretary of State for the Home Department* [2012] UKSC 20, the Supreme Court ruled that in certain circumstances there should be a discretion in exceptional circumstances for judges to extend time for service of appeals against extradition, where the statutory time limits would otherwise operate to prevent an appeal in a manner conflicting with the right of access to an appeal process under Art 6(1) ECHR.

5 *Khan v Government of the USA* [2010] EWHC 1127 (Admin) per Williams J at para 11.

8.06 However, some provisions of the 2003 Act are specifically aimed at providing extradition courts with the duty to refuse extradition in certain specified circumstances traversing the sort of territory with which abuse of process is traditionally concerned.

Extraneous considerations

8.07 Sections 13 and 81 of the 2003 Act provide that a person's extradition will be barred by reason of 'extraneous considerations' if it appears that the Part 1 warrant, or Part 2 request, issued in respect of him, (a) though purporting to be issued on account of the extradition offence, is, in fact, issued for the purpose of prosecuting or punishing him on account of his race, religion, nationality, gender, sexual orientation or political opinions, or (b) if extradited he might be prejudiced at his trial or punished, detained or restricted in his personal liberty by reason of his race, religion, nationality, gender, sexual orientation or political opinions. Speaking in the context of the more restrictively drafted s 3 of the Extradition Act 1870 in *Schtraks v Israel*,[1] Lord Reid observed that '… it appears to me that the provisions … are clearly intended to give effect to the principle that there should in this country be asylum for political refugees' from the Requesting State.[2] Viscount Radcliffe stated that:

> '… in my opinion, the idea that lies behind the phrase 'offence of a political character' is that the fugitive is at odds with the State that applies for his extradition on some issue connected with the political control or government of the country … It does indicate, I think, that the Requesting State is after him for reasons other than the enforcement of the criminal law in its ordinary, what I may call its common or international, aspect'.[3]

1 [1964] AC 556, HL.

2 At 584. See also 582–583. See also Viscount Radcliffe at 591, Lord Evershed at 598. Approved in *Cheng v Governor of Pentonville Prison* [1973] AC 931, HL per Lord Hodson at 942E–H, Lord Diplock at 946F–H, Lord Simon of Glaisdale and Lord Wilberforce at 951A,

953A–E and 954A, Lord Salmon at 961A–D, G–H and 965B–C. See also *R v Governor of Pentonville Prison, ex p Budlong* [1980] 1 WLR 1110, DC per Widgery LCJ and Griffiths J at 1123G–H.

3 At 591. See also Lord Hodson at 612.

8.08 The burden is on the appellant to make out the bar.[1] In the context of s 13(a) of the 2003 Act the requested person must show on the balance of probabilities that 'it appears' that the reason for the issue of the EAW was for the purpose of punishing him on account of one of the '"extraneous considerations" that are identified in section 13(a)'.[2] In the context of s 13(b), he does not have to prove on the balance of probabilities that the events described will take place, but he must show that there is a 'reasonable chance' or 'reasonable grounds for thinking' or a 'serious possibility' that such events will occur (*Fernandez v The Government of Singapore*[3]). In the same case, Lord Parker CJ had observed in the High Court[4] that the central question would be 'was the request, as it were, bona fide for the purposes of prosecuting him for the offence or was it for other purposes on account of his political opinions'.[5] Although s 13(a) enjoins the court to have regard to whether the Pt 1 warrant issued in respect of the person (though purporting to be issued on account of the extradition offence) was in fact issued for the purpose of prosecuting or punishing him on account of his race, religion, nationality, gender, sexual orientation or political opinions, the District Judge is not limited to considering the precise moment when the EAW was issued. He is required to have regard to the underlying process which led to the decision to issue the EAW, so as to consider whether that decision was driven by extraneous considerations: *Adamescu v Bucharest Appeal Court Criminal Division*[6] at para 66. Consideration may extend beyond the state of the mind of the issuing judge to the authorities of the Pt 1 territory: *Slepcik v Governor of HMP Brixton*[7] at [23] per Maurice Kay LJ. The Court in considering these matters is not bound by the ordinary rules of evidence; the appellant may rely on any material in support of a submission based on ss 13 or 81 (*Schtraks v Government of Israel*[8]). The relaxation of the rules of evidence and the protective nature of these bars to extradition does not, however, go so far as to permit the hearing of evidence in a closed material procedure,[9] although evidence from witnesses, whose identities have been withheld from the requesting state and its representatives, may be admitted (see the first instances decisions in *Russian Federation v Trefilov; Turkey v Ipek and others; Azerbaijan v Hajiyeva*).

1 *Antonov & Baranauskas v Prosecutor Generals Office Lithuania* [2015] EWHC 1243 (Admin), at paras 20-21; *Hilali v The Central Court of Criminal Proceedings No 5 of the National Court, Madrid* [2006] 4 All ER 435, DC per Scott Baker LJ at para 62; *Tamarevichute v The Government of the Russian Federation* [2008] EWHC 534 (Admin) per Swift J at para 12; *Ahsan v the Director of Public Prosecutions & others* [2008] EWHC 666 (Admin) per Richards LJ at para 131. *Adamescu v Bucharest Appeal Court Criminal Division* [2020] EWHC 2709 (Admin) at para 65.

2 *Antonov & Baranauskas v Prosecutor Generals Office Lithuania* [2015] EWHC 1243 (Admin), at paras 21; *Adamescu v Bucharest Appeal Court Criminal Division* [2020] EWHC 2709 (Admin) at para 67.

3 [1971] 1 WLR 987, HL per Lord Diplock at 994; *Tamarevichute* (above) per Swift J at para 12. More recently, see *Nikolics v Hungary* [2013] EWHC 2377 (Admin) per Burnett J, at para 11; *Antonov & Baranauskas v Prosecutor Generals Office Lithuania* [2015] EWHC 1243 (Admin), at para 27. In *Adamescu v Bucharest Appeal Court Criminal Division Romania* [2020] EWHC 2709 (Admin) the Court at para 67 summarised: 'the court

is concerned with what may happen in the future if the requested person is extradited. The burden was on the appellant to show that there is a reasonable chance (alternatively expressed as reasonable grounds for thinking, or a serious possibility) that he might be prejudiced at his trial or punished, detained or restricted in his personal liberty on account of his political opinions'.

4 [1971] 1 WLR 459, DC at 466.

5 In *Ahmad v Government of the United States of America* [2006] EWHC 2927 (Admin), the High Court rejected (per Laws LJ at paras 91–100) a submission that the imposition of Special Administrative Measures were applied in America only to Muslim prisoners (and were thus referable to the defendant's religion). See also *Ahsan* at paras 129–141. In *Jaso & others v Central Criminal Court No 2, Madrid* [2007] EWHC 2983 (Admin), the High Court rejected (Per Dyson LJ at paras 59–61) a submission that incommunicado detention policy and a prison dispersal policy were applied only to Muslim prisoners; '[t]here is no basis for a finding other than that all detainees charged with serious offences of terrorism, whatever their political beliefs, will be subject to the same or similar restrictions ...There is no reasonable ground for thinking that there is a causal link between the restrictions on personal liberty and the appellants' political beliefs'. In *Tamarevichute* (above), the High Court rejected a submission that as a person of Romany origin, the appellant might be prejudiced at her trial in Kaliningrad on account of her race. Swift J observed (at para 99) that suffering general prejudice as a result of ethnic origin is not sufficient to constitute a bar to her extradition under the provisions of s 81; specific prejudice is required.

6 [2020] EWHC 2709 (QB).

7 [2004] EWHC 1224 (Admin).

8 [1964] AC 556, HL, at 582 per Lord Reid. *Lodhi v The Governor of Brixton Prison (No 1)* [2001] EWHC Admin 178 at para 89. See, under the 2003 Act, *R (on the application of B) v Westminster Magistrates' Court* [2014] UKSC 59 at paras 21–22; *Hilali* (above) per Scott Baker LJ at para 63; Aikens LJ and Simon J in *Antonov v Prosecutor General's Office, Lithuania* [2015] EWHC 1243 (Admin) at para 21.

9 *B* (above) at paras 27–34.

8.09 The meaning of 'political opinion' is not limited to those persons who have openly and vocally expressed 'political opinions' on specific or general issues, which can be said to be causative of the request. In some instances, adopting the approach taken in the immigration field (*Emilio Gomez v Secretary of State for the Home Department*,[1] the courts have accepted that it properly extends to cases where a person can be said to have a political standpoint, and to cases where the requesting state can be seen to be pursuing a political aim: see *Georgia v Kezerashvili* (21 March 2016, SDJ Riddle) and *Georgia v Gogokhia* (3 March 2017, SDJ Arbuthnot), where in neither case had the defendant in fact expressed any political opinions publicly at all during the period germane to the requests in their cases: see too *Glay Asliturk v Government of Turkey*[2]; *Russian Federation v. Temerko* (23 December 2005, SDJ Workman); *Russian Federation v Azarov* (19 December 2007, DJ N. Evans, para 15); *Russian Federation v Nikitin & Skarga* (8 December 2008, SDJ Workman, para 18); and *Russia Federation v Trefilov Westminster Magistrates' Court* (16 November 2012, DJ Evans).

1 [2000] INLR 549 at §73).

2 [2002] EWHC 2326 (Admin).

8.10 The risk of exposure to 'extraneous considerations' can be indirect. Whilst a defendant is expressly protected under the 2003 Act from illegitimate onward extradition from the Requesting State,[1] he may nonetheless be at risk of refoulement or executive expulsion to another State in which he risks facing 'extraneous considerations'. Non-refoulement[2] is *jus cogens*, ie a peremptory norm of international law. Extradition will be refused by reference to

Art 3 ECHR if a defendant can demonstrate a real risk of refoulement.[3] The fact that the requesting State is a signatory to the ECHR will not be determinative.[4] Moreover, ss 39 and 121 provide that a person must not be extradited before any asylum claim is determined, save where extradition is to a Part 1 territory and where the person is not a national or a citizen of the Part 1 territory and either (a) the Part 1 territory has accepted responsibility for determining the claim, or (b) the Secretary of State is satisfied that the person's life and liberty will not be threatened in that State and that State will not refoule the person in breach of the Refugee Convention.[5]

1 Sections 56–59 and 130–131 of the 2003 Act.

2 Article 33(1) of the 1951 Refugee Convention which confirms: 'No Contracting State shall expel or return ('refouler') a refugee in any manner whatsoever to the frontiers of territories where his life or freedom would be threatened on account of his race, religion, nationality, membership of a particular social group or political opinion.'

3 *Faraj v The Government of Italy* [2004] EWHC 2950 (QB) (no real risk of forcible expulsion to Libya by Italy); *Ramda v Secretary of State for the Home Department* [2005] EWHC 2526 (Admin) at para 60 (risk of forcible expulsion to Algeria by France post-sentence speculative); *Boudhiba v Central Examining Court No. 5 of the High Court of Madrid* [2007] 1 WLR 124, DC at paras 56–57 (risk of forcible expulsion to Tunisia by Spain post-sentence speculative); *Dabas v The High Court of Justice, Madrid* [2007] 1 WLR 145, DC at para 39 (no real risk of forcible expulsion to Syria by Spain and no evidence of risk of persecution were he to be expelled to Syria); *Hilali* (above para **8.08**) at paras 96–106 (risk of forcible expulsion to Morocco by Spain post-sentence speculative); *Ahmad* (above para **8.08**) at paras 87–90 (no real risk of extraordinary rendition by America); *Khemiri & others v The Court of Milan* [2008] EWHC 1988 (Admin) (no real risk of forcible expulsion to Tunisia by Italy); *Spanovic v Croatia* [2009] EWHC 723 (Admin) (no evidence of unfair retrial or inappropriate treatment).

4 *R (Yogathas) v Secretary of State for the Home Department* [2003] 1 AC 920, HL per Lord Bingham of Cornhill at para 9; *Faraj* (above) per Tuckey LJ at para 21.

5 Section 40. Obvious difficulties, and obvious potential for abuse, can arise where the State from which the defendant has been granted asylum, etc is the State requesting his extradition. The asylum provisions of ss 39–40 and 121 of the 2003 Act do not deal with this. It is submitted that, if the CPS and Requesting State have been informed that the requested person holds refugee status as against the Requesting State, but maintain the extradition request nonetheless, then they are liable to be found, subject to specific factual considerations indicating otherwise, to be attempting to circumvent the requested person's asylum protection/appeal procedures and thereby abusing the Court's process.

8.11 These 'extraneous considerations' would, conceptually, amount to instances of abuse of process under domestic law.[1] Before an abuse jurisdiction was acknowledged within the extradition process, in *R v Governor of Belmarsh Prison, ex p Gilligan & Ellis*,[2] the House of Lords observed that the existence of this statutory protection was:

> 'inconsistent with a general abuse of process jurisdiction…If an abuse of process jurisdiction existed there would be no need for such a specific protection.'[3]

The room for overlap in considerations is clear and, in this regard, it is worth noting the case of *Ilia v Greece*[4] in which Underhill LJ commented that the Court did 'not detect [in *Tollman*] any material difference from the approach prescribed in *Hilali*'.[5]

1 *R (Government of the United States of America) v Bow Street Magistrates' Court* [2007] 1 WLR 1157, DC per Lord Phillips CJ at paras 68 and 80. This case is commonly referred to as '*Tollman*'. See more below, at **8.55**.

2 [2001] 1 AC 84, HL.
3 Per Lord Steyn at 97C-D; with whom Lords Browne-Wilkinson, Cooke and Hope agreed. See also, to similar effect, per Lord Clyde at 101E.
4 [2014] EWHC 2372 (Admin), at para 81.
5 [2008] 2 WLR 299, HL (see more below at **8.56**).

Double jeopardy

8.12 Another group of express statutory provisions that cover traditional abuse territory are sections 12 and 80 of the 2003 Act which protect against double jeopardy. In *Fofana & Belize v Deputy Prosecutor Thubin, Tribunal de Grande Instance de Meaux, France,*[1] this protection was held to encompass not only the narrow concepts of *autrefois convict/acquit*, but also the wider abuse jurisdiction acknowledged domestically in *Connelly v DPP*,[2] *DPP v Humphrys*[3] and *R v Beedie*[4] (discussed in detail in **Chapter 7**).

1 [2006] EWHC 744 per Auld LJ at paras 17–23. See also *Maxwell-King v The Government of the United States of America* [2006] EWHC 3033 (Admin) per Lloyd-Jones J at paras 24–31; *John v The Government of the United States of America* [2006] EWHC 3512 (Admin) per Wilkie J at paras 17–24; *Mitchell v France (from High Court of Boulogne Sur Mer)* [2007] EWHC 2006 (Admin) per Collins J at paras 26–28; *Voros v Hungary* [2012] EWHC 518 (Admin) per Keith J para 26. But see *Kulibaba v Government of the United States of America* [2014] EWHC 176 (Admin) for an example of the limitations of this protection.
2 [1964] AC 1254, HL per Lord Pearce at 1365.
3 [1977] AC 1 HL per Lord Hailsham of Marylebone at 41D-E.
4 [1998] QB 356, CA per Rose LJ, at 361–366.

8.13 *Fofana* concerned a French extradition warrant which purported to relate to one offence of fraudulent conduct (the 'Serviware' fraud) but which also described wider allegations of fraud (against other companies) by the two defendants. The defendants had previously been the subject of an indictment in England relating to the same Serviware conduct for which extradition was sought. In the UK, the appellant Fofana pleaded guilty to lesser counts and was sentenced. In respect of the appellant Belize, formal not guilty verdicts were entered. Auld LJ noted[1] that the concept of double jeopardy was 'now a broader concept than a plea in bar of autrefois acquit'. Notwithstanding that the English indictment, confined to the Serviware allegation, 'did not reflect the seriousness and general range of conduct referred to in the [French] warrant',[2] which 'was of a much wider and lengthy course of fraud against a number of French companies, of which the June 2005 Serviware transaction was only part',[3] Auld LJ concluded that:

> '...although the extradition offence specified in the Warrant is not based on exactly, or only partly, the same facts as those charged [in England], there would be such a significant overlap between them as to have required the District Judge to stay the extradition proceedings as an abuse of process.'[4]

More recently, in *Barrs v The Financial Prosecutor of the Republic at the Higher Instance Court of Paris (A French Judicial Authority)*[5] summarised that there are two situations, established in *Fofana*, in which the double jeopardy bar will apply:

'…first, where the subsequent prosecution follows an acquittal or conviction for an offence (or offences) which are the same in fact and law as those previously prosecuted; and secondly, where the subsequent prosecution follows a trial for any offence which was founded on *"the same or substantially the same facts"* as an earlier prosecution, and the court would normally consider it right to stay the prosecution as an abuse of process absent special circumstances being demonstrated as to why another trial should take place.'

1 At para 2.
2 At para 7.
3 At para 11.
4 At para 29.
5 [2019] EWHC 732 (Admin).

8.14 The approach in Fofana continues to be good law, having more recently been applied in a series of cases[1] and applies to both Pt 1 and Pt 2 warrants.[2]

1 *Barrs* (above); *Government of Rwanda v Nteziryayo, Brown (AKA Bajinya), Munyaneza, Mutabaruka, Ugirashebuja v SSHD* [2017] EWHC 1912 (Admin); see also *Heathfield v Germany* [2017] EWHC 2602 (Admin) in which it was said 'The focus of the application of s 12 has to be on the facts that are said to give rise to the offences said to violate the principle of double jeopardy. The authorities which I have discussed show that the key question is whether those facts are the 'same or substantially the same' as the facts which gave rise to the earlier offences. In this case it cannot be said that that test is satisfied' per Knowles J; *Dar v Germany* [2016] EWHC 2405 (Admin); *Ninedeys v District Prosecutor's Office of Varna Bulgaria* [2014] EWHC 4416 (Admin); *Purcell v Ireland* [2012] EWHC 3325 (Admin); *Zdinjak v Croatia* [2012] EWHC 1554 (Admin).
2 *Bohning v Government of the United States of America* [2005] EWHC 2613 (Admin).

Passage of time

8.15 Sections 14 and 82 of the 2003 Act protect a defendant against extradition in circumstances where he may be subject to 'injustice' or 'oppression' by reason of the passage of time since the commission of the offence or, in conviction cases, the conviction.[1] In *Kakis v Government of the Republic of Cyprus*,[2] Lord Diplock observed[3] that 'unjust' is directed to 'the risk of prejudice to the accused in the conduct of the trial itself', whereas 'oppression' is directed to 'hardship to the accused resulting from changes in his circumstances that have occurred during the period to be taken into consideration'. Both propositions may overlap and, together, 'cover all cases where to return him would not be fair'. The relevant period (or 'cradle of events') runs from the last date of the offence to the date of the extradition hearing.[4]

1 Previously s 11(3)(b) of the Extradition Act 1989.
2 [1978] 1 WLR 779, HL.
3 At 782H–783A.
4 At 782G per Lord Diplock; at 790D–E per Lord Scarman; *Government of the United States of America v Tollman (No 2)* [2008] 3 All ER 150, DC per Moses LJ at para 79.

8.16 The protection afforded by ss 14 and 82 is, in practice, significantly wider than that afforded to defendants in domestic criminal proceedings by way of abuse of process (discussed in detail in **Chapter 1**). Unlike the test to be applied in domestic proceedings, the District Judge should not confine imposition of the statutory bar to exceptional or rare cases or circumstances.[1] If it appears that a return will be unjust or oppressive there is no room for any exercise of a residual discretion by the Court – the applicant must be discharged.[2] Therefore, extradition case law under the statutory bar on extradition was observed in *R v Abu Hamza,*[3] in the context of a complaint about pre-trial publicity resulting from unjustified delay, to be neither a close nor helpful analogy to the test to be applied for staying a trial on the grounds of abuse of process in domestic proceedings. Although the converse is not necessarily true,[4] in *Re: Ashley Riddle*, Sedley J observed[5] that the provision:

> 'it should be remembered, is neither a limitation clause nor a disciplinary measure. Its focus is the person sought and the effect on him or her of whatever delay there has been. Thus, excusable delay, if its effect meets the statutory test, may require discharge; and inexcusable delay, if its impact on the person sought is not within the mischief aimed at, may fail to do so. Whether, in either case, this is the result will depend in part on 'all the circumstances', and these may undoubtedly include any good reasons or want of good reasons for the lapse of time, and whether any bad reasons have been the fault of the person sought or the Requesting State.'

1 *Union of India v Manohar lal Narang* [1978] AC 247, HL per Lord Morris of Borth-y-Gest at 279C-E, per Lord Edmund-Davies at 285F–G, per Lord Keith of Kinkell at 293G–294D; *Tollman (No 2)* (above para **8.13**) per Moses LJ at paras 44–47.

2 *Narang* (above) per Viscount Dilhorne at 273A-B, per Lord Edmund-Davies at 283E–284B & 285C-G, per Lord Fraser of Tullybelton at 287F-289B, per Lord Keith of Kinkel at 293C–F

3 [2006] EWCA Crim 2918 per Lord Phillips CJ at paragraph 80.

4 *Tollman (No 2)* (above para **8.15**) per Moses LJ at paras 44–47.

5 [1993] unreported 2 November, DC at transcript p 8. See also *Tollman (No 2)* (above para **8.15**) per Moses LJ at paras 79–80.

8.17 Much of the case law under the 2003 Act concerns the passage of time safeguard and a detailed examination of the case law is beyond the scope of this work. But, ss 14 and 82 reflect long-standing principles of extradition law and have historically been held to cover situations where, by virtue of delay, the passage of time inhibits, by dimming recollection or otherwise, proper consideration of trial issues or inhibits the tracing of witnesses still able to recollect specific events,[1] or cases where witnesses, materials, or certain lines of defence are no longer available,[2] even in cases of relatively short delay.[3] 'Culpable delay' on the part of the Requesting State, will be a relevant factor in 'borderline' cases.[4] Delay on the part of the applicant, ie by fleeing the country, concealing his whereabouts, or evading arrest, cannot – save in the most exceptional circumstances – count towards making his return 'unjust' or 'oppressive'.[5] 'Oppression' may arise where a defendant has lived openly and established family ties in the UK and to remove him would be oppressive. Oppression can also arise in circumstances where the inaction of the Requesting State, or its positive conduct, has caused in the defendant a legitimate sense of false security.[6] Oppression can attach to persons for whom the defendant has responsibility.[7] The assessment is one conducted in the round; '[a]n overall judgment on the merits is required, unshackled by rules with too sharp edges'.[8]

The onus is ultimately on the defendant[9] to demonstrate, on the balance of probabilities, that it would be unjust or oppressive, because of the delay, having regard to all the circumstances, to return him. In seeking to discharge the onus on him, a defendant must produce cogent evidence of injustice or oppression. It is not sufficient to offer mere assertions or speculation. There is no 'cut-off point beyond which extradition must inevitably be regarded as unjust or oppressive'[10] but the authorities establish that the threshold is high.[11] However, even where the applicant is not entitled to rely upon passage of time as a bar, the overall length of the delay is relevant to a possible argument regarding Art 8 ECHR.[12]

1 *Kakis* (above para **8.15**). See, for example, *R v Secretary of State, ex parte Patel* (1995) 7 Admin LR 56 at p70F-G.
2 See, for example, *Narang* (above para **8.16**) at 280G per Lord Morris of Borth-y Gest; *Re: Ashley Riddle* (above para **8.16**) per Sedley J at transcript p 3.
3 See, for example, the absence of an alibi witness in the context of 4½ years' delay in *Kakis* (above para **8.15**) and the absence of witnesses of fact in the context of a four-year delay (three of which were culpable) in *Re: Ashley Riddle* (above para **8.16**).
4 *R v Governor of Brixton Prison, ex p Osman (No 4)* [1992] 1 All ER 579 at 587D–H per Woolf LJ. See also *Garbowski v Poland* [2013] EWHC 3695 (Admin) per Collins J at para 30.
5 *Kakis* (above para **8.15**) per Lord Diplock at 783A. See also the leading case of *Gomes v Trinidad and Tobago* [2009] UKHL 21 per Lord Brown para 29 and at para 64 'If an accused...deliberately flees the jurisdiction in which he has been bailed to appear, it simply does not lie in his mouth to suggest that the Requesting State should share responsibility for the ensuing delay in bringing him to justice because of some subsequent supposed fault on their part, whether this be, as in his case, losing the file, or dilatoriness, or, as will often be the case, mere inaction through pressure of work and limited resources. We would not regard any of these circumstances as breaking the chain of causation...with regard to the effects of the accused's own conduct. Only a deliberate decision by the Requesting State communicated to the accused not to pursue the case against him, or some other circumstances which would similarly justify a sense of security on his part, notwithstanding his own flight from justice, could allow him properly to assert the effects of further delay were not 'of his own choice and making'; *Oprynski v Regional Court In Lublin Poland* [2013] EWHC 3736 (Admin) per Bean J para 6 and *United States v Wood* [2013] EWHC 1971 (Admin) where 'the only proven effect [of the delay] was that it had given the applicant further opportunity to commit serious offences. By "a wide margin", it was not oppressive to extradite', per Mitting J, paras 43–46. The court has also noted that: 'If the question of whether an individual is a fugitive is raised, the District Judge should make a finding whether that is indeed in his view established in any given case': *Kaszowski v Regional Court in Rzeszow, Poland*, [2012] EWHC 2871 (Admin) per Collins J at 11.
6 *Hunt v Court of First Instance, Antwerp* [2006] 2 All ER 735, DC per Newman J at para 25. *Orazio Lettieri v Office of the State Prosecutor, Court of Santa Maria Capua Vetere, Italy* [2013] EWHC 1530 (Admin) per Collins J at para 13.
7 *Re: Ashley-Riddle* (above para **8.16**); *Cookeson v Government of Australia* [2001] EWHC Admin 149; *Hunt* (above); *Tollman (No. 2)* (above para **8.15**) at para 110.
8 *La Torre v Italy* [2007] EWHC 1370 (Admin) at para 37.
9 *Union of India v Manohar lal Narang* (above para **8.15**) per Lord Keith of Kinkel at 293H-294A;
10 Per Simon Brown LJ *Woodcock v Government of New Zealand* [2003] EWHC 2668 (Admin), para 29.
11 *Tappin v United States* [2012] EWHC 22 (Admin) per Cranston J at para 24.
12 *R (on the application of HH) v Westminster City Magistrates' Court* [2012] UKSC 25 per Baroness Hale at para 46.

8.18 Article 8 has been held to be the correct heading under which to consider a passage of time (as opposed to abuse of process), even in situations where the bar may strictly apply but, to so apply it would result in injustice or absurdity. In *Konecny v District Court in Brno-Venkov, Czech Republic*[1] the warrant had been issued as a 'conviction warrant' following the conviction in absentia of the requested person taking place a considerable time after the offences were committed. The effect was to work to the requested person's disadvantage, as the existence of a right to a retrial had the effect of excluding from consideration the passage of time prior to his conviction.[2] The operation of s 14 in this way therefore created a situation where a judicial authority could in essence circumvent the statutory regime.

There have been several attempts address this injustice before the Supreme Court in *Konecny* gave clear guidance on the approach to be taken.

In *Campbell v Public Prosecutor of the Grande Instance Tribunal of St Malo, France*,[3] Keith J thought the answer was to resolve the matter using the abuse of process jurisdiction. In *R (Cousins) v Public Prosecution of the Grande Instance Tribunal of Boulogne sur Mer, France*,[4] Ouseley J had concerns about the use of Art 8 as a 'kitchen sink' and considered the correct resolution of the matter lay in analysing the matter under s 14 but viewing 'injustice' and 'oppression' to the 'full extent' through Art 8.[5] Finally, in *Farzal Rahman v County Court of Boulogne sur Mer, France*,[6] Blake J shared Ouseley J's reservations about Art 8, and considered that construing a person as accused 'unless or until there has been a conviction from which he was required to participate from which he has absconded himself and is therefore a fugitive from justice' was the answer.

Lord Lloyd-Jones, however,[7] determined that 'until such time as section 14 can be amended by Parliament, article 8 provides an appropriate and effective alternative means of addressing passage of time resulting in injustice or oppression in cases where the defendant has been convicted in absentia'.[8] Indeed, part of his reasoning was based on the considerable hurdle presented by abuse of process in extradition proceedings: 'the threshold test to be satisfied would not be one of injustice or oppression but the lower one of disproportionality. This feature also makes reliance on article 8 a more effective solution than abuse of process where the burden on an appellant would be a much heavier one'.[9]

1 [2019] 1 WLR 1586.
2 Ibid at para 54.
3 [2013] EWHC 1288 (Admin).
4 [2014] EWHC 2324 (Admin).
5 Ibid at para 12.
6 [2014] EWHC 4143 (Admin).
7 With whom Lord Kerr, Lord Hodge, Lady Black and Lord Kitchin agreed.
8 See *Konecny* (n 1) at para 57.
9 Ibid.

8.19 The Courts will, however, pay particular regard to any abuse jurisdiction shown to exist in the Requesting State capable of addressing any injustice or oppression alleged. The existence of such a jurisdiction is highly relevant to, but not determinative of, how the UK Courts judge the issues. In *Woodcock v Government of New Zealand*,[1] Simon Brown LJ observed[2] that the applicable statutory provisions:

> '... [require] this court's decision not upon whether, having regard to the passage of time, it would be unjust to *try* the accused, but rather whether it would be unjust to *return* him (albeit, of course, return him for trial). To my mind that entitles, indeed requires, this court to have regard to whatever safeguards may exist in the domestic law of the Requesting State to ensure that the accused would not be subjected to an unjust trial there. There are, it should be borne in mind, clear advantages in having the question whether or not a fair trial is now possible decided in the domestic court rather than by us. That court will have an altogether clearer picture than we have of precisely what evidence is available and the issues likely to arise. For example, the accused is likely to be interviewed on return ... so that more is likely to be known about his defence. If, of course, we were to conclude that the domestic court in the Requesting State would be *bound* to hold that a fair trial of the accused is now impossible, then plainly we would regard it as unjust (and/or oppressive) to return him. Equally, we would have no alternative but to reach our own conclusion on whether a fair trial would now be possible in the Requesting State if we were not persuaded that the courts of that state have what we would regard as satisfactory procedures of their own akin to our (and the New Zealand courts') abuse of process jurisdiction.'[3]

This approach continues to be good law and was recently applied in *PIlarczyk v Poland.*[4]

1 [2004] 1 WLR 1979, DC. See also *Coton v High Court of Dublin, Ireland* [2012] EWHC 3874 (Admin), in which Cranston J at para 13 noted that where a passage of time argument had failed, it was for the Requesting State to consider an abuse application based on delay in the proceedings.

2 At paras 20–21.

3 In *Woodcock*, the court found that extradition was not barred by reason of passage of time because, firstly, the evidence demonstrated that the New Zealand courts have satisfactory procedures for guarding against an unjust trial and, secondly, that, under those procedures, they would certainly not be bound to find a fair trial impossible. The *Woodcock* approach applies under the 2003 Act (*Crean v The Government of Ireland* [2007] EWHC 814 (Admin)). But, where there is no information or evidence as to how the court in the Requesting State would approach an abuse of process argument, it is for this court to consider the risk of hardship or injustice which could arise (*Hunt* (above para **8.17**) per Newman J at para 21). It appears, however, that a different approach will apply in Part 1 cases, where the Requesting State is a signatory to the European Convention on Human Rights. In light of *Lisowski v Regional Court of Bialystok, Poland* [2006] EWHC 3227 (Admin) per Walker J at paras 17–18; *La Torre v The Republic of Italy* [2007] EWHC 1370 (Admin) per Laws LJ at paras 43–45 (bearing in mind the strategic aims of the Council Framework Decision of 2002 and the high level of confidence between EU Member States); *Government of Croatia v Spanovic* [2007] EWHC 1770 (Admin) Hughes LJ at para 24; *Krzyzowski v The Circuit Court in Glewice, Poland* [2007] EWHC 2754 (Admin) per Longmore LJ at para,. 24 and Mitting J at para 31; *Harvey v Judicial Authority of Portugal* [2007] EWHC 3282 (Admin) per Maurice Kay LJ at paras 26–30, *Battistini v Italy* [2009] EWHC 3536 (Admin) per Lord Justice Maurice Kay at paras 7–11. In such cases, the onus is on the defendant to adduce material suggesting deficiencies in the Requesting State's system or justifying a departure from the obligation to give full faith and credence to the legal and judicial system of a fellow European country. In the absence of such a showing, the court is entitled to assume that such procedures exist, and that *Woodcock* applies.

4 [2019] EWHC 3486 (Admin) at para 31.

Trials in absence

8.20 Sections 20 and 85 of the 2003 Act provide that, in cases where a person has been tried in their absence and has not deliberately absented themselves from the trial, extradition of a convicted person shall not lie unless the person is guaranteed a retrial or a review amounting to a retrial. In practice, these provisions give mandatory effect to the line of decisions under previous legislation confirming that it would not be 'in the interests of justice' [1] to extradite in such cases in the absence of an unconditional guarantee of a full and unfettered retrial.[2] In cases where a person has been tried in their absence and has not deliberately absented themselves from the trial, but the trial process remains ongoing (because of, say, an extant appeal), the person will be categorised as an 'accused' person, so that s 20 will not apply. But, Art 6 of the ECHR would, in such a case, provide the same result (via ss 21 and 87).[3]

The leading authority in this area is *Cretu v Romania*.[4] Here the court were considering the impact of the introduction of Art 4a of Council Framework Decision 2009/299/JHA ('the 2009 Framework Decision') on the s 20 provisions. The 2009 Framework Decision changes Box D of the EAW and provides for the circumstances in which the requested person may be deemed not to have been convicted in absentia. As the court in *Cretu* explained 'paragraph 1 of article 4a allows, but does not require, the state in receipt of a request to refuse to surrender if the person did not appear at "the trial resulting in the decision" unless at least one of the four exceptions is established'.[5] The court went on to outline the following principles:

> 'In my judgment, when read in the light of article 4a section 20 of the 2003 Act, by applying a Pupino conforming interpretation, should be interpreted as follows:
>
> i) "Trial" in section 20(3) of the 2003 Act must be read as meaning "trial which resulted in the decision" in conformity with article 4a paragraph 1(a)(i). That suggests an event with a "scheduled date and place" and is not referring to a general prosecution process, Mitting J was right to foreshadow this in Bicioc.
>
> ii) An accused must be taken to be deliberately absent from his trial if he has been summoned as envisaged by article 4a paragraph 1(a)(i) in a manner which, even though he may have been unaware of the scheduled date and place, does not violate article 6 ECHR;
>
> iii) An accused who has instructed ("mandated") a lawyer to represent him in the trial is not, for the purposes of section 20, absent from his trial, however he may have become aware of it;
>
> iv) The question whether an accused is entitled to a retrial or a review amounting to a retrial for the purposes of section 20(5), is to be determined by reference to article 4a paragraph 1(d).
>
> v) Whilst, by virtue of section 206 of the 2003 Act, it remains for the requesting state to satisfy the court conducting the extradition hearing in the United Kingdom to the criminal standard that one (or more) of

> the four exceptions found in article 4a applies, the burden of proof will be discharged to the requisite standard if the information required by article 4a is set out in the EAW.'[6]

The court also discouraged the seeking of further information from the judicial authority on the point unless there was 'confusion, ambiguity or possibly in connection with an argument that the warrant is an abuse of process'.[7]

The executing judicial authority may have regard to the conduct of the person concerned. Where it is the fault of the requested person's own conduct which has led him to be unaware of his trial date, whether through a 'manifest lack of diligence' or otherwise, then he will be taken to have deliberately absented himself.[8]

However, an apparent tension has arisen following the decision in *Stryjecki v Poland.*[9] There, Hickinbottom J restated the principles in *Cretu* but used slightly different language, namely it was said that a manifest lack of diligence on the part of the requested person is merely evidence of, but is not itself proof of, that individual having deliberately absented themselves. Knowles J in *Tyrakowski* acknowledged the apparent tension *Cretu.*[10] Interestingly, in *Szatkowski,*[11] Irwin LJ (who gave judgment in *Cretu)* restated the factors in *Stryjecki* without amendment.[12] In *Dziel v Poland*, Ouseley J commented that Hickinbottom J in *Stryjecki* had restated the propositions in *Cretu* in different language and in doing put the points he made at (vi) or (f) of para 50 of the *Strycjecki* judgment, unintentionally at odds with *Zagrean*[13] and he went on to restate the test in *Zagrean.*[14]

In *Bialkowski v Poland,*[15] Kerr J considered the position in light of all of the above authorities. Rather than seeing a conflict between *Stryjecki* and *Zagrean,* he preferred to resolve the matter thusly:

> '…It is not clear whether the decisions of Julian Knowles J and Ouseley J were cited to the Divisional Court; there is no indication in the judgment of the court that they were.
>
> For my part, I respectfully consider that the seventh proposition is sound and that the sixth proposition can be reconciled with what was said by Cranston J in *Cretu* at [81]. I think Hickinbottom J was simply making the point that the requesting state does not prove that an accused deliberately missed his trial just by proving that he acted evasively in an attempt to avoid receipt of trial information documents. However evasive the accused's conduct, the requesting state must still prove that it took the steps that would acquaint a non-evasive accused with the time and place of trial'.[16]

Therefore, as Lewis J describes in *Ostrzycki v Poland,*[17] 'as a minimum, it will be sufficient if the state has taken the steps that would normally be sufficient under its law to inform a person of the time and place of trial and the accused has by his own conduct prevented the information being served on him'.[18]

The ultimate question for the court in each case is whether the person has knowingly waived his right to a trial.[19]

1 Under s 6(2) of the 1989 Act, or as a matter of jurisdiction under s 26 of the Extradition Act 1870 (and para 20 of Sch 1 to the 1989 Act).

2 For cases under previous statutory provisions in which the right to a re-hearing did not exist or was fettered in some way, see *R v Governor of Brixton Prison & Ors, ex p Caborn-Waterfield* [1960] 2 QB 498; *Athanassiadis v Government of Greece (Note)* [1971] AC 282; *Regina v Governor of Pentonville Prison & Anor, ex p Zezza* [1983] AC 46, HL; *In re Avashilom Sarig* [1993] COD 472; *Regina (Guisto) v Governor of Brixton Prison & Anor.* [2004] 1 AC 101, HL; *R v Governor of Brixton Prison, ex p Cavallo* (unreported) (13 March 1997) DC per Simon Brown LJ at transcript p 4; *R v Governor of Brixton Prison, ex p Barone* (unreported) (7 November 1997) DC, per Kennedy LJ. at transcript pp 10–11; *Peci v Governor of Brixton Prison* (unreported) (5 November 1999) DC, per Moses J at transcript pp 2 and 5–9; *R v Government of Bulgaria, ex p Ratchev* (unreported) (17 May 2000) DC per Henry LJ at paras 8 and 24–35; *Government of Italy v Saia* (unreported) (16 November 2001), DC per Pitchford J at paras 4, 13, 15–17; *Farrow v Government of Italy* (unreported) (14 June 2002) DC, per Rose LJ at paras 9–11; *Sadutto v Governor of HMP Brixton & Anor* [2004] EWHC 563 (Admin).

3 *Stoichkov v Bulgaria* [2005] ECHR 24 June at para 56; *Sejdovic v Italy* [2006] ECHR 1 March at paras 87–88 and 99; *Da An Chen v Government of Romania* [2006] EWHC 1752 (Admin) per Mitting J at para: 10; *Caldarelli v Court of Naples* [2008] 1 WLR 1724, HL; *Bohm v Romania* [2011] EWHC 2671 (Admin) per Irwin J at para 9.

4 [2016] 1 WLR 3344.

5 Ibid at para 23.

6 Ibid at para 34.

7 Ibid at para 35.

8 *Romania v Zagrean* [2016] EWHC 2786 (Admin) at para 81.

9 [2016] EWHC 3309 (Admin) at para 50.

10 *Tyrakowski v Poland* [2017] EWHC 2675 (Admin) at para 30.

11 [2019] EWHC 883 (Admin).

12 Ibid at para 22.

13 [2019] EWHC 351 (Admin) at para 17.

14 Ibid at para 28.

15 [2019] EWHC 1253 (Admin).

16 Ibid at paras 26 and 27.

17 [2020] EWHC 1634 (Admin).

18 Ibid at para 27.

19 *Tyrakowski* (n 10) at para 34; *JK v Poland* [2018] EWHC 197 (Admin) at [49] per Singh LJ.

Physical or mental health

8.21 Sections 25 and 91 protect a defendant against extradition in circumstances where a defendant's physical or mental condition is such that it would be unjust or oppressive to extradite him. Prior to the 2003 Act, issues of physical or mental health fell to be determined pursuant to the overriding discretion afforded to the Secretary of State. It was well-settled law that, in the event that there existed, as between the medical experts instructed by the parties, a live issue to be determined as to fitness to plead/stand trial, that issue should be decided by the courts of the Requesting State.[1] If there is no such live issue, because the respective experts agree that the defendant is unfit, extradition should be refused (*In re Davies*[2]). For a case under the 2003 Act in which s 91 was applied, see *Tollman (No 2)*.[3] 'Oppression' would encompass, amongst other issues, risks associated with travel, see *McCaughey v Government of the United States of America.*[4] Where appropriate, the court may adjourn proceedings to allow for treatment or further investigation rather than discharge when the issue is raised.[5] The application of the protection is highly fact-specific and it has been noted that 'little help is gained by reference to the facts of other cases'.[6] It has been emphasised repeatedly that there can be no 'hard and fast rules' in the operation of these sections.[7]

For a recent restatement of the law in this area see *Surico v Italy*[8] and *Zelenko v Prosecutor Generals Office of the Republic of Latvia.*[9]

For what is required of the content of an assurance from the judicial authority in this context see *Magiera v Poland.*[10]

1 *R (Warren) v Secretary of State for the Home Department* [2003] EWHC 1177. This reasoning has been applied to the 2003 Act, see *Edwards v United States* [2013] EWHC 1906 (Admin) per Wilkie J, at paras 54–58.
2 [1998] COD 1–83, pp 30–32.
3 Above para **8.15**, per Ouseley J at paras 120 et seq.
4 [2006] EWHC 248 (Admin).
5 *Government of the Republic of South Africa v Dewani* [2012] EWHC 842 (Admin) per Sir John Thomas P at paras 73–76.
6 Ibid at para 73. The content of this paragraph continues to be emphasised also see *Surico v Italy* [2018] EWHC 401 (Admin) at para 35.
7 *Government of the Republic of South Africa v Dewani (No. 2)* [2014] 1 WLR 3220 at para 51; *Zelenko v Latvia* [2019] EWHC 3840 (Admin) at para 7.
8 [2018] EWHC 401 (Admin) at paras 34–37.
9 [2019] EWHC 3840 (Admin) at paras 6 and 7.
10 [2017] EWHC 2757 (Admin) at paras 34–35; *Zelenko v Prosecutor's General Office of the Republic of Latvia* [2020] EWHC 1800 (Admin) at paras 59 and 62; *Henriques v Portugal* [2019] EWHC 1998 (Admin) at para 36.

National Security

8.22 Section 208 of the 2003 Act enables the Secretary of State to prevent extradition where the person's extradition in respect of the offence would be against the interests of national security and where the person was either (a) engaging in the conduct constituting (or alleged to constitute) the offence for the purpose of assisting in the exercise of a function conferred or imposed by or under an enactment, or (b) is not liable under the criminal law of any part of the UK for the conduct constituting (or alleged to constitute) the offence, as a result of an authorisation given by the Secretary of State. This could encompass a particular class of entrapment (emanating from the authorities of the UK) that, in a domestic context, would fall to be considered under the principles in *R v Looseley*[1] or *Teixiera de Castro v Portugal,*[2] discussed in detail in **Chapter 6**. For cases where, by contrast, entrapment has been argued to emanate from the authorities of the Requesting State, see below at para **8.127**.

1 [2001] 1 WLR 2060, HL.
2 (1998) 28 EHRR 101.

HUMAN RIGHTS

8.23 The enactment of ss 21 and 87 of the 2003 Act marked a dramatic change in extradition law and practice. For the first time, ECHR rights became an integral part of the extradition machinery. The District Judge is now required in every case to determine whether extradition is Convention-compliant.

Articles 2 & 3 of the ECHR

8.24 Articles 2 and 3 of the ECHR contain fundamental protections against prospective abusive treatment in the Requesting State. Whilst overlapping with the 'extraneous considerations' protections of ss 13 and 81, Arts 2 and 3 apply regardless of the motivation for the treatment or its source in the Requesting State. Art 3 has been expressly held to apply to extradition proceedings. In *Soering v United Kingdom*[1] the European Court of Human Rights held that 'the decision by a Contracting State to extradite a fugitive may give rise to an issue under Art 3, and hence, engage the responsibility of that State under the Convention'.[2] This has been confirmed in numerous cases, for example, in *Ananyev v The Russian Federation.*[3]

The basis for liability of the UK court is that the wanted person is within the State Party's jurisdiction and the State Party is under an obligation to ensure that it has not 'taken action which has, as a direct consequence, caused the exposure of an individual to proscribed ill-treatment'.[4] The test to be applied was outlined in *Soering*, and said to be whether a defendant has 'shown... substantial grounds...for believing' that the person concerned faces a 'real risk' of being subjected to treatment contrary to Art 3 (in *Soering*, the 'death row' phenomenon) if extradited.[5] But the threshold for engaging Art 3 in extradition proceedings is, in practice, a high one.[6] The courts have, however, refused to extradite based on an Art 3 argument in a variety of cases, most commonly those involving appalling detention conditions.[7]

By virtue of the Extradition Act 2003, ss 21, 21A the obligation to consider the compatibility of extradition with the requested person's human rights applies equally to EAW requests made under the Council Framework Decision of 13 June 2002. At EU level (although EU law has no effect after 1 January 2021), the Court of Justice of the European Union confirmed that, notwithstanding that the principle of mutual recognition on which the European arrest warrant system is based is itself founded on the mutual confidence between the member states that their national legal systems are capable of providing equivalent and effective protection of the fundamental rights recognised at EU level, the Framework Decision was not to have the effect of modifying the obligation to respect fundamental rights as enshrined in the *Charter of Fundamental Rights of the European Union* and the *European Convention for the Protection of Human Rights and Fundamental Freedoms European Convention on Human Rights: Aranyosi and Caldararu.*[8] It followed that, where the judicial authority of the executing member state was in possession of evidence of a real risk of inhuman or degrading treatment of individuals detained in the issuing member state, having regard to the standard of protection of fundamental rights guaranteed by EU law and, in particular, by Art 4 of the Charter, that judicial authority was bound to assess the existence of that risk when it is called upon to decide on the surrender to the authorities of the issuing member state of the individual sought by a European arrest warrant: para 88. However, a finding that there is a real risk of inhuman or degrading treatment by virtue of general conditions of detention in the issuing member state could not lead, in itself, to the refusal to execute a European arrest warrant. Whenever the existence of such a risk is identified, it is then necessary that the executing judicial authority make a further assessment, specific and precise, of whether there were substantial grounds to believe that the individual concerned will be exposed to that risk because of the conditions for his detention envisaged in the issuing member state: paras 91, 92. The court must obviously be satisfied that there is a need to seek further information but there is no evidential threshold to be crossed before it can do so. There is therefore no implication from the making of the request for further information that the court has found that Art 3 would be breached on the information currently before it, or that a *prima facie* case to that effect has been made out.[9]

1 (1989) 11 EHRR 439.

2 At para 91. The provisions of Art 3 are absolute. There exists no balancing exercise to be carried out (*Chahal v United Kingdom* (1996) 23 EHRR 413 at paras 79–80; *Saadi v Italy* (Appl No 37201/06) at paras 125–138). In practice, there is no difference between the case law governing asylum/expulsion and that governing extradition. It is irrelevant that the risk is of torture or inhuman or degrading treatment or punishment carried out clandestinely either by the authorities in the Requesting State or by third parties (*HLR v France* (1997) 26 EHRR 29; *D v United Kingdom* (1997) 24 EHRR 423; *R (Bagdanavicius) v Secretary of State for the Home Department* [2005] 2 AC 668, HL; *Mclean v The High Court of Dublin, Ireland* [2008] EWHC 547 (Admin)). It should be noted that Arts 2–4 of Protocol 4 to the European Convention (specific provision for freedom of movement and protection from arbitrary expulsion) have not been ratified by the UK. However, that does not detract from (or limit) the protection provided by other convention rights (*Abdulaziz, Cabales and Balkandali v United Kingdom* (1985) 7 EHRR 471 at para 60).

3 App. No. 2947/06, 24 April 2008. See also *Kasymakhunov v Russia* (2013) App. 29604/12, 14 November 2013 where the risk of ill treatment upon return was based on the general situation in relation to human rights in Uzbekistan (2012) 55 EHRR 18.

4 *Soering* (n.1) (1989) 11 EHRR 439, at paras 90–91.

5 At para 91; *R (Ullah) v Special Adjudicator* [2004] 2 AC 352 per Lord Bingham of Cornhill at para 24. See more recently *Saadi v Italy* (above) at paras 125 and 140.

6 See, for example, *N v Secretary of State for the Home Department* [2005] 2 AC 296, HL. The threshold for engaging Art 2 was thought to be higher still and required a showing of 'near certainty', but the High Court has opined that the same threshold applies for Arts 2 and 3; *Mclean* (above) at paras 5–11.

7 For the authoritative framework for analysis of prison conditions issues, see *Mohammed Elashmawy v Court of Brescia, Italy* [2015] EWHC 28 (Admin) at para 49. See also *Ukraine v Kononko* [2014] EWHC 1420 (Admin). In *Lithuania v Campbell* [2013] NIQB 19, per Girvan LJ at paras 20–26, the conditions at a particular Lithuanian prison were such that there were substantial grounds for believing that an inmate would face a real risk of being subjected to inhuman and degrading treatment. In *Badre v Italy* [2014] EWHC 614 (Admin), the court held that the appellant faced a real risk of treatment contrary to the European Court of Human Rights because there was a systemic problem of overcrowding in Italian prisons and the Italian Government had failed to establish that the appellant would not be affected by this. However, there must be evidence of a specific risk to the applicant rather than generic evidence of unlawful conditions/treatment, eg *Ragul v Azerbaijan* [2013] EWHC 2000 (Admin), per Burnett J at paras 21, 35-36; *Guzeloglu v Government of Republic of Turkey* [2013] EWHC 660 (Admin). In *Lutsyuk v Government of Ukraine* [2013] EWHC 189 (Admin) per Laws LJ, at para 15, the court confirmed that country guidance about conditions from the Asylum and Immigration Tribunal 'is to be treated with respect as the finding of a specialist tribunal': see also *Poland v Dytlow* [2009] EWHC 1009 (Admin) per Keene LJ at paragraph 24. In *Tamarevichute v Russia* [2008] EWHC 534 (Admin), the court accepted it could not go behind the country guidance absent a substantial change in the position. However, country guidance may be updated by later evidence, especially expert evidence (see *Musikyavicius v The Russian Federation* [2011] EWHC 1549 (Admin), per Moses LJ at paras 23–26). The court must consider what the nature of the conditions will be for the duration of the detention: see *Adamescu v Romania* [2020] EWHC 2709 (Admin) at para 165 *et seq*. On the minimum floor space of cells see *Muršić v Croatia* (7334/13) (2017) 65 EHRR 1. For a recent discussion of authorities relating to extradition where a sentence of

life without parole may be imposed see: *Hafeez v Government of the United States* [2020] 1 W.L.R. 1296 and also *Sanchez v Government of the United States* [2020] EWHC 508 (Admin).

8 Cases C-404/15 and C659/15 PPU *Aranyosi and Căldăraru v Generalstaatsanwaltschaft Bremen* [2016] QB 921; *Jane v Lithuania* [2018] EWHC 1122 (Admin) at [43]–[50]; *India v Chawla* [2018] EWHC 1050 (Admin) at paras 29–33. As to what the nature and content of that enquiry ought to be, see *ML (Generalstaatsanwaltschaft Bremen)* C -220/18 PPU [2019] 1 WLR 1052; *Fuzesi v National Crime Agency* [2018] EWHC 3548 (Admin). As to the factors to consider when assessing the adequacy of assurances offered, see *Othman v United Kingdom* (2012) 55 EHRR 1, at para 189. The failure of a Requesting State to comply with assurances offered in this respect may have an impact on future extradition requests, see *Bartulis v Lithuania* [2019] EWHC 3504 (Admin), at para 127.

9 *Purcell v Belgium* [2017] EWHC 1981 (Admin).

8.25 It should be noted that, in relation to EU Member States party to the European Arrest Warrant (EAW) mechanism, the courts have established a rebuttable presumption of compliance with the ECHR. In *R (on the application of Arvdas Klimas) v Prosecutors General Office of Lithuania,* Mitting J held that any 'risk can, in the case of a Convention country, be taken to be eliminated or at least reduced below the level at which it amounts to a real risk by the rights which an individual appellant has in a Convention country and the real and practical obligations which that country owes to him'.[1] However, this assertion was later qualified and restated by Mitting J in *Palczynski v Poland*[2] in the light of the decisions in *Targosinski v Poland*[3] and *MSS v Belgium.*[4] However, the court in *Agius v Malta*[5] concluded that this restatement did not go far enough and held that, although there is an assumption of compliance, 'it is capable of being rebutted by clear and cogent evidence'.[6] The threshold is, however, a high one: *Krzyzak v Poland.*[7] One such example of this presumption being rebutted is in the case of *Grecu v Romania*,[8] following the ECtHR pilot judgment of *Rezmiveş.*[9]

1 [2010] EWHC 2076 (Admin) at para 12.
2 [2011] EWHC 445 (Admin).
3 [2011] EWHC 312 (Admin).
4 (30696/09) (2011) 53 EHRR 2 at paras 7–11.
5 [2011] EWHC 759 (Admin) per Sulvan J at paras 18–19.
6 Ibid at para 18.
7 [2012] EWHC 810 (Admin) per Keith J at paras 7–12.
8 [2017] EWHC 1427 (Admin); [2017] 4 WLR 139 at [48] per Irwin LJ.
9 *Rezmiveş and others v Romania*, App nos. 61467/12, 39516/13, 48231/13 and 68191/13, (ECtHR, 25 April 2014).

Article 5 ECHR

8.26 Article 5(1)(f) of ECHR expressly provides for lawful detention for the purposes of extradition or deportation:

> 'Everyone has the right to liberty and security of person. No one shall be deprived of his liberty save in the following cases and in accordance with a procedure prescribed by law:
>
> …
>
> (f) the lawful arrest or detention of a person … against whom action is being taken with a view to deportation or extradition…'

8.27 Article 5(1) of ECHR requires that the detention of the defendant in the Requested State pursuant to ECHR, Art 5(1)(f), should not be arbitrary or vitiated by misuse of authority or bad faith:

> '...Article 5(1)(f) clearly permits the Commission to decide on the lawfulness ("lawful detention/detention reguliere") of a person against whom action is being taken with a view to extradition (une procedure d'extradition est en cours). The wording of both the French and English texts makes it clear that only the existence of extradition proceedings justifies deprivation of liberty in such a case. It follows that if, for example, the proceedings are not conducted with the requisite diligence, or if the detention results from some misuse of authority, it ceases to be justifiable under Article 5(1)(f)...' (*Lynas v Switzerland*[1]).

1 (1976) 6 DR 141 at 167. Note also ECHR, Art 18 which provides that 'The restrictions permitted under this Convention to the...rights and freedoms [secured in it] shall not be applied for any purpose other than those for which they have been prescribed...'. In *Quinn v France* (1995) 21 EHRR 529, the Court observed that 'the provision (Art 18) afforded specific protection and could be invoked on its own without reference to other articles of the Convention' (at para 57). There, the Court examined the evidence relating to proceedings in France and found no evidence of 'an abuse of procedure' (para 59).

8.28 An applicant's extradition may, therefore, be prevented if there is evidence that s/he would suffer 'a flagrant denial' of the rights enshrined in Art 5(1) in the Requesting State.[1] Such situations are rare and difficult to prove. For example, in *R B (Algeria) v The Secretary of State for the Home Department*, Lord Phillips explained that the term 'a flagrant breach' meant 'a breach whose consequences are so severe that they override the right of a State to expel an alien from its territory'.[2] An example where such an argument was successful is *The Government of the United States v* Giese.[3] In that case, the Court considered whether the risk that the requested person might be subject to a civil commitment order, which was a form of indeterminate confinement for a person deemed to be mentally ill and dangerous, in the USA might amount to a breach of Article 5(1). The Court considered that the definition of 'diagnosed mental disorder' in California, and how it was implemented in practice, was incompatible with the exception under Art 5(1)(e)[4] and that it amounted to a 'flagrant denial' in the circumstances.[5]

1 *Sullivan v The Government of the United States of America & Anor* [2010] EWHC 2076 (Admin), per Moses LJ at para 36.
2 [2010] 2 AC 110, at para 132. See also *Wright (aka Robertson) v Commissioner of the Metropolitan Police* [2012] EWHC 669 (QB) per Silber J, paras 56–57.
3 [2015] EWHC 2733 (Admin).
4 Ibid at paras 60–61.
5 Ibid at paras 62–63.

8.29 Article 5 may also be used in relation to the requirement to act in good faith in detention pending extradition to avoid arbitrariness. In *R v Governor of Brockhill Prison, ex p Evans (No 2)*[1] Lord Hope observed that, '...under Art 5(1), assuming that the detention is lawful under domestic law, the Court must be satisfied that it is nevertheless not open to criticism on the ground that it is arbitrary because, for example, it was resorted to in bad faith or was not proportionate...'.[2] Arbitrariness and bad faith are the keystones of most abuses of process. Although the threshold is high,[3] the jurisprudence of the European Court of Human Rights demonstrates that in cases concerning alleged abuse of extradition procedures and/or executive misconduct in the procuring of the defendant's return, Art 5 may be engaged. As will be seen later, Art 5 has been the foundation upon which the extradition abuse of process jurisdiction has been built.[4] The Court of Justice of the EU similarly noted in *Radu* that:

> 'To avoid being arbitrary, such detention must be carried out in good faith; it must be closely connected to the ground of detention relied on by the executing judicial authority; the place and conditions of detention should be appropriate; and the length of the detention should not exceed that reasonably required for the purpose pursued (thus satisfying the proportionality test)'.[5]

For example, *Bozano v France,*[6] discussed in detail in **Chapter 5**, concerned facts not dissimilar to *R v Bow Street Magistrates' Court, ex p Mackeson,*[7] *R v Plymouth Justices, ex p Driver*[8] and *R v Mullen.*[9] The European Court of Human Rights unanimously found a violation of Art 5, ruling that:

> '… the applicant's deprivation of liberty was neither lawful within the meaning of Article 5(1)(f) nor compatible with the right to security of person. Depriving Mr Bozano of his liberty in this way amounted in fact to a disguised form of extradition designed to circumvent the negative ruling of the Court of Appeal and not detention necessary in the ordinary course of action taken with a view to deportation… the deportation procedure was abused'.[10]

1 [2001] 2 AC 19, HL at p 39B–E.
2 This requirement flows from innumerable decisions of the European Court of Human Rights to the effect that: 'The main issue to be determined is whether the disputed detention was "lawful", including whether it was in accordance with "a procedure prescribed by law". The Convention here refers essentially to national law and establishes the need to apply its rules, but it also requires that any measure depriving the individual of his liberty must be compatible with the purpose of Art 5, namely to protect the individual from arbitrariness… What is at stake here is not only the "right to liberty" but also the "right to security of person"…' (See for example, *Bozano v France* (1986) 9 ECHR 297 at paras 54 and 59). See also *Čonka v Belgium* (2002) 34 E.H.R.R. 54 at para 42 *Khodorkovskiy v Russia*, App. no. 5829/04, 31 May 2011 at para 142, and *Azimov v Russia* (2013) App. No. 67474/11, 18 April 2013, para 163.
3 The test is one of 'flagrant breach'; *R (Ullah) v Special Adjudicator* (above para **8.24**) per Lord Bingham of Cornhill at para 24; *Government of Romani v Ceausescu* [2006] EWHC 2615 (Admin) per Maurice Kay LJ at para 12; *Othman v United Kingdom* (2012) 55 EHRR 1 at paras 231–233.
4 In *A and others v UK* (2009) 49 EHRR 29, the ECtHR said, at para 164, 'To avoid being branded as arbitrary, detention under Art 5(1)(f) must be carried out in good faith; it must be closely connected to the ground of detention relied on by the Government; the place and conditions of detention should be appropriate; and the length of the detention should not exceed that reasonably required for the purpose pursued'. See also *Iskandarov v Russia* (2010) (App. No. 17185/05), 23 September 2010 at para 146 and *Molotchko v Ukraine* (2012) App. No. 12275/10, 26 April 2012, para 143.
5 (Case C-396/11) [2013] 3 W.L.R. 681 at para 62.
6 Above para **8.28**.
7 (1981) 75 Cr App Rep 24, DC.
8 [1986] QB 95, DC.
9 [2000] 1 QB 520, CA.
10 (1986) 9 EHRR 297 at para 60.

8.30 Extradition Acts have historically contained express protection against extradition requests made in bad faith. The test for bad faith has always been a broad one. Under s 11(3)(c) of the 1989 Act,[1] it was stated by Woolf LJ in *In Re Osman*[2] that:

> 'the term good faith has to be given a reasonably generous interpretation so that if the proceedings were brought for a collateral purpose, or with an improper motive and not for the purpose of achieving the proper administration of justice, they would not be regarded as complying with this statutory requirement. Likewise, the accusations would not be made in good faith in the interests of justice if the prosecution deliberately manipulates or misuses the process of the court to deprive the defendant of a protection to which he is entitled by law'.

1 'Without prejudice to the jurisdiction of the High Court apart from this section, the court shall order the person's discharge if it appears to the court in relation to the offence, or each of the offences, in respect of which the applicant's return is sought, that…(c) because the accusation against him is not made in good faith in the interests of justice'. Section 12(2)(a)(iii) gave a like power to the Secretary of State.

2 (25 February 1992, unreported), DC at transcript pp 8–9. Cited by Rose LJ in *R (Saifi) v Governor of Brixton Prison* [2001] 1 WLR 1134 at para 22; Brooke LJ in *Lodhi v Governor of Brixton Prison* [2001] EWHC 178 (Admin) at para 106.

8.31 The 2003 Act contains no 'bad faith' exception. That is because, as was made clear during Parliamentary debate during the passage of the 2003 Act,[1] ECHR, Art 5 would be engaged (via ss 21 or 87 of the 2003 Act) in the case of an extradition request made in bad faith. Such a request would amount to 'arbitrary' extradition contrary to Art 5. Therefore, the developed case law under s 11(3)(c) of the 1989 Act remains applicable. Bad faith may attach to anything in the laying of the allegation/charge that would disclose bad faith on the part of the Requesting State. In *R (Saifi) v Governor of Brixton Prison,*[2] bad faith was found on the part of the Indian prosecuting authorities in circumstances which disclosed a failure to disclose a magistrates' recording that pressure had been applied to the sole witness upon whose evidence the case depended, public attempts on the part of the police to prejudice a fair trial, failure to disclose a retraction statement, and failure to disclose the fact that the witness' statement had been written by a third person. Moreover, Brooke LJ made plain[3] that bad faith is not confined to the Requesting State or its law-enforcement authorities. It may emanate from a witness or complainant. Other examples of successful reliance upon s 11(3)(c) include *Asliturk v Government of Turkey*[4] and *Sutej v Governor of HMP Holloway & another.*[5] For an example of the difficulties in establishing bad faith in a post-conviction extradition request, see *Mariotti v Government of Italy.*[6] The courts have acknowledged the strong presumption that a Requesting State, in making the extradition request, is acting in good faith.[7] It has also noted that the Art 5 ground may be 'parasitic' on an argument of abuse of process for bad faith.[8]

1 Hansard, House of Commons, 25 March 2003, Second Reading, Vol 402, col 188; Hansard, House of Lords, 27 October 2003, Report stage, Vol 654, cols 114–115: 'Can it seriously be said that the High Court has no power to discharge a fugitive where it is plain that the accusation has been made against him in bad faith? Of course not, such a result would bring the whole extradition process into disrepute', per Baroness Scotland of Asthal.

2 Above para **8.30** per Rose LJ at paras 64–66.

3 At para 63.
4 [2002] EWHC 2326 (Admin); extradition of Mayor of Istanbul sought for political reasons.
5 [2003] EWHC 1940 (Admin); allegations made for purposes of bolstering civil proceedings.
6 [2005] EWHC 2745 (Admin) per Maurice Kay LJ at para 27: 'Whether or not the over-enthusiastic and careless statements of Italian officials are also tainted by bad faith (and we do not consider it necessary to make such a finding), we do not believe that it would be appropriate to discharge the applicant in the interests of justice by reference to them. This is a conviction case and we find no bad faith on the part of the Italian authorities or anyone for whom they are responsible in the processes which resulted in the conviction. In circumstances where a conviction for a very grave offence has been obtained by due process, in my judgment it would be a very rare case in which extradition would be refused simply because officials acting on the extradition request have been shown to have overegged the pudding.'
7 *(Ahmad) v Secretary of State* [2006] EWHC 2927 (Admin), Laws LJ at para 101.
8 *Patel v Government of India & Anor* [2013] EWHC 819 (Admin) per Parker J at para 30.

8.32 It is also clear from *Re Murat Calis*[1] that supervening bad faith on the part of the prosecuting/investigating authority is capable of rendering a charge or complaint, albeit initially honest, one of bad faith within s 11(3)(c). In that case, the complainant had visited Mr Calis' lawyer and offered to withdraw his complaint in return for payment. Sedley J held that:

> 'it becomes inescapable in my judgement that the accusation … is no longer being made in good faith, assuming it to have been originally an honest complaint. It is being pursued against the … applicant as a means of blackmail … [T]he facts which establish bad faith in the present case also establish that to return the applicant would be both unjust and oppressive.'[2]

1 (19 November 1993, unreported), DC. See also *Castillo v The Kingdom of Spain* [2005] 1 WLR 1043, DC per Thomas LJ at paras 41–44 (deliberate exaggeration by a Requesting State of the description of conduct in an extradition request capable of evidencing bad faith).
2 At transcript p 10.

Article 6 ECHR

8.33 Article 6 does not generally apply to the Court's examination, under its own domestic law, of an extradition request from a foreign State, even in cases where the Court carries out an assessment of whether there is a case to answer. Extradition proceedings do not involve the determination of guilt or innocence and thus do not amount to the determination of a criminal charge within the meaning of Art 6(1).[1] It is not the function of the Strasbourg authorities to supervise the correct application of extradition law.[2]

Thus Strasbourg has, for example, declined to investigate complaints that extradition proceedings have been vitiated by the length of detention pending extradition in violation of ECHR, Art 6(1),[3] non-service of extradition decisions in violation of ECHR, Art 6(1),[4] non-access to the court file and the inability to advance arguments regarding the characterisation of the offence in violation of ECHR, Art 6(1),[5] inadequate representation and interpretation in violation of ECHR, Arts 6(3)(b) and 6(3)(e),[6] the absence of legal aid in the Requesting State in violation of ECHR, Art 6(3)(c)[7] and the inability to cross-examine in violation of ECHR, Art 6(3)(d).[8] The House of Lords summarised the position in *R (Al-Fawwaz) v Governor of Brixton Prison*:[9]

'... it is clear from the decision of the European Commission of Human Rights in *Kirkwood v United Kingdom* (1984) 37 DR 158 that the provisions of Article 6 do not apply to a committal hearing on an application for extradition, the Commission stating, at p 191, para 9, of its decision: 'Nevertheless, the Commission concludes that these proceedings did not in themselves form part of the determination of the applicant's guilt or innocence, which will be the subject of separate proceedings in the United States which may be expected to conform to standards of fairness equivalent to the requirements of Article 6, including the presumption of innocence, notwithstanding the committal proceedings. In these circumstances, the Commission concludes that the committal proceedings did not form part of or constitute the determination of a criminal charge within the meaning of Article 6 of the Convention.'

However, in *Lukaszewski v District Court in Torun Poland* [2012] UKSC 20, the Supreme Court held that a United Kingdom citizen had a common law right to enter and remain within the United Kingdom, and that extradition proceedings under the 2003 Act could affect that right, and so extradition proceedings against such a person involved the determination of civil rights within the meaning of Art 6(1). Accordingly, pursuant to the Human Rights Act 1998, s 3(1) in the case of a citizen of the United Kingdom, the statutory provisions in the 2003 Act concerning appeals were to be read as being subject to the qualification that the court should have a discretion in exceptional cases to extend the time for filing and serving a notice of appeal.

1 See *Trabelsi v Belgium* (2015) 60 EHRR 21 at para 160; *Monedero Angora v Spain* (dec.) no. 41138/05, 7 October 2008; *Maaouia v France* (2000) App No 39652/98, 5 October 2000 at paras 33–41; *Mamatkulov & Askarov v Turkey* (2005) 18 BHRC 203: 'The Court reiterates that decisions regarding the entry, stay, and deportation of aliens do not concern the determination of an applicant's civil rights or obligations or of a criminal charge against him, within the meaning of Art 6(1) of the Convention' (at para 82).

2 *Altun v Germany* (1983) 36 DR 209 at 231.

3 *Maaouia v France* (above) at paras 33–41; *Raf v Spain* App No 53652/00, 17 June 2003 at para 1; *Albo v Italy* (2004) (dec) App No 56271/00 at para 3(b); *Farmakopoulos v Greece* (1990) 64 DR 52 and *EGM v Luxembourg* (1994) EHRR 144.

4 *Raidl v Austria* 20 E.H.R.R. CD114 at para 3(e); *Raf v Spain* (above).

5 *Mamatkulov & Askarov v Turkey* (above) at paras 81–82.

6 *H v Spain* (1983) 37 DR 93 at 94.

7 *Soering v UK* (above para **8.24**) at para 113

8 *Kirkwood v UK* (1984) 37 DR 158 at 191.

9 [2002] 2 WLR 101, HL per Lord Hutton at para 87.

8.34 However, it was stated in *Soering v United Kingdom*[1] that the act of extradition to a country lacking Art 6 fair trial guarantees can breach the ECHR. That is to say that UK State responsibility may be engaged in circumstances where extradition may be said to have as a direct consequence the exposure of an individual to an Art 6 incompatible trial:

'...the right to a fair trial in criminal proceedings, as embodied in Article 6, holds a prominent place in a democratic society. The court does not exclude that an issue might exceptionally be raised under Article 6 by an extradition decision in circumstances where the fugitive has suffered or risks suffering a flagrant denial of a fair trial in the Requesting State.'[2]

1 Above para **8.24**, at para 113. This principle was subsequently referred to by the European Court in the following terms in *Drozd and Janousek v France and Spain* (1992)

14 EHRR 745 at para 110: 'As the Convention does not require the Contracting Parties to impose its standards on third States or territories, France was not obliged to verify whether the proceedings which resulted in the conviction were compatible with all the requirements of Art 6 of the Convention…would also thwart the current trend towards strengthening international cooperation in the administration of justice, a trend which is in principle in the interests of the persons concerned. The Contracting States are, however, obliged to refuse their co-operation if it emerges that the conviction is the result of a flagrant denial of justice'.

2 See also *R (Al-Fawwaz) v Governor of Brixton Prison* (above para **8.33**) per Lord Scott at 136, para 116: 'But alleged malefactors who are present in this country, whether as permanent residents, as refugees or asylum seekers, or as visitors, are entitled, while they are here, to the protection of our laws and our standards of criminal justice. They should not be exported abroad to face trial under a foreign criminal justice system unless, by our standards, there is a case against them that is fit for trial, and unless, by our standards, they will receive a fair trial in accordance with the requirements of Art 6 of the European Convention for the Protection of Human Rights and Fundamental Freedoms. The … purpose of extradition arrangements is, or should be, to provide the requisite safeguards'.

8.35 The limits on this protection are, however, strict.[1] The matter was put as follows in *R (Ullah) v Special Adjudicator.*[2] Lord Bingham of Cornhill (with whom all other Law Lords agreed) reviewed the ECHR authorities at para 17, and concluded that:

> 'The authority cited in para 17 shows that the court has not excluded the possibility of relying on Article 6, and even Article 5, while fully recognising the great difficulty of doing so and the exceptional nature of such cases …'[3]

and

> '…the Strasbourg jurisprudence…makes it quite clear that successful reliance demands presentation of a very strong case…Where reliance is placed on Article 6 it must be shown that a person has suffered or risks suffering a flagrant denial of a fair trial in the Receiving State…The lack of success of applicants relying on Articles 2, 5 and 6 before the Strasbourg court highlights the difficulty of meeting the stringent test which that court imposes.'[4]

A 'flagrant denial of justice' is 'synonymous with a trial which is manifestly contrary to the provisions of art. 6 or the principles embodied therein': *Othman v UK* (2012) 55 EHRR 1 at [259]. It is the same as establishing a real risk of a 'gross violation' or showing that the deficiencies in the process were such that the trial he would face on his return would be 'so fundamental as to amount to a nullification or destruction of the very essence of the rights [Art 6] guaranteed': *Dudko v Russian Federation* [2010] EWHC 1125 (Admin) at [36].

1 In *Soering* (above para **8.24**), the European Court observed (at para 86) that 'the Convention does not govern the actions of States not Parties to it, nor does it purport to be a means of requiring the Contracting States to impose Convention standards on other States. Article 1 cannot be read as justifying a general principle to the effect that, notwithstanding its extradition obligations, a Contracting State may not surrender an individual unless satisfied that the conditions awaiting him in the country of destination are in full accord with each of the safeguards of the Convention', and (at para 91) that '… [I]nherent in the whole of the Convention is a search for a fair balance between the demands of the general interest of the community and the requirements of the protection of the individual's fundamental rights. As movement about the world becomes easier and crime takes on a larger international dimension, it is increasingly in the interests of all nations that suspected offenders who flee abroad should be brought to justice. Conversely, the establishment of safe havens for fugitives would not only result in danger for the State obliged to harbour the protected person but also tend to undermine the foundations of extradition.'

2 Above para **8.24**.
3 At para 21.
4 At para 24. See also Lord Steyn (with whom all other Law Lords agreed) at para 50: '… a high threshold test will always have to be satisfied. It will be necessary to establish at least a real risk of a flagrant violation of the very essence of the right before other articles could become engaged', and Lord Carswell (with whom all other Law Lords also agreed) at para 63: '… it cannot now be said that persons seeking asylum in a Member State of the Council of Europe are unable to invoke any of the provisions of the Convention when resisting an expulsion decision. I do regard it as important, however, that Member States should not attempt to impose Convention standards on other countries by decisions which have the effect of requiring adherence to those standards in those countries …', and at para 69: 'The concept of a flagrant breach or violation may not always be easy for domestic courts to apply … but it seems to me that it was well expressed by…the criterion that the right in question would be completely denied or nullified in the destination country. This would harmonise with the concept of a fundamental breach, with which courts in this jurisdiction are familiar'. For an early application of those principles under the 2003 Act, see *R (on the application of Bermingham) v Director of the Serious Fraud Office* [2007] QB 727 per Laws LJ at para 111. For a more recent recital of this principle, see *Rwanda v Nteziryayo* [2017] EWHC 1912 (Admin).

8.36 The stringency of this test is increased when one takes into account the strong, albeit rebuttable, presumption that Member States of the EU will abide by their obligations under the ECHR.[1] In *Krolik v Several Judicial Authorities in Poland*, Sir John Thomas P noted 'that something approaching an international consensus is required, if the presumption is to be rebutted'.[2] If the evidence does not pass this significant threshold, extradition may still be granted even in circumstances where there are allegations that the criminal justice system of the Requesting State does not comply with Art 6 standards. Examples include *Altun v Federal Republic of Germany*[3] (military tribunals not independent and impartial); *Mamatkulov & Askarov v Turkey*[4] ('…there may have been reasons for doubting at the time that they would receive a fair trial…') and *Lodhi v Governor of Brixton Prison*[5] ('…features of the judicial system in the UAE which would not be regarded as Convention-compliant…'). By contrast, the possibility of a prospective flagrant breach of Art 6 was recognised in *Okandeji v The Government of the Commonwealth of Australia*[6] (reverse burdens of proof). In *Kapri v The Lord Advocate representing The Government of the Republic of Albania*,[7] the Supreme Court remitted an appeal against extradition for reconsideration on the basis of allegations of systematic judicial corruption in Albania which would constitute a denial of the right to a fair trial in that country. Lord Hope confirmed that "where allegations of corruption are widespread they must be taken seriously' and that they warranted closer examination of the evidence before a final decision was made concerning extradition.[8] Substantial concerns about the conduct of the extradition proceedings (and the prosecution motivating it) may also lead the court to conclude that the proceedings are mala fides and that there is a substantial risk of a flagrant breach of Art 6 if the appellant is extradited.[9]

1 See *Symeou v Public Prosecutor's Office of the Court of Appeals, Patras, Greece* [2009] EWHC 897 (Admin), at para 66.
2 [2012] EWHC 2357 (Admin) at paras 6-8. See also *Sanchez v Spain* [2013] EWHC 2264 (Admin).
3 Above para **8.33**, at para 6 (232).
4 Above para **8.33**, at para 91.
5 Above para **8.30**, at para 105 per Brooke LJ.

6 [2005] EWHC 2925 (Admin).
7 [2013] UKSC 48.
8 Ibid per Lord Hope at paras 28–35.
9 *Ukraine v Kononko* [2014] EWHC 1420 (Admin).

8.37 In *Lis v Poland (No 1)*[1] the court considered the impact of recent legislative changes in Poland on the independence of the Polish judiciary and the decision of the CJEU in *LM: Request for a Preliminary Ruling from High Court (Ireland)*.[2] The question so far as Art 6 was concerned was whether the CJEU had altered the 'flagrant denial of the right to a fair trial' test by holding that:

> 'Accordingly, as long as such a decision has not been adopted by the European Council, the executing judicial authority may refrain, on the basis of Article 1(3) of Framework Decision 2002/584, to give effect to a European arrest warrant issued by a Member State which is the subject of a reasoned proposal as referred to in Article 7(1) TEU only in exceptional circumstances where that authority finds, after carrying out a specific and precise assessment of the particular case, that there are substantial grounds for believing that the person in respect of whom that European arrest warrant has been issued will, following his surrender to the issuing judicial authority, run a real risk of breach of his fundamental right to an independent tribunal and, therefore, of the essence of his fundamental right to a fair trial'[3]

The High Court answered that question in the negative, holding that the CJEU:

> '…referred frequently in the course of its judgment to the potential breach of the "essence" of the applicant's right to a fair trial: see paragraphs [59], [60], [68], [72], [73], [75] and [78]. We are bound to observe that if the Luxembourg Court were seeking to draw a qualitative distinction between that concept and the oft-repeated formulation of the Strasbourg Court of a "flagrant denial of justice" it would have said so in answering question 2. In our judgment there is no sensible distinction to be made between a breach of the essence of a right to a fair trial and the flagrant denial test'.[4]

1 [2018] EWHC 2848 (Admin).
2 Case C-216/18 PPU, dated 25 July 2018.
3 Ibid at para 73.
4 *Lis* (n 1) at para 63.

Article 7 ECHR

8.38 Extradition does not fall within the ambit of ECHR, Art 7.[1] In the absence of trans-national provisions, extradition legislation has retroactive effect. Extradition legislation is procedural in nature. It involves no determination of guilt or innocence. Therefore, the fact that the offence for which extradition is sought was committed at a time when there were no extradition arrangements in place with the Requesting State, will not affect the application of subsequent extradition arrangements. See, in particular, *Marais v Governor of HMP Brixton*.[2] Indeed, that is the very premise upon which ad hoc extradition arrangements may be entered into under s 194 of the 2003 Act. In fact, entire extradition schemes may have retroactive effect.[3]

The position is different, however, in respect of the substantive requirement of dual criminality. In cases where dual criminality is required,[4] the conduct alleged must have been criminal according to the laws of both the Requesting and Requested States at the time it is alleged to have been committed. Thus, if the conduct was, at the time it was committed, not an offence contrary to English law, extradition cannot lie.[5]

The courts have also confirmed that the 'flagrant breach' test applies to Art 7. In *Arranz v Spanish Judicial Authority*, a case concerning Art 7 was pending before the Grand Chamber of the ECtHR which could affect the case.[6] The court held that it would not be right for it to express a view on the issue but proceeded on the basis that the test for UK courts to apply in relation to Art 7 was the same as when considering other provisions of the ECHR.[7] The Court ultimately concluded that, in light of an express undertaking from the Spanish courts to comply with the decision on Art 7 by the Grand Chamber, it would be difficult to see how there could be a real risk of a flagrant breach of Art 7.[8]

1 *X v Netherlands* (1976) 6 DR 184 (Appl 7512/76); *Bakhtiar v Switzerland* (1996) ECHR Appl 27292/95.

2 [2001] EWHC 1051 (Admin).

3 *R v Secretary of State for the Home Department, ex p Hill* [1999] QB 886, per Hooper J at 900–903, per Rose LJ at 918.

4 See ss 63(2) and 64(2) of the 2003 Act for circumstances in which the dual criminality requirement is abrogated in Part 1 cases.

5 *R v Bow Street Metropolitan Stipendiary Magistrate, ex p Pinochet (No 3)* [2000] 1 AC 147, HL per Lord Browne-Wilkinson at p 196; *Dabas v High Court of Madrid* [2007] 2 AC 31, HL per Lord Hope of Craighead at para 46. In *Norris v Government of the United States of America* [2008] 2 WLR 673, this was described by the House of Lords as 'elementary' (at para 63).

6 [2013] EWHC 1662 (Admin).

7 Ibid at paras 33–41.

8 Ibid at paras 43–45. The Grand Chamber in fact upheld the breach of Art 7: see *Del Rio Prada v Spain* (Application no. 42750/09) and the High Court was required in *Spanish Judicial Authority v Arranz* [2015] EWHC 2305 (Admin) to consider the failure by the Spanish Judicial Authority to comply with their earlier undertaking.

Article 8 ECHR

8.39 In *R (Razgar) v Secretary of State for the Home Department,*[1] the House of Lords ruled that the rights protected by Art 8 may be engaged by the foreseeable consequences for health or welfare of removal from the UK pursuant to an expulsion decision, even where such removal does not violate Art 3. In Art 8 terms, the act of extradition constitutes a prima facie interference with the appellant's rights under Art 8(1). Proposed extradition will invariably be 'in accordance with the law' and is sought in pursuance of a legitimate aim, namely 'the prevention of … crime'. Thus, for any extradition to be Art 8(2) (and thus s 87) compliant, it must be shown to be 'necessary in a democratic society' which, in turn, requires the showing of a pressing social need and requires that the interference at issue be proportionate to the legitimate aim pursued.[2] Following *Huang v Secretary of State for the Home Department,*[3] it is not right to apply 'exceptionality' as a formula for determining proportionality.[4] The Supreme Court has confirmed that the court's approach to a case under Art 8 should not be radically different as between extradition and expulsion cases.[5]

1 [2004] 2 AC 368, HL.

2 *Bermingham v Director of Public Prosecutions* (above para **8.35**) per Laws LJ at paras 112 and 118. Note that, in deciding whether extradition is 'necessary in a democratic society in the interests of …public safety …for the prevention of disorder or crime', in *Razgar* (above), Lord Bingham of Cornhill observed, at para 19, that: 'Where removal is proposed in pursuance of a lawful immigration policy, [this] question will almost always fall to be answered affirmatively … In the absence of bad faith, ulterior motive or deliberate abuse of power it is hard to imagine an adjudicator answering this question other than affirmatively'.

3 [2007] 2 WLR 581, HL per Lord Bingham of Cornhill at para 20. The exceptionality test was later dispproved in extradition cases in *Norris v US* [2010] 2 AC 487, per Lord Phillips at para 90.

4 *Jaso* (above para **8.08**) per Dyson LJ at paras 56–57: 'What is required is that the court should decide whether the interference with a person's right to respect for his private or (as the case may be) family life which would result from his or her extradition is proportionate to the legitimate aim of honouring extradition treaties with other States. It is clear that great weight should be accorded to the legitimate aim of honouring extradition treaties made with other States. Thus, although it is wrong to apply an exceptionality test, in an extradition case there will have to be striking and unusual facts to lead to the conclusion that it is disproportionate to interfere with an extraditee's Article 8 rights'.

5 *R (on the application of HH) v Westminster City Magistrates' Court* [2012] UKSC 25, per Baroness Hale at paras 28–31. At para 30, Baroness Hale confirmed 'the court would be well advised to adopt the same structured approach to an Art 8 case as would be applied by the Strasbourg court. First, it asks whether there is or will be an interference with the right to respect for private and family life. Second, it asks whether that interference is in accordance with the law and pursues one or more of the legitimate aims within those listed in Art 8.2. Third, it asks whether the interference is "necessary in a democratic society" in the sense of being a proportionate response to that legitimate aim. In answering that all-important question, it will weigh the nature and gravity of the interference against the importance of the aims pursued. In other words, the balancing exercise is the same in each context: what may differ are the nature and weight of the interests to be put into each side of the scale'.

8.40 The leading authority on the correct analytical approach to Art 8 is the case of *Poland v Celinski*.[1] It was held there that:

> '… it is important in our view that judges hearing cases where reliance is placed on article 8 adopt an approach which clearly sets out an analysis of the facts as found and contains in succinct and clear terms adequate reasoning for the conclusion arrived at by balancing the necessary considerations.
>
> The approach should be one where the judge, after finding the facts, ordinarily sets out each of the "pros" and "cons" in what has aptly been described as a "balance sheet" in some of the cases concerning issues of article 8 which have arisen in the context of care order or adoption: see the cases cited at paras 30–44 of *In re B-S (Children) (Adoption Order: Leave to Oppose)* [2014] 1 WLR 563. The judge should then, having set out the "pros" and "cons" in the "balance sheet" approach, set out his reasoned conclusions as to why extradition should be ordered or the defendant discharged.
>
> We would therefore hope that the judge would list the factors that favoured extradition and then the factors that militated against extradition. The judge would then, on the basis of the identification of the relevant factors, set out his/her conclusion as the result of balancing those factors with reasoning to support that conclusion. As appeals in these cases are, for the reasons we

shall examine, common, such an approach is of the greatest assistance to an appellate court'.[2]

1 [2016] 1 WLR 551, HC.
2 Ibid at paras 15–17.

8.41 Although mostly argued in respect of personal circumstances, in reality, ECHR, Art 8, and in particular its concept of proportionality, is a particularly subtle and potentially effective tool that a defendant is able to wield in most abuse-related scenarios. In certain circumstances, it could, for example, serve to prevent extradition in a case where, although technically available, a Requesting State was exercising an exorbitant jurisdiction,[1] in cases where the UK is the more appropriate trial forum,[2] or in cases of triviality.[3] It is also clear from a number of authorities that a combination of long delay, particularly if unexplained or culpable, and the relative triviality of offences might be sufficient grounds for discharge, even without regard to family or personal circumstances.[4]

1 *R (Al Fawwaz) v Governor of Brixton Prison* (above para **8.33**) per Lord Slynn of Hadley at para 39, per Lord Millett at para 102, per Lord Scott at para 121, per Lord Rodger of Earlsferry at para 149; Boudhiba (above para **8.09**) per Smith LJ at paras 43–44; *Hashmi v Government of the United States of America* [2007] EWHC 564 (Admin) per Scott Baker LJ at paras 24–26.

2 The principles were considered in *Bermingham* (above para **8.35**) per Laws LJ at paras 112–130. Whilst justiciability in this country might be relevant to the Art 8 issue, its application would only be triggered in 'wholly exceptional circumstances' (per Laws LJ at para 118). Where a proposed extradition is properly constituted according to the domestic law of the UK and the relevant bilateral treaty, and its execution is resisted on Art 8 grounds, a wholly exceptional case would have to be shown to justify a finding that the extradition would on the particular facts be disproportionate to its legitimate aim (per Laws LJ at paras 112–118). The starting point is that the prospective extradition (as well as satisfying all relevant formal requirements) is not tainted by abuse (per Laws LJ at para 124). The fact that the appellant could be prosecuted here (and that there would be consequential advantages and disadvantages from the prosecution and defence perspectives) does not amount to an exceptional circumstance (per Laws. LJ at para 129). The fact that the appellant is a UK national does not render the case exceptional (per Laws LJ at paras 120 and 125–130). There can be overlap between the trial forum and personal circumstances, see *BH v The Lord Advocate & Ors* [2012] UK. For other cases in which 'forum' arguments have failed under Pt 2 of the 2003 Act, see *Bentley v Government of the United States of America* [2005] EWHC 1078 (admin) at para 26, *Norris v Government of the United States of America (No 2)* [2007] 1 WLR 1730, DC at paras 157–172. Under Pt 1 of the 2003 Act, see *Hosseini v Head of the Prosecution Department of the Courts of Higher Instance, Paris* [2006] EWHC 1333 (Admin) at paras 49–53. In Scotland, see *Wright v the Scottish Ministers* [2005] SLT 613 at paras 56–70 and *La Torre v Her Majesty's Advocate & another* [2006] HCJAC 56 at paras 78–79, 97–104, and in Strasbourg, see *Raidl v Austria* (above para **8.33**). See also now the 'forum' bar in ss 19B–F and 83A–E of the 2003 Act.

3 *Zak v Regional Court of Bydgoszcz, Poland* [2008] EWHC 470 (Admin) at paras 19–24. Previously, s 11(3)(a) of the Extradition Act 1989 provided that a defendant could be discharged in circumstances of triviality. It must be appreciated that the Extradition Act already prohibits extradition in respect of offences which attract maximum terms of imprisonment of less than 12 months (or for which sentences of less than four months have been imposed). The courts will not impose their own view of sentencing – see *Fridenberga v Public Prosecutor, Prosecutor General's Office for the Republic of Latvia* [2013] EWHC 317 (Admin). Each case is to be decided 'entirely on its facts', per Collins J at para 6. See also *United States of America v Shlesinger* where the applicant had 9 days left to serve on the predicate sentence [2013] EWHC 2671 (Admin).

4 *R. (on the application of Folcik) v Poland* [2014] EWHC 1264 (Admin); *Baturo v Poland* [2014] EWHC 710 (Admin); *Jackowski v Poland* [2012] EWHC 3935 (Admin); *Juchniewicz*

v Poland [2013] EWHC 1529 (Admin) and *Majchrzak v Poland* [2013] EWHC 3584 (Admin). A recent example of the flexibility provided by Art 8 as an alternative to running abuse arguments can be seen in *Konecny* (above).

PACE

8.42 Finally, PACE, ss 76 and 78 apply to extradition proceedings.[1] However, the application of s 78 is confined to cases where a prima facie case is required to be established and is, even then, highly restricted:

> '… when the section is being applied to committal or extradition proceedings, the question is whether the admission of the evidence would have such an adverse effect on the fairness of *those* proceedings that the court ought not to admit it … the magistrates should ordinarily assume that the powers available to the judge at the trial will ensure that the proceedings are fair. The question is, therefore, whether the admission of the evidence would have an adverse effect on the fairness of the decision to commit or extradite the accused for trial, even if the trial is a fair one. I think that the circumstances would have to be very unusual before magistrates could properly come to such a decision … extradition procedure is founded on concepts of comity and reciprocity. It would undermine the effectiveness of international treaty obligations if the courts were to superimpose discretions based on local notions of fairness upon the ordinary rules of admissibility. I do not wish to exclude the possibility that the discretion may be used in extradition proceedings founded upon evidence which, though technically admissible, has been obtained in a way which outrages civilised values. But such cases are also likely to be very rare'.[2]

1 *R v Governor of Brixton Prison, ex p Levin* [1997] AC 741 per Lord Hoffman at 746F. Although note the doubts expressed in *Wellington v The Governor of Her Majesty's Prison Belmarsh* [2004] EWHC 418 (Admin) per Mitting J at paras 16–17 and *Harkins v Secretary of State for the Home Department* [2007] EWHC 639 (Admin) per Lloyd-Jones J at para 38.

2 Per Lord Hoffmann at 748. Accordingly, committals have been upheld even though based upon facts that '..would have caused considerable difficulty' to a domestic prosecution under PACE 1984, s 78, but which did not satisfy the higher *Levin* extradition threshold of 'outrag[ing] civilised values' test. See, for example, *R v Bow Street Magistrates' Court, ex p Proulx* [2001] 1 All ER 57, DC per Mance LJ at para 75; *R (Saifi) v Governor of Brixton Prison* (above para **8.30**) per Rose LJ at para 61.

THE ROLE AND POWERS OF THE SECRETARY OF STATE

8.43 The statutory provisions discussed above therefore constitute a formidable array of safeguards that protect against most species of abusive conduct on the part of a Requesting State. Prior to the 2003 Act, the Secretary of State for the Home Department had an overarching discretion to refuse extradition[1] to refuse extradition. Under the 2003 Act, the executive no longer plays a role in extradition to Category 1 territories, and only a limited role in Category 2 cases (especially following the amendments to ss 70 and 108 of the 2003 Act made by paras 10–15 of the Crime & Courts Act 2013, Sch 20).

1 Sections 12–13 of, and Sch 1, para 8(2) to the 1989 Act. Sections 12(1) and 12(2) provided for his 'general discretion as to the making of an order for the return'. A similar discretion was to be found in Sch 1, para 8(2).

THE SLOW DEVELOPMENT OF AN ABUSE JURISDICTION

8.44 Against this background, numerous attempts were made to read a general common law abuse jurisdiction into the Extradition Acts. Yet, until the very final days of the pre-2003 legislation, the courts remained steadfastly resolute in their reluctance to extend statutory powers by reading a broad abuse of process jurisdiction into extradition legislation on the basis that the overriding executive discretion of the Secretary of State[1] provided sufficient bulwark against abuse. In fact, fewer areas of law can have witnessed such a sustained but unsuccessful attempt to establish a legal principle. In the 30 years between 1971 and 2001, the House of Lords alone entertained, and rejected, eight attempts to establish an extradition abuse jurisdiction.

1 Above para **8.43**.

8.45 In 1971, the House of Lords first ruled that there existed no such jurisdiction in *Atkinson v United States of America.*[1] It was felt to be contrary to the intentions of Parliament[2] and that the necessary safeguard lay with the discretionary powers of the Secretary of State.[3]

1 [1971] AC 197, HL. See also *Royal Government of Greece v Governor of Brixton Prison* [1971] AC 250, HL, sub nom *R v Governor of Brixton Prison, ex p Kotronis* [1969] 3 All ER 304.
2 Per Lord Reid at 232E-G.
3 Per Lord Reid at 232G–233B. See also Lord Morris of Borth-y-Gest at 238G–239A and Lord Guest at 246B–247C.

8.46 However, in 1986, the House of Lords gave judgment in *Re Rees*[1] in terms that indicated that, at least in cases where executive misconduct in the context of English proceedings deprive a defendant of extradition safeguards, an abuse of process jurisdiction did exist.

That decision[2] spawned a small number of decisions between 1986 and 1990 in which the High Court considered abuse of process submissions on their merits[3], whilst some High Court decisions continued to apply *Atkinson.*[4] But in 1991, in *R v Governor of Pentonville Prison, ex p Sinclair*[5] the House of Lords revisited the issue. Lord Ackner[6] observed[7] that, since the decision in *Atkinson,* and since the commencement of proceedings in *Sinclair*'s case, the Extradition Act 1989 had been enacted and drew specific attention to the provisions of s 11(3). Without reference to *Re Rees*, Lord Ackner observed[8] that there was 'no jurisdiction to consider whether such proceedings may be an abuse of the process of the court'. This was further confirmed in *R v Governor of Pentonville Prison, ex p Alves.*[9]

1 [1986] AC 937, HL.
2 And the fact that, contrary to Lord Reid's opinion in *Atkinson*, it had been established that a magistrates' court in domestic proceedings did have jurisdiction to refuse to commit an accused for trial on the ground that it would be unjust or oppressive to require him to be tried (*R v Secretary of State for the Home Department & another, ex p Rees* (unreported) (7 March 1985), DC per Watkins LJ).
3 See *R v Bow Street Magistrates' Court, ex p Van der Holst* (1986) 83 Cr App R. 114, DC per Lloyd LJ at p 124; *R v Governor of Pentonville Prison, ex p Chinoy* [1992] 1 All ER 317, DC per Nolan J.
4 *R v Governor of Pentonville Prison, ex p Parekh* (1988) Times, 19 May, DC; sub nom *In re Parekh* [1988] Crim LR 832, per Stocker LJ (although note the dissenting judgment of Hutchison J).

5 [1991] 2 AC 64, HL.
6 With whom Lords Bridge, Templeman, Griffiths and Goff agreed.
7 At 75–81.
8 At 80–81.
9 [1993] AC 284, HL.

8.47 There then came the House of Lords' landmark ruling in 1993 in *R v Horseferry Road Magistrates' Court, ex p Bennett,*[1] discussed in detail in **Chapter 5**. It appeared from the various wide-ranging and unqualified judgments[2] that the abuse of process jurisdiction (in its now extended form) was equally applicable to extradition proceedings (albeit vested in the High Court rather than the magistrates' court). Therefore, an understandably confident submission was made to the House of Lords the following year in *Re Schmidt,*[3] to the effect that the principles of *Bennett* were applicable in extradition proceedings. It was submitted on Mr Schmidt's behalf that he had been brought before the court of committal by an abuse of process, namely the ruse adopted by the police, and that the Divisional Court possessed an inherent and unlimited supervisory jurisdiction to correct such an abuse. Section 11(3) of the Act of 1989 preserved rather than created the jurisdiction of the High Court. It was submitted that *Atkinson* was out of date and should not be followed and that there was in any event an inherent jurisdiction in the High Court to intervene in such proceedings; which jurisdiction is recognised by the opening words of s 11(3). However, the court re-affirmed the decisions of *Atkinson* and *Sinclair.* This line of authority was again referred to with approval by the House of Lords in 1997 in *R v Secretary of State for the Home Department, ex p Launder*[4] and in 2001 in *R (Al-Fawwaz) v Governor of Brixton Prison*[5] and *R v Governor of Belmarsh Prison, ex p Gilligan.*[6]

1 [1994] 1 AC 42, HL.
2 Per Lord Griffiths at 61–62, per Lord Bridge of Harwich at 67–68, per Lord Lowry at 74 and 76–77.
3 [1995] 1 AC 339, HL.
4 [1997] 1 WLR 839, HL at pp 854–855, per Lord Hope of Craighead (with whom Lords Browne-Wilkinson, Steyn, Clyde and Hutton agreed).
5 [2002] 2 WLR 101, HL, per Lord Slynn of Hadley at para 39, per Lord Millett at para 102, per Lord Scott at para 121, per Lord Rodger of Earlsferry at para 149.
6 [2001] 1 AC 84, HL, per Lord Steyn (with whom Lords Browne-Wilkinson, Cooke and Hope agreed) at 97–98 and Lord Clyde at 101.

THE IMPACT OF THE HUMAN RIGHTS ACT 1998 AND KASHAMU

8.48 Although the courts had described it as a safeguard against unfair extradition, the exercise of supervisory jurisdiction by the Secretary of State had been a matter of significant disquiet for many years. She was plainly the subject of conflicting duties. Her role as ultimate protector against oppression was in conflict with her obligation on behalf of the State to extradite on the basis of extradition treaties (treaties which invariably make no reference to the Secretary of State exercising any general, or supervisory, discretion). Moreover, she was singularly ill-placed to deal with the complex issues of fact that often arose in connection with abuse of process submissions.

8.49 The Extradition Act 2003 eventually addressed this issue by removing the role of the Secretary of State altogether in Part 1 proceedings and significantly limiting it in Part 2 proceedings. The 2003 Act, together with the implementation of the Human Rights Act 1998, transformed the extradition landscape. Extradition proceedings are criminal proceedings 'albeit of a very special kind'.[1] Accordingly, as from October 2000, the Human Rights Act 1998 applied to extradition proceedings. Section 3 of the Human Rights Act 1998 requires that existing legislation 'must be read…in a way which is compatible so far as it is possible to do so' with the Convention. Section 6 of the Human Rights Act 1998 states that it is 'unlawful' for a public authority (prosecution and/or court) 'to act in a way which is incompatible with any Convention right'. Thus, the Human Rights Act significantly changed the way the courts viewed the extradition process.

1 *R (Government of the United States of America) v Bow Street Magistrates' Court* (above para **8.11**) per Lord Phillips CJ at para 76; *R v Governor of Brixton Prison, ex p Levin* [1997] AC 741, HL, per Lord Hoffmann at 746F.

8.50 This was apparent in *R (Kashamu) v Governor of Brixton Prison (No 2),*[1] where the *Atkinson/Schmidt* line of authority was argued to be incompatible with the Human Rights Act 1998. Kashamu was detained under Sch 1 to the 1989 Act in response to an extradition request from the US government in respect of serious drugs offences. On application for habeas corpus, the High Court quashed the committal as a result of material non-disclosure.[2] He was detained immediately on a second warrant. At the second committal proceedings the district judge declined to hear a submission that those committal proceedings constituted an abuse of process. However, on application to the High Court, the court considered whether the coming into force of the Human Rights Act required a different view to be taken.[3]

1 [2002] QB 887.
2 [2001] EWHC 980 (Admin).
3 Per Rose LJ at paras 8–9.

8.51 It was submitted that, following enactment of the Human Rights Act 1998, it must be the courts, rather than the Secretary of State, who should determine the lawfulness of detention under Art 5(1)(f). Rose LJ ruled that:

> '… It is, in my judgment, plain that Article 5 expressly requires the lawfulness of the detention of a person detained with a view to extradition under paragraph (1)(f) to be decided speedily by a court. It is equally plain to my mind that, in the extradition context, the Secretary of State lacks the qualities of independence and impartiality required of the court-like body by the Strasbourg jurisprudence…'[1]
>
> '… it seems to me to be clear that a court and not the Secretary of State is the appropriate forum for a decision as to the lawfulness of a fugitive's detention and, provided the Extradition Act 1989 can be so read, the magistrates' court is to be preferred to the High Court. As I have said, the House of Lords in *Atkinson, Ex p Sinclair* and *Re Schmidt* held that a magistrate has no power to refuse to commit in extradition proceedings because of an abuse of process. The rationale of each of those authorities,

however, is that it is open to the Secretary of State to respond to abuse by refusing to return the fugitive ...'[2]

'... In my judgment, although that is so, it does not now, in the light of the provisions of Article 5(4), provide a rationale for excluding the courts from exercising abuse jurisdiction in relation to the lawfulness of detention... [not providing] sufficient basis on which to oust the jurisdiction of magistrates which, at first blush, is conferred by the wide language of paragraph 6(1), to consider the lawfulness of a fugitive's detention. Put another way, both section 11(3) and paragraph 6(1) of Schedule 1 can, and in my judgment should, be so read as to enable both the High Court and a committing magistrate to consider the lawfulness of detention under Article 5(4) ...'.[3]

1 At para 27. See above paras **8.26–8.32**.
2 At para 29.
3 At para 30.

THE POSITION UNDER THE 2003 ACT

8.52 The 2003 Act removed the supervisory powers of the Secretary of State. In Part 1 cases, the Secretary of State plays no part at all. In Part 2 cases, her role is limited to three confined matters.[1] Moreover, ss 21 and 87 provide that the court of extradition is, in turn, obliged to decide whether the person's extradition would be compatible with the Convention rights within the meaning of the Human Rights Act. In light of these twin developments, it was assumed in early cases that *Kashamu* applied under the 2003 Act and that the judge conducting an extradition hearing under the 2003 Act possessed an implied jurisdiction to hold that the prosecutor is abusing the process of the court and to refuse to order extradition for that reason. For example, in *Okandeji v The Government of the Commonwealth of Australia*[2] and *Jenkins v Government of the United States of America,*[3] 'entrapment' abuse submissions were considered and rejected by the High Court on their merits without detailed consideration of the issue of jurisdiction.[4] In *Government of the Federal Republic of Germany v Kleinschmidt & another,*[5] the High Court (Beatson J) indicated,[6] obiter, that Kashamu applied under the 2003 Act. In *Boudhiba,*[7] where an EAW was issued after the appellant refused to cooperate with a request to be interviewed as a witness, the High Court acknowledged the existence of an abuse jurisdiction to prevent manipulation of the extradition process but rejected the claim on its merits.[8]

1 Sections 94–96A regarding death penalty, specialty and earlier extradition to the UK. The Secretary of State was formerly still susceptible to a human rights challenge by way of judicial review. This arose because the Secretary of State is a public authority within the meaning of the Human Rights Act 1998, s 6 and cannot act incompatibly with the Convention rights set out in Sch 1 to the Act. Accordingly, where the statutory appeals against the decisions of the District Judge and the Secretary of State had been exhausted in Pt 2 cases, but something arose between the determination of such matters and actual extradition to the requesting State (for example, a supervening illness which impacts on the subject's ability to travel to or face trial in the requesting State), the High Court had jurisdiction to entertain an application for judicial review of the Secretary of State's decision to maintain her extradition order on human rights grounds*: McKinnon v. Government of the United States of America and the Secretary of State for the Home Department* [2007] EWHC 762 (Admin). However, the position was

decisively altered by the introduction, with effect from 29 July 2013, of s 108(5)–(8) of the Extradition Act 2003 by the Crime and Courts Act 2013, Sch 20, para 12. These sections provide that a supervening human rights issue may only considered by way of the re-opening of an appeal to the High Court. The threshold is a very high one: '108(7) Where notice of application for leave to appeal is given in accordance with subsections (5) and (6), the High Court is to grant leave only if it appears to the High Court that—(a) the appeal is necessary to avoid real injustice, and (b) the circumstances are exceptional and make it appropriate [for the appeal to be heard'.

2 Above para **8.36**, at paras 28–31.

3 [2005] EWHC 1051 (Admin) at paras 14–23.

4 It was accepted by the US government in *Jenkins* that *Kashamu* 'has resurrected, in the wake of the Human Rights Act 1998, the abuse jurisdiction previously excluded by the decision of the House of Lords in Schmidt' but deemed it unnecessary on the facts to determine a submission that 'the inherent power is limited to such things as refusal of a request made in bad faith'; see paras 31–32.

5 [2006] 1 WLR 1, DC.

6 At para 27.

7 Above para **8.09**.

8 At paras 24–25.

Jurisdiction finally established

8.53 The issue of jurisdiction was fully considered by the High Court in *Bermingham v Director of the Serious Fraud Office.*[1] It was argued by the appellants that abuse arose by virtue of (a) the US government's refusal to disclose any of the evidential material it possessed beyond what was contained in the extradition request, including materials alleged to 'fundamentally undermine' the US case, and (b) deliberate delay in seeking the defendants' extradition so as to take advantage of the 2003 Act and thereby denying the appellants' safeguards they would have enjoyed under the 1989 Act, such as the Secretary of State's discretion and the requirement that the Requesting State should demonstrate a case to answer. It was conceded by the Requesting State that the judge who conducts an extradition hearing under the 2003 Act possesses an implied jurisdiction to hold that the prosecutor is abusing the process of the court and to refuse to order extradition for that reason. Nonetheless, Laws LJ examined and approved the basis upon which that concession was made. Having considered *Atkinson*, *Schmidt* and *Gilligan*, Laws LJ observed[2] that:

> 'In my judgment the reasoning in these cases of high authority has no application in the context of the 2003 Act. Under its provisions the Secretary of State has no statutory discretion to refuse extradition. The safeguard emphasised in *Atkinson* and *Schmidt* is lacking. Moreover in Part I cases, and Part II cases where the category 2 territory has (like the United States) been designated for the purpose of s.84, the prosecutor is not required to establish a *prima facie* case on the evidence. Under the old law that requirement was itself an important discipline. Its absence makes the need for a residual abuse jurisdiction all the plainer ...I should not leave the point without considering the nature of the juridical exercise involved in concluding, as I would, that the judge conducting an extradition hearing under the 2003 Act possesses a jurisdiction to hold that the prosecutor is abusing the process of the court. Lord Reid, in the passage from *Atkinson* which I have cited, would if necessary have *inferred* that the magistrate had power to refuse

to commit. Now, it is plain that the judge's functions under the 2003 Act, and those of the magistrate under the predecessor legislation, are and were wholly statutory. He therefore possesses no inherent powers. But that is not to say that he may not enjoy an *implied* power. The implication arises from the express provisions of the statutory regime which it is his responsibility to administer. It is justified by the imperative that the regime's integrity must not be usurped. Where its integrity is protected by other powers, as in *Atkinson*, *Schmidt* and *Gilligan*, the implication is not justified. But under the 2003 Act that is not the case. The implication of an abuse jurisdiction – Lord Reid's inference – follows'.

1 Above para **8.35.**
2 At paras 96–97.

8.54 In *Knowles v Government of the United States of America & another,*[1] in the context of Bahamian extradition proceedings, the Privy Council ruled[2] that Art 19 of the Bahamian constitution was purposefully drafted in terms that differed from ECHR, Art 5(4), omitting any requirement of speedy decision or of a decision by a court, upon which the decision in *Kashamu* turned. Thus, it was held[3] that the Bahamian courts remained bound by 'the *Atkinson* line of authority' as opposed to *Kashamu*. But, in so ruling, it was clearly apparent from Lord Bingham's opinion[4] that *Kashamu* was regarded as correctly decided and applicable in the UK under the 2003 Act.

1 Above para **8.04**.
2 At paras 26–28.
3 At para 28.
4 With whom Lords Hutton, Rodger, Carswell and Baroness Hale agreed.

8.55 The jurisdiction was affirmed by Lord Phillips CJ in the High Court in *R (Government of the United States of America) v Bow Street Magistrates'* Court ('Tollman')[1] where it was said that:

> 'The 2003 Act places a duty on the judge to decide a large number of matters before acceding to a request for extradition. To these should be added the duty to decide whether the process is being abused, if put on enquiry as to the possibility of this. The judge will usually, though not inevitably, be put on enquiry as to the possibility of abuse of process by allegations made by the person whose extradition is sought'.

Lord Phillips CJ 'would go further' than *Bermingham* and apply to extradition proceedings the statement made by Bingham LJ in *R v Liverpool Stipendiary Magistrate, ex p Ellison,*[2] in relation to conventional criminal proceedings:

> 'If any criminal court at any time has cause to suspect that a prosecutor may be manipulating or using the procedures of the court in order to oppress or unfairly to prejudice a defendant before the court, I have no doubt that it is the duty of the court to inquire into the situation and ensure that its procedure is not being so abused. Usually, no doubt, such inquiry will be prompted by a complaint on the part of the defendant. But the duty of the court in my view exists even in the absence of a complaint'.

1 Above para **8.11**, at paras 81–83.
2 [1990] RTR 220 at p 227.

8.56 In *R (Hilali) v Governor of Whitemoor Prison & another,*[1] Lord Hope of Craighead[2] rejected on its merits[3] a submission that an extradition request continued in the face of acquittal of the principal defendant represented an abuse of process; the issue was relevant only to whether there existed a case to answer in Spain.[4] Similarly, in *Norris v Government of the United States of America,*[5] the joint opinion of the Judicial Committee[6] observed,[7] obiter, that:

> 'In R (Government of the United States of America) v Bow Street Magistrates' Court [2007] 1 WLR 1157, the Divisional Court indicated that such a request might be appropriate where the judge considered that an abuse of process might have occurred. But, again, such cases are likely to be exceptional.'

1 [2008] 2 WLR 299, HL.
2 With whom Lord Bingham, Baroness Hale and Lords Brown and Neuberger agreed.
3 At para 24.
4 'But the Framework Decision makes it clear that the admissibility or sufficiency of the evidence is not for determination by a judge in the Requested State. These issues were not within the jurisdiction of the judge at the extradition hearing in this case' (at para 23).
5 Above para **8.38**.
6 Lords Bingham, Rodger, Carswell, Brown and Neuberger.
7 At para 107.

8.57 The issue of jurisdiction was finally settled in *McKinnon v Government of the United States of America*[1] in which the House of Lords held[2] that:

> 'The district judge also had jurisdiction to consider whether the extradition proceedings constituted an abuse of process so as to protect the integrity of the statutory regime, the Secretary of State having no general discretion to refuse extradition. So much was stated by Laws LJ in the Divisional Court in R (Bermingham) v Director of the Serious Fraud Office [2007] QB 727, para 97 and by Lord Phillips of Worth Matravers CJ in R (Government of the United States of America) v Bow Street Magistrates' Court [2007] 1 WLR 1157, paras 82–83. What was not expressly stated in these decisions but was necessarily implicit was that the abuse of process for consideration was such as to require the extradition proceedings to be permanently stayed and the accused discharged.'

1 [2008] 1 WLR 1739, HL.
2 At para 8, per Lord Brown of Eaton-under-Heywood, with whom Lords Scott, Phillips, Baroness Hale and Lord Neuberger agreed.

Procedure

8.58 In *Tollman,*[1] Lord Phillips CJ ruled[2] that abuse of process submissions fell to be decided inside, and pursuant to, the statutory procedural rubric of the 2003 Act. At para 84, Lord Phillips CJ outlined the procedure to be followed in cases where an abuse issue is raised:

> 'The judge should be alert to the possibility of allegations of abuse of process being made by way of delaying tactics. No steps should be taken to investigate an alleged abuse of process unless the judge is satisfied that there is reason to believe that an abuse may have taken place. Where an allegation

of abuse of process is made, the first step [1] must be to insist on the conduct alleged to constitute the abuse being identified with particularity. The judge must then [2] consider whether the conduct, if established, is capable of amounting to an abuse of process. If it is, he must next [3] consider whether there are reasonable grounds for believing that such conduct may have occurred. If there are, then [4] the judge should not accede to the request for extradition unless he has satisfied himself that such abuse has not occurred.' (numbering added)

1 Above para **8.11** and **8.55**.

2 At para 80: 'Where extradition is challenged on grounds, such as abuse of process, which are not dealt with expressly under the Act, they should nonetheless normally be considered within the extradition hearing. The 2003 Act lays down special rules in relation to extradition that are designed to ensure that extradition proceedings are concluded with expedition. This objective will be torpedoed if allegations of abuse of process are pursued outside the statutory regime'. See also paras 105–109.

STAGE 1: THE CONDUCT ALLEGED TO CONSTITUTE THE ABUSE BEING IDENTIFIED WITH PARTICULARITY

8.59 This requires the defence to set out, usually in writing, exactly what is said to have occurred, and why it is alleged that that constitutes an abuse of the extradition process. Consideration of this issue requires no evidence, merely particulars.

STAGE 2: CONSIDER WHETHER THE CONDUCT, IF ESTABLISHED, IS CAPABLE OF AMOUNTING TO AN ABUSE OF PROCESS

8.60 This requires the court to assume that the conduct identified can be established in evidence, and to determine whether, on that hypothetical assumption, the conduct identified is capable of amounting to an abuse as a matter of law. It is obviously not in the interests of the administration of justice to embark on a lengthy hearing when the application has no chance of success or there is no basis for granting the remedy sought:

> 'The …criterion is self-evident. There is no point in engaging in a lengthy evidentiary inquiry where it cannot in law yield the result sought by the appellant'.[1]

1 *Larosa v Her Majesty the Queen* (2002) 166 CCC (3d) 449, Ont CA, per Doherty JA at para 77. The procedural rubric established by Lord Phillips CJ in 2006 is of relatively recent advent in English extradition proceedings. However, it has been in operation in Canada since at least 2001 and, therefore, the Canadian case law is of particular assistance in its application.

The intrinsic limits of the jurisdiction

8.61 The giving of an answer under stage 2, in any case, requires the practitioner to appreciate the context and limits of the extradition abuse jurisdiction, and the rationale for it being an animal of a different nature to its domestic cousin. Having established the jurisdiction in *Kashamu,*[1] Rose LJ went on[2] to make the following important qualification:

> 'It does not, however, follow that the district judge can be addressed on all the issues which may arise in the course of a summary trial. Extradition proceedings do not, nor does fairness require that they should, involve resolution of trial issues. Self-evidently, extradition contemplates trial in another jurisdiction according to the law there. It is there that questions of admissibility, adequacy of evidence and fairness of the trial itself will be addressed; and, if the Secretary of State has concerns in relation to these or other matters, it is open to him to refuse to order a fugitive's return … *What is pertinent here in the present cases is solely whether the detention is unlawful by English domestic law and/or arbitrary, because of bad faith or deliberate abuse of the English courts' procedure.* The scope of the inquiry is, therefore, narrow. In that connection, it by no means follows, merely because second proceedings have been instituted against Kashamu, following failure of the first proceedings in the circumstances earlier set out, that there has been an abuse. I add that it will only be in a very rare extradition case, *provided the statutory procedures have been followed*, that it will be possible to argue that abuse of process has rendered the detention unlawful under Article 5(4).' (Emphasis added)

1 Above para **8.50**.
2 At paras 33–34. Pitchford J ruled in similar terms at paras 37–38.

8.62 This limitation accords with the Canadian case law, from which the English courts have derived much assistance in establishing the boundaries of the fledgling abuse jurisdiction. In *United States of America v Kwok,*[1] Arbour J ruled[2] that the extradition abuse jurisdiction does '… not confer unlimited *Charter* jurisdiction on the extradition judge and therefore do[es] not render obsolete all previous extradition case law. Section 9(3) clearly confers *Charter* jurisdiction upon the extradition judge insofar as the issues are specific to the functions of the extradition hearing …The added jurisdiction conferred upon the extradition judge must be understood in light of this governing principle'.[3]

1 [2001] 1 SCR 532.
2 At para 54.
3 In *Government of the United States of America v Tollman* [2006] OJ 3672, 14 September (Ont Sup Crt), Malloy J put it this way: 'An extradition judge has the power to stay proceedings for abuse of process both at common law and under the *Charter*...The extent of that power must be analyzed within the context in which it arises…It does not expand the limited role of the extradition judge under the *Extradition Act*, but neither is the power so circumscribed that it applies only where the abuse relates directly to the sufficiency of the evidence issue to be determined by the extradition judge. The focus must be on the Canadian judicial process. The abuse power cannot be used to remedy the actions of foreign States outside our borders, nor can it be invoked in respect of any perceived unfairness of the ultimate trial to be held in the foreign State. However, the power applies to any conduct that reaches into this jurisdiction and undermines the integrity of the judicial system here' (at para 18).

8.63 It is crucial to appreciate the significance of this limitation, which fundamentally distinguishes the extradition abuse jurisdiction from the domestic abuse jurisdiction. It is derived from two interlinked factors that are peculiar to extradition proceedings.

8.64 First, there exists a strong international and public interest in the honouring of extradition treaties. In *R (Warren) v Secretary of State for the Home Department,*[1] Hale LJ observed[2] that:

> 'The object of extradition is to return a person who is properly accused or has been convicted of an extradition crime in a foreign country to face trial or to serve his sentence there … The extradition process is only available for return to friendly foreign states with whom this country has entered into either a multi or a bilateral treaty obligation involving mutually agreed and reciprocal commitments … [T]here is a strong public interest in our respecting such treaty obligations. Such international cooperation is all the more important in modern times, when cross-border problems are becoming ever more common, and the need to provide international solutions for them is ever clearer.'

1 Above para **8.21**.
2 At para 40.

8.65 Allied to that is the duty to construe extradition laws, and conduct extradition proceedings, having full and proper regard to the need to accommodate differences, cultural or legal, between the legal systems of those friendly foreign States with whom the UK has entered into mutual reciprocal extradition arrangements. These principles have been acknowledged by the House Lords to govern extradition proceedings for decades. In *Royal Government of Greece v Governor of Brixton Prison,*[1] Lord Morris of Borth-y-Gest observed[2] that:

> 'Mutual belief and understanding that conditions and undertakings would be honoured and mutual respect for each other's legal systems must be the basis on which extradition treaties are made or are continued in being … I cannot think that it was open to a magistrate or to the court in habeas corpus proceedings to go behind the conviction and to treat it as no conviction for any such reason as that the law and practice in Greece is not the same as the law and practice elsewhere. It is not for the courts to say that a conviction which by authenticated proof is shown to be a conviction in another country is here to be regarded as a nullity because the law of the other country is thought not to be in line with conceptions widely or generally held … We are here concerned with a statutory code which becomes operative consequent upon the making of reciprocal arrangements between friendly states'.

1 Above para **8.45**.
2 At 279C. In *Re Rees* (above para **8.46**), Lord Mackay of Clashfern (with whom Lords Bridge, Brandon, Oliver and Goff agreed) observed (at 959C-D) that: 'The ultimate trial will take place according to the provisions of the judicial system of the State requesting the extradition if the prisoner is handed over. As I said, the fact that an extradition arrangement has been made with such a State may be taken as indicating that her Majesty's government is satisfied with the system of justice under which that trial will take place.'

8.66 In *Re: Ismail*[1] Lord Steyn[2] observed[3] that:

> 'a statute intended to serve the purpose of bringing to justice those accused of serious crimes. There is a transnational interest in the achievement of this aim. Extradition treaties, and extradition statutes, ought, therefore, to be accorded a broad and generous construction so far as the texts permits

it in order to facilitate extradition ...It follows that it would be wrong to approach the problem of construction solely from the perspective of English criminal procedure ... All one can say with confidence is that a purposive interpretation of 'accused' ought to be adopted in order to accommodate the differences between legal systems.'[4]

1 [1999] AC 320, HL.

2 With whom Lords Browne-Wilkinson, Jauncey, Slynn and Hutton agreed.

3 At 327.

4 See, to similar effect, *Government of Belgium v Postlethwaite* [1988] AC 924, HL, per Lord Bridge of Harwich (with whom Lords Templemen, Griffiths, Ackner and Goff agreed) at 947A-D; *R (Al-Fawwaz) v Governor of Brixton Prison* (above para **8.33**) per Lord Millett at para 102(4) and Lord Rodger of Earlsferry at para 148. Under the 2003 Act, mutual respect for, and an accommodation of the differences between, the established legal systems of friendly foreign States with whom the UK has seen fit to enter into international extradition arrangements remain the keystones of extradition law and procedure; whether under Part 1 or Part 2 of the Act. See, for example, *Norris v Government of the United States of America* (above para **8.38**) at para 86 and *McKinnon v Government of the United States of America* (above para **8.57**) per Lord Brown of Eaton-under-Heywood at para 37 (with whom Lords Scott and Phillips, Baroness Hale and Lord Neuberger agreed). Mutual trust is especially crucial within the EAW scheme under which Part 1 extraditions are ordered – see *Assange v Swedish Prosecution Authority (Nos 1 and 2)* [2012] UKSC 22, per Lord Dyson at para 124. In *Zakrzewski v Regional Court in Lodz, Poland* [2013] UKSC 2, Lord Sumption acknowledged the 'mutual trust between States party to the Framework Decision that informs the entire scheme' at para 10, a principle reiterated in *Aranyosi and Căldăraru* Case C-404/15 at paras 75–82 and *LM* Case C-216/18 PPU at paras 35–39.

8.67 Therefore, in *Bermingham*,[1] having established its existence, Laws LJ went on to reiterate the intrinsic limits of the extradition abuse jurisdiction:

> '[98] But the question whether abuse is demonstrated has to be asked and answered in light of the specifics of the statutory scheme. Accordingly, subject to an important qualification which I will explain, no finding of abuse can be justified (in a case like the present where the category 2 territory has been designated for the purpose of s.84) by the prosecutor's refusal or failure to disclose evidential material beyond what was contained in the extradition request. The reason is straightforward. In such an instance, as I have shown, the prosecutor does not have to establish a case to answer. Evidence going to whether there is in fact a case to answer is therefore not relevant to the court's task. Mr Jones submitted that while no doubt the prosecutor was not required to produce evidence of merits, if he failed to do so he would or should be at peril of adverse rulings from the court under s 82 or s 87 of the 2003 Act. Here, Mr Jones makes a like mistake to the major flaw in his argument in the judicial review: his submission looks for a statutory regime which Parliament has chosen not to provide. The prosecutor cannot be penalised, under s.82, 87, or by any other route, for limiting the material he places before the court to what is required for the proper execution of the court's function under ss.78 ff....
>
> [99] Likewise a defendant cannot ordinarily complain of abuse on grounds that if only the prosecutor had acted more promptly the 1989 Act, and not the 2003 Act, would have governed the proceedings, and in that case he (the defendant) would have enjoyed the right to test the prosecutor's case and persuade the court, if he could, that there was no case to answer. We cannot

> entertain any kind of presumption that where in an extradition case the facts arose in the life of the 1989 Act, the defendant should ordinarily have the benefit of that Act and not be fixed with the effects of the supervening statute. Such a presumption would be unconstitutional: it would imply a value judgment by this court that the scheme of the earlier legislation was to be preferred to that of the 2003 Act. We have no authority to propound any such judgment …
>
> [100] I have referred to an important qualification. It applies to both of the points I have discussed: the prosecutor's failure to give more disclosure, and his failure to facilitate the defendant's enjoyment of the relative benefits of the 1989 Act. The prosecutor must act in good faith. Thus if he knew he had no real case, but was pressing the extradition request for some collateral motive and accordingly tailored the choice of documents accompanying the request, there might be a good submission of abuse of process. Again, if he knew he could not (or perhaps, could not without great difficulty) make out a *prima facie* case and so deliberately delayed the extradition process until the 1989 Act had been safely superseded by the 2003 Act, that also might be held to be abusive …'
>
> [127]… the court must feel the weight of what Lord Bingham called 'the great desirability of honouring extradition treaties made with other states'. And given the cross-border nature of the accusation here, these observations of Hale LJ as she then was in *R (Warren) v Secretary of State for the Home Department* [2003] EWHC 1177 are especially in point (at paragraph 40)…'

These limits were echoed in this much-cited passage by Ouseley J in *Symeou v Greece*:

> '33. …The focus of this implied jurisdiction is the abuse of the requested state's duty to extradite those who are properly requested, and who are unable to raise any of the statutory bars to extradition. The residual abuse jurisdiction identified in *Bermingham* and *Tollman* concerns abuse of the extradition process by the prosecuting authority. We emphasise those latter two words. That is the language of those cases. It is the good faith of the requesting authorities which is at issue because it is their request coupled with their perverted intent and purpose which constitutes the abuse. If the authorities of the requesting state seek the extradition of someone for a collateral purpose, or when they know that the trial cannot succeed, they abuse the extradition processes of the requested state.
>
> 34. The abuse jurisdiction of the requested state does not extend to considering misconduct or bad faith by the police of the requesting state in the investigation of the case or the preparation of evidence for trial.
>
> 35. The reason for the distinction lies in the respective functions of the courts of the requested and requesting state in the EAW framework. The former are entitled to ensure that their duties and the functions under the Extradition Act 2003 Part 1 are not being abused. It is the exclusive function of the latter to try the issues relevant to the guilt or otherwise of the individual. This necessarily includes deciding what evidence is admissible, and what weight should be given to particular pieces of evidence having regard to

the way in which an investigation was carried out. It is for the trial court in the requesting state to find the facts about how statements were obtained, which may go to admissibility or weight, both of which are matters for the court conducting the trial. It is the function of that court to decide whether evidence was improperly obtained and if so what the consequences for the trial are. It is for the trial court to decide whether its own procedures have been breached.'[2]

1 Above para **8.35**.
2 [2009] EWHC 897 (Admin), at paras 33–35.

8.68 In *Belbin v France*,[1] Mr Belbin argued that the French Judicial Authority had abused the extradition process by issuing a third, conviction, EAW, which deprived him of a statutory bar to extradition, namely the forum bar, that he could have raised had he been sought under an accusation warrant. The Appellant had previously been sought under such an accusation warrant but that had been discharged pursuant to the 2003 Act, s 4. A second, conviction, warrant was ultimately withdrawn. The third, also a conviction warrant, was the subject of the final proceedings and this appeal. In the interim period, between the first and the last EAWs, Mr Belbin had been convicted in his absence, without knowledge of his trial. In that time, the forum bar had been enacted but, by virtue of the conviction, Mr Belbin could not rely upon it.

The court, on the one hand, broadened the scope of the court's inquiry into abuse arguments by holding that abuse of process by 'prosecuting authority' as discussed in the cases of *Symeou*[2] and *Tollman*[3] must necessarily involve an implied jurisdiction to examine the conduct of a 'judicial authority', in light of the 2002 Framework Decision's requirement that all request be made by a 'judicial authority'.[4] However, the court emphasised the narrow type of conduct which amounts to 'abuse':

> '…it will only amount to an abuse of the extradition process if the statutory regime in the EA is being "usurped" (see [97] of *Bermingham*). It would, for example, be "usurped" by bad faith on the part of the Judicial Authority in the extradition proceedings or a deliberate manipulation of the extradition process… it has also to be shown that, as a result of the "usurpation" of the statutory regime, the requested person will be unfairly prejudiced in his subsequent challenge to extradition in this country or unfairly prejudiced in the proceedings in the requesting country if surrendered there'.[5]

Moreover, the Court were at pains to highlight the limited circumstances in which the abuse jurisdiction will be exercised, stating that:

> 'We wish to emphasise that the circumstances in which the court will consider exercising its implied "abuse of process" jurisdiction in extradition cases are very limited. It will not do so if, first, other bars to extradition are available, because it is a residual, implied jurisdiction. Secondly, the court will only exercise the jurisdiction if it is satisfied, on cogent evidence, that the Judicial Authority concerned has acted in such a way as to "usurp" the statutory regime of the EA or its integrity has been impugned. We say "cogent evidence" because, in the context of the European Arrest Warrant, the UK courts will start from the premise, as set out in the Framework Decision of

> 2002, that there must be mutual trust between Judicial Authorities, although we accept that when the emanation of the Judicial Authority concerned is a prosecuting authority, the UK court is entitled to examine its actions with "rigorous scrutiny". Thirdly, the court has to be satisfied that the abuse of process will cause prejudice to the requested person, either in the extradition process in this country or in the requesting state if he is surrendered'.[6]

On the facts, the Court held that 'there is not and cannot be any suggestion of impropriety or irregularity by the French prosecuting authorities in proceeding as they did against the appellant before or at the trial on 24 October 2011'[7] and, once he had been convicted, the only proper route open to the French authorities was to issue a conviction warrant; there was no obligation on the French authorities to somehow set aside the conviction in the circumstances.[8] When issuing the third EAW, there was no evidence the French authorities were aware of the imminent existence of the forum bar or were endeavouring to take advantage of its absence.[9] As such, '[n]one of the facts points to the French Judicial Authority "usurping" the legislative regime of the EA or misusing it in any way. Its actions were perfectly proper'[10] and the argument was rejected.[11]

1 [2015] EWHC 149 (Admin).
2 Above at **8.67**.
3 Above at **8.11**.
4 *Belbin* (n 1) at para 43.
5 Ibid at para 44.
6 Ibid at para 59.
7 Ibid at para 45.
8 Ibid at para 46.
9 Ibid at para 47.
10 Ibid at para 48.
11 Ibid at para 58.

8.69 A series of cases beginning with *Altun*,[1] which address whether the principles in *Henderson v Henderson*[2] illustrate the limits of abuse of process in extradition.

In *Altun*, Mr Altun had been discharged on an EAW in 2006, having successfully raised double jeopardy as a bar. The judicial authority then issued a second warrant, together with material to rebut the double jeopardy point. It was argued that he should have been discharged on the grounds of abuse of process and that the principle of res judicata or issue estoppel applied in extradition proceedings.

Ouseley J found that the double jeopardy bar had been met in Mr Altun's case and, having dismissed the appeal by the judicial authority on that basis, went on to make obiter remarks on the arguments concerning res judicata and issue estoppel. Ouseley J said that the concept of res judicata does not apply in extradition proceedings. Instead, his Lordship concluded that the conduct of the judicial authority amounted to a type of abuse of process like that in *R v Governor of Pentonville Prison ex parte Tarling*[3] or *Henderson*, namely that 'it becomes an abuse of process to raise in subsequent proceedings matters which could, and therefore should, have been litigated in earlier proceedings'.[4]

The decision therefore appeared to introduce the *Henderson* principle into the law of extradition. It seemed to set down, albeit obiter, that re-issuing an EAW, even if the evidential position had shifted, could amount to an abuse of process. This is problematic in the context of extradition because, as we will see, some of the bars to extradition are based on factual balancing exercises which are subject to change, such as prison conditions, healthcare and the request persons Art 8 rights. To a certain extent the difficulty of the application of the principle was foreshadowed by Ouseley J, although it was primarily in the context of warrants defective for formalities.[5]

1 *Germany v Altun* [2011] EWHC 397 (Admin).
2 (1843) 3 Hare 100 at page 115.
3 [1979] 1 WLR 1417.
4 *R v Governor of Pentonville Prison ex parte Tarling* [1979] 1 WLR 1417 at pp 1422H–1423C, per Gibson J, approved (albeit with the caveat that it was a 'provisional view') by Ousley J in *Altun* at paras 47–49.
5 *Altun* at para 48.

8.70 The position of the Court in *Altun* was examined by the High Court in *Auzins v Latvia*[1]. The facts were similar to *Altun*. The Latvian Judicial Authority had re-issued an EAW after the requested person's extradition on the original warrant had been deemed to be barred by a Scottish court on the basis that the medical treatment he would receive in a Latvian prison would have been so poor that to surrender him would have been oppressive. Mr Auzins relied on, among other things, the remarks in *Altun* to assert that re-issuing the warrant amounted to an abuse of process.

Burnett LJ stated that in his judgment 'there is no basis for excluding extradition proceedings from the general principle stated by the House of Lords in *Humphrys*[2] that issue estoppel has no place in English criminal law'.[3] The court clarified that the abuse must relate to abuse of the EAW statutory scheme because the residual jurisdiction's purpose is not only to protect requested persons from unfair prejudice or oppression, but also to protect the integrity of the scheme under the 2003 Act.[4]

When considering whether such an abuse had been made out however, the court distinguished *Altun*. In that case, the conduct raised arguably amounted to double jeopardy and the evidence sufficient to rebut that assertion was simply not presented by the Judicial Authority. In contrast, in *Auzins*, the underlying circumstances forming the basis of the Scottish court's decision were capable of change such that extradition would no longer be oppressive.[5] The court therefore left open the question of whether Ouseley J's remarks in *Altun* were correct and whether the residual jurisdiction did in fact encompass *Henderson*-type abuse.

1 [2016] 4 WLR 75.
2 [1977] AC 1.
3 At para 36.
4 Ibid at para 44.
5 Ibid at paras 45–47.

8.71 The issue was revisited in *Camaras v Baia Mare Local Court, Romania*[1] in which Ouseley J was asked to consider whether it would be an abuse of process to execute a second EAW in circumstances where extradition had been barred on the previous warrant by virtue of s 20(7) and a lack of evidence of a right to retrial, but there was now a right to retrial in Romanian law. Ouseley J outlined the decision in *Belbin* and emphasised how the instant case was not a matter of 'usurping' the statutory scheme, deliberate manipulation or bad faith. Rather, this was a case of incompetence in putting the correct position before the court on the original warrant.[2]

Ouseley J drew a distinction between the 'residual jurisdiction' of the *Bermingham*, *Tollman* and *Belbin* line of cases, and the *Altun/Henderson* line of authorities.[3] He considered that, of these cases, *Altun* was most similar on the facts and then addressed the provisional comments he made in the case:

> 'I made some obiter and provisional observations, but with the benefit of some argument, to the effect that it was an abuse of process for the second EAW to have been issued and enforced. I feel no particular loyalty towards my observations, nor do I read *Auzins* as an endorsement of them; *Auzins* simply concerned a different point, where there was a change of circumstance, so no further consideration of what I said in *Altun* was necessary, nor is it now'.[4]

He continued:

> 'I am in fact satisfied that it is neither principled nor practical to apply the principle in *Henderson v Henderson* in a straightforward manner to extradition warrant decisions. Extradition involves the issuing of a warrant by a foreign authority which engages the UK's international obligations as well as its domestic legislation. Statutory bars have been enacted which reflect those arrangements, whether Treaty or Framework Decision. There is no scope for more than a residual jurisdiction to preclude the extradition of someone who falls outside the scope of the statutory bars. That is the residual jurisdiction envisaged in the line of cases leading to *Belbin*, where the contention is that the prosecutor or judicial authority has acted in bad faith, deliberately manipulating proceedings, undermining the statutory regime to the unfair prejudice of the defendant. Such a jurisdiction is consistent with those international obligations only because it is obvious that no prosecutor or issuing authority should behave in the manner described in *Belbin* as an abuse of the court's process; it is necessarily implicit in the arrangements, and accepted by all participants, that they would not be allowed to do so'.[5]
>
> 'Any extension of that jurisdiction however would undermine the statutory process itself and the international arrangements to which they give effect. I do not consider that the residual jurisdiction should be expanded to embrace the *Henderson v Henderson* principle. If no bar is made out, it is difficult to see why a person who faces no bars to extradition should then not be extradited, other than as a sanction imposed on the requesting authority for not complying with directions or not getting its case in order'.[6]

Ouseley J held that 'whether the attempted enforcement of a further EAW, in circumstances falling short of Belbin abuse of process, so undermines the interest of the statutory scheme in speedy finality, and in upholding the decisions and orders of the courts, that enforcement should be denied, cannot be answered without consideration of all the circumstances'.[7] In concluding, Ouseley J stated:

> 'In my judgment, the right approach must be a balance reflecting the extent of the public interests at stake, as well as any unfair prejudice caused to the individual in all the circumstances of the case. These will involve the gravity of the actual or alleged offending, the nature and cause of the failure of the issuing authority or CPS which has led to the further EAW, the effect which that might have in consequence on the public interest in that particular extradition, the effect which that has had on the defendant both in his family and private life, and on his trial, retrial, and punishment, whether through change in circumstance or passage of time. In reality, this involves consideration of s14, s21 or s21A oppression and human rights, which is where those balances can be struck. Such an approach, placing this issue within the context of the statutory bars to extradition, avoids extending the residual jurisdiction to areas where its language shows it was not intended to venture.[8]

Ouseley J appears therefore to suggest Henderson type complaints are not in fact an abuse issue at all if they fall short of the terms of the residual jurisdiction. If such an issue is raised, Ouseley J suggest that it is a matter that should be dealt with as a relevant factor in determining the statutory bars to extradition only. The decision therefore ring-fences the abuse of process jurisdiction to Belbin-type abuse. This approach was subsequently approved by Simon LJ in *Malarz v Regional Court of Opole, Poland*.[9]

1 [2016] EWHC 1766 (Admin).
2 At para 16.
3 Ibid at para 20.
4 Ibid at para 26.
5 Ibid at para 27.
6 Ibid at para 28.
7 Ibid at para 32.
8 Ibid at paras 33 and 34.
9 [2018] EWHC 28 (Admin) at para 54.

8.72 However, the position was again revisited in *Giese v Government of the United States of America*.[1] In this case, the first Pt 2 extradition request had failed for want of an assurance that the requested person would not be subject to the civil commitment procedure on return. Once the assurance had been obtained however, the US Government re-issued the request to extradite the appellant. Unlike Ouseley J in *Camaras*, the court considered that *Henderson*-type issues could in fact be a matter of abuse of process.[2] The court went on to outline what they considered to be the correct approach to questions of abuse falling short of the residual jurisdiction:

> 'The key, in our judgment, to cases where it is said that the requesting state failed in the first set of proceedings such that the second set are an abuse of process is to make a "broad, merits-based judgment which takes account of the public and private interest involved and also takes account of all the facts of the case": see *Johnson v Gore Wood & Co* [2002] 2 AC 1, para 31 and *Arranz v Spain* [2016] EWHC 3029 (Admin) at [32]–[33]; [2017] ACD 12. Such a broad, merits-based judgment should take account of the fact that there is no doctrine of res iudicata or issue estoppel in extradition proceedings'.[3]

Therefore, the court appear to set down two different categories of abuse with two different approaches. '*Belbin*-abuse' and '*Henderson*-abuse'.

1 [2018] EWHC 1480 (Admin).
2 Ibid at para 31.
3 Ibid at para 32.

8.73 The matter was recently considered in *Jasvins v General Prosecutor's Office Latvia.*[1] The Court underlined the narrow application of the residual abuse jurisdiction, holding that it is a 'last line of defence, and a line of defence that in any event should not be allowed to subvert any of the statutory bars to extradition'.[2] On the question of whether the rule in *Henderson* fell within the residual jurisdiction, the court was of the view that it did and that Ouseley J's comments in *Camaras* to the effect that abuse considerations merely inform the application of the statutory bars, now had to be read subject to *Giese* and *Auzins*.[3] However, when analysing a situation of *Henderson* abuse, the court emphasised that 'there is no necessary conclusion that proceedings on a second (or later), warrant will amount to an abuse of process with the consequence that those proceedings will be dismissed' and that there could be no 'one-size-fits-all' approach.[4] The court went on to say that:

> 'Where there are successive warrants or successive extradition requests, if proceedings on the subsequent warrants can properly be characterised as a collateral attack on a decision in proceedings on the first warrant, the latter proceedings are capable of amounting to an abuse of process. It may be possible to go further and say that ordinarily this will be the case. But the outcome in any given situation must depend on the overall merits-based assessment of public interests and careful evaluation of the facts, referred to at paragraph 32 in judgment of *Giese*'.[5]

1 [2020] EWHC 602 (Admin).
2 Ibid at para 15.
3 Ibid at para 16.
4 Ibid at para 17.
5 Ibid at para 20.

The applicable threshold

8.74 For these interlinked reasons, whatever the position in a domestic context, the courts will require exceptional facts to be made out to warrant a finding of abuse in an extradition context. In *McKinnon v Government of the United States of America,*[1] the House of Lords held[2] that the question to be asked is whether extradition would 'violate those fundamental principles of justice which underlie the community's sense of fair play and decency'? and noted[3] that it would require a 'wholly extreme case' to do so.[4]

1 Above para **8.57**.
2 At para 33 per Lord Brown of Eaton-under-Heywood.
3 At para 41. See also *Hilali v The Central Court of Criminal Proceedings No 5 of the National Court, Madrid* (above para **8.08**) per Scott Baker LJ at para 107: '... such circumstances are likely to be rare and there would have to be bad faith or something of that kind'.
4 In *Aswat & Ahmad v Government of the United States of America* (above para **8.08**), Laws LJ observed (at para 101) that '...the starting-point: Kennedy LJ's observation in *Serbeh* that 'there is (still) a fundamental assumption that the Requesting State is acting in good

faith'. This is a premise of effective relations between sovereign States. As I have said the assumption may be contradicted by evidence; and it is the court's plain duty to consider such evidence (where it is presented) on a statutory appeal under the 2003 Act. But where the Requesting State is one in which the UK has for many years reposed the confidence not only of general good relations, but also of successive bilateral treaties consistently honoured, the evidence required to displace good faith must possess special force'.

8.75 That approach mirrors the '...outrag[ing] civilised values' test identified by the House of Lords in applying s 78 of the Police & Criminal Evidence Act 1984 to extradition proceedings.[1] It also correlates to the limited exception to the principle of non-enquiry in the US, enunciated in *Gallina v Fraser* of 'procedures or punishment so antipathetic to a Federal Court's sense of decency'.[2]

1 Above para **8.42**.
2 (1960) 278 F.2d 77 (2nd Cir) at 79.

Not concerned with the prospective trial process

8.76 The first point to note is that extradition abuse is not concerned with the ultimate trial process. Mitting J noted in *Wellington*[1] that: 'The fairness of the use of evidence at trial is a question for the trial court, not for the committing magistrate'.

1 Above para **8.42**, at para 17(3). This too accords with the Canadian position. See *Canada v Schmidt* [1987] 1 SCR 500 per La Forest J at paras 47–49 and 54–55. In *Cobb & Grossman v USA* [2001] 1 SCR 587, the Supreme Court of Canada noted that: 'The issue is not whether the appellants will have a fair trial if extradited, but whether they are having a fair extradition hearing in light of the threats and inducements imposed upon them, by those involved in their extradition, to force them to abandon their right to such a hearing.' (Arbour J at para 33). For an illustration of this principle in operation in Canada, see *United States of America v Kinsella (2006) NBQB 435* concerning allegations of attempts by the US prosecutor to oppress and intimidate the defendant during pre-trial hearings in the US. Clear evidence of *mala fides* or improper motive is required; *France v Diab*, 2014 ONCA 374 (CanLII).

8.77 For an example of a case, albeit decided under the 1989 Act, of this principle in operation, see *R (Harkins) v Secretary of State for the Home Department.*[1] In 1999, Harkins was arrested in Florida on suspicion of the murder and attempted robbery of Joshua Hayes. He was interviewed and he informed the police that he had spent the night at home with his fiancé, having been dropped there by an acquaintance by the name of Glover. Glover was arrested and interviewed. In the third different version of events provided by Glover, he alleged that Harkins had, in fact, carried out the murder. As a result of further enquiries, the case was dropped against Harkins and he was notified that the District Attorney was not going to prosecute him for any involvement in the killing of Hayes. A formal notice was entered on the record as to the discontinuance of the prosecution. In 2000, a different Assistant State Attorney revisited the case. Glover was re-interviewed, following which a written agreement was produced in which Glover agreed to co-operate fully with the prosecution against Harkins and on terms that Glover's co-operation could not be used against himself, in return for Glover's plea to offences of robbery with a weapon and being an accessory after the fact to first degree murder (punishable with up to 15 years in a Florida State prison). Harkins was charged again with capital murder and attempted robbery. It was alleged that the Assistant State Attorney had offered a witness (exculpating Harkins) the discontinuance of unrelated charges and immunity in respect of the index offence, in return for falsely implicating Harkins. Harkins left America and was arrested in Scotland as a result of the provisional arrest warrant issued by the Bow Street Magistrates' Court pursuant to the Extradition Act 1989. Harkins alleged that the manner in which the evidence of Glover was obtained was an abuse of process by the prosecution.

1 Above para **8.42**.

8.78 In refusing to stay the proceedings, the High Court (Lloyd-Jones J) held[1] that:

> '... questions as to the admissibility or fairness of evidence at trial are, in general, matters for the court of the trial, in this case Florida ... Furthermore, there is evidence before this court that it would be open to the claimant to file a motion before the Florida court challenging the admissibility of this evidence ... In these circumstances I consider that it was open to the Secretary of State to conclude that arguments in relation to the admissibility of the evidence of Glover should more appropriately be left for consideration by the courts of Florida. Moreover, for these reasons I consider that the Secretary of State was entitled to conclude that this was not a case in which the claimant's extradition is barred because the application of his return is not made in good faith in the interests of justice'.[2]

1 At paras 4–43.

2 See also *Jaso* (above para **8.08**) in which it was submitted that material showed that there was a real possibility that, at least in part, the evidence on which the prosecution against the appellants was based was obtained by torture, and therefore an abuse of process. The High Court ruled (per Dyson LJ at paras 34 and 39) that 'the relevant question in the present context is not whether there is a real possibility that evidence implicating all or any of the appellants was obtained from Mr Cillero by torture. Rather it is whether there is a real possibility that, if such evidence was obtained by torture, the Spanish court will admit it. Unless there is a real possibility that the evidence will be deployed against the appellants in the Spanish courts, it cannot be an abuse of process to extradite them to Spain. That is why this abuse of process argument is closely linked to the question whether there is a risk that the appellants' Article 6 rights will be violated if they are extradited. In my judgment, the decision in *A v Secretary of State for the Home Department (No 2)* [2006] 2 AC 221 is not relevant ... There is jurisdiction under Spanish law to exclude unlawfully obtained evidence ... The correct forum for determining whether the evidence was in fact so obtained is the Spanish courts. The district judge was not required to investigate the allegation of torture herself'. See also *Mustafa (aka Hamza) v Government of the United States of America & another* [2008] EWHC 1357 (Admin) at paras 8 and 37–41; *Symeou v Greece* above at para **8.67**.

8.79 A more recent example can be found in *Pakstys v Lithuania*.[1] The Appellant had been arrested on an allegation EAW from Lithuania relating to an incident in 2012 where it is said he possessed 500g of cannabis with intent to supply. The EAW was based on a ruling of the Siauliai District Court. At the time of the extradition proceedings, Lithuanian press reports emerged of an investigation into the activities of a number of police officers in the area of Siauliai County.[2] In a Further Information provided, it was confirmed that 'there were reasonable grounds to believe that police officers had added between 20g and 50g of cannabis to the quantity seized at the time it is alleged the claimant was driving the car. It also confirmed that the Panevezys Regional Court was conducting hearings against corrupt officers, including the officers identified as Ruchtinas, Pocius and Ivanovas. Ruchtinas and Ivanovas are said to have admitted adding the cannabis to the package found'.[3] A later document containing further information confirmed that 'the outcome of the officers' case cannot have any influence on a decision to refer the material of the criminal case …to court'[4] and a further document confirmed that 'The pre-trial investigation file contains service reports by chief Investigator R Pocius and senior investigator G Aina about the fact that on 22 November 2012 the police received intelligence information that Vygandas Pakstys … may be illegally disposing of narcotic substances and transporting them by car. In order to verify this information, the officer met the said car as soon as it entered Siauliai from the direction of Kelme Town'.[5] It was argued that extradition in such circumstances would amount to an abuse of process as, were the Appellant to be returned, Lithuania would rely upon the evidence of corrupt police officers. Thirlwall J concluded:

> '34. Mr Hall asserts that the Respondent's steadfast position that they will prosecute the appellant as soon as he is surrendered is abusive as it demonstrates that they are not prepared to listen to the Appellant's evidence or defence and reassess the case in the light of it or in the light of the evidence about the police corruption. I do not agree with that analysis. There is nothing to suggest that the Respondent will not review its decision to prosecute in the light of new evidence. The fact that as of January they did not consider that the outcome of the case in respect of the two police officers would affect a decision to refer the case to court may reflect their view of the strength of the evidence independent of those two officers. Whether they are right will be a matter for the court in Lithuania. It is not a matter for this court. As Burnett LJ made clear in *Auzins v Latvia* [2016] EWHC 802 the underlying purpose of the abuse jurisdiction in extradition cases
>
> > "is to protect the integrity of the statutory scheme of the 2003 and the integrity of the EAW system, as well as to protect a requested person from oppression and unfair prejudice."
>
> He was there summarising the discussions in *R (Bermingham and Others) v Director of the Serious Fraud Office* [2007] 2 WLR 635, *Belbin v France* [2015] EWHC 149 and *Italy v Barone* [2010] EWHC 3004 (Admin).
>
> 35. There is nothing in this case which begins to undermine the statutory scheme or the integrity of the EAW system. The complaints about police corruption are already being considered by the Lithuanian courts, and the effect of any corruption on the integrity of the evidence will be for them. As Ouseley J said in *Symeou v Greece* [2009] EWHC 897 (Admin) it is essential to recognise the respective functions of the courts of the requesting State and the requested state…. I agree. In this case the courts of the requesting state will deal with all such matters and it is not for the courts of England and Wales to seek to police that process. That would be wholly contrary to Framework Decision.'[6]

1 [2017] EWHC 47 (Admin).
2 Ibid at para 4.
3 Ibid at para 5.
4 Ibid at para 6.
5 Ibid at para 33.
6 Ibid at paras 34–35.

Pre-2004 case law

8.80 Because of the absence of jurisdiction until 2004, examples of pre-2004 abuse allegations considered on their merits are few and far between, but do exist. In *Re Rees*,[1] the defendant was the subject of an extradition request made by the Federal Republic of Germany in respect of hostage-taking offences in Bolivia. Evidence was received from Bolivia and the magistrate commenced committal proceedings. During the course of those proceedings, further statements were received from Bolivia. Their admission into evidence was subject to technical difficulties. To avoid those difficulties, on the day of the extradition hearing, and outside the applicable time limit for receipt of evidence, a second order to proceed was procured from the Secretary of State in respect of the same offences (no further request having been received from Germany). The first committal proceedings were then terminated, and the defendant was discharged. On leaving the dock, he was immediately re-arrested on a warrant issued by the magistrate in accordance with the second order to proceed. Proceedings re-commenced (and the latest Bolivian statements were adduced without hindrance). The magistrate entertained and rejected a submission that the renewed proceedings constituted an abuse of process. The House of Lords declined to decide whether an abuse jurisdiction existed,[2] holding that, on the facts, even if the extradition court did possess an abuse jurisdiction, the tactics employed were 'perfectly proper'[3] and that such an application was 'without merit'.[4]

1 Above para **8.46**.
2 Certified questions 6 and 7 listed at p 941G–H.
3 At 963G–H per Lord Mackay of Clashfern, with whom Lords Bridge, Brandon, Oliver and Goff agreed.
4 At 964C–D.

8.81 *Re Schmidt*[1] concerned a German national living in the Republic of Ireland. Tentative German requests to Ireland to issue a provisional arrest warrant had failed. In 1992, an officer of the extradition squad of the International and Organised Crime Branch of the Metropolitan Police telephoned Schmidt and his solicitor in Ireland and (wrongly) said that he was investigating a cheque fraud and was anxious to exclude Schmidt from his inquiries. He invited Schmidt to come to England to be interviewed and went so far as to tell Schmidt's solicitor that, if Schmidt did not come, his name would probably be circulated as that of a suspect, a warrant would be issued for his arrest and he would be liable to be arrested when he next came to the UK. This was all repeated to Schmidt's Irish solicitor. It was all a lie. There was no allegation of cheque fraud. It was simply a device to persuade Schmidt to enter the UK. In fact, the UK had received an extradition request from Germany in respect of 58 charges of supplying and possessing over 386kg of cannabis between 1987 and 1991. Germany had no extradition treaty with the Republic of Ireland and, therefore, needed to get Schmidt into the UK (with whom it did). In November 1992, Schmidt and his Irish solicitor met the police officer in London. Schmidt accompanied the officer to a police station where he was arrested on a provisional warrant under the Extradition Act 1989 issued that morning. Lord Jauncey of Tullichettle[2] ruled[3] that, even if the court did have jurisdiction to entertain an application for abuse of process, it would be rejected on the merits:

> 'At the very worst, he was tricked into coming to England but not coerced … The 58 German charges outstanding against the applicant suggest that he may be a substantial international dealer in drugs. As such, his frequent visits to England are unlikely to be in the public interest. To bring such a person to justice the police and other drug enforcement agencies may from time to time have to tempt him to enter their fief. In my view, what was done by D.S. Jones was far more akin to the enticement of the drug enforcement agent in *Liangsiriprasert* than to the forceable abduction in *Reg v Horseferry Road Magistrates' Court, Ex parte Bennett* [1994] 1 A.C. 42. I agree with Roch LJ that the detective sergeant's conduct was not so grave or serious as would have warranted the intervention of the High Court had it possessed such a power'.

1 Above para **8.47**.
2 With whom Lords Templeman, Ackner, Slynn and Lloyd agreed.
3 At pp 379–380.

8.82 In *R v Bow Street Magistrates' Court, ex p Van der Holst,*[1] failure, categorised as 'stupid' and 'irregular' but falling short of bad faith, to bring a defendant before the court as soon as possible following arrest pursuant to an extradition request, so as to frustrate statutory and treaty time limits, was held not to constitute a deliberate manipulation of the court's process. In *R v Governor of Pentonville Prison, ex parte Chinoy,*[2] it was held that reliance by the US upon telephone intercept evidence obtained in France in breach of French law and sovereignty was not an abuse where the unlawful conduct had occurred prior to the matter coming within the jurisdiction of the English Court. *R v Governor of Brixton Prison, ex p Cuoghi*[3] was a case in which submissions were advanced as to authentication. The defence had sought an adjournment, and counsel for the Requesting State had indicated that the adjournment would not be used to obtain properly authenticated documents. The High Court held[4] no abuse to have occurred where the Requesting State, of its own volition, had supplied properly authenticated documents in the interim period.

1 Above para **8.46**, per Lloyd LJ at 124.
2 Above para **8.46**, per Nolan J (with whom Farquharson LJ agreed) at 327A–330J.
3 [1998] 1 WLR 1513, DC.
4 Per Kennedy LJ at 1521G–1522B.

8.83 In respect of successive requests for extradition, in *R (Kashamu) v Governor of Brixton Prison (No 2),*[1] the High Court held that immediate detention on a second warrant extradition request following dismissal of the first by the High Court as a result of material non-disclosure did not constitute an abuse.[2] In a decision soon after the fledgling *Kashamu* abuse jurisdiction had been established, the High Court in *Lodhi v Governor of Brixton Prison (No 2)* [3] gave short shrift to the argument based on *R v Horsham Justices, ex p Reeves*[4] that a second extradition request amounted to an abuse of process.[5]

1 Above para **8.50**.
2 Rose LJ at para 34.
3 (9 October 2002), unreported.
4 (1980) 75 Cr App Rep 236.
5 These cases should not, however, be seen as laying down a principle that successive requests will never be abusive. See *Central Examining Court of the National Court of Madrid v City of Westminster Magistrates' Court* discussed below at para **8.88**.

CASE LAW UNDER THE 2003 ACT

8.84 In *R v Horseferry Road Magistrates' Court, ex p Bennett,*[1] the House of Lords postulated two species of abuse of process in a domestic context, which can be summarised as: (i) where the conduct complained of prejudices the defence to such an extent that it is not possible to have a fair trial, or (ii) where, no matter how fair the trial may be, circumstances exist which render it offensive to justice and propriety to try the defendant at all. Neither of these translate directly into an extradition context. Limb (i) does not fall within the scope of the narrow extradition abuse jurisdiction at all; insofar as an extradition defendant seeks to raise issues as to the fairness of his prospective trial in the Requesting State, he must do so under ss 21 or 87 via the medium of ECHR, Art 6 and satisfy the 'flagrant denial of justice' test.[2] Limb (ii) must be modified so as to focus not upon the propriety or manipulation of the prospective trial but rather upon the propriety or manipulation of the extradition process.

1 [1994] 1 AC 42, HL.
2 Above paras **8.33–8.36**.

8.85 Whilst there is clearly overlap, the need to translate the domestic abuse jurisdiction to the extradition context has led the Court of Appeal of Ontario[1] to re-formulate the *Bennett* test:

(i) where the conduct complained of prejudices the conduct of the defence to such an extent that it is not possible to have a fair *extradition* hearing; or

(ii) where, no matter how fairly an extradition hearing could be conducted, circumstances exist which render it offensive to justice and propriety to proceed at all.

1 *Larosa v Her Majesty The Queen* (above para **8.60**) per Doherty JA at para 52.

Manipulation of the extradition machinery

8.86 Here, the practitioner is concerned with a case in which the extradition request has been (or has attempted to have been) implemented or enforced in a manner involving deliberate manipulation of the extradition machinery to the advantage of the Requesting State and the prejudice of the requested person. The result is that the conduct complained of prejudices the conduct of the defence to such an extent that it is not possible to have a fair *extradition* hearing. Something more than incompetence will generally be required.[1] The focus of enquiry will not be upon the underlying foreign process but will be upon the conduct of the Requesting State in the UK proceedings. *Re Rees*[2] and *R v Bow Street Magistrates' Court, ex p Van der Holst*[3] (alleged manipulation of applicable time limits), *In re Schmidt*[4] (luring a defendant by deceit into the UK from which he might be extradited), *R v Governor of Brixton Prison, ex p Cuoghi*[5] (alleged misuse of adjournment/alleged breach of undertaking), *R (Kashamu) v Governor of Brixton Prison (No 2)*[6] and *Lohdi v Governor of British Prison (No 2)*[7] (repetitive requests), *Hajda v Poland* (application for extension of time after application for discharge filed)[8] are all examples of allegations of deliberate manipulation of the extradition machinery, all refused on their facts. It should also be noted that the courts have established a high threshold for arguments from EU Member States, asserting that 'The court must start from the premise that the judicial authorities of an EU Member State act with all the good faith that the judicial authorities of the United Kingdom deploy'.[9]

1 In *R (Jackowski) v Regional Court of Ostroleka, Poland* [2012] EWHC 3935 (Admin) Collins J noted, at para 14, 'I do not say it is impossible for incompetence to result in an abuse of process but it would take a strong case, in my judgment, to reach that state of affairs'; see also to this effect *Camaras* (above).

2 Above para **8.46**.

3 Above para **8.46**.

4 Above para **8.47**.

5 Above para **8.82**.

6 Above para **8.50**.

7 Above para **8.30**.

8 [2013] EWHC 1080 (Admin).

9 *Campbell v Spain* [2010] EWHC 3316 (Admin) per Ouseley J at para 10. See also *Louca v Germany* [2009] UKSC 4, [2009] 1 W.L.R. 2550.

8.87 Unless it can be shown that a prosecutor 'knew he could not, or perhaps, could not without great difficulty, make out a *prima facie* case and so deliberately delayed the extradition process until the 1989 Act had been safely superseded by the 2003 Act', it is, in principle, not abusive to delay an extradition request until such time as more favourable extradition laws are in force (*Bermingham*[1]) or even to withdraw an extant request so as to proceed under a different extradition regime. In *R (Government of the United States of America) v Bow Street Magistrates' Court,*[2] it was argued there had been deliberate delay in seeking the defendants' extradition so as to take advantage of the 2003 Act thereby denying the appellants safeguards that they would have enjoyed under the 1989 Act (such as the Secretary of State's discretion and the requirement that the Requesting State should demonstrate a case to answer). Lord Phillips CJ held[3] that:

> 'We think that it is clear from all of this that the United States Government decided to withdraw the first requests, not because it had decided not to proceed with their attempts to extradite Mr. and Mrs Tollman under the 1989 Act, but because they had concluded that this could be more satisfactorily achieved under the 2003 Act … We do not consider that these facts, of themselves, constitute an abuse of process. If the present requests could properly have been made had the earlier requests never been made, we cannot see how the fact that the earlier requests were made, but not pursued, materially affects the position. If Mr and Mrs Tollman are to demonstrate an arguable case of abuse of process they need to demonstrate that there are grounds for suspecting that the present proceedings are being pursued for some improper motive, or are otherwise abusive.'[4]

1 Above para **8.32**, per Laws LJ at paras 99–100. See also *R v Bow Street Magistrates' Court, ex p Odoli* (unreported) (26 January 1999), DC per Ralph-Gibson LJ at transcript 16C–D: 'There is, in my judgment, nothing in the point that, if the application had been made on an earlier date, it would have been made under different legal provisions. If Parliament had thought it right to provide that the new provisions should not apply to alleged offences said to have been committed before the coming into force of the new provisions, it could, and would, have so provided'. See, to similar effect, *McKinnon v Government of the United States of America* [2007] EWHC 762 (Admin) per Maurice Kay LJ at para 39.

2 Above at para **8.11**, per Lord Phillips CJ at paras 113–117. It is also not abusive to discontinue extant domestic criminal charges to make way for extradition proceedings, even where both sets of proceedings relate to the same conduct (*Larosa v Her Majesty the Queen* (above para **8.60**) per Doherty JA at para 60). The Ontario Court of Appeal did recognise, however,

that an arguable abuse would be made out if there existed some evidential basis for finding that the domestic charges were a ruse or were manipulated to hold the defendant in custody pending the submission of the extradition request (at para 62). Equally, if a person is detained under immigration powers in order to keep him in custody until the US authorities could commence extradition proceedings, that is also improper (*Government of the United States of America v Tollman* (above para **8.62**) per Malloy J at para 128).

3 At paras 116–117.

4 Neither should extradition proceedings be stayed because the evidentiary provisions of the Extradition Act create a different standard for the person sought in tendering evidence from that which the extradition partner must meet (*United States of America v Ferras* [2006] 2 SCR 77 at para 50; *United States of America v Kinsella* (above para **8.76**) at paras 39–44.

8.88 Unless acting without instructions, and so long as the extradition request, or European Arrest warrant, is ultimately approved and issued ('not merely rubber-stamped') by the Requesting State, or Part 1 Issuing Judicial Authority, it is, in principle, not abusive to assist a Requesting State in the drafting of an extradition request so as to ensure compliance with legislative requirements; *Central Examining Court of the National Court of Madrid v City of Westminster Magistrates' Court*[1] per Sedley LJ:[2]

> '... the partial drafting of the Spanish court's warrants by the CPS... represents neither an abdication of its functions by the [Issuing Judicial Authority] nor a usurpation of the IJA's functions by the CPS. It is a practical and, in my judgment, legitimate endeavour on the part of one country to get a suitable form of extradition process before the courts of another country... the material was not capable of founding or generating a rational suspicion of abusive conduct on the part of the IJA or the CPS...The simple provision of drafting assistance to the IJA is not, in law, capable of constituting an abuse. It impacts neither on the principle of equality of arms, nor on the visible independence and impartiality of the Spanish Judicial Authority'.

1 [2007] EWHC 2059 (Admin).

2 At paras 24 and 31–35.

8.89 In *R (Ahsan) v Director of Public Prosecutions & another,*[1] it was argued that failure to consider guidance agreed between the Attorney General of the US and the Attorney General of the UK in respect of handling criminal cases with concurrent jurisdiction (in respect of forum) rendered extradition proceedings abusive. Richards LJ ruled[2] that the guidance did not apply where there had been no investigation initiated in the UK but observed in any event that: 'Even if the guidance had applied and there had been a failure to consider it, the failure would not be capable of rendering the extradition proceedings an abuse of process'.

1 Above para **8.08**.

2 At para 128.

8.90 In *Lopetas v Minister of Justice for Lithuania,*[1] the appellant was arrested in Cornwall on a European Arrest Warrant. Because of a difficulty in transporting him to court, he was not produced at the City of Westminster Magistrates' Court until three days later, and so fell to be discharged under s 4(3) and (5) of the 2003 Act because he had not been brought to court, in the words of the provision, 'as soon as practicable'. That led the Lithuanian authorities to issue a further European Arrest Warrant, certified by the Serious Organised Crime Agency (SOCA) pursuant to s 2(7) of the Act, which was executed immediately upon the appellant's discharge. However, the appellant fell to be discharged for a second time, this time under s 4(2) and (4) of the Act, because he had not been handed a copy of the warrant as soon as practicable after his arrest. However, a member of the SOCA, present at court that day, observing that second error, wrongly took the view that it could be dealt with by issuing a new certificate under s 2(7) of the Act.[2] The result was that the appellant remained in custody awaiting hearing of the extradition proceedings for 14 days on an unlawful basis until a third warrant was issued and certified. At the extradition hearing, it was argued that the unlawful re-certification of the second warrant had constituted an abuse of process, or alternatively that once it was realised by those representing the Lithuanian authorities that the appellant's continued detention was unlawful, failure to have been listed (instead, the Crown Prosecution Service advised the Lithuanian authorities to re-issue the warrant) was abusive. The District Judge held that 'the course of conduct could have been abusive if known to be unlawful and done to detain the defendant', but found no evidence to suggest that that had been the motivation. The decision plainly envisages that, had there been evidence from which manipulative intent might reasonably have been inferred, then an abuse would have been made out. The High Court reached a similar conclusion. Before the High Court, the appellant disclaimed any suggestion of bad faith. The High Court proceeded on the basis that (but declined to decide whether) the re-certification of the second warrant had been unlawful. Assuming that it had been, it was held[3] by Auld LJ that:

> '... it cannot, given the circumstances, possibly be regarded in itself as an abuse of process so as to taint in any way the reinstitution of proceedings following the issue of the third properly-certified warrant. [In respect of a submission that the High Court should mark what happened ... as an abuse of process by discharging [the Appellant] to condone the unlawfulness] ... Such a submission is totally inappropriate to the circumstances of this case, the facts of which disclose, whether lawful or unlawful, no error in the way in which the proceedings were reinstituted. This does not approach the type of egregious conduct that the court has considered, notably that in Bennett ... there was clearly no basis for suspicion [of some skulduggery] ... Quite plainly that it had been a mistake and one which, as soon as the Crown Prosecution Service appreciated it, they corrected properly by the reissue of proceedings'.

1 [2007] EWHC 2407 (Admin). See also *Popa v Czech Republic* [2011] EWHC 329 (Admin) per Lloyd Jones J at paras 50 to 53 where 'Incompetent as it undoubtedly was, the conduct of the CPS in the present case does not approach the high threshold that must be reached before executive conduct may amount to an abuse of process' at para 52.

2 There should have been a reissue of the warrant, properly certified, not certification of an old warrant that was no longer valid: see s 213.

3 At paras 16–17.

8.91 It would, however, be abusive for those representing a Requesting State deliberately to withhold service of its extradition request until the commencement of the extradition hearing so as to ambush a defendant and deprive him of a proper opportunity to contest them: *Government of the Federal Republic of Germany v Kleinschmidt & another*.[1]

1 Above para **8.52**.

8.92 It has also been held to be an abuse of the process for a Requesting State to deliberately use a conviction warrant (usually after convicting the accused in their absence) in place of an accusation warrant so as to gain a procedural advantage.[1] In *Belgium v Bartlett*, it was an abuse of process for a Requesting State to issue a conviction warrant against an individual following a trial in absentia because he had not absented himself from the proceedings but had been legitimately awaiting a pending decision on his extradition in England.[2] The decision to issue the conviction warrant was tactical and was not taken fairly and impartially in the interests of justice, and accordingly it could not stand.[3]

1 See *Campbell v Public Prosecutor of Grande Instance Tribunal of St Malo France* [2013] EWHC 1288 (Admin) and *Federal Public Prosecutor of Brussels, Belgium v Bartlett* [2012] EWHC 2480 (Admin). However, in *Cakollari v Albania* [2011] EWHC 132 (Admin) it was not an abuse of process to issue an accusation extradition request in respect of an extraditee where his trial was already under way as the extraditee had deliberately absented himself from the judicial process in the Requesting State.
2 [2012] EWHC 2480 (Admin).
3 Ibid per Sir John Thomas at paras 30–31, 34–35 and 37.

8.93 In *Boudhiba*,[1] Smith LJ observed[2] that the court would have been prepared to hold extradition proceedings to be an abuse of process if a defendant had been tricked into prejudicing himself by making admissions in an interview in the UK (conducted under the auspices of the mutual legal assistance provisions of the Crime (International Cooperation) Act 2003) whilst under the false impression that he was being interviewed as a witness, even in the absence of bad faith on the part of the Requesting State or interviewing authorities

1 Above para **8.10**.
2 At paras 24–25.

8.94 In relation to conviction warrants, it is now well-established that it is an abuse of process for a Requesting State to seek to pursue extradition where a defendant has already served the whole of the sentence on remand waiting for the extradition as the 'application for extradition in those circumstances is substantively empty'.[1] It is also a breach of Art 8. However, if the suggestion is that the sentence is now time-barred under the Requesting State's law then the court will require 'the clearest possible evidence of bad faith … coupled with unequivocal evidence that the sentence was indeed time-barred'.[2]

1 Per Hickinbottom J at para 5 *Kulka v Regional Court of Piotrkow Trybunalski, Poland* [2013] EWHC 3034 (Admin). See also *Newman v District Court of Krako, Poland* [2012] EWHC 2931 (Admin); *Wysocki v Poland* [2010] EWHC 3430 (Admin).
2 *Mohammed v The Court of Appeal, Paris* [2013] EWHC 1768 (Admin) (21 June 2013), Foskett J at para 12. See also *Konuksever v The Government of Turkey* [2012] EWHC 2166 (Admin).

8.95 As regards repetitive extradition requests, in *Central Examining Court of the National Court of Madrid v City of Westminster Magistrates' Court*,[1] Sedley LJ observed[2] that: 'I do not doubt that a point may come at which an [Issuing Judicial Authority] can be stopped from repeated use of the European arrest warrant process if it is turning into a form of harassment'. This will depend on the facts of the case. In *R (on the application of Folcik) v Poland*,[3] for example, it was not disproportionate to extradite a Polish man convicted of dishonesty offences committed ten years earlier, even though he had very recently been extradited to Poland on separate matters and allowed to return to the United Kingdom. Although the Polish authorities could have extradited for the conviction matter at the same time, there was no mala fides and it was not an abuse of process because 'the omission [was] in good faith; that is to say it is as a result of incompetence or unawareness by the requesting authority that the other charges or convictions are outstanding rather than a deliberate omission to put them to one side'.[4] In another case, It was not an abuse of process for two European arrest warrants to be issued by two different prosecuting authorities within the same country faced with similar criminal conduct.[5] However, in *Germany v Altun*, the issue of a second warrant after the court had discharged the first warrant on the grounds of double jeopardy was an abuse of process.[6] It was also an abuse of process for Italian authorities effectively to ignore a ruling of the Divisional Court refusing a pre-2003 extradition request because of concerns over the extraditee's conviction by simply issuing another request after the post-2003 regime was introduced.[7] It had made no attempt to address the evidential defects identified by that court.

1 [2007] EWHC 2059 (Admin).
2 At para 21.
3 [2014] EWHC 1264 (Admin).
4 Para 9 per Bean J.
5 *Borowski v Regional Court in Wloclawek, Poland* [2012] EWHC 3568 (Admin).
6 Above para **8.69**. The case had a very complicated history, and the court concluded that not every second warrant would be an abuse but that 'prosecutors should not think that, because so many defects in procedure can be dealt with after discharge by a fresh warrant, that all grounds for discharge can be remedied by further evidence on a fresh warrant' per Ouseley J para 52.
7 *Office of the prosecutor General of Turin v Barone (No. 2)* [2010] EWHC 3004 (Admin), per Moses LJ at paras 38–39.

8.96 An infamous example of abuse of the extradition process is to be found in the Canadian Supreme Court decision of *Cobb & Grossman v USA*.[1] In that case, the appellants, Canadian citizens, allegedly defrauded American residents of some $22 million through a telemarketing scheme executed from Canada concerning illegal sale of gemstones. Canadian police declined to initiate proceedings but instead provided the materials gathered by them to the US authorities. The US requested extradition on charges of fraud and conspiracy to commit fraud. While many of the co-conspirators voluntarily returned to the jurisdiction of Pennsylvania, the appellants contested their extradition on the basis that extraditing them would unjustifiedly violate their rights under the Canadian Charter of Rights and Freedoms in the light of statements made by the American judge and prosecuting attorney with conduct of the matter in the US. First, as he was sentencing a co-conspirator in the scheme, the American judge assigned to their trial had stated that: 'I want you to believe me that, as to those people who don't come in and cooperate and if we get them extradited and they're found guilty, as far as I'm concerned they're going to get the absolute maximum jail sentence that the law permits me to give'. Secondly, the prosecuting attorney subsequently said during a television interview that: 'I have told some of these individuals, "Look, you can come down and you can put this behind you by serving your time in prison and making restitution to the victims, or you can wind up serving a great deal longer sentence under much more stringent conditions", and described those conditions to them [as] "'You're going to be the boyfriend of a very bad man if you wait out your extradition," out of the 89 people we've indicted so far, approximately 55 of them have said "'We give up"'.

1 Above para **8.65**.

8.97 The extradition Judge (Hawkins J) stayed the extradition proceedings as an abuse of process, finding that the Judge's remark was 'nothing short of a bold, undisguised, threat intended to intimidate the applicants and others into abandoning their right to resist extradition by lawful means' and, in respect of the comments of the prosecutor, that 'I believe and hope I can safely say that no right-thinking Canadian would endorse the use of a threat of homosexual rape as a means of persuading Canadian residents to abandon their rights to a full extradition hearing'. Hawkins J concluded that:

> 'In my view, to commit these fugitives for surrender to be tried before a judge who has publicly threatened them with the imposition of a maximum sentence before having commenced their trial and to be prosecuted by a prosecutor who has publicly threatened them with homosexual rape (boasting at the same time how effective the technique has been) "shocks the Canadian conscience" and is "simply not acceptable"'.

8.98 That decision was overturned by the Court of Appeal for Ontario but reinstated by the Canadian Supreme Court. On issues of jurisdiction, the Supreme Court, overturning prior authority,[1] held that the extradition judge is competent to grant *Charter* remedies, including a stay of proceedings, on the basis of a *Charter* violation but only insofar as the *Charter* breach pertains directly to the circumscribed issues relevant at the committal stage of the extradition process.[2] The issue is not whether the appellants will have a fair trial if extradited, but whether they are having a fair extradition hearing in the light of the threats and inducements imposed upon them, by those involved in requesting their extradition, to force them to abandon their right to such a hearing. Conduct by the Requesting State, or by its representatives, agents or officials, which interferes or attempts to interfere with the conduct of judicial proceedings in Canada is a matter that directly concerns the extradition judge.[3] The Requesting State is a party to judicial proceedings before a Canadian court and is subject to the application of rules and remedies that serve to control the conduct of parties who turn to the courts for assistance. Even aside from any claim of *Charter* protection, litigants are protected from unfair, abusive, proceedings through the doctrine of abuse of process, which bars litigants – and not only the State – from pursuing frivolous or vexatious proceedings, or otherwise abusing the process of the courts.[4] A stay of proceedings will be entered only in the clearest of cases and is always better dealt with by the court where the abuse occurs.[5]

1 *Argentina v Mellino* [1987] 1 SCR 536.
2 Per Arbour J at para 26.
3 At para 33.
4 At para 35.
5 At para 38.

8.99 But in this case, a stay of proceedings was justified either as a remedy based on s 7 of the Canadian *Charter*[1] or on the basis of the doctrine of abuse of process.[2] The statements made by the American Judge and the US Attorney may properly be visited upon the Requesting State itself, who was a party before the court. One interpretation of the Judge's statement, and any interpretation of the prosecutor's 'sinister' statement, were an attempt to influence the unfolding of Canadian judicial proceedings by putting undue pressure on the appellants to desist from their objections to the extradition request. The pressures were not only inappropriate but also, in the case of the statements made by the prosecutor on the eve of the opening of the judicial hearing in Canada, amounted unequivocally to an abuse of the process of the court. Litigants should not be expected to overcome well-founded fears of violent reprisals in order to be participants in a judicial process. Aside from such intimidation itself, it is plain that a committal order requiring a fugitive to return to face such an ominous climate – which was created by those who would play a large, if not decisive, role in determining the fugitive's ultimate fate – would not be consistent with the principles of fundamental justice The intimidation bore directly upon the very proceedings before the extradition judge. Aside from the intimidation itself, a committal order obtained in the present circumstances would clearly not be consistent with the principles of fundamental justice.[3] Whilst 'foreign' conduct may not attract *Charter* scrutiny, conduct attributable to a litigant before a Canadian court is sufficient to trigger the application of the common law doctrine of abuse of process.[4]

1 The right to life, liberty, and security of the person and the right not to be deprived thereof except in accordance with the principles of fundamental justice.
2 At para 40.
3 At para 43.
4 At para 49. The Supreme Court further held that the existence of potential remedies at the executive stage does not oust the jurisdiction of the courts to control their own process (at paras 42 and 44).

8.100 The threats from the American authorities did not in fact induce the persons sought to abandon their right to resist extradition. The Supreme Court of Canada found this to be immaterial. It was the attempt to interfere with the due process of the court that mattered, not the success or failure of that attempt.[1] The Supreme Court concluded[2] that:

> 'By placing undue pressure on Canadian citizens to forego due legal process in Canada, the foreign State has disentitled itself from pursuing its recourse before the courts and attempting to show why extradition should legally proceed. The intimidation bore directly upon the very proceedings before the extradition judge, thus engaging the appellants' right to fundamental justice at common law, under the doctrine of abuse of process … this was one of the clearest of cases where to proceed further with the extradition hearing would violate "those fundamental principles of justice which underlie the community's sense of fair play and decency", since the Requesting State in the proceedings, represented by the Attorney General of Canada, had not repudiated the statements of some of its officials that an unconscionable price would be paid by the appellants for having insisted on exercising their rights under Canadian law.'

1 At para 50.
2 At paras 52–53.

8.101 It should be noted, however, that a partially different result was reached in the linked case of *Shulman v USA*[1] concerning one of Cobb's co-conspirators. Here, by contrast, the appellant received a fair extradition hearing. He was not subjected to undue pressure by American officials before or during his committal hearing because he was not aware of the American Judge's statement and the prosecuting attorney's threat had not yet been uttered. The Supreme Court held[2] that the comments could not in any way have had any impact on the fairness of the committal hearing, and thus the extradition judge was correct in denying the appellant's application for a stay of proceedings. However, by the time Shulman's appeal had been listed, he had become aware of the American Judge's statement and the prosecuting attorney's threat had been uttered. Whilst holding that the extradition appeal court also has an implied, if not inherent, jurisdiction to control its own process, including through the application of the common law doctrine of abuse of process,[3] in light of the fact that the ambiguous statement was made by the American Judge a few months before the appellant's extradition hearing and had gone unnoticed by the appellant until it was raised by others in related proceedings, the Supreme Court was not bound by any factual findings of the extradition judge and was able to come to its own conclusions about the nature of the American Judge's statement. The Supreme Court ruled that:

> 'It is quite possible that the Judge did not mean that he would impose the maximum sentence regardless of any other relevant factor, but simply that he would discount the maximum sentence by any other legally relevant factor, and then give no additional reduction in light of the absence of cooperation. This is, I would have thought, all that the law permits[3] … his remarks, made in the course of a sentencing hearing, may not necessarily be construed as a threat of judicial retaliation directed at those who avail themselves of the Canadian judicial system to oppose an extradition request, as is their right. Taken alone, and in their proper context, these comments, in my judgment, would not be sufficient to sustain a claim of abuse of process'.[4]

1 [2001] 1 SCR 616.
2 At para 24.
3 At para 38.
4 At para 50. By contrast, the 'unambiguous' prosecutor's statement was of a different nature and properly characterised as a shocking use of threats by a US official attempting to induce Canadian citizens to renounce the exercise of their lawful access to courts in Canada in order to resist a US extradition request. The statement was made almost two years after Shulman had been committed for surrender by the extradition judge, but before the hearing of his appeal by the Court of Appeal. The statement was properly attributed to the Requesting State, the respondent in the Court of Appeal. The Appeal Court should have received evidence as to its utterance and, having received that evidence, and the respondent having made no efforts to distance itself from the impugned statements, should have stayed the proceedings as an abuse of the ongoing judicial process.

8.102 In *McKinnon v Government of the United States of America*,[1] the House of Lords adopted and applied *Cobb*. The appellant, a British citizen, was alleged to have hacked into US government computers and installed unauthorised software which enabled him to access, alter, and delete, data on those computers, causing damage. When interviewed under caution, the defendant admitted responsibility although not that he had caused damage.

Grand jury indictments were returned against him alleging seven counts of fraud and related activity in connection with computers, and warrants issued for his arrest. But, before making a request for the appellant's extradition, the US prosecutors informed his legal representatives that, if he went voluntarily to the US without contesting extradition and if he pleaded guilty to two counts, the prosecution would be prepared to limit its allegations of monetary damage and not pursue allegations of endangering national security, thus enabling them to make a recommendation to the court which was likely to result in the appellant receiving a sentence of 37–46 months' imprisonment, probably at the shorter end of that bracket, and, after serving six to twelve months in the US, the prosecutor would recommend to the Department of Justice that the appellant be repatriated to serve the rest of his sentence in the UK, and that that recommendation was likely to be accepted (the practical effect being that the appellant's release date would then be determined by the UK rules on remission, such that he might serve a total of eighteen months to two years in prison). The appellant was offered a plea agreement on those terms. The appellant alleged that he was also informed through his legal representatives that, if he chose not to co-operate and was extradited to the US and convicted by a jury after pleading not guilty, he could expect to receive a sentence of at least eight to ten years' imprisonment (based upon the extant allegations of monetary damage and endangering national security), possibly longer, and would not be repatriated to the UK to serve any part of it, so that he would serve the whole sentence in the US, possibly in a high security prison, with at best some 15 per cent remission. The defendant took advice from an American defence lawyer and refused the 'deal'. Extradition proceedings were commenced.

1 Above para **8.57**.

8.103 The appellant relied on *Cobb*[1] and argued that, where the respondent government is seeking the assistance of the English courts to extradite an accused, it must comply with the legal principles of this jurisdiction. That he has in fact resisted the pressure improperly put upon him is no answer to the contention that it constituted an abuse of process; it was calculated to interfere with the extradition proceedings. Lord Brown of Eaton-under-Heywood[2] ruled[3] that:

> 'The district judge…had jurisdiction to consider whether the extradition proceedings constituted an abuse of process so as to protect the integrity of the statutory regime, the Secretary of State having no general discretion to refuse extradition. So much was stated by Laws LJ in…R (Bermingham) v Director of the Serious Fraud Office … and by Lord Phillips of Worth Matravers CJ in R (Government of the United States of America) v Bow Street Magistrates' Court…What was not expressly stated in these decisions but was necessarily implicit was that the abuse of process for consideration was such as to require the extradition proceedings to be permanently stayed and the accused discharged'.

1 Discussed above at paras **8.96–8.102**.
2 With whom Lords Scott and Phillips and Baroness Hale and Lord Neuberger agreed.
3 At para 8.

8.104 Approving[1] (at paras 30–32) the principles laid down in *Cobb*, the House of Lords stated[2] that the 'essential questions underlying' the determination of whether it is an abuse of process in the circumstances of this case were:

> 'Did the US prosecuting authority here "attempt to interfere with the due process of the court"? Did it place "undue pressure [on the appellant] to forego due legal process" in the UK and so disentitle itself from pursuing extradition proceedings? Would extradition in this case "violate those fundamental principles of justice which underlie the community's sense of fair play and decency"? Would the appellant following extradition be paying "an unconscionable price … having insisted on exercising [his] rights under [English] law"?'

1 At paras 30–32.
2 At para 33.

8.105 However, the House of Lords found differences between the alleged conduct in this case, and the conduct in *Cobb*, to be striking. In respect of the disparity between the predicted sentences, the House of Lords observed[1] that the discount would have to be very substantially more generous than anything promised here (as to the way the case would be put and the likely outcome) before it constituted unlawful pressure such as to vitiate the process. So too would the predicted consequences of non-co-operation need to go significantly beyond what could properly be regarded as the defendant's just deserts on conviction for that to constitute unlawful pressure. As regards the allegation that the US authorities had threatened to oppose repatriation, the House of Lords observed that, even were it to be regarded as an unlawful threat, it has now been expressly repudiated by the US prosecutor, again in marked contrast to the position in *Cobb*.[2] Lord Brown concluded[3] that:

> 'it would only be in a wholly extreme case like *Cobb* itself that the court should properly regard any encouragement to accused persons to surrender for trial and plead guilty, in particular if made by a prosecutor during a regulated process of plea bargaining, as so unconscionable as to constitute an abuse of process justifying the Requested State's refusal to extradite the accused. It is difficult, indeed, to think of anything other than the threat of unlawful action which could fairly be said so to imperil the integrity of the extradition process as to require the accused, notwithstanding his having resisted the undue pressure, to be discharged irrespective of the strength of the case against him.'

1 At para 38.
2 At para 40.
3 At para 41.

Conduct of UK authorities

8.106 In *R (Raissi) v Secretary of State for the Home Department*,[1] in addition to finding abuse by reason of ulterior motive,[2] the Court of Appeal additionally, and separately, held in the same case that, independent of the actions or motive of a Requesting State, extradition proceedings had been abused by the legal representative of the Requesting State in the UK. The Court of Appeal examined the status of the Crown Prosecution Service when acting in its capacity as legal representative of a Requesting State in extradition proceedings and concluded that, even though the CPS was acting as representative of the Requesting State, that did not mean that it did not owe a duty to the UK Court.[3] The CPS's duty to the court might require it not to 'act unquestioningly' on its instructions.[4] In the event of conflict between its instructions from the Requesting State and its duty to the court, the CPS's primary duty was to the court.[5] The duty of the CPS to the court extended also to a duty not to take part in proceedings which it knew or ought to know were an abuse of the process of the court.[6] In this case, the preliminary[7] findings of the Court of Appeal disclosed that the CPS had abused the process of the court. The extradition request related to what can only be described as minor charges, for which the appellant would normally have been entitled to bail. He was remanded in custody because it was said that he was a terrorist involved in the 9/11 atrocities, and that the charges were only 'holding charges'. The material available to CPS did not support such an allegation and/or the CPS were being reckless as to its accuracy. In the circumstances, the Court of Appeal[8] held[9] that:

> 'We also consider that the way in which the extradition proceedings were conducted in this country, with opposition to bail based on allegations which appear unfounded in evidence amounted to an abuse of process … the opposition to bail, based on unsubstantiated assertions, was also an abuse' (para 146).

1 [2008] EWCA Civ 72.
2 See below paras **8.122–8.123**.
3 At para 135.
4 At para 138.
5 At para 139.
6 At para 141.
7 See below para **8.123**.
8 Sir Anthony Clarke MR, Smith LJ and Hooper LJ.
9 At paras 144 and 146.

8.107 However, in *MacDonald v Czech Republic*,[1] the court noted, in relation to extradition cases, that false information given by the authority who will actually prosecute the case could amount to an abuse of process but that there was no authority which confirmed that misleading information given by UK police, independent of the judicial authority, was capable of amounting to an abuse of process. It would be contrary to what lay behind the EAW procedure if an error made by the English authorities could mean that an otherwise perfectly proper extradition could be prevented.[2]

1 [2014] EWHC 945 (Admin).
2 Per Collins J at para 53.

8.108 *Tague v Governor of Full Sutton Prison*[1] concerned an import EAW. The UK had sought the extradition of Mr Tague from Spain. Spain ordered the extradition of Mr Tague on the condition that he be given a full re-trial. Under UK law, Mr Tague was not entitled to a re-trial. SOCA (now the NCA) failed to pick up on this inconsistency when it could and should have done so.[2] Mr Tague argued that there had been an abuse of process on the basis that execution of the EAW in these circumstances offended the court's sense of justice and propriety.

The court held that it was not SOCA's responsibility to check that the Spanish court understood that such a restriction was not available; that was a job for whoever appeared on behalf of the judicial authority at the Spanish court.[3] The conduct of the UK authorities amounted to no more than a lack of care and precision and did not amount to a deliberate bad faith policy to ignore or exercise wilful blindness to conditions placed on EAW extraditions by executing Member States.[4] The court considered that because the condition imposed by the Spanish court was in fact in contravention of EU law,[5] this case lay at the less serious end of the spectrum.[6] It was said that ultimately the decision the court had to make in a case such as this, was a single value judgment which should be undertaken 'untrammelled by any rigid rules and considering all the factors'.[7]

1 [2015] EWHC 3576 (Admin).
2 Ibid at para 28.
3 Ibid at para 51.
4 Ibid at 58.
5 *Melloni v Ministerio Fiscal* [2013] QB 1067.
6 *Tague* (n 1) at para 57.
7 Ibid at para 60.

Disguised extradition: deportation and extradition

8.109 Before coming to 'ulterior motive' or 'bad faith' category of cases, it is instructive to consider one particular species of conduct of abuse that straddles both categories of abuse: disguised extradition.

8.110 Both the Extradition Act and the international treaties which it implements contemplate that a foreign State, wishing to have a person returned to it from the UK to face charges must proceed under the Extradition Act. An individual has greater procedural protections in an extradition proceeding than in a deportation proceeding. Deportation and extradition have different underlying objectives. Deportation, which is a discretionary decision of the immigration authorities, is aimed at protecting the public good. It is unilateral in nature and reflects national law and the sovereign right of the State. Extradition, which is initiated by foreign authorities, is enshrined in international treaties (multilateral and bilateral). It reflects international cooperation in criminal matters and is aimed at delivering a person sought for prosecution to the appropriate jurisdiction. Generally, the extradition process engages more rigorous standards in terms of the kind of process that UK authorities are obliged to undertake in order to return the person to a foreign State and the safeguards available to the individual. Specifically, one significant advantage of extradition over deportation to the person sought is in the long-established rule of international law that, following extradition, a Requesting State may only prosecute for the conduct in respect of which extradition has been granted; the rule of 'specialty'. The rule, and the various exceptions to it, is reflected in every international extradition treaty, and under the 2003 Act is reflected in ss 17 and 95. A fugitive, returned pursuant to deportation procedures, is deprived of this fundamental protection because the purpose of deportation is not the prosecution of crime. Therefore, to the State that wants a particular individual returned, deportation is more advantageous. There are fewer safeguards (although the rights enshrined in the ECHR apply in both procedures) and no restrictions in terms of what the person, once deported to that State, can be prosecuted for. The assistance of the host State is, however, required for disguised extradition by way of deportation since deportation is a unilateral exercise of its sovereignty.

8.111 Issues of disguised extradition arise in the context of domestic criminal proceedings where the practitioner will be concerned with an allegation that his or her client's very presence before the UK courts has been obtained in breach of extradition arrangements between the UK and the State in which he or she was previously situated. The client may have been duped into entering the country unlawfully. She may have been lured or tricked from a State with whom the UK has no extradition arrangements into a third State with whom it has for the purposes of onward extradition to the UK.[1] These issues are discussed in **Chapter 5**. But, while less common, issues of disguised extradition can arise in deportation[2] or extradition proceedings. In an extradition context, cases do occur in which a Requesting State has attempted, but failed, to secure illegitimately a person's deportation in circumvention of extradition procedure, and is then forced to resort to an extradition request. In such a case, it is possible to argue that the subsequent extradition proceedings are tainted by the prior attempt to interfere with the due process of the court and by doubts about the underlying motive of the Requesting State. This scenario has yet to arise in an extradition case in the UK. Although English case law has established the principle, to ascertain the factors that underlie such a submission, the practitioner must turn to Canadian case law.

1 *Somchai Liangsirisprasert v Government of the United States of America* [1991] 1 AC 225, PC.
2 In immigration proceedings, the issue will arise in circumstances where the Requesting State has failed to prove its case in an extradition context, and is therefore seeking to achieve the return of the person through another forum (where the individual receives less procedural protections). However, as stated at **8.110**, this requires the assistance of the host State.

8.112 In practical terms, there is significant overlap between extradition and deportation, which is not, in and of itself, improper. A host State may well have an entirely legitimate basis, irrespective of any prospective prosecution, for deporting an individual in the public interest. There can be no abuse of process if the deportation accords with the requirements of national law and (in the case of State Parties) complies with the ECHR. There is, in principle, nothing improper or abusive in a host State deporting such an individual, even if the practical effect of that deportation will be removal to a foreign State where he will face prosecution for offences allegedly committed there. The end result of extradition, namely the return of a person to a place where he or she is wanted for prosecution, may be legitimately achieved through deportation, if the removal of that person from the UK is conducive to the public good and consistent with the requirements of UK law and the ECHR:[1]

> 'the fact that the present applicant will serve an existing sentence of imprisonment, if he is sent to the United States, does not mean that an act

which otherwise would be deportation and nothing else becomes instead not deportation but the surrender of a fugitive criminal. To hold otherwise would be to give assent to the proposition that the quality of an act is determined by its consequence, which is obviously untrue; otherwise cause would become the same thing as effect. There may, it is true, be no practical difference from the applicant's point of view between a deportation which gives the United States authorities the power to make him serve his sentence, and an illegal surrender having the same effect. But that cannot involve that in law the two things must be regarded as the same. If, therefore, this deportation order is to be regarded as invalid, it must be for some other reason than the consequence to which it will lead.'

1 *R v Governor of Brixton Prison, ex p Soblen* [1963] 2 QB 243, CA per Donovan LJ at p 307. See also Lord Denning MR at 301–302; *Government of the United States of America v Tollman* (above para **8.62**) per Malloy J para 26). See also *Halm v Canada (Minister of Employment and Immigration)* [1996] 1 FC 547 (TD) per Rothstein J at paras 18–23; *Kissell v The Attorney-General of Canada on behalf of the United States of America* [2006] 47314 (Ont. Supr. Crt.) per Beaulieu J at paras 142–143.

8.113 What, in contrast, is not permissible is use of the power of deportation to remove a foreign national to another country *for the purpose of* enabling that foreign state to prosecute him or her for offences allegedly committed. It is an abuse of process to exercise a statutory power for a reason that is unrelated to the purpose for which that power was granted.[1] The guiding principle was clearly stated by Lord Denning in *R v Governor of Brixton Prison, ex p Soblen.*[2] The powers of deportation and extradition must each be exercised for their own distinct purpose. Where a proceeding is undertaken professedly for an authorised purpose, but in fact with an ulterior object, it is unlawful. In appropriate cases, the courts will, therefore, be duty-bound to inquire into this purpose, engaging in a factual inquiry which focuses on the purposes for which immigration procedures were engaged.[3] Lord Denning MR observed[4] that:

> 'So there we have in this case the two principles: on the one hand the principle arising out of the law of extradition under which the officers of the Crown cannot and must not surrender a fugitive criminal to another country at its request except in accordance with the Extradition Acts duly fulfilled; on the other hand the principle arising out of the law of deportation, under which the Secretary of State can deport an alien and put him on board a ship or aircraft bound for his own country if he considers it conducive to the public good that that should be done. How are we to decide between these two principles? It seems to me that it depends on the purpose [for] which the act is done. If it was done for an authorised purpose, it was lawful. If it was done professedly for an authorised purpose, but in fact for a different purpose with an ulterior object, it was unlawful. If, therefore, the purpose of the Home Secretary in this case was to surrender the applicant as a fugitive criminal to the United States of America, because they had asked for him, then it would be unlawful; but if his purpose was to deport him to his home country because he considered his presence here to be not conducive to the public good, then his action is lawful. It is open to these courts to inquire whether the purpose of the Home Secretary was a lawful or an unlawful purpose. Was there a misuse of the power or not? The courts can always go

behind the face of the deportation order in order to see whether the powers entrusted by Parliament have been exercised lawfully or not.'[5]

1 See *Government of the United States of America v Tollman* (above para **8.62**) per Malloy J at para 26: '… if a foreign state seeks the assistance of Canada to have a fugitive returned there for prosecution, that foreign state must bring the appropriate extradition application through diplomatic channels pursuant to the treaty and the *Extradition Act.* It would be improper for Canadian immigration authorities to apprehend a person and return him to the United States solely because they were requested to do so by the United States, for to do so would be to completely circumvent the *Extradition Act* and the safeguards built into that legislative scheme', and para 121: 'There is clear and binding authority that it is an abuse of process to use the immigration system for the purpose of effecting extradition. We have extradition treaties and extradition legislation for a purpose, just as we have immigration legislation for a purpose.'

2 Above para **8.112**.

3 See, to similar effect, *Moore v Minister of Manpower and Immigration* [1968] SCR 839, in which the Supreme Court of Canada held, at para 12, that: 'To decide that the deportation proceedings are a sham or not bona fide, it would be necessary to hold that the Minister did not genuinely consider it in the public interest to expel the appellant', and held on the facts of that case that the applicant had failed to discharge his onus of showing that the deportation proceedings taken were in fact a sham designed to effect the applicant's extradition to Panama rather than for a legitimate purpose under the Immigration Act. In that case, Mr Moore had previously been deported from Canada, was illegally in this country, and had been travelling under a false passport. See also *Kindler v Minister of Employment and Immigration* (1985) 47 CR (3d) 225 (Fed Ct). Mr. Kindler had been convicted of first-degree murder in Pennsylvania and the jury had recommended the death penalty. He escaped the jurisdiction before sentencing and had been living and working illegally in Quebec. Rouleau J concluded that on the facts of that case, there was insufficient evidence to prove that the Minister did not genuinely consider it in the public interest to order the deportation. Having made that determination, however, he noted (at p 234) that: 'I should add that, if the petitioner had been able to show that the real purpose of the deportation proceedings was to surrender him to a foreign State because he is a fugitive criminal sought by such foreign State, this would have been an abuse of the power to deport and as such would have been restrained by the court. Parliament has set up, in the Extradition Act, a special procedure for the surrender of foreign criminals and the general discretionary power to deport cannot be utilized to replace this special procedure. *Generalia specialibus non derogant.*'

4 At 302.

5 See also *Caddoux v Bow Street Magistrates' Court* [2004] EWHC 642 (Admin) per Kennedy LJ at paras 11–12, where it is observed that, even in a case where a deportation order may legitimately be made 'once the request for extradition was received I accept that there were powerful reasons of comity for giving it priority. The fact then was that a person wanted by the French authorities was still on English soil. If he were to be deported without notice to the French authorities, and that would we were told be the normal practice, they might well be deprived of the opportunity to require him to stand trial in France, so, as it seems to me, the Secretary of State was right to allow the extradition proceedings to go ahead, leaving the deportation order to be implemented if necessary at the conclusion of these proceedings'.

8.114 Therefore, the lynchpin of an abuse of process argument based on this type of disguised extradition is whether the UK authorities had, from the outset, legitimate grounds in seeking to deport the person sought. Where the authorities undertake deportation in order to surrender the person as a fugitive criminal in response to a request from another State, their purpose is unlawful. However, where the authorities seek to deport in order to protect domestic public good, the action is legitimate. The fact that there is a practical overlap between the outcome of these two proceedings and that an accused is wanted by another country does not preclude a sovereign State from making legitimate decisions about its power to deport individuals. In order to show impropriety, the defendant must bring enough evidence to show, or at least strongly to suggest, that the deportation proceedings were undertaken by UK authorities in bad faith and with an ulterior motive.[1] This is a difficult argument to make. The threshold is high, and a finding of bad faith is reserved only for exceptional cases.[2]

1 *Kissell* (above para **8.112**) at paras 144 and 154.
2 *Soblen* (above para **8.112**) *at* 307–308 per Donovan LJ; *Moore* (above para **8.113**) at para 11; *Halm* (above para **8.112**) at para 21; *Government of the United States of America v Tollman* (Above para **8.62**) at para 22.

8.115 Consequently, there is nothing improper in a Requesting State making a tactical or strategic decision about extradition, for example by withholding an extradition request because a deportation was likely to be effective or asking for extradition if it was not, so long as the immigration authorities of the host State have a legitimate basis to pursue deportation. Put another way, if a host State is proposing legitimately to deport a fugitive, there is nothing abusive in the Requesting State accepting the fugitive on that basis or even facilitating those proceedings.[1]

1 *Kissell* (above para **8.112**) at paras 151 and 160–161: '… there are not sufficient grounds for inferring that the American authorities decided to pursue extradition because they somehow "knew" that the immigration process would not go their way. Yet, even if this was the case, there would not be anything illegitimate about it, to the extent that…the American authorities are entitled to make any strategic choices that they wish, so long as domestic deportation proceedings were founded on a legitimate basis'. See also *Bembenek v Canada (MEI)* (1991) 69 CCC (3d) 34 (Ont Ct Gen Div). This decision is also authority for the proposition that there is nothing improper about pursuing extradition when deportation proceedings are also pending.

8.116 Equally, there is nothing improper in the Requesting State providing the host State with information and assistance in ongoing legitimate deportation proceedings. Co-operation and communication between State authorities with respect to a certain individual who is sought for prosecution does not, by itself, suggest bad faith or improper motive. Indeed, such communication and cooperation is necessary in order for authorities of the host State successfully to pursue the objectives of immigration law.[1] There is even nothing improper about the Requesting State notifying the host State of the presence of a person wanted for criminal charges, thereby effectively initiating a process of investigation under the host State's immigration law, or co-operating with the host State in locating and arresting that person.[2]

1 *Kissell* (above para **8.112**) para 152, 156. See also *Soblen* (above para **8.112**) per Donovan LJ at pp 309–310; *Bembenek* (above para **8.115**) per Campbell J at pp 11–13: 'there is nothing sinister or improper in assisting the Canadian authorities in their own opposition to the refugee claim, so long as the Canadian authorities are acting in good faith in pursuit of legitimate Canadian objectives'; *Halm* (above para **8.112**) per Rothstein J at para 25: 'The fact that the United States wanted the applicant back or that there were communications between U.S. and Canadian officials is also not evidence of bad faith or improper motive' and *Attorney General of Canada on behalf of the United States of America v Welsh & Romero* (2007) BCSC 1567 at para 39.
2 *Kissell* (above para **8.112**) at paras 153 and 156.

8.117 The dividing line is, however, crossed when the Requesting State and the host State collude so as to bring about deportation proceedings *for the purpose of* enabling that foreign State to prosecute him or her for offences allegedly committed. Thus, to make good a *Cobb*-type abuse submission in a disguised extradition case of this type, it will be necessary for the defendant to show not only that deportation proceedings have been attempted, but that their purpose was to avoid or circumvent extradition. This will require showing, not only that this was the purpose of the Requesting State, but also that the UK authorities colluded in such a plan.[1] Collusion is of course necessary because deportation is a decision of the host State and mala fides in the exercise of that power would have to be demonstrated. In *Halm,*[2] Rothstein J adopted[3] the following principles as a guideline for distinguishing between a legitimate deportation and a disguised extradition:

(1) If the purpose of the exercise is to deport the person because his presence is not conducive to the public good, that is a legitimate exercise of the power of deportation.

(2) If the purpose is to surrender the person as a fugitive criminal to a State because it asked for him, that is not a legitimate exercise of the power of deportation.

(3) It is open to the courts to inquire whether the purpose of the government was lawful or otherwise.

(4) The onus is on the party alleging an unlawful exercise of power. It is a heavy onus.

(5) To succeed, it would be necessary to hold that the Minister did not genuinely consider it in the public interest to expel the person in question.

1 *Kissell* (above para **8.12**) at para 136.
2 Above para **8.12**.
3 At para 21.

8.118 *Government of the United States of America v Tollman*[1] is a clear illustration of how the authorities can cross this line by engaging in an extra-legal process that flouts established norms and rules. Mr Tollman, a US citizen, was wanted by the US authorities on allegations of income tax evasion. To the knowledge of the US authorities, he was permanently resident in London. The US authorities took no steps until they received information that Mr Tollman would be travelling on business to Bermuda via Toronto. The US authorities took no steps to bring extradition proceedings against Mr Tollman in the UK or in Canada. Instead, they contacted Canadian immigration authorities and asked them to detain Mr Tollman as soon as he entered Canada and to deliver him to the US border where US authorities would be waiting to take him into custody to face the charges against him. The sole basis for this request was the outstanding charges against Mr Tollman in the US. This was an attempt to use the Canadian immigration system to effect Mr Tollman's removal to the US to face trial, improperly ignoring the extradition process. Initially, Canadian immigration authorities agreed to assist and Mr Tollman was detained by Canadian immigration authorities. However, despite objection by the Canadian immigration authorities, Mr Tollman's release was ordered on bail by the Immigration Review Board (IRB) pending a full immigration hearing. A Canadian immigration official unilaterally took the position that the IRB order was made without jurisdiction and refused to release Mr Tollman. During the time thus afforded, the US authorities sought and obtained a provisional arrest warrant under the Extradition Act. Although the material filed in support of that application may not have been overtly false, it was characterised by 'strategic omissions'. It was misleading in many respects and many material facts were either not disclosed or were buried in attachments and not referred to in the main affidavit. The Superior Court of Justice of Ontario[2] concluded that the US deliberately set out to thwart the Canadian extradition process and to deny him the protections afforded to him under Canadian legislation and concluded[3] that:

> 'It would appear that the intention behind all of this was to bring maximum pressure to bear upon Mr. Tollman in the hopes that he would simply agree to deportation and give up his rights under the *Extradition Act.* The fact that none of these efforts was successful is irrelevant. The conduct of the United States constitutes an affront to the processes of this court that cannot be condoned. This case falls squarely within the principles enunciated by the Supreme Court of Canada in *United States of America v Cobb* … By attempting to thwart the appropriate legal process in Canada in the hopes of having Mr. Tollman abandon his rights under Canadian law, the foreign state has disentitled itself to any relief from this court. This is conduct that offends this community's sense of fair play and decency and constitutes an abuse of process. The only suitable remedy in these circumstances is a stay of proceedings.'

1 Above para **8.62**.

2 Malloy J.

3 At para 13. The core findings in this case (at paras 120–132) were that there was a discernible overall plan by the US authorities to engineer a situation that avoided a legal process altogether (at paras 120–121), whether extradition (from the UK or Canada) or deportation. The US deliberately tried to pressure Canadian immigration authorities into swiftly detaining Mr Tollman at the airport, and 'delivering' him to the US border without due process. Secondly, the American authorities were found to have actually pressured immigration authorities deliberately to disobey a court order, thereby preventing the lawful release of the applicant from detention (at para 132). Further, it was found by Molloy J that the underlying intent of the American authorities was to pressure the applicant into relinquishing his rights under the extradition process. To this end, the American authorities deliberately chose to seek to apprehend Mr Tollman in Canada, a jurisdiction to which he did not have many ties, instead of at his regular place of residence (the UK) so that he would become more willing to surrender if he became caught up in lengthy proceedings (at para 129). To this end, the American authorities were also found to have deliberately instructed immigration authorities to put him in unjustifiably harsh conditions of detention with the purpose of ensuring that his detention was as unpleasant as possible so as to pressure him into abandoning his rights and surrendering to the US (at paras 129–130). 'The actions taken by the United States against Gavin Tollman in this country speak loudly of a deliberate plan to engineer the return of Mr. Tollman to the United States to face tax fraud charges without having to go through the nuisance of an extradition proceeding. The fall-back plan was that if extradition had to be resorted to at all, it would be pursued in this country where Mr. Tollman had no ties to the community, away from his wife, his children, his friends and his work; a place where he was more likely to be held in custody or to have his freedom severely curtailed, and therefore more likely to waive his rights and simply surrender to the United States' (at para 120).

8.119 In respect of a specific submission advanced on behalf of the Requesting State, that there can be no prejudice to Mr Tollman once the extradition arrest warrant is issued, that ultimately he got what claims he is entitled to – an extradition hearing rather than a deportation hearing, with all of the rights that that entails – Malloy J observed[1] that:

'First of all, the success or failure of the abusive steps taken is irrelevant: *Cobb.* The US hoped to obtain custody of Mr. Tollman without having to undergo an extradition proceeding; they have not been successful. However, the Canadian judicial system was engaged when the US attempted to achieve extradition through the immigration process. It is not open to a party to excuse previous abusive actions by eventually resorting to the appropriate legal processes'.

1 At para 142. See also para 146. For *Cobb*, see above paras **8.96–8.100**.

8.120 Malloy J concluded that:

'this is a situation, as recognized by the Ontario Court of Appeal in *Larosa*, where proceeding with the extradition committal hearing would be a breach of fundamental justice, no matter how fairly that hearing might be conducted[1] … In addition to the personal impact on Mr. Tollman, the conduct here must be condemned as contrary to the fundamental principles upon which our justice system is based. The justice system must be fair for all who become enmeshed in it, regardless of intellect, wealth or station in life. Mr. Tollman was able to insist on his rights, albeit at considerable personal and financial cost. However, he was armed with intelligence, stamina, a social position of power and prestige, and enormous personal wealth. Very few people would have been able to do what he has done. If the system went awry for him, what hope is there for the weak, the poor and those less powerful? The answer must be in the vigilance of the justice system itself. Misconduct of this sort cannot ever be tolerated, for to do so is to condone, perhaps even to invite, similar conduct in the future. This is the kind of conduct that offends this community's sense of fair play and decency. Having conducted itself in this manner, the Requesting State is disentitled to any relief from this court. Accordingly, this extradition proceeding is permanently stayed'.[2]

1 At para 145.
2 At para 149. By contrast, facts found to fall on the correct side of the line are to be found in *Kissell* (above at para **8.112**).

Ulterior motive or purpose

8.121 Allegations of bad faith in the investigation of an offence and prosecution are ordinarily matters for the court in the Requesting State, so the requested court will not generally examine them.[1] However, in exceptional circumstances, the court will examine the conduct of the Requesting State and the circumstances giving rise to the underlying criminal allegation. *R v Governor of Pentonville Prison, ex p Chinoy*[2] is an example of such a category of allegation (alleged reliance upon evidence unlawfully obtained in a third State). Moreover, the principles upon which the Court will act pursuant to an abuse of process application are likely to be materially identical to those which previously applied under s 11(3)(c) of the 1989 Act, and the case law outlined above at paragraphs **8.30–8.32** remains of considerable importance in establishing the relevant benchmark.

1 *Symeou* (above at **8.67**).
2 Discussed above at para **8.82**.

8.122 Facts giving rise to a proper inference of ulterior intent are to be found in the provisional[1] findings of the Court of Appeal in *R (Raissi) v Secretary of State for the Home Department.*[2] It was here held[3] that extradition proceedings had been used for an ulterior purpose, namely to secure the defendant's detention in custody on trivial charges to allow time for the US authorities to gather or provide evidence of another more serious offence, or alternatively, to secure the defendant's presence in the US for the purpose of investigating that more serious offence. The initial intention of the US authorities was that the UK police should make some preliminary discreet enquiries about the appellant, without arresting him. However, within a short time, the appellant had been arrested by the UK domestic authorities on suspicion of terrorism, involvement in 9/11. During the seven-day period for which he could lawfully be held without charge, a case for extradition was put together by the US authorities and sent to London. Following questioning by the UK authorities, the appellant was 'de-arrested' and immediately re-arrested on a provisional extradition warrant where the charges (making false statements to obtain a pilot's licence) were of a trivial nature and were only obliquely capable of being related to any act of terrorism. The US government sought a remand in custody on the ground that the appellant would be charged with an offence of terrorism connected with 9/11, the present charges being merely 'holding charges'. The appellant spent over four months in custody until he was discharged in respect of the minor charges (no prima facie case having been established) and no alternative terrorism charges having materialised. In an application for judicial review of a refusal of ex gratia compensation, the appellant contended that the extradition charges which he faced were a device to enable him to be detained in custody whilst the US authorities investigated whether he was involved in 9/11. They were trivial and, of themselves, would never have warranted extradition proceedings or detention in custody. The appellant contended that his detention on trivial extradition charges was a breach of Art 5 of the ECHR and a device to get round the law of this country which prevented him from being held without charge as a suspect for terrorism offences for more than seven days (as the law then stood). As such, it was an abuse of the process of the court. It was finally submitted that the extradition proceedings were also a device to enable the US authorities to bring the appellant back to the US for intelligence-gathering purposes.

1 Provisional because the Court proceeded without receiving counter-evidence from the US government and because the case was decided in the context of an ex gratia compensation application.
2 Above para **8.106**.
3 At paras 139–146.

8.123 The Court of Appeal held[1] that:

> 'it appears … likely that the extradition proceedings were used for an ulterior purpose, namely to secure the appellant's detention in custody in order to allow time for the US authorities to provide evidence of a terrorist offence. It should be noted that it would have been unlawful for the UK police to detain the appellant any longer [than 7 days] without evidence to justify a charge; such evidence did not exist … We think it almost inconceivable that the US authorities would have bothered to bring extradition proceedings

on the charges alleged. We note as a matter of interest that the charges had not been brought by the grand jury when the extradition proceedings were begun. The grand jury made its decisions on 27 November, the very day on which the extradition case had to be presented in the UK court. It looks very much as though events in London were driving events in Arizona. In addition, if the quotation from the Washington Post be accurate, it would appear that at least part of the motive of the US Government behind the extradition proceedings was not to secure the appellant's attendance at a trial of the non-disclosure offences but to secure his presence in the US for the purposes of questioning about 9/11. We do not for a moment doubt the honesty of the belief of either the US Government or the CPS as to need to investigate the appellant's possible involvement in 9/11 and we fully recognise the heightened emotional atmosphere of late 2001. But having said that, it seems to us that the extradition proceedings themselves were a device to secure the appellant's presence in the US for the purpose of investigating 9/11 rather than for the purpose of putting him on trial for non-disclosure offences … The proceedings were used as a device to circumvent the rule of English law that a terrorist suspect could (at that time) be held without charge for only 7 days.'

1 At para 144.

8.124 By contrast, in *Knowles v Government of the United States of America,*[1] following the defeat of an extradition request based upon one Grand Jury indictment, the US government deployed a second extradition request based upon an earlier Grand Jury indictment relating to earlier events. It was argued that the US government had deliberately held the second indictment/request back and its conduct constituted an abuse of process. Lord Bingham observed[2] that:

> 'The appellant faces an uphill task in seeking to dislodge the conclusion of three courts below that the Government's conduct in proceeding on the second extradition request was not abusive. The Board would be very slow to intervene in the absence of a clear legal misdirection, and it finds none … it is, within broad limits, for a prosecutor to decide what charges he will prefer, and how he will frame his charges. In the absence of unfairness or oppression, this is not a matter for the Requested State and not a matter which calls for explanation. Since the appellant did not know of the first grand jury indictment, he was not misled by the Government's initial decision not to rely on it and it cannot be said that the Government made any implied representation to him'.

1 Above para **8.04**.
2 At para 25.

8.125 In *Tonge & Yarrow v Public Prosecutor's Office of Appeal, Crete,*[1] the appellants contended that their flight from Greece had been the result of ill-treatment having occurred while they were in custody in Crete (about which they complained at the time). The alleged ill-treatment was held not to be sufficient to meet the test of showing that there were material grounds for believing that there was a real risk of ECHR, Art 3 ill-treatment of these two appellants if either of them were returned to Greece. Nor did the evidence establish that psychological or psychiatric harm would result in either appellant being extradited to a place where they may have been ill-treated in the past. In those circumstances, in respect of an alternative submission that the alleged ill-treatment in the past rendered their return to Greece an abuse of process, Keene LJ ruled[2] that:

> 'I cannot see that the extradition of these two appellants would amount to an abuse of process. They have not been identified or arrested because of such ill-treatment. Nor does it seem that their availability now to be returned to Greece to stand trial has been the result of anything that can amount to an abuse of process. However regrettable any such ill- treatment that occurred may have been, I cannot see that it gives rise to any potential breach of their Article 5(4) rights if extradition is now ordered'.

1 [2006] EWHC 3388 (Admin).
2 At para 20.

8.126 In *Bulgaria v Atanasova-Kalaidzhieva*,[1] the High court had previously refused to extradite the suspect because it had concluded that the prosecutor had been acting in bad faith and that the investigation into the alleged offence had been tainted. Requests for further information from the Requesting State had been ignored. The issue of a second warrant was, therefore, an abuse of process in the absence of any reassurance that the prosecution was being conducted in good faith or that a fair trial was now possible. Pitchford LJ noted that the Bulgarian court owed to the UK court a mutual obligation of respect but had ignored the court's concerns.[2]

1 [2011] EWHC 2335 (Admin).
2 At paras 35–36.

8.127 As regards entrapment, *Okandeji v The Government of the Commonwealth of Australia*,[1] *Jenkins v Government of the United States of America*,[2] *Stepp v Government of the United States of America*,[3] *R (Ahsan) v Director of Public Prosecutions & another*,[4] and *Tappin v Government of the United States of America*,[5] are all examples of allegations of the underlying criminal allegation being tainted by abusive entrapment; all being considered but failing on their merits. In this area, perhaps above all others, the weight of the cross-jurisdictional nature of extradition proceedings is most profoundly felt. In *Somchai Liangsiriprasert v Government of the United States of America*,[6] a drug dealer was persuaded by a US drug enforcement agent to travel from Thailand to Hong Kong in order to receive payment for drugs exported from Thailand to the US. There was no extradition between the two countries for drug offences. On arrival in Hong Kong, the applicant was arrested and proceedings for his extradition to the US were commenced. He submitted, inter alia, that it would be oppressive and an abuse of process for a government agency to entice a criminal to a jurisdiction from which extradition was available. In answer to this submission, Lord Griffiths said:[7]

> 'As to the suggestion that it was oppressive or an abuse of process, the short answer is that international crime has to be fought by international co-operation between law enforcement agencies. It is notoriously difficult to apprehend those at the centre of the drug trade; it is only their couriers

who are usually caught. If the courts were to regard the penetration of a drug-dealing organisation by the agents of a law enforcement agency and a plan to tempt the criminals into a jurisdiction from which they could be extradited as an abuse of process it would indeed be a red letter day for the drug barons … In the present case the applicant and S.C. came to Hong Kong of their own free will to collect, as they thought, the illicit profits of their heroin trade. They were present in Hong Kong not because of any unlawful conduct of the authorities but because of their own criminality and greed. The proper extradition procedures have been observed and their Lordships reject without hesitation that it is in the circumstances of this case oppressive or an abuse of the judicial process for the United States to seek their extradition'.

1 Above para **8.36**.
2 Above para **8.52**.
3 [2006] EWHC 1033 (Admin).
4 Above para **8.08** at paras 109–126.
5 [2012] EWHC 22 (Admin).
6 Above para **8.111**.
7 At 242–243.

8.128 Subject to those matters discussed below at paragraphs **8.131–8.132**, and a defendant being able to positively demonstrate that the evidence,[1] or description of conduct,[2] provided by the Requesting State is deliberately false or exaggerated, it is not open to a defendant to argue abuse based upon the strength, or perceived strength, of evidence against him or co-defendants, in the underlying criminal proceedings in the Requesting State.[3] In *Kashamu (No 2)*,[4] Rose LJ observed[5] that 'extradition contemplates trial in another jurisdiction according to the law there. It is there that questions of admissibility, adequacy of evidence and fairness of the trial itself will be addressed'. In *Jaso*,[6] the appellants were arrested upon a European Arrest warrant alleging membership of 'Urederra', a cell of ETA. It was submitted that a recent comprehensive investigation of *Urederra* membership had been carried out by another investigating magistrate which made no mention of the appellants. It was, therefore, submitted that there existed cause for suspecting that abuse of process may have occurred and the decision to issue the EAWs had been taken in bad faith. The High Court held[7] that:

'The allegation of bad faith against the Spanish authorities is very serious. It amounts to saying that the prosecution is being brought by the authorities knowing that the case against the appellants is without foundation. In my judgment, the appellants have fallen far short of establishing even a *prima facie* case of bad faith … it was no part of the function of the district judge to examine the evidential basis for the issue of the EAWs, still less to reach any conclusion as to whether the prosecutions have any prospect of success. To require her to do this would be to undermine the trust in the integrity and fairness of the judicial institutions of member states to which I have earlier referred. Under the guise of an abuse of process argument, that is precisely what the appellants are seeking to do …In any event, the case against the appellants of membership of ETA does not wholly depend on showing that they were members of the *Urederra* …Thus, even if it were appropriate for the district judge to consider whether the appellants were members of *Urederra* and she decided that there was no evidence of such membership, that would not raise a prima facie case of abuse of process'.

1 *United States of America v Vreeland* (2002) 164 CCC (3d) 266 (Ont SC); there exists jurisdiction to consider whether the State requesting extradition has knowingly presented false or fabricated evidence to the court of the Requested State. In a procedural ruling given in *Government of the United States of America v Tollman* (above para **8.62**) dated 1 June 2006, the matter was put this way per Malloy J at paras 65 & 70: '… the court should be particularly sedulous to ensure that the abuse of process application is not merely being used to obtain disclosure of, or to attack the weight of, the evidence in support of the charges underlying the extradition. Otherwise, there is a risk that extradition proceedings will become mired in procedural motions for disclosure of the evidence in the hands of the foreign authorities, brought in the guise of abuse of process proceedings. This is not to say that the allegations that the evidence against an individual is untrue can never be made in an abuse of process proceeding. However, the allegations must go further than attacking the truth or reliability of the evidence; it will be necessary to show additional evidence of wrongdoing by the foreign authority, over and above an attack on the accuracy of the evidence in the Record of Case. Evidence that the foreign authorities knew the evidence in the Record of Case was untrue at the time of certification is, however, capable of supporting a finding of abuse of process … prosecutorial bad faith in misrepresenting facts to the court. A finding of abuse of process by prosecutorial misconduct will only be made in the clearest of circumstances. Singling out an inaccuracy or exaggeration of one small part of the evidence stated in a case of this nature is not, in my view, sufficient to give rise to a remedy for abuse of process'.

2 *Castillo v The Kingdom of Spain* (above at para **8.32**).

3 *R (Hilali) v Governor of Whitemoor Prison & another* (above para **8.56**) per Lord Hope of Craighead at paras 23–24.

4 Above para **8.50**.

5 At para 33.

6 Above para **8.08**.

7 Dyson LJ at paras 73–74.

8.129 Neither is it, in principle, abusive for a Requesting State to continue with an extradition request in the face of acquittal of the principal defendant.[1]

1 *R (Hilali) v Governor of Whitemoor Prison & another* (above para **8.56**) per Lord Hope of Craighead at paras 23–24.

8.130 However, it was a clear and profound abuse of process when the prosecutor behind the extradition request was patently not conducting the investigation. In *Ukraine v Kononko*,[1] Ukraine had instructed private solicitors to act to pursue 'enormous sums'[2] resulting from the defrauding of a bank in Kazakhstan. The bank had lost so much money that it had be nationalised as a result. Ukrainian lawyers acting for the bank sought criminal prosecutions and to recover the money. Ukrainian law did not permit private prosecutions paid for by the bank or Republic of Kazakhstan. The suggestion in this case was that the Ukrainian prosecutor's office (who had initially instructed City solicitors for the extradition) was being used by the bank to effect this extradition. The District Judge had accepted that extradition would lead to a breach of Art 3 (appalling prison conditions) and Art 6, but had not accepted the abuse of process argument. Further information had then been uncovered which confirmed communications between the Ukrainian prosecutor and the legal team acting for the Government of Kazakhstan.[3] The District Judge had not been aware of this material. Letters had also been written by the prosecutor's office to a journalist denying the Government had sought the assistance of Ukrainian lawyers or instructed a city firm in relation to the extradition. Collins

J concluded that this was clearly untrue and that it was 'fatal so far as the abuse of process argument is concerned'.[4] The judge noted that 'it is said – and there is strong evidence to support this – that, effectively, the prosecution in this case is indeed being paid for by Ilyashev [the Ukrainian law firm], no doubt funded by the Republic of Kazakhstan or the bank that is left in Kazakhstan'.[5] The court concluded that there was clear evidence of an abuse of process, including evidence that the prosecutor behind the extradition request had not conducted the investigation.

1 [2014] EWHC 1420 (Admin).
2 At para 4.
3 At paras 11 and 18.
4 At para 27.
5 At para 7.

Non-disclosure as evidence of bad faith

8.131 It is now fairly well established that, although a defendant cannot compel a Requesting State to make disclosure, if he is otherwise able to gain access to documentation that demonstrates material non-disclosure on the part of the Requesting State, then that may, depending upon the nature of the non-disclosure, constitute, of itself, evidence of bad faith or abuse.[1] In *R v Governor of Brixton Prison, ex p Kashamu (No 1)*,[2] the government of the US conceded that disclosure should have been made in respect of evidence to the effect that the witness, upon whom the government's case rested had attended an identification procedure and failed to identify Mr Kashamu from a photograph line-up (in fact he had picked out a volunteer). No reference was made to this fact in any of the material provided by the US government in support of its extradition request. The US government accepted that the effect of the failure had been to vitiate the committal and render it void. Application for habeas corpus was, accordingly granted. Pill LJ was prepared to categorise the failure to supply the material as:

> '... a misjudgement of the extent of the legal requirement of disclosure in an extradition request ... the decision of the magistrate had been taken in ignorance of crucial information, and the failure to supply that information to the magistrate might have resulted in injustice to the defendant[3] ... It had a fundamental effect on the proceedings before the magistrate ... the proceedings before the magistrate were unfair'.[3]

1 For recent examples of this type of abuse see *Chawla v India* [2020] EWHC 102 (Admin); *Kapoor v India* [2015] EWHC 1378 (Admin).
2 Above para **8.50**.
3 At paras 23, 26. See also *The Attorney General of the Bahamas v Kozeny*, Cais no.92 of 2007 where the Bahamas Court of Appeal held that the duty of good faith underlying extradition requires disclosure in a timely fashion (at para 51).

8.132 In *R (Kashamu) v Governor of Brixton Prison No 2)*,[1] Pitchford J referred[2] to the facts of *ex p Kashamu (No 1)* as an example of the newly-established narrow abuse definition:[3] '... the claimant had been deprived of the opportunity of addressing the district judge upon all the material which should have been before him'. In *R (Saifi) v Governor of Brixton Prison*,[4]

Rose LJ placed significant reliance upon non-disclosure in the context of a finding of bad faith under s 11(3)(c) of the 1989 Act[5]. In *Bermingham,*[6] it was acknowledged by Laws LJ that a tenable case of abuse might lie if a defendant can show that a prosecutor 'knew he had no real case, but was pressing the extradition request for some collateral motive and accordingly tailored the choice of documents accompanying the request'.[7] Thus, it has been repeatedly recognised that a Requesting State has an underlying duty of candour in making requests for extradition.[8] The same principle applies to cases where the obligation to provide a prima facie case is abrogated. If a defendant is able, independently, to show deliberate exaggeration of the description of conduct, that is capable of evidencing bad faith.[9] Similarly, misinformation given to the court is capable of constituting an abuse of process.[10]

1 Above para **8.50**.
2 At para 39.
3 Set out at paras 37–38.
4 Above para **8.30.**
5 '... this non-disclosure [of the circumstances surrounding the confession made by Ali Sheikh] on such a central feature of the case has not been explained. It is to be inferred that it was deliberate and calculated to leave those considering the case with the impression that it was stronger than the true facts merited' at para 64(3).
6 Above para **8.35**.
7 At paras 98 and 100, set out above at para **8.67**.
8 *Wellington v Governor of HMP Belmarsh* (above para **8.42**) per Mitting J at para 26. In *Jenkins v Government of the United States of America* (above para **8.52**), Sedley LJ observed (at para 29) that 'there is a general duty on a Requesting State to be candid about vitiating factors in its case ... If the defence is able independently to establish a case of breach of the accused's Convention rights, the court must of course entertain it'. In *Knowles v Government of the United States of America* (above para **8.04**), Lord Bingham of Cornhill observed (at para 35), that a Requesting State 'does ... owe the court of the Requested State a duty of candour and good faith. While it is for the Requesting State to decide what evidence it will rely on to seek a committal, it must in pursuance of that duty disclose evidence which destroys or very severely undermines the evidence on which it relies. It is for the party seeking to resist an order to establish a breach of duty by the Requesting State. The Board would endorse the general approach laid down by Mitting J (sitting with Lord Woolf CJ in the Divisional Court) in *Wellington* "... In the present case the appellant has failed to discharge the burden lying on him ...".' For a more recent application of this duty, see *Bartulis v Panevezys Regional Court (Lithuania)* [2019] EWHC 3504 (Admin), at paras 131–133.
9 See *Castillo v Kingdom of Spain* (above para **8.32**) per Thomas LJ at para 25 and 37–44: 'a description of the conduct in the request which was deliberately exaggerated would form part of the accusation for the purposes of determining whether or not the accusation had been made in good faith ... given the fact there is no enquiry into evidential sufficiency, it is of the utmost importance that the description of conduct alleged is framed with the greatest care; it is an essential protection to the person whose extradition is sought'.
10 *Konuksever v The government of Turkey* [2012] EWHC 2166 (Admin) per Irwin J at paras 62–63.

Prescribed particulars in the warrant are incorrect

8.133 In *Zakrzewski v The Regional Court in Lodz, Poland,*[1] the Supreme Court established that extradition could be refused even where there was no mala fides. However, this will occur only in exceptional and very specific circumstances. Mr Zakrzewski had been arrested under a conviction warrant for four sentences totalling 45 months. Before the extradition hearing, on application from Zakrzewski, a Polish court aggregated the sentences, imposing a cumulative prison sentence of 22 months. The Supreme Court considered whether this change invalidated the EAW on the grounds that it no longer gave the particulars required by s 2(6)(e) of the Extradition Act 2003 or reflected the operative sentence (ie the aggregated sentence).[2] The district judge rejected this argument but the High Court had found that a EAW must relate to the 'current operative sentence'.

1 [2013] UKSC 2.
2 The purpose of s 2(6)(e) is to enable the court to confirm that the sentence constitutes an extradition offence.

8.134 Before the Supreme Court, Lord Sumption acknowledged that the court could correct particulars that became incorrect when deciding whether to extradite and that, in this context, there were two safeguards against unjustified extradition. The 'first and main one is the mutual trust between States party to the Framework Decision that informs the entire scheme'[1] and:

> 'The second safeguard lies in the inherent right of an English court, as the executing court, to ensure that its process is not abused. One form of abuse of process is the fortunately rare case in which the prosecutor has manipulated the process of the executing court for a collateral and improper purpose: see *R (Government of the United States of America) v Bow Street Magistrates' Court* [2007] 1 WLR 1157. We are not concerned with anything of that kind on this appeal. Another category comprises cases, rather less rare, in which the prescribed particulars are given in the warrant but they are wrong. In *Caldarelli v Judge for Preliminary Investigations of the Court of Naples, Italy* [2008] 1 WLR 1724, para 24, Lord Bingham observed that "it might in some circumstances be necessary to question statements made in the EAW", notwithstanding the general rule. The question is in what circumstances is the power envisaged by Lord Bingham exercisable.'[2]

1 [2013] UKSC 2 at para 10.
2 At para 11.

8.135 Lord Sumption considered the case of *Criminal Court at the National High Court, First Division v Murua*[1] and noted that it would be inconsistent with the statutory scheme to refuse to act on a warrant which included the prescribed particulars, merely because those particulars contained immaterial errors. Consequently, there are strict limits on the power to find abuse in such circumstances where the process had not been manipulated. Lord Sumption set out the following criteria:

> 'The first is that the jurisdiction is exceptional. The statements in the warrant must comprise statutory particulars which are wrong or incomplete in some respect which is misleading (though not necessarily intentionally). Secondly, the true facts required to correct the error or omission must be clear and beyond legitimate dispute. The power of the court to prevent abuse of its process must be exercised in the light of the purposes of that process. In extradition cases, it must have regard, as Sir Anthony May observed, to the scheme and purpose of the legislation. It is not therefore to be used as an indirect way of mounting a contentious challenge to the factual or evidential basis for the conduct alleged in the warrant, this being a matter

for the requesting court. Third, the error or omission must be material to the operation of the statutory scheme. No doubt errors in some particulars (such as the identity of the defendant or the offence charged) would by their very nature be material. In other cases, the materiality of the error will depend on its impact on the decision whether or not to order extradition. The fourth observation follows from the third. In my view, Ms Cumberland was right to submit to Sir Anthony May in Murua that the sole juridical basis for the inquiry into the accuracy of the particulars in the warrant is abuse of process. I do not think that it goes to the validity of the warrant. This is because in considering whether to refuse extradition on the ground of abuse of process, the materiality of the error in the warrant will be of critical importance, whereas if the error goes to the validity of the warrant, no question of materiality can arise. An invalid warrant is incapable of initiating extradition proceedings. I do not think that it is consistent with the scheme of the Framework Decision to refuse to act on a warrant in which the prescribed particulars were included, merely because those particulars contain immaterial errors.'[2]

1 [2010] EWHC 2609 (Admin).
2 At para 13.

8.136 On the facts of this case, the 'error' in the warrant was not material to the statutory scheme. Whilst, the particulars of sentence were no longer complete, they were not wrong.[1] The fact that the imprisonment period, which would satisfy the four original sentences, was shortened was immaterial, because even the shorter sentences were longer than the minimum of 4 months required to be an extradition offence under the Act.[2] Lord Sumption noted that 'the sentence of the court will rarely be the 'current operative sentence', since the period to be served will commonly be affected by a variety of factors such as remission or parole'.[3] The EAW had, therefore, been withdrawn by the court. Lord Sumption's approach has since been applied in a series of subsequent cases.[4]

It is important to note, however, that since *Zakrzewski* there has been considerable judicial reconsideration on the circumstances in which a Judicial Authority can supplement an otherwise deficient warrant with additional information, which is likely to limit further the circumstances in which the *Zakrzewski* style abuse may exist. In *Goluchowski v District Court in Elblag,* Poland,[5] Lord Mance cast doubt upon Lord Sumption's position in *Zakrewski* that information in the warrant should be taken at face value. Lord Mance had in mind the then recent decision of the CJEU in *archetul de pe lângă Curtea de Apel Cluj v Bob-Dogi*[6] and concluded[7] that 'under European Union law that, if information obtained under article 15 subsequently to the EAW shows that a European arrest warrant was in fact based on an 'enforceable judgment' or equivalent judicial decision, even though this was not fully or accurately 'evidenced' on its face, the EAW will be valid and enforceable. On the other hand, if subsequently obtained information undermines in a fundamental respect a statement in an EAW which on its face evidences an enforceable judgment or equivalent judicial decision, it could not be right to give effect to the EAW 'willy-nilly'. The position was affirmed and clarified further in *Alexander v The*

Public Prosecutor's Office, Marseille District Court of First Instance, France,[8] in which the Court confirmed that it was open to a Requesting Judicial Authority to supplement a deficient European arrest warrant with missing information so as to establish the validity of the warrant, albeit 'The system of mutual respect and cooperation between states does not mean that the English Court should set about requesting all the required information in the face of a wholly deficient warrant'.[9] This is not to say that the abuse envisaged in Zakrzewski could no longer exist at all, but simply that its application is likely to be further confined. This was demonstrated recently in *Podolak v Poland*,[10] where the Court found, in the circumstances and applying *Alexander*, that the District Judge had been right to admit evidence that the limitation period in issue had been extended[11] before concluding that 'the application by the Respondent to admit evidence of the extension of the limitation period cannot plausibly be characterised as something that undermines any purpose or principle on which the provisions of Part I of the 2003 Act rests' and as such the Appellant's abuse of process argument failed. In so concluding, Swift J observed:[12]

> 'Given the approach now taken to section 2 cases and the relevance of supplementary information following the judgment of the Divisional Court in *Alexander*, it is at least arguable that the part of the abuse process jurisdiction relied on by Lord Sumption in that case [*Zakrzewski*] (see paragraph 11 at C-D) has been rendered redundant. However, on the assumption it has not, I do not consider that it affords this Appellant any assistance. The change of circumstances from the statement in the warrant about the limitation period to the information about the extension admitted into evidence by the District Judge does not disclose any matter that is material so as to render the extradition request abusive. Because the Appellant had absconded, events moved on. The decision to extend the limitation period was, no doubt, premised at least in part, on the Appellant's absconding from the extradition process in 2014 and 2015.'

1 At para 14. Under Polish law, the original sentences remained valid but the cumulative one determined what period of imprisonment would be treated as satisfying them. Note also the comments in *Karaqi (aka Fejzullahu) v Public Prosecutor's Office of the Athens' Court of Appeal, Greece* [2020] EWHC 2650 (Admin) at para 58, that if, contrary to the position of the Judicial Authority, the District Judge found the sentence for which surrender under an EAW was sought had become unenforceable, that could amount to an abuse of process.

2 At para 15.

3 At para 16.

4 See *Arranz v Spanish Judicial Authority* [2013] EWHC 1662 (Admin) ([2013] ACD 324); *Dabrowski v Regional Court in Lublin, Poland; District Court in Zamosc, Poland* [2013] EWHC 1469 (Admin); *Marzurkiewicz v District Court In Rzeszow, Poland* [2013] EWHC 1332 (Admin); *Artola v The 6th Section of the National High Court of Madrid, Spain* [2013] EWHC 524 (Admin); *Bicioc v Baia Mare Local Court Romania* [2014] EWHC 628 (Admin); *King v France* [2015] EWHC 3670 (Admin); *Goluchowski v District Court in Elblag, Poland* [2016] UKSC 36, at paras 37, 48, 50–52; *Cretu v Romania* [2016] EWHC 353 (Admin), at para 53–54; *Romania v Sovaiala* [2016] EWHC 1489 (Admin); *Stedman v France* [2017] EWHC 2673 (Admin) at para 65; *Sulaiman v France* [2017] Lloyd's Rep FC 111; *Imre v District Court in Szolnok (Hungary)* [2018] EWHC 218 (Admin); *Lewicki v Italy* [2018] EWHC 1160 (Admin).

5 See *Goluchowski v District Court in Elblag, Poland* [2016] UKSC 36, at paras 37–38 and *Zakrzewski* at para 8.

6 (Case C-241/15.)

7 *Goluchowski* at para 40. See also Lord Neuberger at paras 50–52.

8 [2017] EWHC 1392 (Admin), at paras 73–74.
9 At para 75.
10 [2020] EWHC 2830 (Admin).
11 At paras 20–21.
12 At para 27.

EXTRADITION OFFENCE

Actions of a third-party state

8.137 In an unusual case, which may be confined to its particular facts, the actions of a third-party state were sufficient to cause an extradition request to be considered abusive, event absent any bad faith or ulterior motive on part of the UK authorities or the Requesting State. In *R (Ristea) v Italy*,[1] the Requested Person had been convicted in Italy in his absence in 2011 and sentenced to nine years' imprisonment. Later in 2011, he was convicted in Romania of a separate offence and sentenced there to a period of seven years' imprisonment. The Requested Person applied to the Bucharest Tribunal to transfer the sentence he was required to serve in Italy, and a 20-month sentence from Germany, under the procedure set out in the 2008 Framework Decision 2008/909HJA. A Romanian Court accepted his request and considered that the sentences met the criteria for being merged. That Court therefore determined to impose a concurrent sentence of nine years' imprisonment, from which it deducted the various periods of time spent on remand. The Requested Person served just under three-quarters of that time before being conditionally released by Romania in December 2016, after which time he travelled to the UK. He was then arrested a year later, in December 2017, pursuant to an EAW issued by Italy. The EAW specified that the sentence 'is still valid and takes effect with reference to the term of imprisonment of nine years as Italy has never requested or in any way authorised the recognition of the aforementioned judgment and such recognition took place outside the scope of community law as laid down in [the 2008 Framework Decision] (implemented in Italy by legislative decree 161/20010)'.[2] Italy's position was that Romania had not properly complied with the 2008 Framework Decision; the Appellant's position was obviously that he had served the time required by the sentence. There was no suggestion of bad faith by any party. On whether extradition in these circumstances amounted to an abuse of process, Laing J held:

> '64. That leads me to the second ground of appeal, which is the abuse of process argument. I consider that it is regrettable, if indeed it is the case, that the Romanian Court did not comply with the 2008 Framework Decision and that it, nonetheless, purported to merge the sentences and to impose upon the appellant a longer sentence than the sentence which he would have had to serve in respect of the crime which he had committed in Romania. It is not for me to say whether or not the sentence which was imposed by the Romanian Court and the Romanian Court's decision to permit that the sentences should run concurrently or indeed the Romanian Court's decision to release conditionally after serving 74 per cent of the sentence was right. That is a matter for the Romanian court, but it has left the appellant in the position where, as far as he was concerned, at his request, the Bucharest

Tribunal purported to, or in fact did, merge the sentences and ordered him to serve a longer sentence than he would have had to serve in respect of the Romanian offence only, a sentence which he has served subject to conditional released.

65. I consider that, on the particular facts of this case, it would be an abuse of the extradition processes for the appellant now to be extradited to Italy to serve the nine-year sentence and for him to be, required to negotiate with the Italian authorities as to how much of that sentence he has served, in circumstances where he thought, acting in accordance with Romanian law, that he had already served the sentence in Romania. For those reasons, I consider that the second ground of appeal succeeds'.[3]

This decision seems to be in tension with the explicit statements in earlier authorities that the Requesting State itself is acting in a way which impugns the integrity of the extradition process.[4]

1 [2018] EWHC 1876 (Admin)
2 At para 17.
3 At paras 64–65.
4 See, e.g. *Camaras* (above at **8.71**) at para 27 and *Malarz* (also above at **8.71**), where, at para 54, Simon LJ confirmed 'Mistakes made in extradition proceedings may invalidate them but mistakes as such are not abuses of the process, not even egregious mistakes, unless the abuse undermines the very nature of the extradition jurisdiction. The court will only exercise the jurisdiction to stay the extradition proceedings as abuse of process if satisfied on (a) cogent evidence that (b) the requesting authority has acted in a way that subverts or impugns (the word "usurped" is sometimes used) the integrity of the domestic process, acting in breach of the mutual trust that exists between Judicial Authorities'.

'STAGE 3': WHETHER THERE ARE REASONABLE GROUNDS FOR BELIEVING THAT SUCH CONDUCT MAY HAVE OCCURRED

8.138 No steps should be taken to investigate an alleged abuse of process unless the judge is satisfied that there is reason to believe that an abuse may have taken place.[1] As regards 'stage 3', Canadian case law makes it clear that this stage requires the court to be satisfied that the appellant's evidence possesses an 'air of reality'.[2] In *Larosa v Her Majesty The Queen,*[3] Doherty JA observed[4] that '... [t]he appellant bears the burden of demonstrating the "air of reality" and may do so by reference to the appeal record or to evidence, normally by way of affidavit, tendered in support ... A bald assertion in the notice of motion will not suffice to trigger the evidentiary inquiry sought by the appellant'. Doherty further observed[5] that:

'In order to ask the court to delve into the circumstances surrounding the exercise of the Crown's discretion, or to inquire into the motivation of the Crown officers responsible for advising the Attorney-General, the accused bears the burden of making a tenable allegation of *mala fides* on the part of the Crown. Such an allegation must be supportable by the record before the court, or if the record is lacking or insufficient, by an offer of proof. Without such an allegation, the court is entitled to assume what is inherent in the process, that the Crown exercised its discretion properly, and not for improper or arbitrary motives. [T]he allegation of improper or arbitrary motives cannot be an irresponsible allegation made solely for the purpose of initiating a "fishing expedition" in the hope that something of value will accrue to the defence'.[6]

1 *R (Government of the United States of America) v Bow Street Magistrates' Court* (above para **8.11**) per Lord Phillips CJ at para 84). In *Bziom v Poland* [2013] EWHC 2587 (Admin), Ouseley J at paras 15–21 confirmed that a District judge was entitled to reject allegations as incapable of belief. At para 15, he continued: 'If, however, the way in which he came to that conclusion had prevented the appellant giving evidence, or made it obviously pointless to do so as the judge's mind was made up, or so discouraged [counsel] from calling him that no proper professional judgment could be exercised, there might be an arguable case that that had been unfair'.

2 *Larosa v Her Majesty The Queen* (above para **8.60**) per Doherty JA at paras 76 and 78–81. See also *United States of America v Kwok* (above para **8.62**) at para 88).

3 Above para **8.60**.

4 At paras 81 and 85.

5 At para 795.

6 In the *United States v Freimuth* (2004) 183 CCC (3d) 296 (BCSC), Romilly J said (at para 56) that: 'Allegations of misconduct by foreign authorities should not be given any credence without further proof. In the absence of such evidence, entertaining allegations that foreign officials are misleading our Courts conveys a reflection of the gravest possible kind, not only upon the motives and actions of the responsible government, but also impliedly upon the judicial authorities of a neighbouring and friendly power.'

8.139

'The function of the "air of reality" test is two-fold. First, it provides a mechanism to weed out frivolous applications before incurring the expense and delay of a lengthy evidentiary hearing. Second, it imposes a threshold of plausibility before the applicant will be entitled to relief such as production of documents, particulars, or the compelling of viva voce testimony. The level of plausibility required to survive the air of reality test is somewhat amorphous. Typically, when cases are dismissed as having no air of reality, the allegations can fairly be described as ludicrous or preposterous. However, in my opinion, the actual test is, and must be, higher than that. Obviously, at this point, the applicant cannot be expected to reach the standard of proof on a balance of probabilities, as this is the ultimate standard to be applied at the abuse of process hearing itself. However, it is not enough for the applicant to show that his allegations are not ridiculous; he must be able to show some reasonable prospect of success on the application. The Ontario Court of Appeal's decision in *Larosa* contains the best working definition of the test I have found, namely that the applicant must demonstrate "some realistic possibility that the allegations can be substantiated".'[1]

1 *United States of America v Tollman (procedural ruling)* (above para **8.128**) per Malloy J at para 21.

No right to disclosure at stage 3

8.140 It has long been recognised that a significant, and often insurmountable, practical hurdle in the way of mounting abuse submissions in extradition proceedings will be the absence of any disclosure from the Requesting State. Donovan LJ recognised the difficulty of this task in *R v Brixton Prison (Governor), ex parte Soblen*:[1]

'The task of the subject who seeks to establish such an allegation as this is indeed heavy. On the face of it, the [deportation] order which he wished the court to quash will look perfectly valid on its face, and to get behind it and to demonstrate its alleged true character he will need to have revealed to him the communications, oral and written, which have passed between the home and the foreign authorities. But if the appropriate minister here certifies, as he has done in this case, that such disclosure will be contrary to the public interest, then, as a rule, the subject will not obtain it. He will be left to do his best without such assistance, and in the nature of things, therefore, he will seldom be able to raise a prima facie case, or alternatively to sow such substantial and disquieting doubts in the minds of the court as to the bona fides of the order he is challenging that the court will consider that some answer is called for. If that answer is withheld, or being furnished is found unsatisfactory, then in my view, the order challenged ought not to be upheld, for otherwise there would be virtually no protection for the subject against the illegal order which had been clothed with the garments of legality simply for the sake of appearances and where discovery was resisted'.[2]

1 Above para **8.112**, at 307–308.

2 See, to similar effect, *Government of the United States of America v Tollman* (above para **8.62**) at para 22: 'The onus is on [a defendant] to establish his allegations of abuse. The applicable standard is the balance of probabilities, but abuse will only be found in the "clearest of cases" and the case law has repeatedly described this as a "heavy onus", particularly where prosecutorial misconduct is alleged. That said, it is virtually impossible for one person to prove by direct evidence the motive or intent behind the acts of another. In the absence of some direct evidence from the person whose conduct is challenged, the motivation behind that conduct must typically be inferred from the surrounding circumstances. The onus, however, remains on the person alleging the misconduct to prove the improper motivation.'

8.141 There was thus recognised two interlinked principles by the Court of Appeal:

(1) A person resisting extradition has no right to seek disclosure so as to assist in his establishing a prima facie case of abuse (now stage 3). But,

(2) If he can raise a prima facie case of abuse notwithstanding this (now stage 4 below), then the Court may expect an answer from the Requesting State and, if none is forthcoming or the answer is not satisfactory, then the order for extradition will not be upheld. With modification, that remains the position today.

The second principle is discussed below at paragraphs **8.150–8.152**. In respect of the first principle, in extradition proceedings, it had been held[1] that the Requesting State alone is the sole arbiter of such material as it chooses to place before the court. Neither principles of comity nor the express terms of the Act afford the court in this country any right – still less power – to request further material from the Requesting State as a condition precedent to committal.[2]

1 *R v Governor of Pentonville Prison, ex p Lee* [1993] 1 WLR 1294 at 1298 per Ognall J: 'It is important to remember that the conduct of extradition proceedings is entirely the creature of statute. This has a number of consequences… The Requesting State must be the sole arbiter of such material as it chooses to place before the court in support of its application and in purported compliance with the relevant domestic extradition legislation. It alone will decide what material in support of its allegations it places before the Secretary of State and the court under sections 7 and 9 of the Act of 1989. If it furnishes inadequate evidence, then it takes

the risk that its request will be refused, in which event it will be up to the Requesting State to determine whether it starts fresh proceedings or not.'

2 At p 1300 Ognall J further observed that: 'Provided that there has been compliance with the terms of the Extradition Act 1989, fairness is not a criterion relevant to the function of the committing court'. Therefore, an application to adjourn for the purposes of seeking documentation to throw doubt upon the credibility of accomplice evidence was refused.

8.142 *Ex parte Lee* was doubted by Pill LJ In *Kashamu (No 1).*[1] However, the Divisional Court revisited the issue in *Lodhi v Governor of Brixton Prison.*[2] Brooke LJ ruled that *ex parte Lee* is 'clearly right … still good law'.[3] No duty of disclosure exists. And in *Serbeh v Governor of Brixton Prison,*[4] Kennedy LJ, with whom Pitchford J agreed, reviewed the above authorities[5] and concluded[6] that:

> 'I can find nothing in the authorities to support [the] proposition that even where, as here, there is not even a suspicion of bad faith the Requesting Country must now, as a result of the implementation of the Human Rights Act, make full disclosure of its prosecution case, and of any relevant unused material or be at risk of having the proceedings struck out as an abuse of process … In my judgment, as was made clear by Ognall J in *ex p Lee* and by the European Commission in *Kirkwood*, extradition proceedings are not to be equated with criminal proceedings before domestic courts. In extradition proceedings it is still for the Requesting State to decide what material it chooses to place before the Court … there is a fundamental assumption that the Requesting State is acting in good faith. If there is reason … to call that assumption into question, then the reason can be examined, and, if appropriate, acted upon, but there was and is no such reason in this case, and accordingly, in my judgment the complaints of non–disclosure and abuse of process are misconceived.'

1 Above para **8.50**, at paras 38–39.
2 Above para **8.30**.
3 At paras 108–115.
4 [2002] EWHC 2356 (QB).
5 At paras 31–38.
6 At paras 39–40.

8.143 In *Wellington v Governor of Her Majesty's Prison Belmarsh,*[1] Mitting J again reviewed the authorities[2] and summarised their effect[3] as follows: '(1) It is for the Requesting State alone to determine the evidence upon which it relies to seek a committal. (2) The Requesting State is not under any general duty of disclosure similar to that imposed on the prosecution at any stage in domestic criminal proceedings'. Having observed that a provable breach of a Requesting State's duty of candour may constitute an abuse,[4] Mitting J observed that: 'it is for the person subject to the extradition process to establish that the Requesting State is abusing the process of the court'.

1 Above para **8.42**.
2 At paras 15(5)(iii) and (7) and 20–25.
3 At para 26.
4 Above para **8.128**.

8.144 Under the 2003 Act, in *Jenkins,*[1] Sedley LJ approved[2] a concession made to the effect that no power to order disclosure exists. In *Bermingham,*[3] Laws LJ observed[4] that: 'The prosecutor cannot be penalised, under s 82, 87, or by any other route, for limiting the material he places before the court to what is required for the proper execution of the court's function under ss 78 ff. The observations of Ognall J in *Lee* … are in point'. In *R (Government of the United States of America) v Bow Street Magistrates' Court*,[5] Lord Phillips CJ reiterated[6] that there exists no power to order disclosure in extradition proceedings:

> 'Neither the rules governing disclosure in a civil action, nor those governing disclosure in a criminal trial can be applied to an extradition hearing. Furthermore, those rules form part of an adversarial process which differs from extradition proceedings. Where an order for disclosure is made, it requires one party to disclose documents to the other, not to the court. But where extradition is sought, the court is under a duty to satisfy itself that all the requirements for making the order are satisfied and that none of the bars to making the order exists … There is a further objection to ordering disclosure. The order will be made either against a judicial authority within the European Union or against a foreign Sovereign State that is requesting the Secretary of State to comply with treaty obligations. In neither case would it be appropriate to order discovery.'

1 Above para **8.52**.
2 At para 29.
3 Above para **8.35**.
4 At para 98.
5 Above para **8.11**.
6 At paras 85–86.

8.145 In *Knowles v Government of the United States of America,*[1] Lord Bingham of Cornhill reiterated[2] that it is for the party seeking to resist an order to establish a breach of duty (of candour to disclose evidence which destroys or very severely undermines the evidence on which it relies) by the Requesting State. In *R (Raissi) v Secretary of State for the Home Department,*[3] the Court of Appeal extended *Knowles* to apply to the Crown Prosecution Service (as agent for the Requesting State) 'a duty to disclose evidence about which it knows and which destroys or severely undermines the evidence on which the Requesting State relies',[4] but again recognised[5] that this duty of candour is not enforceable by means of order for disclosure.

1 Above para **8.04**.
2 At para 35.
3 Above para **8.96**.
4 The Court observed that this duty would also apply in the context of contested applications for bail.
5 Per Hooper LJ at paras 139–143.

8.146 In *Norris v Government of the United States of America,*[1] the House of Lords observed[2] that:

> 'The system of extradition under Part 2 of the 2003 Act does not require the Requesting State to provide details of the evidence (witnesses, documents etc) on which the prosecution would rely at trial. Nor does the district judge have any occasion to inquire into it. It is well settled that, consistently with that approach, in extradition proceedings the accused has no right to disclosure of the kind that would be available in domestic proceedings'.[3]

1 Above para **8.38**.
2 At para 107.
3 Approving *Wellington, Jenkins* and *R (Government of the United States of America) v Bow Street Magistrates' Court.*

'STAGE 4': THE JUDGE SHOULD NOT ACCEDE TO THE REQUEST FOR EXTRADITION UNLESS HE HAS SATISFIED HIMSELF THAT SUCH ABUSE HAS NOT OCCURRED

8.147 As regards 'stage 4', it is at this stage that the judge will conduct a full evidential enquiry. The defence will here be obliged to substantiate its allegations by evidence. The defence and Requesting State may call such evidence as they wish. Both sides are entitled to submit written evidence[1] in lieu of live evidence. In extradition proceedings, there exists no right to cross-examine the foreign prosecutor. The foreign State is permitted to file its evidence in the form required by the 2003 Act and cannot be forced to do otherwise. As a matter of reality, there may be cases where the person sought is able to establish an air of reality to his allegations, but where all of the direct evidence is within the knowledge of the foreign State authorities, and unfairness might arise where the person sought testifies under oath as to one version of facts and the Requesting State seeks to contradict that evidence by written evidence untested by cross-examination. The English and Canadian Courts, both recognising this problem, have addressed it in different ways. The Canadian Courts have held that the evidential abuse hearing held at this stage is not part of the extradition hearing and, therefore, carries with it the ability of the judge to order cross-examination of the foreign prosecutor.[2] However, in England, that approach is precluded by the ruling of Lord Phillips CJ in *R (Government of the United States of America) v Bow Street Magistrates' Court*[3] to the effect that a 'stage 4' hearing falls to be determined within the rubric of the extradition hearing. Therefore, in *Tollman (No 2)*,[4] Moses LJ observed[5] that, absent oral evidence, there is always the risk that the judge will credit the complaints made by those whom the opposing party has called live.

1 Properly authenticated under s 202.
2 *United States of America v Tollman (procedural ruling)* (above para **8.128**) per Malloy J at paras 30–35.
3 Above para **8.58**.
4 Above para **8.15**.
5 At para 100.

8.148 When abuse is raised for the first time in the appellate court (as in *Shulman*[1]), and the appellate court determines that steps 1–3 have been established, then the appropriate course is to remit to the Magistrates' Court.[2]

1 Above para **8.101**.
2 *Larosa v Her Majesty The Queen* (above para **8.60**) per Doherty JA at para 83.

The disclosure position at stage 4

8.149 If a defendant has reached 'stage 4', he will have demonstrated that there is reason to believe that an abuse of process may have occurred. Pursuant to *Government of the United States of America) v Bow Street Magistrates' Court*,[1] it is now open to the District Judge to 'call upon the judicial authority that has issued the arrest warrant, or the State seeking extradition in a Part 2 case, for whatever information or evidence the Judge requires in order to determine whether an abuse of process has occurred or not'.[2] The Magistrate has no authority to invoke the power unless and until he finds that the material already available to him is capable of founding or generating a rational suspicion of abusive conduct on the part of the Issuing Judicial Authority ('IJA') or the CPS (*Central Examining Court of the National Court of Madrid v City of Westminster Magistrates' Court*[3]). And, where triggered, 'the Magistrates' Court has no power to make any coercive order against an IJA. What the magistrate can do is "call upon" the IJA for such information as is needed to decide whether a reasonably suspected or apparent abuse has in fact occurred. What he or she cannot do is to make a speculative request in order to see if any indications of abuse of process can be found'.[4] In *Norris v Government of the United States of America*,[5] the House of Lords observed[6] that such requests will be exceptional.

1 Above para **8.11**, per Lord Phillips CJ at paras 85–89. This is an exercise of the powers given to the Requested State by most extradition treaties, including, for example, Art 15(2) of the European Council Framework Decision 2002/584/JHA of 13 June 2002 on the European arrest warrant and the surrender procedures between Member States and Art 10 of the 2003 US-UK extradition treaty. The first recognition of this power is to be found in the judgment of Mitting J in *Wellington* (above para **8.42**) at paras 25–26, where it is stated that, where 'there was evidence that the process of the court was being abused, the court would have been entitled, in my view, to ask the United Kingdom authorities to request the United States Government that it provide further evidence relevant to that question under … Article [IX(2)] of the Order in Council'. However, in the same case, Lord Woolf CJ 'remain[ed] to be persuaded that Article IX(2) is intended to give to the judge hearing the extradition proceedings a discretion to require the appropriate authorities to obtain information from the requesting party. If such a power does exist, certainly it should only be exercised in the most exceptional cases. The district judge hearing extradition proceedings should determine them in the ordinary way on the material placed before him and come to the appropriate conclusion on that evidence' (at para 29). In *Jenkins v Government of the United States of America* (above para **8.52**), it was conceded, under the 2003 Act, that the Court may ask the Home Secretary to exercise his power under Art IX(2) and that 'it may be appropriate to use it … where there is before the court of the Requested State sufficient evidence of an abuse of its process to call for more information before a decision is arrived at'.

2 The position is different in Canada where the Canadian Courts exercise a power to order disclosure once a defendant establishes that 'the allegations must be capable of supporting the remedy sought [stage 2 above], there must be an air of reality to the allegations [stage 3 above], and it must be likely that the documents sought and the testimony sought would be relevant to the allegations' (*Larosa v Her Majesty The Queen* (above para **8.60**) per Doherty JA at para 76). Whilst the extent of the power is not settled (see *The Attorney General of Canada on behalf of the Government of the United States of America v Welsh & Romero* (above para **8.116**) at paras 50–51), the power has been exercised to order production of documents outside Canada on the basis that an abuse hearing is fundamentally different to an extradition hearing and more akin to a trial of an issue to which the Requesting State is a party litigant (*United States of America v Tollman (procedural ruling)* (above para **8.128**) per Malloy J at paras 58–63).

3 Above para **8.88**, per Sedley LJ at para 25.

4 At para 30.

5 Above para **8.38**.

6 At para 107.

8.150 The information and evidence obtained should be made available to the party contesting extradition since equality of arms requires that, in normal circumstances, the party contesting extradition should be aware of, and thus able to comment on, the material upon which the court will be basing its decision.[1] There may be occasions where a judicial authority or Requesting State is content that the court should see evidence but, on reasonable grounds, is not prepared that this should be disclosed to the person whose extradition is sought. The evidence might, for instance, disclose details of ongoing investigations into suspected co-defendants. The judge will be capable of evaluating the material that is provided to him, whether it is favourable or unfavourable to the person resisting extradition. The issue will then be whether, if a decision is reached without allowing that person the chance to comment on the material, the procedure will fail to satisfy the requirement of fairness. That question will be fact-specific and must be left to the judge to decide on the particular facts. If the judge concludes that fairness requires that the material be disclosed, but the Requesting Authority or State is not prepared to agree to this, then the appropriate course will be for the judge to hold that fair process is impossible, that to grant the application for extradition in the circumstances would involve an abuse of process, and to discharge the person whose extradition is sought.[2]

1 *Government of the United States of America v Bow Street Magistrates' Court* (above para **8.11**) per Lord Phillips CJ at para 90.
2 At para 92.

8.151 If, on the other hand, a Requesting State fails or refuses to comply with such a request altogether, 'the overwhelming inference' would be that matters had occurred as alleged by the defence.[1]

1 *Government of the United States of America) v Bow Street Magistrates' Court* (above para **8.11**) per Lord Phillips CJ at para 122. For an example of a case in which such an inference was drawn, see *Government of the United States of America v Tollman* (above para **8.62**) per Malloy J at para 132.

8.152 'Stage 4', as currently formulated,[1] might appear to reverse the established burden of proof. Indeed, at least one High Court decision assumes this.[2] But, the burden of establishing an abuse in any criminal proceedings rests on the defendant on the balance of probabilities. Section 206 of the 2003 Act applies that principle to extradition proceedings.[3] Therefore, the authors respectfully submit that the ultimate test must be that the judge should accede to the request for extradition unless he has satisfied himself, on the balance of probabilities, that such abuse has occurred. Perhaps a true reflection of the reality of the position lies in the statement of Bealieu J in *Kissell v The Attorney General on behalf of the Government of the United States of America*[4] to the effect that a reversal of the burden is only legitimate in a case where a defendant has gone beyond showing an 'air of reality' and has, in fact, shown a 'very strong circumstantial' case:

> 'I take into account the admonition of British and Canadian courts that, while the onus is on the Applicant, he or she may not always be able to bring direct evidence, and therefore may ask the court to draw certain inferences (*Tollman*, at para 22). However, I also agree with the submission of the Respondent that to draw a negative inference based on the responding state's failure to produce further evidence to justify its position can only be done in rare cases, where the Applicant has made a very strong circumstantial case suggesting impropriety. This is not the case here, as, for example, it was in *Tollman*, where Molloy J held not only that there was an 'air of reality' to the Applicant's allegations, but that he made a 'prima facie' case'.[5]

1 Above para 8.**58**.

2 *Central Examining Court of the National Court of Madrid v City of Westminster Magistrates' Court* (above para **8.88**) per Sedley LJ at para 25: '… where there is reason to suspect departure from these principles – but not otherwise – the examining judicial authority in this country may seek further information with a view to satisfying itself, as in law it must, that there has not been an abuse of process. In other words, the burden shifts'.

3 *Kociukow v District Court of Bialystok III Penal Division* [2006] 1 WLR 3061, DC per Jack J at para 9; *Mitoi v Government of Romania* [2006] EWHC 1977 (Admin) per Mitting J at para 23.

4 Above para **8.112**.

5 At para 155. An example of this is found in the case of *Bulgaria v Atanasova-Kalaidzhieva* [2011] EWHC 2335 (Admin) – see para **8.126** above. This was the second time that Bulgaria had sought the extradition of the respondent. The first request for extradition was made in 2001 and had failed. The court held that the applicant was entitled to the relief sought because the allegation of bad faith was made out. See also, *Office of the Prosecutor General of Turin v Barone (No. 2)* [2010] EWHC 3004 (Admin).

Chapter 9

Adverse publicity

9.01 Judicial anxiety concerning the prejudicial effect of pre-trial publicity on criminal trials is not of a recent vintage. A cursory glance at nineteenth century newspapers suggests that coverage of the same sort of crimes that are newsworthy today, for example hooliganism, sexual violence and homicide, was lurid and sensational then. The earliest reported authority of judicial concern on this subject is the judgment of Lord Ellenborough in *R v Fisher*[1] which concerned a rape trial where a newspaper reported that the defendant was guilty of the offence charged. Lord Ellenborough said:

> 'if anything is more important than another in the administration of justice, it is that jurymen should come to the trial of those persons on whose guilt or innocence they are to decide, with minds pure and unprejudiced. Is it possible that they should do so, after having read for weeks and months before, ex parte statements of the evidence against the accused, which the latter have no opportunity to disprove or to controvert?'

Similar nineteenth century judicial anxiety was expressed in *A-G v Parnell*[2] and by Alverstone CJ in *R v Tibbits*.[3]

1 (1811) 2 Camp 563.
2 (1880) 14 Cox CC 474.
3 [1902] 1 KB 77.

9.02 Traditionally, the responsibility for ensuring that defendants do not suffer 'undue' prejudice from media reported comment is not that of the individual defendant but that of the State itself. A public interest has always been recognised in ensuring that conduct in any form which tends to interfere with the course of justice in particular legal proceedings should be deterred and, if necessary, punished. This has spawned the jurisprudence of criminal contempt of court whereby the State in the personage of the Attorney-General has issued proceedings, especially against newspapers, where it is felt that reportage has interfered with or perverted the course of justice. While a full consideration of the law relating to criminal contempt is beyond the scope of this chapter, it is important to appreciate that this jurisprudence was the forerunner to that relating to abuse of process. Furthermore, the interrelationship is more than just historical. In seeking to understand the court's abuse of process jurisdiction in the context of pre-trial publicity, it is vital to appreciate that the law on criminal contempt has both shaped and promoted the law relating to pre-trial publicity.

9.03 The law on abuse as it relates to pre-trial publicity is relatively new. Only since the early 1990s have there been decisions on the power and responsibility of the courts, as part of their abuse jurisdiction, to stay criminal proceedings on the ground of prejudicial pre-trial publicity. Previously, in the absence of proceedings brought by the Attorney-General for such contempt, the courts were unwilling to intervene and accept on the basis of submissions made by the defendant alone that even before the criminal proceedings had begun, there was a risk of unfairness arising out of prior publicity. Why this sudden development or willingness? This is perhaps the result of first, an acceptance that modern media is able to create and orchestrate an unprecedented level of hostility towards a particular defendant, media 'abuses' thus becoming more powerful and insidious. Secondly, a perception that the State can no longer be relied on exclusively to deter and punish such abuses via actions for contempt or by other means: this perception perhaps going hand in hand with the development of new remedies by the courts especially in the field of public law, recognising that the State alone cannot any longer be regarded as the sole guardian of individual rights. Thirdly, in view of the high evidential threshold for contempt introduced by the Contempt of Court Act 1981 and in particular the requirement that each allegedly contemptuous item of publicity be judged in isolation from any others, which together have probably created a climate of prejudice, the test for contempt has increasingly been regarded as less relevant or helpful in an abuse context.

PUBLICITY AND JURY DECISION-MAKING

9.04 In our jurisdiction all serious criminal cases are decided on by a jury and not by professional judges. Juries are never asked to provide reasons for their verdicts and indeed it is a criminal offence under the Contempt of Court Act 1981 for individual jurors to be interviewed after a verdict has been delivered as to how it was arrived at. This absence of reasons or inscrutability is in stark contrast to jurisdictions where a judge sits as the tribunal of fact, for example under the Diplock Court regime in Northern Ireland where a High Court Judge sits as the tribunal of fact. If a defendant is convicted, the judge always provides reasons which, furthermore, are directly appealable.

9.05 In proceedings against a particular defendant which have attracted substantial, predominantly hostile publicity and where he is convicted, one can readily appreciate why that defendant may feel he did not receive a fair trial or hearing by the jury. The inscrutability of the jury verdict can do nothing to alleviate this grievance. However, against this is the stark fact that public confidence in the criminal justice system would surely be undermined if notorious defendants accused of horrific crimes could escape justice, not even stand trial, because of adverse publicity.

9.06 Confronting this dilemma, the courts have tenaciously grasped the axiom that in criminal trials a jury of ordinary and randomly selected people can be empanelled to try the case objectively. Time and again, English judges have vouchsafed the objectivity and robustness of the traditional English jury where the danger of undesirable 'bias' is excluded.[1] This traditional and endemic view of the English jury is so entrenched by our system that attempts in highly publicised trials to exclude potentially biased jurors by means of questionnaires and so on, have almost always been rejected by trial judges holding that the jury system untouched can be relied on to act dispassionately. Nonetheless, since the early 1990s this conventional wisdom has come under direct attack. There have been cases, to be considered later, where proceedings have been halted or convictions been quashed, at least in part, because of a judicial acceptance that pre-trial publicity rendered a fair trial impossible.

1 Interestingly, the original jury system comprised people from the area where the defendant lived who were expected to use their local knowledge, including their knowledge of the defendant, to judge the plausibility of the prosecution and defence cases.

CONTEMPT OF COURT IN THE CONTEXT OF PRE-TRIAL PUBLICITY

9.07 It has long been recognised by the common law in the realm of contempt that adverse pre-trial publicity can inhibit a fair trial. Perhaps the most famous judicial statement of this is the judgment of Lord Diplock in *A-G v Times Newspapers Ltd*[1] which was concerned with pre-trial reportage by the *Sunday Times* of the thalidomide scandal. That newspaper intended to print a full story about the scandal and the consequent litigation between the manufacturers, Distillers, and the affected children. Distillers complained about this to the Attorney-General who then sought an injunction banning publication. Lord Diplock, in granting the Attorney-General's application said:

> 'the due administration of justice requires … that all citizens … should be able to rely upon obtaining in the courts the arbitrament of a tribunal which is free from bias against any party and whose decision be based upon those facts only that have been proved in evidence and deduced before it in accordance with the procedure adopted in courts of law; and … that, once the dispute has been submitted to a court of law, they should be able to rely upon there being no usurpation by any other person of the function of the court to decide it according to law'.[2]

Lord Diplock was therefore of the view that if the due administration of justice is hindered or usurped then the result must be that the trial will be unfair.

1 [1974] AC 273.
2 [1974] AC 273 at 309.

9.08 In a later case, *A-G v English*, Lord Diplock said:[1]

> 'trial by newspaper, or as it should be more compendiously expressed today, trial by the media is not to be permitted in this country … the true course of justice must not at any stage be put at risk'.

1 [1983] 1 AC 116 at 141.

9.09 In the same case, but sitting in the Divisional Court Watkins LJ expressed the issue in more florid language:[1]

> 'everyone surely agrees that the well of justice must remain clear. Thus, by one means or another the poison of prejudice must be kept away from it. If it is not, then the possibility of a miscarriage of justice inevitably

accompanies prejudice. No-one will know what harm is done except the jury whose verdict, whatever it be, will not inform others as to whether or not it is tainted by prejudice.'

1 [1983] 1 AC 116 at 125.

9.10 The courts' power to prevent or punish instances of prejudicial pre-trial publicity is now governed by the Contempt of Court Act 1981. Pursuant to s 4(2) a judge seised of active proceedings is empowered to make an order banning publication for a defined period of those proceedings. Section 4(2) provides:

> 'in any such proceedings the court may, where it appears to be necessary for avoiding a substantial risk of prejudice to the administration of justice in those proceedings … order that the publication of any report of the proceedings be postponed for such period as the court think necessary for that purpose'.

9.11 There must therefore be a substantial risk of prejudice, which would be caused by publicity. In relation to the jurors being affected by prejudice, in *R v Horsham Justice, ex p Farquharson*[1] Denning MR held that the risk really must be substantial:

> 'in considering to make an Order under section 4(2), the sole consideration is the risk of prejudice to be the administration of justice. Whoever has to consider it should remember that at a trial judges are not influenced by what they may have read in the newspapers. Nor are the ordinary folk who sit on juries, they are good sensible people … the risk of them being influenced is so slight that it can usually be disregarded as insubstantial—and therefore not the subject of an order under s 4(2)'.[2]

1 [1982] QB 762.
2 [1982] QB 762 at 794.

9.12 In cases concerned with the application of a s 4(2) order, and in particular with the meaning of a substantial risk of prejudice, the appellate courts have emphasised the need for judicial restraint. Such restraint has been encouraged first, by emphasising in general terms the competing public interests involved, in particular the desirability of ensuring freedom of expression and open justice. Secondly, as the quote from Denning MR in para **9.11** shows, the courts have also evinced a belief that judges and jurors are able to discard from their thinking, prejudicial publicity. Eleven years after Denning MR's views in *Farquharson,* Lord Taylor in *R v Central Criminal Court ex p Telegraph plc*[1] said in this context:

> 'In determining whether publication of matter would cause a substantial risk of prejudice to a future trial, a court should credit the jury with the will and ability to provide by the judge's direction to decide the case only on the evidence before them. The court should also bear in mind the staying power and the detail of publicity, even in case of notoriety, are limited and that the nature of the trial is to focus the jury's minds on the evidence before them rather than matters outside the courtroom'.[2]

1 [1993] 1 WLR 980.
2 [1993] 1 WLR 980 at 987.

9.13 However, the courts have on occasions accepted that a banning order under s 4(2) is required, otherwise the anticipated publicity would imperil the fairness of future criminal proceedings. For example, in *A-G v Steadman*[1] Bell J granted an injunction against any performances of 'Maxwell; the Musical' a satirical and disparaging play about the life of the late Robert Maxwell on the grounds that it would prejudice the forthcoming trial of his sons, Kevin and Ian.

1 (February 1995, unreported).

9.14 In addition to giving the courts a preventative power pursuant to s 4, the Act also provides a 'strict liability' rule of contempt. An intention to cause prejudice is not an essential element of the contempt. What matters is the effect of the publicity on active proceedings. By s 2(2) this rule, 'applies only to a publication which creates a substantial risk that the course of justice in the proceedings in question will be seriously impeded or prejudiced'. There has been a great deal of jurisprudence on the meaning of the terms 'substantial risk' and 'serious prejudice'.

9.15 In *A-G v Hat Trick Productions Ltd*[1] Auld LJ said:

> 'Serious prejudice is not capable of useful paraphrase save possibly as something which puts the course of justice at risk, as, in a criminal trial, by affecting its outcome or necessitating the discharge of the jury'.[2]

In that case Auld LJ held that a broadcast from an episode of 'Have I Got News for You' which denigrated Ian and Kevin Maxwell six months before their trial did create a substantial risk of serious prejudice against them. During the programme Angus Deayton had said: 'The BBC are in fact cracking down on references to Ian and Kevin Maxwell just in case programme makers appear biased in their treatment of these two heartless scheming bastards'.

1 [1997] EMLR 76.
2 At 81.

9.16 In *A-G v Associated Newspapers*[1] a contempt was held arising out of prejudicial publicity in the *Evening Standard* against various defendants who were, at the date of publication, on trial for serious offences. The newspaper correctly informed its readers that those defendants currently on trial for prison escape were convicted IRA terrorists. The trial judge held this disclosure was very prejudicial to the defendants and stayed the trial. Subsequently the High Court in effect upheld this view by holding pursuant to s 2(2) that the newspaper had committed a contempt.

The issue of contempt arising out of publicity was considered from a different perspective in *AG v MGN Ltd and News Group International Ltd.*[2] The case concerned the vilification of a suspect during a criminal investigation. The man was arrested on suspicion of murdering a young woman to whom he had been renting a property. The man was never charged and shortly after another man was arrested and confessed to the murder. Therefore the issue was one of publicity impeding the course of justice outside the trial process.

In this case the Court rejected the view that contempt could not be made out unless it was likely to lead to a successful appeal on conviction by the defendant, expressed by Sedley LJ in *Attorney General v Guardian Newspapers Ltd.*[3] Instead it adopted a wider approach considering whether the publicity constituted a potential impediment to the course of justice. It found that:

> 'the vilification of a suspect under arrest readily falls within the protective ambit of s.2(2) of the 1981 Act as a potential impediment to the course of justice. At the simplest level, publication of such material may deter or discourage witnesses from coming forward and providing information helpful to the suspect, which may, (depending on the circumstances) help immediately to clear him of suspicion or enable his defence to be fully developed at trial'.[4]

1 [1998] EMLR 711.
2 [2012] 1 Cr App R 1.
3 [1999] EMLR 904 at 905.
4 [2012] 1 Cr App R 1 at para 31.

9.17 These cases demonstrate the existence of a concern which the courts have regarding the prejudicial effects of media coverage. Using the test of s 2(2), the courts have on occasions been satisfied beyond reasonable doubt that pre-trial publicity has created a serious risk of substantial prejudice.

The use of the internet and social media

9.18 The issue of contempt of court was re-visited in 2013 in light of problems encountered through the rise of modern media. The reform of the laws of contempt was referred to the Law Commission[1] and raised as a priority by the Attorney General.[2]

The Law Commission began its review of this area by publishing a report recommending abolition of the archaic offence of scandalising the court,[3] a recommendation subsequently implemented in section 33 of the Crime and Courts Act 2013. In December 2013, the Law Commission published the first of a series of three consultation paperson the contempt of court. That same month, the then Attorney General, Dominic Grieve QC MP, in a change of policy designed to help inform the public about the legal pitfalls of commenting in a way which could be seen as prejudicial to a court case, outlined his future policy to publish AG advisory notes on the Government website and on twitter. The Attorney General said:

> 'Blogs and social media sites like Twitter and Facebook mean that individuals can now reach thousands of people with a single tweet or post. This is an exciting prospect, but it can pose certain challenges to the criminal justice system. In days gone by, it was only the mainstream media that had the opportunity to bring information relating to a court case to such a large group of people that it could put a court case at risk. That is no longer the case, and is why I have decided to publish the advisories that I have previously only issued to the media. This is not about telling people what they can or cannot talk about on social media; quite the opposite in fact, it's designed to help facilitate commentary in a lawful way. I hope that by making this information available to the public at large, we can help stop

people from inadvertently breaking the law, and make sure that cases are tried on the evidence, not what people have found online.'

In June 2021 a further Attorney General launched an innovative new campaign,[4] entitled '#ThinkBeforeYouPost' to again warn of the legal consequences of prejudicing the judicial process via social media. As part of the campaign the AG's office published two highly practical documents, the first described as a factsheet, entitled 'Contempt of court and social media', and the second, taking the form of a case studies document. In the course of the factsheet, warnings are given as to how certain posts could delay, impede or even abort court proceedings, the emphasis being on protecting the fairness of the proceedings.

1 Eleventh Programme of Reform (2011) Law Com No 330.
2 In January 2012 the Attorney General emphasised the need to urgently reform contempt laws and asked the Commission to prioritise work on this project.
3 Contempt of Court: Scandalising the Court (2012), Law Com No 207.
4 Between 28 June and 2 July 2021.

Abuse of process

9.19 The Court of Appeal's judgment in the 2006 case of *R v Abu Hamza*[1] should be the starting point for any lawyer contemplating an abuse of process argument based on adverse publicity. In the course of this judgment, the then Lord Chief Justice, reviewed the history of the case law, from the 1969 *Kray* decision, through to *In re B*.[2] Whilst the court acknowledged that such applications were now a growth area for lawyers, nevertheless, it made it quite clear that few such applications were ever likely to succeed.

The court further emphasised in *Abu Hamza* that there was no different or discreet abuse of process test for arguments based on the effect of adverse publicity. The authors suggest that where a fair trial is no longer possible, on account of adverse publicity, or where the conduct offends the court's sense of propriety in the revised limb 2 test the proceedings may be stayed. This is the classic abuse of process test. The Lord Chief Justice in *Abu Hamza* further described the test thus:[3] 'Only where the effect of the publicity has been so extreme that it is not possible to expect the jury to disregard it will it be appropriate to stay a trial on the ground of abuse of process'.

1 *R v Abu Hamza* [2007] 1Cr App R 27.
2 [2006] EWCA Crim 2692.
3 See para 78 of the judgment.

9.20 In the abuse context, just as in the cases on contempt considered in paras **9.07–9.17**, judicial faith in the will and the ability of jurors to ignore any potential prejudicial effect of publicity has always been expressed. This is hardly surprising in view of it being a fundamental tenet of our system that jury trial provides the fairest and most reliable method of determining guilt or innocence. It must be presupposed that the jury will try the case according to the evidence. Perhaps the most frequently quoted reference of this faith in the jury is the robust judgment of Lawton J in *R v Kray*[1] where the notorious Kray twins were on trial only one month after they had been convicted for murder, that first trial having attracted massive media publicity. In rejecting the Kray twins' application for a stay of the second trial against them arising out of this publicity Lawton J said:

> 'I have enough confidence in my fellow-countryman to think that they have got newspapers sized up just as they have got other public institutions sized up, and they are capable in normal circumstances of looking at a matter fairly and without prejudice even though they have to disregard what they may have read in a newspaper … it is, however, a matter of human experience, and certainly a matter of the experience of those who practice in the criminal court, first, that the public's recollection is short, and, secondly, that the drama, if I may use that term, of a trial will almost have the effect of excluding from recollection that which went before. A person summoned for the case would not, in my judgment, disqualify himself merely because he had read any of the newspapers containing allegation of the kind I have referred to; but the position would be different if, as a result of reading what he had, his mind had become so clogged with prejudice that he was unable to try the case impartially'.[2]

1 (1969) 53 Cr App Rep 412.
2 (1969) 53 Cr App Rep 412 at 414–415.

9.21 Later as Lawton LJ in *R v Coughlan*[1] he expressed a similar view:

> 'it is our experience that juries in general understand the responsibility which rests upon them … Juries are capable of disregarding that which is not properly before them. They are expected to disregard what one accused says about another in his absence. If they can do that, which is far from easy, they can disregard what is said in the newspapers.'

1 (1976) 64 Cr App R 11.

9.22 The views of Lawton LJ have, it is submitted, been followed by the courts thereafter. In *Ex p B*[1] for example Scott Baker J held that Lawton J's observations in *Kray* about juries are as true in 1994 as they were 25 years ago. Similar sentiments have been expressed in a contempt of court context by Denning MR and Taylor CJ in the cases reported in paras **9.11–9.12**.

1 (17 February 1994, unreported).

9.23 In *Abu Hamza* the Court of Appeal recognised that, in general:

> 'the courts have not been prepared to accede to submissions that publicity before a trial has made a fair trial impossible. Rather they have held that directions from the judge coupled with the effect of the trial process itself will result in the jury disregarding such publicity'.[1]

Having noted exceptions to the general rule, in the shape of the *McCann* and *Taylor and Taylor* decisions, the court went on to review the case law, which demonstrated a confidence in the integrity of juries to act fairly.

1 See para 89 of the judgment.

Trust in the jury

9.24 The Court of Appeal in *Abu Hamza* made reference to the *West*, *Kray* and *Young and Coughlan* decisions, before endorsing the statement made by the President of the Queen's Bench Division, Sir Igor Judge, as he then was, in the 2006 case of *In re B*[1] which read as follows:

> 'There is a feature of our trial system which is sometimes overlooked or taken for granted … that juries up and down the country have a passionate and profound belief in, and a commitment to, the right of the defendant to be given a fair trial. They know that it is integral to their responsibility. It is, when all is said and done, their birthright; it is shared by each one of them with the defendant. They guard it faithfully. The integrity of the jury is an essential feature of our trial process. Juries follow the directions which the judge will give them to focus exclusively on the evidence and to ignore anything they may have heard or read out of court … the directions themselves will appeal directly to their own instinctive and fundamental belief in the need for the trial process to be fair.'

1 [2006] EWCA Crim 2692.

9.25 Further on in the judgment, the Court of Appeal noted the observations of Lord Hope of Craighead in *Montgomery*, who acknowledged the obvious point that:

> ' … the entire system of trial by jury is based upon the assumption that the jury will follow the instructions which they receive from the judge and that they will return a true verdict in accordance with the evidence'.[1]

The judiciary naturally must have confidence in the assumption that their faith in juries is well placed. The authors suggest that the challenges the judiciary will face, when confronted with adverse publicity in high-profile cases, will continue to grow, with the advancements in technology which allow public access to all manner of information. The principal threat to the fairness of trials will come from the internet, which will prove to be much more difficult to regulate than media broadcasts on the television or reports in newspapers.

1 *Montgomery v HM Advocate* [2003] 1 AC 641 PC.

9.26 It is within the direct experience of the authors, for example, that, during the course of the Afghan Hijacking trial at the Central Criminal Court,[1] Mr Justice Butterfield was faced with a genuine problem posed by the internet, when it was drawn to the court's, and counsels' attention, that a bundle of a juror's internet reports on an aspect of the case, but not part of the evidence, were found inside the actual jury room. Butterfield J dealt with the problem swiftly, with a strong direction that they ignore such material, and refrain from any further research on the internet. The reality is, however, that jurors now have instant access to a library of material, and in circumstances which are not currently capable of being policed. Jurors who choose not to follow judicial directions, are now perfectly able to research information about a defendant, much of which may be prejudicial, irrelevant, and inadmissible for trial purposes.

1 *R v Safi and others* (2001).

The risk of prejudice

9.27 The *Abu Hamza* decision is of particular interest for the Court of Appeal's guidance to judges in relation to the approach a court should take, in adverse publicity cases, where there is a proven risk of prejudice. In para 92 of the judgment it states:

> 'The risk that members of a jury may be affected by prejudice is one that cannot wholly be eliminated. Any member may bring personal prejudices to the jury room and equally there will be a risk that a jury may disregard the directions of the judge when they consider that they are contrary to what justice requires. Our legal principles are designed to reduce such risks to the minimum, but they cannot obviate them altogether if those reasonably suspected of criminal conduct are to be brought to trial … Prejudicial publicity renders more difficult the task of the court, that is of the judge and jury together, in trying the case fairly. Our laws of contempt of court are designed to prevent the media from interfering with the due process of justice by making it more difficult to conduct a fair trial. The fact, however, that adverse publicity may have risked prejudicing a fair trial is no reason for not proceeding with the trial if the judge concludes that, with his assistance, it will be possible to have a fair trial.'

From this statement, the court is making it clear that certain levels of proven prejudice, or risks of prejudice, will have to be tolerated, so long as the trial judge maintains the view that a fair trial is still achievable. It will be for individual judges to make a judgement call, based on their experience, their assessment of the prejudice, and its likely effect on the fairness of the proceedings.

Proximity to trial – the fade factor

9.28 In *A-G v News Group Newspapers*[1] Sir John Donaldson MR said:

> 'proximity to the trial is clearly a factor of great importance and this trial will not have taken place for another ten months, by which time many wickets will have fallen, not to mention much water having flowed under many bridges, all of which would blunt the impact of publications'.[2]

1 [1987] QB 1.
2 [1987] QB 1 at 16.

9.29 The courts, as this quotation explains, have adopted the belief that a 'fade factor' is an effective diluter of prejudice. Part of this belief is how juries behave especially in longer complex trials: a gradual focusing of the jury's mind on the evidence before it to the exclusion of all information which has been communicated outside the courtroom. Sir John Donaldson MR said:

> 'the fact is that for one reason or another a trial by its very nature, seems to cause all concerned to be become progressively more inward looking, studying the evidence given and submissions made to the exclusion of all other sources of enlightenment. This is a well known phenomenon'.[1]

A similar view was expressed by Taylor CJ in *Ex p Telegraph plc*[2] quoted in para **9.12**.

1 [1987] QB 1 at 16.
2 [1993] 1 WLR 980.

9.30 Belief in this fade factor was confidently asserted by Scott Baker J in *Ex p B:*[1]

> 'in most cases, one day's headline news is the next day's fire lighter. Most members of the public do not remember in any detail what they have seen on television, heard on the radio or read in the newspaper except for a very short period of time … In this country public trust and confidence is placed in juries to decide the facts in all serious criminal cases, and jurors are well able to put out of their minds extraneous material and try the case on the evidence they hear in court.'

1 (17 February 1994, unreported).

9.31 In *Abu Hamza*, the court took note of the Scottish position on pre-trial publicity, set out in the judgment of Lord Hope of Craighead in the Privy Council decision of *Montgomery v HM Advocate:*[1]

> 'Recent research conducted for the New Zealand Law Commission suggests that the impact of pre-trial publicity and of prejudicial media coverage during the trial, even in high profile cases, is minimal: Young, Cameron and Tinsley, Juries in Criminal trials: part Two, vol 1, ch 9, para 287 (New Zealand Law Commission preliminary paper no 37, November 1999).The lapse of time since the last exposure may increasingly be regarded, with each month that passes, in itself as some kind of a safeguard. Nevertheless the risk that the widespread, prolonged and prejudicial publicity that occurred in this case will have a residual effect on the minds of at least some members of the jury cannot be regarded as negligible. The principal safeguards of the objective impartiality of the tribunal lie in the trial process itself and the conduct of the trial by the trial judge. On the one hand there is the discipline to which the jury will be subjected of listening to and thinking about the evidence. The actions of seeing and hearing the witnesses may be expected to have a far greater impact on their minds than such residual recollections as may exist about reports about the case in the media. This impact can be expected to be reinforced on the other hand by such warnings and directions as the trial judge may think it appropriate to give them as the trial proceeds, in particular when he delivers his charge before they retire to consider their verdicts.'

Based on this line of authorities, there is clearly a widespread judicial scepticism in the context of abuse of process as to pre-trial publicity having any lasting or corrupting effect on the fairness of criminal trials. Such scepticism, for reasons described in this chapter already, is unsurprising. Furthermore, until the 1990s it appears that no criminal trial was stayed on this ground. This disbelief in a criminal context as to the effect of publicity after it has occurred, created a disjuncture with the approach of judges in a contempt context. The authorities considered above, in paras **9.11–9.17**, evidence this difference of approach between the older abuse of process decisions, and the contempt cases. It is, however, submitted that since the early 1990s this disbelief has been superseded by a more flexible and pragmatic approach, albeit that the instances where defence arguments will succeed are expected to continue to remain few and far between.

1 [2003] 1 AC 641.

A REVIEW OF THE CASE LAW

9.32 It is submitted that since the early 1990s there has been an increased judicial willingness to recognise that, in criminal trials, pre-trial publicity can cause a risk of substantial prejudice. The earliest case was *R v McCann*[1] where the Court of Appeal quashed the conviction of alleged Irish terrorists because the trial judge failed to discharge the jury following a sudden wave of publicity as it retired to consider its verdict. In *McCann* the alleged target of the terrorist plot, Tom King MP, and also Denning LJ made widely publicised comments suggesting that people who refuse to answer police questions are probably guilty. McCann and others had refused to answer such questions. In his judgment Beldam LJ stated that:

> 'we are left with a definite impression that the impact which those statements and the television interviews may well have had on the fairness of the trial could not be overcome by any direction to the jury'.[2]

Notice, however, that *McCann* is concerned with publicity from senior or authoritative figures occurring at the crucial moment when the jury was about to retire. *McCann* is therefore easy to distinguish on its facts.

1 (1991) 92 Cr App R 239.
2 (1991) 92 Cr App R 239 at 253.

9.33 A case of far greater significance is the judgment of the Court of Appeal in *R v Taylor and Taylor.*[1] In that case the court took special notice of the adverse publicity which in its view rendered it, 'quite impossible to say that the jury were not influenced in their decision by what they had read in the press'.[2] While the court did not quash the convictions of the defendants simply on the publicity ground alone, it is significant to note that it declined to order a re-trial because, 'by reason of the view taken of the way in which this case was reported, we do not think that a fair trial could now take place'.[3] In his description of the pre-trial publicity itself McCowan LJ said this:

> 'in giving leave to appeal, the single judge described that coverage as "unremitting, extensive, sensational, inaccurate and misleading". Having had the opportunity of reading a substantial selection of the newspaper reports in question, we see no reason to dissent from that view'.[4]

1 (1993) 98 Cr App R 361.
2 (1993) 98 Cr App R 361 at 368.
3 (1993) 98 Cr App R 361 at 369.
4 (1993) 98 Cr App R 361 at 368.

9.34 The Court of Appeal's judgment in *Taylor* was followed by the ruling of Garland J in *R v Reade.*[1] Garland J stayed the trial of police officers who were accused of extracting false confessions from members of the Birmingham Six in 1974. Again, as with *Taylor,* the judge in part stayed the trial on the grounds of pre-trial publicity. Two aspects of Garland J's judgment are worthy of special note. First, Garland J accepted that the volume intensity and continuing nature of the publicity against the defendant had a 'snowball effect'. This snowball effect was the antithesis of the fade factor because in the view of Garland J, each extra bit of added adverse publicity served to fuel and continue the effect of past adverse publicity. Secondly, because of the enormous publicity concerning the quashing of the convictions of the Birmingham Six, it would be impossible to avoid a jury from having the impression that in quashing those convictions, the Court of Appeal was, as a matter of fact, finding the police officer defendants guilty of conspiracy and perjury.

1 (1993) Independent, 19 October.

9.35 One further aspect of this judgment which deserves mention is the acceptance by Garland J that the prejudice need not be specifically directed at the actual defendants personally. Garland J accepted that the identities of the Birmingham Six police officers was of itself unimportant because the prejudice was generalised and aimed at whichever police officers it was who had allegedly beaten confessions out of the Birmingham Six. Garland J's acceptance of generalised prejudice in this regard can be contrasted with the view of Turner J in *R v Alcindor*[1] which concerned publicity arising out of the capsize of the 'Herald of Free Enterprise'. Here, Turner J held that because the publicity was generalised there was no serious risk of prejudice against the individual defendants.

1 (11 June 1990, unreported).

R v Maxwell

9.36 Perhaps the most elaborate attempt ever made to persuade a judge to stay proceedings on the grounds of pre-trial publicity was that of Kevin and Ian Maxwell in May 1995. In addition to placing before the trial judge, Phillips J, evidence of allegedly prejudicial newspaper reports and videos of television programmes, the defendants also sought to adduce direct evidence of prejudice by means of findings gathered by opinion polls which they had commissioned from a polling organisation. They commissioned three separate polls in an effort to gauge the public's attitude and depth of prejudice. This was the first time in criminal proceedings that evidence of opinion polls was admitted (although in trademark and passing-off cases such evidence is routinely admissible).[1]

1 See for example *Customglass Boats Ltd v Sorthouse Bros Ltd* [1976] RPC 589 and *Lego System A/S v Lego M Lemelstrich* [1983] FSR 155. Phillips J was not persuaded by the evidence of the opinion pollsters: 'I do not believe I would have reached a significantly different conclusion as to the effects of publicity without the assistance of these [opinion polls] and I hope that their use in this case will not be taken as a precedent in future.'

9.37 After an extensive hearing of the abuse application Phillips J rejected it, holding that the Maxwell brothers could receive a fair trial.[1] However, Phillips J took the opportunity to consider the jurisdiction to stay proceedings on the grounds of pre-trial publicity:

> 'No stay should be imposed unless the defendant shows on the balance of probabilities that owing to the extent and the nature of the pre-trial publicity he will suffer serious prejudice to the extent that no fair trial can be held. I would accept this test, so far as it goes, but it remains necessary to identify the essential aspects of a fair trial for the purpose of the test. If it were enough to render a trial unfair that publicity has created the risk of prejudice against the defendant our system of criminal justice would be seriously flawed. There will inevitably be cases where the facts are so dramatic that almost everyone in the land will know of them. There will be circumstances when arrests are made of defendants whose guilt will, or may, appear likely. Intense media coverage may well take place before a suspect is identified or apprehended. If in the most notorious cases defendants were to claim immunity from trial because of the risk of prejudice public confidence in the criminal justice system would be destroyed'.

1 In the event, Phillips J was proved right because, of course, the brothers were both acquitted.

9.38 The judge continued:

> 'Our system of criminal justice is founded on the belief that the jury trial provides the fairest and most reliable method of determining whether guilt is established. This belief is based on the premise that the jury will do their best to be true to their oath and to try the case according to the evidence. The ability of the jury to disregard extrinsic material has been repeatedly emphasised by judges of great experience'.

9.39 Phillips J then quoted from *Kray*[1] and concluded:

> 'It seems to me that the court will only be justified in staying a trial on the ground of adverse pre-trial publicity if satisfied on a balance of probabilities that if the jury return a verdict of guilty the effect of the pre-trial publicity will be such as to render that verdict unsafe and unsatisfactory. In considering this question the court has to consider the likely length of time the jury will be subject to the trial process, the issues that are likely to arise and the evidence that is likely to be called in order to form a view as to whether it is probable that—try as they may to disregard the pre-trial publicity—the jury's verdict will be rendered unsafe on account of it'.

1 See para **9.29** above.

9.40 On a more general point concerning the *Maxwell* case, it would, it is submitted, be overly simplistic to deduce from the acquittal of the Maxwell brothers that the views of, for example, Lawton J considered in paras **9.20–9.21**, have been vindicated; ie that the jury can be trusted to exclude all kinds of prejudice. While refusing the application for a stay in *Maxwell* it is to be recalled that Phillips J did allow the use of an extensive questionnaire, consisting of 40 questions, in order to sift out from the jury panel those persons who evinced any prejudice. The eventual jury was therefore only drawn from the 'survivors' of the much larger panel. How efficacious this highly unusual exercise really was is of course unknown.

9.41 In *R v Andrews*[1] a similar attempt to permit jury questionnaires was made by the defence but rejected by the trial judge. This was upheld by the

Court of Appeal, who said that the questioning of jurors 'whether orally or by the use of questionnaires was to be avoided save in the most exceptional circumstances'. The court further held that questionnaires were a flawed instrument as answers were likely to be vague and questions would tend to remind jurors of issues which they would be told to disregard.

1 [1999] Crim LR 156.

Post-Maxwell authorities

9.42 In *R v Knights*[1] HH Judge Sanders granted a stay of proceedings against the defendant. The judge held that:

> 'the reporting was unlawful, misleading and scandalous … certain reporters were determined to run a hate campaign against Knights unchecked by their editors and without any regard to the interests of justice. I have absolutely no doubt that the massive media publicity in this case was unfair, outrageous and oppressive'.

Interestingly, following this determination of the criminal proceedings the Attorney-General consequently brought contempt proceedings against five newspapers whose reportage had been denounced by the judge. However, the High Court dismissed all the actions holding that they had not caused a substantial risk of serious prejudice.

1 (1995, unreported), Harrow Crown Court.

9.43 In *R v Hassan and Caldon*[1] HH Judge Colgan stayed the proceedings. This case arose out of a 'sting' operation carried out by the *News of the World*. That newspaper gave wide prominence to its article concerning the defendants in September 1994. It described the defendants as 'veteran villains' with 'long criminal records' etc. At the start of the trial in July 1995 the trial was stayed. The judge held the article was grossly prejudicial, 'especially in attributing criminal records to the accused'. Subsequently, the Attorney-General cited the *News of the World* for contempt which was upheld by the Divisional Court, who imposed a fine of £50,000.[2] To avoid the problem of being held so liable again, the newspaper publishes stories about crime before any proceedings or investigations are undertaken by police. This, therefore, prevents the test of 'active proceedings' in the Contempt of Court Act 1981 being triggered.

1 (July 1995, unreported), Isleworth Crown Court.
2 *A-G v News Group Newspapers* (1997) *Independent*, 17 July.

9.44 The 'Cromwell Street murders' and the cases against Fred and Rosemary West attracted massive pre-trial and during trial publicity. Following her conviction for 10 murders, Rosemary West appealed partly on the ground of adverse publicity.[1] However Taylor LCJ roundly dismissed this ground, holding that it would be absurd for a defendant to escape a trial on most grave charges on the ground of pre-trial publicity. He held that only adverse and prejudicial publicity during the trial itself could possibly justify a stay. However, Taylor LCJ accepted that the incidence of such publicity could be such that a judicial direction to the jury to disregard it may be an inadequate means of removing the effect of it from jurors' minds. This dicta was subsequently applied in the 2001 Leeds footballer prosecution, *R v Woodgate*.[2] Here the judge stayed the trial on the basis of a single article published in the *Sunday Mirror* when the jury had retired.

1 [1996] 2 Cr App Rep 374.
2 (Unreported).

9.45 Taylor LCJ's dichotomy in *West* was adopted by Kay J in *R v Magee*.[1] Kay J stayed proceedings against six defendants arising out of newspaper reports concerning their criminal backgrounds during the trial. He held that there was 'a real difference between pre-trial publicity and publicity which comes to the attention of the jury after they have been selected'. Consistent with his dichotomy Kay J refused applications to stay the proceedings based on publicity which occurred before the trial had, which he accepted was prejudicial because it had publicised the criminal past of the defendants. In this regard he held that the jury could be expected to disregard such publicity. However, when it again occurred during the trial this faith was undermined.

1 (January 1997, unreported), Woolwich Crown Court.

R v Stone[1]

9.46 This case raises a novel issue concerning adverse publicity following a conviction which is then subsequently quashed by the Court of Appeal. However the court went further and also reconsidered whether trials should be stayed on this ground of abuse.

1 [2001] EWCA 297, (2001) 145 Sol Jo LB 68.

9.47 In relation to post-conviction publicity about criminal trials generally it is important to bear in mind that such post-conviction publicity, freed from the constraints of contempt of court and sub judice restrictions, will inevitably tend to communicate information about the accused which would not have occurred pre-conviction. Such restrictions intended to keep a jury in ignorance of various facts normally concerned with an accused's previous bad character, fall away or lose their rationale once he/she has been convicted. Accordingly, information which would have been deemed highly prejudicial pre-conviction can be freely published.

9.48 In *Stone* a ghastly double murder of mother and daughter occurred in July 1996. They attracted massive publicity. A year later Stone was charged with the murders and ultimately was convicted in October 1988. In the following days there was extensive publicity about Stone, much of which was related to his alleged antecedence. Much which was detrimental was publicised which had not been known to the trial jury. For example, he was described as a childhood depraved psychopath, details of his previous convictions for violent crime were reported and he was said to fantasise about killing. In other words, there was clearly publicity post-conviction which was highly adverse to Stone.

9.49 Following the successful appeal on grounds unrelated to abuse, the prosecution applied for leave to have Stone retried. This was resisted on the ground that the post-trial publicity meant that he could not now receive a fair (re)trial. The prosecution, however, submitted that the adverse publicity was restricted to late 1998 and moreover there had been substantial publicity that had been in favour of Stone's appeal. Accordingly, its overall likely prejudicial effect due to the elapse of time had been so diluted as to have become insignificant.

9.50 Prior to *Stone* the only other occasion when the court directly considered a retrial in the circumstance of adverse publicity was in *Taylor and Taylor* considered at para **9.33** above. Here the court had declined to order a retrial, although no reasons for this were given. In *Stone* however, Kennedy LJ was critical of this earlier decision, holding that a justification for this decision against a retrial ought to have been given and therefore the case was of little relevance. Instead, Kennedy LJ was much more impressed with the approach of Philips J in *Maxwell* (see para **9.36** above) which he regarded as a 'valuable approach'.

9.51 Kennedy LJ also took advantage to emphasise the courts' reluctance to ever stay a trial for a serious offence on the ground of adverse publicity. First, in a section of his judgment marked 'Caveat' he sought to deride the proposition that a right to a fair trial equated with keeping a jury in ignorance of various facts about the accused. He listed examples of how a jury may become properly aware of such information without it ever being alleged that this had caused an unfair trial. Second, he held that in almost all cases, pre-trial adverse publicity could never properly found a stay. Only if it occurred during the actual trial might a stay be granted:

> 'Mr Clegg submits that in the light of decisions such as *McCann, Taylor*, and *Reade* it must now be accepted that there can be situations where an appropriate direction will not suffice. It is unreasonable to expect a jury to put the adverse publicity out of their minds. We agree, but that can only happen rarely, and usually in relation to adverse publicity which occurs during the course of the trial'.[1]

Kennedy LJ quoted with approval the opinion of Schiemann LJ in *A-G v MGN Ltd*;[2] the ability of a jury 'not to accept as true the contents of a publication just because it has been published'. Accordingly, a retrial was ordered and duly occurred in late 2001. Stone was convicted again.

1 [2001] EWCA 297, para 58.
2 [1997] 1 All ER 456 at 461.

R v Ali (Ahmed) and others[1]

9.52 The issue of adverse publicity following a conviction was later considered in *Ahmed*. The Crown's case was that the defendants had agreed to detonate improvised explosive on a transatlantic flight. At the end of the trial the jury was unable to reach verdicts on a number of the defendants. The trial attracted a great deal of media attention and the verdicts were well publicised. In particular the media published reports of the defendants' alleged links with prominent Al Qaeda members, an issue not relied upon at trial. The defendants faced two subsequent re-trials on counts that the jury were unable to reach verdicts on. At the end of the second retrial, the defendants appealed raising, *inter alia*, that in light of the media interest the retrials were unfair or not in the interests of justice.

The judgment endorsed the approach adopted in *Abu Hamza* and *Re: B.*[2] However, it did recognise that a distinction can be drawn between pre and post-trial publicity:

> 'The fact that it was a trial following a conviction on one count in our view is an important factor that may be viewed as more significant than pre-trial publicity.'[3]

The judgment also considered the role of the Crown and Attorney General with regards to responding to the publicity garnered by the trial, without making any recommendations. Instead, the judgment reiterated that the question to be resolved in an application for contempt differs to that raised by an appeal of this kind.[4]

1 [2011] EWCA Crim 1260.
2 [2011] EWCA Crim 1260 at para 89.
3 [2011] EWCA Crim 1260 at para 105.
4 [2011] EWCA Crim 1260 at para 101.

R v Abu Hamza

9.53 On the facts, the Court of Appeal considered the evidence upon which the defence contended the trial judge should have stayed proceedings against this Imam of a London mosque. There were 600 pages of newspaper reports, and articles spanning a two-year period, which were put before the trial judge, who treated them as samples of a sustained campaign against the defendant, which were almost entirely hostile to him. The Court of Appeal agreed there had been a prolonged barrage of adverse publicity, some of which had characterised the appellant as an ogre, and a public enemy. Indeed, the court agreed with the trial judge's assessment that the publicity had put at risk the fairness of the trial.

The court described the trial judge's position as follows:

> 'The challenge posed to the judge of taking appropriate steps to neutralise the effect of these matters by appropriate directions and guidance in the course of his summing up was considerable. The task was an exacting one'.

Having acknowledged the difficulties, the court went on to find that the judge's detailed, careful and skilful directions on the media coverage had lived up to the task. There had been no requirement to stay the proceedings.

9.54 In the subsequent case of *R v Dobson (Gary)*[1] the prosecution applied for the acquittal of the respondent (Dobson) to be quashed and for a retrial to be ordered, in relation to the murder of Mr. Stephen Lawrence. The defence, inter alia, submitted that a fair trial was no longer possible in light of the constant adverse publicity and identification of those suspected of having committed the murder. The Court of Appeal disagreed and, taking into consideration the *Hamza* and other related decisions, found that any prejudice suffered did not render him immune from prosecution. The court concluded that the potentially prejudicial publicity was unlikely to render the subsequent properly conducted trial unfair, the test being whether the publicity's impact would make a fair trial unlikely.

More recently, in the 2017 decision of *R v C(PM)*,[2] the court of appeal applied the *Hamza* principles. The case involved an incident which occurred during the course of the trial proceedings at Southwark crown court where Mr. C was on trial for corruption offences, which significantly involved Nigeria and Nigerian financial transactions. While the jury were in retirement deliberating upon their verdicts, the news media widely reported part of a conversation said to be between the then Prime Minister and the Queen on the eve of an international summit in London about global corruption, in the context of who would be attending the summit: 'We've got the Nigerians…actually we've got the leaders of some fantastically corrupt countries coming to Britain… Nigeria and Afghanistan, possibly the two most corrupt countries in the world'. Following his refusal to accede to a defence request to discharge the jury, the Judge, in response to the defence arguments on prejudice, directed the jury to ignore the reported remarks of the Prime Minister. The court of appeal held that, although the risk of prejudice would often be increased where the adverse publicity occurred unexpectedly occurred during a trial, rather than before it, the guiding principle remains that stated in *Hamza*, namely that the jury could be trusted to follow judicial direction and to strive to try the defendant fairly.

1 [2011] 2 Cr App R 8.
2 [2017] EWCA Crim 557.

9.55 The Court of Appeal's earlier judgments in *Stone* and *West* can be regarded as an attempt to curtail the nascent, largely 1990s, jurisprudence concerning the right of an accused to avoid trial on the ground of prejudicial publicity. Underlying this approach is a belief concerning the shortness of human memory or strength of the fade factor. Kennedy LJ held in the final paragraph of his judgment: '… people do forget. Even if they do not forget entirely, the passage of time makes it easier for them to set aside that which they are told to disregard'.

9.56 It is submitted that the approach adopted by Taylor LCJ and Kennedy LJ is not without difficulty. First, it assumes that the prejudice engendered by publicity is liable to be grossly exaggerated by defendants. Ultimately, short of the opinion poll evidence adduced by the Maxwells in their case, this subject is largely one of conjecture. However, both the traditional approach of the law on contempt considered above and contemporary fears regarding the power of the media are based on the view that adverse publicity can engender bias in the mind of a decision-maker. As Lord Goff said in *R v Gough*[1], 'bias is such an insidious thing that, even though a person may in good faith believe that he was acting impartially, his mind may unconsciously be affected by bias'. Kennedy LJ's lofty dismissal of the proposition concerning prejudice sits uneasily with this.

1 (1993) 97 Cr App Rep 188 at 191.

9.57 Second, this view runs the risk of encouraging the media on the one hand to believe that they enjoy, pre-trial at least, a relatively free licence to publish what they like, and the accused on the other to believe that the courts will not protect their right to a fair trial. Such a loss of faith will create a vacuum which, it is submitted, will quickly be filled with the defence team feeling the need to engage with the media to help obtain a more friendly portrayal. In *R v Andrews*[1] the Court of Appeal criticised the role played by the defence solicitors in holding a press conference with their client which understandably they regarded as unsavoury. Such actions may become more common, even if unattractive and alien to English legal tradition, if the courts refuse to accept a view held by many that prejudice can engender an unfair trial.

1 [1999] Crim LR 156.

9.58 The policy underlying the judgments in *West* and *Stone* is readily understandable. If jury trial is to survive in an age of formidable media power, high-profile and notorious defendants cannot be seen to escape justice. Far from blaming itself, the media outcry in the event of such a stay would be frenzied and with this a substantial danger of public disquiet about the criminal justice system would be caused. Against this backdrop the position, or rather compromise, established in these two cases can be understood.

9.59 But compromises are generally unstable and fragile. Recent reportage of allegations of paedophilia against TV celebrities seems sufficient to destroy their careers even before any charge is laid. Worse still is the branding of unconvicted defendants charged with offences of terrorism as, quite simply, terrorists. They are assumed to be and labelled as that which they are subsequently tried for. Any prospect that the media might have acted with self-restraint in the reporting of police investigations and charges in such cases seems unfounded.

9.60 The perennial problem will thus return to haunt trial judges and the Court of Appeal. Absent rigorous action by the Attorney-General, a politician who by nature will always be reluctant to create enemies in the media camp, any solution will have to come from the courts.

ALTERNATIVE TO A STAY – REMEDIES TO REDUCE THE RISK OF PREJUDICE

9.61 There are remedies available to a trial judge short of exercising a stay which can dilute or remove the risk of prejudice. Such remedies include:

(1) Moving the trial venue to a different geographical location if the risk of prejudice has predominantly been caused by local publicity. Accordingly in *Stone* the appellant who had originally been tried in Maidstone was retried in Nottingham. Of course, if the publicity is national, there is nowhere to go.

(2) As in *Maxwell*, questioning potential jurors to weed out the most prejudiced. It is submitted that there are two difficulties with this remedy, one principled and the other practical. The principled objection is that questioning a potential jury for the purpose of weeding out members constitutes a derogation from the principle that members of the jury should be selected at random, this to ensure fairness and that the jury is a cross-section of society. Secondly, it creates the insoluble problem of determining how prejudiced

a potential juror should be before he is removed from the panel; on what empirical basis is the court to decide that one level of prejudice is acceptable but another not? As Phillips J said in *R v Maxwell*, 'the fact that a juror may have read or heard prejudicial matter about a defendant, and even formed an adverse opinion of him on the basis of it, does not of itself disqualify the juror on the ground of bias'. The view of the Ontario Court of Appeal in *R v Hubbert*[1] is also constructive:

> 'in this era of rapid dissemination of the news by the various media, it would be naïve to think that in the case of a crime involving considerable notoriety, it would be impossible to select 12 jurors who have not heard anything about the case, information about a case, and even the holding of a tentative opinion about it, does make partial juror sworn to render a true verdict according to the evidence'.

The exercise, it is submitted, is entirely speculative. Moreover, the questioning process may of itself create further problems. First, will the prejudice in fact be identified or elicited as a result of the screening process? As Mason CJ and Toohey J in *Murphy v R* put it:

> 'the challenge for cause based on partiality run into an obvious difficulty; it seems unlikely that a prejudiced juror will recognise his own personal prejudice, or, knowing it, would admit it'.[2]

Secondly, the process may be self-defeating in that it brings to the attention of a juror those matters which the parties would wish him to disregard.

(3) Delaying the start of the trial to allow feelings of prejudice to subside. However, this remedy is only likely to succeed if it can be safely assumed that during the 'cooling-off' period no further prejudicial publicity occurs. In *Stone* the Court of Appeal took into account the date of a possible re-trial holding that the delay would further reduce the risk of prejudice. Hamza's original trial date was postponed given the obvious prejudice of the timing of his trial at the time of the London bombings of 7 July 2005.

This is the most commonly used remedy whereby at any time during the course of the trial, probably more than once, the judge directs the jury to base its verdict on the evidence it hears in court and nothing else. Depending on the nature of the prejudicial publicity and its specificity a judge is also able to comment in detail informing the jury that various allegations made in the media are, for example, totally false and to be disregarded. In *R v Andrews*[3] the trial judge directed prosecution counsel, before opening his case to the jury, to inform it that certain allegations made in newspapers were entirely bogus and formed no part of the Crown's case. While it is unknown as to whether such directions have the desired effect, based on the presupposition that juries do act fairly, it is presumed that they do so.

1 (1975) 29 CCC (2d) 279.
2 (1989) 167 CLR 94 at 103.
3 [1999] Crim LR 156. See para **9.57**.

JURISPRUDENCE OF THE ECHR

9.62 It is submitted that there is only sparse ECHR jurisprudence concerned with this subject. Unsurprisingly as a general principle the Strasbourg Court has held that pre-trial publicity can adversely affect the fairness of criminal proceedings,[1] particularly where such publicity is instigated or encouraged by those in authority. Accordingly, the court has accepted that press freedom may be curtailed in order to ensure a fair trial and protect members of the jury from exposure to prejudicial influences.[2] Furthermore the Commission has accepted that publicity which creates an atmosphere of animosity or a virulent press campaign can prejudice a fair trial.[3] Finally, the court will also assess whether the effect of prejudicial coverage has been appropriately dealt with by judicial directions to a jury to ignore the same.[4]

The issue of pre-trial publicity was recently raised in *Ali and Others v The United Kingdom*,[5] in which the applicants contended that due to the publicity between their trial and two retrials, the applicants did not receive a fair trial by an impartial tribunal. The merit of the appeal was not considered, with the Court ruling that all but one of the applications had been lodged outside the time limit and thus could not be accepted. The matter was adjourned with regards to one of the applicants as it was impossible to determine the admissibility of the complaint on the basis of the case file. In these later proceedings[6] the court made it clear it will be rare indeed that prejudicial publicity will make a fair trial, at some future date, impossible.

1 See *X v Austria* [1963] 1476/62.
2 See *Hodgson v United Kingdom* (1987) 10 EHRR 503.
3 See *Berns and Ewart v Luxembourg* (1991) 68 DR 137.
4 See *X v UK* (1978) App No 7542/76, and see *Noye v UK* (2003) 36 EHRRCD 231.
5 *Abdulla Ahmed Ali and others v United Kingdom*, ECtHR, Application no. 30971/12, Decision.
6 *Ali v UK* (2016) 62 EHRR 7.

Chapter 10

Procedural considerations

INTRODUCTION

10.01 In this chapter the various options open to practitioners seeking to make submissions on abuse of process, from the magistrates' court level up to the Court of Appeal, and beyond will be analysed. The procedural opportunities, and constraints, relevant to practitioners will be considered, in order to answer the various issues of when, where and how such applications may be made. In addition, the aim is to assist the practitioner with practical advice on how best to either present, or respond to, an abuse submission.

10.02 The starting point naturally is to satisfy oneself that a proper argument exists on the merits, and that the case meets the stringent criterion required. While this may sound self-evident the courts continue to sound out regular warnings to practitioners as to the need for self-restraint before embarking. Indeed, since *Attorney-General's Reference (No 1 of 1990)*[1] the courts have, in the face of an ever-burgeoning body of abuse case law, sought to encourage practitioners to exercise greater self-restraint, in the light of a history of what some courts clearly consider to be a significant number of unmeritorious applications.

1 [1992] QB 630.

10.03 Lord Bingham CJ in *Environment Agency v Stanford*[1] stated that the courts have repeatedly emphasised how the jurisdiction to stay proceedings as an abuse of process ought to be exercised with the very greatest caution. His Lordship commented that the lower courts were too often invited to stay proceedings in inappropriate circumstances, for example where a prosecution was merely ill-advised or unwise, issues which in his view were more properly relied on as mitigation.

1 [1999] Env LR 286, QB.

10.04 In *R v Childs*[1] Lord Chief Justice Woolf issued the following judicial warning to those advocates who advance unwarranted abuse applications:

> 'If they were advanced when they were not warranted, courts should make it clear that that was inappropriate conduct, and would take appropriate steps where, as sometimes happened, a huge amount of court time was wasted in consequence.'

Whilst the Court of Appeal will no doubt continue to dispose swiftly of unmeritorious abuse appeals, trial courts have been generally unsuccessful in holding back the tide of applications. In the light of the ever-expanding nature of the doctrine, the judiciary will further expect that, at the very least, the parties use the correct procedures.

1 *R v Childs* (2002) Times, 30 November.

10.05 Finally, any observer of recent judicial policy in the criminal courts will notice an increased willingness to use wasted costs orders as a means of punishing unmeritorious defence applications and to deter others. Practitioners should bear this possibility closely in mind.

THE MAGISTRATES' COURT: JURISDICTION

The legal context

10.06 Magistrates' courts may encounter defence applications to stay the proceedings on the grounds of abuse in two sets of circumstances. First, in relation to a summary trial to be heard before them and secondly, in relation to their duty under the transfer procedure in the Crime and Disorder Act 1998, s 51 to send an offence to the Crown Court for trial, which has now replaced committal proceedings. In practice, as summary proceedings rarely give rise to abuse of process issues and they are, in any event, never concerned with serious crime, it was in the context of the former committal proceedings, and now in the context of sending offences to the Crown Court for trial, that the issue arises of whether magistrates should have the power to halt a prosecution: in effect, to stigmatise it as an abuse of process at this preliminary stage and prior to any member of the judiciary being able to decide the issue.

10.07 Bearing in mind that the law concerning abuse of process is exclusively derived from the common law and that magistrates are inferior tribunals wholly subject to the supervisory jurisdiction of the High Court, the issue of whether magistrates should enjoy a jurisdiction to rule on abuse applications is ultimately a policy issue to be decided by the High Court. As abuse applications frequently involve complex matrices of fact and law, usually accompanied by defence complaints of prosecution impropriety in the context of serious allegations of criminality against the defendant, it is understandable that the High Court has, in various cases which have come before it, wanted to consider carefully the wisdom of allowing magistrates jurisdiction in this area.

The general position

10.08 In *R v Derby Magistrates' Court, ex p Brooks*[1] Sir Roger Ormrod said:

> 'The discretionary power of a magistrates' court to stop a prosecution has only recently been recognised by this court, and this development of the law is in a phase of rapid growth. It has no statutory basis …'

1 (1985) 80 Cr App Rep 164.

10.09 Sir Roger Ormrod then referred to various authorities and held that a magistrates' court did have this discretionary power. He observed:

'the ultimate objective of this discretionary power is to ensure that there should be a fair trial according to law, which involves fairness both to the defendant and the prosecution'.

10.10 Another useful statement of general principal in this regard is the statement of general principle laid down by Mann LJ in *R v Telford Justices, ex p Badhan.*[1] In that case Mann LJ affirmed that magistrates did enjoy an abuse jurisdiction:

> 'We...can see no reason why examining justices (even one examining magistrate; see the Act of 1980, s 4(1)) should not be able to decide that an initiation of the process of committal is an abuse of that process. A question of abuse is one which is within the ability of justices to decide, and it is one they admittedly have power to determine on summary trial'.

1 (1991) 93 Cr App Rep 171.

The creation of a split jurisdiction in Bennett

10.11 In *R v Horseferry Road Magistrates' Court, ex p Bennett*[1] the House of Lords followed the principle of the *Telford Justices* case, holding that magistrates enjoy a power to stay proceedings on the grounds of abuse in relation to both summary trials and committal proceedings. However, bearing in mind that in *Bennett* the House of Lords had significantly pushed outwards the boundaries of the abuse jurisdiction generally, the question naturally arose as to whether it was wise to vest in magistrates, in common with the judiciary, a full jurisdiction over abuse matters. In the context of the facts in *Bennett* which are recounted elsewhere in this book,[2] it was understandable that various speeches in that case were concerned in part with whether magistrates really were a competent tribunal to determine complex matters concerned with alleged international lawlessness by the executive and breach of extradition procedures, neither of these matters strictly having an impact on the fairness of the trial. It was one thing for the House, as it did in *Bennett,* to widen the circumstances in which a Crown Court could stay proceedings and another to provide the same ambit of discretion to legally unqualified persons sitting as part-time magistrates in the context of a committal.

1 [1994] AC 42.
2 See paras **5.39–5.55**.

10.12 The result of such concerns in *Bennett* led to the creation of a split jurisdiction in relation to abuse matters. Whereas the judiciary would enjoy a full jurisdiction, magistrates would not and their jurisdiction would be made more narrow. In *Bennett* Lord Griffiths held that magistrates' jurisdiction in this context 'should be strictly confined to matters directly affecting the fairness of the trial of the particular accused'.[1] Examples of matters falling within this category were, according to Lord Griffiths, those concerning delay or the unfair manipulation of court procedures.

1 (1994) 98 Cr App Rep 114 at 127.

10.13 According to Lord Griffiths, a line could be drawn between this and a special exclusive category of abuse concerned with upholding the rule of law, which he held should be confined to the jurisdiction of the High Court. Accordingly, when an allegation of abuse akin to that made in *Bennett* arose then magistrates were not competent to decide the matter. The remedy in this situation was for magistrates to exercise their discretion to allow an adjournment of the proceedings before them in order to enable the defence to then immediately make an application to the Divisional Court which would be empowered to rule.

Problems arising from the split jurisdiction

10.14 Before considering the relevant authorities subsequent to *Bennett* it should be appreciated that the creation of this split jurisdiction in the context of abuse and the powers of magistrates creates two practical difficulties. First, is it really possible in practice to draw a line between what Lord Griffiths said were 'matters directly affecting the fairness of the trial of the particular accused' and avowedly more policy-type issues concerned with upholding the rule of law? On what side of the line, for example, does an allegation of prosecution mala fides or oppressive conduct fall? Second, by creating a system whereby in the context of committal proceedings, now replaced with the transfer procedure in the CDA 1998, s 51(1), abuse applications concerned with the rule of law category are to be remitted for consideration to the High Court, a problem is thereby created in relation to the powers of a trial judge sitting in the Crown Court. If a complaint of abuse is referred to the High Court and rejected following which the accused was committed, or now sent, for trial to the Crown Court, what is a trial judge to do when he becomes seized of the case and the defence then makes a similar abuse application? In the context of a prior adverse ruling by magistrates, there is no difficulty in principle as a Crown Court judge can examine the issues afresh and reach a different conclusion. His discretion is unfettered in this respect. The problem, however, arises when the High Court composed of a Lord Justice of Appeal and a High Court judge has ruled against the defendant and the trial judge is then in effect being asked to reconsider the matter.

10.15 To this problem there appears only one principled solution, that the trial judge abide by the ruling of the High Court even though generally speaking the High Court as a court of review is less equipped to give careful consideration to the complex issues of fact and law which generally surround abuse applications than a trial judge before whom, for example, live evidence can be called and be cross-examined. But in a less clear-cut situation, what is a trial judge to do when the defence submit that there have been supervening matters between the ruling of the High Court and the application before him which had they occurred or been known about at the time of the High Court application, could have led that court to have reached an opposite conclusion. If such supervening matters really have arisen, can a trial judge de facto or de jure confine consideration of abuse to only these events posing the theoretical question of what would the High Court have done if it had been aware of such events?

10.16 Bearing in mind that international lawlessness or *Bennett*-type abuse applications are rare, the problems in paras **10.14** and **10.15** do not appear in practice to have caused real difficulty. However, from time to time the High Court is called on to clarify whether a magistrates' court should have jurisdiction to entertain a particular abuse application. For example, in *R v Belmarsh Magistrates' Court, ex p Watts*[1] the defendant made an abuse application at committal on the ground that the prosecution fell foul of the *Hunter*[2] rule. This rule is discussed fully in **Chapter 4**. In *Watts* the magistrate found that he did not as a matter of law have jurisdiction to entertain this application. In the Divisional Court Buxton LJ disagreed: 'We are indeed satisfied that the magistrate was wrong to think that he lacked jurisdiction to act on a finding of abuse of process on *Hunter* grounds'. The judgment in *Watts* is more fully considered at para **10.19**.

1 [1999] 2 Cr App Rep 188.
2 *Hunter v Chief Constable of West Midlands Police* [1982] AC 529.

Post-Bennett authorities – widening of magistrates' jurisdiction

10.17 Post-*Bennett* the next relevant authority is the judgment of Lord Bingham CJ in *R v Staines Magistrates' Court, ex p Westfallen*.[1] In his judgment Lord Bingham considered the 'narrow category' of *Bennett*-type abuse and concluded that Lord Griffiths was there 'plainly concerned with a flouting of the rule of law and abuse of power by police and prosecuting authorities'.

10.18 By the time of the judgment of Rose LJ sitting in the Court of Appeal in *R v Mullen* the area of abuse jurisdiction beyond that of magistrates had become characterised or described as a useful shorthand as '*Bennett*-type abuse'. In *Mullen* Rose LJ described *Bennett*-type abuse as follows:

> 'it seems to us that *Bennett*-type abuse, where it would be offensive to justice and propriety to try the defendant at all, is different both from the type of abuse which renders a fair trial impossible and from all other cases where an exercise of judicial discretion is called for. It arises not from the relationship between the prosecution and the defendant but from the relationship between the prosecution and the court. It arises from the courts' need to exercise control over executive involvement in the whole prosecution process, not limited to the trial itself'.[2]

The import of this definition was an attempt to clarify the dividing line between the abuse categories available to magistrates and those which are not. Respecting the dichotomy created by the House in *Bennett*, Rose LJ was perhaps seeking to helpfully explain the parameters in a more clear and useful way.

1 [1998] 1 WLR 652 at 662.
2 [1999] 3 WLR 777 at 791C.

10.19 In *R v Belmarsh Magistrates' Court, ex p Watts*,[1] Watts, an HM Customs and Excise officer, had been an important prosecution witness in a trial leading to the conviction for drugs trafficking offences of the defendant. Subsequently and presumably as a reaction to later confiscation proceedings initiated against him, the defendant launched a private prosecution of Ms Watts alleging false defamatory libel and misfeasance. Following issuance of the summonses Watts contended that they were an abuse of process and the (private) prosecution should be stayed. The particular abuse alleged was that the defendant was in fact seeking to reopen the safety of his conviction and was therefore in breach of the rule established by the House of Lords in *Hunter v Chief Constable of the West Midlands Police.*[2]

1 [1999] 2 Cr App Rep 188.
2 [1982] AC 529.

10.20 While the magistrate held that the defendant's summonses did amount to a violation of the rule in *Hunter* he also held that because of the dichotomy of jurisdiction created in *Bennett* this meant that he had no jurisdiction to stay the proceedings as an abuse, this being a matter exclusively for the High Court. Accordingly, the magistrate declined to stay the proceedings and Ms Watts then appealed to the High Court in part contending that the magistrate was wrong in law to hold that he lacked the power to stay the proceedings. The ruling of the court was given by Buxton LJ. Buxton LJ concluded:

> 'Within the general jurisdiction … there is a limited category of cases, involving infractions of the rule of law outside the narrow confines of the actual trial or court process, where the magistrates do not have jurisdiction, or alternatively as a matter of law should not exercise such jurisdiction as they may have … Such cases should, as in *Bennett*, be addressed by … the Divisional Court. That category is however a narrow one. It excludes every complaint that is directed at the fairness or propriety of the trial process itself[1].'

1 [1999] 2 Cr App Rep 188 at 195C.

10.21 Buxton LJ held that in all circumstances of alleged abuse short of *Bennett*-type abuse, magistrates did enjoy a jurisdiction. On the facts of the case before him, Buxton LJ held that the magistrate did have jurisdiction to inquire into allegations concerning the bona fides of the prosecution and whether the prosecution had been commenced oppressively or unfairly. This would include an allegation of abuse arising out of a purported breach of the rule in *Hunter* and accordingly, the magistrate had wrongly decided that he lacked the jurisdiction to deal with that complaint. Having established this point of principle, Buxton LJ held that the defendant summonses were an abuse and stayed the proceedings.

Significance of Watts

10.22 In addition to seeking to clarify the dividing line between *Bennett*-type abuse and all other types of abuse with only the former being beyond the jurisdiction of magistrates, Buxton LJ's clear policy was to seek as far as possible to allow magistrates a discretion to determine abuse applications. Moreover, the High Court does not wish to find itself regularly embroiled in abuse applications arising out of magistrates declining jurisdiction believing that they are unable to rule on an application. Magistrates should therefore accept, except in extreme and hopefully very rare circumstances, the role of dealing with abuse applications while respecting the split jurisdiction created in *Bennett.*

10.23 While holding that magistrates did enjoy a wide jurisdiction in this context Buxton LJ also made two further pronouncements. First, that where there was uncertainty as to which side of the dividing line an abuse application fell, then magistrates should remit the matter to the High Court adjourning the proceedings in the meantime. Secondly, in relation to cases which clearly did not fall into the *Bennett*-type abuse category Buxton LJ made clear that magistrates who still felt themselves unsuited to determining a particularly difficult or convoluted abuse application always possessed the discretion to decline jurisdiction and in effect tell the defendant to refer his complaint to the Divisional Court instead. The court will act as a sort of safety net or last resort for troubled magistrates, for as Buxton LJ stated:

> 'It will however, always be open to magistrates in cases that do not fall within the narrow *Bennett* category to decline jurisdiction, and require the matter to be pursued in the Divisional Court, whether because of the complexity or novelty of the point, or because of the length of investigation that is required. Any such decision by a magistrate, being one taken within the limits of his judgment, will be unlikely to be overturned in this court'.

10.24 Although such instances will be extremely rare, one largely pragmatic advantage of allowing magistrates jurisdiction here is the obvious saving of time and legal cost gained by staying a case at the earliest opportunity. If there is an abuse which should result in the proceedings being stayed, then there is advantage to all concerned in magistrates being able to do so. From a defendant's perspective, it is probably also correct in principle that he should be able to complain about the proceedings being brought at the earliest opportunity.

Conclusions

10.25 On the basis of all the authorities listed above it is submitted that magistrates have jurisdiction to consider abuse applications in almost all circumstances. These circumstances can be categorised as follows:

(1) abuse complaints directed at the propriety or fairness of the trial process or procedure;

(2) abuse complaints concerning mala fides of the prosecution, investigations of the bona fides of the prosecution, or investigations into whether the prosecution had been instituted oppressively or unfairly;

(3) in cases of delay;

(4) in cases of alleged unfair manipulation of court procedures.

10.26 Further examples of instances where jurisdiction would exist, given the above headings, are non-availability of evidence type abuses, non-disclosure abuses and double jeopardy species of abuse. Finally, it is contended that a magistrate does not have jurisdiction in these particular areas:

(1) instances of abuse of process under the narrow category of *ex p Bennett*;

(2) illegality and abuse of power by police, prosecution authorities or government officials pursuant to ulterior motives or wrongful purposes in violation of international law and for fundamental human rights.

SENDING CASES UNDER S 51[1]

10.27 The provisions of s 51 have now substantially curtailed defence opportunities to make abuse of process applications in the magistrates' courts in relation to indictable only offences and either-way offences, where the accused indicates (or is deemed to indicate) a not guilty plea and at the mode of trial hearing the magistrates decline jurisdiction or the accused elects trial on indictment. The legislation has now abolished committal proceedings for these offences. This curtailment was inevitable given that:

> 'The purpose of sending defendants to the Crown Court pursuant to s 51 of the 1998 Act was to reduce delay in dealing with indictable only offences and related either-way offences or serious summary offences, so that the Crown Court was enabled to deal with management and progress of a trial from an early stage'.[2]

1 Crime and Disorder Act 1998, s 51.
2 See *Fehily v Governor of Wandsworth Prison* (2002) Times, 18 July, DC.

10.28 In the decision of *R v Salubi,*[1] however, Auld LJ held that the magistrates still retained a limited jurisdiction to stay cases for abuse even where their s 51(1) duty was to send indictable-only cases 'forthwith' to the Crown Court, albeit that 'such a case would be very rare' and that it should be borne in mind that 'the matter may be the subject of an abuse application immediately after it has arrived [in the Crown Court].' Whilst identifying what may constitute such a rare circumstance, Auld LJ stated:

> 'Even in the rare cases where it might be appropriate to make an abuse of process application to a magistrates' court at the sending stage, it should be remembered that the onus is on the defence to establish bad faith or serious misconduct and that incorrect procedure based on lack of judgment does not suffice; … In most cases the Crown Court is likely to be better equipped to make such value judgments. Instances of possible bad faith might be the addition of an unmeritorious indictable-only charge in the late stages of committal proceedings for either-way offences, solely with the object of overcoming custody time limits or of overcoming evidential difficulties that would otherwise delay or defeat a committal'.[2]

An example of such a rare case is *R (Craik, Chief Constable of Northumbria Police) v Newcastle upon Tyne Magistrates' Court,*[3] where it was held that the District Judge had been required to stay the case for abuse and should not have issued a summons for a private prosecution against a former Chief Constable or sent him for trial for unlawfully imprisoning a defendant, on what can only have been the basis of vicarious liability. The proceedings were hopelessly misconceived, vexatious and an abuse of process. To pursue such a case was to be guilty of the kind of serious misconduct that required the exercise by the magistrates' court of its power to stay proceedings as an abuse of process.

1 [2002] EWHC 919 (Admin), [2002] 2 Cr App R 40 at 660.
2 At 670, para 21.
3 [2010] A C D 55; [2010] 5 Archbold Review 2.

Summary trials

10.29 The timing of the making of any such application obviously depends on a variety of factors, the most important of which is usually the timing of service by the prosecution of its evidence on the defence.

Whilst the court and the parties will be keen to manage proceedings in accordance with the overriding objective of the Criminal Procedure Rules and to respect custody time limits, there is no statutory timetable for the service of evidence in summary trials.

In the context of disclosure, the practitioner should have regard to the disclosure provisions set out in Pt 15 of the Criminal Procedure Rules 2015.[1] In addition to this, Practice Direction IV, para 15A.1 makes clear that parties must comply with the recently revised Judicial Protocol on Disclosure of Unused Material in Criminal Cases and the Attorney General's Guidelines on Disclosure, 2020.[2] These documents should be 'read together as complementary, comprehensive guidance'. Practitioners would be wise also to consider the Criminal Procedure and Investigations Act 1996 Code of Practice (pursuant to s 23(1) of that Act), particularly in the context of abuse of process in relation to evidence gathering or lack of evidence. The general position is that the prosecution are not under an obligation to serve 'initial disclosure', i.e. material meeting the test in s 3 of the 1996 Act, until the defendant has entered a not guilty plea in the magistrates court.[3] Prior to the defendant entering a not guilty plea at the magistrates' court, the common law duty of disclosure will apply, as it does throughout proceedings. Under the common law, the Crown will be under an obligation to serve only material which may assist the accused in relation to bail or the early preparation of his case, and if no such material exists then the Crown should certify that such is the case.[4] The prosecution must also, as prescribed by Pt 8 of the CPR, serve initial details of the prosecution case ('IDPC'). The IDPC must be served on the court officer (and the defence if they request the IDPC) as soon as practicable, and in any event no later than the beginning of the day of the first hearing. If the defence do not request the IDPC, then 'the prosecutor must make them available to the defendant at, or before, the beginning of the day of the first hearing'. Practitioners will be familiar with receiving these papers on the morning of the first appearance, particularly in the case of overnight remands.

However, it is anticipated that initial disclosure will be served prior to the entering of a not guilty plea in certain circumstances. Where a matter is charged following an application of the Full Code Test and a not guilty plea is anticipated, the Crown can be expected to make initial disclosure prior to the first hearing.[5] Furthermore, where the accused is charged following application of the Threshold Test, initial disclosure should be made as soon as possible after charge.[6]

1 SI 2020/759.
2 At the time of writing, only the latter has been published.
3 See CPIA 1996, s 1(1) and the Attorney General's Guidelines 2020 at para 102.
4 *R v DPP Ex p. Lee* [1999] 2 Cr App R 304.
5 Attorney General's Guidelines on Disclosure (2020), para 101.
6 Ibid at para 103.

10.30 The prosecution may find themselves in circumstances where, at the time of the first appearance they have not complied with CrimPR 8.3. In these circumstances what is the magistrates' court empowered to do?

Under the old procedure rules, it had been consistently held that magistrates do not, in these circumstances, have the jurisdiction to stay the proceedings as an abuse of process.[1] Given that the abuse jurisdiction of magistrates is essentially a common law creation following *ex parte Bennett*, it is submitted that the first element of the analysis in the old case law remains good law. The remedy, prescribed by the old procedure rules, was that the magistrates should either to proceed having decided there would be no prejudice to the defendant, or to adjourn.[2]

The current Pt 8 does not provide a sanction in the event that the Part is not complied with. It is submitted that the correct course where the IDPC is not provided, or where it is inadequate, remains the same as under the old law, namely either to adjourn for to allow compliance (with any sanction being by way of costs[3]) or to proceed whilst respecting CrimPR 8.4. A decision refusing to adjourn which thereby compels a prosecutor to proceed immediately to trial on that occasion is likely to be subject to a successful judicial review on the basis that it was unreasonable.[4]

1 See *King v Kucharz* (1989) 153 JP 336; *R (on the application of AP) v Leeds Youth Court* (2001) 165 JP 684; and *R v Calderdale Magistrates' Court, ex p Donahue and Cutler* [2001] Crim LR 141.
2 See the Magistrates Courts (Advance Information) Rules SI 1985/601, r 7.
3 See generally the Criminal Procedure Rules 2020/759, Part 45
4 *DPP v Radziwilowicz and Wanas* [2014] EWHC 2283 (Admin); (2014)178 J.P. 432.

10.31 There have been several authorities concerned with alleged abuse arising from non-disclosure by the prosecution of unused material and evidence that is relevant to the issue. Two important cases are *R v Stratford Magistrates, ex p Imbert*[1] and *R v DPP, ex p Lee.*[2]

R v Stratford Magistrates, ex p Imbert held that the right to a fair trial under Art 6 of the ECHR does not require that prosecution witness statements in summary proceedings have to be disclosed to the defence before trial.

However, *Daventry District Council v Olins*[3] held that a prosecuting authority, including local government authorities, should reveal the identity of a complainant to a defendant at an early stage and well before advance disclosure.

1 [1999] 2 Cr App Rep 276, QBD.
2 [1999] 2 All ER 737.
3 [1990] COD 244.

10.32 In *R v DPP, ex p Lee* the fairness of the prosecution's refusal to make disclosure pre-committal to the defence was considered by the High Court. The prosecution contended that the code of practice did not require disclosure of unused material until post-committal when it would be regulated by the provisions of the code and CPIA. The defence contended that their case would be prejudiced if no disclosure was made until a subsequent stage in the proceedings, i.e. post-committal, because it would delay defence preparation generally and hinder the making of a successful contested bail application.

10.33 Faced with compelling arguments from both sides, Kennedy LJ held that the prosecution did have a residual common law obligation to make pre-committal disclosure. Kennedy LJ provided examples of circumstances where such an obligation would arise. Two relevant examples were first, where the disclosure of unused material could reasonably be expected to assist in making an application for bail and secondly, where such material could assist an application made in the magistrates' court for a stay based on abuse. While Kennedy LJ was concerned to prevent the notion arising that 'full-blown' common law disclosure is required pre-committal, he was also anxious to ensure that the defence were not unfairly prejudiced by the provisions of the CPIA.

10.34 *Ex p Lee* is therefore authority for the proposition that there is a common law duty of disclosure from the prosecution to make disclosure of material which would assist defence preparation at the earliest possible opportunity in the proceedings. Accordingly, a failure to abide by this duty may subsequently found an application for a stay. Since the commencement of s 41 and Sch 3 of the CJA 2003 and the abolition of committal proceedings, there will be little scope for disclosure before the 'relevant time' is reached. Nevertheless, it is submitted that the prosecutor must still consider what immediate disclosure is required in the interests of justice, such as where the disclosure of unused material could reasonably be expected to assist in making an application for bail.

R (Barons Pub Co. Ltd) v Staines Magistrates' Court[1] held that the magistrates' court has no power of review of a prosecution other than through an abuse of process application.

1 [2013] Crim LR 758.

CASE STATED AND JUDICIAL REVIEW OF THE MAGISTRATES' COURT

10.35 Case stated is a remedy of ancient origin. It developed at a time when there was no Court of Appeal in criminal cases. It was a facility whereby the opinion of the High Court could be taken on a difficult area of law by a quarter session. In the Crown Court the procedure is now governed by the Supreme Court Act 1981, s 28(1). No appeal lies by way of case stated on an interlocutory matter from the Crown Court. In *Loade v DPP*[1] the court decided that 'any order, judgment or decision' in s 28(1) meant the final decision.

1 [1990] 1 QB 1052.

Appeal by way of case stated

10.36 An appeal by way of case stated is a procedure whereby the High Court is able to review the decisions of inferior courts in relation to points of law. Unlike judicial review, case stated is not generally concerned with how a decision was reached, but only as to its legal merit. If an appeal was therefore to be based for instance on an alleged breach of natural justice by magistrates, the general rule suggests that judicial review is the appropriate option. In *Moss and*

Son Ltd v Crown Prosecution Service,[1] the High Court held that misconduct or oppression of the type explained in Ex p Bennett had to be shown whether the challenge was by way of an application for a stay for abuse of process or by judicial review.

1 [2012] EWHC 3658 (Admin); (2013) 177 J.P. 221.

10.37 This right to apply to the justices composing the court to state a case for the opinion of the High Court on the question of law or jurisdiction involved, under the Magistrates' Courts Act 1980, s 111(1), states that an aggrieved person may question the proceeding on the ground that:

(1) it is wrong in law; or

(2) it is in excess of jurisdiction.

The procedure for making an application under s 111 is contained within Part 64 of the Criminal Procedure Rules.

Availability of case stated

10.38 In *Atkinson v United States Government*,[1] a case concerned with extradition proceedings, Lord Reid opined that there was no power to state a case unless there had first been some final adjudication.[2] However, it is submitted that the Magistrates' Court Act 1980, s 111(1) does provide for the possibility of the availability of this remedy. In *Environment Agency v Stanford*[3] it was held that in summary proceedings a decision against the prosecution on grounds of abuse is final and is therefore capable of being the subject of case stated.

1 [1971] AC 197.
2 [1971] AC 197 at 234.
3 [1999] Env LR 286, QB.

10.39 The procedure is applicable where there are no factual disputes, for the High Court is bound by the findings of fact as stated by the magistrates' court (except where it is contended there was no evidence on which one could have arrived at a particular finding of fact).[1] The aggrieved party may question 'the conviction, order, determination or other proceeding of the court' and the remedy is available to both prosecution and defence. The majority of appeals by way of case stated are based on attempts to overturn either a summary conviction or a summary acquittal. Indeed, it is only available where there has been a final determination in the proceedings, such as a conviction, sentence, acquittal, or (as in abuse cases) an order to stay proceedings.[2] Given this restriction, where a magistrates' court has ruled against the defence at a pre-trial review or preliminary hearing, it has no jurisdiction to state what is, in essence, an 'interlocutory' case throughout the hearing.[3]

1 *Bracegirdle v Oxley* [1947] KB 349.
2 See *DPP v Karl Metten* (22 January 1999, unreported); and *Environment Agency v Stanford* [1998] COD 373.
3 See *Streames v Copping* (1985) 149 JP 305; which was followed in *R v Greater Manchester Justices, ex p Aldi GmbH & Co KG* (1994) 159 JP 717. See also *Gillian v DPP* [2007] 2 Cr App R 12; *Downes v RSPCA* [2017] EWHC 3622 (Admin), [2018] 2 Cr App R 3 (25); *Winder v DPP* [2020] EWHC 1611 (Admin).

10.40 For examples of cases where the prosecution were successful in appealing, by way of case stated, against magistrates' decisions to stay proceedings for abuse of process, see *DPP v Jimale*[1] and also *DPP v Chalmers*.[2] In a further decision of the High Court, where an issue arose as to whether case stated or judicial review was the more appropriate remedy for challenging a magistrates' decision to stay, Sullivan J in the *Sevenoaks Magistrates' Court* case[3] stated that:

> 'In many cases it may well be more convenient to challenge the alleged irregularity by way of case stated, because there will then be no room for doubt as to the facts found by the magistrates and their reasons for allowing the application'.

1 [2001] Crim LR 138.
2 [2000] COD 2. See also *DPP v Gowring* [2013] EWHC 4614 (Admin); *DPP v Jarman* [2013] EWHC 4391 (Admin); *DPP v Fell* [2013] EWHC 562 (Admin); *East Riding of Yorkshire Council v Dearlove* [2012] RTR 29.
3 *R (on the application of Tunbridge Wells Borough Council) v Sevenoaks Magistrates' Court* [2001] EWHC Admin 897.

10.41 It is submitted, however, that as the prosecution in practice very rarely accept all the factual assertions made by the defence in abuse applications, so the case stated route is generally inappropriate and the judicial review route is almost always to be preferred. On a purely tactical point, however, if it is felt that the case stated is available the question then arises of whether the route should be pursued in respect of the magistrates' ruling. Alternatively, should the matter be left for the judgment of the trial judge?

10.42 There seems, in principle, only two advantages why the case stated route might be preferred. First, if the magistrate has not provided any reasoning when rejecting an abuse submission or holding it, this remedy can be used to expose the underlying reasoning. Secondly, the case stated procedure does not require leave from any superior court prior to the hearing.

JUDICIAL REVIEW

Applications for judicial review

10.43 An application to the High Court for judicial review may be made by either the defence or the prosecution, in respect of any ruling or decision of the magistrates' court. Judicial review, which is designed to be expeditious, is not an appeal from a decision, but rather a review of the manner in which it was made.[1]

1 See *Chief Constable of North Wales Police v Evans* [1982] 1 WLR 1155; the procedure for judicial review is governed by the Supreme Court Act 1981, ss 29 and 31, Pt 54 of the Civil Procedure Rules 1998 and the Pt 54 Practice Direction. A party proposing to make an application for judicial review is required to follow the Pre-Action Protocol for Judicial Review.

10.44 In the context of abuse of process applications, the case law suggests that the two most sought after forms of relief are prohibiting orders (formerly known as orders of prohibition)[1] and quashing orders (formerly known as orders of certiorari).[2] The prohibiting order would have the effect, in essence, of having the proceedings stayed, for such an order would prevent magistrates from starting or continuing with a hearing. The object of the order is to prevent magistrates from acting in a manner which is either inconsistent with or in excess of their jurisdiction. In practice this may be used, for example, to challenge a decision to commence or continue with a summary trial or committal proceedings, the abuse of process arguments having been rejected, possibly at an earlier preliminary hearing. The quashing order, by way of contrast, would have the effect of quashing the magistrates' decision to permit the proceedings to continue. Less common remedies in the abuse context would be found in mandatory orders (formerly known as orders of mandamus) and in declarations. The case of *R v Newcastle-upon-Tyne Justices, ex p Hindle*[3] is an example of a case where an order of mandamus was sought to oblige the magistrate to exercise the abuse of process discretion to stay proceedings.

1 See *R v Brentford Justices, ex p Wong* (1980) 73 Cr App R 67; *R v Horsham Justices, ex p Reeves* (1980) 75 Cr App R 236n; *R v Derby Magistrates' Court, ex p Brooks* (1984) 80 Cr App R 164; *R v Willesden Justices, ex p Clemmings* (1987) 87 Cr App R 280; *R v Telford Justices, ex p Badham* [1991] 2 WLR 866.

2 See *R v Guildford Magistrates' Court, ex p Healy* [1983] 1 WLR 108; *R v Liverpool Stipendiary Magistrate, ex p Ellison* [1990] RTR 220n; *R v Rotherham Justices, ex p Brough* [1991] Crim LR 522; *R v Croydon Justices, ex p Dean* (1993) 98 Cr App R 76.

3 [1984] 1 All ER 770.

10.45 Where magistrates have ruled that it is permissible for proceedings to continue, there have also been instances of defendants seeking declarations that such decisions were unlawful.[1] The prosecution, on the other hand, also have an interest in the remedies available through judicial review. Such interest would normally lie in mandatory and quashing orders. For example, they may seek a mandatory order to oblige a magistrate to allow proceedings to continue, or they may seek a quashing order to quash a magistrate's decision to stay proceedings.[2]

1 See *R v Colwyn Justices, ex p DPP* (1990) 154 JP 989; *R v Bow Street Stipendiary Magistrate, ex p DPP and Cherry* (1990) 91 Cr App R 283; *R v Bow Street Metropolitan Stipendiary Magistrate, ex p DPP* (1992) 95 Cr App R 9.

2 See *Ex p DPP and Cherry*; *R v Bow Street MSM, ex p DPP;* and *R v Haringey Justices, ex p DPP* [1996] 2 WLR 114.

The grounds for judicial review

10.46 The grounds on which the High Court may grant relief fall broadly into the following three categories, namely:

(1) *Illegality* – where the magistrates' court has exceeded or abused its powers, or made an error in law;[1]

(2) *Procedural impropriety* – where the court has acted in breach of the rules of natural justice;[2]

(3) *Irrationality* – where the court has reached a decision, which no reasonable tribunal, properly directed and on the evidence, could have reached.[3]

1 See for example, *Croydon Youth Court, ex p DPP* [1997] 2 Cr App R 411.
2 *Warley Magistrates' Court, ex p DPP* [1998] 2 Cr app R 307.
3 *Associated Provincial Picture House Ltd v Wednesbury Corpn* [1948] 1 KB 223.

10.47 Defendants seeking a review of a failed abuse application in the magistrates' court will be seeking to argue that the magistrates acted irrationally or were *Wednesbury* unreasonable. In other words, on the merits of the application put forward by the defence, the application ought to have succeeded.

Approach of the High Court

10.48 On numerous occasions the High Court has resisted becoming a de facto Court of Appeal in relation to failed abuse applications made in the magistrates' court. The overall policy of the High Court in relation to judicial review proceedings arising out of criminal proceedings was set out by Lord Bingham CJ in *R v DPP, ex p Kebilene*:[1]

> 'Where the grant of leave to move judicial review would delay or obstruct the conduct of criminal proceedings which ought, in the public interest, to be resolved with all appropriate expedition, the court will always scrutinise the application with the greatest care, both to satisfy itself that there are sound reasons for making the application and satisfy itself that there are no discretionary grounds (such as delay or the availability of alternative remedies or vexatious conduct by the applicant) which should lead it to refuse leave. The court would be very slow to intervene where the applicant's complaint is one that can be met by appropriate orders or directions in the criminal proceedings …'.[2]

1 [1999] 3 WLR 175; see also the House of Lords' judgment *R v DPP, ex p Kebilene* [2000] 2 AC 326. For a recent restatement, see *R (Baron's Pub Co. Ltd) v Staines Magistrates' Court* [2013] Crim L R 758.
2 [1999] 3 WLR 175 at p 183.

10.49 Commenting on this principle, Lord Steyn in *Kebeline* said:

> 'There is a common law principle … which provides a strong presumption against the Divisional Court entertaining a judicial review application where the complaint can be raised within the criminal trial and appeal process'.

Judicial review is, therefore, available in an appropriate case regarding a decision not to prosecute, as no other remedy is available.[1]

Issues of disclosure will generally not be appropriate for judicial review and are better suited to resolution in the criminal courts.[2]

1 *R (E) v DPP; R (S and R) v DPP* [2012] 1 Cr App R 6.
2 *R (L) v Serious Fraud Office* [2018] 1 WLR 4557.

10.50 It is submitted that the root of this principle can be traced to the judgment of Lord Mustill in *Neill v North Antrim Magistrates' Court*:[1]

> 'it is, however, one thing to hold that it is for the magistrates to rule on admissibility, if invited to do so, so that a decision on the issue must in principle be reviewable, and quite another to say that the grant of relief

should follow as a matter of course. I wholly share the sentiments of those who, over the years, have exclaimed in dismay at the vision of the streams of applications by persons committed for trial seeking to put off the evil day by drawing attention to supposed errors in the application at the committal stage of the high technical rules of criminal evidence. It is only in the case of a really substantial error leading to a demonstrable injustice that the judge in the Divisional Court should contemplate the granting of leave to move'.[2]

1 (1992) 97 Cr App R 121.
2 (1992) 97 Cr App R 121 at 131.

10.51 The principle expressed in this case was reaffirmed by the House of Lords in *R v Bedwellty Justices, ex p Williams.*[1]

1 [1997] AC 225.

10.52 With regard to applications for judicial review based on an alleged abuse of process application which has failed before the magistrates, two authorities make the position plain. First, the judgment of Brook LJ in *R v Liverpool City Justices and Crown Prosecution Service, ex p Price*:[1]

> 'It still did not seem sufficiently well-known that it is only in a very exceptional case that the High Court will exercise its supervisory jurisdiction to intervene and quash a decision by justices in the exercise of their discretion not to stay criminal proceedings for abuse of process. The test was not whether the court agreed with the decision which the magistrates reached, but whether their decision was so plainly irrational and untenable that no reasonable bench of justices, properly directed, could have reached it'.[2]

1 (1998) 162 JP 766, [1998] COD 453.
2 Ibid at p 455. See also *R v Willesden Justices, ex p Clemmings* (1987) 87 Cr App R 280; *R v Barry Magistrates' Court, ex p Malpas* [1998] COD 90; *R v Canterbury and St Augustine Justices, ex p Turner* (1983) 147 JP 193.

10.53 The High Court is, therefore, expressing the view that the burden of proof on the defence is high and necessarily higher than the burden which it will face in the Crown Court where, if a Crown Court judge disagrees with a magistrate's decision, he can overrule it.

10.54 In *R v Bow Street Magistrates' Court, ex p Finch and Bossino*[1] an application was made for judicial review of the committal, in part because of the magistrates' rejection of abuse submission, where Auld LJ held:

> 'the courts have made plain that stays by any court on the ground of abuse of process should only be granted in the most exceptional circumstances and where a defendant is able to demonstrate that he has suffered serious prejudice. This is particularly so in committal proceedings before magistrates where the final airing of the evidence and decision at trial are yet to come'.[2]

1 (9 June 1999, unreported).
2 At p 9 of the transcript. Here a complaint of covert non-disclosure by the prosecution at committal of edited parts of tapes was relied on. Auld LJ held that the court of trial would be best placed to determine the propriety and effect of this alleged non-disclosure.

A procedural note

10.55 In *Ebrahim*[1] Brooke LJ, in the High Court, set out the following procedural guidance for practitioners and magistrates alike, namely:

> 'If a ruling on a stay application is made in a lower court, the court should give its reasons, however briefly, and it is the professional duty of the advocates for the parties to take a note of these. If the decision is to be challenged on judicial review, this court will expect to see a note of the lower court's reasons before deciding whether to grant permission for the application to proceed. If any relevant oral evidence was given, this court will hope that an agreed note can be prepared, summarising its effect'.

1 *R (Ebrahim) v Feltham Magistrates' Court*; *Monat v DPP* [2001] EWHC Admin 130, [2001] 1 WLR 1293, DC.

Procedural tactics in summary cases

10.56 An accused in summary proceedings who has made a failed abuse application before magistrates faces a choice of avenues. He can seek judicial review of the refusal in the High Court or instead exercise the right for a retrial in the Crown Court. The existence of an accused having this choice was doubted in *R v Peterborough Magistrates' Court, ex p Dowler*[1] which questioned whether an accused should have a right to apply for judicial review when there was a subsisting right of appeal to the Crown Court. However, in *R v Hereford Magistrates' Court, ex p Rowlands*,[2] *Dowler* in this regard was doubted and the existence of a choice affirmed. However, the court cautioned that permission should only be granted where the applicant advanced an apparently plausible case, which if made good might be held to vitiate the proceedings in the lower court, and that the granting of relief was discretionary and many factors would be relevant. Bearing in mind the present largely unwelcoming attitude of the High Court as considered above, in most cases and unless the accused feels very confident as to the strength of his abuse claim, it would seem that the accused should opt for the Crown Court over the High Court.

1 [1996] 2 Cr App R 561.
2 [1998] QB 110.

10.57 There are also other disadvantages which appertain to the High Court practice which favour the Crown Court. Judicial review is not a suitable forum for a re-examination of facts found by justices and a detailed reassessment of how such findings should determine the final determination. The High Court by its nature has a need for expedition in its hearings and it will not be sympathetic to being asked to reconsider complex facts especially when it is probably known that there is a judge in the Crown Court available with greater ability and time to consider such matters. The authors have experienced judges sitting in the High Court stating that while it would seem that the applicant has an arguable abuse case on the merits, it is the trial judge who will be best suited to determining this and accordingly so have refused leave to move for judicial review.

10.58 It should also be appreciated that before a Crown Court judge, the accused has the potential to request a voir dire and therefore the calling of live evidence, a facility unavailable in the High Court which is purely based on statement of truth or affidavit evidence. Where facts emerge after conviction, an appeal to the Crown Court is the correct procedure, as the Crown Court has the power to investigate facts.[1] Finally, it can rarely be in the defendant's interest to embark on a judicial review application which is unlikely to succeed and thereon renew it in the Crown Court. An adverse finding in the High Court, even if it is only at the permission stage,[2] with admittedly there being no detailed consideration of the facts, is still nonetheless unlikely to seem appealing to a Crown Court judge.

1 *R v Huyton JJ, ex p Roberts* [1988] COD 43.
2 Civil Procedure Rules 1998, r 54.4.

10.59 However, if the judicial review is to be pursued then applications must be made promptly and, in any event, not later than 3 months after the grounds to make the claim first arose.[1] The prosecution must always be named as an interested party where the claim is for judicial review of a decision of a magistrates' court or the Crown Court.[2]

1 Civil Procedure Rules 1998, r 54.5.
2 Civil Procedure Rules 1998, PD 54A, para 5.2.

CHALLENGING INTERLOCUTORY DECISIONS BY JUDICIAL REVIEW

10.60 Generally, the practitioner should wait until the conclusion of the case in the magistrates' court before making an application for judicial review. In *R (Parashar) v Sunderland Magistrates' Court*,[1] the Divisional Court set out the limited set of circumstances when it would be appropriate to apply to the High Court for a review at an interlocutory stage. They are:

> '(1) where it is properly arguable that the ability of the defendant to present his defence is so seriously compromised by the decision under challenge that an unfair trial is inevitable; (2) where an important point of principle is raised, likely to affect other cases; and (3) where the case has some other exceptional feature which justifies the intervention of the High Court'.[2]

1 [2019] EWHC 514 (Admin).
2 Ibid at para 42.

THE CROWN COURT

Appeals to the Crown Court

10.61 A defendant who has been convicted, after summary proceedings before the justices, may appeal to the Crown Court against his conviction.[1] The appeal is by way of rehearing and, consequently, there would be nothing to prevent the defence practitioner from raising the same abuse of process argument as adopted in the lower court, or indeed in amending the same, or trying a new approach altogether. Likewise, there is no obligation on the prosecution to put their case forward, on the same basis or in the same manner, as was the case before the justices.[2]

1 See Magistrates Court Act 1980, ss 108–110, Criminal Procedure Rules 2020, Pt 34, and Supreme Court Act 1981, s 79(3).
2 See *Hingley-Finch v DPP* (1998) 1 Archbold News 2, DC.

10.62 If either or both of the parties seek to call evidence in support of an abuse of process application, it is contended that they must first, if a short voir dire is to be held at the outset of the appeal, seek the court's leave so to do (as with any other such application before a Crown Court judge). It will be within the judge's discretion as to what evidence may be allowed or not, whether or not it was called in the lower court, the criteria for such discretion presumably being one of relevance. As is the case with any appeal against conviction, the practitioner will no doubt want to advise the appellant that the appeal will put the sentence at large together with a possible liability as to costs, in the event of an adverse finding or conviction. A notice of appeal must be given in writing to the relevant magistrates' court and every other party within 21 days of sentence being passed or deferred. The notice must state whether the appeal is against conviction, sentence, order or failure to make an order, and must summarise the issues. In an appeal against conviction it must specify witnesses the appellant wishes to question and estimate the length of the appeal.[1]

1 Criminal Procedure Rules 2020, Pt 34, rr 34.2, 34.3.

10.63 In the *Ebrahim* decision Brooke LJ opined that the Crown Court appellant, raising a complaint of abuse of process, should not apply for the proceedings to be stayed. The appropriate course rather was to apply for an order allowing the appeal and quashing the conviction on the grounds that the original trial was unfair, and that the unfairness was of such a nature that it could not be remedied on appeal.

Abuse of process applications in the Crown Court

10.64 Once a case has been sent for trial in the Crown Court, the first occasion on which it would be appropriate to raise the question of an abuse of process application is at a preliminary hearing or as soon as practicable after the case has been sent. At a Plea and Trial Preparation Hearing (PTPH) (or a preparatory hearing) the defence is expected to inform the court of legal issues in addition to a list of other obligations which both parties have in relation to general matters of case management and preparation.[1] *R v Penner*[2] held that it was essential that the issues in a case are carefully examined and identified at the plea and case management hearing. Dealing with a case justly, as required by the Criminal Procedure Rules, includes not allowing some perceived procedural advantage by obstructing or delaying the preparation of a case for trial or by taking unfair advantage of another's mistake.[3]

A similar situation applies to the preparatory hearings regime whether they be for serious or complex cases under Pt III of the Criminal Procedure and

Investigations Act 1996 or serious or complex fraud cases under the Criminal Justice Act 1987, as amended by CJA 2003.

1 See Criminal Procedure Rules 2020, Pt 3; Criminal Practice Directions (General matters) 3A.
2 [2010] Crim L R 936.
3 Criminal Practice Direction (General Matters) 1A.

10.65 In relation to pre-trial hearings, which are now governed by the CPIA 1996, s 39 (as amended by CJA 2003), the special feature that rulings made in such hearings have, pursuant to s 40 of that Act, is that they are binding until the determination of all the proceedings. Section 40(3)–(5) reads as follows:

> '(3) Subject to subsection (4), a ruling made under this section has binding effect from the time it is made until the case against the accused or, if there is more than one, against each of them is disposed of; and the case against an accused is disposed of if—
>
> (a) he is acquitted or convicted, or
>
> (b) the prosecutor decides not to proceed with the case against him.
>
> (4) A judge may discharge or vary (or further vary) a ruling made under this section if it appears to him that it is in the interests of justice to do so; and a judge may act under this subsection—
>
> (a) on an application by a party to the case, or
>
> (b) of the judge's own motion.
>
> (5) No application may be made under subsection (4) unless there has been a material change of circumstances since the ruling was made or if a previous application has been made, since the application (or last application) was made.'

10.66 It is submitted that the effect of this more formalised regime is that while a trial judge always has the discretion to review a pre-trial ruling made by him, it means that the defence, if they wish to renew a previously unsuccessful abuse application, will have to establish pursuant to subs (5) a material change of circumstances. This may not be easy and so it is submitted that an abuse application should not be mounted until the optimum moment when all material evidence has been gathered and arguments refined.

Challenging adverse rulings of the Crown Court

10.67 Whether the High Court has power to entertain an application for judicial review arising out of a ruling made by a Crown Court judge is governed by section 29(3) of the Supreme Court Act 1981 which provides that:

> 'In relation to the jurisdiction of the Crown Court, other than its jurisdiction in matters relating to trial on indictment, the High Court shall have all such jurisdiction to make mandatory, prohibiting or quashing orders as the High Court possesses in relation to the jurisdiction of an inferior court'.

10.68 Section 29(3) therefore prevents a decision made by the Crown Court from being challenged by an application for judicial review if it was deemed to be relating to a matter relating to trial on indictment. The same rule is applicable to appeals by way of case stated from the Crown Court.[1]

1 Supreme Court Act 1981, s 28.

10.69 The rationale for s 29(3) was explained by Lord Bridge in *Re Smalley*[1] as follows:

> 'it is not difficult to discern a sensible legislative purpose in excluding appeal or judicial review of any decision affecting the conduct of a trial on indictment, whether given in the course of the trial or by way of pre-trial directions. In any such case to allow an appellate or review process might … seriously delay the trial. If it is the prosecutor who is aggrieved by such a decision, it is no way surprising that he has no remedy, since prosecutors have never enjoyed rights of appeal or review when unsuccessful in trials on indictment. If, on the other hand, the defendant is so aggrieved, he will have his remedy by way of appeal against conviction …'[2].

1 [1985] AC 622.
2 Ibid at 642–643.

10.70 This explanation was approved by Lord Slynn (speaking for a unanimous House) in *Re Ashton.*[1] In *Ashton* the trial judge had refused an application to stay the trial for grounds of abuse and judicial review of this refusal was sought. The decisions of *Re Ashton* and *Re Smalley* were applied in *R (Snelgrove) v Woolwich Crown Court* in the context of a failed attempt to judicially review an unsuccessful dismissal application.[2] *Snelgrove* held that once a case has been sent by the magistrates to the Crown Court, the Crown Court is seized of the matter and all decisions concerning the issue between the accused and the Crown were 'matters relating to a trial on indictment'. As such they were excepted from judicial review by s 29(3) of the 1981 Act.

While the position which Lord Bridge commented upon above has changed, given that prosecutors do now enjoy the right to appeal a terminating ruling, the authors do not anticipate any movement in the current position. Crown Court Judges' rulings on abuse of process are likely to continue to remain outside the ambit of any application for judicial review.

1 [1994] 1 AC 9.
2 [2005] 1 Cr App R 18.

10.71 In relation to a future application for judicial review where a Crown Court judge is refusing to hold a prosecution to be an abuse of process, by reason of an alleged breach of the European Convention, the House of Lords held in *R v DPP, ex p Kebilene* that s 29(3) would likewise prohibit such an application.[1]

1 See for example the judgment of Lord Steyn at p 9 of transcript (1999) *Times*, 2 November.

Preparatory hearings and interlocutory appeals

10.72 The preparatory hearing regime introduced by the Criminal Justice Act 1987 was a central part of the new scheme for serious fraud trials. One of the radical concepts introduced by the Act was that of interlocutory appeals allowing the parties to appeal to the Court of Appeal pre-trial any ruling on a point of law which could affect the outcome of a trial. Section 9(11) of the Act granted this right of interlocutory appeal in respect of such rulings made during a preparatory hearing.

10.73 In the House of Lords decision of *R v H*[1] a significantly new approach was adopted to the scope of these interlocutory appeals. Their Lordships overruled the previous line of authority of *Re Gunarwardena,*[2] which had held abuse of process applications fell outside CJA 1987, s 7(1).

1 [2007] 2 WLR 364.
2 [1990] 91 Cr App R 55.

10.74 In *R v H* it was held that the purposes for which a preparatory hearing could be held, pursuant to s 7(1) of the 1987 Act, should be given a broad and generous interpretation, and that the aim of those purposes was the efficient and expeditious disposal of criminal proceedings so as to reduce the amount of time which would otherwise be wasted. In his commentary on this decision, Professor Ormerod[1] discussed this apparent right of defence appeal, as follows:

> 'A majority of the House has arguably accepted that a decision to stay or make other terminating rulings may be made at a preparatory hearing, under s.9, and as a consequence, be appealed by the defence if rejected. This might be seen as a useful balance to the Crown's right of appeal under section 58 of the Criminal Justice Act 2003, but arguments will now no doubt arise as to whether an application to stay for abuse should be delayed until a preparatory hearing occurs (and D has been arraigned) in order to secure the chance of a defence appeal if rejected.'

However, in *R v V J A*,[2] the Court of Appeal held that the judge's determination on the application to stay the proceedings against V as being an abuse of process did not constitute a ruling on 'any other question of law relating to the case' under s 9(3)(c) of the 1987 Act within *R v H.* The right to an interlocutory appeal was an exceptional right in Crown Court trials, and even where a question of law falling within the ambit of s 9(3)(c) was raised, the court could exercise its discretion in refusing to grant leave.

R v I(C)[3] held that the changes in the Crown Court's general case management powers and disclosure rules since 1996 meant that 'it is emphatically not the case that most heavy fraud or similar cases will nowadays call for a preparatory hearing'. Virtually the only reason for directing such a hearing is if the judge is going to have to give a ruling which ought to be the subject of an interlocutory appeal; which would be justified only very exceptionally, as where the point was discrete, novel, certain to arise, involved no factual dispute and needed to be authoritatively determined lest the trial proceed on what might turn out to be a false footing.

1 [2007] Crim LR 731–735.
2 [2011] Lloyd's Rep F C 113, CA.
3 [2010] 1 Cr App R 10, at para 21; see also *R v Berry* [2014] EWCA Crim 505; and *R v Lear* [2018] 2 Cr App R 11.

Decisions which do not relate to trial on indictment

10.75 Appeal by way of case stated or judicial review are both possible options open to an applicant seeking to question a Crown Court decision in a matter not relating to trial on indictment.[1] A Crown Court decision to allow or dismiss an appeal from a magistrates' court would clearly fall within that category and thus allow the unsuccessful party a further appeal, from the Crown Court to the Divisional Court, by case stated. This also applies to an aggrieved prosecutor who had a summary conviction overturned, or else, to a defendant who was convicted for the second time, on appeal to the Crown Court. An appellant contemplating an appeal by case stated, on the basis of some form of abuse of process submission, must have regard to the fact that an appeal would only lie on the ground that the Crown Court decision was either wrong in law or in excess of jurisdiction. The principles which govern the granting of relief by way of judicial review of a Crown Court decision, are broadly the same as those discussed above at para **10.46** in relation to judicial review of magistrates' courts decisions.[2]

1 See the Supreme Court Act 1981, ss 28 and 29(3).
2 See also, in relation to the powers of the High Court, *R v Chelmsford Crown Court, ex p Chief Constable of Essex Police* [1994] 99 Cr App R 59, DC, and *R v Leeds Crown Court, ex p Barlow* [1989] RTR 246, DC.

APPEALS TO THE COURT OF APPEAL AGAINST ADVERSE RULINGS IN THE CROWN COURT

10.76 As a result of the amendment to the Criminal Appeal Act 1968, s 2[1] the single criterion for interference by the Court of Appeal with a conviction reached by a jury is now its unsafety. The amended s 2(1) is as follows:

> 'Subject to the provisions of this Act, the Court of Appeal—
>
> (a) shall allow an appeal against conviction if they think that the conviction is unsafe; and
>
> (b) shall dismiss such an appeal in any other case'.

1 By virtue of the Criminal Appeal Act 1995.

10.77 The court's jurisdiction is entirely statutory and it depends on interpretation of the word 'unsafe'. What does 'unsafe' mean? In the absence of any statutory definition, this crucial word has been the subject of debate by lawyers, academics and judges alike. Sir John Smith, in his prescient 1995 article, predicted that the powers of the Court of Appeal to allow an appeal against conviction were in danger of being severely curtailed (albeit that was never the intention of the Royal Commission, the Home Office or Parliament) on the basis of the simple rules of statutory construction.[1] As it was to transpire, the deletion by the Criminal Appeal Act 1995 of the second limb criteria 'or unsatisfactory', 'wrong decision of any question of law' and 'material irregularity' found in the 1968 Act was to cause significant difficulties in the years to come for practitioners seeking to argue abuse of process as a ground of appeal. This was largely because the Court of Appeal in some cases drew a restrictive and narrow definition of 'unsafe' which appeared to rule out certain forms of abuse of process as a route to appeal.

1 See Sir John Smith 'The Criminal Appeal Act 1995' [1995] Crim LR 920, his commentary at 1997 CLR 48 and Professor JR Spencer 'When is a conviction 'unsafe'' (1998) 5 Archbold News.

10.78 Against a background of uncertainty and ambiguity in the case law, the lowest point for abuse of process as a ground of appeal, was the decision of *R v Chalkley and Jeffries*[1] which defined 'unsafe' in a most narrow fashion. Recently, however, the pendulum appears to have swung strongly back in favour of a broader interpretation of 'unsafe' as in the case of *R v Mullen*[2] where the Court of Appeal acknowledged the various circumstances in which abuse of process submissions could lead to successful appeals against conviction.

1 (1998) 2 Cr App R 79.
2 [2000] QB 520, CA.

10.79 Before turning to an analysis of the recent case law on the subject, it is proposed to start by briefly looking at the pre-1995 Act practice of the Court of Appeal (which is still of relevance in the light of *R v Mullen*).

Pre-1995 Act practice

10.80 In the 1984 decision in *R v Heston-Francois,*[1] the Court of Appeal acknowledged abuse of process as a ground of appeal. Lord Justice Watkins stated that:

> 'Where there has been oppressive conduct savouring of abuse of process, it seems clear that the Court of Appeal … may quash a conviction on the ground that it is "unsatisfactory" or "unsafe".'

He added that the Court of Appeal was well placed to decide whether or not a particular accused suffered any actual prejudice in the course of a trial. In 1992, the court reaffirmed this doctrine as a ground of appeal in the *Attorney-General's Reference (No 1 of 1990)*.[2]

1 (1984) 78 Cr App R 209.
2 [1992] QB 630; (1992) 95 Cr App R 296.

10.81 One of the other popular catch phrases of the Court of Appeal pre-1995 was the 'lurking doubt' approach formulated by Widgery LJ in *R v Cooper.*[1] This was an alternative approach to considering a conviction as being unsafe or unsatisfactory. However, in *R v F*[2] the court denigrated the continued use of this phrase, arguing that 'unsafety' was a simpler, briefer, and therefore a superior, concept.

1 [1969] 1 QB 267; 53 Cr App R 82.
2 [1999] Crim LR 306.

10.82 The other significant issue which concerned the role of the court was its jurisdiction to hold a conviction unsafe or unsatisfactory when the defendant has unequivocally pleaded guilty. As a plea of guilty is said to be the best evidence of a defendant's guilt, how then could the court seek to upset this? In suitable circumstances this paradox did not trouble the court. For example, in two cases concerned with the cause celebre of the Arms to Iraq affair, *R v Schlesinger*[1] and *R v Blackledge*,[2] the appellants had pleaded guilty. The investigation by Sir Richard Scott however, revealed that prior to the respective trials, important evidence which undermined the prosecution's case had not been disclosed and accordingly when the defendants had decided to plead guilty they had done so without knowledge of this abuse by the prosecution. In *Schlesinger* and *Blackledge* the court was in no doubt that the appellant's convictions were unsafe and unsatisfactory. Prosecution machinations had deprived the appellants of their right to a fair trial, they had pleaded guilty on a false basis and therefore their convictions could be overturned.

1 [1995] Crim L R 137.
2 [1996] 1 Cr App R 326.

Post-1995 Act but pre-Mullen case law

10.83 A better understanding of the *Mullen* decision will no doubt be reached by a brief review of the earlier authorities, which place it in a proper context. In *R v Graham*[1] the Court of Appeal held that the amended version of s 2(1) pursuant to the 1995 Act, was intended to focus attention on one question only, namely whether the court considered the conviction unsafe. Where the court was satisfied, despite any misdirection or irregularity in the conduct of the trial or any fresh evidence, that the conviction was nonetheless safe the appeal would be dismissed. So arguably if the court felt that the trial judge should have granted an abuse application and stayed the proceedings on the evidence before him but nonetheless the trial was fair then according to this logic, the conviction could still nonetheless be safe.

1 [1997] 1 Cr App R 302.

10.84 In *R v Chalkley* the appellant had pleaded guilty following an adverse s 78 ruling as to the admissibility of certain highly damaging evidence. It was contended that if the ruling of the trial judge was wrong in law then this should lead to the quashing of his conviction. The court found this argument legally erroneous. An irregularity in the trial procedure including an error of law by the judge, which might prior to amendment by the 1995 Act have rendered a conviction unsatisfactory, is not of itself a ground for quashing a conviction. Now it is only a ground if it leads on to the conclusion that the conviction is for some reason unsafe. The Court of Appeal held that, when considering an appeal against conviction the previous tests of 'unsatisfactoriness' and 'material irregularity' were no longer at the disposal of the court, save as aids in determining the safety of a conviction. Accordingly, the court held that it had no power to allow an appeal against conviction which was not considered unsafe, albeit that in some regard the conviction was unsatisfactory.

10.85 In relation to a plea of guilty the court held that a conviction here would only be unsafe where the consequence of an incorrect ruling of law on admitted facts was to leave an accused with no legal escape from a verdict of guilty on those facts. A conviction, however, would not normally be unsafe, per Auld LJ, where an accused was influenced to change his plea to guilty having recognised that, as a result of a ruling to admit damning evidence against him, a defence was hopeless. 'The court has no power under the substituted s 2(1) to allow an appeal if it does not think the conviction unsafe but is dissatisfied in some way with what went on at the trial'. The court did not consider the scenario of whether a conviction may be held to be unsafe where there has been an abuse of process. In other words, can a conviction be regarded as unsafe where the appellant has had a fair trial but it was for some reason unfair to try him? Better in such a circumstance that the accused was never tried at all but the accused was and had a fair trial and was properly convicted. Is such a conviction 'safe'? The approach of the court in *Chalkley* was that even if the court held there was an abuse, the conviction could still be safe.

10.86 In *R v Martin*[1] the House considered obiter the same issue and there was a difference of opinion. Lord Hope in an abuse context, adopted a broader interpretation of 'unsafe':

> 'I do not think it can be doubted that the Appeal Court … have power to declare a conviction to be unsafe and to quash a conviction if they find that the course of proceedings leading to what would otherwise have been a fair trial has been such as to threaten either basic human rights or the rule of law'.

1 [1998] AC 917, HL.

10.87 Lord Lloyd, however, felt that it would not be sufficient for the appellant to establish that the proceedings constituted an abuse of process for the conviction to be quashed.

10.88 Two other cases were decided by the court soon after *Chalkley* and *Martin*. In *R v Simpson*[1] the court pondered whether it could ever quash a conviction as unsafe arising out of a prosecution abuse if no abuse application had ever been made at the trial. In *R v MacDonald*[2] Auld LJ took the opportunity to withdraw from the position which he had adopted in *Chalkley*. Considering what should happen in a *Bennett*-type abuse situation Auld LJ said:

> 'It may be that a conviction in a trial which should never have taken place is to be regarded as unsafe for that reason. It may be that, despite the statutory basis of the court's jurisdiction, it also has some inherent or ancillary jurisdictional basis for intervening to mark abuse of process by quashing a conviction when it considers that the court below should have stayed the proceeding. Or it may be that the recent amendment to the 1968 Act has removed the supervisory role of this court over abuse of criminal process where the affront to justice, however, outrageous, has not so prejudiced a defendant in his trial as to render his conviction unsafe. All that is for decision by another court in an appropriate case'.

The *Mullen* decision (see para **10.89** below) neatly fits the description of that 'appropriate case'.

1 [1998] Crim LR 481.
2 [1998] Crim LR 808.

The decision in Mullen

10.89 Until the Court of Appeal decision in *Mullen*[1] the state of the case law in relation to post-amendment appeals on abuse of process, was highly unsatisfactory. The pre-*Mullen* case law was frequently in a state of ambiguity and uncertainty where certain decisions were, it is submitted, decided on an overly restrictive interpretation of the word 'unsafe', the *Chalkley* case being a prime example. It is submitted that the *Mullen* decision is a landmark case, of fundamental importance to the question of abuse of process in the context of appeals to the Court of Appeal.

1 [2000] QB 520, CA.

10.90 In the judgment of the Vice President, Rose LJ, considerable attention was given to the proper meaning of the amendment to the Criminal Appeal Act 1968, and the correct interpretation of the word 'unsafe'. Rose LJ held that:

> '… for a conviction to be safe it must be lawful; and if it results from a trial which should never have taken place it can hardly be regarded as "safe". Indeed the Oxford Dictionary gives the legal meaning of "unsafe" as "likely to constitute a miscarriage of justice". Sir John Smith's article to which we have referred does not deal with "unsafe" in relation to abuse, though his commentary on *Simpson* … raises directly pertinent questions. But, for the reasons which we have given, we agree with his 1995 conclusion that "unsafe" bears a broad meaning and one which is apt to embrace abuse of process of the *Bennett*–type or any other kind.'

10.91 While Rose LJ stressed, elsewhere in the judgment[1], that there may be certain circumstances where a finding of abuse of process by the Court of Appeal may not necessarily lead to the quashing of a conviction on appeal, nevertheless this judgment clearly opens up many avenues for arguing abuse of process as a ground of appeal. It is of considerable significance that Rose LJ ended the above passage with reference, not only to the *Bennett*-type abuse (ie where it would be unfair for a defendant to be tried, for example, by reason of procedural unfairness by the prosecution) situation, but also to abuse of 'any other kind'. This must presumably include the first main limb of abuse of process (using the two limb test in *R v Beckford*[2]), where the circumstances are such that it is not possible for a defendant to receive a fair trial.

It is worth noting that the importation of the concept of 'fairness' in the second limb of the *Beckford* test, where it would be unfair for the defendant to be tried even though a fair trial could be conducted, was considered unhelpful in *Warren v Attorney General for Jersey*,[3] which reviewed authorities including the Supreme Court case of *R v Maxwell*.[4] In *Maxwell* it was held that it is well established that the court has the power to stay proceedings in two categories of case. The first category is where it will be impossible to give the accused a fair trial and the second is where it offends the court's sense of justice and propriety to be asked to try the accused in the particular circumstances of the case; where the court is concerned to protect the integrity of the criminal justice system.

1 [2000] QB 520, CA at p 536H.
2 [1996] 1 Cr App R 94.
3 [2012] 1 AC 22, PC; see, in particular the judgments of Lord Dyson at para 35 and Lord Kerr at paras 83–86.
4 *R v Maxwell* [2011] 1 WLR 1837.

10.92 A number of points of principle and procedure emerge from this important judgment. First, the Court of Appeal reaffirmed that it has a supervisory discretion to oversee appeals on the ground of abuse of process. Secondly, that it will entertain appeals which cover all species of abuse of process, that is, consider appeals on the basis that the trial was unfair or that the court's sense of justice and propriety is offended or public confidence in the criminal justice system would be undermined by the trial. Thirdly, that not all findings of abuse of process by the court will necessarily lead to a conviction being quashed or a retrial avoided. Rose LJ explained that in this circumstance the court would not exercise its power to quash convictions automatically: 'In each case it is a matter of discretionary balance, to be approached with regard to the particular conduct complained of and the particular offence charged'. Furthermore he added:

> 'In arriving at this conclusion we strongly emphasise that nothing in this judgment should be taken to suggest that there may not be cases, such as *Latif*, in which the seriousness of the crime is so great relative to the nature of the abuse of process that it would be a proper exercise of judicial discretion to permit a prosecution to proceed or to allow a conviction to stand notwithstanding an abuse of process of this kind'.

10.93 The *Latif* case[1] which Rose LJ referred to in the above passage involved strong public policy considerations in relation to the fight against organised crime, in the context of a serious drugs case (where customs officers arranged for the appellant to be lured from Pakistan to the UK by trickery and deception and also committed criminal offences). The 'discretionary balance' mentioned by Rose LJ was in *Latif* described by Lord Steyn in the following terms:

> 'If the court always refuses to stay such proceedings, the perception will be that the court condones criminal conduct and malpractice by law enforcement agencies. That would undermine public confidence in the criminal justice system and bring it into disrepute. On the other hand, if the court were always to stay proceedings in such cases, it would incur the reproach that it is failing to protect the public from serious crime. The weakness of both extreme positions leaves only one principled solution. The court has a discretion; it has to perform a balancing exercise'.

1 *R v Latif; R v Shahzad* [1996] 1 All ER 353, HL.

10.94 Weighing up the public policy considerations involved, the House held that the officer's conduct was not so unworthy or shameful that it was an affront to the public conscience to allow the prosecution to proceed. Lord Steyn observed 'realistically any criminal behaviour of the customs officer was venial compared to that of *Shahzad*' who was said to have been an organiser in the heroin trade.[1]

1 See WG Roser 'Entrapment: have the courts found a solution to this fundamental dilemma to the criminal justice system? [1993] 67 ALJ 722 and Andrew L-T Choo 'Halting criminal prosecutions: The abuse of process doctrine revisited' [1995] Crim LR 864 as referred to in *Latif*.

10.95 It is submitted that *R v Mullen* should be regarded as the authoritative decision on appeals to the Court of Appeal. The judgment of Rose LJ both answers the questions posed by *Chalkley* and rids us of the ambiguities it created.[1] Indeed, not only has *Mullen* given effect, to a large extent, to the intention of the Home Office, the Royal Commission and Parliament (in conferring a broad meaning to 'unsafe') it has also rejuvenated the pre-amendment case law and resurrected, after their temporary demise at the hands of *Chalkley,* the decisions of *R v Bloomfield,*[2] *R v Mahdi*[3] and *Blackledge.*[4] The test of whether a conviction is safe no longer simply depends on whether the court is satisfied that the appellant is guilty on the evidence. The court now has a discretion to consider issues such as procedural unfairness by the prosecution, for example, non-disclosure, material irregularities and abuse.

1 Note Professor Smith's commentary on *Mullen* at [1999] Crim LR 562.
2 [1997] 1 Cr App R 135.
3 [1993] Crim LR 793.
4 [1996] 1 Cr App R 326.

The approval of Mullen

10.96 In the decision of *R v Togher*[1] the Court of Appeal resoundingly approved the *Mullen* decision, Lord Woolf CJ, at para 30 of his judgment, stating the following:

> 'Applying the broader approach identified by Rose LJ, we consider that if a defendant has been denied a fair trial it will almost be inevitable that the conviction will be regarded as unsafe. For this reason we endorse the approach of Rose LJ in *Mullen* and prefer the broader approach to the narrower approach supported by Auld LJ. Certainly, if it would be right to stop a prosecution on the basis that it was an abuse of process, this court would be most unlikely to conclude that if there was a conviction despite this fact, the conviction should not be set aside'.

The authors respectfully agree with the Lord Chief Justice's judgment for, if an appellate court has decided either that it was unfair for an appellant to have been tried, or that a fair trial was not possible, it is difficult to conceive of proper circumstances where the court can nevertheless maintain the safety of the conviction.

1 [2001] 1 Cr App R 33.

What is the effect of pleading guilty on an appeal to the Court of Appeal?

10.97 In *Mullen* the Court of Appeal made plain that pursuant to its statutory jurisdiction to entertain appeals against conviction pursuant to the Criminal Appeal Act 1995, it was able to entertain such appeals based on the ground that the fairness of the trial was negated by an abuse of process. What, however, is the position where a defendant unsuccessfully argues abuse of process before the trial court, subsequently changes his plea to guilty, before appealing against the conviction on the grounds of the adverse abuse ruling? Does the Court of Appeal have jurisdiction to entertain such an appeal, or is the defendant required to maintain the not guilty plea in order to preserve his subsequent appeal rights? It appears that this question can be answered in the affirmative. Although *Chalkley* initially offered a position to the contrary, the decisions of *Togher* and *R v Early*[1] have thrown much light on this subject and it seems it is this line of authority which has prevailed.

1 [2003] 1 Cr App R 19.

10.98 It will be recalled that in *Chalkley*[1] the court held that a conviction following a plea of guilty will not normally be deemed in any circumstances to be unsafe, even if the proceedings had been irregular in some significant way or amounted to an abuse of process. So far as the court was concerned in *Chalkley*, the decisive factor overriding all others was if the defendant had entered a valid plea of guilty.[2] Following *Chalkley* in *Rajcoomar,* which was a post-*Mullen* case, the court ruled that *Mullen* did not affect the court's ruling in *Chalkley*. The court pointed out in *Rajcoomar* that in *Mullen* the defendant had pleaded not guilty and had contested his trial.

1 [1998] 2 Cr App R 79.
2 For example, a plea which is not vitiated by mistake or duress.

10.99 The opposing school of thought, based principally on a construction of the court's judgment in *Mullen,* is that the court does have a jurisdiction to consider appeals against conviction even after valid guilty pleas. In his commentary on *Rajcoomar*, Professor Smith succinctly sets out the argument:

> '… But if, as the court said in *Mullen*, … for a conviction to be safe, it must be lawful; and, if it results from a trial which should never have taken place, it can hardly be regarded as safe, what does it matter whether the conviction results from a plea of guilty or a verdict of guilty by the jury? In both cases the defendant is in law guilty of the offence charged, but in neither case should the trial have taken place at all. According to the reasoning in *Mullen*, it is safe in both, or it is safe in neither'.[1]

1 [1999] Crim LR 728.

10.100 In *Togher* the Court of Appeal followed the decision in *Mullen* and held that an appeal against conviction after a plea of guilty could be allowed if the proceedings constituted an abuse of process such that it would be inconsistent with the due administration of justice to allow the guilty plea to stand. The actual appeals were dismissed in *Togher*, however. The court was wholly unimpressed with the argument that there had in fact been an abuse of process in the related trial proceedings. On the facts of that case there was found to be no justification for interfering with the freely-entered pleas of guilty. Whilst the court accepted that the appellants had been deprived of certain prosecution disclosure, the non-disclosure did not amount to an abuse of process, for, as the Lord Chief Justice said:

> 'They were never ignorant of any evidence which went directly to their innocence or guilt. They were only unaware of material which could, but for their pleas, have been used in order to attack the credibility of the prosecution witnesses. Ignorance of this nature does not justify reopening their pleas of guilty'.[1]

1 [2001] 1 Cr App R 33 at para 59.

10.101 By contrast, the non-disclosure and misconduct in *Early* was so significant that the convictions of all eight appellants (who had pleaded guilty) were quashed in the Court of Appeal. Lord Justice Rose, in *Early*, stated that the Court of Appeal would approach the question of the safety of convictions, following pleas of guilty, in accordance with the *Mullen* and *Togher* decisions. In *Early* the court clearly had no doubt that the non-disclosure impinged upon issues relating to 'innocence or guilt'. Indeed, in relation to two of the appellants, the court declared that, had the trial judge been aware of the true position, he may well have decided not to refuse the abuse of process applications.

10.102 In *Early* Rose LJ made it clear that prosecution witnesses who perjure themselves in a public interest immunity or abuse voir dire are likely to 'taint beyond redemption' a prosecution case, irrespective of the strength of the case against a particular defendant. This decision suggests therefore that situations 'where it would be inconsistent with the due administration of justice to allow the pleas of guilty to stand'[1] include, first, proven instances of gross misconduct by the prosecution and/or, second, significant prosecution non-disclosure, at the time the pleas were entered.

1 Per Woolf CJ in *R v Togher* [2001] 1 Cr App R 457 at 468, para 33.

10.103 The issue has been considered more recently in the case of *R v Asiedu*.[1] In that case, the defendant entered a basis of plea at the beginning of his retrial for terrorism related offences following a Goodyear indication. Following this, he complained that there had been an abuse of process by virtue of lack of prosecution disclosure.

Albeit on the facts, the appellant was unsuccessful, the authority is of assistance as Lord Hughes reviewed the authorities in this area and confirmed the circumstances in which a guilty plea will not affect a defendant's ability to appeal against his conviction. The first is where the plea of guilty was compelled as a matter of law by an adverse ruling by the trial judge which left no arguable defence to be put before the jury.[2] i.e. if a judge ruled that even on the defence case he had no defence in law, he will not be precluded from appealing the correctness of that ruling and his conviction. His Lordship continued:

> 'The second situation in which a plea of guilty will not prevent an appeal is where, even if on the admitted or assumed facts the defendant was guilty, there was a legal obstacle to his being tried for the offence. That will be true in those cases, rare as they are, where his prosecution would be stayed on the grounds that it is offensive to justice to bring him to trial. Such cases are generally described, conveniently if not entirely accurately, as cases of "abuse of process". The classical example of such is *R. v Horseferry Road Magistrates' Court Ex p. Bennett* (1994) 98 Cr. App. R. 114; [1994] A.C. 42…As this court [in Mullen] said, at 161 and 540: "… for a conviction to be safe, it must be lawful; and if it results from a trial which should never have taken place, it can hardly be regarded as safe". By parity of reasoning, if the trial process should never have taken place because it is offensive to justice, a conviction upon a plea of guilty is as unsafe as one following trial'.[3]

Lord Hughes then went on to distinguish *Chalkley* and held that 'the court there went too far in offering, obiter, the opinion that a plea of guilty would prevent an appeal [in cases where there has been an abuse of process]. That dictum was inconsistent with the reasoning in the later case of *Mullen* (although there had been no plea of guilty there) and it was corrected in *R v Togher* [2001] 1 Cr App R 33 (p 457)'.[4]

1 [2015] EWCA Crim 714; [2015] 2 Cr App R 8.
2 Ibid at para 20.
3 Ibid at para 21.
4 Ibid at para 22.

10.104 It is submitted that the decision in *Asiedu* confirms that the *Togher / Early* line of authority, is to be preferred over *Chalkley* and *Rajcoomar*, to the extent that the latter cases suggest that a guilty plea following a failed abuse of process argument precludes an appeal against conviction to the Court of Appeal.

10.105 Finally, it is relevant to consider the position of the court pre-implementation of the 1995 Act. For example, in *Schlesinger*[1] there was an unequivocal plea of guilty at the trial. Nonetheless, the court unhesitatingly quashed the conviction holding that the entire prosecution of the defendant was an abuse.[2] It is submitted that the decision in *Mullen* is in conformity with the decision in *Schlesinger*.

1 *R v Schlesinger* [1995] Crim LR 137.
2 Here the defendant had entered a guilty plea in ignorance of abusive behaviour committed by the prosecution. See paras **5.147–5.148** for further consideration of this case.

10.106 It is submitted that to deprive an appellant who has pleaded guilty from any avenue of appeal would be wrong in principle and inconsistent with the interests of justice. Moreover, on pragmatic grounds it would mean that a defendant, properly advised, would contest every prosecution no matter how hopeless his defence or how legally inescapable his conviction. A defendant pleading not guilty in such circumstances would result in his trial being almost a farce with defence counsel simply adopting a formalistic role. Nonetheless, bearing in mind the prevailing ambiguity in the authorities, it seems that for the purpose of preserving appeal rights, every defendant must be advised to plead not guilty for fear that otherwise appeal rights may be precluded.

Abuse of process as a novel ground of appeal

10.107 In the Court of Appeal can it be argued that the trial was unfair because of a specific abuse which was known to the defence at the trial but never complained about?

10.108 In *Mullen* the court held that, where no ruling is sought by the defence on a matter within the trial judge's discretion, this will 'usually be fatal to any subsequent attempt to rely on that matter by way of appeal to this court'. In these circumstances practitioners would be well advised to make their abuse of process application at the appropriate time in the Crown Court, in order to avoid being precluded from arguing it on appeal. In *Mullen* itself the court excused the defence's failure to argue abuse at trial for two reasons. First, the prosecution were responsible for non-disclosure of documents which were at the time of trial relevant to the abuse issue and secondly, the state of the law on this species of abuse was not so favourable to the defence at the time, the trial having occurred in 1990 pre-*Bennett.*[1]

1 At that time there were conflicting authorities on the issue of whether a court should ever inquire into circumstances concerning how a defendant had come into the jurisdiction.

Prosecution appeals to the Court of Appeal

10.109 The prosecution have a right of appeal against a Crown Court judge's ruling to stay a case for abuse of process. This right of appeal was introduced by ss 58–61 of the Criminal Justice Act 2003, whose provisions came into force on 4 April 2005.[1] The appeal procedure is available on the basis that a stay of proceedings amounts to a 'Terminating Ruling.' The Court of Appeal has no inherent jurisdiction to hear an appeal by the prosecution against a terminating ruling, thus for jurisdiction to arise the prosecution must have complied with the pre-conditions under ss 58(4) and 58(8).[2]

1 See Criminal Justice Act 2003 (Commencement No 8 and Transitional and Saving Provisions) Order 2005 (SI 2005/950).

2 *R v T (N)* [2010] 2 Cr App R 12. See also Arch Rev (2010), 4, 2; the strictures of these rules are apparent from the decision in *R v C* [2017] EWCA Crim 2257.

10.110 The limitations upon this right, however, were highlighted in the decision of *R v B.*[1] On the facts of the case, Sir Igor Judge, as he then was, dismissed the prosecution's appeal, and found that there was no possible basis for interfering with the trial judge's decision to stay. The case had involved the alleged attempted abduction of a child, the issue being identification. On appeal, the Court accepted that critical evidence, which had been destroyed, relating to identification, justified the trial judge's ruling that a fair trial was then no longer possible. The only issue taken with the trial judge, by the Court of Appeal, related to his decision to give the prosecution leave to appeal in the first place.

1 See [2008] EWCA Crim 1144, CA, judgment of 1 May 2008.

10.111 The court held that when a judge exercised his discretion or made his judgment in the course of a trial, the 'very fact that he has had carefully to balance conflicting considerations will almost inevitably mean that he might reasonably have reached a different, or the opposite conclusion to the one he did reach'.[1] The mere fact, however, that there were valid opposing arguments does not begin to provide the prosecution with the basis for a successful appeal. The Court held that an application for leave to appeal will not be given unless it is seriously arguable that it had been unreasonable for the judge to have made his decision on the ruling in the manner that he did. Section 67 of the Criminal Justice Act 2003 expressly sets out the Appeal Court's powers to reverse a ruling.

1 See para 19 of Sir Igor Judge's judgment.

10.112 Where the prosecution fail to obtain leave to appeal, or abandon the appeal, then the proper course, pursuant to CJA 2003, s 58(8) will be for the

Appeal Court to order an acquittal in respect of the offence or offences which are the subject of appeal.[1]

1 See *R v R* [2008] 3 Archbold News 2, CA on the 'acquittal agreement'; for other examples of terminating ruling appeals in abuse of process cases, see *R v O* [2007] EWCA Crim 3483, and *R v Arnold* [2008] EWCA Crim 1034, in relation to a Courts-Martial appeal.

RETRIALS

10.113 A less common area where abuse arguments arise is in relation to retrials. They occur either after a first trial has had a 'hung' or discharged jury,[1] or by direction of the Court of Appeal. By the very nature of a retrial, 'delay' will commonly be an issue, particularly where serious and complex proceedings are involved, but are there any additional abuse factors peculiar to retrial situations?

1 See *R v Piggott and Litwin* [1999] 2 Cr App R 320 for an example of a retrial amounting to an abuse of process (where late prosecution amendments to the first trial's indictment significantly affected the fairness of proceeding to a second trial).

10.114 The Privy Council decision of *Charles v State of Trinidad and Tobago*[1] contains important statements of principle in this regard. In *Charles* the Privy Council found an abuse of process where a defendant had to endure a third trial for murder some nine years after the event, in circumstances where he had remained in custody under sentence of death. In the course of his judgment Slynn LJ made it clear that the Board ought to have regard both to the history of the protracted proceedings and, more significantly, to the personal concerns and anxieties that may be left by an accused. Lord Slynn emphasised the importance of the principles enunciated in the decision of *Barker v Wingo*[2] whereby:

> '… the United States Supreme Court considered that the right to speedy trial was designed to protect three interests of defendants, namely (i) to prevent oppressive pre-trial incarceration; (ii) to minimise anxiety and concern of the accused; and (iii) to limit the possibility that the defence will be impaired'.

1 [2000] 1 WLR 384.
2 407 US 514 (1972).

10.115 While the facts of *Charles* are clearly in the extreme, nevertheless it is suggested that the general principle, namely that we should have regard to the personal distress of an accused, is of more general application.

10.116 In the subsequent decision of *R v Henworth*[1] however, the Court of Appeal made it clear that there was no principle of law that, where a prosecution had failed twice, it was necessarily an abuse of process to hold a third trial. Having emphasised the clear public interest in juries deciding serious criminal cases, one way or the other, Kennedy LJ in *Henworth*[2] nevertheless stated that:

> '… we recognise the possibility that in any given case a time may come when it would be an abuse of process for the prosecution to try again.

Whether that situation arises must depend on the facts of the case which include, first, the overall period of delay and the reasons for the delay; second, the results of previous trials; thirdly, the seriousness of the offence or offences under consideration; and, fourthly, possibly, the extent to which the case now to be met has changed from that which was considered in previous trials'.

1 [2001] EWCA Crim 120, [2001] 2 Cr App R 47.
2 [2001] EWCA Crim 120, [2001] 2 Cr App R 47 at 52, para 26.

10.117 The Privy Council adopted a similar stance, to this vexed question of second retrials, in the decision of *Bowe v R.*[1] In *Bowe* it was held that whether a second retrial should be allowed depended on an informed and dispassionate assessment of how the interests of justice, in the broadest sense, could best be served. On the one hand, the court should take into account the defendant's interests, particularly where there has been a long delay or where the defence may be prejudiced in some significant way, whilst on the other hand, however, the court must take account of the public interest in convicting the guilty, deterring violent crime and maintaining confidence in the efficacy of our system of criminal justice.

The Court of Appeal endorsed this expression of principle in *R v Byrne* and *R v Benguit.*[2] In *R v Bell*[3] the Court of Appeal reiterated that the jurisdiction which permits a second re-trial after two jury disagreements must be exercised with extreme caution. The broad public interest in the administration of criminal justice meant that a second re-trial should be confined to a very small number of cases in which the jury is being invited to address a crime of extreme gravity which has undoubtedly occurred and in which the evidence that the defendant had committed the crime on any fair-minded objective judgment remains very powerful.

1 *Bowe v R* [2001] UKPC 19, [2001] 4 LRC 372.
2 *R v Byrne* [2002] EWCA Crim 632; *R v Benguit* [2005] EWCA Crim 1953.
3 *R v Bell* [2010] 1 Cr App R 27. See also *R v Ali* [2011] 2 Cr App R 22; and *R v Burton* [2016] 1 Cr App R 7.

Where the Crown adopt a change of stance at the retrial

10.118 In *R v Mercer*[1] the Court of Appeal held that where fresh evidence becomes available to the prosecution between trial and retrial, it is entirely acceptable for them to take it into account. Where the Crown therefore choose to act on it, and subsequently put their case against an accused on a different basis, this was held not to constitute circumstances giving rise to an abuse of process. On the facts of *Mercer* two males entered and robbed a building society, whilst a third drove the getaway car. At the first trial the Crown's case had been that the appellant entered the building society, whereas on the retrial the suggestion was that he acted as the getaway driver. The change of stance arose as a result of new evidence having come to light, which identified the second robber who entered the premises, the identity of the first having been clear throughout.

1 *R v Mercer* [2001] EWCA Crim 638, [2001] All ER (D) 187 (Mar).

Where the Court of Appeal orders a retrial

10.119 Section 7 of the Criminal Appeal Act 1968 states that the power to order a retrial is as follows:

> '(1) Where the Court of Appeal allows an appeal against conviction and it appears to the court that the interests of justice so require, they may order the appellant to be retried'.

The simple question thus arises: does this prevent one from arguing abuse of process on a retrial?

10.120 In *Charles* Lord Slynn noted the potential for overlap between the two freestanding decisions: the decision to order a stay and to order a retrial:

> 'Whether a stay should be granted raised some questions analogous to those which arise when a decision has to be taken as to whether there should be a retrial. In *Reid v R* ([1980] AC 343, 350) the Board gave general guidance as to the factors which might be relevant in the exercise of the Court of Appeal's function in deciding whether to order a retrial; "The seriousness or otherwise of the offence must always be a relevant factor; so may its prevalence; and where the previous trial was prolonged and complex, the expense and the length of time for which the court and jury would be involved in a fresh hearing may also be relevant considerations".
>
> So too is the consideration that any criminal trial is to some extent an ordeal for the defendant, which the defendant ought not to be condemned to undergo for a second time through no fault of his own unless the interests of justice require that he should do so.'

10.121 The authors suggest that, where the Court of Appeal have fully and properly considered the abuse-type arguments, before making the order for retrial, the defence will have considerable problems in even persuading the trial judge to entertain the abuse argument. Where the Court of Appeal have, for example, rejected a defence delay argument on the order of a retrial, one would not expect a Crown Court judge (where the timetable for the retrial has been followed) to allow the defence to resurrect the self-same argument as to abuse of process. This was the approach adopted by Turner J in the case of *R v Doran*[1] in relation to defence submissions which had previously been argued and ruled on:

> 'Not only has a court of competent jurisdiction ruled on those matters which were at present before it as issues, but that decision is one which is plainly binding this court in respect of matters which were raised in the higher court'.

1 (6 July 1999, unreported), Bristol Crown Court.

10.122 In *Doran* Turner J, however, naturally adopted a contrary position in relation to arguments which had not previously been advanced or ruled on. Indeed, it is further suggested that an abuse of process submission could still be made after an order for retrial where there had been a material change of circumstances, such as a significant unexpected delay in the listing of the retrial, which had not been within the contemplation of the Court of Appeal.

In *Maxwell*, Dyson JSC held that,

> 'the interests of justice is not a hard-edged concept. A decision as to what the interests of justice requires calls for an exercise of judgment in which a number of relevant factors have to be taken into account and weighed in the balance. In difficult borderline cases, there may be scope for legitimate differences of opinion. I do not believe it to be controversial that a decision under section 7 of the 1968 Act as to whether the interests of justice require a retrial calls for an exercise of judgment which should only be upset on appeal if it was plainly wrong in the sense that it is one which no reasonable court could have made or if the court took account of immaterial factors or failed to take into account material factors.'[1]

1 *R v Maxwell* [2011] 1 WLR 1837, per Dyson JSC at 19.

Compensation in miscarriage cases

10.123 It is now beyond doubt that where a conviction is quashed in circumstances of abuse of process, this will not fall within the meaning of 'miscarriage of justice' for the purposes of the Criminal Justice Act 1988, s 133.

It had previously been thought that in the case of *Mullen,*[1] Lord Bingham had established that 'miscarriage of justice' included both cases where the person was demonstrably innocent, but also cases where, innocent or not, the defendant should not have been convicted i.e. in circumstances of abuse of process.[2]

In *R (Adams) v Secretary of State for Justice (JUSTICE and another intervening),*[3] the question was considered afresh.

The Supreme Court adopted the framework of analysis of Dyson LJ in the court below,[4] positing that there were four categories of case which may come within the meaning of 'miscarriage of justice'. These were:

> "(1) Where the fresh evidence shows clearly that the defendant is innocent of the crime of which he has been convicted. (2) Where the fresh evidence is such that, had it been available at the time of the trial, no reasonable jury could properly have convicted the defendant. (3) Where the fresh evidence renders the conviction unsafe in that, had it been available at the time of the trial, a reasonable jury might or might not have convicted the defendant. (4) Where something has gone seriously wrong in the investigation of the offence or the conduct of the trial, resulting in the conviction of someone who should not have been convicted.".[5]

A 5:4 majority in the Supreme Court held that 'miscarriage of justice' encompassed only the first of the two situations posited above.[6] The four dissenting judgments favoured the approach of Lord Steyn in *Mullen,* namely that only proof of innocence would amount to it having been a 'miscarriage of justice' within the meaning of the Act.[7] Lord Clarke was the only judge who specifically considered that circumstances of an abuse of process may fall within category 2.[8]

However, subsequent to the judgment in *Adams*, Criminal Justice Act 1988, s 133 was enacted to codify in statute the view of the dissenting justices in *Adams*, namely that compensation would only be awarded 'if and only if the new or newly discovered fact shows beyond reasonable doubt that the person did not commit the offence' (i.e. that the applicant was innocent of the crimes of which he was convicted').

Attempts to have this position declared incompatible with Art 6(2) ECHR have been unsuccessful.[9]

1 See *R v Secretary of State for the Home Department, ex p Mullen* [2004] UKHL 18, [2005] 1 AC 1.
2 Ibid at para 9.
3 [2012] 1 AC 48.
4 [2010] QB 460 at para 19.
5 [2012] 1 AC 48 at para 9.
6 Ibid per Lord Phillips, Lord Hope, Lady Hale, Lord Kerr, and Lord Clarke.
7 Ibid per Lord Judge CJ, Lord Brown, Lord Roger, and Lord Walker.
8 Ibid at para 212.
9 *R (Hallam) v Secretary of State for Justice (JUSTICE intervening)* [2020] AC 279.

THE ABUSE OF PROCESS HEARING

Rules of procedure

10.124 The procedural requirements for making an application to stay an indictment on the grounds of abuse of process in the Crown Court are governed by the Criminal Procedure Rules 2020, r 3.28 and Criminal Practice Directions 2015 I (General Matters) 3C (as amended by Criminal Practice Directions 2015 (Amendment no. 11) [2020] EWCA Crim 1347. The CrimPR r 3.28 provides that:

> '3.28.— Application to stay case for abuse of process
>
> (1) This rule applies where a defendant wants the Crown Court to stay the case on the grounds that the proceedings are an abuse of the court, or otherwise unfair.
>
> (2) Such a defendant must—
>
> (a) apply in writing—
>
> (i) as soon as practicable after becoming aware of the grounds for doing so,
>
> (ii) at a pre-trial hearing, unless the grounds for the application do not arise until trial, and
>
> (iii) in any event, before the defendant pleads guilty or the jury (if there is one) retires to consider its verdict at trial;
>
> (b) serve the application on—
>
> (i) the court officer, and
>
> (ii) each other party; and

(c) in the application—

(i) explain the grounds on which it is made,

(ii) include, attach or identify all supporting material,

(iii) specify relevant events, dates and propositions of law, and

(iv) identify any witness the applicant wants to call to give evidence in person.

(3) A party who wants to make representations in response to the application must serve the representations on—

(a) the court officer; and

(b) each other party,

not more than 10 business days after service of the application.'

The Crim PD 1 3C provides that:

'3C.1 In all cases where a defendant in the Crown Court proposes to make an application to stay an indictment on the grounds of abuse of process, written notice of such application must be given to the prosecuting authority and to any co-defendant as soon as practicable after the defendant becomes aware of the grounds for doing so and not later than 14 days before the date fixed or warned for trial ("the relevant date"). Such notice must:

(a) give the name of the case and the indictment number;

(b) state the fixed date or the warned date as appropriate;

(c) specify the nature of the application;

(d) set out in numbered sub-paragraphs the grounds upon which the application is to be made;

(e) be copied to the chief listing officer at the court centre where the case is due to be heard.

3C.2 Any co-defendant who wishes to make a like application must give a like notice not later than seven days before the relevant date, setting out any additional grounds relied upon.

3C.3 In relation to such applications, the following automatic directions shall apply:

(a) the advocate for the applicant(s) must lodge with the court and serve on all other parties a skeleton argument in support of the application, at least five clear working days before the relevant date. If reference is to be made to any document not in the existing trial documents, a paginated and indexed bundle of such documents is to be provided with the skeleton argument;

(b) the advocate for the prosecution must lodge with the court and serve on all other parties a responsive skeleton argument at least two clear working days before the relevant date, together with a supplementary bundle if appropriate.

3C.4 Paragraphs XII D.17 to D.23 of these Practice Directions set out the general requirements for skeleton arguments. All skeleton arguments must specify any propositions of law to be advanced (together with the authorities relied upon in support, with paragraph references to passages relied upon) and, where appropriate, include a chronology of events and a list of dramatis personae. In all instances where reference is made to a document, the reference in the trial documents or supplementary bundle is to be given.

3C.5 The above time limits are minimum time limits. In appropriate cases, the court will order longer lead times. To this end, in all cases where defence advocates are, at the time of the preliminary hearing or as soon as practicable after the case has been sent, considering the possibility of an abuse of process application, this must be raised with the judge dealing with the matter, who will order a different timetable if appropriate, and may wish, in any event, to give additional directions about the conduct of the application. If the trial judge has not been identified, the matter should be raised with the Resident Judge.'

10.125 The obligation upon defence advocates, who are 'considering the possibility' of an abuse application, to raise the matter with a judge at a preliminary hearing or as soon as practicable after the case has been sent, is consistent with the Crown Court rules requirement to give advance notice of a question of law which would attract a binding ruling (see CPIA 1996, s 40). A similar requirement is found in the standard case management forms in both the Magistrates' and Crown Court. Whilst the above practice direction assists with efficient case management in the Crown Court, in the Magistrates' Court, the 'Preparation for Effective Trial, or 'PET', form is used to ensure such applications are dealt with efficiently and in accordance with Criminal Procedure Rules, rr 3.3 and 3.8. The form requires parties to identify points of law, including abuse of process, and requires any skeleton argument to be served at least 14 days before the trial.[1]

1 Magistrates' Courts Preparation for Effective Trial form, November 2015, http://www.justice.gov.uk/courts/procedure-rules/criminal/formspage; see also Criminal Procedure Rules Pts 1 and 3.

The Protocol for the Control and Management of Heavy Fraud and other Complex Criminal Cases

10.126 On 22 March 2005 Lord Woolf CJ issued this protocol with the avowed aim of promoting good practice and efficient case management, with a view to the reduction in the length of court hearings. One particular section of the protocol directly focuses on abuse of process. The protocol, which supplements the Criminal Procedure Rules, is primarily directed towards cases which are estimated to last eight weeks or longer, but should also be followed in all cases estimated to last more than four weeks. The abuse of process section states as follows:

'5. Abuse of process

i Applications to stay or dismiss for abuse of process have become a normal feature of heavy and complex cases. Such applications may be based on delay and the health of defendants.

ii Applications in relation to absent special circumstances [sic] tend to be unsuccessful and not to be pursued on appeal. For this reason there is comparatively little Court of Appeal guidance: but see *Harris and Howells* [2003] EWCA Crim 486. It should be noted that abuse of process is not there to discipline the prosecution or the police.

iii The arguments on both sides must be reduced to writing. Oral evidence is seldom relevant.

iv The Judge should direct full written submissions (rather than "skeleton arguments") on any abuse application in accordance with a timetable set by him; these should identify any element of prejudice the defendant is alleged to have suffered.

v The judge should normally aim to conclude the hearing within an absolute maximum of one day, if necessary in accordance with a timetable. The parties should therefore prepare their papers on this basis and not expect the judge to allow the oral hearing to be anything more than an occasion to highlight concisely their arguments and answer any questions the court may have of them; applications will not be allowed to drag on.'

10.127 In the introduction to the above, a flexibility of application of the protocol according to the needs of each case was deemed to be essential, given that it was 'designed to inform but not to proscribe'. Having taken account of that, however, the protocol serves as a clear warning to practitioners who are involved in abuse applications relating to trials of more than four weeks in length, to set out their detailed written arguments in full, for there will generally be a strictly limited time allowed by judges for oral submissions. This is consistent with the general cultural trend towards much tighter control over advocates' opportunities to address the court.

Nevertheless, in *DPP v Ayers*[1] the Divisional Court held that criminal proceedings are essentially proceedings conducted through oral submissions. However serious a party's default had been in general terms in the course of a case, it was essentially unjust to deprive that party of the opportunity of making oral submissions. It was difficult, although perhaps not impossible, to imagine a case where a court in criminal proceedings would be entitled to shut out a party that had failed to serve a skeleton argument from making oral submissions.

1 *See DPP v Ayers* [2006] Crim LR 62.

10.128 The application is normally instigated by the defence. However, it would appear there is some authority to suggest that where the court itself has some reason to suspect there is a ground for staying proceedings, it has a duty to raise it of its own motion, irrespective of the lack of any defence application.[1]

1 *See R v City of Liverpool Stipendiary Magistrate, ex p Ellison* [1990] RTR 220, 227 per Bingham LJ; and *Gillick v West Norfolk and Wisbech Area Health Authority* [1986] AC 112.

Timing of application

10.129 An application to stay proceedings is obviously a preliminary issue which should be raised either pre-trial or at the outset of the trial. Self-evidently, as a successful abuse application may bring an end to the entire proceedings (although this is not necessarily so, for a successful abuse application may only relate to a stay of part of the prosecution's case), it ought to be heard at the earliest opportunity. In *R v Aldershot Youth Court, ex p A*[1] the Divisional Court held that by its nature an application to stay proceedings as an abuse is a plea in bar and as with a plea of autrefois acquit or convict, the plea was to be taken and determined before the accused pleaded to the indictment/charge.

1 (1997) 3 Archbold News 2, QBD.

10.130 The Court of Appeal in *Smolinski*[1] directed that any application to stay a trial as an abuse of process on the grounds of delay should not be made at the beginning of the trial, but rather should be made after the Crown has put its case. Lord Woolf concluded his judgment:

> 'We hope to have made clear two things in the court of hearing this appeal. One is that we discourage applications based on abuse in cases of this sort. Secondly, where evidence is given after so many years, the court should exercise very careful scrutiny at the end of the evidence to see whether or not the case is safe to be left to the jury'.

1 [2004] 2 Cr App R 40.

10.131 The approach in *Smolinkski* is an attractive one to the extent that it allows the judge to consider the complainant's evidence and cross examination in light of the defence submission to stay. However, that approach was heavily criticised in the case of *F*,[1] which overruled the *Smolinski* line of authorities and held that an abuse application should take place before any trial of the substantive offence.

1 See above, para **1.28**.

10.132 The Court in *F* laid down the following principles:

(a) An application to stay a prosecution as an abuse of process on grounds of delay and a submission of 'no case to answer' are two distinct matters which require separate consideration.[1]

(b) Any such application must be determined in accordance with *Attorney General's Reference (No 1 of 1990)*. That application should not succeed unless, exceptionally, a fair trial is no longer possible owing to prejudice to the defendant occasioned by the delay which cannot fairly be addressed in the normal trial process. The presence or absence of explanation or justification for delay is relevant only insofar as it bears on that question.[2]

(c) An application to stop the case on the grounds that there is no case to answer must be determined in accordance with *R v Galbraith*. For the reasons there explained, it is dangerous to ask the question in terms of whether a conviction would be safe, or the jury can safely convict, because that invites that judge to evaluate the weight and reliability of the evidence, which is the task of the evidence. The question is whether the evidence, viewed overall, is such that the jury could properly convict.[3]

(d) There is no different Galbraith test for offences which are alleged to have been committed some years ago, whether or not they are sexual offences.[4]

(e) An application to stay for abuse of process ought ordinarily to be heard and determined at the outset of the case, and before the evidence is heard, unless there is a specific reason to defer it because the question of prejudice and fair trial can better be determined at a later stage.[5]

1 [2012] QB 703 at [39]–[40].
2 Ibid at [38]–[40].
3 Ibid at [36]–[37].
4 Ibid at [41].
5 Ibid at [43]–[45]; one example such an exception is in instances of missing evidence where the judge will be concerned to see what actual prejudice is caused to the defendant in practice, rather than in theory, see *R v Hewitt* [2020] EWCA Crim 1247 at para 130.

10.133 Lord Judge CJ stated:

> 'Where there are genuine grounds for an application to stay on the basis that a fair trial will be impossible because of incurable prejudice to the defendant caused by delay, that application is, by its nature, preliminary to rather than part of the trial process. The contention is that the trial should not take place at all. If it is to be made, notice should be given before the trial begins.... If the ruling is deferred, there is, as this case demonstrates and as Lord Lane envisaged, a significant danger that the submissions to the judge would conflate *Galbraith* principles with the issue of abuse of process. If the application succeeds, it will almost inevitably appear that the judge has usurped the function of the jury..... But perhaps most important of all, as all the authorities underline, it is only in the exceptional cases where a fair trial is not possible that these applications are justified on the grounds of delay, even when the precondition to a successful application, serious prejudice, may have occurred, the best safeguard against unfairness to either side in such cases is the trial process itself, and an evaluation by the jury of the evidence'.[1]

1 At [45].

10.134 It is therefore now settled law that an abuse application to stay a prosecution on the grounds of delay should be made during a preliminary hearing before the trial commences. This approach avoids placing a potentially unnecessary financial and emotional burden on defendants, witnesses and complainants. A complainant, who, even in the event of a successful application to stay, may be telling the truth, will not have to go through the distress of giving evidence at trial only to subsequently have the case stayed as an abuse of process. There are also financial advantages to this approach, in that the legal costs of prosecuting or defending the trial would not be wasted as they would in the event of a subsequent application to stay.

Must the trial judge conduct an inquiry into an abuse submission?

10.135 If, after hearing from the defence, the trial judge concludes that the submission has no justification or hope of success either because it is wrong in law or the facts appear very far from an abuse situation, it is submitted that the judge has no duty to conduct any inquiry.

10.136 In *R v Heston-Francois*[1] the question arose as to whether there was a general duty on the trial judge to conduct such an inquiry when it was *justifiably* requested by the defence. The facts were that the defendant was on bail awaiting trial and the police, in the course of conducting another investigation, searched his home and seized legally privileged documents (documents prepared for use in his defence to the trial he was already facing). These documents were not only seized but they were then handed to the investigators who were involved in the prosecution of the defendant's imminent trial. At this trial the defence submitted abuse arguing that the conduct of the officers had been oppressive and justified a stay. The trial judge however, declined to conduct any inquiry into this, ruling that all relevant matters could be adequately explored during the course of the trial, and so a ruling could be made later in the proceedings. Post-conviction, the defendant appealed to the Court of Appeal.

1 (1984) 78 Cr App R 209.

10.137 The Court of Appeal emphasised that in circumstances such as an abuse application, a trial judge should be the master of his own procedure and therefore enjoy a wide discretion as to how to conduct an abuse inquiry. If the trial judge exercised his discretion wrongly or behaved unfairly, then of course this could be reviewed subsequently by the Court of Appeal and, in the view of the court, it was well placed to conduct such a review.

10.138 A perusal of the judgment of Watkins LJ in this case reveals that the court was concerned by several policy considerations which clearly led it to reach the conclusion that it did. Watkins LJ suggested that if a trial judge was to have a duty always to conduct a pre-trial inquiry into allegations of abuse, then this would tend to suggest that it was part of a court's duty to regulate the conduct of police officers. As no such duty existed then neither should there be a duty to always conduct a pre-trial inquiry. In relation to the trial process itself, Watkins LJ agreed with the trial judge's view that the trial was the best forum or procedure for eliciting facts relevant to an abuse application. Moreover, a trial judge having heard the relevant evidence had a variety of remedies available to him. Reprehensible conduct by the police could be dealt with within the context of the trial by judicial control over admissibility of evidence, the power to direct a verdict of not guilty and the ability of a jury having heard all the evidence to return a verdict of not guilty.

10.139 As a matter of practice Watkins LJ also pointed to several problems which would arise if a general duty on a trial judge was held to exist:

> '… for example, (i) of defining the issues claimed to exist, which may be very complex, (ii) of providing for representation of persons whose conduct is impugned, (iii) of ensuring that the persons affected are sufficiently aware

of the case they have to meet. Whilst these problems may be overcome, the issues referred to are best left, we think, to be dealt with during the course of the trial and; if necessary, later by the Court of Appeal.'

10.140 In relation to such problems Watkins LJ also observed that:

'A pre-trial inquiry such as the appellant contends the judge in this case was under a duty to embark on would itself be open to abuse by unscrupulous and dishonest accused persons. The criminal trial system would be placed in jeopardy'.

10.141 In *A-G's Reference* Lane CJ expressly approved the view of Watkins LJ expressed in *Heston-Francois.*[1] He held that the trial process is equipped to deal with most complaints of abuse, for example the ability to ensure that all relevant evidence of this is presented during the trial and the ability of the judge to give directions to the jury.

R v (Ebrahim) v Feltham Magistrates' Court adopted the point made in *Heston-Francois* that a stay will not be granted where the trial process is itself equipped to deal with the matters complained of.

1 (1984) 78 Cr App R 209.

10.142 On the basis of these authorities therefore, it appears that there is no obligation on a trial judge to hold a pre-trial hearing even when it is justifiably requested by the defence. It is however, submitted that both of these authorities have now largely been overtaken by subsequent developments and perhaps by the growth of abuse applications generally. Certainly, it is the experience of the authors that where, for example, an allegation of mala fides is made against police officers, it would be extremely unusual for a trial judge to hold that this matter need not be investigated until the relevant officers gave their evidence in the ordinary way in the course of the trial. Furthermore, there has been an increased awareness on the part of the judiciary as to their responsibility to ensure that abuses do not go uncorrected, together with the growth generally in our criminal justice system of pre-trial or preparatory hearings.

Voir dires

10.143 It is normal for applications concerned with the exclusion of prosecution evidence under PACE, s 78 or for a stay of the proceedings to be considered in a voir dire or a 'trial within a trial' held in the absence of the jury.[1] The usual procedure is for the prosecution to call witnesses to testify as to the circumstances about which the defence has made complaint, for the defence to cross-examine these witnesses and then for the defence to call any evidence it considers necessary. Judges will only expect the calling of live evidence in an abuse voir dire where it is absolutely necessary, however. The parties will generally be encouraged to make the arguments on the face of the documentation, unless this is simply not possible. There is no obligation on the accused to give evidence although there is antiquated authority to the effect that he is not entitled to do so. However, it is submitted that if a fair determination of the issues makes it desirable for the accused to give evidence, and he wished to do so, it would be wrong to refuse this.

It should be borne in mind that if the accused does give evidence and the abuse application fails, the prosecution may lead evidence in the trial proper regarding this previous testimony. Prosecution cross-examination of the accused before the jury can be directed to expose any discrepancies and inconsistencies between the two testimonies in order to attack the credibility of the accused.

1 In *R v Barry Magistrates' Court, ex p Malpas* [1998] COD 90, DC, the Divisional Court acknowledged the Crown Court's use of abuse voir dires for dealing with disputed facts.

No power to order disclosure

10.144 The position of a trial judge conducting an abuse hearing was described by Watkins LJ in *R v Manchester Crown Court, ex p Cunningham*:[1]

> 'He is not in a trial situation nor is his role an inquisitorial one. He cannot compel any other evidential material to be provided'.

1 [1992] COD 23. This case is also known as *R v Manchester Crown Court, ex p Brokenbrow* (1991) Times, 31 October.

10.145 It was held in *ex p Cunningham* that a trial judge has no power to compel disclosure of documents from any party, including the prosecution, if such documents purely relate to the abuse application and do not fall under the prosecution's general duty of disclosure in relation to the trial. In relation to third parties, the trial judge has no power to issue a witness summons either for documents or for the giving of witness testimony pursuant to the Criminal Procedure (Attendance of Witnesses) Act 1965 (which has now been greatly amended by the Criminal Procedure and Investigations Act 1996, s 66). In *R v Gokal*[1] the Court of Appeal upheld the refusal of the trial judge to make orders under the Criminal Justice (International Co-operation) Act 1990 in relation to the seeking of foreign evidence in order to support a forthcoming abuse application to be made by the defence.

1 [1997] 2 Cr App R 266, CA.

Argument and giving of reasons

10.146 In practice, a considerable number of abuse applications tend to be made in circumstances where, at the appropriate hearing, the defence and prosecution present the facts and argument without the necessity of calling any evidence. This is largely because the dispute between the parties will generally lie over the proper inference to be drawn from the facts, as opposed to the facts themselves. Alternatively, the prosecution may contend that, even if the defence's arguments or allegations are made out, they do not in law amount to an abuse. Where the defence do contemplate calling evidence in a voir dire, as part of the abuse application, they need to be ever mindful of the inherent dangers of exposing their witnesses to prosecution cross-examination. Indeed, practitioners are cautioned against the calling of defence evidence, unless they are confident first, that it is necessary and secondly, that it would be of positive assistance to the application.

10.147 The burden of proving assertions as to the alleged abuse and/or establishing the evidential foundations rests on the defence. In *ex p Cunningham* the court considered how a judge should rule on an abuse application. Watkins LJ said: 'In rejecting or granting an application the judge need only deliver a short judgment showing his command of the law and a summary of the reasons for his decision'. While it makes for good practice for magistrates to similarly provide reasons, there is no legal obligation on them to do so.

Divisible indictments

10.148 In *R v Munro*[1] the Court of Appeal held that the power to stay proceedings exists in order to enable a court to regulate the efficient and fair disposal of criminal cases. Lord Justice Steyn went on to acknowledge the good sense in a court having an inherent jurisdiction to stay an indictment in part; whether that meant staying some counts and not others, or staying (in a multi-handed case) as against some defendants and not others. To that end, Steyn LJ held that it was 'an illusion to regard an indictment as an indivisible entity'.

1 (1993) 97 Cr App R 183.

Defence evidence at sending hearings in the Magistrates' courts

10.149 In *R v Clerkenwell Stipendiary Magistrate, ex p Bell*[1] the applicant, B, was alleged to have committed an offence of theft at some time before May 1987. He was charged with the offence on 26 September 1989. On 22 January 1990 at, what were previously called committal proceedings, it was contended on his behalf that given the delay the magistrate should not commit him for trial because of abuse of process. The magistrate proceeded to hear evidence from a police officer explaining the delay, in relation to B moving address, but refused to hear evidence from B himself. He committed B for trial, which decision was then subject to a judicial review application. The High Court granted the application and quashed the committal. It was held that the magistrate should have heard evidence from B, because any possible prejudice to B caused by the delay was a relevant matter and clearly B could give evidence as to this.[2] In short, the refusal to hear evidence from B amounted to a breach of natural justice.

1 [1991] Crim LR 468, QBD.
2 *R v Telford Justices, ex p Badham* was cited in support of this proposition.

Fairness to the prosecution

10.150 In *R v Derby Crown Court, ex p Brooks*[1] Sir Roger Ormrod in his famous dictum concerning the abuse of process said in relation to this subject as follows:

> 'the power to stop a prosecution arises when it is an abuse of the process of the court … the ultimate objective of this discretionary power is to ensure that there should be a fair trial according to law, which involves fairness to both the defendant and to the prosecution …'.

In *R (Ebrahim) v Feltham Magistrates' Court*, the court reiterated the principle that a fair trial involves fairness to both the defendant and the prosecution, and that the trial process itself is equipped to deal with the bulk of complaints on which applications for a stay are founded.

1 (1984) 80 Cr App R 164 at 168.

10.151 Lane CJ in *Attorney-General's Reference (No 1 of 1990)*[1] emphasised that the court's power to stay proceedings should never be used as a means of punishing the prosecution. This concern was similarly expressed in the course of the Lord Woolf CJ 2005 Protocol on the Control and Management of Heavy Fraud and Other Complex Criminal Cases.

Now the overriding objective, contained in Rule 1.1 of the Criminal Procedure Rules 2020, requires criminal cases to be dealt with justly, including (2)(b) dealing with the prosecution and the defence fairly.

1 (1992) 95 Cr App R 296, CA.

10.152 The issue of whether the prosecution have been fairly heard in answer to a defendant's abuse application usually rises in the context of a magistrate's decision to stay proceedings about which the prosecution subsequently seek judicial review arguing that this was irrational. In *R v Crawley Justices, ex p DPP*[1] the Divisional Court heard a prosecution application for judicial review arising out of a justice's decision to dismiss the charges against the defendant on the grounds of prosecution delay. The justices held that the delay was so protracted and unjustifiable that it constituted an abuse. For its part the prosecution, while it did not deny the facts concerning delay, submitted that it had not received a fair hearing because the magistrates had not directed themselves to the essential issue of whether the delay had in fact prejudiced a fair trial. Furthermore, the magistrates had not considered who was responsible for the delay and the prosecution had argued that some of the responsibility lay with the accused. It transpired that at the particular hearing complained of, the justices had refused to hear any submissions from the prosecution and immediately proceeded to dismiss the charges. Unsurprisingly, the High Court granted the application finding in effect that the tenets of natural justice had been broken and the prosecution had been treated unfairly.[2] Moreover, in the opinion of the court, had the magistrates heard all the facts they probably would not have decided that there was an abuse.

1 [1991] COD 365, DC.
2 See also *King v Kucharz* [1989] COD 469, DC.

10.153 In the case of *Director of Public Prosecutions v Ayres*[1] the prosecution also found themselves in some difficulty with the Justices. While the prosecution would appear to have rightly attracted certain criticism for failing to comply with various disclosure directions, nevertheless, the net result was that the Justices allowed a defence application that the prosecution not be permitted to respond to the abuse of process application, which application to stay succeeded. The High Court allowed an appeal by way of case stated by the prosecution. The Court held that, however serious a party's default had been in general terms in the course of a case, it was essentially unjust to deprive that party of the opportunity of putting forward an explanation for the default and/or of making submissions on the important issue of abuse of process.

1 See the report at [2006] Crim LR 62–63.

Fairness to third parties

10.154 Principles of even-handedness and fairness have also been held to apply, in the context of an abuse of process hearing where evidence is called, to the position of witnesses. In *A-G v Morgan; A-G v News Group Newspapers Ltd*[1] the Divisional Court held that where an application to stay had been founded on allegedly prejudicial publicity, it was irregular to have allowed the author of the criticised article (who was expecting to be a witness for the prosecution in the substantive trial) to be called as a witness on the application for a stay and then cross-examined at length as to his entire conduct vis-à-vis the article. The author should have first, been provided with an opportunity to take legal advice and second, having given evidence, should have been warned as to his privilege against self-incrimination.

The overriding objective in the Criminal Procedure Rules 2020, rr 1.1(2)(d) requires participants in a criminal case to respect the interests of witnesses, victims and jurors.

1 [1998] EMLR 294, DC.

Third party abuse

10.155 In the light of the extensive disclosure obligations on the prosecution, in relation to third parties, and given the duties of disclosure incumbent upon the third parties themselves, it was not surprising to see judicial recognition of the concept of third party abuse in the decision of *R v Momodou*.[1] On the facts of the case, the third party who came in for criticism was a private company who ran an immigration detention centre, whose employees became prosecution witnesses in a criminal trial, there having been an arson and violent disorder at the centre. The abuse application arose from the fact that the third party employer had arranged for witness training for certain of its employees, some of whom were significant witnesses in the case. The Crown accepted that defence criticism of the witness training was justified.

1 [2005] 2 All ER 571.

10.156 The Court of Appeal found, on the facts of the case, that the trial judge properly dealt with the defence complaints by fully ventilating them before the jury, in the course of directions, which raised the potential difficulties they caused. In the course of his judgment Lord Justice Judge held as follows:

> 'The steady development of the abuse of process jurisdiction suggests that, notwithstanding that the prosecution or prosecuting authority may be blameless, as a matter of principle, the judge is vested with jurisdiction to order that proceedings should be stayed. The activities of third parties may constitute an abuse of process making a fair trial impossible, and if so, in an extreme case, this discretion is available to be exercised.'[1]

1 [2005] 2 All ER 571 at para 54.

The use of intermediaries

10.157 The use of intermediaries is one of the discretionary special measures created by the Youth Justice and Criminal Evidence Act 1999. In *R v Cox*,[1] the Court of Appeal held that:

> 'in the context of a defendant with communication problems, when every sensible step taken to identify an available intermediary has been unsuccessful, the next stage is not for the proceedings to be stayed, which in case like [Cox, where the appellant had been convicted of rape,] would represent a gross unfairness to the complainant, but for the judge to make an informed assessment of whether the absence of an intermediary would make the proposed trial an unfair trial. It would, in fact, be a most unusual case for a defendant who is fit to plead to be found to be so disadvantaged by his condition that a properly brought prosecution would have to be stayed. That would be an unjust outcome where, on the face of the evidence, a genuine complaint has properly been brought against the defendant.'

In *Cox*, the judge had from start to finish conducted the proceedings with appropriate and necessary caution such that the appellant had received a fair trial.

1 *R v Cox* [2012] 2 Cr App R 6. See also *R (C) v Sevenoaks Youth Court* [2010] 1 All ER 735, DC; *R v Thomas* [2020] EWCA Crim 117.

Legal representation

10.158 In Campbell the court had stayed confiscation proceedings as an abuse, on the grounds that since, despite a representation order having been made in her favour, she was unable to find a suitably qualified counsel to represent her at the rate of remuneration applicable under the graduated fee structure and the Legal Services Commission had refused to make an exception to provide adequate funding for counsel, she could not have a fair trial without representation. In the 2014 case of *Crawley & others* at Southwark Crown Court HHJ Leonard QC similarly stayed a complex serious fraud trial on the grounds that no Barristers could be found to defend the proceedings. Upon a prosecution appeal however, the Court of Appeal reversed the trial Judge's ruling under section 66 CJA 2003 and ordered that the trial proceedings be resumed.[1] Their Lordships evidently considered that far greater efforts needed to be made to secure counsel before the judge could properly reach the conclusion a stay was appropriate.

1 *R v Crawley (Operation Cotton)* [2014] EWCA Crim 1028.

The burden of proof

10.159 The applicant making the abuse of process submission has the burden of proving it, and the standard of proof is the balance of probabilities.[1] As Mann LJ commented, in *Telford Justices,* the manner in which the applicant discharges such an onus will depend on all the circumstances of the particular case. The applicant must carefully decide whether to make the submission on the papers, and agreed facts, or whether some initial calling of evidence, perhaps in a voir dire, is required.

1 *R v Telford Justices, ex p Badhan* [1991] 2 QB 78; *Attorney-General's Reference (No 1 of 1990)* [1992] QB 630; and *R v Cardiff Magistrates' Court, ex p Hole* [1997] COD 84.

10.160 It may well be essential for applicants to lay an evidential foundation for the intended submission. Indeed, the Crown may take issue with the evidence presented, forcing the tribunal to make an initial determination as to the facts. The evidential burden would lie on the applicant. An example of such a situation might apply where a defence witness is called to testify to the effect that a number of important defence witnesses are unavailable by reason of the delay. The prosecution may challenge first, the assertion that they are important, second, the assertion that they are unavailable, and third, that their alleged unavailability had anything to do with supposed prosecution led delay.

10.161 The *ex p Hole* decision provides clear guidance to applicants as to the manner in which the burden may be discharged. The Divisional Court there held that:

> 'If one is considering whether, on a balance of probabilities, the applicants are able to show that because of the delay they cannot fairly defend themselves against the charges, it is necessary to look at the charges and see exactly what defence it is that they are impeded from advancing'.

In essence, the burden is to specify the alleged prejudice or unfairness and whether or not it applies to oral or documentary evidence, for example, to directly relate such matters to the particular charge(s) against a defendant. In the above non-availability of evidence type submission, the burden would clearly be on the applicant to identify the witnesses he would have wished to call.

10.162 While the actual burden on applicants may in practice be less onerous in delay cases where there has been an exceptionally long delay, the burden of proof always remains on the applicant. In the *Tan v Cameron* decision[1] the Privy Counsel considered the vexed question as to whether there should be shifting burdens of proof, reversals of the burden of proof and rebuttable presumptions. The court held that the question as to whether proceedings ought to be stayed is a question to be considered 'in the round' and that nothing was to be gained by the introduction of shifting burdens of proof. The court was clearly not prepared to accept that in a case of substantial delay, prejudice was presumed to exist to the extent that the prosecution took on a burden to rebut such a presumption of prejudice.[2]

1 [1992] 2 AC 205, PC.
2 See also *R v Bow Street Magistrates, ex p DPP* (1989) 91 Cr App R 283.

10.163 What was described as a 'heavy' burden in the *Tan* decision, which was a delay case, may well be an even greater burden on the applicant who seeks a stay on the basis of alleged mala fides. In the case of *ex p Thomas*[1] the added evidential difficulties of proving dishonesty were considered by the Divisional Court. The essence of the defence case was an allegation that the prosecutor, who had unsuccessfully sought to extend custody time limits for defendants charged with a drugs importation offence, had dishonestly contrived to manipulate the prosecution process. The prosecutor had the defendants re-arrested, before they could leave the court building, on new charges of possession with intent to supply the self same drugs. The Divisional Court, remitting the case back to the magistrates, stated that the justices must bear in mind that the burden of establishing dishonesty lay fairly and squarely on the defence, and that it was a 'heavy' burden. Where the defence take on the mantle of proving dishonesty, as opposed to an error of judgment for example, the evidential hurdle is an obviously high one given the seriousness of the allegation.

1 See *R v Great Yarmouth Magistrates, ex p Thomas, Davis and Darlington* [1992] Crim LR 116; and *R v Rotherham Justices, ex p Brough* [1991] Crim LR 522.

The standard of proof

10.164 In cases where it is appropriate to consider the 'standard of proof', the applicant will have to satisfy a particular court or tribunal on the basis of the 'balance of probabilities' test. In *R (TP) v West London Youth Court*[1] the defence sought to judicially review an adverse ruling on abuse of process on the grounds that the District Judge should have applied a lesser standard of proof. In the context of an abuse application on fitness to stand trial, the defence contended that the judge should have asked himself whether there 'was a real possibility that the claimant would not be able to participate effectively'. The Divisional Court dismissed the application, and, in so doing, pointed out how 'It would be odd in the extreme if one species of abuse [referring to fitness to stand trial]… requires proof of a lesser standard'.[2] In the course of his judgment, Scott Baker LJ went on to make the important point that any trial judge who had concerns over a defendant's fitness to stand trial has a continuing jurisdiction, and that, should the stage be reached where it is apparent a defendant is unable to effectively participate, the proceedings may then be stayed.

1 [2006] 1 Cr App R 25.
2 See Scott Baker LJ, p 408, at para 14 of the judgment.

Judicial discretion in delay cases

10.165 The language of burden and standard of proof has, however, been described as potentially misleading in relation to the exercise of judicial discretion in the case of applications to stay based on delay grounds. The Court of Appeal in the decision of *R v S (SP)*,[1] held that 'the discretionary decision whether or not to grant a stay as an abuse of process, because of delay, is an exercise in judicial assessment dependent on judgment rather than on any conclusion as to fact based on evidence'.[2] The court disapproved of the use of burden and standard terminology in these cases on the basis that such language was more apt to an evidence-based fact-finding process, which is clearly not necessarily the case in all delay abuse applications.

1 [2006] 2 Cr App R 23; 170 JP 434.
2 See the judgment of Rose LJ (Vice President) at para 20.

Presentation

10.166 Before presenting the abuse arguments at court, the practitioner is well advised to have already taken specific client instructions on the matters raised. Certain species of abuse are clearly more directly connected than others to the clients' own particular recollection of a set of events; breach of promise or substantial delay cases being prime examples. The practitioner may also wish to question and take statements from defence witnesses in relation to abuse matters. Even if the client and his witnesses provide a long series of negative answers in relation to their ability to, for example, recall material events in the distant past, the same should be noted in their witness statements.

10.167 If an enquiry agent has, for example, also been used to investigate important aspects of a client's defence, the result of such investigation (if relevant to the abuse application) may also be reduced into an evidential format, possibly for use in a voir dire or in argument. Likewise, a compendious way of summarising the extensive efforts to prepare a client's case, which may have met with abject failure given the delay for example, could be for the solicitor in question to prepare a full, accurate and detailed witness statement.

10.168 In a sexual abuse delay case, for example, the solicitor could, in such a witness statement, succinctly set out matters such as:

(1) the names of defence witnesses who were to be traced; an outline of their relevance; the results of efforts to trace and proof the same;

(2) details of the disclosure sought from the prosecution (such as unused material); an outline of its relevance; the results of efforts to receive the same and/or the availability;

(3) details of efforts made to seek voluntary or other disclosure from third parties (such as social service files, medical records, educational records); an outline of the relevance of the same; the results of efforts to receive the same and/or the availability.

10.169 Such a solicitor could also annex to the statement the copy exhibits, such as letters or documents, which evidence the above-mentioned inquiries and their results. If the case has been thoroughly prepared and the solicitor's evidence is sufficiently relevant and material, such a document could clearly be of assistance to the court. Not only would it possibly save the court's valuable time, in terms of obviating the need for the calling of live evidence, it is presentationally more attractive, with more evidential weight than simple bland assertions in open court. If it is intended to contain certain disclosure from the clients' instructions, or from his witness statements (for example, re their inability to remember), the solicitor is advised to ask for the clients' specific consent to such a course.

10.170 The Practice Directions make it clear that the practitioner is expected to have his or her documentation well in order, be it a skeleton argument, bundle of trial documents and/or supplementary material, in readiness for such an application. In addition to the skeleton argument's submissions on law, possibly with a chronology of events and list of dramatis personae attached, it is sometimes helpful to annex copies of particularly pertinent abuse authorities. Having said that, practitioners are cautioned against the excessive citation of abuse authorities, which has been expressly disapproved of by the Divisional Court.[1]

1 See *R v Sheffield Stipendiary Magistrate, ex p Stephens* [1992] Crim LR 873.

Chapter 11

Confiscation proceedings

INTRODUCTION

11.01 At the beginning of this chapter in the previous edition of this work, it was predicted, following the decision in *R v Shabir*,[1] that the court's power to stay was likely to be invoked more frequently in order to prevent a truly oppressive confiscation order being made. In the event, the scope for arguing abuse in confiscation proceedings has been significantly narrowed by decisions of the Court of Appeal and the Supreme Court.[2] However, as one door closes, another opens; the court can now avoid making a confiscation order of the type held to be an abuse of the process in *Shabir*[3] by applying Art 1 of the First Protocol to the European Convention on Human Rights (A1P1).

1 [2009] 1 Cr App R (S) 497, CA; [2008] EWCA Crim 1809.
2 *R v Nelson* [2010] 1 Cr App R (S) 82, CA; *R v Waya* [2012] UKSC 51; [2012] 3 WLR 1188.
3 Op cit.

11.02 The court retains jurisdiction to stay an application for confiscation where it amounts to an abuse of the court's process. In *R v Mahmood and Shahin*[1] Thomas LJ said this [at 36]:

> 'It was accepted on behalf of the Crown that a judge had in principle a discretion to stay proceedings if what the Crown was proceeding to do amounted to an abuse of process. We consider that that concession was rightly made by the Crown.'[2]

The few reported cases in which a stay has been upheld have concerned confiscation orders that were not merely harsh but 'truly oppressive'. What is now clear is that the judge should refuse to make such an order on the ground that to do so would be wholly disproportionate and a breach of A1P1. There is no need to invoke the abuse of process. In the years that followed, this trend continued.

1 [2005] EWCA Crim 2168; [2006] Cr App R (S) 96, CA at 570.
2 See also *R v Farquhar* [2008] EWCA Crim 806 and *R v Neild* [2007] EWCA Crim 993.

11.03 Nevertheless, the confiscation regime continues to tolerate a significant measure of harshness. The practitioner must understand the 'legislative intention' in order to identify circumstances in which an order will be oppressive (and therefore disproportionate) and not merely harsh. To do this, it is important to examine the development of the law of confiscation, so before discussing the likely impact of the decision in *R v Waya*[1] on the jurisdiction, it is helpful to consider the statutory confiscation scheme.

1 *R v Waya* [2012] UKSC 51; [2012] 3 WLR 1188.

PROCEEDS OF CRIME ACT 2002, PART 2

11.04 Part 2 of the Proceeds of Crime Act 2002 ('PoCA') provides a comprehensive system for the making and enforcement of confiscation orders. The PoCA regime replaces the previous legislation[1] and applies to offences committed on or after 24 March 2003. Although the focus of this chapter is the 2002 Act, the discussion below is equally applicable to the earlier confiscation regimes.

1 Criminal Justice Act 1988 Part IV; Drug Trafficking Act 1994.

11.05 PoCA provides for the confiscation of assets from defendants convicted of offences from which they have benefited. The Act requires a defendant who has benefited from his offending to pay a sum of money equal to the amount of his benefit, but not exceeding the value of his realisable assets. The scheme is 'value-based', to be contrasted with schemes which require an offender to surrender the actual proceeds of his crime. It is not confiscation in the sense in which schoolchildren and others understand it.[1]

1 *R v May* [2008] 1 AC 1028, HL *per* Lord Bingham at para 9.

11.06 The purposes of confiscation are to punish convicted offenders, to deter the commission of further offences and to reduce the profits available to fund further criminal enterprises: *R v Rezvi*[1] (a case under the Criminal Justice Act 1988). The legislative purpose of PoCA is to ensure that criminals (and especially professional criminals engaged in serious organised crime) do not profit from their crimes, and it sends a strong deterrent message to that effect.[2] The statutory language must be given a fair and purposive construction in order to give effect to its legislative policy.

1 [2003] 1 AC 1099.
2 *R v Waya* op cit at s 2.

11.07 A confiscation order is an *in personam* order made in the Crown Court requiring a convicted defendant to pay a sum of money within a given period of time, in default of which he must serve a term of imprisonment. Confiscation orders are not intended to be restitutionary measures.[1] A criminal who has benefited financially from crime but no longer possesses the specific proceeds will be deprived of assets he has up to the value of his criminal benefit. The object is to deprive him, directly or indirectly, of what he has gained.

1 *R v May* [2008] 1 AC 1028, HL.

11.08 Throughout the complex legislative history, the essential structure of the confiscation regime first introduced by the Drug Trafficking Offences Act 1986 has been retained. Confiscation entails a three-stage process: benefit from criminal conduct; determining the quantum of that benefit; and, identifying the recoverable amount. The Crown Court is required to answer three distinct questions summarised by Lord Bingham in *R v May*:[1]

(1) Has the defendant (D) benefited from the relevant criminal conduct?

(2) If so, what is the value of the benefit D has so obtained?

(3) What sum is recoverable from D?

1 Op cit at [8].

11.09 If the prosecution asks the court to proceed with confiscation, it must do so pursuant to s 6(1) of PoCA. Although the court was originally given a discretion as to whether to make a confiscation order, this was removed by Parliament[1] so the making of an order was converted to a duty and not just a power. Though see the subsequent amendment to s 6 discussed below in the final section of this chapter.

1 By the amendments made to the Criminal Justice Act 1988 by the Proceeds of Crime Act 1995.

11.10 Although the method adopted by Parliament for calculating the amount of a confiscation order produces results which those subject to them doubtless consider grossly unfair, in *R v Hockey*,[1] the Court of Appeal pointed out:

> 'The Parliamentary intention is, in our judgment clear, and has been stated to be clear in decisions of the House of Lords and this court … There is a borderline between legislative powers and judicial powers, and it is sometimes open to argument where that borderline should run. The intention of this statute is clear. It was not open to the judge to frustrate the intention of Parliament, as expressed in the statute, as he purported to do [by refusing to make a confiscation order].'[1]

1 [2008] 1 Cr App R (S) 50, CA at para 18.

11.11 This caution was reiterated in *R v Paulet*[1] in which it was observed:

> 'The abuse of process jurisdiction is one which needs to be exercised with great circumspection. The jurisdiction cannot be converted on a case-by-case basis into a structure which involves, on proper analysis, something like wholesale undermining of the statutory provisions. It is not easy to conclude that it is an abuse of process for those responsible for enforcing legislation to see that it is indeed properly enforced.'
>
> Paulet went on to complain to the European Court of Human Rights (see below).

1 [2009] EWCA Crim 288 at para 23; see also *R v Nelson* [2010] 1 Cr App R (S) 82.

The 'intention of Parliament'

11.12 Until legislative intervention beginning in 1986, the courts' powers of confiscation were narrow. So, in *R v Cuthbertson*[1] the House of Lords held[2] that the power of forfeiture and destruction conferred by s 27 of the Misuse of Drugs Act 1971[3] applied only to tangible property (including drugs, apparatus, vehicles and 'cash ready to be, or having just been, handed over for them') and did *not* attach to intangible property, or to property situated abroad. In particular, s 27 did not authorise the court to follow or trace assets which had been acquired with the property (e.g. cash) that could have been forfeited. As a means of stripping professional drug-traffickers of the profits of their unlawful enterprises (some £750,000 in that case), the powers of forfeiture were clearly inadequate.

1 [1981] AC 470, HL.
2 With an expression of 'considerable regret' (at 479).
3 Under s 27 of the Misuse of Drugs Act 1971, 'anything shown to relate to the offence' is subject to forfeiture.

11.13 The decision in *Cuthbertson* prompted the establishment of a committee under the chairmanship of the Hon Mr Justice Hodgson.[1] The Committee's recommendations led to the enactment of the Drug Trafficking Offences Act 1986[2] which made provision for confiscation of the benefit of drug trafficking. Two years later, the court was given power to make a confiscation order against those convicted of crimes other than drug trafficking by s 71 of the Criminal Justice Act 1988. Parliament also gave effect to the UK's obligations under the Vienna Convention against Illicit Traffic in Narcotic Drugs and Psychotropic Substances (1988)[3] and the Council of Europe Convention on Laundering, Search, Seizure and Confiscation of the Proceeds of Crime (1991).[4] Part 5 of the Vienna Convention required parties to 'adopt such measures as may be necessary to enable confiscation of '... [the] proceeds derived from offences established in accordance with Art 1, or property the value of which corresponds to that of such proceeds'. Article 5.7 provided for the reversal of the burden of proof.[5] Over time, the confiscation regimes were modified, extended (so as to include a distinct regime for terrorist offences: Terrorism Act 2000, Pt III) and tightened.

1 See Report of the Committee: *The Profits of Crime and their Recovery* (Heineman, 1984).
2 The Drug Trafficking Offences Act was repealed by the Drug Trafficking Act 1994 which extended the confiscation regime in relation to drug trafficking offences: see Pt 1.
3 United Nations Convention against Illicit Traffic in Narcotic Drugs and Psychotropic Substances (Vienna, 20 December 1988).
4 Council of Europe Convention on Laundering, Search, Seizure and Confiscation of the Proceeds of Crime (Strasbourg, 8 November 1990; ETS No 141). The convention aimed to facilitate international cooperation and mutual assistance in investigating crime and tracking down, seizing and confiscating the proceeds thereof.
5 Each Party may consider ensuring that the onus of proof be reversed regarding the lawful origin of alleged proceeds or other property liable to confiscation, to the extent that such action is consistent with the principles of its domestic law and with the nature of judicial and other proceedings.

The statutory assumptions

11.14 Under each successive confiscation regime, in determining the value of the defendant's 'benefit', the courts have been able to assume that all property that has passed through his hands during the six years preceding his conviction derived from the commission of criminal offences by him with which he has not been charged, still less convicted.[1] Thus the legislation, driven by international conventions, has reversed the burden of proof, requiring the defendant show that his entire assets do not derive from criminal conduct.

1 DTOA, s 2(3); CJA, s 72AA(4); DTA, s 4(3); PoCA, s 10. As Lord Bingham CJ explained in *R v Clarke and Bentham* [1997] 2 Cr App R (S) 99, CA at 102 (a drug trafficking case): 'The object of [the DTOA] is to strip drug traffickers of their ill-gotten gains, whether or not those gains are the product of the offence giving rise to the enquiry'.

11.15 It follows that the powers have not been restricted to confiscating the proceeds of the particular offence of which the defendant was convicted. The practical effect of the assumption is to require the court to presume that the defendant is a career criminal whose acquisitions and expenditure in the preceding six years represent the proceeds of his criminal activity. It is up to the defendant to prove (on the balance of probabilities) that they were not. The rationale of the confiscation regime was explained by Lord Woolf CJ in *R v Benjafield*[1] as follows:

'The reason the legislation gives the courts the power to make confiscation orders and the reason why it creates statutory assumptions which interfere with the onus and burden of proof which normally exist in criminal proceedings is obvious and illustrated by the facts of these appeals. The provisions of the 1988 Act are aimed at depriving repeat offenders of the fruits of their crimes. The 1994 Act is aimed at achieving the same objective in relation to those who profit from drug trafficking. Both in the case of repeat offenders and drug traffickers, it is very much in the public interest that they are not able to profit from their crimes. If offenders are likely to lose their ill-gotten benefits, then this in itself will be a significant deterrent to the commission of further offences. In particular in relation to drug trafficking, justice requires that the profits made by the commission of those especially antisocial offences should be confiscated. Their profits are usually achieved at immense cost to those to whom the drugs are ultimately supplied. It is notoriously difficult to combat the traffickers' activities and the dangers that they create for society provide a justification for action out of the ordinary. In addition, those at whom the legislation is aimed, whether repeat offenders or drug traffickers, are usually adept at concealing their profits and unless they are called upon to explain the source of their assets, it will be frequently difficult and often impossible to identify the proceeds of their crimes.'

1 [2001] 3 WLR 75, CA at para 43.

11.16 In *R v Dickens*,[1] Lord Lane characterised the DTOA confiscation regime as follows:

'It is plain that the object of the Act is to ensure, so far as is possible, that the convicted drug trafficker is parted from the proceeds of any drug trafficking which he has carried out. The provisions are intentionally *Draconian*. Since the amount of those proceeds and the size of his realisable assets at the time of conviction are likely to be peculiarly within the defendant's knowledge, it is not surprising perhaps if evidential burdens are cast upon him of a kind which are, to say the least, unusual in the area of the criminal law and this, despite the fact that the confiscation order and the penalties for failing to comply with it may be rigorous.'

1 [1990] 2 QB 102, CA.

11.17 Part 2 of the Proceeds of Crime Act 2002 is, if anything, intended to be more 'draconian'. Nevertheless, the confiscation legislation has survived repeated challenges in the House of Lords and the European Court of Human Rights ('ECtHR'). It is important to have this history and these statutory purposes in mind when considering if a given set of circumstances are likely to reach the threshold at which they could be stayed as an abuse of process.

Draconian but ECHR compliant?

11.18 There have been several challenges in the ECtHR to the confiscation regime directed at the compatibility of the assumptions. In the first of these, *Welch v UK*,[1] the court concluded that a confiscation order amounted to a penalty, and so could not have retrospective application (Art 7(1)). However, the court made it plain that:

> '... this conclusion concerns only the retrospective application of the relevant legislation and does not call into question in any respect the powers of confiscation conferred on the courts in a weapon in the fight against the scourge of drug trafficking.'

1 *Welch v UK* (1995) 20 EHRR 247.

11.19 *In Phillips v UK*,[1] following the applicant's conviction for a drug trafficking offence, a confiscation order was made under the DTA 1994 in the sum of £91,400. Although he had no declared taxable source of income, P had deposited considerable sums of cash in his building society accounts in the period running up to his arrest; he had also purchased a property that he converted into four flats, invested in a newsagent business and was the registered owner of five cars including a recently acquired BMW. He gave evidence at the confiscation hearing that the judge rejected as untruthful. In assessing the amount of the benefit, the judge applied the assumptions in DTA, s 4(3). Before the ECtHR, P claimed that the statutory assumptions breached his right to the presumption of innocence under Art 6.2. The UK Government argued that Art 6.2 was not engaged at all (though it conceded that Art 6.1 applied to confiscation).

1 European Court of Human Rights, Fourth Section: 5 July 2001.

11.20 The Court held that the purpose of the confiscation procedure was not the conviction or acquittal of the applicant for any other drug-related offence, but was 'to enable the national court to assess the amount at which the confiscation order should properly be fixed'.[1] Article 6.2 had no application, because the procedure, which was analogous to the determination of the amount of a fine or the length of imprisonment to be served, was part of the sentencing process and did not involve a new 'charge'. However, Art 6.1 applied throughout the entirety of the criminal proceedings and included a right to be presumed innocent and to require the prosecution to prove the allegations against the defendant (c.f. *Saunders v UK*[2]). The question of compatibility was not to be answered in the abstract, but rather by examining whether the way the assumptions applied in the applicant's case offended the basic principles of a fair trial procedure inherent in Art 6.1.[3] The confiscation process was fair because, although the application of the assumptions[4] was mandatory, there were proper safeguards to protect a defendant: judicial proceeding; public hearing; advance disclosure; a measure of judicial discretion etc. In particular, a defendant had the opportunity to rebut the presumption by giving and calling evidence to show that the property in question was legitimately obtained. The applicant's complaint that the confiscation powers under the DTA 1994 were unreasonably extensive and in breach of A1P1 was also dismissed. The interference with the applicant's right to peaceful enjoyment of property guaranteed by Art 1 was proportionate given the importance of the aim pursued by the legislation, namely the serious problem of drug trafficking.

1 At para 34.
2 European Court of Human Rights, Fourth Section: 17 December 1996, para 68.
3 At para 40.
4 In DTA, s 4(3).

11.21 Soon after *Phillips*, confiscation under both the CJA 1988 and the DTA 1994 was considered by the House of Lords in *R v Benjafield*; *R v Rezvi*.[1] Again, the issue was whether the statutory confiscation regimes under the DTA and CJA were compatible with the ECHR. The House of Lords (unanimously) held that the assumptions were not wider than was necessary to achieve the legitimate (and internationally recognised) aim in the public interest of depriving professional and habitual criminals of the proceeds of their criminal conduct and so were not incompatible with Convention rights. It was a notorious fact that such criminals frequently take steps to conceal their profits from crime; putting a burden on the defendant was not disproportionate to the objective. Article 6.2 was not engaged because the confiscation proceedings did not amount to a 'charge' but were part of the sentencing process following a conviction for a relevant offence. Parliament had devised 'a precise, fair and proportionate response to the important need to protect the public'.[2]

1 [2003] 1 AC 1099, HL. See also *McIntosh v Lord Advocate* [2003] 1 AC 1078, PC.
2 *Per* Lord Steyn at p.1161.

11.22 Significantly though, Lord Steyn considered that one reason why the means adopted by the legislation to accomplish the legitimate aim were not wider than necessary was 'the role of the court in standing back and deciding whether there is or might be a risk of serious or real injustice and, if there is, or might be, in emphasising that a confiscation order ought not be made'.[1] However, as the Court of Appeal explained in *R v Ahmed*[2] this remark is confined to the application of the assumptions and was not intended to suggest that the court has a surviving general discretion.

1 *Per* Lord Steyn at 1153.
2 [2005] 1 WLR 122, CA at para 10.

11.23 Once the court has determined the value of the defendant's benefit, it must assess the value of the realisable property available. Whilst the burden of proving benefit is on the prosecution, it is for the defendant to establish, on the balance of probabilities, that the amount that might be realised is less. In *Grayson and Barnham v UK*[1] it was argued in the European Court of Human Rights that the fact that a legal burden was placed on a defendant to show he did not have realisable assets equivalent to the benefit figure offended the basic principles of a fair procedure in contravention of Art 6 and A1P1. The court concluded that the legislation did *not* violate the applicants' Convention rights. Noting the safeguards built into the system, it was not unreasonable to expect a convicted person to explain what had happened to the money shown by the prosecution to have been in his possession. Such matters fell within the applicants' particular knowledge and the burden would not have been difficult to meet had the accounts of their financial affairs been true.

However, in *Paulet v United Kingdom*,[2] a complaint to the European Court of Human Rights succeeded on the ground that while an interference with A1P1 could be justified, and PoCA was in pursuance of a justifiable aim, to be ECHR compliant the interference had to be proportionate. The legislation as drafted at the time and prior to the guidance given in *Waya* made no refence to proportionality. When anlaysing Protcol 1, the Court held that:

'this provision must be construed in the light of the general principle set out in the first sentence of the first paragraph and there must, therefore, exist a reasonable relationship of proportionality between the means employed and the aim sought to be realised.'[3]

The central conclusion was:

> 'Consequently, the Court cannot but conclude that at the time the applicant brought the domestic proceedings, the scope of the review carried out by the domestic courts was too narrow to satisfy the requirement of seeking the "fair balance" inherent in the second paragraph of art.1 of Protocol No.1.'[4]

1 European Court of Human Rights, Fourth Section: 23 September 2008.
2 (2015) 61 EHRR 39.
3 Op cit para 64.
4 Op cit para 68.

11.24 In the passage from *Benjafield* quoted above,[1] Lord Steyn was referring to DTA, s 4(4), but PoCA, s 10(6) is in the same terms:[2]

> 'But the court must not make a required assumption in relation to particular property or expenditure if: (a) the assumption is shown to be incorrect, or (b) there will be a serious risk of injustice if the assumption were made.'

1 Above para **11.21**.
2 CJA, s 72AA(5) is also to identical effect.

11.25 It is by this method that the court is given a measure of discretion in relation to the assumptions. To the extent that a confiscation order in a 'criminal lifestyle' case is based on assumptions it ought not, except in very unusual circumstances, to court the danger of being disproportionate because those assumptions will only be applied if they can be made without risk of serious injustice. However, s 10(6)(b) does not give the court a general discretion not to make a confiscation order where it might cause hardship; rather, it applies only where a risk of injustice arises from the operation of the assumptions in the calculation of benefit.

11.26 So, in *R v Lunnon*,[1] where the defendant had submitted a detailed basis of plea and the prosecution had explicitly conceded that he had no prior involvement in drug trafficking, it was inconsistent with that concession for the court to assume all property that passed through his hands during the six years preceding his conviction derived from drug trafficking (s 4(3)). Accordingly, unless the concession was withdrawn, there would be an apparent injustice if the assumption was applied; s 4(4)(b) enabled the court to avoid the risk of injustice by disapplying the assumption. The Court of Appeal stressed that the obligation on the court under s 4(4)(b) to 'stand back' and make its own independent assessment was of fundamental importance, since this was what rendered the reverse burden of proof compatible with the requirements of Art 6 of the European Convention on Human Rights.

1 [2005] 1 Cr App R (S) 111, CA; cf *R v Lazarus* [2005] Crim LR 64, CA.

CONFISCATION AND A1P1

11.27 By its very nature, confiscation involves a deprivation of property. Article 1 of the First Protocol to the European Convention provides:

> 'Every natural or legal person is entitled to the peaceful enjoyment of his possessions. No one shall be deprived of his possessions except in the public interest and subject to the conditions provided for by law and by the general principles of international law. The preceding provisions shall not, however, in any way impair the right of a state to enforce such laws as it deems necessary to control the use of property in accordance with the general interest or to secure the payment of taxes or other contributions or penalties.'

11.28 The general purpose of A1P1 is to protect the individual from arbitrary deprivation of possession of property. Any deprivation of possession of property must be in the public interest and subject to the conditions provided for by law.

11.29 A1P1 contains three separate and distinct rules. The first rule is a rule of general application which recognises every person's right to peaceful enjoyment of his possessions. The second rule deals with measures which deprive a person of his possessions. Deprivation is permissible if, but only if, it is 'in the public interest and subject to the conditions provided for by law and by the general principles of international law'. The reference to international law is irrelevant in the case of a taking by a state of the property of its own nationals. The third rule deals with the state's power to enforce laws controlling the use by a person of his property but is not relevant to cases of deprivation of property, which are governed by a combination of rules 1 and 2.[1]

1 *Sporrong and Lonnroth v Sweden* (1982) 5 EHRR 35.

11.30 A taking of property in pursuance of legitimate social, economic or other policies may be 'in the public interest' but to be compliant with A1P1, the measure under which the property is taken must pursue a legitimate aim in the public interest and there must be a reasonable relationship of proportionality between the means employed and the aim sought to be realised.

11.31 In the context of criminal confiscation, A1P1 imports the requirement that there must be a reasonable relationship of proportionality between the means employed by the state in, *inter alia*, the deprivation of property as a form of penalty, and the legitimate aim which is sought to be realised by the deprivation. The critical questions are:

(1) whether the proposed taking is in accordance with 'conditions provided for by law'; if so

(2) whether the measure relied upon to justify the taking has a legitimate aim;

(3) if the first and second conditions are each satisfied, whether the taking strikes a fair balance between the general interest of the community and the requirements of the protection of the companies' right to peaceful enjoyment of their possessions.

The Court must determine:

> '…whether a fair balance was struck between the demands of the general interest of the community and the requirements of the protection of the

individual's fundamental rights. The search for this balance is inherent in the whole of the Convention and is also reflected in the structure of article 1.'[1]

1 *Sporrong and Lonnroth* (above) at §69.

11.32 The Strasbourg Court has adopted a generous approach to the 'public interest' test, allowing a wide margin of appreciation to a national legislature with regard both to choosing the means of enforcement and to ascertaining whether the consequences of enforcement are justified in the general interest for the purpose of achieving the object of the law in question.[1]

1 *Jahn v Germany* (2006) 42 EHRR 1084, para 93; see also *James v UK* (1986) 8 EHRR 123.

11.33 In *R v Shabir*,[1] Hughes LJ observed that:

> 'Even if it be accepted that [A1P1] may be capable of being infringed by a truly oppressive and thus disproportionate individual order for confiscation (as to which we express no opinion), it is clear that the court's power to stay for oppression provides the remedy.'

On the very unusual and exceptional facts of the case, the Court was sure that, if application had been made to the judge to stay the confiscation application for abuse of process, it would have been granted. The confiscation order was quashed because the Prosecution's application (applying the assumptions) in the amount of £212,464.17 (when the benefit from the particular offences of which S was convicted was only £464) was oppressive. A compensation order in the sum of £464 was substituted.

1 *R v Shabir* [2008] EWCA Crim 1809; [2009] 1 Cr App R (S) 497, CA.

11.34 In *Shabir*, although A1P1 was referred to in argument, there was no consideration in the judgment of whether a fair balance was struck between the demands of the general interest of the community and the requirements of the protection of S's A1P1 rights. However, in *R v Waya*,[1] the question as to whether A1P1 may be infringed by a truly oppressive and thus disproportionate individual order was reconsidered by Hughes LJ. sitting as a Justice of the Supreme Court.

1 [2012] UKSC 51; [2012] 3 WLR 1188.

11.35 The factual issue in the case concerned what if any benefit a defendant convicted of 'mortgage fraud' obtains. However, after the first hearing, the Supreme Court invited submissions from the parties as to: (a) whether the PoCA confiscation regime is capable of operating in a manner which is oppressive and/or an abuse of process; and (b) if so, whether the court ought to give any (and if so what) guidance on when that might occur. In the event, the decision began with a detailed analysis of the interplay between Pt 2 of the 2002 Act and A1P1.

11.36 Given that A1P1 is one of the Convention rights to which the Human Rights Act 1998 applies,[1] section 3(1) requires that so far as it is possible to do so, legislation must be 'read and given effect in a way which is compatible' with it. This means that:

(a) the confiscation regime in Pt 2 of PoCA must be read and given effect in a manner which avoids a violation of A1P1;

(b) a confiscation order which does not conform to the test of proportionality will constitute such a violation;

(c) it is incumbent upon the domestic court to provide a remedy for any such violation; and

(d) the appropriate remedy lies in the duty of the Crown Court judge not to make an order which involves such a violation.

1 Section 1(1)(b) of the Human Rights Act 1998.

11.37 The purpose of confiscation proceedings is 'to recover the financial benefit that the offender has obtained from his criminal conduct' rather than the imposition of fines or deterrence. It follows that a confiscation order must therefore bear a proportionate relationship to this purpose to avoid an infringement of A1P1. Although the overall confiscation scheme is A1P1 'compliant', in any particular case, the court might be asked to make an order which does not strike a fair balance between the demands of the general interest of the community and the requirements of the protection of the defendant's fundamental rights.

11.38 The court must refuse to make a confiscation order which would be disproportionate. In order to avoid infringing the defendant's A1P1 rights, s 6(5) of PoCA must be interpreted ('read down') as if it provided as follows [emphasis added]:

> 'If the court decides under subsection (4)(b) or (c) that the defendant has benefited from the conduct referred to it must— (a) decide the recoverable amount, and (b) make an order (a confiscation order) requiring him to pay that amount *except in so far as such an order would be a breach of article 1, Protocol 1*.'

11.39 In a 'criminal lifestyle' case, the assumptions must not be made if they (or any of them) are shown to be incorrect or if making them would give rise to a risk of serious injustice: ss 10(6)(a) & (b). Although(b) is not couched in the language of the Convention, it is plain that if applying the assumptions would produce a disproportionate order, the court is provided with the means to avoid it.

11.40 However, the judge's responsibility to refuse to make a disproportionate confiscation order is not the same as the re-creation by another route of the general discretion once available under the earliest confiscation statute but deliberately removed by Parliament. An order which the judge would not have made as a matter of discretion does not thereby *ipso facto* become disproportionate.

Repayment by the defendant

11.41 Confiscation orders are not intended to be restitutionary measures. The victim may seek damages in the civil courts and, for this reason, Parliament has acknowledged that payment to the victim should have priority over a confiscation order. Although the making of a confiscation order is mandatory provided the conditions are met (s 6(1)), an exception is made where the victim of the offending has launched a civil claim to recover his or her losses (or intends to do so). In that event, the confiscation order is discretionary (s 6(6); below); the judge has a discretion as to whether to make an order and if so, in what amount (s 7(3)).

11.42 There is every reason, in the public interest, to encourage the prompt and voluntary repayment by the criminal of the benefit derived from the crime.[1] If before sentence, the defendant has made full restitution, there will be no occasion for the victim to make a civil claim. However, without either the fact or prospect of such proceedings, s 6(6) is not engaged; a person making full restitution in those circumstances has no protection. If the prosecution applies, a confiscation order will be made for the full sum of benefit obtained, up to the amount of the defendant's realisable/available assets. If the only benefit the defendant has obtained is the amount which he has already repaid to the loser, this has the consequence that there must be a confiscation order for the same sum again, so long as the defendant has assets to meet it. That means he pays up to double the benefit he has obtained from crime.

1 See *R v Mahmood & Shahin* (above para **11.02**); *R v Farquhar* (above para **11.02**).

11.43 In the conjoined appeals of *R v Morgan; R v Bygrave*[1] this issue was considered by the Court of Appeal. The Court held that it *could* amount to an abuse of process for the Crown to seek a confiscation order which would result in an order to pay up to double the full restitution which the defendant has made or is willing immediately to make, and which would thus deter him from making it. However, this would only be so where:

(a) the defendant's crimes are limited to offences causing loss to one or more identifiable loser(s);

(b) his benefit is limited to those crimes;

(c) the loser has neither brought nor intends any civil proceedings to recover the loss; but

(d) the defendant either has repaid the loser, or stands ready willing and able immediately to repay him, the full amount of the loss.[2]

1 [2008] EWCA Crim 1323; [2008] 4 All ER 890, CA.
2 It is likely to be difficult to establish the latter unless the defendant has either already made restitution in full or is in a position to tender it immediately in a guaranteed form, such as a banker's draft or funds in a solicitor's hands.

11.44 Like *Shabir*, *Morgan* was also reconsidered by the Supreme Court in *Waya*. Although the observations of the Court of Appeal in *Morgan* were correct, the Justices decided that this was another situation properly to be treated as disproportionate rather than an abuse. To make a confiscation order in his case, when he had already restored to the loser any proceeds of crime which he ever had, was disproportionate. It would not achieve the statutory objective of removing his proceeds of crime but would simply be an additional financial penalty.

11.45 Section 6(6) of PoCA gives the court a discretion as to whether to make a confiscation order wherever the loser whose property represents the defendant's proceeds of crime either has brought, or proposes to bring, civil proceedings to recover his loss. However, if the defendant has already repaid whatever he obtained to the victim, s 6(6) has no application. The Supreme Court considered that it would be unfair and capricious, and thus disproportionate, to distinguish between a defendant whose victim was about to sue him and a defendant who had already repaid.

11.46 However, only where there is 'full restoration' of whatever was obtained by the defendant as a result of or in connection with his criminal conduct (s 76(4) PoCA) will it be disproportionate to make a confiscation order. *Morgan* itself was such a case; the defendant cheated an elderly lady out of a total of £279,872.02. Between his arrest and the confiscation hearing he repaid about five-sixths of what he had obtained; he said that he stood ready to repay the balance although it was not clear that he would be able to do so. His appeal was dismissed.

11.47 In *R v Harvey*,[1] the Court of Appeal had another opportunity to consider 'partial restoration' in the light of *Waya*. H was convicted of handling stolen property, namely heavy plant and machinery used in road construction. Some items of plant were restored but only after years of use by H (who operated a plant hire business). Relying on *Waya* (on the facts a partial restoration case) to argue that the value of the plant when recovered by the police should be deducted from the benefit figure.

1 [2014] 1 WLR 124, CA.

11.48 Having reviewed various decision involving 'restoration', the court that if:

(i) D obtains chattels as a result of his criminal conduct;

(ii) D uses those chattels for a substantial period, thereby materially reducing their value;

(iii) the chattels are ultimately restored to their true owners,

then the court in assessing D's benefit should not give credit for the residual value of those chattels. If a person steals or otherwise unlawfully obtains someone else's property and uses it for a number of years thereby materially reducing its value, a confiscation order based upon the original value of that property without any deduction is not disproportionate. A1P1 does not require a deduction be made.

ABUSE OF PROCESS AND CONFISCATION?

11.49 As we have seen, in *Shabir* the court concluded that the order made by the judge, on the particular fact of the case, was truly oppressive and thus disproportionate. In *Morgan* the court said it would be an abuse of the process for the prosecution to seek a confiscation order where the defendant had made full restoration to the victim of whatever he had obtained by his crime.

Were the cases to be argued today, the court decisions would be the same (the court should refuse to make the order sought) but on the basis of A1P1, not abuse.[1] It is the writer's view that there will be few, if any cases in the future where it will be necessary to stay for abuse. As Hughes LJ said in *R v Beazley*[2] (a post-*Waya* decision of the Court of Appeal):

> 'Resort to a stay for abuse of process is no longer either appropriate or required.'

In particular, the jurisdiction to stay for abuse cannot be invoked where the judge feels unhappy about the consequences of a statutory regime which has been put in place by Parliament.

Following the decision in *Waya*, PoCA was amended so that s 6(5)[3] now includes the words at the end of the subsection: 'Paragraph (b) applies only if, or to the extent that, it would not be disproportionate to require the defendant to pay the recoverable amount.' Through this statutory amendment, the utility of the abuse of process jurisdiction had been further eroded as what might otherwise be challenged as an abuse can be accommodated within the concept of proportionality and the remedy that would be provided by a stay of proceedings is unnecessary if the court has the discretion not to make an order on the ground that it would be disproportionate.

This dynamic can be seen in *R v Andrewes*[4] which concerned the obtaining of a pecuniary advantage by deception (Theft Act 1968, s 16) and fraud (Fraud Act 2006, s 1) in which the defendant had secured lucrative employment through false assertions about his education and employment history. The criminal benefit had been assessed as the income derived from the dishonestly obtained positions, net of tax and national insurance. This sun totalled £643,602. The recoverable amount was agreed to be £96,737.24. The principal grounds of appeal against the propriety of confiscation order at all were remoteness and proportionality. Remoteness was rejected on the basis that the defendant had through his pleas accepted benefiting from his offences, the evidence was that the offences were causative of the offers of employment and the offences were ongoing.

The following observations were made about the concept of proportionality. First, it does not reintroduce by the back door the notion of residual judicial discretion. An assessment of disproportionality is not to be made by balancing competing factors in the manner of a public law case. Third, proportionality in this context is not concerned with the ratio between the criminal benefit and the recoverable amount.[5] Davis LJ went on to explain that disproportionality in this context is to be measured with reference to the statutory objective of depriving criminals of the proceeds of their criminality. The 'underpinning, even if not the absolute principle' for determining what disproportionate does mean is 'indicated by reference to whether such an order will constitute double recovery from or double penalty on, the defendant and will not achieve an expropriation of the proceeds of his crime.'[6]

Andrewes succeeded in his appeal on the proportionality ground, which was reasoned as follows:

> 'In all the circumstances, he is, in our judgment, to be taken as having given full value for his remuneration. He is thereby taken to have made full restoration. A confiscation order would accordingly be disproportionate to the aim of the 2002 Act: it would involve a double penalty.'

In an earlier part of the judgment, in a discussion of the authorities bearing on the issue of proportionality, the David LJ emphasised the need for caution when considering pre-*Waya* cases and then said this:

> '…in *Shabir* [2008] EWCA Crim 1809, [2009] 1 Cr. App. App. R. (S) 84 an outrageously unjust result was averted by resort to principles of oppression and abuse of process. It is doubtful whether resort to such principles would be necessary nowadays, if such facts ever to recur.'[7]

The point is not that *Shabir* is no longer good law but that the change in the legislation, whereby a discretionary gloss has been added to the s 6 duty, means that the threshold of abuse of process is unlikely to be reached.

An attempt to secure the stay of proceedings by reference to the abuse jurisdiction was considered by the Privy Council in Attorney-General for the Attorney-General for the *Isle of Man v Darroch*.[8] In this case the issue was whether it was an abuse of process for the prosecution, having taken a deliberate decision not to seek costs and announced that decision in open court, to then seek to change course and pursue an order for substantial costs. The defendant and his legal representatives were not present when the prosecution announced its intention not to seek costs. The court concluded therefore that there could be no question of the defendant having relied to his detriment on the statement by the prosecution. It was said that while it was unattractive for the prosecution to change its position, that decision had to be assessed on the particular facts of the case. The case fell short of the '*high threshold required to establish an abuse of process*'.[9]

1 *Waya* at para 18.
2 *Beazley* [2013] 1 WLR 567, CA.
3 Added by the Serious Crime Act 2015.
4 [2020] Crim LR 1085; [2020] EWCA Crim 1055.
5 Op cit para 79.
6 Op cit para 84.
7 Op cit para 49.
8 [2019] 1 WLR 4211.
9 Op cit 4219.

Chapter 12

Abuse of process doctrine in international criminal proceedings

INTRODUCTION

12.01 As discussed in previous chapters of this book, the abuse of process doctrine has developed from a common law basis in order to remedy serious prejudice to the rights of an accused in criminal proceedings, deter future misconduct and enhance the integrity of the judicial process. In order to address these same issues, the international criminal tribunals first applied the abuse of process doctrine by looking to its application in various common law systems. This inquiry has resulted in a set of applicable principles which are relatively uniform across the international criminal tribunals.

AD HOC TRIBUNALS: INTERNATIONAL CRIMINAL TRIBUNAL FOR THE FORMER YUGOSLAVIA AND THE INTERNATIONAL CRIMINAL TRIBUNAL FOR RWANDA

Applicable principles

12.02 The possibility of a stay of proceedings occasioned by the frustration of a fair trial was first discussed by the ICTY Appeals Chamber in the case of *Prosecutor v Dušco Tadić* in July 1999. When faced with Defence submissions that Mr. Tadić did not receive a fair trial because relevant and admissible evidence was not presented due to a lack of cooperation of the authorities in the Republika Srpska, the ICTY Appeals Chamber considered that it could:

> 'conceive of situations where a fair trial is not possible because witnesses central to the defence case do not appear due to the obstructionist efforts of a State. In such circumstances, the defence, after exhausting all the other measures mentioned above, has the option of submitting a motion for a stay of proceedings.'[1]

However, the Appeals Chamber noted that it was the obligation of the complaining party to bring such difficulties and violations to the attention of the Trial Chamber forthwith so that the latter can determine whether any assistance could be provided under the Rules or Statute to relieve the situation.[2] As the appellant had remained silent on the matter before the Trial Chamber, the Appeals Chamber ruled that the Defence could not raise this argument on appeal.[3] No further discussion was therefore had on the mechanics of staying such proceedings.

1 ICTY, Appeals Chamber, *Prosecutor v Dusko Tadić*, IT-94-1-A, Judgment, 15 July 1999, ('Tadić Appeals') at para 55.
2 Ibid.
3 Tadić Appeals at para 55.

12.03 In *Prosecutor v Jean Bosco Barayagwiza*, the ICTR Appeals Chamber subsequently formulated the applicable standard of the abuse of process doctrine in its decision of 3 November 1999.[1] The Appeals Chamber was faced with, *inter alia*, the question as to whether the detention and arrest of an accused, prior to his transfer to the custody of the ICTR, could affect proceedings before the Tribunal.

1 ICTR, Appeals Chamber, *Jean-Bosco Barayagwiza v Prosecutor*, ICTR-97-52, Decision, 3 November 1999, ('Barayagwiza Decision of 3 November 1999').

12.04 Mr. Barayagwiza had been detained for a period of 19 months between 15 April 1996 when he was initially detained in Cameroon and 19 November 1997, when he was transferred to the Tribunal's detention unit. His first appearance before ICTR Trial Chamber II was not scheduled until 23 February 1998.[1]

1 Barayagwiza Decision of 3 November 1999 at paras 2–3.

12.05 The ICTR Appeals Chamber looked at whether the following rights of the accused were violated, namely: (i) Mr. Barayagwiza's right to be promptly charged under Rule 40*bis* of the ICTR Rules of Procedure and Evidence; and (ii) his right to be brought before a Judge without delay.

12.06 With respect to the first issue, the ICTR Appeals Chamber found that Mr. Barayagwiza was detained 'at the request of the Prosecutor from 17 April 1996 through 16 May 1996 [...] [t]his detention – for 29 days – violated the 20-day limitation in Rule 40.'[1] The ICTR Appeals Chamber held that the length of time that Barayagwiza was detained in Cameroon at the behest of the Tribunal without being indicted violated Rule 40*bis* and established human rights jurisprudence governing the detention of suspects.[2]

1 Barayagwiza Decision of 3 November 1999 at para 52. In doing so, the Appeals Chamber noted that the Tribunal had issued a valid request for provisional detention which were honoured by Cameroon and but for those requests, Barayagwiza would have been released on 21 February 1997, when the Cameroon Court of Appeals denied the Rwandan extradition request and ordered for his immediate release.
2 Barayagwiza Decision of 3 November 1999 at para 67.

12.07 With respect to the second issue, the Appeals Chamber took the plain meaning of 'without delay' in order to find that the 96 day delay between Mr. Barayagwiza's transfer to the Tribunal's detention unit and his initial appearance was a violation of his fundamental rights.[1] On this basis, the Appeals Chamber opined that to proceed with Mr. Barayagwiza's trial would amount to an act of injustice and therefore declined to exercise jurisdiction over Mr. Barayagwiza on the basis of the abuse of process doctrine.[2]

1 Barayagwiza Decision of 3 November 1999 at para 71.
2 Barayagwiza Decision of 3 November 1999 at para 72.

12.08 In doing so, the ICTR Appeals Chamber accepted that it had an inherent power to decline to adjudicate a case which would be oppressive highlighting that:

> '[T]he abuse of process doctrine may be invoked as a matter of discretion. It is a process by which Judges may decline to exercise the court's jurisdiction in cases where to exercise that jurisdiction in light of serious and egregious violations of the accused's rights would prove detrimental to the court's integrity.'[1]

It found that the abuse of process doctrine was applicable in two distinct situations:

> '(1) where delay has made a fair trial for the accused impossible; and (2) where in the circumstances of a particular case, proceeding with the trial of the accused would contravene the court's sense of justice, due to pre-trial impropriety or misconduct [...]'[2]

Additionally, the Appeals Chamber held that it was irrelevant as to which entity or entities were responsible for the alleged violations of an accused's rights and that the application of the abuse of process doctrine is case specific and limited to egregious circumstances.[3]

1 Barayagwiza Decision of 3 November 1999 at para 74. In particular, the Appeals Chamber relied on leading principles established in *R. Horseferry Road ex parte Bennett* [1994] 1 A.C. 42 as to when a court would enjoy discretion to stay any criminal proceedings, followed by an analysis of the four guidelines set out in *Bell v DPP of Jamaica* [1985] AC 937 (Privy Council) in order to determine whether a delay would deprive the accused of a fair trial.

2 Barayagwiza Decision of 3 November 1999 at para 77.

3 Barayagwiza Decision of 3 November 1999 at para 73.

12.09 These principles became the applicable law for the abuse of process doctrine in international criminal proceedings.

Having set out these principles, the ICTR Appeals Chamber concluded on the facts that Mr. Barayagwiza:

> 'was in the constructive custody of the Tribunal from 4 March 1997 until his transfer to the Tribunal's detention unit on 19 November 1997. However, international human rights standards comport with the requirements of Rule 40*bis*. Thus, even if he was not in the constructive custody of the Tribunal, the period of provisional detention was impermissibly lengthy. Pursuant to that Rule, the indictment against the Appellant had to be confirmed within 90 days from 4 March 1997. However, the indictment was not confirmed in this case until 23 October 1997. [The Appeals Chamber] find[s], therefore, that the Appellant's right to be promptly charged pursuant to international standards as reflected in Rule 40bis was violated. Moreover, [the Appeals Chamber] find[s] that the Appellant's right to an initial appearance, without delay upon his transfer to the Tribunal's detention unit under Rule 62, was violated.'[1]

The abuse of process doctrine was found to be applicable under these facts.[2]

1 Barayagwiza Decision of 3 November 1999 at para 100.

2 Whilst not central to the Appeals Chambers findings, the Chamber also concluded that: (i) Mr. Barayagwiza's writ of habeas corpus was a distinct issue from the underlying legality of

his initial detention and that therefore he enjoyed the right for the writ to be heard upon filing. The failure to provide Mr. Barayagwiza a hearing on the writ therefore violated his right to challenge the legality of his continued detention in Cameroon during the periods when he was held at the behest of the Tribunal; and (ii) the Prosecutor has certain responsibilities to ensure that accused persons appearing before the Tribunal are guaranteed a fair and expeditious trial. The Appeals Chamber found that the Prosecutor failed to take steps to encourage the Registry or Chambers to place Mr. Barayagwiza's initial appearance on the docket and therefore failed in her duty to diligently prosecute the case. See Barayagwiza Decision of 3 November 1999 at paras 87–99.

12.10 At the time, the Appeals Chamber concluded that the only appropriate remedy to rectify the serious and egregious violations of Mr. Barayagwiza's right was to order for his immediate release and dismissal of all charges against him with prejudice to the Prosecutor.[1]

1 Barayagwiza Decision of 3 November 1999 at para 106.

12.11 Although the ICTR Appeals Chamber upheld the principles on the abuse of process doctrine, it ultimately reversed its disposition in its decision of 31 March 2000,[1] finding that, although Mr. Barayagwiza's rights had been violated, it was not as severe as had been originally determined.[2] It therefore concluded that Mr. Barayagwiza could be tried before the Tribunal and that the appropriate remedy would be a reduction in sentence upon conviction or financial compensation upon acquittal.[3]

1 ICTR, Appeals Chamber, *Jean-Bosco Barayagwiza v Prosecutor*, ICTR-97-19-AR72, Decision (Prosecutor's Request for Review or Reconsideration), 31 March 2000 ('Barayagwiza Decision of 31 March 2000'). On 25 November 1999, the Appeals Chamber had suspended the effect of Barayagwiza Decision of 3 November 1999 at the request of the Prosecution. On 1 December 1999 the Prosecutor filed a motion for review of the Barayagwiza Decision of 3 November 1999 requesting Appeals Chamber to consider 'new facts' leading to the Barayagwiza Decision of 31 March 2000.

2 Although it exceeds the scope of this chapter the reasons for Appeals Chamber's reversal has been much discussed following the Prosecutor's submissions that 'her ability to continue with prosecutions and investigations depends on the Government of Rwanda and that, unless [Mr. Barayagwiza] is tried, the Rwandan Government will no longer be "involved in any manner"'. See Barayagwiza Decision of 31 March 2000 at para 24.

3 Barayagwiza Decision of 31 March 2000 at para 75.

12.12 Following Mr. Barayagwiza's conviction, the ICTR Appeals Chamber's reversal was subsequently raised on appeal by Mr. Barayagwiza,[1] with the Defence submitting that political pressure was exerted in order to have the Appeal Chamber's decision of 3 November 1999 reversed. The Appeals Chamber ultimately found that Mr. Barayagwiza was unable to establish that the Judges or the Appeals Chamber was influenced by such pressures and subsequently upheld the position adopted in its decision of 31 March 2000.[2]

1 ICTR, Appeals Chamber, *Nahimana et al v Prosecutor*, ICTR-99-52-A, Judgment, 28 November 2007 ('Barayagwiza Appeals Judgment').

2 Barayagwiza Appeals Judgment at para 32.

ICTY/ICTR fact patterns

12.13 The core principles of the abuse of process doctrine as established by the Appeals Chamber in *Prosecutor v Barayagwiza* have stood the test of time.

Abuse of process motions tend to be filed in response to certain specific fact patterns. For the *ad hoc* tribunals, these fact patterns can be broadly described as: (i) violations of undue delay; (ii) violations arising from Prosecutorial misconduct; (iii) violations arising from conduct of national authorities; (iv) violations arising out of an inability for the Defence to prepare; and (v) violations of the right to be tried by an impartial tribunal.

Undue delay

12.14 The length of undue delay is assessed on a case-by-case basis in light of several criteria including *inter alia*: the complexity of proceedings; the charges against the accused; the conduct of the accused; and the conduct of organs of the Tribunal.

12.15 As discussed, in *Prosecutor v Barayagwiza*, the ICTR Appeals Chamber found that the abuse of process doctrine is applicable where an accused spends an inordinate amount of time spent in provisional detention without knowledge of the general nature of the charges against him.[1]

1 Barayagwiza Decision of 3 November 1999 at para 85. The Appeals Chamber had found that the Prosecutor's failure to prosecute the case was tantamount to negligence.

12.16 The ICTR Appeals Chamber was faced with similar facts in *Prosecutor v Jean-Paul Akayesu* in June 2001.[1] Here Mr. Akayesu submitted that he had been arrested and detained on 10 October 1995 at the request of the Rwandan Government, followed by a request for his detention by the Prosecutor of the Tribunal on 22 November 1995. Mr. Akayesu was eventually transferred to the Tribunal's detention unit on 26 May 1996.

1 ICTR, Appeals Chamber, *Prosecutor v Jean-Paul Akayesu*, ICTR-96-4, Judgment, 1 June 2001, ('Akayesu Appeals').

12.17 According to Mr. Akayesu, he was only informed of the ICTR's arrest warrant against him on 29 March 1996 with his initial appearance scheduled on 30 May 1996. The Akayesu Defence asserted that this sequence of event culminated in the violation of his right to be promptly charged and informed of the nature of charges against him, resulting in his unlawful detention under ICTR Rule 40.[1]

1 Akayesu Appeals at para 354 and fn. 641.

12.18 In contrast to its approach in *Prosecutor v Jean Bosco Barayagwiza*, here the ICTR Appeals Chamber focused on the procedural aspect of the doctrine, finding that as Mr. Akayesu had not raised either violation before the Trial Chamber he therefore had waived his right to raise it on appeal.[1]

1 Akayesu Appeals at paras 359–362 and 370, 375. *See also* Tadić Appeals at para 55.

12.19 ICTR Trial Chamber II adopted a similar position in *Prosecutor v Pauline Nyiramasuhuko* in which it stated that the accused's allegations of undue delay since arrest were unfounded because she had made no effort to request provisional release.[1]

1 ICTR, Trial Chamber II, *Prosecutor v Pauline Nyiramasuhuko*, ICTR-97-21-T, Decision on Defence Motion for a Stay of Proceedings and Abuse of Process, 20 February 2004.

On 25 June 2003, the Defence for Nyiramasuhuko submitted that the accused had been detained on remand for an unreasonable period given that she had been arrested on 18 July 1997 and on 21 March 2003, the Prosecutor had stated that it required a further 16 months for the remainder of the Prosecution's case. The Defence asserted that this, along with fact that Ms. Nyiramasuhuko had not been promptly informed of charges against her during arrest, amounted to a violation of her right to be expeditiously tried, the right to be brought before a judge and the right to be informed of the nature of charges against her without undue delay.

12.20 The *ad hoc* international tribunals have routinely considered the meaning of 'undue' in this context. In *Prosecutor v André Rwamakuba*, the ICTR Trial Chamber III concluded that a period of time of more than seven years does not necessarily amount to an excessive delay in the proceedings.[1] The Chamber confirmed that the reasonableness of the period of the proceedings could not be translated into a fixed number of days, months or years,[2] ultimately finding that in the particular circumstances of the case and its complexity, no undue could be found.[3]

1 ICTR, Trial Chamber III, *Prosecutor v André Rwamakuba*, ICTR-98-44C-PT, Decision on Defence Motion for Stay of Proceedings, 3 June 2005, ('Rwamakuba Decision') at para 26. Depending on the relevant time, the Defence for Rwamakuba had contended that the total length of delay would be nine years and nine and a half months from the moment of first arrest of the accused on 2 August 1995; nine years and four and a half months from the date the Prosecutor wrote to the Namibian Government on 22 December 1995; seven years and three and a half months running from the time the accused was seen by UN investigators; or six and a half years from the time the accused was transferred to the Tribunal.
2 Rwamakuba Decision at para 26.
3 Rwamakuba Decision at para 37.

12.21 In particular, the Trial Chamber reasoned that the delays encountered either on account of: (i) the Prosecution's motions for leave to amend the indictment or seeking severance; or (ii) subsequent assignment of the Presiding judge, were unavoidable to ensure a fair and expeditious rehearing of the case.[1] It concluded that it did not consider a fair trial to be impossible, or that the continuation of proceedings would contravene the sense of justice of the Tribunal.[2]

1 Rwamakuba Decision at paras 31–35.
2 Rwamakuba Decision at para 39.

12.22 Similar facts were dealt with by ICTY Trial Chamber III in *Prosecutor v Vojislav Šešelj* where, in 2009, Mr. Šešelj orally requested the termination of his proceedings on account of serious violations amounting to an abuse of process.[1] He alleged that he had waited five years before the commencement of his trial and that his detention of six years and eight months whilst awaiting judgment exceeded the standard of reasonable limits.[2] Trial Chamber III found that the complexity of trial and the seriousness of charges could not be overstated and that each interruption was justified by a higher interest aimed at preserving the fairness of proceedings.[3]

1 ICTY, Trial Chamber III, *Prosecutor v Vojislav* Šešelj, IT-03-67-T, Decision on Oral Request of the Accused for Abuse of Process, 10 February 2010 (Šešelj Decision of 10 February 2010).
2 Šešelj Decision of 10 February 2010 at para 14.
3 Šešelj Decision of 10 February 2010 at para 29.

Prosecutorial misconduct

12.23 The conduct of the Prosecutor does not solely arise in the context of allegations of undue delay. As held by the ICTR Appeals Chamber in *Prosecutor v Jean Bosco Barayagwiza*, given that the Prosecutor is seen as the engine behind proceedings, s/he is under an obligation to ensure that, within the scope of his/her authority, the case proceeds to trial in a way that respects the rights of the accused.[1]

1 Barayagwiza Decision of 3 November 1999 at para 92.

12.24 As well as submitting that the length of time spent in detention and at trial was excessive, Vojislav Šešelj also alleged that his selective prosecution was politically motivated and therefore an abuse of process.[1] In particular, he stated that the indictment brought against him was solely as a result of an agreement between the former Prosecutor of the Tribunal, Carla Del Ponte, and the former Prime Minister of Serbia, Zoran Đinđić.[2] ICTY Trial Chamber III refused to substantively address these allegations on the basis that they were already the subject of a request by the accused[3] and had been dealt with by the Trial Chamber in its decision of 18 September 2008.[4]

1 Šešelj Decision of 10 February 2010 at para 7.
2 Šešelj had also, inter alia, alleged that the Prosecution had interfered with a potential witness.
3 Šešelj Decision of 10 February 2010 at para 24.
4 *Ibid*. The Trial Chamber therefore dismissed Šešelj's submissions on the basis that he had not presented any new fact that would justify reconsideration.

12.25 The importance of determining prosecutorial misconduct under the abuse of process doctrine was previously clarified by the ICTY Appeals Chamber in *Prosecutor v Radovan Karadžić*, in its Decision on Karadžić's Appeal Of Trial Chamber's Decision on Alleged Holbrooke Agreement.[1] The facts concerned an alleged agreement that Karadžić had allegedly made on 18–19 July 1996 with Mr. Richard Holbrooke, the United States special negotiator, which stipulated that, in exchange for completely withdrawing from public life, he would not be subject to prosecution by the Tribunal.[2] Karadžić had asserted that because of this agreement, the Tribunal lacked jurisdiction and, in the alternative, it had no jurisdiction under the abuse of process doctrine.[3]

1 ICTY, Appeals Chamber, *Prosecutor v Radovan Karadžić*, IT-95-5/18-AR73.4, Decision on Karadžić's Appeal of Trial Chamber's Decision on Alleged Holbrooke Agreement, 12 October 2009 ('Karadžić Appeals Decision of 12 October 2009').
2 Karadžić Appeals Decision of 12 October 2009 at para 5.
3 Karadžić Appeals Decision of 12 October 2009 at para 4.

12.26 The ICTY Appeals Chamber agreed with the Defence's submission on the point that the jurisprudence of the Appeals Chamber did not require misconduct from the ICTY Prosecutor in order to make a finding of an abuse of process.[1]

1 Karadžić Appeals Decision of 12 October 2009 at para 47.

12.27 However, the ICTY Appeals Chamber ultimately found that, even if Karadžić's allegations were proved correct, it would not trigger the doctrine of abuse of process justifying a stay of the proceedings. In this regard, the Appeals Chamber highlighted that the fundamental aims of international criminal courts and tribunals is to end impunity and ensure that serious violations of international humanitarian law are prosecuted and punished. The Appeals Chamber held that individuals accused of such crimes can have no legitimate expectation of immunity from prosecution.[1]

1 Karadžić Appeals Decision of 12 October 2009 at para 52.

12.28 In *Prosecutor v Pauline Rwamakuba*, ICTR Trial Chamber III was faced with allegations of prosecutorial bias. Here, the Defence had contended that the appearance of bias continued by virtue of the participation of the Prosecution Counsel Ms. Dior Fall Sow.[1] The Defence had on previous occasion submitted that Senegalese Judge Vaz knew the Senegalese Prosecutor Ms. Dior Fall Sow for many years and that the latter had resided with the Judge when first arriving in Arusha.[2] The Trial Chamber found that the Defence's contention of an alleged appearance of bias on behalf of the Prosecution Counsel was not supported. In particular, it cited to the fact that the Prosecution acted independently and, moreover, a new panel of judges had already been assigned to the case.[3]

1 Rwamakuba Decision at para 13.
2 ICTR, Trial Chamber III, *Prosecutor v Karemera et al*, ICTR-98-44-AR15*bis*, Reasons for Decision on Interlocutory Appeals Regarding the Continuation of the Proceedings with a Substitute Judge and on Nzirorera's Motion for Leave to Consider New Material, 22 October 2004 at para 2.
3 Rwamakuba Decision at para 41.

12.29 In *Prosecutor v Édouard Karemera et al.* ICTR Trial Chamber III had concluded that payments to a prosecution witness went beyond that which is reasonably required for the management of witnesses and victims and ordered for records of payments to be disclosed to the Defence as evidence which may affect the credibility of the witness in question. The Defence for Joseph Nzirorera subsequently sought to move the Chamber for an order dismissing the indictment against him on the grounds that payments to Prosecution witnesses by the Prosecution were excessive and amounted to an abuse of process.[1]

1 ICTR, Trial Chamber III, *Prosecutor v Karemera et al.*, ICTR-98-44-T, Decision on Joseph Nzirorera's Motion to Dismiss for Abuse of Process: Payments to Prosecution Witnesses and 'Requete de Mathieu Ngirumpatse en Retrait de L'Acte D'Accusation', 27 October 2008 ('Nzirorera Decision of 27 October 2008'). Mathieu Ngirumpatse had also filed submissions on 13 August 2008.

12.30 The Chamber came to the conclusion that the payments were not made for the purposes of 'inducing' testimony against Joseph Nzirorera and that rather the payments and benefits were made as part of a witness protection programme.[1] It further stated that the Defence for Nzirorera had failed to demonstrate how the benefits had influenced witnesses to align their testimony and behaviour with the interests of the Prosecution.[2]

1 Nzirorera Decision of 27 October 2008 at para 5.
2 Ibid.

12.31 As part of the Prosecution's obligation to ensure a fair process and minimise the disparity of resources between itself and the defence, it is subjected to various disclosure obligations. Violation of the Prosecution's disclosure obligations will therefore amount to an inequality of arms with significant prejudice caused to the defence.

12.32 In *Prosecutor v Laurent Semanza*, the Defence submitted that the Prosecution had persistently and continuously violated such disclosure obligations.[1] ICTR Trial Chamber III ultimately dismissed the request for dismissal of the entire proceedings on the basis that:

(1) the Defence had failed to show that the materials which the Prosecutor had allegedly disclosed late were more than mere copies of the supporting materials which accompanied the Indictment when the Prosecutor sought confirmation;[2]

(2) the rules of procedure and evidence of the ICTR do not require the Prosecutor to disclose materials in a language which an accused understands;[3]

(3) the second and third 'amendments' to the indictment were not strict amendments but rather corrections pursuant to the Tribunal's oral and written orders;[4]

(4) contrary to the defence's arguments, the Prosecutor had indeed filed a list of witnesses that she intends to call to testify at trial within prescribed timeframe;[5] and

(5) the Prosecutor had provided redacted witness statements subject to decision of the Chamber, and therefore there was no disclosure violation for failing to disclose unredacted statements.[6]

1 ICTR, Trial Chamber III, *Prosecutor v Laurent Semanza*, ICTR-97-20-I, Decision on the Defence Motion for dismissal of the entire proceedings due to persistent and continuing violations of the rights of the Accused, Rules of Procedure and Evidence and the Statute of the Tribunal and Abuse of Process, 11 September 2000 ('Semanza Decision of 11 September 2000'). Defence submissions included: failing to provide full supporting materials to the indictment as opposed to summaries of the supporting material; failing to provide the indictment and supporting material in a language the accused understands; failing to obtain leave to amend the indictment on two separate occasions; failing to disclose copies of statements of witnesses scheduled to testify at trial within the statutory timeframe; and failing to provide unredacted versions of seventeen statements for witness that were not the subject of any protective measures and consequently remained unintelligible in form.

2 Semanza Decision of 11 September 2000 at para 18.

3 Semanza Decision of 11 September 2000 at para 19.

4 Semanza Decision of 11 September 2000 at para 26.

5 Semanza Decision of 11 September 2000 at para 27.

6 Semanza Decision of 11 September 2000 at para 28.

12.33 ICTR Trial Chamber I had to deal with similar disclosure issues in *Prosecutor v Tharcisse Renzaho*.[1] As part of the allegations of denial of fair trial, the Defence for Mr. Renzaho submitted that the Prosecution had violated its affirmative and ongoing obligations to disclose exculpatory evidence throughout the trial.[2] The Trial Chamber found that the Defence for Renzaho had, in large part, failed to identify the exculpatory material with specificity.[3] With regard to specific documents that should have been disclosed to the Defence, the Chamber found there to be no prejudice suffered by the accused and dismissed allegations that this amounted to an unfair trial.[4]

1 ICTR, Trial Chamber I, *Prosecutor v Tharcisse Renzaho*, ICTR-97-31-T, Judgment and Sentence, 14 July 2009 ('Renzaho Trial Judgment').

2 Renzaho Trial Judgment at para 36.
3 Renzaho Trial Judgment at paras 39–51.
4 Ibid.

12.34 The practice of investigative authorities has also been the subject of motions concerning the abuse of process doctrine. In contempt proceedings against Florence Hartmann, the Defence filed a motion for stay of proceedings for abuse of process on the basis that a number of serious violations had occurred in the course of the investigation that were attributable to the *Amicus Curiae* investigator.[1] The Defence had divided the allegations into several categories including, *inter alia*, the complete failure to investigate both incriminatory and exculpatory facts and a failure to abide by basic standards of investigative diligence in the process of collecting evidence.[2]

1 ICTY, *In the Case Against Florence Hartmann*, IT-02-54-R77.5, Reasons for Decision on the Defence Motion for Stay of Proceedings for Abuse of Process, 3 February 2009 ('Hartmann Decision of 3 February 2009').
2 Hartmann Decision of 3 February 2009 at para 1.

12.35 The specially appointed Chamber concluded that to the extent that the Defence allegations were problematic they did not amount to an abuse of process when taken either individually or cumulatively.[1] In particular, the Chamber stated that it had already dealt with the alleged investigative flaws in prior decisions.[2]

1 Hartmann Decision of 3 February 2009 at para 13.
2 Hartmann Decision of 3 February 2009 at para 5.

12.36 In *Prosecutor v Eliezer Niyitegeka*, the Defence submitted that the Prosecutor had conducted an interrogation of the accused without recordings being made and in the absence of a lawyer and that, during the course of the interrogation, the Prosecutor had attempted to compel the accused to admit guilt to all charges alleged against him in the indictment.[1] ICTR Trial Chamber II considered the issue of abuse of process to be unfounded. Although the Chamber had accepted that parties had met and that plea agreements had been made in other cases, it determined that the Defence had only raised the issue in April 2000 despite the interrogation occurring in February 1999.[2] In these circumstances, the Chamber found the allegations made by the Accused to be unfounded.

1 ICTR, Trial Chamber II, *Prosecutor v Eliezer Niyitegeka*, ICTR-96-14-T, Decision on the Preliminary Motion of the Defence (Objections Based on Lack of Jurisdiction and Defects in the Form of the Indictment) and on the Urgent Defence Motion Seeking Stay of Proceedings, 21 June 2000 ('Niyitegeka Decision of 21 June 2000') at para 6. The Defence alleged that in order to encourage a guilty plea, the Prosecutor had made mention of certain promises and inducements, including: (i) that some of the charges proffered against the Accused would be removed; (ii) that if the Accused accepted the demands, the Prosecutor would arrange for the family of the Accused to be transferred, without delay, receiving financial assistance for at least six months, whilst awaiting intervention of UNHCR; and (iii) that if the Accused refused to co-operate, the Prosecutor could proceed to amend the Indictment and include, *inter alia*, the additional charge of rape even though she knew that the Accused had not raped anyone and that there was no credible evidence to prove such a charge.
2 Niyitegeka Decision of 21 June 2000 at para 61.

12.37 Concerns regarding the practice of the Prosecution in relation to the abuse of process doctrine are not limited to submissions raised by the defence.

In *Prosecutor v Janko Bobetko*, the Republic of Croatia sought to submit an interlocutory appeal against the warrant of arrest and order for surrender of Janko Bobetko.[1] Croatia had submitted that the warrant of arrest and subsequent order to surrender were unlawful on grounds that: (i) the Prosecution must interview or offer to interview every proposed accused person before seeking a confirmation of an indictment; and (ii) the confirming Judge should have requested the prosecution to submit evidence which would demonstrate the necessity to arrest the accused.[2]

1 ICTY, Appeals Chamber, *Prosecutor v Bobetko*, IT-02-62-AR54 bis, Decision on Challenge by Croatia to Decision and Orders of Confirming Judge, 29 November 2002 ('Bobetko Decision of 29 November 2002').

2 Bobetko Decision of 29 November 2002 at para 13.

12.38 Croatia's request was ultimately dismissed on the basis that the statutory provisions of the Tribunal did not provide for a right to appeal or to seek a review of a decision of a confirming Judge and even if it did, Croatia had no standing to make such an application.[1] The Chamber also found there to be no requirement obliging the Prosecution to interview every proposed accused or to submit evidence before the Judge confirming the indictment on the necessity of arrest.[2]

1 Bobetko Decision of 29 November 2002 at paras 7–11.

2 Ibid at para 13.

Conduct of national authorities

12.39 The *ad hoc* Tribunals have also considered the conduct of various national authorities as part of allegations of abuse of process.

12.40 In *Prosecutor v Dragan Nikolić*, the ICTY Appeals Chamber was confronted with the question as to whether it could exercise jurisdiction over Dragan Nikolić, notwithstanding the alleged violations of Serbia and Montenegro's sovereignty and of the accused's human rights violations committed by the NATO-led Stabilization Force (SFOR).[1] The Nikolić Defence had submitted that when he was arrested by SFOR in Bosnia and Herzegovina, SFOR was aware that he had been kidnapped and that by taking him into custody, SFOR had effectively accepted the kidnapping in breach of sovereign rights of Serbia and Montenegro and the accused's human rights.[2] The Defence concluded that SFRO, and by extension the Prosecutor, had acted in collusion with the individuals who had kidnapped the accused and that therefore jurisdiction should be set aside.[3]

1 ICTY, Appeals Chamber, *Prosecutor v Dragan Nikolić*, IT-94-2-AR73, 'Decision on Interlocutory Appeal concerning Legality of Arrest', 5 June 2003 ('Nikolić Appeals Decision').

2 Nikolić Appeals Decision at para 6.

3 *Ibid.* Although finding that Dragan Nikolic had been allegedly illegally arrested and abducted from the territory of FRY by some unknown individuals and transferred to territory of Bosnia and Herzegovina, the ICTY Trial Chamber II did not find that either SFOR or the ICTY Office of the Prosecutor (OTP) were be involved in such acts. On this basis the Trial Chamber concluded there to be no violation of sovereignty of Serbia and Montenegro attributable to the SFOR or OTP, nor a violation of the accused's human rights or fundamental principle of due process, and that therefore the events did not egregiously violate the accused's rights.

12.41 The ICTY Appeals Chamber went on to consider the circumstances in which violations of state sovereignty would require jurisdiction to be set aside. Relying on the various jurisprudence of national courts,[1] the Appeals Chamber held there to be two general principles:

(1) Cases concerning genocide, crimes against humanity and war crimes were universally recognised and of such seriousness and special character that arguably there was good reason not to set aside jurisdiction; and

(2) Absent a complaint by the State whose sovereignty had been breached it was easier for courts to accept jurisdiction.[2]

1 See for example, Supreme Court of Israel, *People of Israel v Eichmann*, Judgment of 29 May 1962 in ILR, Vol. 36, p.306; Court of Cassation (Criminal Chamber), *La Fédération Nationale pour les Déportés et Internes Resistants et Patriotes and Others v Barbie,* Judgment of 6 October 1983 in ILR, Vol. 78, pp 130–131.
2 Nikolić Appeals Decision at paras 24–26.

12.42 On this basis, ICTY Appeals Chamber stated that it did not consider that in cases of universally condemned offences, jurisdiction should be set aside on the ground that there was a violation of state sovereignty of a state, when the violation is brought by the apprehension of fugitives from international justice.[1] Moreover, the ICTY Appeals Chamber found there to be no egregious violation of the accused's rights upon arrest and, even assuming that the conduct of the kidnappers could be attributed to SFOR so that it was responsible for breach of the accused's rights, the Appeals Chamber found no basis upon which jurisdiction should not be exercised.[2]

1 Nikolić Appeals Decision at para 26.
2 Nikolić Appeals Decision at para 27.

12.43 In *Prosecutor v Radovan Karadžić*, the accused had asserted that the alleged raids of his wife's home and sister-in-law's home conducted by NATO troops were a breach of his right to prepare his defence and to have a fair trial.[1] In particular, he stated that the raids were conducted on behalf of the Tribunal and with the assistance of two employees from the ICTY Office of the Prosecutor, the purpose being to 'intimidate and discourage potential witness in Bosnia'.[2]

1 ICTY, Trial Chamber, *Prosecutor v Radovan Karadžić*, IT-95-5/18-PT, Decision on Motion to Dismiss for Abuse of Process, 12 May 2009 ('Karadžić Decision of 12 May 2009').
2 Karadžić Decision of 12 May 2009 at para 3.

12.44 The ICTY Trial Chamber ultimately found that the accused had brought no evidence before the Chamber to show that the Prosecution, or anybody else in the Tribunal or under its jurisdiction, was involved in the operation at his family's property.[1] In addition, it held that the accused had failed to make any specific allegations of misconduct by the authorities performing such searches and, subsequently, there was no question of an egregious violation of the accused's rights justifying a finding of an abuse of process.[2]

1 Karadžić Decision of 12 May 2009 at para 13.
2 Karadžić Decision of 12 May 2009 at para 14.

Obstacles to preparation of the defence

12.45 The right to adequate time and facilities is enshrined in various human rights instruments, as well as the Statutes of both the ICTY and ICTR. It is a fundamental right seen to be an extension of the principle of equality of arms.

12.46 Linked to the section above, infringements of this right can be caused by obstructionist efforts on behalf of a third-party State. This was the case in *Prosecutor v Dušco Tadić*, whereby the ICTY Appeals Chamber was faced with submissions that Dušco Tadić had not received a fair trial because relevant and admissible evidence was not presented due to a lack of Republika Srpska's cooperation in securing the attendance of certain witnesses.

12.47 The lack of cooperation from state or regional authorities was also the subject of three decisions in *Prosecutor v Milan Milutonović et al.*[1] Here the Defence for Dragoljub Ojdanić requested a stay of proceedings on the basis that the Defence team were unsuccessful in its efforts to investigate in Kosovo in view of the violence at the time.

1 ICTY, Trial Chamber III, *Prosecutor v Milutonović et al.*, IT-05-87-PT, Decision on Ojdanić Motion for Stay of Proceedings, 9 June 2006 ('First Ojdanić Decision'); ICTY, Trial Chamber III, *Prosecutor v Milutonović et al.*, IT-05-87-PT, Decision on Second Ojdanić Motion for Stay of Proceedings, 19 October 2006 ('Second Ojdanić Decision'); and ICTY, Trial Chamber III, *Prosecutor v Milutonović et al.*, IT-05-87-PT, Decision on Third Ojdanić Motion for Stay of Proceedings, 27 August 2007 ('Third Ojdanić Decision').

12.48 In its First Ojdanić Decision, ICTY Trial Chamber III considered that, although the Defence team were unable to complete its investigations during its last visit to Kosovo, this did not mean that it would continue indefinitely to be unable to do so.[1] The Chamber focused on efforts made by UNMIK to arrange further visits for the Defence to visit Kosovo and ultimately found that it could not be said that the accused would not have a fair trial.[2]

1 First Ojdanić Decision at para 4.
2 First Ojdanić Decision at para 5.

12.49 In the Second Ojdanić Decision, the Trial Chamber was seized of the same matter. The Defence submitted that it had done everything it could to arrange a visit to Kosovo before the trial recommenced but its efforts had failed.[1] The Trial Chamber again noted the efforts that had been made by UNMIK to take all reasonable and necessary measures, as soon as possible, in order to assist the Defence in its investigations in Kosovo.[2] For those visits which could not be facilitated by UNMIK at the time, the Chamber placed the burden on the Defence to propose alternative methods to accomplish its investigative demand.[3] In this context, the Chamber found that it was the Defence that had unilaterally broken off cooperative efforts with UNMIK and that simply because the Ojdanić Defence was not satisfied with the arrangements for its visit to Kosovo, would necessarily lead to the conclusion that the accused's rights were violated.[4]

1 Second Ojdanić Decision at para 2.
2 Second Ojdanić Decision at para 9.
3 Second Ojdanić Decision at para 10.
4 Ibid.

12.50 The Trial Chamber maintained this position in its Third Ojdanić Decision, whereby the Defence had submitted that as the security situation had not improved in Kosovo, it remained unable to contact 730 individuals who resided in Kosovo.[1] The Trial Chamber reiterated that the Defence should take up efforts taken by UNMIK and that the submission of a list of names did not add significant weight to the request.[2]

1 Third Ojdanić Decision at para 30.
2 Third Ojdanić Decision at para 42.

12.51 In both *Prosecutor v André Rwamakuba* and *Prosecutor v Tharcisse Renzaho*, the obstacles to the defence investigations were caused by the death of its witnesses.

12.52 In *Prosecutor v André Rwamakuba*, the Defence had submitted that it had suffered prejudice due to an excessive delay in proceedings and that, in the elapsed time, some witness would have died and others had lost interest in their testimonies.[1] ICTR Trial Chamber III concluded that it did not consider that a fair trial had become impossible, or that the continuation of proceedings would contravene the sense of justice of the Tribunal.[2] It stated that the effect of the elapsed period of time on the witness testimonies was not particular to the Defence and could apply to the Prosecution and other accused as well.[3]

1 Rwamakuba Decision at para 11.
2 Rwamakuba Decision at para 39.
3 Rwamakuba Decision at para 40.

12.53 In *Prosecutor v Tharcisse Renzaho*, the Defence submitted that it been denied a fair trial due to *inter alia*: the death of two witnesses; the refusal of others to testify; and interference by a former Defence investigator who had allegedly discouraged witnesses from testifying.[1] ICTR Trial Chamber I addressed the concerns of the Defence during its Trial Judgment and ultimately found that the Defence had failed to demonstrate that it had suffered material prejudice by the death of witnesses; witness intimidation or witness interference.[2]

1 Renzaho Trial Judgment at para 57.
2 Renzaho Trial Judgment at para 60.

12.54 In *Prosecutor v Radoslav Brđanin*, the Defence filed a motion seeking dismissal of the indictment based on complaints that the Tribunal had failed to honour the principle of equality of arms and provide sufficient resources to the Defence.[1] In particular, the Defence asserted that Mr. Brđanin was at a significant disadvantage in preparing for trial because the prosecution enjoyed access to greater resources.[2]

1 ICTY, Trial Chamber III, *Prosecutor v Radoslav Brđanin*, IT-98-36, Decision on Second Motion by Brdjanin to Dismiss the Indictment, 16 May 2001 ('Brđanin Decision of 16 May 2001').
2 Brđanin Decision of 16 May 2001 at para 1.

12.55 ICTY Trial Chamber II dismissed the motion, finding it was appropriate for the Defence to exhaust the avenues of redress available prior to seizing the Trial Chamber.[1] This included redress from other organs of the Tribunal, including the Registry.[2]

1 Brđanin Decision of 16 May 2001 at para 3.
2 Ibid.

12.56 *In the Case against Florence Hartmann*, the Defence had submitted that its right to equality of arms and adequate time and resources to prepare had been obstructed by the *Amicus Curiae* investigator. The Defence complained that the *Amicus Curiae*, in his role as investigator and prosecutor, had: (i) failed and declined to provide information about those persons who assisted him in identifying potential witnesses, (ii) failed and declined to provide information pertaining to the chain and custody of some of the proposed exhibits; (iii) declined to provide the Defence request to be interviewed; (iv) declined to explain nature of its case, thereby denying Defence ability to prepare; and (v) declined to respond to repeated requests by the Defence for waiver/lifting of immunities of potential witnesses.[1]

1 ICTY, *In the Case of Florence Hartmann*, IT-02-54-R77.5, Motion for Stay of Proceedings for Abuse of Process, 23 January 2009.

12.57 The specially appointed Chamber ultimately considered the various requests of the Defence to fall outside the disclosure obligations of the *Amicus Curiae*.[1]

1 Hartmann Decision of 3 February 2009 at para 11.

Impartiality of proceedings

12.58 The right to be tried by a competent, independent and impartial tribunal remains a cornerstone of fair proceedings. Violations of these rights go to the core of abuse of process challenges.

12.59 In *Prosecutor v Stanišić & Župljanin*,[1] the Defence submitted that appeal proceedings should be terminated following interlocutory review of a denial of the rights of the Accused. This was grounded on the allegation that Trial Chamber II, which had convicted the Accused, was not a properly constituted trial chamber consisting of three impartial judges.[2] The allegation followed the publication of a letter written by Judge Harhoff, which the Defence had argued reasonably established bias in favour of conviction on the part of Judge Harhoff.[3] It was the Defence's position that the presence of a judge whose impartiality has been rebutted inevitably taints the entire trial process and therefore the only remedy was to vacate the trial judgment as soon as practicable.[4]

1 ICTY, Appeals Chamber, *Prosecutor v Stanišić & Župljanin*, IT-08-91-A, Stojan Župljanin's Motion to Vacate Trial Judgment, 21 October 2013; ICTY, Appeals Chamber, *Prosecutor v Stanišić & Župljanin*, IT-08-91-A, Motion on Behalf of Mićo Stanišić Requesting a Declaration of Mistrial, 23 October 2013.

2 ICTY, Appeals Chamber, *Prosecutor v Stanišić & Župljanin*, IT-08-91-A, Stojan Župljanin's Motion to Vacate Trial Judgment, 21 October 2013, paras 2, 26.

3 ICTY, Appeals Chamber, *Prosecutor v Stanišić & Župljanin*, IT-08-91-A, Motion on Behalf of Mićo Stanišić Requesting a Declaration of Mistrial, 23 October 2013, paras 2, 6-19, 30, 34; ICTY, Appeals Chamber, *Prosecutor v Stanišić & Župljanin*, IT-08-91-A, Stojan Župljanin's Motion to Vacate Trial Judgment, 21 October 2013, paras 1–2, 22, 26.

4 ICTY, Appeals Chamber, *Prosecutor v Stanišić & Župljanin*, IT-08-91-A, Stojan Župljanin's Motion to Vacate Trial Judgment, 21 October 2013, paras 2, 16–19, 24–25.

12.60 Having recognised that the doctrine of 'abuse of process' allows a court to decline to exercise jurisdiction either because it will be impossible to give the accused a fair trial or because it offends the court's sense of justice and propriety to try the accused in the circumstances of a particular case, the Appeals Chamber set out that the question in cases of abuse of process is not whether it is 'necessary' for a court to issue an interlocutory decision terminating proceedings but whether a court should continue to exercise jurisdiction over a case in light of serious and egregious violations of the accused's rights that would prove detrimental to the court's integrity.[1]

1 ICTY, Appeals Chamber, *Prosecutor v Stanišić & Župljanin*, IT-08-91-A, Decision on Mićo Stanišić's Motion Requesting a Declaration of Mistrial and Stojan Župljanin's Motion to Vacate Trial Judgment, 2 April 2014, para 35.

12.61 However, the Appeals Chamber found that the discretionary power of a court to stay or terminate proceedings by reason of abuse of process applies during the trial phase of a case since its main purpose is to prevent wrongful convictions and preserve the integrity of the judicial system.[1] As such, the Appeals Chamber considered that an allegation of partiality of a trial judge is a ground to appeal a conviction on the basis that it is unsafe,[2] and had permitted the Defence to the respective Notices of Appeal to include the issue of Judge Harhoff's alleged partiality and its impact on the Trial Judgment.[3]

1 ICTY, Appeals Chamber, *Prosecutor v Stanišić & Župljanin*, IT-08-91-A, Decision on Mićo Stanišić's Motion Requesting a Declaration of Mistrial and Stojan Župljanin's Motion to Vacate Trial Judgment, 2 April 2014, para 35.
2 Ibid.
3 Ibid.

12.62 In *Prosecutor v. Mladić*,[1] the Defence had requested an indefinite stay of proceedings on the basis that there was an alleged institutional bias against the Accused given that, *inter alia*, the President of the Tribunal, three Appeals Chamber judges, and two of the three judges of the Chamber have already found the Accused guilty in other proceedings before the Tribunal. Having been seized of similar requests, both the President and Trial Chamber I found that in the absence of request or relief under article 15(B) of the Rules concerning the disqualification of judges, there was no basis for a stay of proceedings.[2]

1 ICTY, *Prosecutor v Ratko Mladić*, IT-09-92-T, Defence Motion for Stay of Proceedings for Systemic Bias, 20 July 2016 filed before both the President and Trial Chamber I.
2 ICTY, *Presidency, Prosecutor v Ratko Mladić*, IT-09-92-T, Decision on Defence Motion for Stay of Proceedings for Systemic Bias, 14 September 2016; ICTY, Trial Chamber I, *Prosecutor v Ratko Mladić*, IT-09-92-T, Decision on Defence Motion for Stay of Proceedings for Systemic Bias or in the alternative a Mistrial, 22 September 2016.

INTERNATIONAL RESIDUAL MECHANISM FOR CRIMINAL TRIBUNALS

12.63 Mandated to continue the work of the ICTY and ICTR, the IRMCT has not yet had to substantially address allegations of abuse of process. Where it has been seized of similar complaints, it has endorsed the aforementioned approach adopted by the *ad hoc* tribunals.

12.64 In *Prosecutor v. Stanišić and Simatović*,[1] the Stanišić Defence argued that the Prosecution's approach to the retrial gravely undermines the Accused's rights through: (i) systemic violations of the *res judicata* and *non bis in* *idem* principles; and (ii) violation of the Appeals Chamber's order for retrial through the impermissible addition to, or expansion of, the charges which constituted an abuse of process. The Trial Chamber recognised its discretion to stay proceedings noting that this was an exceptional measure designed to avoid prejudice to a party and for which a chamber must consider whether the continuation of the proceedings would have an impact on the fairness or integrity of the trial.[2] Having dismissed the Defence's submissions in relation to the *res judicata* and *non bis in idem* principles, the Trial Chamber decided to exercise its discretion to limit the Prosecution's evidence to that presented during the original trial and, only if necessary, to allow the Prosecution to present new evidence in certain limited instances.[3] As such the abuse of process doctrine was not further discussed and a stay of proceedings was not considered necessary to ensure the fairness or integrity of the trial.[4]

1 IRMCT, Trial Chamber, *Prosecutor v Stanišić and Simatović*, MICT-15-96-PT, Stanišić Defence Request to Stay the Proceedings until the Prosecution respects the Principle of Finality and the Appeal Chamber's Order for Retrial, 27 October 2016, paras 15–16.
2 Ibid, para 26.
3 Ibid, para 27.
4 Ibid, para 28.

12.65 In *Prosecutor v Turinabo et al.*,[1] the Defence had sought a permanent stay of proceedings on the basis that the Prosecution had initiated contempt investigations in the absence of prior judicial authorisation which it stated: (i) was required under the statutory framework, (ii) was in accordance with jurisprudence of the *ad hoc* tribunals and (iii) was necessary where the Prosecution had a conflict of interest.

1 MICT, Single Judge, *Prosecutor v Turinabo et al*, MICT-18-116-PT, Joint Motion to Quash Indictment or Enter a Permanent Stay of Proceedings, 25 January 2019.

12.66 Whilst disagreeing with the Defence's interpretation of the statutory framework and finding that there was no showing of a conflict of interest, the Single Judge further held that the relief sought by the Defence was disproportionate when considering that had the Defence demonstrated a conflict of interest, the case would not be dismissed and instead referred to an *amicus curiae* for prosecution.[1]

1 MICT, Single Judge, *Prosecutor v Turinabo et al*, MICT-18-116-PT, Decision on Joint Motion to Quash Indictment or Enter a Permanent Stay of Proceedings, 13 March 2019.

HYBRID TRIBUNALS: SPECIAL COURT FOR SIERRA LEONE; EXTRAORDINARY CHAMBERS IN THE COURTS OF CAMBODIA AND THE SPECIAL TRIBUNAL FOR LEBANON

SCSL

12.67 At the second plenary hearing in March 2003, the doctrine of abuse of process was incorporated into the SCSL Rules of Procedure and Evidence. This codification makes the SCSL the only international criminal tribunal to have an express statutory provision concerning abuse of process. SCSL Rule 72(B)(v) allows for objections based on abuse of process to be made as a preliminary motion. No further definition or guidelines as to what constitutes abuse of process is provided for in the SCSL statutory provisions. As a result, the Special Court relied on the jurisprudence of the *ad hoc* international tribunals.

Conduct of national authorities

12.68 One of the main triggers for applications of the abuse of process doctrine before the SCSL concerned article 9 of the Lomè Accord- the peace treaty signed between the Government of Sierra Leone and the Revolutionary United Front of Sierra Leone on 7 July 1999. Article 9 of the Lomè Accord allowed for pardon and amnesties to 'all combatants and collaborators in respect of anything done by them in pursuit of their objectives, up to the time of the signing of the Lomè Accord.'[1]

1 Peace Agreement between the Government of Sierra Leone and the Revolutionary United Front of Sierra Leone, 3 June 1999 see S/1999/777, Annex to Letter Dated 12 July 1999 from the Chargé D'Affaires Ad Interim of the Permanent Mission of Togo to the United Nations Addressed to the President of the Security Council.

12.69 On the basis of article 9 of the Lomè Accord, several of the accused asserted that the Special Court did not enjoy jurisdiction over crimes committed in Sierra Leone prior to July 1999 and that it would be an abuse of process to allow the prosecution of any of the alleged crimes pre-dating the Lomè Accord.

12.70 The SCSL Appeals Chamber addressed such submissions in its 'Decision on Challenge of Jurisdiction: Lomè Accord Amnesty', after it was seized of the matter on behalf of Defence representing Morris Kallon and Brima Brazzy Kamara.[1]

1 SCSL, Appeals Chamber, *Prosecutor v Kallon and Kamara*, SCSL-2004-15-AR72(E), Decision on Challenge to Jurisdiction: Lomé Accord Amnesty, 13 March 2004 ('Kallon Decision of 13 March 2004').

12.71 The SCSL Appeals Chamber engaged in lengthy analysis as to the establishment of the Special Court and the legitimacy of amnesties in international law, ultimately finding that amnesties were not applicable to crimes under international law, which are covered by universal jurisdiction.[1] There being no bar to its jurisdiction, the Appeals Chamber subsequently questioned whether the Lomè Accord justified a finding of abuse of process, seemingly agreeing that the undertaking itself was in breach of a state's obligation towards the international community as a whole.[2] Although the Appeals Chamber recognised it had an inherent power to stay proceedings, it found there to be no abuse of process.

1 Kallon Decision of 13 March 2004 at para 88.
2 Kallon Decision of 13 March 2004 at para 73.

12.72 In *Prosecutor v Alex Tamba Brima et al.*, the Defence for Santigie Borbor Kanu asserted that crimes against humanity were not part of domestic law during the alleged time of commission of the crime and that an abuse of process resulted from breach of the *nullem crimen sige lege* principle.[1]

1 SCSL, Trial Chamber, *Prosecutor v Brima et al.*, SCSL-2004-16-PT, Written Reasons for the Trial Chamber's Oral Decision on the Defence Motion on Abuse of Process Due to Infringement of Principles of *Nullum Crimen Sine Lege* and Non-Retroactivity as to Several Counts, 31 March 2004 ('Kanu Decision of 31 March 2004').

12.73 The SCSL Trial Chamber noted that the SCSL Rules of Procedure and Evidence did not provide guidance as to what constitutes an abuse of process and therefore found it imperative to look towards the application of the doctrine in international and national context.[1] In doing so, the Chamber noted the main principles, acknowledging the breadth and latitude of the discretionary authority available to it.[2]

1 Kanu Decision of 31 March 2004 at paras 19–26.
2 Kanu Decision of 31 March 2004 at para 24.

12.74 The Chamber ultimately dismissed the motion in its entirety on the basis that the Defence had incorrectly brought the application under SCSL Rule 72(B)(v) when it actually considered it to be a jurisdictional issue and ought to have been presented under SCSL Rule 72(B)(i).[1] The Chamber found that neither the Prosecution or the Designated Judge had committed or contributed to an abuse of process given that the Prosecution had lawfully exercised its powers to issue an indictment.[2]

1 Kanu Decision of 31 March 2004 at para 28.
2 Kanu Decision of 31 March 2004 at paras 29–30.

Prosecutorial misconduct

12.75 Proceedings against Charles Taylor, former President of Liberia, raised a number of allegations against the conduct of the Prosecution amounting to prosecutorial abuse of process.

12.76 In particular, the Defence asserted that the prosecution of Taylor had from the outset been selective and vindictive in nature arguing that Mr. Taylor was singled out for prosecution on the basis of improper political motives of the United States, and that other individuals who are similarly situated to Mr. Taylor were not prosecuted.[1] As evidence, the Defence relied on comments made by Prosecutor David Crane to the US Congress and his disclosure of the sealed Indictment to the U.S. Government.[2]

1 SCSL, Trial Chamber II, *Prosecutor v Charles Taylor*, SCSL-03-01-T, Judgment, 18 May 2012 ('Taylor Trial Judgment') at paras 73–74.
2 Ibid. On 8 February 2005, in a statement to the US Congressional Subcommittee on Africa, Global Human Rights and International Operations, Prosecutor Crane had revealed that States financially supporting the Special Court insisted to prosecute Taylor because of his support to the civil war in Sierra Leone.

12.77 Following an application of the facts to the selective prosecution test as set out in *Prosecutor v Zejnil Delalić et al.*,[1] the SCSL Chamber found that however inappropriate the Prosecutor's actions may have been, such actions did not constitute clear evidence of the intent of the Prosecutor to discriminate on improper motives. The dismissal of all charges was therefore considered to be an entirely disproportionate response.[2]

1 In order to establish that there has been selective prosecution, the Defence must establish: (i) an unlawful or improper (including discriminatory) motive for the prosecution; and (ii) that other similarly situated persons were not prosecuted see ICTY, Appeals Chamber, *Prosecutor v Zejnil Delalić et al.*, IT-96-21-A, Judgment, 20 February 2001 at para. 611.
2 Taylor Trial Judgment at paras 81–83.

12.78 The Defence for Mr. Taylor also accused the Prosecutor of making discretionary payments and other inducements to witnesses amounting to prosecutorial abuse of process, which deprived the accused of a fair trial.[1] In particular, the Defence alleged that the Prosecution's Witness Management Unit had made large payments on a systematic basis to Prosecution witnesses, and that this tainted the overall credibility of Prosecution evidence especially given that in the light of the realities of life in Sierra Leone, such sums could have a significant effect on the lives of witnesses.[2] The Chamber concluded that the payments and incentives made available to Prosecution witness were in accordance with the statutory framework of the court. The remedy of such was therefore to address the matter when analysing witness credibility.[3]

1 Taylor Trial Judgment at para 148.
2 Taylor Trial Judgment at para 185.
3 Taylor Trial Judgment at paras 194–195.

12.79 In *Prosecutor v Augustine Gbao*, the Prosecution was alleged to have abused the process of the Court by holding a highly exculpatory document for the entirety of its case and that the late disclosure had caused material prejudice by depriving the accused of an opportunity to cross-examine several critical Prosecution witnesses.

12.80 Whilst SCSL Trial Chamber I agreed that the delayed disclosure of the exculpatory statement was done in breach of the Prosecution's disclosure obligations, it ultimately dismissed Mr. Gbao's request for a judicial finding of an abuse of process. The Chamber observed that Mr. Gbao had in his possession the statement for a period of over twenty months before he filed his motion on abuse of process. It considered that, if the prejudice claimed from the late disclosure was the absence of the statement for the cross-examination of select Prosecution witnesses, then an application for the recall of the witness or for some other relief should have been made at the time of disclosure or as soon as practicable.[1] The Trial Chamber accordingly stated that available remedies existed for Mr. Gbao to remove or mitigate any such prejudice.

1 See SCSL, Trial Chamber, *Prosecutor v Sesay* et al., SCSL-04-15-T, Written Reasoned Decision on Gbao Motion Requesting the Trial Chamber to Stay Trial Proceedings of Counts 15-18 against the Third Accused for Prosecution's Violation of Rule 68 and Abuse of Process, 22 July 2008 (made public by SCSL, *Prosecutor v Sesay et al.*, SCSL-04-15-T, Trial Chamber Consequential Order regarding Written Reasoned Decision on Gbao Motion Requesting the Trial Chamber to Stay Proceedings of Count 15-18 against the Third Accused for Prosecution's Violation of Rule 68 and Abuse of Process, 28 July 2008).

ECCC

12.81 Unlike the SCSL, the ECCC did not develop or include the abuse of process doctrine in its statutory framework. It has however accepted that it has the discretion to decline to exercise its jurisdiction in cases where the accused's rights have been so seriously violated, that a continuation of the proceedings would contravene the court's sense of justice. In cases where the serious violation has been caused by other authorities than the court itself, it has found that the abuse of process doctrine would normally only be applied if: (i) the offending authority acted in concert with the court; or (ii) if the defendant was subject to torture or other serious mistreatment by the offending authority.

Lack of independence and impartiality

12.82 Motions under the abuse of process doctrine primarily arose before the ECCC Pre-Trial Chamber following a statement given by Prime Minister Hun Sen on 9 September 2009 in an address in Takeo Province that 'some foreign judges and prosecutors [of the ECCC] have received orders from their governments to create problems here...There is no doubt that they received advice from their government to do so'.[1]

1 Associated Press, Cambodia PM Accuses Other Countries of Stirring Unrest, 10 September 2009.

12.83 In *Prosecutor v Ieng Thirith*, the Co-Lawyers for Ieng Thirith sought a stay of proceedings on the basis that the statements of the Cambodian Prime Minister had shown a lack of impartiality within the Office of the Co-investigating Judge (OCIJ) and that the OCIJ lacked independence from the Office of the Prosecutor.[1]

1 ECCC, Pre-Trial Chamber, Case 002, Decision on Ieng Thirith's appeal against the Co-investigating judges' order rejecting the request for stay of proceedings on the basic of abuse of process, 8 August 2010 brought before Pre-Trial Chamber, 10 August 2010 ('Thirith Decision of 10 August 2010').

12.84 The ECCC Pre-Trial Chamber noted that Cambodian law did not provide for an abuse of procedure mechanism.[1] However, the Pre-Trial Chamber felt bound to follow international practice accepting that the abuse of process doctrine was based upon its inherent jurisdiction to ensure an accused person is accorded a fair trial.[2] The ECCC Pre-Trial Chamber therefore applied the applicable principles for a finding of an abuse of process as established within the *ad hoc* tribunals.

1 Thirith Decision of 10 August 2010 at paras 10–14.
2 Ibid.

12.85 In its assessment as to whether the accused had suffered a serious mistreatment or if there was any other egregious violation of her rights, the ECCC Pre-Trial Chamber was cognisant of the fact that in cases containing allegations of violations that result mainly from a lack of impartiality or integrity of a Judge or his office, no direct evidence may be available especially when it comes to prove the intention of the author of such a violation.[1] However, the Pre-Trial Chamber stated that statements of a person as quoted by the press do not amount to reliable evidence.[2] It was therefore not satisfied that the alleged interference was proven or that it would amount to a violation of the rights of the Charged Person's which would warrant a finding of abuse of process.[3]

1 Thirith Decision of 10 August 2010 at para 26.
2 Thirith Decision of 10 August 2010 at para 38.
3 Ibid.

Conduct of national authorities

12.86 As with cases before the ICTY and ICTR, the ECCC agreed that it has the authority to consider whether the legality of prior detention of an accused would amount to an abuse of process that would justify a stay of proceedings and release of the accused.

12.87 In *Prosecutor v Kaing Guek Eav*, the ECCC Trial Chamber did find that the accused's prior detention before the Military Court constituted a violation of Cambodian domestic law applicable at the time.[1] The Chamber held that the prior detention contravened an accused's internationally recognised right to a trial within a reasonable time and detention in accordance with the law.[2] However, following jurisprudence of the ICTY, ICTR and ICC, the Chamber recognised that a finding of abuse of process was only justified in exceptional circumstances, namely in instances of torture or serious mistreatment.[3] The Chamber therefore dismissed the accused's request for release on the basis that the abuse of process doctrine was not applicable in his case. However, it did find that the accused could seek some remedy during the sentencing stage, namely consideration for time spent in detention upon conviction or compensation upon acquittal.[4]

1 ECCC, Trial Chamber, Case 001, Decision on Request for Release, 15 June 2009 ('Duch Decision of 15 June 2009'). See also ECCC, Case 001, 001/18-07-2007-ECCC-OCIJ (PTC01), Pre-Trial Chamber, Decision on Appeal Against Provisional Detention Order of Kaing Guek Eav alias 'Duch', 3 December 2007 ('Duch Decision of 3 December 2007').
2 Duch Decision of 15 June 2009 at para 21.
3 Duch Decision of 15 June 2009 at para 33.
4 Duch Decision of 15 June 2009 at paras 35–37.

Obstacles to preparation of the defence

12.88 As with *Prosecutor v Radoslav Brđanin*, Co-Lawyers for Khieu Sampan also raised the abuse of process doctrine in connection with translation issues. Here, the Co-Lawyers asserted that an order of the Co-Investigating Judges gave rise to a substantial procedural defect which allowed for only portions of the case file to be translated from Khmer to English.[1] The Co-Lawyers complained that this procedural defect infringed upon a charged person's right to a lawyer of his choice; the lawyer's right to have access to the case file; the charged person's right to effective representation and the principle of equality of arms.[2] The Pre-Trial Chamber found that the Co-Lawyers had only enunciated which rights had been infringed, without substantiating or explaining how they have been affected.[3] It also found that the Co-Lawyers had failed to make reasoned submissions as to how abuse of process doctrine would apply and thereby rejected the application.[4]

1 ECCC, Pre-Trial Chamber, Case 002, Decision on Khieu Samphan's Appeal Against the Order on the Request for Annulment for Abuse of Process, 4 May 2010 ('Samphan Decision of 4 May 2010').
2 Samphan Decision of 4 May 2010 at paras 15–16.
3 Samphan Decision of 4 May 2010 at paras 23–24. ECCC, Pre-Trial Chamber, Case 002, Decision on Khieu Samphan's Interlocutory Application for an Immediate and Final Stay of Proceedings for Abuse of Process, 12 January 2011.
4 Samphan Decision of 4 May 2010 at paras 23–24.

12.89 Issues concerning an accused's right to lawyer of his/her own choice were also brought to the attention of the Pre-Trial Chamber in *Prosecutor v Kaing Guek Eav*.[1] Here, the Trial Chamber considered whether or not the accused had been provided with a lawyer of his own choice, despite making it clear that he wanted the assistance of an international lawyer as well as a national lawyer.[2] The Pre-Trial Chamber found that the facts of the case made clear that the international lawyer was present and that he was allowed to defend the accused via the national lawyer.[3] It therefore considered that the rights of the accused had not been violated.

1 Duch Decision of 3 December 2007.
2 Duch Decision of 3 December 2007 at para 11.
3 Ibid.

12.90 As part of the same decision, the Pre-Trial Chamber further examined whether the Co-investigating Judges had failed to remind the accused of his right to remain silent at every stage of the proceedings.[1] Although the Pre-Trial Chamber found that it was apparent that the accused had only been informed of his right to remain silent at the commencement of the initial hearing he attended, it ultimately found that any right to request an annulment of the proceedings based on this procedural defect had been waived by the accused.[2]

1 Duch Decision of 3 December 2007 at para 10.
2 Ibid.

STL

12.91 The abuse of process doctrine was substantially addressed before the Tribunal following complaints concerning the lack of cooperation of the Government of the Lebanese Republic to the Defence in October 2013. In its 'Motion for Stay of Proceedings Due to Lebanon's Failure to Cooperate', the Defence for Assad Sabra argued that the systematic failure of the Lebanese authorities to effectively cooperate with the defence – contrary to its clear legal obligation to do so under statutory provisions and concerning material that is essential to preparation on wide variety of topics – frustrated article 15 of the agreement between the UN and the Government of the Lebanese Republic and had seriously prejudiced the investigations of the Defence and its ability to prepare. The Defence further submitted that the issue was exacerbated by fact that no other state or organisation had provided any information as sought by the Defence.[1]

1 STL, Pre-Trial Judge, *Prosecutor v Ayyash et al.,* STL-11/01/PT/PTJ, Motion for Stay of Proceedings, 11 October 2013.

12.92 The STL Trial Chamber confirmed that the STL Statute and Rules of Procedure and Evidence do not refer to the power to order a stay of proceedings.[1] However, the Chamber did cite to the STL Appeals Chamber decision *In the Matter of El Sayed*, in which the Appeals Chamber had explicitly found that that it could exercise its inherent jurisdiction in various situations including requests for stay of proceedings.[2]

1 STL, Trial Chamber, *Prosecutor v Ayyash et al.,* STL-11/01/PT/TC, Decision on Defence Motion to Stay the Proceedings, 17 December 2013 ('Sabra Decision of 17 December 2013') at para 9.
2 *Ibid*, citing to STL, Appeals Chamber, *In the Matter of El Sayed*, CH/AC/2010/02, Decision on Appeal of Pre-Trial Judge's Order regarding Jurisdiction and Standing, 10 November 2010 at para 46.

12.93 Having acknowledged that it was a discretionary move, the Chamber considered that requests for stay of proceedings involved an exercise of judicial assessment dependent on judgment rather than on any conclusion as to fact based on evidence and that it enjoyed a margin of appreciation, based on its intimate understanding of the process thus far.[1]

1 Sabra Decision of 17 December 2013 at para 10.

12.94 The Chamber subsequently relied on the jurisprudence of the *ad hoc* tribunals and the ICC in its assessment of the abuse of process doctrine, finding that it consisted of the following principles:

(1) a stay of proceedings on a finding of abuse of process was a drastic remedy necessary only if essential preconditions of fair trial are missing and there is no sufficient indication that it be resolved during trial process;[1]

(2) conditional stay of proceedings was possible whereby the unfairness to the accused may be of such a nature that-at least theoretically – a fair trial might become possible at a later stage because of change in situation that led to the stay. However, in certain circumstances a conditional stay could be tantamount to a permanent stay;[2]

(3) the impossibility of receiving a fair trial means that at the outset it is clear that the essential preconditions of a fair trial are missing, and insufficient indication exists that this will be resolved during the trial process. In those circumstances the proceedings should be stayed;[3]

(4) in situations involving unavailable evidence– while the evidence should relate to the 'heart of the case', its absence does not have to have a 'decisive impact' on the outcome of the case. Whether the impact is decisive is contingent upon the entirety of the available evidence and the proceedings. Before the trial, where no evidence has been submitted, requiring the defence to prove 'decisive impact' on the outcome of the case would be too onerous, however defence will not have properly substantiated its request if the unavailable evidence is not identified with sufficient specificity.[4]

1 Sabra Decision of 17 December 2013 at para 12.
2 Sabra Decision of 17 December 2013 at para 13.
3 Ibid.
4 Sabra Decision of 17 December 2013 at para 14.

12.95 When applying the principles to the facts as alleged by the Defence for Sabra, the Chamber held that the threshold for issuing an order against the Government of the Lebanese Republic for its non-compliance with a request for assistance is lower than that for an order of stay of proceedings.[1] In particular it noted that an order for compliance could be issued where the Government of Lebanon had failed to provide relevant documents required for investigation, whereas an order for stay of proceedings required a finding that the essential preconditions of a fair trial are missing and that there is insufficient indication that the issue will be resolved during trial process.[2]

1 Sabra Decision of 17 December 2013 at para 17.
2 Sabra Decision of 17 December 2013 at para 18.

12.96 The STL Trial Chamber ultimately concluded that it would not issue an order for a stay of proceedings without first issuing an order for compliance under STL Rule 20(A), thus finding the Defence motion to be premature.[1]

1 Ibid.

INTERNATIONAL CRIMINAL COURT

12.97 As the first permanent international criminal court, the jurisprudence of the ICC is key to any practitioner in the field. Whilst the drafters of the Rome Statute may not have envisaged a statutory provision detailing the abuse of process doctrine, noting that the conclusion of the Rome Statute pre-dates the Barayagwiza Decision, the Court has not shied away from applying the doctrine in proceedings before it.

Applicable principles

12.98 The jurisprudence of the Court has developed the following principles under the abuse of process doctrine. They are applicable to every situation in which a party to the proceedings requests a permanent stay of the proceedings:

(1) a stay of proceedings is available where it would be repugnant or odious to the administration of justice to allow the case to continue, or where the rights of the accused have been breached to such an extent that a fair trial has been rendered impossible;[1]

(2) in imposing a stay of proceedings, it is not necessary to find that the Prosecution acted in bad faith;[2] it is sufficient to show that:

   (a) the rights of the accused have been violated to such an extent that the essential preconditions of a fair trial are missing; and

   (b) there is no sufficient indication that this will be resolved during the trial process;[3]

(3) a stay of proceedings is an exceptional remedy to be applied as a last resort; not every violation of fair trial rights will justify the imposition of a stay of proceedings;[4]

(4) to 'conceive of a stay of proceedings' as an appropriate remedy for any difficulties encountered in accessing information or facilities during trial preparation 'would run contrary to the responsibility of trial judges to relieve unfairness as part of the trial process';[5] and

(5) the Appeals Chamber held that if the unfairness to the accused person is of such nature that – at least theoretically – a fair trial might become possible at a later stage because of a change in the situation that led to the stay, a conditional stay of the proceedings may be the appropriate remedy and that such a conditional stay is not entirely irreversible.[6]

As above, the fact patterns before the ICC can also be grouped into the following three categories: (i) conduct of national authorities; (ii) prosecutorial misconduct; and (iii) obstacles to the preparation of the defence.

1 ICC, Appeals Chamber, *Prosecutor v Thomas Lubanga Dyilo*, Judgment on the Appeal of Mr. Thomas Lubanga Dyilo against the Decision on the Defence Challenge to the Jurisdiction

of the Court pursuant to article 19 (2) (a) of the Statute of 3 October 2006, 14 December 2006, ICC-01/04-01/06-772 (OA 4) ('Lubanga OA4'); ICC, Appeals Chamber, *Prosecutor v Thomas Lubanga Dyilo*, Judgment on the appeal of the Prosecutor against the decision of Trial Chamber I entitled 'Decision on the consequences of non-disclosure of exculpatory materials covered by article 54(3)(e) agreements and the application to stay the prosecution of the accused, together with certain other issues raised at the Status Conference on 10 June 2008', 21 October 2008, ICC-01/04-01/06-1486 (OA 13) ('Lubanga OA13'); ICC, Trial Chamber I, *Prosecutor v Thomas Lubanga Dyilo*, Redacted Decision on the 'Defence Application Seeking a Permanent Stay of the Proceedings', 7 March 2011, ICC-01/04-01/06-2690-Red2 ('Lubanga Trial Decision of 7 March 2011').

2 ICC, Trial Chamber V, *Prosecutor v Uhuru Mugnai Kenyatta*, Decision on Defence Application Pursuant to Article 64(4) and Related Requests, 26 April 2013, ICC-01/09-02/11-728 at para 76.

3 ICC, Trial Chamber I, *Prosecutor v Thomas Lubanga Dyilo*, Decision on the consequences of non-disclosure of exculpatory materials covered by Article 54(3)(e) agreements and the application to stay the prosecution of the accused, together with certain other issues raised at the Status Conference on 10 June 2008, 13 June 2008, ICC-01/04-01/06-1401 ('Lubanga Trial Decision of 13 June 2008') at para 91.

4 ICC, Appeals Chamber, *Prosecutor v Thomas Lubanga Dyilo*, Judgment on the appeal of the Prosecutor against the decision of Trial Chamber I of 8 July 2010 entitled 'Decision on the Prosecution's Urgent Request for Variation of the Time-Limit to Disclose the Identity of Intermediary 143 or Alternatively to Stay Proceedings Pending Further Consultations with the VWU', 8 October 2010, ICC-01/04-01/06-2582 (OA 18) at para 55 (a stay is a 'drastic' remedy which 'potentially frustrat[es] the objective of the trial of delivering justice in a particular case as well as affecting the broader purposes expressed in the preamble to the Rome Statute').

5 ICC, Trial Chamber IV, *Prosecutor v Abdallah Banda Abakaer Nourain and Saleh Mohammed Jerbo Jamus*, Decision on the defence request for a temporary stay of proceedings, 26 October 2012, ICC-02/05-03/09-410 at para 79.

6 ICC, Appeals Chamber, *Prosecutor v Thomas Lubanga Dyilo*, Judgment on the appeal of the Prosecutor against the decision of Trial Chamber I entitled 'Decision on the consequences of non-disclosure of exculpatory materials covered by Article 54(3)(e) agreements and the application to stay the prosecution of the accused, together with certain other issues raised at the Status Conference on 10 June 2008', 21 October 2008, ICC-01/04-01/06-1486 (OA 13) ('Lubanga OA13').

Conduct of national authorities

12.99 The ICC has had to consider the abuse of process doctrine in the context of alleged violations of due process in the domestic country where a suspect has been detained.

Lubanga OA4[1]

12.100 The first application of the abuse of process doctrine before the ICC was as a result of an application by the Lubanga Defence in which it asserted that prior to his arrest under the warrant of the Court, Mr. Lubanga was unlawfully detained and ill-treated by the Congolese authorities. The Defence asserted that the Prosecutor had been privy to Mr. Lubanga's prior illegal detention by the Congolese authorities with a view to facilitating his unimpeded arrest under the warrant of the Court. In the submissions of the Lubanga Defence, this amounted to complicity on the part of the Prosecutor in the actions of the Congolese authorities.

1 ICC, Appeals Chamber, *Prosecutor v Thomas Lubanga Dyilo*, Judgment on the Appeal of Mr. Thomas Lubanga Dyilo against the Decision on the Defence Challenge to the Jurisdiction of the Court pursuant to Article 19(2)(a) of the Statute of 3 October 2006, 14 December 2006, ICC-01/04-01/06-772 (OA 4) ('Lubanga OA4').

12.101 In its preliminary considerations, the ICC Appeals Chamber disagreed with the Pre-Trial Chamber's findings[1] that issue concerned the Court's 'jurisdiction'. In doing so, the Appeals Chamber stated that a request for stay of proceedings was a *sui generis* application conveying a procedural step not envisaged by the Rules of Procedure and Evidence or the Regulations of the Court.[2]

1 ICC, Pre-Trial Chamber I, *Prosecutor v Thomas Lubanga Dyilo,* Decision on the Defence Challenge to the Jurisdiction of the Court pursuant to Article 19(2)(a) of the Statute, 3 October 2006, ICC-01/04-01/06-512.

2 Lubanga OA4 at para 24.

12.102 The ICC Appeals Chamber went on to assess the abuse of process doctrine and its applicability in proceedings before the ICC. In particular it assessed the application of the doctrine in various common law jurisdictions in order to identify key principles. This included, *inter alia*, the fact that the authority to stay proceedings under the abuse of process doctrine was a discretionary power involving an exercise of judicial assessment dependent on judgment rather than on any conclusion as to fact based on evidence.[1] The Chamber also recognised that not every infraction of the law or breach of the rights of the accused in the process of bringing him/her to justice would justify a stay of proceedings so that the illegal conduct must be such as to make it otiose or repugnant to the rule of law to put the accused on trial.[2]

1 Lubanga OA4 at para 28.

2 Lubanga OA4 at para 30.

12.103 The Chamber considered that where a fair trial became impossible because of breaches of the fundamental rights of the suspect or the accused by his/her accusers, it would be a contradiction in terms to put the person on trial as justice could not be done.[1]

1 Lubanga OA4 at para 37.

12.104 In conclusion, the Appeals Chamber ultimately found that the Pre-Trial Chamber's analysis had side-lined the main point as to whether the accused could still have a fair trial and failed to provide specific consideration as to whether a fair trial remained possible in the particular circumstances of the case. However, the Appeals Chamber also found that there was neither any evidence to suggest that the accused had been detained illegally under Congolese law nor anything to indicate that his arrest or appearance before the Congolese authority involved or entailed any violation of his rights.[1] The Lubanga Defence's appeal was therefore rejected.

1 Lubanga OA4 at para 41.

Katanga OA10[1]

12.105 Following Lubanga OA4, the Defence for Germain Katanga requested Trial Chamber II to declare that the arrest and detention of the accused in the DRC was unlawful asserting that his fundamental rights were violated, including his right to liberty, his right to be brought promptly before the judicial authorities, his right to be informed of the charges, and his right to assistance of counsel. The Defence subsequently requested the termination of proceedings.

1 ICC, Appeals Chamber, *Prosecutor v Germain Katanga and Mathieu Ngudjolo Chui*, Judgment on the Appeal of Mr Katanga Against the Decision of Trial Chamber II of 20 November 2009 Entitled 'Decision on the Motion of the Defence for Germain Katanga for a Declaration on Unlawful Detention and Stay of Proceedings', 12 July 2010, ICC-01/04-01/07-2259 (OA 10) ('Katanga OA10').

12.106 The Trial Chamber rejected the Defence application – finding that a challenge to the lawfulness of the pre-surrender arrest and detention of an accused, in particular where such a challenge is accompanied by an application to stay or terminate the proceedings, must be submitted in the initial phase of the proceedings and not during trial stage.[1] Upon appeal, the Katanga Defence submitted that the retrospective time limit for such an application was unfair. The Defence further complained that given that it was a sui generis application, coupled with the serious nature of violations, the time limit was both inapplicable and disproportionate.

1 ICC, Trial Chamber II, *Prosecutor v Germain Katanga and Mathieu Ngudjolo Chui,* Decision on the Motion of the Defence for Germain Katanga for a Declaration on Unlawful Detention and Stay of Proceedings, 20 November 2009, ICC-01/04-01-07-1666-Conf-Exp-tENG.

12.107 Whilst the Appeals Chamber did note that none of the time limits stipulated in the Statute, the Rules of Procedure and Evidence or the Regulations of the Court directly apply to motions alleging unlawful pre-surrender arrest and detention and seeking a stay of proceedings, it did find that the approach adopted by the Trial Chamber was correct.[1] The Chamber focused on the fact that matters alleging unlawful pre-surrender arrest and detention are given prominence before the Pre-Trial Chamber, finding that the matter could only be raised at trial stage if there existed circumstances whereby the accused person could not reasonably have been expected to raise the matter before the Pre-Trial Chamber.[2]

1 Katanga OA10 at paras 39 and 40.
2 Katanga OA10 at para 48.

12.108 Trial Chamber III ultimately found that that the Defence had failed to properly substantiate its allegations[1] in particular finding 'no application was made to the Chamber to call witnesses or to admit documentary evidence [...].'[2] The abuse of process challenge was therefore dismissed as being without foundation.[3]

1 Bemba Decision of 24 June 2010 at paras 250–260.
2 Bemba Decision of 24 June 2010 at para 254.
3 Bemba Decision of 24 June 2010 at para 262.

12.109 Whilst the Bemba Decision of 24 June 2010 was appealed, the Trial Chamber's remarks concerning the abuse of process challenge were not subject of the appeal.[1]

1 ICC, Appeals Chamber, *Prosecutor v Jean-Pierre Bemba Gombo*, Judgment on the appeal of Mr Jean-Pierre Bemba Gombo against the Decision of Trial Chamber III of 24 June 2010 entitled 'Decision on the Admissibility and Abuse of Process Challenges', 19 October 2010, ICC-01/05-01/08-962-Corr ('Bemba OA3'). This is not to be confused with the Trial Chamber's admonishment of the Defence for its 'extremely late filings' submitted before the CAR courts which constituted 'an abuse of this court's process'. Whilst this admonishment

was the subject of Bemba OA3 it does not address the substantive points of the abuse of process doctrine see Bemba OA3 at 103–104, 106 and 133–135.

Gbagbo OA2[1]

12.110 In *Prosecutor v Laurent Gbagbo*, the Defence argued that proceedings against the accused should be stayed due to alleged violations of his rights that occurred from the time of his arrest by the domestic authorities on 11 April 2011, to his transfer to the Court on 29 November 2011. In particular, the Defence complained that prior to his transfer, Mr. Gbagbo was subjected to arbitrary arrest and detention by the Ivorian authorities and that, during the abovementioned period of time, he was subjected to conditions of detention amounting to inhuman and degrading treatment as well as torture.

1 ICC, Appeals Chamber, *Prosecutor v Laurent Koudou Gbagbo*, Judgment on the appeal of Mr Laurent Koudou Gbagbo against the decision of Pre-Trial Chamber I on jurisdiction and stay of the proceedings, 12 December 2012, ICC-02/11-01/11-321 (OA 2) ('Gbagbo OA2').

12.111 The ICC Pre-Trial Chamber I found that Mr. Gbagbo had not been detained at the behest of the Court, nor did the Court have any involvement with the domestic proceedings of the Ivorian authorities.[1] It stated that the mere fact that the Prosecutor had been in contact with Ivorian authorities did not suggest that there was any involvement by the Prosecutor in Mr. Gbagbo's detention.[2] The Chamber further dismissed the argument that the Prosecutor had a duty of care during Mr Gbagbo's detention by national authorities on the basis that the powers of the Prosecutor may only be exercised in the context of, or in relation to, proceedings before the Court.[3]

1 ICC, Pre-Trial Chamber I, *Prosecutor v Laurent Koudou Gbagbo*, Decision on the Corrigendum of the challenge to the jurisdiction of the International Criminal Court on the basis of Articles 12(3), 19(2), 21(3), 55 and 59 of the Rome Statute filed by the Defence for President Gbagbo (ICC-02/11-01/11-129, 15 August 2012, ICC-02/11-01/11-212 at para 108.
2 Ibid at para 109.
3 ICC, Pre-Trial Chamber I, *Prosecutor v Laurent Gbagbo*, Decision on the Corrigendum of the challenge to the jurisdiction of the International Criminal Court on the basis of Articles 12(3), 19(2), 21(3), 55 and 59 of the Rome Statute filed by the Defence for President Gbagbo (ICC-02/11-01/11-129), 15 August 2012, ICC-02/11-01/11-212 at para 111.

12.112 The Defence for Mr. Gbagbo appealed on the basis that the Pre-Trial Chamber had erred in how it addressed his arguments in the jurisdictional challenge. Notably, the Defence did not seek leave to appeal this decision, arguing instead that the Pre-Trial Chamber had rendered a decision on jurisdiction which could be appealed as of right pursuant to article 82(1)(a) of the Statute.

12.113 The ICC Appeals Chamber reiterated its position in Lubanga OA4, and distinguished requests for a stay of proceedings based on an alleged violation of a suspect's fundamental rights from jurisdictional challenges. Accordingly, the Appeals Chamber held that the Pre-Trial Chamber's decision to reject Mr Gbagbo's request for a stay of proceedings was not a 'decision with respect to jurisdiction' in terms of ICC article 82(1)(a). Rather, it was a separate decision which was unrelated to the question of the jurisdiction of the Court.[1] As a result the Appeals Chamber dismissed the abuse of process grounds *in limine*.

1 Gbagbo OA2 at paras 101–06.

12.114

Al Hassan Decision of 24 August 2020[1]

On 16 June 2020, the Defence for Mr. Al Hassan invoked the abuse of process doctrine in its request before Trial Chamber X for the termination of proceedings and immediate release of Mr. Al Hassan. The Defence asserted that Mr. Al Hassan had been interrogated under highly coercive and abusive circumstances, and/or subjected to severe detention abuses, which were likely to meet the threshold of torture following his arrest and detention in Mali by French and Malian authorities.[2] In particular, the Defence complained that the Prosecution had aggravated and compounded the effects of the torture undergone by Mr. Al Hassan to such an extent that the constituent elements of a fair trial could not be pieced together.[3]

1 ICC, Trial Chamber X, *Prosecutor v Al Hassan Ag Abdoul Aziz Ag Mohamed Ag Mahmoud*, ICC-01/12-01/18-1009-Red, Public redacted version of 'Decision on the Defence request to terminate the proceedings and related requests' dated 24 August 2020, 29 October 2020 ("Al Hassan Decision").

2 ICC, Trial Chamber X, *Prosecutor v Al Hassan Ag Abdoul Aziz Ag Mohamed Ag Mahmoud*, ICC-01/12-01/18-885-Corr-Red3, Public redacted version of 'Corrigendum to "Defence Request to terminate the proceedings"' dated 16 June 2020, 28 July 2020, para 1.

3 Al Hassan Decision at para 3.

12.115 Having been seized of the request, Trial Chamber acknowledged the applicable principles as set out in prior jurisprudence of the Court with regard to the remedy of a stay of proceedings for abuse of process. In doing so, it further emphasised the following principles.

12.116 First, it recalled the Appeals Chamber's finding that: (i) a trial chamber has discretion under article 64(2) of the Statute to determine the timeliness of motions alleging pre-surrender unlawful arrest and detention and seeking a stay of proceedings; (ii) these motions must, as a general rule, be brought before the pre-trial chamber; and (iii) '[o]nly in circumstances where the accused person could not reasonably be expected to raise the matter at that stage will he or she be permitted to raise it at the trial stage'.[1] Whilst Trial Chamber X had considered that the request before it was filed at a late stage it proceeded to analyse the request on its merit when considering the seriousness of the allegations and in line with its obligations under articles 21(3), 67 and 68 of the Statute.

1 Al Hassan Decision at para 44.

12.117 Second, Trial Chamber X noted that other chambers of this Court adjudicating motions of similar nature determined, explicitly or implicitly, that the burden of proving the allegations underlying such a motion falls upon the Defence, and not the Prosecution.[1]

1 Al Hassan Decision at para 71.

12.118 Third, the Chamber endorsed prior jurisprudence in its finding that violations of fundamental rights, however serious, can have the requisite impact on proceedings to constitute an abuse of process only insofar as they can be attributed to the Court.[1] In particular, Trial Chamber X reiterated that attribution in this sense means that the act of violation of fundamental rights is: (i) either directly perpetrated by persons associated with the Court; or

(ii) perpetrated by third persons in collusion with the Court. It further noted the Appeals Chamber's finding that '[m]ere knowledge on the part of the Prosecutor of the investigations carried out by the [national] authorities is no proof of involvement on his part in the way they were conducted or the means used for the purpose.[2] In analysing the approach of the *ad hoc* tribunals with regard to allegations of serious mistreatment of an accused by a third party, the Chamber considered that this was consistent with the position endorsed before the Court whereby the abuse of process doctrine was envisaged to be invoked in exceptional cases only where serious violations of the right of the accused could not be directly attributed to an organ of the Court.[3]

1 Al Hassan Decision at para 57.
2 Ibid.
3 Al Hassan Decision at para 61.

12.119 Applying these principles, Trial Chamber found that the alleged torture and cruel, inhuman and degrading treatment could not be attributed to the Prosecution on the basis that: (i) Mr. Al Hassan was not detained at the behest of the Prosecution or the Court, at least prior to the notification to the competent Malian authorities of the request for provisional arrest of Mr .Al Hassan on 28 March 2018;[1] (ii) cooperation or agreement between the Malian authorities and the Prosecution to investigate the events of 2012 did not establish collusion on the part of the Prosecution in the alleged acts of torture by French or Malian authorities;[2] and (iii) the Prosecution had undertaken safeguards within its competence during its interviews of Mr. Al Hassan.[3]

1 Al Hassan Decision at para 92.
2 Al Hassan Decision at para 95.
3 Al Hassan Decision at paras 96–98.

12.120 Having found that the high threshold required to justify a stay of proceedings had not been met, Trial Chamber X noted the availability of alternative remedies to address abuse of process complaints including the exclusion of certain evidence or a determination that certain evidence be given little to no weight at the end of the trial.[1]

1 Al Hassan Decision at para 119.

12.121 The Defence's request for leave to appeal was subsequently denied.[1]

1 ICC, Trial Chamber X, *Prosecutor v Al Hassan Ag Abdoul Aziz Ag Mohamed Ag Mahmoud*, ICC-01/12-01/18-1009-Red, Public redacted version of 'Decision on Defence request for leave to appeal the "Decision on the Defence request to terminate the proceedings and related requests"' dated 12 October 2020, 29 October 2020.

Prosecutorial misconduct

Lubanga OA13[1]

12.122 The decision in Lubanga OA13 is the first instance whereby a conditional stay of proceedings and immediate release of the accused was ordered as a result of misconduct by the ICC Chief Prosecutor.

1 ICC, Appeals Chamber, *Prosecutor v Thomas Lubanga Dyilo*, Judgment on the appeal of the Prosecutor against the Decision of Trial Chamber I entitled 'Decision on the consequences

of non-disclosure of exculpatory materials covered by Article 54(3)(e) agreements and the application to stay the prosecution of the accused, together with certain other issues raised at the Status Conference on 10 June 2008', 21 October 2008, ICC-01/04-01/06-1486 (OA 13) ('Lubanga OA13').

12.123 On 13 June 2008, Trial Chamber I rendered its 'Decision on the consequences of non-disclosure of exculpatory materials covered by article 54(3)(e) agreements and the application to stay the prosecution of the accused, together with certain other issues raised at the Status Conference on 10 June 2008' in which it stayed proceedings before the Chamber in respect of Mr. Lubanga and halted the trial process in all respects as, in the view of the Trial Chamber, the non-disclosure of certain documents by the Prosecutor to the Defence had made a fair trial impossible.[1]

1 Lubanga Trial Decision of 13 June 2008.

12.124 The Trial Chamber had noted that in the case of Mr. Lubanga, the Prosecutor was unable to disclose to the Defence more than 200 documents which contained potentially exculpatory information or information that was potentially material to the preparation of the defence.[1] This was caused by the Prosecutor's retrieval of the documents on conditions of confidentiality in accordance with ICC article 54(3)(e)[2] so that the information providers had subsequently withheld consent for their disclosure in court proceedings.

1 Ibid para 63.
2 ICC Rome Statute article 54(3)(e) 'The Prosecutor may [...] agree not to disclose, at any stage of the proceedings, documents or information that the Prosecutor obtains on the condition of confidentiality and solely for the purpose of generating new evidence, unless the provider of the information consents'.

12.125 As a result, the Trial Chamber came to the conclusion that a substantial amount of material containing potentially exculpatory information and information material to the preparation of the defence could not be disclosed to the defence, or indeed the Trial Chamber, because it had been obtained by the Prosecutor under article 54(3)(e) of the Statute. It reiterated the fact that the information providers had not consented to the lifting of the confidentiality and that the Prosecution was unable to demonstrate that such deficiencies could be corrected.[1]

1 Lubanga Trial Decision of 13 June 2008 at para 91.

12.126 When confronted with the same facts, the Appeals Chamber first analysed the Prosecution's conduct prior to determining whether the abuse of process doctrine had been triggered.

12.127 At the outset, the ICC Appeals Chamber agreed that the use of ICC article 54(3)(e) of the Statute must not lead to breaches of the obligations of the Prosecutor *vis-à-vis* the suspect or the accused person.[1] The Appeals Chamber also found that a fundamental right of the accused person in proceedings before the Court is the right to disclosure of exculpatory evidence. It therefore concluded that the Prosecutor's reliance on ICC article 54(3)(e) led to direct tensions with his disclosure obligations.[2]

1 Lubanga OA13 at para 42.
2 Lubanga OA13 at paras 43–55.

12.128 In discussing whether the Trial Chamber's decision to stay proceedings was premature and excessive, the ICC Appeals Chamber found that it was clear that the Trial Chamber intended to impose a stay that was conditional and that could be reversed in the event that information providers alter their position and give their consent to the disclosure of the documents in question.[1] The Appeals Chamber held that if the unfairness to the accused person is of such nature that – at least theoretically – a fair trial might become possible at a later stage because of a change in the situation that led to the stay, a conditional stay of the proceedings may be the appropriate remedy and that such a conditional stay is not entirely irreversible.[2]

1 Lubanga OA13 at para 75.
2 Lubanga OA13 at para 80.

12.129 At the same time, the Appeals Chamber noted that an accused had an on-going right to be tried without undue delay so that a conditional stay could not be imposed indefinitely.[1] It therefore concluded that a Chamber that has imposed a conditional stay must, from time to time, review its decision and determine whether a fair trial has become possible or whether, in particular because of the time that has elapsed, a fair trial may have become permanently and incurably impossible.[2] In the latter case, the Chamber may have to modify its decision and permanently stay the proceedings.

1 Lubanga OA13 at para 81.
2 Lubanga OA13 at para 81.

12.130 Ultimately therefore, the Appeals Chamber upheld that proceedings could be stayed in these instances. However, in the time that the Trial Chamber had issued its decision, and prior to the Appeals Chamber's judgment, the information provider had granted consent for the documents obtained pursuant to ICC article 54(3)(e) to be disclosed. As a result, the Appeals Chamber upheld the Trial Chamber's order to stay proceedings[1] whilst at the same time directing the Trial Chamber to decide anew whether Mr. Lubanga should remain in detention or whether he should be released, with or without conditions.[2]

1 Lubanga OA13 at para 52.
2 ICC, Appeals Chamber, *Prosecutor v Thomas Lubanga Dyilo*, Judgment on the appeal of the Prosecutor against the decision of Trial Chamber I entitled 'Decision on the release of Thomas Lubanga Dyilo', 21 October 2008, ICC-01/04-01/06-1487.

Lubanga OA18[1]

12.131 In 2010, the Trial Chamber once again found that misconduct on the part of the Prosecution had led to an abuse of process. On 12 May 2010, the Trial Chamber ordered the Prosecution to, inter alia, disclose the identity of intermediary 143 to Mr. Lubanga Dyilo once the necessary protective measures were implemented.[2]

1 ICC, Appeals Chamber, *Prosecutor v Thomas Lubanga Dyilo*, Judgment on the appeal of the Prosecutor against the decision of Trial Chamber I of 8 July 2010 entitled 'Decision on the Prosecution's Urgent Request for Variation of the Time-Limit to Disclose the Identity of Intermediary 143 or Alternatively to Stay Proceedings Pending Further Consultations with the VWU', 8 October 2010, ICC-01/04-01/06-2582 (OA 18) ('Lubanga OA18').
2 ICC, Trial Chamber I, *Prosecutor v Thomas Lubanga Dyilo*, Decision on Intermediaries, 12 May 2010, ICC-01/04-01/06-2434-Conf-Exp (public redacted version issued 31 May 2010, ICC-01/04-01/-6-2434-Red2).

12.132 On 6 July 2010, as Mr. Lubanga Dyilo was about to commence his questioning of intermediary 321, the Prosecutor informed the Trial Chamber that intermediary 143 was requesting protective measures and that the disclosure of his identity might be further delayed until 16 July 2010 or later.[1] The Trial Chamber considered that, for Mr. Lubanga Dyilo to properly question intermediary 321, he needed to know the identity of intermediary 143. The Chamber repeatedly ordered the Prosecution to disclose the identity of intermediary 143 to the defence team, only for the Prosecution to refuse to effect the disclosure on grounds of security.

1 ICC, Trial Chamber I, *Prosecutor v Thomas Lubanga* Dyilo, Transcript, ICC-01/04-01/06-T-310-RED-ENG, p 56, line 13 to p 59, line 3.

12.133 On 8 July 2010, ICC Trial Chamber I ordered a stay of proceedings on a *propio motu* basis under the abuse of process doctrine due to the Prosecutor's material non-compliance with the Chamber's orders and, more generally, because of the Prosecutor's clearly evinced intention not to implement the Chamber's orders.[1]

1 ICC, Trial Chamber I, *Prosecutor v Thomas Lubanga Dyilo*, Decision on the Prosecution's Urgent Request for Variation of the Time-Limit to Disclose the Identity of Intermediary 143 or Alternatively to Stay Proceedings Pending Further Consultations with the VWU, 8 July 2010, ICC-01/04-01/06-2517-Red.

12.134 On appeal, the ICC Appeals Chamber held that it was undisputed that the Prosecutor did not fulfil the terms of the disclosure orders issued by the Trial Chamber within the specified time limit.[1] The Appeals Chamber noted that Prosecutor did not contend that his non-compliance was caused by any external factor, and thereby found that such wilful non-compliance constituted a clear refusal to implement the orders of the Chamber.[2]

1 Lubanga OA18 at para 46.
2 Lubanga OA18 at para 46.

12.135 Having found that there was a violation of fairness by the Prosecution, the Appeals Chamber then discussed whether a stay of proceedings was the appropriate remedy. In this regard, it re-iterated that a stay of proceedings is a drastic remedy, bringing about a halt to the proceedings. It therefore considered that there was a high threshold for a Trial Chamber to impose a stay of proceedings, requiring that it be impossible to piece together the constituent elements of a fair trial.[1]

1 Lubanga OA18 at para 55.

12.136 At the same time, the Appeals Chamber recalled its previous findings that a Trial Chamber ordering a stay of the proceedings enjoys a margin of appreciation based on its innate understanding of the proceedings.[1] In this regard, it noted that the Trial Chamber did not impose the stay of proceedings solely on the basis of the non-disclosure of the intermediary's identity, but that it relied also, and as a necessary part of its decision, on its determination that the Prosecutor clearly evinced the intention not to implement orders of the Trial Chamber.[2]

1 Lubanga OA18 at para 56 citing to Lubanga OA13.
2 Lubanga OA18 at para 57.

12.137 The ICC Appeals Chamber emphasised the importance of disclosure and considered that, if a Trial Chamber loses control of such a significant and fundamental part of proceedings because of the Prosecutor's refusal to comply with its orders, it would indeed be impossible to ensure a fair trial and a stay of proceedings would then be justified.[1] However, the Appeals Chamber found that with the facts before it, the Trial Chamber had yet to lose control of the proceedings as it had the option to impose sanctions on the Prosecution in accordance with ICC article 71, the purpose of which was not only to punish the offending party, but also to bring about compliance.[2]

1 Lubanga OA18 at para 58.
2 Lubanga OA18 at para 59.

12.138 The Appeals Chamber therefore remanded the case back to the Chamber. During the pendency of the appeal the identity of intermediary 143 had been disclosed to the defence, so that the trial was able to proceed. The Lubanga Defence subsequently requested a stay of proceedings on grounds that the Prosecution's use of intermediaries had rendered a fair trial impossible. Trial Chamber I rejected this argument and held that any intermediary related impropriety could be addressed when evaluating the credibility of Prosecution witnesses.[1]

1 Lubanga Trial Decision of 7 March 2011.

Mbarushimana Decision of 1 July 2011[1]

12.139 In *Prosecutor v Mbarushimana*, the Defence requested a permanent stay of proceedings on the basis that the Prosecutor had misled the Pre-Trial Chamber as to the nature of the proceedings conducted against Mr. Mbarushimana in the Federal Republic of Germany at the time it requested an arrest warrant. The Defence complained that, as Mr. Mbarushimana was the concrete subject of an active police/intelligence agency investigation in Germany, his case was actually inadmissible at the time the ICC arrest warrant was issued. By failing to inform the Pre-Trial Chamber of this German investigation at the time the arrest warrant was being considered, the Defence argued that the Prosecutor's conduct constituted an abuse of process.

1 ICC, Pre-Trial Chamber I, *Prosecutor v Callixte Mbarushimana*, Decision on the 'Defence request for a permanent stay of proceedings', 1 July 2011, ICC-01/04-01/10-264 ('Mbarushimana Decision of 1 July 2011').

12.140 Taking into account previous findings of the Appeals Chamber, Pre-Trial Chamber I noted that not each and every breach of the rights of the suspect and/or the accused is tantamount to an abuse of process.[1] The Pre-Trial Chamber held that, even if it were to be determined that the Prosecutor erred in characterising the nature of the German proceedings concerning Mr. Mbarushimana, such behaviour cannot be equated to the types of conduct that usually form a basis for a stay of proceedings due to an abuse of judicial process (which typically include delays in bringing the accused to justice, broken promises to the accused with regard to his prosecution and bringing the accused to justice by illegal or devious means).[2]

1 Mbarushimana Decision of 1 July 2011 at p.7 relying on Lubanga OA4; Lubanga Trial Decision of 13 June 2008; Lubanga OA13; Lubanga OA18 and Lubanga Trial Decision of 7 March 2011.
2 Mbarushimana Decision of 1 July 2011 at p 6.

Kenyatta Decision of 26 April 2013[1]

12.141 On 5 February 2013, the Defence for Uhuru Kenyatta filed an application requesting that the preliminary issue of the validity of the confirmation decision be referred to the Pre-Trial Chamber for reconsideration pursuant to article 64(4),[2] and that the trial date be vacated. The Defence alleged that the confirmation decision was rendered invalid as a result of the Prosecution's failure to disclose a potentially exculpatory affidavit made by Witness 4, a witness who allegedly provided key evidence relied upon by the Prosecution during the confirmation hearing. As the litigation proceeded, the Kenyatta Defence modified its relief to request the following: termination of proceedings; stay of proceedings or remission of the case back to the Pre-Trial Chamber pursuant to ICC article 64(4) for reconsideration.

1 ICC, Trial Chamber V, *Prosecutor v Uhuru Muigai Kenyatta*, Decision on defence application pursuant to article 64(4) and related requests, 26 April 2013, ICC-01/09-02/11-728 ('Kenyatta Decision of 26 April 2013').

2 ICC Rome Statute article 64(4): 'The Trial Chamber may, if necessary for its effective and fair functioning, refer preliminary issues to the Pre-Trial Chamber or, if necessary, to another available judge of the Pre-Trial Division.'

12.142 Trial Chamber V firstly considered the relief for termination or stay to be interchangeable remedies, as they would have the effect of permanently halting the proceedings without prospect of recommencement.[1]

1 Kenyatta Decision of 26 April 2013 at para 70.

12.143 The Chamber than applied the test for a stay of proceedings. The Trial Chamber concluded that there was no information before it that members of the Prosecution had purposely tried to withhold the affidavit from the Defence until post confirmation decision.[1] Nevertheless, it did find that the Prosecution had made a grave mistake when it wrongly classified the affidavit.

1 Kenyatta Decision of 26 April 2013 at para 93.

12.144 Recalling Trial Chamber I's finding[1] that disclosure of potentially exculpatory material is a fundamental aspect of the accused's right to a fair trial, the Chamber found the Prosecution's conduct in failing to disclose the affidavit and other documents related to Witness 4 to be a cause for serious concern.[2] In her concurring opinion, Judge van den Wyngaert went further to find that the accused's rights had been violated by the extremely late and piecemeal disclosure of an inordinate amount of totally new evidence, which was the immediate consequence of the Prosecution's failure to investigate properly prior to confirmation.[3]

1 Lubanga Trial Decision of 13 June 2008, at paras 77 and 92.

2 Kenyatta Decision of 26 April 2013 at para 95.

3 Concurring Opinion of Judge Christine Van den Wyngaert, ICC-01/09-02/11-728-Anx2.

12.145 In terms of relief, the Chamber noted that, unlike in Lubanga OA18, where the Prosecution was refusing to disclose the materials concerned at the time the stay was ordered, the situation in the case before it very different because the documents at issue had since been disclosed.[1] The Chamber considered the prejudice the non-disclosure caused could be rectified at trial as the Prosecution no longer intended to call Witness 4 and the Defence would have the opportunity to challenge the credibility of other evidence relied upon by the Prosecution at confirmation in corroboration of Witness 4's evidence.[2] The Chamber concluded that it would have been disproportionate to terminate or stay the proceedings as a result of the non-disclosure.

1 Kenyatta Decision of 26 April 2013 at para 96.
2 Kenyatta Decision of 26 April 2013 at para 96.

Kenyatta Decision of 5 December 2013[1]

12.146 On 10 October 2013, the Defence filed its 'Defence Application for a Permanent Stay of the Proceedings due to Abuse of Process'. As part of its application the Defence alleged that the evidence of ten Prosecution witnesses has been irremediably tainted by the actions of Witness 118 and a Prosecution intermediary. Furthermore, the Defence submitted that the Witness 118 and the Intermediary both directly and indirectly intimidated and interfered with specific individuals to stop the cooperation of these witnesses with the Defence. The Kenyatta Defence argued that it would be repugnant to the rule of law and seriously prejudicial to the integrity of the trial process to put Uhuru Kenyatta on trial in these circumstances.

1 ICC, Trial Chamber V, *Prosecutor v Uhuru Muigai Kenyatta*, Decision on Defence application for a permanent stay of the proceedings due to abuse of process, 5 December 2013, ICC-01/09-02/11-868-Red ('Kenyatta Decision of 5 December 2013').

12.147 Trial Chamber V(b) considered the Defence allegations to be more appropriately addressed in the course of the trial or proceedings commenced by the Prosecution under article 70 of the Statute. The Chamber was not persuaded that it was appropriate or safe to evaluate the truth or falsity of the testimony of the named Prosecution witnesses on the basis of the supporting materials, or pre-trial submissions, alone. The Chamber did not accept that these were issues that could be assessed in isolation from the evidence as a whole and that rather they were ultimately issued to be resolved at trial.[1]

1 Kenyatta Decision of 5 December 2013 at para 39.

12.148 In relation to the allegations of witness intimidation and interference, the Trial Chamber found the allegations to be largely unsubstantiated. In particular, the Chamber noted that the Defence's own supporting material demonstrated that the Defence was able to investigate and compile materials which would go to the credibility of Prosecution witnesses and could find its own witnesses in support of its case.[1] The Chamber found that a variety of steps could be taken to address whatever unfairness, if any, the Defence faced in its trial preparation, including: (i) ruling certain testimony and other materials inadmissible; (ii) determining that certain evidence be given little to no weight at the end of the trial; (iii) making evidentiary inferences to counterbalance the fact that the Defence may have been wrongfully deprived of access to specific evidence; (iv) adjourning the trial to allow for additional investigations; and (v) ensuring that appropriate measures are taken to protect Defence witnesses.[2]

1 Kenyatta Decision of 5 December 2013 at para 101.
2 Ibid.

12.149 Trial Chamber V(b) therefore concluded that there was no indication that the essential conditions of fair trial were missing or that there was insufficient indication that this will be resolved during the trial process.

Banda Decision of 30 January 2014[1]

12.150 In *Prosecutor v Abdallah Banda Abakaer Nourain et al.* a similar fact pattern to the Kenyatta Decision of 26 April 2013 arose. Here, the Defence for Abdallah Banda asserted that the Prosecution had failed to disclose exonerating evidence that was highly relevant to the contested issues in the case and that the Prosecution's failure to disclose the statements of Witnesses 467 and 471 prior to the confirmation of charges hearing was a flagrant violation of its obligations under article 67(2) of the Statute and a serious violation of the fair trial rights of Mr. Banda. The Defence submitted that the late disclosure of the disputed material and the failure to investigate exonerating materials equally was prejudicial to it and, in particular, to its own investigations. The Defence concluded that the Prosecution's failures had severely prejudiced the Defence's investigation, obstructed the administration of justice and violated the right to a fair trial of the accused and therefore, the case should be terminated.

1 ICC, Trial Chamber IV, *Prosecutor v Abdallah Banda Abakaer Nourain*, Public redacted 'Decision on the "Defence request for termination of proceedings"', 30 January 2014, ICC-02/05-03/09-535-Red ('Banda Decision of 30 January 2014').

12.151 Whilst finding that the Prosecution could have reasonably assessed that the two statements at issue were at least material to the preparation of the Defence at the confirmation stage, Trial Chamber IV did not consider this failure to be odious or repugnant to the administration of justice such that the proceedings could not continue.[1] The Chamber further concluded that the Defence allegations could also be rectified at trial.

1 Banda Decision of 30 January 2014 at para 41. Similarly, the Chamber found that whilst the declarations of two screened individuals may have warranted further investigation by the Prosecution, the alleged failures did not amount to conduct that could be considered odious or repugnant to the administration of justice such as to constitute an abuse of process see Banda Decision of 30 January 2014 at para 52.

Bemba Decision of 24 June 2010[1]

12.152 On 25 February 2010, the Defence for Jean-Pierre Bemba Gombo simultaneously submitted an admissibility challenge and an abuse of process challenge.[2]

The latter was predicated upon three grounds: (i) the Prosecution's failure to disclose evidence relating to its contact with members of the Central African Republic (CAR) Government and the judiciary, as regards the issue of complementarity; (ii) the misuse of the judicial process for political purposes; and (iii) the unlawful means by which the accused was brought to the Court.[3]

1 ICC, Trial Chamber III, *Prosecutor v Jean-Pierre Bemba Gombo*, Decision on the Admissibility and Abuse of Process Challenges, 24 June 2010, ICC-01/05-01/08 ("Bemba Decision of 24 June 2010").

2 Bemba Decision of 24 June 2010 at para 23.

3 Bemba Decision of 24 June 2010 at para 148.

12.153 Trial Chamber III found there to be no evidence that the Prosecution was in breach of its responsibilities and it had no reason to doubt the undertaking by lead counsel that she had complied with her obligations.[1] In particular, the Chamber noted that the main national judicial decisions relevant to the matter were all disclosed on 3 October 2008 and therefore found the Defence complaints about material non- disclosure as regards the admissibility challenge to be essentially speculative.[2]

1 Bemba Decision of 24 June 2010 at para 215.
2 Bemba Decision of 24 June 2010 at para 216.

Bemba Decision of 17 June 2015[1]

12.154 On 15 December 2014, the Defence for Mr. Bemba seized Trial Chamber III of its request for relief for abuse of process.[2] The Defence's challenge was rooted in the Prosecution's *ex parte* investigation of contempt allegations during the Defence case. In particular, the Defence argued that in conducting its investigation into the credibility of Defence witnesses and evidence, the Prosecution: (i) had requested States to perform actions which violated defence privileges and immunities; (ii) had access to privileged information relating to the Bemba case; (iii) failed to disclose crucial information in a timely manner; and (iv) contaminated the appearance of the impartiality of the proceedings.[3]

1 ICC, Trial Chamber III, *Prosecutor v Jean-Pierre Bemba Gomba*, ICC-01/05-01/08-3255, Decision on 'Defence Request for Relief for Abuse of Process', 17 June 2015.
2 ICC, Trial Chamber III, *Prosecutor v Jean-Pierre Bemba Gomba*, ICC-01/05-01/08-3217-Red2, Public Redacted Version of 'Defence Request for Relief for Abuse of Process' dated 15 December 2014, 30 January 2014. The Defence had originally filed a lengthier submission see ICC, Trial Chamber III, *Prosecutor v Jean-Pierre Bemba Gomba*, ICC-01/05-01/08-3203-Red2, Public Redacted Version of 'Defence Request for Relief for Abuse of Process' dated 11 November 2014, 25 November 2014.
3 ICC, Trial Chamber III, *Prosecutor v Jean-Pierre Bemba Gomba*, ICC-01/05-01/08-3217-Red2, Public Redacted Version of 'Defence Request for Relief for Abuse of Process' dated 15 December 2014, 30 January 2014, para 7.

12.155 In considering the request, Trial Chamber III recognised that whilst the Rome Statute does not expressly provide for a stay of proceedings as a remedy for an abuse of process, the jurisprudence of the Court has confirmed the availability of a stay of proceedings in certain circumstances.[1] Further, whilst the Chamber did not consider itself competent to make any determinations as to the legality or propriety of measures conducted in the article 70 Investigation or the subsequent contempt proceedings, it reiterated that it was bound by the duty to ensure full respect for the fundamental rights of the Accused, including his right to a fair trial in the Bemba case.[2]

1 Bemba Decision of 17 June 2015 at paras 8–11.
2 Bemba Decision of 17 June 2015 at paras 17–18.

12.156 However, Trial Chamber III ultimately denied the Defence's request primarily finding that a motion alleging abuse of process and requesting a stay of proceedings must substantiate how the alleged infraction of the law of violation of the Accused's rights entail the conclusion that it would be 'impossible to piece together the constituent elements of a fair trial' or that it would be 'repugnant or odious' to the administration of justice to allow the case to continue.[1]

1 Bemba Decision of 17 June 2015 at para 30.

12.157 The Chamber made further findings in relation to, inter alia: (i) the lack of reason to doubt the Prosecution's assertion that it was not privy to any information that is protected by legitimate professional privilege;1 (ii) the minimal prejudice arising from delayed disclosure following: judicial orders clarifying the Prosecution's disclosure obligations, the fact that the relevant material was subsequently disclosed and the Defence's failure to make timely submissions on the basis of the material once disclosed;[2] and (iii) the lack of doubt as to its impartiality on the basis that: it made no assessment of the merit of any *ex parte* allegations put before it, the trial judgment would be based solely on evidence submitted and discussed before it at trial and further, that it was composed of professional judges who, unlike a lay jury, are 'sufficiently capable of evaluating the value of any allegations brought before it and [disregarding] them as necessary'.[3]

1 Bemba Decision of 17 June 2015 at para 73.
2 Bemba Decision of 17 June 2015 at paras 82–90.
3 Bemba Decision of 17 June 2015 at paras 99–102.

12.158 The Defence's request for leave to appeal was subsequently denied.[1]

1 ICC, Trial Chamber III, *Prosecutor v Jean-Pierre Bemba Gomba*, ICC-01/05-01/08-3273, Decision on 'Defence Request for Leave to Appeal the "Decision on Defence Request for Relief for Abuse of Process"', 24 July 2015.

Bemba Decision of 7 March 20161

12.159 Trial Chamber III was again seized of an abuse of process challenge on the basis of the delayed disclosure by the Prosecution of two investigative reports which the Defence submitted, related to the credibility of witnesses who appeared on the Defence list that would have aided the Defence in its preparations.[1] In particular, the Defence put forward a number of actions which it stated it could have taken had disclosure been properly effected during its Defence case and that the delayed disclosure had hindered the Defence in substantiating its allegation as to abuse of process.[2] The Defence submitted that the late disclosure and stage of proceedings meant that the only appropriate and available remedy for the Prosecution's non-disclosure is a stay of the proceedings.[3]

1 ICC, Trial Chamber III, *Prosecutor v Jean-Pierre Bemba Gomba*, ICC-01/05-01/08-3257-Red, Defence request for a stay of proceedings and request for further disclosure, 19 June 2015.
2 ICC, Trial Chamber III, *Prosecutor v Jean-Pierre Bemba Gomba*, ICC-01/05-01/08-3257-Red, Defence request for a stay of proceedings and request for further disclosure, 19 June 2015, paras 20, 24, and 26.
3 ICC, Trial Chamber III, *Prosecutor v Jean-Pierre Bemba Gomba*, ICC-01/05-01/08-3257-Red, Defence request for a stay of proceedings and request for further disclosure, 19 June 2015, paras 7 and 31–34.

12.160 Having reviewed the investigative reports, Trial Chamber III found that minimal, if any, prejudice was caused to the Defence by the timing of the disclosure on that basis that, inter alia, (i) the limited and general information therein; (ii) similar information was contained in other disclosed material; (iii) similar information was provided during course of witness testimony; (iii) the Defence had gained access to the reports in the related contempt proceedings.[1] In these circumstances, the Trial Chamber did not consider that any remedy was necessary, warranted, or appropriate.[2]

1 Bemba Decision of 7 March 2016 at paras 23–25, 29–34.
2 Bemba Decision of 7 March 2016 at para 25.

Ntaganda Decision of 28 April 2017[1]

12.161 Trial Chamber VI was seized of an abuse of process challenge on 21 March 2017 following the initiation of *ex parte* contempt investigations by the Prosecution.[2] In particular, the Defence submitted that the acquisition by the Prosecution team in the Ntaganda case of 4,684 conversations of Mr. Ntaganda, concurrent with trial proceedings, given the high relevance of those conversations to Defence strategy as well as to Mr. Ntaganda's personal knowledge of the case amounted to an abuse of the Court's process, as a result of which Mr. Ntaganda could not receive a fair trial.[3]

1 ICC, Trial Chamber VI, *Prosecutor v Bosco Ntaganda*, ICC-01/04-02/06-1883, Decision on Defence request for stay of proceedings with prejudice to the Prosecution, 28 April 2017.
2 ICC, Trial Chamber VI, *Prosecutor v Bosco Ntaganda*, ICC-01/04-02/06-1830-Red, Public redacted version of 'Defence Request for stay of proceedings with prejudice to the Prosecutor' dated 20 March 2017, 21 March 2017.
3 ICC, Trial Chamber VI, *Prosecutor v Bosco Ntaganda*, ICC-01/04-02/06-1830-Red, Public redacted version of 'Defence Request for stay of proceedings with prejudice to the Prosecutor' dated 20 March 2017, 21 March 2017, para 2.

12.162 Trial Chamber VI observed prior jurisprudence of the Court which consistently confirmed the availability of the remedy of a permanent stay of proceedings where it would be 'repugnant or odious to the administration of justice to allow the case to continue, or where the rights of the accused have been breached to such an extent that a fair trial has been rendered impossible'.[1] The Chamber further set out that a determination to stay proceedings was not necessitated on a finding that the Prosecution had acted in bad faith but rather, it was sufficient to show that: (i) the rights of the accused have been violated to such an extent that the essential preconditions of a fair trial are missing; and (ii) there is no sufficient indication that this will be resolved during the trial process.[2]

1 Ntaganda Decision of 28 April 2017 at para 20.
2 Ntaganda Decision of 28 April 2017 at para 21. Noting further the comparable factual situation in the Bemba case, Trial Chamber VI considered it was not competent to determine those issues related to measures taken in the context of article 70 proceedings see Ntaganda Decision of 28 April 2017, para 24.

12.163 Whilst Trial Chamber VI did find that it would have been preferable for the Prosecution to have engaged a separate team to conduct the Art 70 investigations flowing from the Ntaganda case, it held that this failure to follow best practices did not in and of itself amount to an abuse of process rendering a fair trial impossible.[1] Rather it stated that the proper assessment was whether the Prosecution gained any actual advantage, and whether any undue prejudice resulting therefrom amounts to a violation of the rights of the accused to such an extent that the essential preconditions of a fair trial are missing, and is such that it cannot be remedied during the course of the trial.[2]

1 Ntaganda Decision of 28 April 2017 at para 32.
2 Ibid.

12.164 In this regard Trial Chamber VI found that the Prosecution's access to detailed confidential Defence information had placed the Prosecution in an unduly advantageous position *vis-à-vis* the Defence. However, the prejudice arising from this access did not meet the requisite threshold for a stay of proceedings on the basis that the information relevant to defence strategy was limited and the Defence had not yet identified any concrete instances of the Prosecution having used the information in a manner resulting in undue prejudice to the accused.[1]

1 Ntaganda Decision of 28 April 2017 at para 43.

12.165 With regard to the prejudice arising from the prolonged *ex parte* nature of the Art 70 proceedings, the Chamber found that a stay of proceedings was not warranted on the basis that the statutory framework specifically provides for material to be withheld from the Defence where it may compromise ongoing investigations. Moreover, the Chamber considered, *inter alia*, that it was not in position to question the legality or propriety of the *ex parte* nature of the Art 70 investigations as a whole but in any case, had provided specific instructions to the Prosecution to conclude the investigations swiftly and effecting relevant disclosure in the Ntaganda case, with the specific purpose of minimising any prejudice to the accused.

12.166 Finally, the Chamber found that the Defence had failed to substantiate its allegation that the Prosecution had created an irremediable situation of apprehension of bias on the part of the Chamber in light of the fact it was composed of professional judges and therefore able to assess the information in the relevant context.[1]

1 Ntaganda Decision of 28 April 2017 at para 57.

12.167 Although dismissing the Defence's request for a permanent stay of proceedings, Trial Chamber VI proposed alternative measures in response to the abuse of process challenge and to ensure the fair and expeditious conduct of the proceedings. Namely, the Prosecution were not permitted to use material obtained in the context of the Art 70 proceedings during the Defence's presentation of evidence unless specifically authorised by the Chamber as necessary for the determination of the truth and any further reviews of Mr. Ntaganda's conversations were urged to be conducted by Prosecution members who were not part of the Ntaganda trial team.[1] The Chamber further considered additional measures including the recalling of Prosecution witnesses and/or disregarding of certain evidence upon receipt of concrete instances of prejudice as a result of the Prosecution having unduly benefited from its access to Mr. Ntaganda's conversations.[2]

1 Ntaganda Decision of 28 April 2017 at para 61.
2 Ntaganda Decision of 28 April 2017 at para 62.

12.168 The Defence's request for leave to appeal was subsequently denied.[1]

1 ICC, Trial Chamber VI, *Prosecutor v Bosco Ntaganda*, ICC-01/04-02/06-1955, Decision on Defence request for leave to appeal the 'Decision on Defence request for stay of proceedings with prejudice to the Prosecution', 13 June 2017.

Obstacles to preparation of Defence

Banda Decision of 26 October 2012[1]

12.169 On 6 January 2012, the Defence for Abdallah Banda Abakaer Nourain and Saleh Mohammed Jerbo Jamus filed a request for a temporary stay of proceedings on the basis that it has suffered severe restrictions on its investigations due to, inter alia, the conduct of the Government of Sudan. The Defence asserted that it had made multiple unsuccessful efforts to gain access to the Republic of the Sudan in order to access numerous, identified potential defence witnesses believed to have resided in Darfur. It complained that it had been unable to travel to Darfur in order conduct interviews or to identify and locate other potential witnesses as the Government of Sudan had denied access to the Defence and had even criminalised cooperation with the Court. The Defence invited the Chamber to stay the proceedings until such time as the minimum guarantees of a fair trial could be met and when the Prosecution was able to fully discharge its art 54 duties so that the Trial Chamber was able to determine the truth.

1 ICC, Trial Chamber IV, *Prosecutor v Abdallah Banda Abakaer Nourain and Saleh Mohammed Jerbo Jamus*, Decision on the defence request for a temporary stay of proceedings, 26 October 2012, ICC-02/05-03/09-410 ('Banda Decision of 26 October 2012').

12.170 In discussing the limits of its discretionary powers, Trial Chamber IV was of the view that the facts supporting the application for a request for stay of proceedings need to be 'properly substantiated'.[1] Trial Chamber IV considered that the evidence which the accused persons claimed was unavailable to them must be relevant to the contested issues, given the Chamber's previous findings that the trial will proceed only on the basis of a narrow number of contested issues.[2] The Chamber did not consider that this would amount to a requirement that the absence of the evidence must have 'a decisive impact' on the outcome of the case.[3]

1 Banda Decision of 26 October 2012 at para 90.
2 See ICC, Trial Chamber IV, *Prosecutor v Abdallah Banda Abakaer Nourain and Saleh Mohammed Jerbo Jamus,* Decision on the Joint Submission regarding the contested issues and the agreed facts, 28 September 2011, ICC-02/05-03/09-227.
3 Banda Decision of 26 October 2012 at para 92.

12.171 However, the Chamber opined that the Defence would not have 'properly substantiated' its request for stay of proceedings if the unavailable evidence was not identified with sufficient specificity by the Defence in light of the information available to it at the time.[1] As a result the Chamber concluded that because the Defence merely claimed that it had indications that some materials or information could exist and that the existence of others could be inferred, it held that the Defence has failed to establish that the materials were in fact available.[2] Moreover, the Chamber noted that national jurisdictions had been careful to avoid granting applications of stay of proceedings on grounds of speculative or vague claims of impeded defence investigations.[3]

1 Banda Decision of 26 October 2012 at para 93.
2 Banda Decision of 26 October 2012 at para 94 relying on ICTR, *Prosecutor v Nahimana et al.*, ICTR-99-52-T, Decision on the Motion to Stay the Proceedings in the Trial of Ferdinand Nahimana, 5 June 2003 at para 13.
3 Banda Decision of 26 October 2012 at para 95.

12.172 With regard to the infringement of the Defence's right to adequate time and facilities and right to secure attendance of witnesses, the Trial Chamber again considered that the Defence had failed to properly substantiate this part of its request in order to show that other lines of defence were inaccessible as a result of the obstructionist efforts of the Government of Sudan.[1]

1 Banda Decision of 26 October 2012 at para 108.

12.173 The Chamber further found that some degree of investigation in the Sudan did appear to be possible, in spite of the Defence's inability to travel to the Sudan. In particular, it concluded that, whilst not obliged to, the Defence could consider revealing lines of investigations to the Prosecution in order to facilitate the search for, and disclosure of, relevant evidence and the investigation thereof.[1] In light of these alternative remedies, Trial Chamber IV found that any stay of proceedings would be premature, not least because the matter could be resolved during and after trial when the Chamber would be able to analyse the entirety of the evidence at the close of trial proceedings.

1 Banda Decision of 26 October 2012 at para 113.

Kenyatta Decision of 26 April 2013[1]

12.174 As part of its application pursuant to ICC article 64(4), the Kenyatta Defence also alleged that: the Prosecution's on going and protracted investigation; the manner in which it had disclosed evidence to the Defence (e.g. in various versions of redactions); and the inclusion of new or radically altered post confirmation allegations had led to an ever-shifting case which had consequently put pressure on the Defence and required it to expend considerable investigative resources. As such, the Defence asserted that it had not been afforded adequate time to prepare for trial as it had to answer a wholly different case than the one confirmed by the Pre-Trial Chamber.

1 ICC, Trial Chamber V, *Prosecutor v Uhuru Muigai Kenyatta*, Decision on defence application pursuant to article 64(4) and related requests, 26 April 2013, ICC-01/09-02/11-728 ('Kenyatta Decision of 26 April 2013').

12.175 Trial Chamber V clarified that the Prosecution is not necessarily required to rely on entirely the same evidence at trial as it did at the confirmation of charges stage, thereby stressing that it is the charges as confirmed by the Pre-Trial Chamber and subsequently set out in the updated Document Containing Charges, and not the information contained in the Pre-Trial Brief, that serves as the basis for trial.[1] The Chamber found that the Prosecution had not exceeded the facts and circumstances described in the confirmed charges and reflected in the updated Document Containing Charges.[2] Trial Chamber V therefore concluded that a termination or stay of the proceedings was unwarranted due to issues arising from post-confirmation investigation.

1 Kenyatta Decision of 26 April 2013 at para 107.
2 Kenyatta Decision of 26 April 2013 at para 110.

Abd-Al-Rahman Decision of 16 October 2020[1]

12.176 On 5 October 2020, the Abd-Al-Rahman Defence requested a stay or termination of proceedings on the basis that: (i) there is no indication that a postponement of the confirmation hearing would resolve the difficulties faced by the Prosecutor, particularly those in relation to a lack of resources and the Government of Sudan's lack of cooperation; (ii) to postpone the confirmation hearing would infringe upon Mr. Abd-Al-Rahman's right to be tried without undue delay, pursuant to Art 67(1)(c) of the Statute; (iii) the Chamber has the power to halt the proceedings if it considers this solution to be the only option, as found in the Kenyatta case; (iv) considering that the suspect is currently in detention, this militates all the more in favour of granting a stay of proceedings; and (v) the Banda case should be considered, in which a temporary, conditional suspension of the proceedings was ordered due to issues surrounding Sudan's lack of cooperation, with the case still on hold to this day.[2]

1 ICC, *Prosecutor v Ali Muhammad Ali Abd-Al-Rahman ('Ali Kushayb')*, ICC-02/05-01/20-186, Decision on Defence Request for a Stay of Proceedings, 16 October 2020.
2 ICC, *Prosecutor v Ali Muhammad Ali Abd-Al-Rahman ('Ali Kushayb')*, ICC-02/05-01/20-174, Requête aux fins d'arrêt ou de suspension temporaire des procedures, 5 October 2020.

12.177 Seized with the request, the Single Judge recalled that the Rome Statute did not provide for the concept of stay of proceedings and that whilst other chambers had previously resorted to this as an exceptional remedy, he considered it disputable whether this could be validly applied in the Court's system.[1] The Single Judge went on to deny the request considering that whilst a decision postponing the confirmation hearing had not been taken, any request for postponement could not be prejudicial in and of itself noting that such a request was permitted under the statutory framework.[2] Further the Single Judge found that if granted, the requested relief of a stay of proceedings would itself result in a delay to the proceedings, thus harming the interests of the suspect.

1 Abd-Al-Rahman Decision of 16 October 2020 at para 7.
2 Abd-Al-Rahman Decision of 16 October 2020 at paras 9–10.

FINAL REMARKS

12.178 The doctrine of abuse of process has been applied in a broad range of circumstances and at various stages of proceedings in international criminal proceedings. Whilst common principles have been shared between the tribunals, the most notable difference of the application of the doctrine concerns the issue as to whether a finding of abuse prevents the tribunal in question from exercising jurisdiction over the entirety of proceedings. Whilst the ICTY, ICTR and SCSL viewed the doctrine through the jurisdictional lens, the ICC was clear from the outset in establishing that the doctrine was a *sui generis* application that did not go towards the jurisdictional powers of the court. To some extent, the lack of bar to the court's jurisdiction over proceedings allowed the ICC to develop the use of a conditional stay of proceedings as a temporary remedy to a finding of abuse of process which has been subsequently accepted as a remedy at the STL.

12.179 The continued development and application of the doctrine is underscored by the fact that it remains the foundation upon which a tribunal can safeguard the rights of an accused. Each tribunal has, to a certain extent, demonstrated a willingness to entertain applications for a stay of proceedings, regardless of the character of the tribunal or indeed the magnitude of the consequence of any stay of its proceedings. The ICC's willingness to permanently stay its first ever case has invariably been recognised as a bold step, irrespective of any position as to the correctness of such a decision. The doctrine is therefore a testament to the fact that proceedings can be stayed where the minimum requirements of due process are not met even in proceedings that are concerned with 'the most serious crimes of concern to the international community'.

Appendix A

The Code for Crown Prosecutors

October 2018

INTRODUCTION

1.1. The Code for Crown Prosecutors (the Code) is issued by the Director of Public Prosecutions (DPP) under section 10 of the Prosecution of Offences Act 1985. This is the eighth edition of the Code and replaces all earlier versions.

1.2. The DPP is the head of the Crown Prosecution Service (CPS), which is the principal public prosecution service for England and Wales. The DPP operates independently, under the superintendence of the Attorney General who is accountable to Parliament for the work of the CPS.

1.3. The Code gives guidance to prosecutors on the general principles to be applied when making decisions about prosecutions. The Code is issued primarily for prosecutors in the CPS but other prosecutors follow the Code, either through convention or because they are required to do so by law.

1.4. In this Code:

- "suspect" is used to describe a person who is under consideration as the subject of formal criminal proceedings;
- "defendant" is used to describe a person who has been charged or summonsed;
- "offender" is used to describe a person who has admitted guilt as to the commission of an offence, or who has been found guilty in a court of law;
- "victim" is used to describe a person against whom an offence has been committed, or the complainant in a case being considered or prosecuted by the CPS.

GENERAL PRINCIPLES

2.1. The independence of the prosecutor is central to the criminal justice system of a democratic society. Prosecutors are independent from persons or agencies that are not part of the prosecution decision-making process. CPS prosecutors are also independent from the police and other investigators. Prosecutors must be free to carry out their professional duties without political interference and must not be affected by improper or undue pressure or influence from any source.

2.2. It is not the function of the CPS to decide whether a person is guilty of a criminal offence, but to make assessments about whether it is appropriate to present charges for the criminal court to consider. The CPS assessment of any case is not in any sense a finding of, or implication of, any guilt or criminal conduct. A finding of guilt can only be made by a court.

2.3. Similarly, a decision not to bring criminal charges does not necessarily mean that an individual has not been a victim of crime. It is not the role of the CPS to make such determinations.

2.4. The decision to prosecute or to recommend an out-of-court disposal is a serious step that affects suspects, victims, witnesses and the public at large and must be undertaken with the utmost care.

2.5. It is the duty of prosecutors to make sure that the right person is prosecuted for the right offence and to bring offenders to justice wherever possible. Casework decisions taken fairly, impartially and with integrity help to secure justice for victims, witnesses, suspects, defendants and the public. Prosecutors must ensure that the law is properly applied, that relevant evidence is put before the court and that obligations of disclosure are complied with.

2.6. Although each case must be considered on its own facts and on its own merits, there are general principles that apply in every case.

2.7. When making decisions, prosecutors must be fair and objective. They must not let any personal views about the ethnic or national origin, gender, disability, age, religion or belief, sexual orientation or gender identity of the suspect, defendant, victim or any witness influence their decisions. Neither must they be motivated by political considerations. Prosecutors must always act in the interests of justice and not solely for the purpose of obtaining a conviction.

2.8. Prosecutors must be even-handed in their approach to every case, and have a duty to protect the rights of suspects and defendants, while providing the best possible service to victims.

2.9. The CPS is a public authority for the purposes of current, relevant equality legislation. Prosecutors are bound by the duties set out in this legislation.

2.10. Prosecutors must apply the principles of the European Convention on Human Rights, in accordance with the Human Rights Act 1998, at each stage of a case. They must comply with any guidelines issued by the Attorney General and with the policies and guidance of the CPS issued on behalf of the DPP, unless it is determined that there are exceptional circumstances. CPS guidance contains further evidential and public interest factors for specific offences and offenders and is available for the public to view on the CPS website. Prosecutors must also comply with the Criminal Procedure Rules and Criminal Practice Directions, and have regard to the Sentencing Council Guidelines and the obligations arising from international conventions.

2.11. The CPS prosecutes on behalf of some other Government departments. In such cases, prosecutors should have regard to any relevant enforcement policies of those departments.

2.12. Some offences may be prosecuted by either the CPS or by other prosecutors in England and Wales. When making decisions in these cases, CPS prosecutors may, where they think it appropriate, have regard to any relevant enforcement or prosecution policy or code of the other prosecutor.

2.13. Where the law differs in England and Wales prosecutors must apply the Code and have regard to any relevant policy, guidance or charging standard.

THE DECISION WHETHER TO PROSECUTE

3.1. In more serious or complex cases, prosecutors decide whether a person should be charged with a criminal offence and, if so, what that offence should be. Prosecutors may also advise on or authorise out-of-court disposals as an alternative to prosecution. They make their decisions in accordance with this Code, the DPP's Guidance on Charging and any relevant legal guidance or policy. The police apply the same principles in deciding whether to start criminal proceedings against a person in those cases for which they are responsible.

3.2. The police and other investigators are responsible for conducting inquiries into any alleged crime and for deciding how to deploy their resources. This includes decisions to start or continue an investigation and on the scope of the investigation. Prosecutors should advise the police and other investigators about possible reasonable lines of inquiry, evidential requirements, pre-charge procedures, disclosure management and the overall investigation strategy. This can include decisions to refine or narrow the scope of the criminal conduct and the number of suspects under investigation. Such advice assists the police and other investigators to complete the investigation within a reasonable period of time and to build the most effective prosecution case.

3.3. Prosecutors cannot direct the police or other investigators. However, prosecutors must have regard to the impact of any failure to pursue an advised reasonable line of inquiry or to comply with a request for information, when deciding whether the application of the Full Code Test should be deferred or whether the test can be met at all.

3.4. Prosecutors should identify and, where possible, seek to rectify evidential weaknesses but, subject to the Threshold Test (see section 5), they should quickly stop cases which do not meet the evidential stage of the Full Code Test (see section 4) and which cannot be strengthened by further investigation, or where the public interest clearly does not require a prosecution (see section 4). Although prosecutors primarily consider the evidence and information supplied by the police and other investigators, the suspect or those acting on their behalf may also submit evidence or information to the prosecutor, before or after charge, to help inform the prosecutor's decision. In appropriate cases, the prosecutor may invite the suspect or their representative to do so.

3.5. Prosecutors should not start or continue a prosecution where their view is that it is highly likely that a court will rule that a prosecution is an abuse of its process, and stay the proceedings.

3.6. Prosecutors review every case they receive from the police or other investigators. Review is a continuing process and prosecutors must take account of any change in circumstances that occurs as the case develops. This includes what becomes known of the defence case, any further reasonable lines of inquiry that should be pursued, and receipt of any unused material that may undermine the prosecution case or assist the defence case, to the extent that charges should be altered or discontinued or the prosecution should not proceed. If a case is to be stopped, care should be taken when choosing the method of termination, as this can affect the victim's position under the Victims' Right to Review scheme. Wherever possible, prosecutors should consult the investigator when considering changing the charges or stopping the case. Prosecutors and investigators work closely together, but the final responsibility for the decision whether or not a case should go ahead rests with the CPS.

3.7. Parliament has decided that a limited number of offences should only be taken to court with the agreement of the DPP. These are called consent cases. In such cases the DPP, or a prosecutor acting on their behalf, applies the Code in deciding whether to give consent to a prosecution.

3.8. There are also certain offences that can only be taken to court with the consent of the Attorney General. Prosecutors must follow current guidance when referring any such cases to the Attorney General. Some offences require the consent of a Secretary of State before a prosecution is started. Prosecutors must obtain such consent prior to charge and apply any relevant guidance in these cases. Additionally, the Attorney General will be kept informed of certain cases as part of their superintendence of the CPS and accountability to Parliament for its actions.

THE FULL CODE TEST

4.1. Prosecutors must only start or continue a prosecution when the case has passed both stages of the Full Code Test. The exception is when the Threshold Test may be applied (see section 5).

4.2. The Full Code Test has two stages: (i) the evidential stage; followed by (ii) the public interest stage.

4.3. The Full Code Test should be applied:

(a) when all outstanding reasonable lines of inquiry have been pursued; or

(b) prior to the investigation being completed, if the prosecutor is satisfied that any further evidence or material is unlikely to affect the application of the Full Code Test, whether in favour of or against a prosecution.

4.4. In most cases prosecutors should only consider whether a prosecution is in the public interest after considering whether there is sufficient evidence to prosecute. However, there will be cases where it is clear, prior to reviewing all the evidence, that the public interest does not require a prosecution. In these instances, prosecutors may decide that the case should not proceed further.

4.5. Prosecutors should only take such a decision when they are satisfied that the broad extent of the criminality has been determined and that they are able to make a fully informed assessment of the public interest. If prosecutors do not have sufficient information to take such a decision, the investigation should continue and a decision taken later in accordance with the Full Code Test set out in this section.

THE EVIDENTIAL STAGE

4.6. Prosecutors must be satisfied that there is sufficient evidence to provide a realistic prospect of conviction against each suspect on each charge. They must consider what the defence case may be, and how it is likely to affect the prospects of conviction. A case which does not pass the evidential stage must not proceed, no matter how serious or sensitive it may be.

4.7. The finding that there is a realistic prospect of conviction is based on the prosecutor's objective assessment of the evidence, including the impact of any defence and any other information that the suspect has put forward or on which they might rely. It means that an objective, impartial and reasonable jury or bench of magistrates or judge hearing a case alone, properly directed and acting in accordance with the law, is more likely than not to convict the defendant of the charge alleged. This is a different test from the one that the criminal courts themselves must apply. A court may only convict if it is sure that the defendant is guilty.

4.8. When deciding whether there is sufficient evidence to prosecute, prosecutors should ask themselves the following:

Can the evidence be used in court?

Prosecutors should consider whether there is any question over the admissibility of certain evidence. In doing so, prosecutors should assess:

- the likelihood of that evidence being held as inadmissible by the court; and
- the importance of that evidence in relation to the evidence as a whole.

Is the evidence reliable?

Prosecutors should consider whether there are any reasons to question the reliability of the evidence, including its accuracy or integrity.

Is the evidence credible?

Prosecutors should consider whether there are any reasons to doubt the credibility of the evidence.

Is there any other material that might affect the sufficiency of evidence?

Prosecutors must consider at this stage and throughout the case whether there is any material that may affect the assessment of the sufficiency of evidence, including examined and unexamined material in the possession of the police, and material that may be obtained through further reasonable lines of inquiry.

THE PUBLIC INTEREST STAGE

4.9. In every case where there is sufficient evidence to justify a prosecution or to offer an out-of-court disposal, prosecutors must go on to consider whether a prosecution is required in the public interest.

4.10. It has never been the rule that a prosecution will automatically take place once the evidential stage is met. A prosecution will usually take place unless the prosecutor is satisfied that there are public interest factors tending against prosecution which outweigh those tending in favour. In some cases the prosecutor may be satisfied that the public interest can be properly served by offering the offender the opportunity to have the matter dealt with by an out-of-court disposal rather than bringing a prosecution.

4.11. When deciding the public interest, prosecutors should consider each of the questions set out below in paragraphs 4.14 a) to g) so as to identify and determine the relevant public interest factors tending for and against prosecution. These factors, together with any public interest factors set out in relevant guidance or policy issued by the DPP, should enable prosecutors to form an overall assessment of the public interest.

4.12. The explanatory text below each question in paragraphs 4.14 a) to g) provides guidance to prosecutors when addressing each particular question and determining whether it identifies public interest factors for or against prosecution. The questions identified are not exhaustive, and not all the questions may be relevant in every case. The weight to be attached to each of the questions, and the factors identified, will also vary according to the facts and merits of each case.

4.13. It is quite possible that one public interest factor alone may outweigh a number of other factors which tend in the opposite direction. Although there may be public interest factors tending against prosecution in a particular case, prosecutors should consider whether nonetheless a prosecution should go ahead and those factors put to the court for consideration when sentence is passed.

4.14. Prosecutors should consider each of the following questions:

a) How serious is the offence committed?

- The more serious the offence, the more likely it is that a prosecution is required.
- When assessing the seriousness of an offence, prosecutors should include in their consideration the suspect's culpability and the harm caused, by asking themselves the questions at b) and c).

b) What is the level of culpability of the suspect?

- The greater the suspect's level of culpability, the more likely it is that a prosecution is required.
- Culpability is likely to be determined by:
  - i. the suspect's level of involvement;
  - ii. the extent to which the offending was premeditated and/or planned;
  - iii. the extent to which the suspect has benefitted from criminal conduct;
  - iv. whether the suspect has previous criminal convictions and/ or out-of-court disposals and any offending whilst on bail or whilst subject to a court order;
  - v. whether the offending was or is likely to be continued, repeated or escalated;
  - vi. the suspect's age and maturity (see paragraph d below).
- A suspect is likely to have a much lower level of culpability if the suspect has been compelled, coerced or exploited, particularly if they are the victim of a crime that is linked to their offending.
- Prosecutors should also have regard to whether the suspect is, or was at the time of the offence, affected by any significant mental or physical ill health or disability, as in some circumstances this may mean that it is less likely that a prosecution is required. However, prosecutors will also need to consider how serious the offence was, whether the suspect is likely to re-offend and the need to safeguard the public or those providing care to such persons.

c) **What are the circumstances of and the harm caused to the victim?**

- The circumstances of the victim are highly relevant. The more vulnerable the victim's situation, or the greater the perceived vulnerability of the victim, the more likely it is that a prosecution is required.
- This includes where a position of trust or authority exists between the suspect and victim.
- A prosecution is also more likely if the offence has been committed against a victim who was at the time a person serving the public.
- It is more likely that prosecution is required if the offence was motivated by any form of prejudice against the victim's actual or presumed ethnic or national origin, gender, disability, age, religion or belief, sexual orientation or gender identity; or if the suspect targeted or exploited the victim, or demonstrated hostility towards the victim, based on any of those characteristics.
- Prosecutors also need to consider if a prosecution is likely to have an adverse effect on the victim's physical or mental health, always bearing in mind the seriousness of the offence, the availability of special measures and the possibility of a prosecution without the participation of the victim.
- Prosecutors should take into account the views expressed by the victim about the impact that the offence has had. In appropriate cases, this may also include the views of the victim's family.
- However, the CPS does not act for victims or their families in the same way as solicitors act for their clients, and prosecutors must form an overall view of the public interest.

d) **What was the suspect's age and maturity at the time of the offence?**

- The criminal justice system treats children and young people differently from adults and significant weight must be attached to the age of the suspect if they are a child or young person under 18.
- The best interests and welfare of the child or young person must be considered, including whether a prosecution is likely to have an adverse impact on their future prospects that is disproportionate to the seriousness of the offending.
- Prosecutors must have regard to the principal aim of the youth justice system, which is to prevent offending by children and young people. Prosecutors must also have regard to the obligations arising under the United Nations 1989 Convention on the Rights of the Child.

- Prosecutors should consider the suspect's maturity, as well as their chronological age, as young adults will continue to mature into their mid-twenties.
- As a starting point, the younger the suspect, the less likely it is that a prosecution is required.
- However, there may be circumstances which mean that, notwithstanding the fact that the suspect is under 18 or lacks maturity, a prosecution is in the public interest. These include where:

  i. the offence committed is serious;

  ii. the suspect's past record suggests that there are no suitable alternatives to prosecution; and

  iii. the absence of an admission means that out-of-court disposals that might have addressed the offending behaviour are not available.

e) **What is the impact on the community?**

- The greater the impact of the offending on the community, the more likely it is that a prosecution is required.
- The prevalence of an offence in a community may cause particular harm to that community, increasing the seriousness of the offending.
- Community is not restricted to communities defined by location and may relate to a group of people who share certain characteristics, experiences or backgrounds, including an occupational group.
- Evidence of impact on a community may be obtained by way of a Community Impact Statement.

f) **Is prosecution a proportionate response?**

- In considering whether prosecution is proportionate to the likely outcome, the following may be relevant:

  i. The cost to the CPS and the wider criminal justice system, especially where it could be regarded as excessive when weighed against any likely penalty. Prosecutors should not decide the public interest on the basis of this factor alone. It is essential that regard is also given to the public interest factors identified when considering the other questions in paragraphs 4.14 a) to g), but cost can be a relevant factor when making an overall assessment of the public interest.

  ii. Cases should be prosecuted in accordance with principles of effective case management. For example, in a case involving multiple suspects, prosecution might be reserved for the main participants in order to avoid excessively long and complex proceedings.

g) **Do sources of information require protecting?**

- In cases where public interest immunity does not apply, special care should be taken when proceeding with a prosecution where details may need to be made public that could harm sources of information, ongoing investigations, international relations or national security. It is essential that such cases are kept under continuing review.

THE THRESHOLD TEST

5.1. In limited circumstances, where the Full Code Test is not met, the Threshold Test may be applied to charge a suspect. The seriousness or circumstances of the case must justify the making of an immediate charging decision, and there must be substantial grounds to object to bail.

5.2. There must be a rigorous examination of the five conditions of the Threshold Test, to ensure that it is only applied when necessary and that cases are not charged prematurely. All five conditions must be met before the Threshold Test can be applied. Where any of the conditions are not met, there is no need to consider any of the other conditions, as the Threshold Test cannot be applied and the suspect cannot be charged.

First condition – There are reasonable grounds to suspect that the person to be charged has committed the offence

5.3. Prosecutors must be satisfied, on an objective assessment of the evidence, that there are reasonable grounds to suspect that the person to be charged has committed the offence. The assessment must consider the impact of any defence or information that the suspect has put forward or on which they might rely.

5.4. In determining whether there are reasonable grounds to suspect, prosecutors must consider all of the material or information available, whether in evidential format or otherwise. Prosecutors must be satisfied that the material to be relied on at this stage is capable of being:

- put into an admissible format for presentation in court;
- reliable; and
- credible.

Second condition – Further evidence can be obtained to provide a realistic prospect of conviction

5.5. Prosecutors must be satisfied that there are reasonable grounds to believe that the continuing investigation will provide further evidence, within a reasonable period of time, so that when all the evidence is considered together, including material which may point away from as well as towards a particular suspect, it is capable of establishing a realistic prospect of conviction in accordance with the Full Code Test.

5.6. The likely further evidence must be identifiable and not merely speculative.

5.7. In reaching this decision prosecutors must consider:

- the nature, extent and admissibility of any likely further evidence and the impact it will have on the case;
- the charges that all the evidence will support;
- the reasons why the evidence is not already available;
- the time required to obtain the further evidence, including whether it could be obtained within any available detention period; and
- whether the delay in applying the Full Code Test is reasonable in all the circumstances.

Third condition – The seriousness or the circumstances of the case justifies the making of an immediate charging decision

5.8. The seriousness and the circumstances of the case should be assessed in relation to the alleged offending and should be linked to the level of risk created by granting bail.

Fourth condition – There are continuing substantial grounds to object to bail in accordance with the Bail Act 1976 and in all the circumstances of the case it is proper to do so

5.9. This determination must be based on a proper risk assessment, which reveals that the suspect is not suitable to be bailed, even with substantial conditions. For example, a dangerous suspect who poses a serious risk of harm to a particular person or the public, or a suspect who poses a serious risk of absconding or interfering with witnesses. Prosecutors should not accept, without careful enquiry, any unjustified or unsupported assertions about risk if release on bail were to take place.

Fifth condition – It is in the public interest to charge the suspect

5.10. Prosecutors must apply the public interest stage of the Full Code Test based on the information available at that time.

REVIEWING THE THRESHOLD TEST

5.11. A decision to charge under the Threshold Test must be kept under review. The prosecutor should be proactive to secure from the police the identified outstanding evidence or other material in accordance with an agreed timetable. The evidence must be regularly assessed to ensure that the charge is still appropriate and that continued objection to bail is justified. The Full Code Test must be applied as soon as the anticipated further evidence or material is received and, in any event, in Crown Court cases, usually before the formal service of the prosecution case.

SELECTION OF CHARGES

6.1. Prosecutors should select charges which:

- reflect the seriousness and extent of the offending;
- give the court adequate powers to sentence and impose appropriate post-conviction orders;
- allow a confiscation order to be made in appropriate cases, where a defendant has benefitted from criminal conduct; and
- enable the case to be presented in a clear and simple way.

6.2. This means that prosecutors may not always choose or continue with the most serious charge where there is a choice and the interests of justice are met by selecting the lesser charge.

6.3. Prosecutors should never proceed with more charges than are necessary just to encourage a defendant to plead guilty to a few. In the same way, they should never proceed with a more serious charge just to encourage a defendant to plead guilty to a less serious one.

6.4. Prosecutors should not change the charge simply because of the decision made by the court or the defendant about where the case will be heard.

6.5. Prosecutors must take account of any relevant change in circumstances as the case progresses after charge.

OUT-OF-COURT DISPOSALS

7.1. An out-of-court disposal may take the place of a prosecution if it is an appropriate response to the offender and/or the seriousness and consequences of the offending.

7.2. Prosecutors must follow any relevant guidance when asked to advise on or authorise an out-of-court disposal, including any appropriate regulatory proceedings, a punitive or civil penalty, or other disposal. They should ensure that the appropriate evidential standard for the specific out-of-court disposal is met including, where required, a clear admission of guilt, and that the public interest would be properly served by such a disposal.

COURT VENUE

8.1. Prosecutors must have regard to the guidelines on sentencing and allocation when making submissions to the magistrates' court about where the defendant should be tried.

8.2. Speed must never be the only reason for asking for a case to stay in the magistrates' court. But prosecutors should consider the effect of any likely delay if a case is sent to the Crown Court, including the possible effect on any victim or witness.

8.3. Prosecutors should bear in mind that if confiscation proceedings are required, these may only take place in the Crown Court. Summary proceedings may be committed for that purpose, where appropriate.

Venue for Trial in Cases Involving Children and Young People

8.4. Prosecutors must bear in mind that children and young people (under 18s) should be tried in the youth court wherever possible. It is the court which is best designed to meet their specific needs. A trial of a child or young person in the Crown Court should be reserved for the most serious cases or where the interests of justice require a child or young person to be jointly tried with an adult.

ACCEPTING GUILTY PLEAS

9.1. Defendants may want to plead guilty to some, but not all, of the charges. Alternatively, they may want to plead guilty to a different, possibly less serious, charge because they are admitting only part of the crime.

9.2. Prosecutors should only accept the defendant's plea if:

- the court is able to pass a sentence that matches the seriousness of the offending, particularly where there are aggravating features;
- it enables the court to make a confiscation order in appropriate cases, where a defendant has benefitted from criminal conduct; and
- it provides the court with adequate powers to impose other ancillary orders, bearing in mind that these can be made with some offences but not with others.

9.3. Particular care must be taken when considering pleas which would enable the defendant to avoid the imposition of a mandatory minimum sentence.

9.4. Prosecutors must never accept a guilty plea just because it is convenient.

9.5. In considering whether the pleas offered are acceptable, prosecutors should ensure that the interests and, where possible, the views of the victim, or in appropriate cases the views of the victim's family, are taken into account when deciding whether it is in the public interest to accept the plea. However, the decision rests with the prosecutor.

9.6. It must be made clear to the court on what basis any plea is advanced and accepted. In cases where a defendant pleads guilty to the charges but on the basis of facts that are different from the prosecution case, and where this may significantly affect sentence, the court should be invited to hear evidence to determine what happened, and then sentence on that basis.

9.7. Where a defendant has previously indicated that they will ask the court to take an offence into consideration when sentencing, but then declines to admit that offence at court, prosecutors will consider whether a prosecution is required for that offence. Prosecutors should explain to the defence advocate and the court that the prosecution of that offence may be subject to further review, in consultation with the police or other investigators wherever possible.

RECONSIDERING A PROSECUTION DECISION

10.1. People should be able to rely on decisions taken by the CPS. Normally, if the CPS tells a suspect or defendant that there will not be a prosecution, or that the prosecution has been stopped, the case will not start again. But occasionally there are cases where the CPS will overturn a decision not to prosecute or to deal with the case by way of an out-of-court disposal or when it will restart the prosecution, particularly if the case is serious.

10.2. These cases include:

- cases where a further review of the original decision shows that it was wrong and, in order to maintain confidence in the criminal justice system, a prosecution should be brought despite the earlier decision;
- cases which are stopped so that further anticipated evidence, which is likely to become available in the fairly near future, can be collected and prepared. In these cases, the prosecutor will tell the defendant that the prosecution may well start again;
- cases which are not prosecuted or are stopped because of a lack of evidence but where more significant evidence is discovered later; and
- cases involving a death in which a review following the findings of an inquest concludes that a prosecution should be brought, notwithstanding any earlier decision not to prosecute.

10.3. Victims may seek a review of certain CPS decisions not to start a prosecution or to stop a prosecution, under the Victims' Right to Review Scheme.

Appendix B

Attorney General's Guidelines on Disclosure For investigators, prosecutors and defence practitioners 2020

December 2020

FOREWORD

Proper disclosure of unused material remains a crucial part of a fair trial and is essential to avoiding miscarriages of justice. Disclosure remains one of the most important and complex issues in the criminal justice system, and it is a priority for this Government to encourage improvements in disclosure practice in order to ensure the disclosure regime operates effectively, fairly and justly.

In November 2018, the Attorney General's *Review of the efficiency and effectiveness of disclosure in the criminal justice system* ('the Review') highlighted significant concerns with the culture around disclosure, engagement between prosecutors, investigators and defence practitioners, and the challenge of the exponential increase in digital data. The Review made a series of practical recommendations, crucially recognising that the systemic nature of the problem would demand a system-wide approach to improve disclosure obligations. These recommendations included: earlier engagement between the prosecution and defence, harnessing the use of technology, and culture change.

We are pleased to publish a revised version of the Attorney General's Guidelines on Disclosure and CPIA Code of Practice, which have been prepared following the recommendations made in the Review. These documents have been prepared so that they complement each other.

The Rt. Hon. Suella Braverman QC MP Attorney General

The Rt. Hon. Robert Buckland QC MP Lord Chancellor

INTRODUCTION

These Guidelines are issued by the Attorney General for investigators, prosecutors and defence practitioners on the application of the disclosure regime contained in the Criminal Procedure and Investigations Act 1996 ('CPIA') Code of Practice Order 2020.

These Guidelines replace the existing Attorney General's Guidelines on Disclosure issued in 2013 and the Supplementary Guidelines on Digital Material issued in 2013, which is an annex to the general guidelines.

The Guidelines outline the high level principles which should be followed when the disclosure regime is applied throughout England and Wales. They are not designed to be an unequivocal statement of the law at any one time, nor are they a substitute for a thorough understanding of the relevant legislation, codes of practice, case law and procedure.

IMPORTANT PRINCIPLES

1. Every accused person has a right to a fair trial. This right is a fundamental part of our legal system and is guaranteed by Article 6 of the European Convention on Human Rights (ECHR). The disclosure process secures the right to a fair trial.

2. The statutory framework for criminal investigations and disclosure is contained in the Criminal Procedure and Investigations Act 1996 (the CPIA 1996). The CPIA 1996 is an important part of the system that ensures criminal investigations and trials are conducted in a fair, objective and thorough manner.

3. A fair trial does not require consideration of irrelevant material. It does not require irrelevant material to be obtained or reviewed. It should not involve spurious applications or arguments which aim to divert the trial process from examining the real issues before the court.

4. The statutory disclosure regime does not require the prosecutor to make available to the accused either neutral material or material which is adverse to the accused. This material may be listed on the schedule, alerting the accused to its existence, but does not need to be disclosed: prosecutors should not disclose material which they are not required to, as this would overburden the participants in the trial process, divert attention away from the relevant issues and may lead to unjustifiable delays. **Disclosure should be completed in a thinking manner, in light of the issues in the case, and not simply as a schedule completing exercise**. Prosecutors need to think about what the case is about, what the likely issues for trial are going to be and how this affects the reasonable lines of inquiry, what material is relevant, and whether material meets the test for disclosure.

5. There will always be a number of participants in prosecutions and investigations. Communication within the prosecution team is vital to ensure that all disclosure issues are given sufficient attention by the right person. The respective roles of an investigator, the officer in charge of an investigation, disclosure officer, and prosecutor are set out in the CPIA Code.

6. A full log of disclosure decisions and the reasons for those decisions must be kept on file and made available to the prosecution team. Any prosecutor must be able to see and understand previous disclosure decisions before carrying out their continuous review function.

7. The role of the reviewing lawyer is central to ensuring that all members of the prosecution team are aware of their role and their duties. Where prosecution advocates are instructed, they should be provided with clear written instructions about disclosure and provided with copies of any unused material which has been disclosed to the defence.

8. Investigators and disclosure officers must be fair and objective and must work together with prosecutors to ensure that disclosure obligations are met. Investigators and disclosure officers should be familiar with the CPIA Code of Practice – in particular their obligations to **retain and record** the relevant material, to **review** it and to **reveal** it to the prosecutor (see paragraphs 3-7 of the Code).

9. Investigators and disclosure officers should be deployed on cases which are commensurate with their training, skills and experience. The conduct of an investigation provides the foundation for the entire case, and may even impact on linked cases. The specific strategy and approach to disclosure that will be taken must always be considered at the start of each investigation.

10. Where there are a number of disclosure officers assigned to a case there should be a lead disclosure officer who is the focus for enquiries and whose responsibility it is to ensure that the investigator's disclosure obligations are complied with. Regular case conferences should be held, as required, to ensure that prosecutors are apprised of all relevant developments. Full records, including detailed minutes, should be kept of any such meetings. The parties involved should agree at the outset whose responsibility it will be to record the case conferences.

The balance between the right to a fair trial (Article 6 of the European Convention of Human Rights) and the right to private and family life (Article 8 of the European Convention of Human Rights)

11. Investigators and prosecutors need to be aware of the delicate questions which arise when both the right to a fair trial and the privacy of complainants and witnesses are engaged.

12. Fulfilling disclosure obligations is part of ensuring a fair trial in accordance with Article 6 of the ECHR. To comply with Article 6, during the course of an investigation, the investigator or prosecutor may decide that it is necessary to request and/or process personal or private information from a complainant or witness to pursue a reasonable line of inquiry; this includes, but is not limited to, digital material.

13. When seeking to obtain and review such material, investigators and prosecutors should be aware that these lines of inquiry may engage that individual's Article 8 rights and those rights in respect of other parties within that material. Such material may also include sensitive data. When seeking to satisfy their disclosure obligations in these circumstances, investigators and prosecutors should apply the following principles:

    a. Collecting and/or processing personal or private material can only be done when in accordance with the law, strictly necessary, and proportionate.

    b. In order to be in accordance with the law and strictly necessary, an investigator must be pursuing a reasonable line of inquiry in seeking to obtain the material. What constitutes a reasonable line of inquiry may be informed by others, including the prosecutor and the defendant. Seeking the personal or private information of a complainant or witness will not be a reasonable line of inquiry in every case – an assessment of reasonableness is required (see below for an example).

    c. The assessment of reasonableness must be made on a case-by-case basis and regard may be had to:

        (i) the prospect of obtaining relevant material; and

        (ii) what the perceived relevance of that material is, having regard to the identifiable facts and issues in the individual case;

d. If, by following a reasonable line of inquiry, it becomes necessary to obtain personal or private material, investigators will also need to consider:

   (i) what review is required;

   (ii) how the review of this material should be conducted;

   (iii) what is the least intrusive method which will nonetheless secure relevant material;

   (iv) are particular parameters for searching best suited to the identification of relevant material;

   (v) is provision of the material in its entirety to the investigator strictly necessary; or alternatively, could the material be obtained from other sources, or by the investigator viewing and/or capturing the material in situ? An incremental approach should be taken to the degree of intrusion.

e. The rationale for pursuing the reasonable line of inquiry and the scope of the review it necessitates should be open and transparent. It should be capable of articulation by the investigator making the decision. It should provide the basis for:

   (i) consultation with the prosecutor,

   (ii) engagement with the defence and,

   (iii) the provision of information to the witness about how their material is to be handled.

f. The refusal by a witness to provide private or personal material requires an investigator and prosecutor to consider the information the witness has been provided (and could be provided) with regard to the use of their personal material, the reasons for refusal, and how the trial process could address the absence of the material.

g. Disclosure of such material to the defence is in accordance with the law and necessary if, but only if, the material meets the disclosure test in the CPIA 1996. Personal information which does not meet this test but is contained within the material to be disclosed should be redacted.

h. Where there is a conflict between both of these rights, investigators and prosecutors should bear in mind that the right to a fair trial is an absolute right. Where prosecutors and investigators work within the framework provided by the CPIA, any unavoidable intrusion into privacy rights is likely to be justified, so long as any intrusion is no more than necessary.

For retention of data, see paragraphs 21-25 of Annex A on Digital Material and paragraph 5(a) and (b) of the Code.

Example

There will be cases where there is no requirement for the police to take the devices of a complainant/witness or others at all, and no requirement for any examination to be undertaken.

Examples of this could include sexual offences committed opportunistically against strangers, or historic allegations where there is considered to be no prospect that the complainant's phone will contain any material relevant to the period in which the conduct is said to have occurred and/or the complainant through age or other circumstances did not have access to a phone at that time.

However, decisions will depend on the facts of the case in question. For example, in the case of a sexual offence committed opportunistically against a stranger, a mobile phone could contain first complaint evidence. Investigators should always carefully consider what is relevant for the case in question.

A case might, for example, involve a complainant contacting the police to make an allegation of an offence against a person they had met that same day. The suspect may accept that they met the complainant but deny the allegation. The complainant and suspect communicated on a single medium. The investigator may consider it is a reasonable line of enquiry to view the messages from the day on which the two persons met as, before and after, they are highly likely to be relevant. They may contain material about what was expected or not expected when complainant and suspect met, the nature of their relationship, and the response after they met, all of which may cast light on the complainant's account and the suspect's account. That is unlikely to require the investigator taking custody of the phone or obtaining a large volume of data. If, by way of example and contrast, the complainant alleged coercive and controlling behaviour over a period of years, including manipulative conduct over various platforms, a larger quantity of data may be relevant and require review and retention by the investigator by different means.

THE INVESTIGATION

14. Consideration of disclosure issues is an integral part of an investigation and is not something that should be considered in isolation.

15. Investigators should approach the investigation with a view to establishing what actually happened. They are to be fair and objective.

16. The following diagram illustrates how material that forms part of an investigation may be categorised and consequently treated. Further information on sensitive material can be found at paragraph 65.

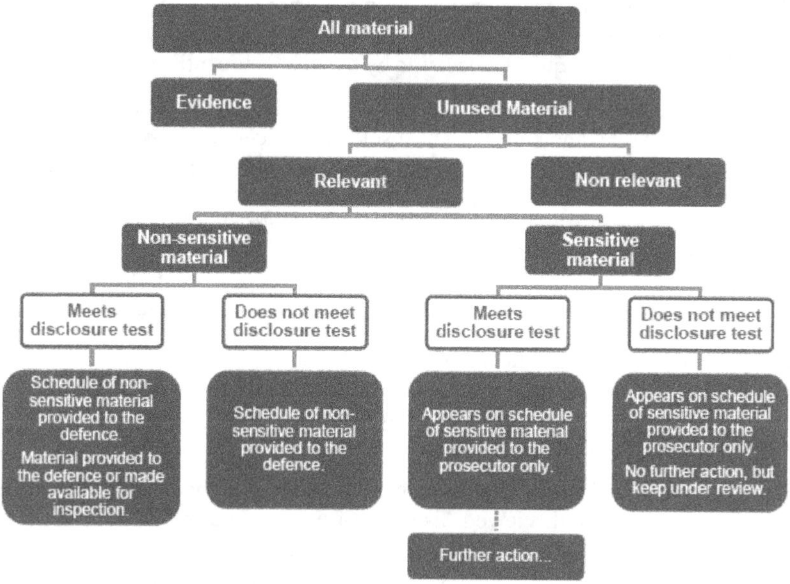

17. Investigators should ensure that all reasonable lines of inquiry are investigated, whether they point towards or away from the suspect. What is 'reasonable' will depend on the context of the case. A fair investigation does not mean an endless investigation. Investigators and disclosure officers must give thought to defining, and articulating the limits of the scope of their investigations. When assessing what is reasonable, thought should be given to what is likely to be obtained as a result of the line of inquiry and how it can be obtained. An investigator may seek the advice of the prosecutor when considering which lines of inquiry should be pursued where appropriate.

18. When conducting an investigation, an investigator should always have in mind their obligation to retain and record all relevant material. Material which is presumed to meet the test for disclosure, as set out in paragraph 87 of these guidelines, must always be retained and recorded. All relevant material must be retained, whereas non-relevant material does not need to be retained.

The definition of relevant material

Material may be relevant to an investigation if it appears to an investigator, or to the officer in charge of an investigation, or to the disclosure officer, that it has some bearing on any offence under investigation or any person being investigated, or on the surrounding circumstances of the case, unless it is incapable of having any impact on the case.

19. The decision as to relevance requires an exercise of judgment and, although some material may plainly be relevant or non-relevant, ultimately this requires a decision by the disclosure officer or investigator.

20. Disclosure officers and/or investigators must inspect, view, listen to, or search all relevant material. The disclosure officer must provide a personal declaration that this task has been completed. In some cases a detailed examination of every item of material seized would be disproportionate. In these cases the disclosure officer can apply search techniques using the principles contained in Annex A. Whatever the approach taken by disclosure officers in examining material, it is crucial that disclosure officers record their reasons for a particular approach in writing.

21. Disclosure officers should seek the advice and assistance of prosecutors when in doubt as to their responsibility as early as possible. They must deal expeditiously with requests by the prosecutor for further information on material, which may lead to disclosure.

22. Where prosecutors have reason to believe that the disclosure officer has not inspected, viewed, listened to or searched relevant material, or has not done so sufficiently or has not articulated a reason for doing so, they should raise this issue with the disclosure officer and request that it is addressed. Prosecutors should also assist disclosure officers and investigators in defining the parameters of review and the methodology to be adopted.

23. It may become apparent to an investigator that some material obtained in the course of an investigation, either because it was considered to be potentially relevant, or because it was inextricably linked to material that was relevant, is in fact incapable of impacting on the case. It is not necessary to retain such material. However, the investigator should also exercise considerable caution in reaching that conclusion. The investigator should be particularly mindful of the fact that some investigations continue over some time. Material that is incapable of impact may change over time and it may not be possible to foresee what the issues in the case will be. The advice of the prosecutor may be sought where necessary. Ultimately, however, the decision on whether to retain material is one for the investigator, and should always be based on their assessment of the relevance of the material and the likelihood of it having any impact on the case in future.

24. Prosecutors must be alert to the need to provide advice to and, where necessary, probe actions taken by the investigator to ensure that disclosure obligations are capable of being met. This should include advice on potential further reasonable lines of inquiry. There should be no aspects of an investigation about which prosecutors are unable to ask probing questions.

25. In some investigations it may be appropriate for the officer in charge of the investigation to seek engagement with the defence at the pre-charge stage. This is likely to be where it is possible that such engagement will lead to the defence volunteering additional information which may assist

in identifying new lines of inquiry. Annex B sets out the process for any such pre-charge engagement.

Third party material

26. Third party material is material held by a person, organisation, or government department other than the investigator and prosecutor, either within the UK or outside the UK. Third parties are not directly involved in the case in question, but may hold information relevant to it.

27. The CPIA Code and these guidelines make clear the obligation on the investigator to pursue all reasonable lines of inquiry in relation to material held by third parties within the UK.

28. It is for investigators, in consultation or discussion with prosecutors where appropriate, to pursue all reasonable lines of inquiry. Prosecutors can advise on additional reasonable lines of inquiry and should satisfy themselves that such reasonable lines of inquiry have been pursued.

29. If as a result of the duty to pursue all reasonable lines of inquiry, the investigator or prosecutor obtains or receives material from a third party, then it must be dealt with in accordance with the CPIA 1996, (i.e. the prosecutor must disclose material if it meets the disclosure tests, subject to any public interest immunity claim). The person who has an interest in the material (the third party) may make representations to the court concerning public interest immunity (see section 16 of the CPIA 1996).

30. Material not in the possession of an investigator or prosecutor falls outside the CPIA. In such cases these guidelines prescribe the approach to be taken to disclosure of material held by third parties.

Material held by Government departments

31. During an investigation or prosecution it may become apparent that a Government department or another Crown body has material that may be relevant to an issue in the case.

32. The investigator or prosecutor should inform the Government department or Crown body at the earliest opportunity of the nature of the case and the relevant issues in the case, and ask whether it has any relevant material. They should assist the Government department or Crown body in understanding what may be relevant in the context of the case in question.

33. Crown Servants have a duty to support the administration of justice and should take reasonable steps to identify and consider such material. This extends to revealing to the investigator or prosecutor the extent of the searches conducted and the existence of any information which they believe may be relevant to the issues in the case, to supply them with that information unless it is protected to the issues in the case, and to supply them with that information unless it is protected in law, subject to legal professional privilege or attracts public interest immunity.

34. If access is denied to relevant material, the investigator or prosecutor should consider the reasons given by the Government department or Crown body and what, if any, further steps might be taken to obtain the material. The final decision on further steps rests with the prosecutor.

35. Investigators and prosecutors cannot be regarded to be in constructive possession of material held by Government departments or Crown bodies simply by virtue of their status as Government departments or Crown bodies.

36. The steps taken to identify and obtain relevant material held by a Government department or Crown body should be recorded by the investigator and the prosecutor.

37. Where appropriate, the defence should be informed of the steps taken to obtain material and the results of the line of inquiry.

Other domestic bodies

38. An investigator, disclosure officer or a prosecutor may believe that a third party (for example a local authority, social services department, hospital, doctor, school, provider of forensic services, or CCTV operator) has material or information which might be relevant to the case. If so, then reasonable steps should be taken to secure and consider the material held by the third party where it appears that such material exists and that it may be relevant to an issue in the case.

39. The investigator, disclosure officer or prosecutor should follow the steps in paragraphs 32, 34 and 36 above when engaging with the relevant domestic body.

40. A third party has no obligation under the CPIA to reveal material to investigators or prosecutors. There is also no duty on the third party to retain material which may be relevant to the investigation and, in some circumstances, the third party may not be aware of the investigation or prosecution.

41. If access to the material is refused and, despite the reasons given for refusal of access, it is still believed that it is reasonable to seek production of the material or information and that the requirements of a witness summons are satisfied (or any other relevant power), then the prosecutor or investigator should apply for the summons causing a representative of the third party to produce the material to court.

42. When the third party material in question is personal data, investigators and prosecutors must refer to paragraphs 11 – 13 of these guidelines to ensure that there is no unjust intrusion of privacy.

43. Further guidance and best practice on obtaining third party material can be found in the Joint Protocol on Third Party Material and Chapter 5 of the CPS Disclosure Manual.

44. The defence should be informed of what steps have been taken to obtain material and what the results of the inquiry have been.

International enquiries

45. The obligations under the CPIA Code to pursue all reasonable lines of inquiry apply to material held overseas.

46. Where it appears that there is relevant material, the investigator or prosecutor must take reasonable steps to obtain it, either informally or by making use of the powers contained in the Crime (International Co-operation) Act 2003, the Criminal Justice (European Investigation Order) Regulations 2017 and any international conventions.

47. There may be cases where a foreign state or court refuses to make the material available to the investigator or prosecutor. There may be other cases where the foreign state, though willing to show the material to investigators, will not allow the material to be copied or otherwise made available and the courts of the foreign state will not order its provision.

48. It is for these reasons that there is no absolute duty on the prosecutor to disclose relevant material held overseas by entities not subject to the jurisdiction of the courts in England and Wales. However, consideration should be given to whether the type of material believed to be held can be provided to the defence.

49. The obligation on the investigator and prosecutor under the CPIA Code is to take reasonable steps. Where investigators are allowed to examine the files of a foreign state but are not allowed to take copies, take notes or list the documents held, there is no breach by the prosecution in its duty of disclosure by reason of its failure to obtain such material, provided reasonable steps have been taken to try and obtain it. Prosecutors have a margin of consideration as to what steps are appropriate in the particular case, but prosecutors must be alive to their duties and there may be some circumstances where these duties cannot be met. Whether or not a prosecutor has taken reasonable steps is for the court to determine in each case if the matter is raised.

50. Where it is apparent during the investigation that there may be relevant material held overseas then investigators and prosecutors should consider engaging with the defence at the pre-charge stage, applying the principles contained in Annex B, to ensure that all reasonable lines of inquiry are followed.

51. It is important that the position taken in relation to any material held overseas is clearly set out in a document such as a disclosure management document (DMD) so that the court and the defence know what the position is. Further information on DMDs can be found below, at paragraph 92.

52. In the DMD, investigators and prosecutors must record and explain the situation and set out, insofar as they are permitted by the foreign state, such information as they can and the steps they have taken to obtain it.

53. The defence should be informed of what steps have been taken to obtain material and what the results of the enquiry have been.

Electronic material

54. The exponential increase in the use of technology in society means that many routine investigations are increasingly likely to have to engage with digital material of some form. It is not only in large and complex investigations where there may be large quantities of such material. When dealing with large quantities of digital material prosecutors and investigators should apply the principles contained in Annex A to these guidelines.

55. Where investigations involve a large quantity of digital material it may be impossible for investigators to examine every item of such material individually. Therefore there should be no expectation that this should happen. Investigators and disclosure officers will need to decide how best to pursue a reasonable line of inquiry in relation to the relevant digital material, and ensure that the extent and manner of the examination are appropriate to the issues in the case. In reaching any such decisions, investigators and disclosure officers must bear in mind the overriding obligation to ensure a fair trial of any suspect who is charged and the requirement to provide disclosure in the trial process.

56. Prosecutors and investigators must ensure that any line of inquiry pursued in relation to the digital devices of victims and witnesses are reasonable in the context of the likely issues in the case. Digital devices should not be obtained as a matter of course and the decision to obtain and examine a digital device will be a fact-specific decision to be made in each and every case[14]. Where digital devices are obtained, if it becomes apparent that they do not contain relevant material they should be returned at the earliest opportunity.

57. Prosecutors should be consulted, where appropriate, to agree a strategy for dealing with digital material. This strategy should be set out in a disclosure management document (DMD) and shared with the defence at the appropriate time.

REVELATION OF MATERIAL TO A PROSECUTOR

58. Prosecutors only have knowledge of the matters which are revealed to them by investigators and disclosure officers. The schedules are the means by which that revelation takes place. Therefore it is crucial that the schedules detail all of the relevant material and that the material is adequately described. This process will also enable defence practitioners to become appraised of relevant material at the appropriate stage of the

investigation. More detail on what constitutes relevant material can be found here.

59. Schedules must be completed in a form which not only reveals sufficient information to the prosecutor, but which demonstrates a transparent and thinking approach to the disclosure exercise. The speed with which the schedule is produced should not reduce the quality of the material contained therein.

60. Descriptions on the schedules must be clear and accurate and must contain sufficient detail to enable the prosecutor to make an informed decision on disclosure. Abbreviations and acronyms should be avoided as they risk significant material being overlooked.

61. Investigators and disclosure officers must ensure that material which is presumed to meet the test for disclosure, as set out in paragraph 87 of these guidelines and paragraph 6.6 of the CPIA Code, is placed on the schedules. The requirement to schedule this material is in addition to the requirement to schedule all other relevant unused material.

62. Where relevant unused material has been omitted from the schedule or where material is not described sufficiently, and the prosecutor asks the disclosure officer to rectify the schedule, the disclosure officer must comply with this request in a timely manner.

63. Disclosure officers must bring to the prosecutor's attention any material which is potentially capable of meeting the test for disclosure. This material should be provided to the prosecutor along with the reasons why it is thought to meet the test.

64. Disclosure officers must also draw material to the attention of the prosecutor for consideration where they have doubt as to whether it might reasonably be considered capable of undermining the prosecution case or of assisting the case for the accused.

Revelation of sensitive material

What is sensitive material?

65. Sensitive material is material that, if disclosed, would give rise to a real risk of serious prejudice to an important public interest. Investigators must ensure that all relevant unused sensitive material is retained, reviewed and revealed to the prosecutor. Sensitive material should be revealed to a prosecutor on a separate schedule to the non-sensitive material.

Examples of sensitive material can be found in paragraph 6.14 of the CPIA Code.

66. When making a decision about the sensitivity of an item, investigators should have regard to the types of material listed in paragraph 6.14 of the

CPIA Code. The disclosure officer must ensure that the sensitive material schedule include the reasons why it is asserted that items on the schedule are considered sensitive.

67. Where a document contains a mix of sensitive and non-sensitive material, the sensitive material must be redacted, with a copy of the redacted document placed on the non-sensitive unused material schedule and the original placed on the sensitive schedule.

68. Investigators must ensure that the descriptions of sensitive unused material are sufficiently clear to enable the prosecutor to make an informed decision as to whether or not the material itself should be viewed, to the extent possible without compromising the confidentiality of the information.

69. Prosecutors must carefully review the sensitive unused material schedule in order to be satisfied that there are no omissions, that the items have been correctly identified as sensitive, and that the items are adequately described. If a prosecutor identifies that a schedule is inadequate, the investigator must provide an adequate schedule as soon as possible. This may involve items being moved from the sensitive unused material schedule to the non-sensitive unused material schedule.

The timing of revelation

70. In order to support prosecutors' assessment of the impact of unused material on any proposed prosecution, it is essential that prosecutors are provided with the schedule of unused material at an early stage, as well as any material which the disclosure officer considers potentially capable of meeting the test for disclosure. This will allow for a thorough review of the case, and will enable the prosecutor to consider what the disclosure strategy should be.

71. The timing of revelation of material should be in accordance with paragraph 7.1 of the Code. The point at which the case file is submitted to the CPS will depend on the circumstances of the charging decision and on the anticipated plea:

    a. Where the police are seeking a charging decision under the Full Code Test from the CPS, and it is anticipated that the defendant will plead not guilty, the unused material schedules should be provided to the prosecutor by the disclosure officer at the same time as seeking this charging decision.

    b. Where the police have charged a suspect on the Full Code Test under the arrangements contained in the Director's Guidance on Charging, and a not guilty plea is anticipated, then the unused material schedule should be provided to the prosecutor at the point at which the case file is submitted to the CPS.

    c. In all other cases the disclosure officer must provide the schedules as soon as possible after a not guilty plea has either been indicated or entered.

72. There may be instances where an investigator is seeking a charging decision on the Full Code Test and anticipating a not guilty plea, but where it is not feasible to provide the unused material schedules to the prosecutor at the same time as seeking a charging decision. This may be the case where an arrest is not planned, and the suspect cannot be bailed.

73. For large and complex investigations, particularly those conducted by the Serious Fraud Office, it is recognised that the preparation of schedules continues beyond the point of charge due to the quantity and complexity of data to be analysed, and that it may not be feasible or necessary to provide the schedules at the same time that a charging decision is sought.

74. Disclosure officers should apply the criteria contained in the Director's Guidance on Charging when making a decision about a suspect's likely plea, and must follow any additional guidance provided by the prosecutor.

THE CHARGING DECISION

75. Prosecutors must ensure that all reasonable lines of inquiry likely to affect the application of the Full Code Test have been pursued before the Test is applied, unless the prosecutor is satisfied that any further evidence or material is unlikely to affect the application of the Full Code Test. The failure to pursue reasonable lines of inquiry may result in the application of the Full Code Test being deferred, or in a decision that the Test cannot be met.

76. If a decision is made to charge a case under the Threshold Test, then prosecutors and investigators need to be proactive in ensuring that any outstanding lines of inquiry are pursued and that the case is kept under continuous review.

COMMON LAW DISCLOSURE

77. A prosecutor's statutory duty of disclosure applies from the point of a not guilty plea in the magistrates' court and from the point a case is sent to the Crown Court. However prosecutors must also consider their duties under the common law, which apply at all stages of a case, from charge to sentence and post-conviction (see paragraphs 137 and 138), and regardless of anticipated or actual plea.

78. These duties may require the prosecutor to disclose material to the accused outside the statutory scheme in accordance with the interests of justice and fairness. An example of this is where it would assist the accused in the preparation of the defence case, prior to plea and regardless of anticipated plea. This would include material which would assist in the making of a bail application, material which may enable the accused to make an early application to stay the proceedings as an abuse of process, material which may enable the accused to make representations about the trial venue or a lesser charge, or material which would enable an accused to prepare for trial effectively.

INITIAL DISCLOSURE

79. The defence must be provided with copies of, or access to, any prosecution material not previously disclosed, which might reasonably be considered capable of undermining the case for the prosecution against the accused, or of assisting the case for the accused. Paragraphs 100-107 of these Guidelines contain guidance as to when initial disclosure should be served.

80. In order for the prosecutor to comply with their duty of initial disclosure they must analyse the case for the prosecution, the defence case, and the likely trial issues. A prosecutor can anticipate the likely issues on the basis of information available (such as any explanation provided by the accused in interview).

81. The prosecutor must also encourage dialogue and prompt engagement with the defence about the likely issues for trial.

82. The defence are under a duty to engage with the prosecutor in order to aid understanding about the defence case and the likely issues for trial at this early stage. This engagement assists in ensuring compliance with the overriding objective of the Criminal Procedure Rules.

83. Prosecutors must review schedules prepared by disclosure officers thoroughly at an early stage and must be alert to the possibility that relevant material may exist which has not been revealed to them or material included which should not have been. If no schedules are provided, if there are apparent omissions from the schedules, or if documents or other items are inadequately described or are unclear, the prosecutor must request properly completed schedules from the investigator. Investigators must comply with any such request. A log of such communications should be kept by the prosecutor.

84. In deciding whether material satisfies the disclosure test, consideration should include:

    a. The use that might be made of it in cross-examination;

    b. Its capacity to support submissions that could lead to:

        i. The exclusion of evidence;

        ii. A stay of proceedings, where the material is required to allow a proper application to be made;

        iii. A court or tribunal finding that any public authority had acted incompatibly with the accused's rights under the European Convention of Human Rights;

    c. Its capacity to suggest an explanation or partial explanation of the accused's actions;

    d. Its capacity to undermine the reliability or credibility of a prosecution witness;

    e. The capacity of the material to have a bearing on scientific or medical evidence in the case.

85. Material relating to the accused's mental or physical health, intellectual capacity, or to any ill treatment which the accused may have suffered when in the investigator's custody is likely to meet the test for disclosure.

86. Material should not be viewed in isolation as, whilst items taken alone may not be reasonably considered capable of undermining the prosecution case or assisting the case for the accused, several items together can have that effect.

Material which is likely to meet the test for disclosure

87. The following material is likely to include information which meets the test for disclosure:

   a) records which are derived from tapes or recordings of telephone messages (for example 999 calls) containing descriptions of an alleged offence or offender;

   b) any incident logs relating to the allegation;

   c) contemporaneous records of the incident, such as:

      - crime reports and crime report forms;
      - an investigation log;
      - any record or note made by an investigator (including police notebook entries and other handwritten notes) on which they later make a statement or which relates to contact with suspects, victims or witnesses;
      - an account of an incident or information relevant to an incident noted by an investigator in manuscript or electronically;
      - records of actions carried out by officers (such as house-to-house interviews, CCTV or forensic enquiries) noted by a police officer in manuscript or electronically;
      - CCTV footage, or other imagery, of the incident in action;

   d) the defendant's custody record or voluntary attendance record;

   e) any previous accounts made by a complainant or by any other witnesses;

   f) interview records (written records, or audio or video tapes, of interviews with actual or potential witnesses or suspects);

   g) any material casting doubt on the reliability of a witness e. g. relevant previous convictions and relevant cautions of any prosecution witnesses and any co-accused.

88. This list is reflected in paragraph 5.4 and 6.6 of the Code. This material, in addition to all other material which may be relevant to an investigation, must be retained and listed on the schedule by the investigator. It is likely that some of this material will need to be redacted (see paragraph 6(c) of the Code and paragraph 65 of these guidelines for redaction and revelation of sensitive material.)

89. As this material is likely to contain information which meets the test for disclosure, prosecutors should start their review of the material with a presumption that this material should be disclosed to the defence. However, in every instance the disclosure test should be applied in a thinking manner.

90. After applying the disclosure test, a prosecutor must record on the unused material schedule whether each item of this material does or does not meet the test for disclosure and they must record the reason for that decision.

91. This list of material is not intended to cause automatic disclosure – investigators and prosecutors should always apply the disclosure test and consider each list of material carefully in the context of the case in question.

Disclosure management document (DMD)

What is a disclosure management document?

92. A disclosure management document (DMD) outlines the strategy and approach taken in relation to disclosure and should be served to the defence and the court at an early stage. DMDs will require careful preparation and presentation which is tailored to the individual case. The investigator should provide information for use in the DMD and the prosecutor should prepare it.

93. A DMD is a living document which should be amended in light of developments in the case and kept up to date as the case progresses. DMDs are intended to assist the court in case management and will also enable the defence to engage from an early stage with the prosecution's proposed approach to disclosure.

94. DMDs may set out:

a. Where prosecutors and investigators operate in an integrated office, an explanation as to how the disclosure responsibilities have been managed.

b. A brief summary of the prosecution case and a statement outlining how the prosecutor's general approach will comply with the CPIA 1996 regime and these guidelines

c. The prosecutor's understanding of the defence case, including information revealed during interview. The prosecutor may wish to explain their understanding of what is in dispute and what is not in dispute, the lines of inquiry that have been pursued in light of these issues, and specific disclosure decisions that have been taken.

d. An outline of the prosecution's general approach to disclosure, which may include detail relating to:

   i. The lines of inquiry pursued, particularly those which may assist the defence.

   ii. The timescales for disclosure and, where relevant, how the review of unused material has been prioritised.

   iii. The method and extent of examination of digital material, in accordance with the Annex A to these guidelines.

   iv. Any potential video footage.

   v. Any linked investigations, including an explanation of the nexus between investigations and any memoranda of understanding and disclosure agreements between investigators.

   vi. Any third party material, including the steps taken to obtain the material.

   vii. Any international material, including the steps taken to obtain the material.

   viii. Credibility of prosecution witnesses (including professional witnesses).

95. In cases heard in the magistrates' court and the youth court, prosecutors should always consider whether or not a disclosure management document (DMD) would be beneficial. DMDs are most likely to be beneficial in cases with the following features:

a. Substantial or complex third party material;

b. Digital material in which parameters of search, examination or analysis have been set;

c. Cases involving international enquiries;

d. Cases where there are linked operations;

e. Non-recent offending;

f. Cases involving material held or sought by the investigation that is susceptible to a claim of legal professional privilege.

96. DMDs should be prepared in all Crown Court cases.

97. In order for the prosecutor to complete a DMD at an early stage, the investigator should, at the point of or prior to charge, provide written details as to the lines of inquiry that have been pursued.

98. Where a DMD has been prepared, it should be served at the same time as initial disclosure.

99. An example template for a DMD is contained in Annex C.

The timing of initial disclosure

100. In all cases it is essential that the prosecution takes a grip on the case and its disclosure requirements at an early stage. Prosecutors must adopt a considered and appropriately resourced approach to providing initial disclosure. Initial disclosure in this context refers to the period post-charge; more detailed timings for this are set out below.

Cases expected to be tried in the magistrates' courts

101. Where a case is charged on the Full Code Test and a not guilty plea is anticipated, initial disclosure should be served in advance of the first hearing.

102. Where a guilty plea was originally anticipated but a not guilty plea is entered then initial disclosure should be served as soon as possible after a not guilty plea is entered.

103. Where a case is charged on the Threshold Test, initial disclosure should be served as soon as possible after the Full Code Test is applied and in accordance with any order made by the court.

Cases sent to the Crown Court for trial

104. Where it is expected that the accused will maintain a not guilty plea, it is encouraged as a matter of best practice for initial disclosure to be served prior to the Plea and Trial Preparation Hearing (PTPH).

105. It is accepted that it may not be appropriate or possible to serve initial disclosure prior to the PTPH for cases charged on the Threshold Test. Where initial disclosure has not been served at the PTPH it should be served as soon as possible after that hearing and in accordance with any direction made by the court.

106. In cases prosecuted by the Serious Fraud Office, or other similarly large or complex cases, it is accepted that full initial disclosure may not be capable of being served prior to the PTPH. In such cases, best practice is to adopt a phased approach to disclosure, ensuring that robust judicial case management during Further Case Management Hearings, and in line with the Criminal Procedure Rules and Criminal Practice Directions, manages the on-going disclosure process. Utilising an initial DMD at the PTPH which outlines the intended plan for onwards

staged disclosure of remaining materials and associated schedules, can be an effective mechanism for this approach and is to adopted where possible.

107. Nothing in these guidelines should undermine the established principles of the Better Case Management Framework.

CASE MANAGEMENT

108. In order for the statutory disclosure regime to work effectively all parties should ensure compliance with the Criminal Procedure Rules. The rules require the court to actively manage the case by identifying the real issues. Each party is obliged to assist the court with this duty.

109. It is important that prosecutors keep a record of all correspondence which relates to disclosure and keep a record of any disclosure decisions made.

Magistrates' court

110. Following a not guilty plea being entered in the magistrates' court, the defence must ensure that the trial issues are clearly identified both in court and on the preparation for effective trial form. Prosecutors should ensure that any issues of dispute that are raised are noted on file. The preparation for effective trial form should be carefully reviewed, alongside the DMD (where this is exists). Consideration of any issues raised in court or on the form will assist in deciding whether any further material undermines the prosecution case or assists the accused.

Crown Court

111. A focus of the Plea and Trial Preparation Hearing (PTPH) must be on the disclosure strategy. This will involve the defence identifying the likely trial issues, a discussion of any additional lines of inquiry, and scrutiny of the DMD.

112. Prosecutors must ensure that the disclosure strategy and any disclosure decisions taken previously are reviewed in light of any issues raised at the PTPH and on the plea and trial preparation form.

113. Where the defence do not feel that the prosecution have adequately discharged their obligations then this must be brought to the court's attention at an early stage. The defence should be proactive in ensuring that any issue is addressed, and must not delay raising these issues until a late stage in the proceedings. The DMD may be relevant in any challenge raised.

114. Where any party has not complied with their obligations, the court will consider giving any direction appropriate to ensure compliance and progression of the case.

Applications for non-disclosure in the public interest

115. The CPIA 1996 allows prosecutors to apply to the court for an order to withhold material which would otherwise fall to be disclosed if disclosure would give rise to a real risk of serious prejudice to an important public interest. Before making such an application, prosecutors should aim to disclose as much of the material as they properly can (for example, by giving the defence redacted or edited copies or summaries). Neutral material or material damaging to the defendant should not be disclosed, and should not be brought to the attention of the court. Only in truly borderline cases should the prosecution seek a judicial ruling on whether material in its possession should be disclosed.

116. Prior to the hearing, the prosecutor and the prosecution advocate must examine all material which is the subject matter of the application and make any necessary enquiries of the investigator. There is an additional duty of candour on the advocate at this hearing, given the defendant will not be present. In order to assist the court, it is best practice for the advocate to prepare a note that is either written in conjunction, or agreed with, the prosecutor and disclosure officer.

117. The investigator must also be frank with the prosecutor about the full extent of the sensitive material. Prior to or at the hearing the court must be provided with full and accurate information about the material.

118. The prosecutor and/or investigator should attend such applications. Section 16 of the CPIA 1996 allows a person claiming to have an interest in the sensitive material to apply to the court for the opportunity to be heard at the application.

119. The prosecutor should carefully consider the series of questions contained in paragraph 36 of *R v H and others* [2004] UKHL 3. These are the questions that the court must address before it makes a decision to withhold material. It is essential that these principles are scrupulously adhered to, to ensure that the procedure for examination of material in the absence of the accused is compliant with Article 6 of the ECHR.

120. If the prosecutor concludes that a fair trial cannot take place because material which satisfies the test for disclosure cannot be disclosed and that this cannot be remedied by an application for non-disclosure in the public interest, through altering the presentation of the case or by any other means, then they should not continue with the case.

THE DEFENCE STATEMENT

121. Defence statements are an integral part of the statutory disclosure regime. A defence statement should help to focus the attention of the prosecutor, court and co-defendants on the relevant issues in order to identify material which may meet the test for disclosure. The defence must serve their defence statement in a timely manner, in accordance with any court directions made.

122. There is no requirement for a defence statement to be served in the magistrates' court but it should be noted that if one is not provided the court does not have a power to hear an application for further prosecution disclosure under section 8 of the CPIA 1996.

123. Defence practitioners should ensure that defence statements are drafted in accordance with the requirements in the CPIA 1996. Defence statements should not make general and unspecified allegations in order to seek far reaching disclosure and should not describe the defence in ambiguous or limited terms (such as self-defence, mistaken identify, consent).

124. It is vital that prosecutors consider defence statements thoroughly. Prosecutors should challenge the lack of (in the Crown Court) or inadequate defence statements in writing, copying the document to the court and the defence and seeking directions from the court to require the provision of an adequate defence statement from the defence.

125. Prosecutors must send a copy of the defence statement to the investigator as soon as reasonably practicable after receipt and, at the same time, provide guidance to the disclosure officer about the key issues. The advice should contain guidance on whether any further reasonable lines of inquiry need to be pursued, guidance on what to look for when reviewing the unused material and guidance on what further material may need to be disclosed. On receipt of a defence statement, disclosure officers must re-review retained unused material and draw to the attention of the prosecutor any material which is potentially capable of meeting the test for disclosure and consider whether any further reasonable lines of inquiry need to be pursued. They should address the matters raised in guidance given by the prosecutor.

126. Defence requests for further disclosure should ordinarily only be answered by the prosecution if the request is relevant to, and directed to, an issue identified in the defence statement. If it is not, then a further or amended defence statement should be sought and obtained by the prosecutor before considering the request for further disclosure.

CONTINUING DISCLOSURE

127. The obligation of continuing disclosure is crucial and particular attention must be paid to understanding the significance of developments in the case on the unused material and earlier disclosure decisions. After service of initial disclosure, a prosecutor must keep under review whether or not there is prosecution material which might reasonably be considered capable of undermining the case for the prosecution against the accused, or of assisting the case for the accused, which has not been previously been disclosed. This obligation is a continuous one, and it can be beneficial for it to take place in tranches, particularly in large and/or complex cases.

128. In particular, prosecutors should consider any issues raised by the defence at the first hearing in the magistrates' court or the PTPH in the Crown Court, as well as during any further hearings and after receipt of a defence statement. Any matters raised on the preparation for effective trial form or the PTPH form should also be carefully considered.

APPLICATIONS FOR DISCLOSURE UNDER SECTION 8 OF THE CPIA

129. An application for disclosure can only be made if the defence have provided an adequate defence statement.

130. Any application for disclosure must describe the material which is subject to the application and explain why there is reasonable cause to believe that the prosecutor has the material and why it meets the test for disclosure.

131. Prosecutors must carefully review any application for disclosure and consider whether any items described in the application meet the test for disclosure. This may require the prosecutor asking the disclosure officer for copies of the items or inspecting the items.

THE TRIAL

132. Prosecutors must ensure that advocates in court are provided with sufficient instructions regarding the disclosure strategy and any disclosure decisions taken.

133. Prosecution advocates should ensure that all material which ought to be disclosed under the CPIA 1996 is disclosed to the defence. Prosecution advocates must ensure that they are fully informed about disclosure so that they are able to make decisions. Prosecution advocates must consider, in every case, whether they can be satisfied that they are in possession of all relevant documentation and that they have been fully instructed regarding disclosure matters. If the advocate considers that further information or action is required then written advice should be provided setting out the aspects that need clarification or action.

134. All decisions regarding disclosure must be kept under review until the conclusion of the trial, whenever possible in consultation with the reviewing prosecutor. The prosecution advocate must in every case specifically consider whether they can satisfactorily discharge the duty of continuing review on the basis of the material supplied already, or whether it is necessary to reconsider the unused material schedule and/or unused material.

135. Prosecution advocates must not abrogate their responsibility under the CPIA 1996 by disclosing material which does not pass the test for disclosure. This is especially so where it is proposed to disclose material engaging Article 8 rights.

136. There is no basis in practice or law for counsel-to-counsel disclosure. It is of critical importance that, even where prosecution counsel is advising and leading on disclosure, the duty to disclose material that meets the test for disclosure remains with the prosecutor. A record of material disclosed made must be kept, not least in the event of an appeal or a re-trial.

MATERIAL RELEVANT TO SENTENCE

137. At sentence, the prosecutor should disclose any material which might reasonably be considered capable of ensuring fairness in the sentencing process. This material could include information which might mitigate the seriousness of the offence or the level of the defendant's involvement.

POST-CONVICTION

138. Where, at any stage after the conclusion of the proceedings, material comes to light which might reasonably be considered capable of casting doubt upon the safety of the conviction, the prosecutor should disclose such material.

CONFISCATION PROCEEDINGS

139. The disclosure regime in the CPIA ceases to have effect post-conviction and the continuing duty of disclosure does not apply to confiscation proceedings (see section 7A(1)(b) of the CPIA).

140. Part 2 of the Proceeds of Crime Act 2002 provides the legislative scheme for confiscation in the Crown Court following a conviction. The prosecutor is required to set out relevant matters in accordance with Section 16 of the Proceeds of Crime Act 2002 apply and the disclosure requirements at common law also apply meaning that there may be a requirement to disclose material in the interests of justice and fairness in the proceedings.

ANNEX A – DIGITAL MATERIAL

A1. This annex is intended to supplement the Attorney General's Guidelines on Disclosure. It is not intended to be a detailed operational guide but is intended to set out a common approach to be adopted when seeking to obtain and handle digital material, whether that be from a suspect or from a complainant. This annex aims to set out how relevant material and consequently material satisfying the test for disclosure can best be identified, revealed and if necessary disclosed to the defence without imposing unrealistic or disproportionate demands on the investigator and prosecutor. This annex also seeks to recognise the considerations investigators and prosecutors should have when obtaining and handling sensitive personal information, in accordance with obligations under data protection legislation.

A2. In cases involving large amounts of digital material, investigators should complete an investigation management document (IMD) which will inform the disclosure management document (DMD) that prosecutors should complete. The DMD allows prosecutors to be open and transparent with the defence and the court about how the prosecution has approached complying with its disclosure obligations in the specific context of the individual case.

A3. In cases where there may be a large amount of digital material, the investigator should consult the prosecutor, ideally before it is seized, and in turn they may consider seeking the advice of a digital forensic specialist on the strategy for the identification and review of digital material, including potential timings for this.

A4. The defence must also play their part in defining the real issues in the case. This is required by the overriding objective of the Criminal Procedure Rules. The defence should be invited by the prosecution at an early stage to participate in defining the scope of the reasonable searches that may be made of digital material in order to identify material that might reasonably be expected to undermine the prosecution case or assist the case for the defence.

A5. This approach enables the court to use its case management powers robustly to ensure that the prosecution's obligation of disclosure is discharged effectively.

General principles for investigators

A6. These general principles must be followed by investigators in handling and examining digital material:

a. No action should be taken which changes data on a device which may subsequently be relied upon in court.

b. If it is necessary to access original data then that data should only be accessed by someone who is competent to do so and is able to explain the relevance and implications of their actions to a court.

c. An audit trail should be kept of all processes followed. Another practitioner should be able to follow the audit trail and achieve the same results.

d. The investigator in charge of the investigation has responsibility for ensuring that the law and these principles are followed.

A7. Where an investigator has reasonable grounds for believing that digital material may contain material subject to legal professional privilege then this may not be seized unless the provisions of the Criminal Justice and Police Act 2001 apply. This is addressed in more detail later on in this Annex.

A8. The legal obligations in relation to seizure, relevance and retention are found in the Police and Criminal Evidence Act 1984, the Criminal Justice and Police Act 2001 and the Criminal Procedure and Investigations Act 1996.

Obtaining devices by seizure or co-operation

A9. Digital material may be seized from suspects using legal powers but this material may be obtained from suspects and witnesses with their cooperation as well. Before searching a suspect's premises where digital material is likely to be found, consideration must be given to:

a. What sort of material is likely to be found, and in what volume;

b. Whether it is likely that relevant material at the location will be able to be viewed and copied; and

c. What should be seized.

A10. Investigators will need to consider the practicalities of requesting/seizing digital devices, especially where there are a large number of devices. They will also need to consider the effect that taking possession/seizure will have on a business, organisation or individual; and where it is not feasible to obtain an image of the digital material, the likely timescale for returning the obtained items.

A11. In deciding whether to obtain and retain digital material, it is important that the investigator either complies with the procedure under the relevant statutory authority, relying on statutory powers or a search warrant, or obtains the owner's permission.

A12. When seeking to obtain digital material, whether from a suspect or a witness/complainant, investigators should be guided by the principles set out in paragraphs 11-13 in the Attorney General's Guidelines. Any intrusion into the personal and private lives of individuals should be carried out only where deemed necessary and using the least intrusive means possible to obtain the material required, adopting an incremental approach. Further guidance has been published by the CPS which has been endorsed by the Court of Appeal

A13. A computer hard drive is a single storage entity. This means that if any digital material found on the hard drive can lawfully be obtained or seized, the computer hard drive may, if appropriate, be seized or imaged. In some circumstances investigators may wish to image specific folders, files or categories of data where it is feasible to do so without seizing the hard drive or other media. Digital material may also be contained across a number of digital devices and so more than one device may be required in order to access the information sought.

A14. Digital material must not be requested or seized if an investigator has reasonable grounds for believing it is subject to legal professional privilege, other than where sections 50 or 51 of the Criminal Justice and Police Act 2001 apply. If such material is seized it must be isolated from other seized material and any other investigation material in the possession of the investigation authority.

The Police and Criminal Evidence Act 1984

A15. The Police and Criminal Evidence Act 1984 provides the power to seize anything from a suspect in the following circumstances:

a. Where a search has been authorised pursuant to a warrant – the search must fall within the scope of the warrant issued;

b. After arrest;

c. Where evidence or anything used in the commission of an offence is on a premises and it is necessary to seize it to prevent it being concealed, lost, altered or destroyed.

A16. An image of the digital material may be taken at the location of the search. Where an image is taken the original does not need to be seized. Where it is not possible to image the digital material it will need to be removed from the location for examination elsewhere. This allows the investigator to seize and sift material for the purpose of identifying material which meets the test of retention. If digital material is seized in its original form, investigators must be prepared to copy or image the material for the owners of that material when reasonably practicable.

The Criminal Justice and Police Act 2001

A17. The additional powers of seizure in sections 50 and 51 of the Criminal Justice and Police Act 2001 (CJPA 2001) only extend the scope of existing powers of search and seizure under the Police and Criminal Evidence Act 1984 and other specified statutory authorities where the relevant conditions and circumstances specified in the legislation apply.

A18. Investigators must be careful to only exercise powers under the CJPA 2001 when it is necessary and to not remove any more material than is justified. The removal of large volumes of material, much of which may not ultimately be retainable, may have serious consequences for the owner of the material, particularly when they are involved in business or other commercial activities.

A19. A written notice must be given to the occupier of the premises where items are seized under sections 50 and 51.

A20. Until material seized under the CJPA 2001 has been examined, it must be kept securely and separately from any material seized under other powers. Any such material must be examined as soon as reasonably practicable to determine which elements may be retained and which should be returned. Consideration should be given as to whether the person from whom the property was seized, or a person with interest in the property, should be given an opportunity of being present or represented at the examination.

Retention

A21. Where material is seized under the powers conferred by PACE 1984 the duty to retain it under the Code is subject to the provisions on retention under section 22 of PACE 1984. Material seized under sections 50 and 51 of the CJPA 2001 may be retained or returned in accordance with sections 53 to 58 of the CJPA 2001. Where material is obtained through co-operation and not using powers conferred on investigators by legislation, these principles should also be observed, including retaining the material for only as long as is necessary (see paragraph 5(b) of the Code).

A22. Retention is limited to evidence and relevant material (as defined in the CPIA Code). Where either evidence or relevant material is inextricably linked to non-relevant material which it is not reasonably practicable to separate from the other linked material without prejudicing the use of that other material in any investigation or proceedings, that material can also be retained.

A23. However, inextricably linked material must not be examined, imaged, copied or used for any purpose other than for providing the source of or the integrity of the linked material.

A24. There are four categories of material that may be retained:

a. Material that is evidence or potential evidence in the case. Where material is retained for evidential purposes there will be a strong argument that the whole thing (or an authenticated image or copy) should be retained for the purpose of proving provenance and continuity.

b. Where evidential material has been retained, inextricably linked non-relevant material which it is not reasonably practicable to separate can also be retained (PACE Code B paragraph 7).

c. An investigator should retain material that is relevant to the investigation and required to be scheduled as unused material. This is broader than but includes the duty to retain material which may satisfy the test for prosecution disclosure. The general duty to retain relevant material is set out in the CPIA Code at paragraph 5.

d. Material which is inextricably linked to relevant unused material which of itself may not be relevant material. Such material should be retained (PACE Code B paragraph 7).

A25. The balance of any digital material should be returned in accordance with sections 53-55 of the CJPA 2001 if seized under that Act.

Legal professional privilege

A26. No digital material may be requested or seized which an investigator has reasonable grounds for believing to be subject to legal professional privilege (LPP), other than under the additional powers of seizure in the CJPA 2001.

A27. The CJPA 2001 enables an investigator to seize relevant items which contain LPP material where it is not reasonably practicable on the search premises to separate LPP material from non-LPP material.

A28. Where LPP material or material suspected of containing LPP is seized, it must be isolated from the other material which has been seized in the investigation. Where suspected LPP material is discovered when reviewing material, and it was not anticipated that this material existed, again it must be isolated from the other material and the steps outlined below taken. The prosecution will need to decide on a case by case basis if the material is LPP material or not – defence may be able to assist with this.

A29. Where material has been identified as potentially containing LPP it must be reviewed by a lawyer independent of the prosecuting authority. No member of the investigative or prosecution team involved in either the current investigation or, if the LPP material relates to other criminal proceedings, in those proceedings should have sight of or access to the LPP material.

A30. If the material is voluminous, search terms or other filters may have to be used to identify the LPP material. If so this will also have to be done by someone independent and not connected with the investigation.

A31. It is essential that anyone dealing with LPP material maintains proper records showing the way in which the material has been handled and those who have had access to it, as well as decisions taken in relation to that material.

A32. LPP material can only be retained in specific circumstances in accordance with section 54 of the CJPA 2001. It can only be retained where the property which comprises the LPP material has been lawfully seized and it is not reasonably practicable for the item to be separated from the rest of the property without prejudicing the use of the rest of the property. LPP material which cannot be retained must be returned as soon as practicable after the seizure without waiting for the whole examination of the seized material.

Excluded and special procedure material

A33. Similar principles to those that apply to LPP material apply to excluded or special procedure material . By way of example, this may include material a journalist holds in confidence from a source.

Encryption

A34. Part III of the Regulation of Investigatory Powers Act 2000 (RIPA 2000) and the Investigation of Protected Electronic Information Code of Practice govern encryption.

A35. RIPA enables specified law enforcement agencies to compel individuals or companies to provide passwords or encryption keys for the purpose of rendering protected material readable. Failure to comply with RIPA 2000 Part III orders is a criminal offence. The Code of Practice provides guidance when exercising powers under RIPA, to require disclosure of protected electronic data in an intelligible form or to acquire the means by which protected electronic data may be accessed or put in an intelligible form.

Sifting and examination

A36. In complying with its duty of disclosure, the prosecution should follow the procedure as outlined below.

A37. Where digital material is examined, the extent and manner of inspecting, viewing or listening will depend on the nature of the material and its form.

A38. It is important for investigators and prosecutors to remember that the duty under the CPIA Code is to "pursue all reasonable lines of inquiry including those that point away from the suspect".

A39. Lines of inquiry, of whatever kind, should be pursued only if they are reasonable in the context of the individual case. It is not the duty of the prosecution to comb through all the material in its possession (e.g. every word or byte of computer material) on the lookout for anything which might conceivably or speculatively undermine the case or assist the defence. The duty of the prosecution is to disclose material which might reasonably be considered capable of undermining its case or assisting the case for the accused which they become aware of, or to which their attention is drawn.

A40. In some cases, the sift may be conducted by an investigator and/or disclosure officer manually assessing the content of the computer or other digital material from its directory and determining which files are relevant and should be retained for evidence or unused material.

A41. In other cases, such an approach may not be feasible. Where there is a large volume of material, it is perfectly proper for the investigator and/or disclosure officer to search by sample, key words, or other appropriate search tools or analytical techniques to locate relevant passages, phrases and identifiers. For the avoidance of any doubt, mobile phones are capable of storing a large volume of material. Technology that takes the form of search tools which use unambiguous calculations to perform problem-solving operations, such as algorithms or predictive coding, are an acceptable method of examining and reviewing material for disclosure purposes.

A42. In cases involving very large quantities of data, the person in charge of the investigation will develop a strategy setting out how the material should be analysed or searched to identify categories of data. This strategy may include an initial scoping exercise of the material obtained to ascertain the most effective strategy for reviewing relevant material. Any such strategy should be agreed with the prosecutor and communicated to the court and defence using a DMD

A43. Where search terms are to be used, investigators and prosecutors should consider whether engagement with the defence at the pre-charge stage would assist in the identification of relevant search terms. It will usually be appropriate to provide to the accused and their legal representative with a copy of the reasonable search terms used, or to be used, and to invite them to suggest any further reasonable search terms. If search terms are suggested which the investigator or prosecutor believes will not be productive, for example where the use of common words is likely to identify a mass of irrelevant material, the investigator or prosecutor should discuss the issues with the defence in order to agree sensible refinements.

A44. The digital strategy must be set out in an IMD and subsequently a DMD. This should include the details of any sampling techniques used (including key word searches) and how the material identified as a result was examined.

A45. It may be necessary to carry out sampling and searches on more than one occasion, especially as there is a duty on the prosecutor to keep duties of disclosure under review. To comply with this duty, further sampling and searches may be appropriate (and should be considered) where:

a. Further evidence or unused material is obtained in the course of the investigation; and/or

b. The defence statement is served on the prosecutor; and/or

c. The defendant makes an application under section 8 of the CPIA 1996 for disclosure; and/or

d. The defendant requests that further sampling or searches be carried out (provided it is a reasonable line of inquiry).

Record keeping

A46. A record or log must be made of all digital material seized or imaged and subsequently retained as relevant to the investigation.

A47. In cases involving large quantities of data where the person in charge of the investigation has developed a strategy setting out how the material should be analysed or searched to identify categories of data, a record should be made of the strategy and the analytical techniques used to search the data, including the software used. The record should include details of the person who has carried out the process and the date and time it was carried out. In such cases the strategy should record the reasons why certain categories have been searched for (such as names, companies, dates etc.).

A48. It is important that any searching or analytical processing of digital material, as well as the data identified by that process, is properly recorded. So far as is practicable, what is required is a record of the terms of the searches or processing that has been carried out. This means that in principle the following details may be recorded:

a. A record of all searches carried out, including the date of each search and the person(s) who conducted it.

b. A record of all search words or terms used on each search. However, where it is impracticable to record each word or term it will usually be sufficient to record each broad category of search.

c. A log of the key judgements made while refining the search strategy in light of what is found, or deciding not to carry out further searches.

d. Where material relating to a "hit" is not examined, the decision not to examine should be explained in the record of examination or in a statement. For instance, a large number of "hits" may be obtained in relation to a particular search word or term, but material relating to the "hits" is not examined because they do not appear to be relevant to the investigation. Any subsequent refinement of the search terms and further hits should also be noted and explained as above.

A49. Just as it is not necessary for the investigator or prosecutor to produce records of every search made of hard copy material, it is not necessary to produce records of what may be many hundreds of searches or analyses that have been carried out on digitally stored material simply to demonstrate that these have been done. Instead, the investigator and the prosecutor should ensure that they are able to explain how the disclosure exercise has been approached and to give the accused or suspect's legal representative an opportunity to participate in defining the reasonable searches to be made, as described in the section on sifting/examination.

Scheduling

A50. The disclosure officer should ensure that scheduling of relevant material is carried out in accordance with the CPIA Code of Practice. This may require each item of unused material to be listed separately on the unused material schedule and numbered consecutively (which may include numbering by volume and sub-volume). The description of each item should make clear the nature of the item and should contain sufficient detail to enable the prosecutor to decide whether they need to inspect the material before deciding whether or not it should be disclosed.

A51. It will generally be disproportionate in cases involving large quantities of digital data to list each item of material separately. Unless it is necessary or otherwise appropriate to separately list each item, the material should be listed in a block or blocks and described by quantity and generic title. Where the material is listed in a block or blocks, the search terms used and any items of material which might satisfy the disclosure test should be listed and described separately. In practical terms this will mean, where appropriate, cross referencing the schedules to the DMD.

A52. Where material has been listed in a block and metadata is available for the material within the block, consideration should be given to creating a file of that metadata and listing this separately and linked to the block listing to which it relates.

A53. Where continuation sheets of the unused material schedule are used, or additional schedules are sent subsequently, the item numbering must be, where possible, sequential to all other items on earlier schedules. This may include numbering by volume or sub-volume.

ANNEX B – PRE-CHARGE ENGAGEMENT

The scope of pre-charge engagement

B1. These Guidelines are intended to assist prosecutors, investigators, suspects and suspect's legal representatives who wish to enter into discussions about an investigation at any time after the first PACE interview, up until the commencement of criminal proceedings.

B2. These Guidelines are not intended to cover discussions regarding pleas to an allegation of serious or complex fraud. Nor do they apply to formal agreements relating to the provision of information or evidence about the criminal activities of others. In such cases, where appropriate, the parties should refer to the relevant guidance and follow the advised procedures:

a. In cases of serious or complex fraud, see the Attorney General's Guidelines on Plea discussions in cases of serious or complex fraud.

b. In cases where the suspect wishes to enter into a formal agreement to provide information or evidence, see sections 71-75 of the Serious Organised Crime and Police Act (SOCPA) 2005 and the CPS legal guidance on SOCPA 2005 – Queen's Evidence.

What is pre-charge engagement?

B3. Pre-charge engagement in these guidelines refers to voluntary engagement between the parties to an investigation after the first PACE interview, and before any suspect has been formally charged. Pre-charge engagement is a voluntary process and it may be terminated at any time. It does not refer to engagement between the parties to an investigation by way of further PACE interviews, and none of the guidance in this Annex is intended to apply to such circumstances. Should a defendant choose not to engage at this stage, that decision should not be held against him at a later stage in the proceedings.

B4. Pre-charge engagement may, among other things, involve:

a. Giving the suspect the opportunity to comment on any proposed further lines of inquiry.

b. Ascertaining whether the suspect can identify any other lines of inquiry.

c. Asking whether the suspect is aware of, or can provide access to, digital material that has a bearing on the allegation.

d. Discussing ways to overcome barriers to obtaining potential evidence, such as revealing encryption keys.

e. Agreeing any key word searches of digital material that the suspect would like carried out.

f. Obtaining a suspect's consent to access medical records.

g. The suspect identifying and providing contact details of any potential witnesses.

h. Clarifying whether any expert or forensic evidence is agreed and, if not, whether the suspect's representatives intend to instruct their own expert, including timescales for this.

B5. Pre-charge engagement is encouraged by the Code for Crown Prosecutors and may impact decisions as to charge.

When is pre-charge engagement appropriate?

B6. It may take place whenever it is agreed between the parties that it may assist the investigation. Where a suspect is not yet represented, an investigator should take care to ensure that the suspect understands their right to legal advice before the pre charge engagement process commences. Sufficient time should be given to enable a suspect to access this advice if they wish to do so.

B7. Pre-charge engagement should not, however, be considered a replacement to a further interview with a suspect. Investigators and prosecutors should be conscious that adverse inferences under section 34 of the Criminal Justice and Public Order Act 1994 are not available at trial where a suspect failed to mention a fact when asked about a matter in pre-charge engagement. An adverse inference may only be drawn where the suspect failed to mention a fact while being questioned under caution by a constable trying to discover whether or by whom the offence had been committed. Moreover, investigators and prosecutors should be aware of the advantages of holding a further formal interview, including the fact that suspects will have been appropriately cautioned and that any answers given will be recorded.

B8. Accordingly, investigators and prosecutors should not seek to initiate, or agree to, pre-charge engagement in respect of matters where they are likely to seek to rely on the contents of the suspect's answers as evidence at trial. Pre-charge engagement should not therefore be used for putting new summaries of the case to the defence, and where deemed necessary such accounts should be put to the suspect in a further interview.

B9. A no comment interview does not preclude the possibility of pre-charge engagement. When taking into account paragraph 8 above, while a no comment interview may limit the scope of any such discussions, pre-charge engagement may still be pursued where appropriate, but consideration should be given to a further PACE interview with the suspect before there is any agreement to engage in pre-charge engagement.

B10. There are a number of potential benefits that may arise from pre-charge engagement:

a. Suspects who maintain their innocence will be aided by early identification of lines of inquiry which may lead to evidence or material that points away from the suspect or points towards another suspect.

b. Pre-charge engagement can help inform a prosecutor's charging decision. It might avoid a case being charged that would otherwise be stopped later in proceedings, when further information becomes available.

c. The issues in dispute may be narrowed, so that unnecessary inquiries are not pursued, and if a case is charged and proceeds to trial, it can be managed more efficiently.

d. Early resolution of a case may reduce anxiety and uncertainty for suspects and complainants.

e. The cost of the matter to the criminal justice system may be reduced, including potentially avoiding or mitigating the cost of criminal proceedings.

WHO MAY INITIATE AND CONDUCT PRE-CHARGE ENGAGEMENT?

B11. Depending on the circumstances, it may be appropriate for an investigator, the prosecutor, the suspect's representative or an unrepresented suspect to initiate pre-charge engagement.

B12. When referring a case to a prosecutor, the investigator should inform the prosecutor if any pre-charge engagement has already taken place and should indicate if they believe pre-charge engagement would benefit the case.

B13. The prosecutor may advise the investigator to initiate and carry out pre-charge engagement, or do so themselves.

B14. In cases in which statutory time limits on charging apply, it will usually be more practical for the investigator, rather than the prosecutor, to initiate and conduct pre-charge engagement.

B15. Prosecutors and investigators should be alert to use pre-charge engagement as a means to frustrate or delay the investigation unnecessarily. Engagement should not be initiated or continued where this is apparent. In particular, pre-charge engagement is not intended to provide an opportunity for the suspect to make unfounded allegations against the complainant, so that the complainant becomes unjustly subject to investigation. Prosecutors and investigators should be alert to prevent this happening and investigators are not obliged to follow any line of inquiry suggested by the suspect's representative: a line of inquiry should be reasonable in the circumstances of the case. What is reasonable is a matter for an investigator to decide, with the assistance of a prosecutor if required. Refer to Annex A and paragraphs A11-13 for more guidance on reasonable lines of inquiry, particularly in relation to the obtaining of a complainant's mobile or other personal devices.

Information on pre-charge engagement

B16. The investigator should provide information on pre-charge engagement to the suspect or their representative either before or after interview.

B17. The pre-charge engagement process should be explained orally or in writing, in simple terms.

B18. The explanation may include the aim and benefits of the process, any relevant timescales and a police point of contact to make any future representations at the pre-charge stage.

Conducting pre-charge engagement

B19. Pre-charge engagement discussions may take place face to face or via correspondence.

B20. It need not always be undertaken via a formal process, but a written record should always be made and kept. For instance, the process may be initiated immediately after interview, when the investigator and suspect's representative may agree on the further lines of inquiry that have arisen from interview.

B21. However, in some circumstances the parties will require a more formal mechanism to enable them to begin the process at any stage post-interview and before charge. This may be done by the investigator, prosecutor or suspect's representative sending a letter of invitation to the other party, which:

a. Asks whether the other party wishes to enter into pre-charge engagement in accordance with these Guidelines.

b. Explains in what way the engagement may assist the investigation. The prosecutor or investigator may wish to include the information sought, or sought to be discussed.

Disclosure during PCE

B22. Since pre-charge engagement takes place prior to the institution of any proceedings, the statutory disclosure rules will not be engaged. However, disclosure of unused material must be considered as part of the pre-charge engagement process, to ensure that the discussions are fair and that the suspect is not misled as to the strength of the prosecution case.

B23. Accordingly, before, during and after pre-charge engagement, the investigator/prosecutor should consider whether any further material, additional to that contained in the summary of the allegation, falls to be disclosed to the suspect. The investigator/prosecutor should at all stages bear in mind the potential need to cease pre-charge engagement and to put further evidence to the suspect in a PACE interview.

B24. As the suspect provides information during the process, the investigator/prosecutor should continually be alive to the potential need to make any further disclosure.

RECORDING THE DISCUSSIONS

B25. A full written, signed record of the pre-charge engagement discussions should be made.

B26. Additionally, the prosecutor and/or investigator should record every key action involved in the process, such as the provision of written information on pre-charge engagement to the suspect, any informal discussions with the suspect's representative about entering into the process, or any formal letter of invitation sent or received.

B27. A record should be made of all information provided by the suspect's representative, such as potential lines of inquiry, suggested key word searches of digital material and any witness details.

B28. The law may require the prosecutor to disclose any information provided by the suspect's representative to another party, including a defendant in criminal proceedings.

B29. A record should also be made of all information and material provided to the suspect's representative, including any disclosure material.

B30. The prosecutor and investigator should ensure that the records of the pre-charge engagement are provided to each other. Information or material generated by the process will need to be assessed for evidential and disclosure purposes.

ANNEX C – DISCLOSURE MANAGEMENT DOCUMENTS (DMDS)

Template "Disclosure Management Document"

This Disclosure Management Document sets out the approach of the prosecution to relevant non-sensitive material in this case. Unless otherwise indicated, all the material on the non-sensitive schedule has been inspected by the disclosure officer.

R v [Name]

Prosecutor:

Disclosure officer:

Prosecution counsel instructed:

1. Reasonable lines of inquiry

The rationale for the identification and scheduling of relevant material is based upon the reasonable lines of inquiry that were conducted within this investigation. The Disclosure Officer's understanding of the defence case is as follows;

- [What explanation has been offered by the accused, whether in formal interview, defence statement or otherwise. How has this been followed up? This should be set out.]
- [What are the identified/likely issues in the case e.g identification, alibi, factual dispute, no intention etc]
- [Insert summary of reasonable lines of inquiry pursued, particularly those that point away from the suspect, or which may assist the defence]
- The time frame selected is considered to be a reasonable line of inquiry, and represents [e.g. the date that the victim first met the suspect to a month after the suspect's arrest]

2. Electronic material

This section should cover the following issues:

- What mobile telephones/communication devices/computers were seized during the investigation (from all suspects, complainants, witnesses).
- Identify the items with reference to the schedule of materials – i.e. telephone, download
- Have the devices been downloaded? If not, why not. If so, what type of download?
- Set out the method of examination of each download – were key words deployed, was the entire download inspected, were date parameters employed?
- What social media accounts of suspect/complaint/witness have been considered a reasonable line of inquiry.
- Were any phones from the complainant or suspect not seized? If not, why not?
- Set out the method by which the defence will be given disclosure of material that satisfies the disclosure test explaining, if relevant, why the whole item is not being provided.
- What CCTV/multi-media evidence has been seized and how it has been examined?

Appendix B

A suggested presentation and wording of the information is set out below:

<table>
<tr><th>Exhibit ref</th><th>Description</th><th>Inquiry undertaken</th><th>Result</th></tr>
<tr><td rowspan="7">AB/1</td><td rowspan="7">I-phone seized from defendant</td><td rowspan="2">This telephone has been downloaded using the XRY software. This has resulted in 40,000 pages of data which includes telephone calls to and from the suspect, contact list, text messages, WhatsApp messages and internet search history. No further data has been downloaded from the phone.</td><td>Relevant evidential material has been served.</td></tr>
<tr><td rowspan="6">Material which has been identified through keyword searching has been collated and scheduled. The defence are invited to identify any further keywords which might represent a reasonable line of inquiry. If further interrogation of the telephone is considered to be necessary the defence are invited to identify what enquiries should be undertaken and identify the relevance of such enquiries to the issues in this case.</td></tr>
<tr><td>The internet search history does not appear to be relevant to the issues in the case and has not been reviewed.</td></tr>
<tr><td>The contact list has been reviewed to identify whether the complainant is a contact, no further checks have been made.</td></tr>
<tr><td>The telephone call list has been reviewed for any contact between the suspect and complainant between dates × and Y. All identified contact has been produced as exhibit AB/2.</td></tr>
<tr><td>Text messages and WhatsApp messages have been searched using the following keywords [A, B, C, D] all responsive messages which correspond with the keywords have been disclosed.</td></tr>
<tr><td>No further checks have been conducted upon the phone.</td></tr>
</table>

3. Third Party Material

The prosecution believe that the following third parties have relevant non sensitive material that might satisfy the disclosure test if it were in the possession of the prosecution (e.g. Medical and dental records, Records held by other agencies, Records/material held by Social Services or local authority):

The reason for this belief is …

The type of relevant material is…

The following steps have been taken to obtain this material:

The defence have a critical role in ensuring that the prosecution are directed to material that meets the disclosure test. Any representations by the defence on the contents of this document, including identifying issues in the case and why material meets the test for disclosure should be received by *[insert date/ timescale]*

Signed:

Dated:

Appendix C

Criminal Procedure and Investigations Act 1996 (section 23(1)) Code of Practice

Revised in accordance with section 25(4) of the Criminal Procedure and Investigations Act 1996 and presented to Parliament pursuant to section 25(2) of the Act

September 2020

PREAMBLE

This code of practice is issued under Part II of the Criminal Procedure and Investigations Act 1996 ('the Act'). It sets out the manner in which police officers are to record, retain and reveal to the prosecutor material obtained in a criminal investigation and which may be relevant to the investigation, and related matters.

INTRODUCTION

1.1 This code of practice applies in respect of criminal investigations conducted by police officers which begin on or after the day on which this code comes into effect. Persons other than police officers who are charged with the duty of conducting an investigation as defined in the Act are to have regard to the relevant provisions of the code, and should take these into account in applying their own operating procedures.

1.2 This code does not apply to persons who are not charged with the duty of conducting an investigation as defined in the Act.

1.3 Nothing in this code applies to material intercepted in obedience to a warrant issued under section 2 of the Interception of Communications Act 1985 or section 5 of the Regulation of Investigatory Powers Act 2000, or to any copy of that material as defined in section 10 of the 1985 Act or section 15 of the 2000 Act and by sections of the Investigatory Powers Act 2016.

1.4 This code extends only to England and Wales.

DEFINITIONS

2.1 In this code:

1. *a criminal investigation* is an investigation conducted by police officers with a view to it being ascertained whether a person should be charged with an offence, or whether a person charged with an offence is guilty of it. This will include:

   - investigations into crimes that have been committed;
   - investigations whose purpose is to ascertain whether a crime has been committed, with a view to the possible institution of criminal proceedings; and
   - investigations which begin in the belief that a crime may be committed, for example when the police keep premises or individuals under observation for a period of time, with a view to the possible institution of criminal proceedings;

2. charging a person with an offence includes prosecution by way of summons or postal requisition;

3. *an investigator* is any police officer involved in the conduct of a criminal investigation. All investigators have a responsibility for carrying out the duties imposed on them under this code, including in particular recording information, and retaining records of information and other material;

4. the *officer in charge of an investigation* is the police officer responsible for directing a criminal investigation. They are also responsible for ensuring that proper procedures are in place for recording information, and retaining records of information and other material, in the investigation;

5. the *disclosure officer* is the person responsible for examining material retained by the police during the investigation; revealing material to the prosecutor during the investigation and any criminal proceedings resulting from it, and certifying that they have done this; and disclosing material to the accused at the request of the prosecutor;

6. the *prosecutor* is the authority responsible for the conduct, on behalf of the Crown, of criminal proceedings resulting from a specific criminal investigation;

7. *material* is material of any kind, including information and objects, which is obtained or inspected in the course of a criminal investigation and which may be relevant to the investigation. This includes not only material coming into the possession of the investigator (such as documents seized in the course of searching premises) but also material generated by them (such as interview records);

8. material may be *relevant to an investigation* if it appears to an investigator, or to the officer in charge of an investigation, or to the disclosure officer, that it has some bearing on any offence under investigation or any person being investigated, or on the surrounding circumstances of the case, unless it is incapable of having any impact on the case;

9. *sensitive material* is material, the disclosure of which the disclosure officer believes would give rise to a real risk of serious prejudice to an important public interest;

10. references to *prosecution disclosure* are to the duty of the prosecutor under sections 3 and 7A of the Act to disclose material which is in their possession or which they have inspected in pursuance of this code, and which might reasonably be considered capable of undermining the case against the accused, or of assisting the case for the accused;

11. references to the disclosure of material to a person accused of an offence include references to the disclosure of material to their legal representative;

12. references to police officers and to the chief officer of police include those employed in a police force as defined in section 3(3) of the Prosecution of Offences Act 1985.

GENERAL RESPONSIBILITIES

3.1 The functions of the investigator, the officer in charge of an investigation and the disclosure officer are separate. Whether they are undertaken by one, two or more persons will depend on the complexity of the case and the administrative arrangements within each police force. Where they are undertaken by more than one person, close consultation between them is essential to the effective performance of the duties imposed by this code.

3.2 In any criminal investigation, one or more deputy disclosure officers may be appointed to assist the disclosure officer, and a deputy disclosure officer may perform any function of a disclosure officer as defined in paragraph 2.1.

3.3 The chief officer of police for each police force is responsible for putting in place arrangements to ensure that in every investigation the identity of the officer in charge of an investigation and the disclosure officer is recorded. The chief officer of police for each police force shall ensure that disclosure officers and deputy disclosure officers have sufficient skills and authority, commensurate with the complexity of the investigation, to discharge their functions effectively. An individual must not be appointed as disclosure officer, or continue in that role, if that is likely to result in a conflict of interest, for instance, if the disclosure officer is the victim of the alleged crime which is the subject of the investigation. The advice of a more senior officer must always be sought if there is doubt as to whether a conflict of interest precludes an individual acting as disclosure officer. If thereafter the doubt remains, the advice of a prosecutor should be sought.

3.4 The officer in charge of an investigation may delegate tasks to another investigator, to civilians employed by the police force, or to other persons participating in the investigation under arrangements for joint investigations, but they remain responsible for ensuring that these have been carried out and for accounting for any general policies followed in the investigation. In particular, it is an essential part of their duties to ensure that all material which may be relevant to an investigation is retained, and either made available to the disclosure officer or (in exceptional circumstances) revealed directly to the prosecutor.

3.5 In conducting an investigation, the investigator should pursue all reasonable lines of inquiry, whether these point towards or away from the suspect. What is reasonable in each case will depend on the particular circumstances. It is a matter for the investigator, with the assistance of the prosecutor if required, to decide what constitutes a reasonable line of inquiry in each case.

3.6 If the officer in charge of an investigation believes that other persons may be in possession of material that may be relevant to the investigation, and if this has not been obtained under paragraph 3.5 above, they should ask the disclosure officer to inform them of the existence of the investigation and to invite them to retain the material in case they receive a request for its disclosure. The disclosure officer should inform the prosecutor that they may have such material. However, the officer in charge of an investigation is not required to make speculative enquiries of other persons; there must be some reason to believe that they may have relevant material. That reason may come from information provided to the police by the accused or from other inquiries made or from some other source.

3.7 If, during a criminal investigation, the officer in charge of an investigation or disclosure officer for any reason no longer has responsibility for the functions falling to them, either their supervisor or the police officer in charge of criminal investigations for the police force concerned must assign someone else to assume that responsibility. That person's identity must be recorded, as with those initially responsible for these functions in each investigation.

RECORDING OF INFORMATION

4.1 If material which may be relevant to the investigation consists of information which is not recorded in any form, the officer in charge of an investigation must ensure that it is recorded in a durable or retrievable form.

4.2 Where it is not practicable to retain the initial record of information because it forms part of a larger record which is to be destroyed, its contents should be transferred as a true record to a durable and more easily-stored form before that happens.

4.3 Negative information is often relevant to an investigation. If it may be relevant it must be recorded. An example might be a number of people present in a particular place at a particular time who state that they saw nothing unusual.

4.4 Where information which may be relevant is obtained, it must be recorded at the time it is obtained or as soon as practicable after that time. This includes, for example, information obtained in house-to-house enquiries, although the requirement to record information promptly does not require an investigator to take a statement from a potential witness where it would not otherwise be taken.

RETENTION OF MATERIAL

(a) Duty to retain material

5.1 The investigator must retain material obtained in a criminal investigation which may be relevant to the investigation. Material may be photographed, video-recorded, captured digitally or otherwise retained in the form of a copy rather than the original at any time, if the original is perishable; the original was supplied to the investigator rather than generated by them and is to be returned to its owner; or the retention of a copy rather than the original is reasonable in all the circumstances.

5.2 Where material has been seized in the exercise of the powers of seizure conferred by the Police and Criminal Evidence Act 1984, the duty to retain it under this code is subject to the provisions on the retention of seized material in section 22 of that Act.

5.3 If the officer in charge of an investigation becomes aware as a result of developments in the case that material previously examined but not retained (because it was not thought to be relevant) may now be relevant to the investigation, they should, wherever practicable, take steps to obtain it or ensure that it is retained for further inspection or for production in court if required.

5.4 The duty to retain material includes in particular the duty to retain material falling into the following categories:

- Records which are derived from tapes or recordings of telephone messages (for example, 999 calls) containing descriptions of an alleged offence or offender;
- Any incident logs relating to the allegation;
- Contemporaneous records of the incident, such as:
    - crime reports and crime report forms;
    - an investigation log;

  - any record or note made by an investigator (including police notebook entries and other handwritten notes) on which they later make a statement or which relates to contact with suspects, victims or witnesses;
  - an account of an incident or information relevant to an incident noted by an investigator in manuscript or electronically;
  - records of actions carried out by officers (such as house-to-house interviews, CCTV or forensic enquiries) noted by a police officer in manuscript or electronically;
  - CCTV footage, or other imagery, of the incident in action;
- The defendant's custody record or voluntary attendance record;
- Any previous accounts made by a complainant or any other witnesses;
- Interview records (written records, or audio or video tapes, of interviews with actual or potential witnesses or suspects);
- Any material casting doubt on the reliability of a witness e.g. relevant previous convictions and relevant cautions of any prosecution witnesses and any co-accused;
- Final versions of witness statements (and draft versions where their content differs from the final version), including any exhibits mentioned (unless these have been returned to their owner on the understanding that they will be produced in court if required);
- Material relating to other suspects in the investigation;
- Communications between the police and experts such as forensic scientists, reports of work carried out by experts, and schedules of scientific material prepared by the expert for the investigator, for the purposes of criminal proceedings;
- Records of the first description of a suspect by each potential witness who purports to identify or describe the suspect, whether or not the description differs from that of subsequent descriptions by that or other witnesses.

5.5 The duty to retain material where it may be relevant to the investigation also includes in particular the duty to retain any material which may satisfy the test for prosecution disclosure in the Act, such as:

- information provided by an accused person which indicates an explanation for the offence with which they have been charged;
- any material casting doubt on the reliability of a confession;
- any material casting doubt on the reliability of a prosecution witness.

5.6 The duty to retain material falling into these categories does not extend to items which are purely ancillary to such material and possess no independent significance (for example, duplicate copies of records or reports).

(b) Length of time for which material is to be retained

5.7 All material which may be relevant to the investigation must be retained until a decision is taken whether to institute proceedings against a person for an offence.

5.8 If a criminal investigation results in proceedings being instituted, all material which may be relevant must be retained at least until the accused is acquitted or convicted or the prosecutor decides not to proceed with the case.

5.9 Where the accused is convicted, all material which may be relevant must be retained at least until:

- the convicted person is released from custody, or discharged from hospital, in cases where the court imposes a custodial sentence or a hospital order;
- six months from the date of conviction, in all other cases.

If the court imposes a custodial sentence or hospital order and the convicted person is released from custody or discharged from hospital earlier than six months from the date of conviction, all material which may be relevant must be retained at least until six months from the date of conviction.

5.10 If an appeal against conviction is in progress when the release or discharge occurs, or at the end of the period of six months specified in paragraph 5.9, all material which may be relevant must be retained until the appeal is determined. Similarly, if the Criminal Cases Review Commission is considering an application at that point in time, all material which may be relevant must be retained at least until the Commission decides not to refer the case to the Court.

PREPARATION OF MATERIAL FOR PROSECUTOR

(a) Schedules of unused material

6.1 The officer in charge of the investigation, the disclosure officer or an investigator may seek advice from the prosecutor about whether any particular item of material may be relevant to the investigation.

6.2 Material which may be relevant to an investigation and has been retained in accordance with this code, and which the disclosure officer believes will not form part of the prosecution case, must be listed on the appropriate schedule of unused material.

6.3 The disclosure officer must ensure that the appropriate schedule of unused material is prepared in the following circumstances:

- the accused is charged with an offence which is triable only on indictment;
- the accused is charged with an offence which is triable either way, and it is considered that the case is likely to be tried on indictment;
- the accused is charged with an either-way offence that is likely to remain in the magistrates' court, and it is considered that they are likely to plead not guilty;
- the accused is charged with a summary offence and it is considered that they are likely to plead not guilty.

6.4 Where, however, the accused is charged with a summary offence or an either-way offence, and it is considered that they are likely to plead guilty (e.g. because they have admitted the offence), a schedule is *not* required unless a not guilty plea is subsequently entered or indicated.

6.5 Irrespective of the anticipated plea, the Common Law test for disclosure requires material to be disclosed if there is material known to the disclosure officer that might assist the defence with the early preparation of their case or at a bail hearing (for example, a key prosecution witness has relevant previous convictions or a witness has withdrawn their statement). A note must be made on the case summary for the prosecutor of any such material, which must be revealed to the prosecutor who will review it and consider whether it is disclosable. Where there is no such material, a certificate to that effect must be completed.

6.6 Material in the following list (which where it exists will have been retained or recorded in accordance with paragraph 5.4) is likely to include information which meets the test for prosecution disclosure. This material must therefore, subject to the exception at 6.4 above, be scheduled and provided to the prosecutor. In reviewing this material, disclosure officers and prosecutors are to start with a presumption that it is likely to meet the disclosure test, although the material will need to be carefully considered and the disclosure test applied before a decision is made:

a) records which are derived from tapes or recordings of telephone messages (for example 999 calls) containing descriptions of an alleged offence or offender;

b) any incident logs relating to the allegation;

c) contemporaneous records of the incident, such as:

   - crime reports and crime report forms;
   - an investigation log;
   - any record or note made by an investigator (including police notebook entries and other handwritten notes) on which they later make a statement or which relates to contact with suspects, victims or witnesses;

- an account of an incident or information relevant to an incident noted by an investigator in manuscript or electronically;
- records of actions carried out by officers (such as house-to-house interviews, CCTV or forensic enquiries) noted by a police officer in manuscript or electronically;
- CCTV footage, or other imagery, of the incident in action;

d) the defendant's custody record or voluntary attendance record;

e) any previous accounts made by a complainant or by any other witnesses;

f) interview records (written records, or audio or video tapes, of interviews with actual or potential witnesses or suspects);

g) any material casting doubt on the reliability of a witness e. g. relevant previous convictions and relevant cautions of any prosecution witnesses and any co-accused.

This material must be listed on the schedule by the disclosure officer in addition to all other material which may be relevant to an investigation; it is likely that some of this material will need to be redacted (see 6.12).

(b) Way in which material is to be listed on schedule

6.7 Material which the disclosure officer does not believe is sensitive must be listed on a schedule of non-sensitive material, which must include a statement that the disclosure officer does not believe the material is sensitive. Where there is sensitive unused material, see para 6.13 below.

6.8 The disclosure officer should ensure, subject to paras 6.10-6.11 below, that each item of material is listed separately on the schedule, and is numbered consecutively (which may include numbering by volume and sub-volume).

6.9 The description of each item should make clear the nature of the item and should contain sufficient detail to enable the prosecutor to decide whether they need to inspect the material before deciding whether or not it should be disclosed.

6.10 In some investigations it may be disproportionate to list each item of material separately. These may be listed in a block or blocks and described by quantity and generic title.

6.11 Even if some material is listed in a block, the disclosure officer must ensure that any items among that material which might satisfy the test for prosecution disclosure are listed and described individually.

(c) Redaction of sensitive material

6.12 The disclosure officer should redact any sensitive information contained in material that is likely to satisfy the test for prosecution disclosure.

The disclosure officer should also redact any personal, confidential information in material that is to be disclosed. Such could include a person's date of birth, address, email address and phone number.

6.13 Any material which is believed to be sensitive must be listed on a schedule of sensitive material. If there is no sensitive material, the disclosure officer must record this fact on a schedule of sensitive material, or otherwise so indicate.

6.14 Subject to paragraph 6.15 below, the disclosure officer must list on a sensitive schedule any material the disclosure of which they believe would give rise to a real risk of serious prejudice to an important public interest, and the reason for that belief. The schedule must include a statement that the disclosure officer believes the material is sensitive. Depending on the circumstances, examples of such material may include the following, among others:

- material relating to national security;
- material received from the intelligence and security agencies;
- material relating to intelligence from foreign sources which reveals sensitive intelligence gathering methods;
- material given in confidence;
- material relating to the identity or activities of informants, or undercover police officers, or witnesses, or other persons supplying information to the police who may be in danger if their identities are revealed;
- material revealing the location of any premises or other place used for police surveillance, or the identity of any person allowing a police officer to use them for surveillance;
- material revealing, either directly or indirectly, techniques and methods relied upon by a police officer in the course of a criminal investigation, for example covert surveillance techniques, or other methods of detecting crime;
- material whose disclosure might facilitate the commission of other offences or hinder the prevention and detection of crime;
- material upon the strength of which search warrants were obtained;
- material containing details of persons taking part in identification parades;
- material supplied to an investigator during a criminal investigation which has been generated by an official of a body concerned with the regulation or supervision of bodies corporate or of persons engaged in financial activities, or which has been generated by a person retained by such a body;
- material supplied to an investigator during a criminal investigation which relates to a child or young person and which has been

generated by a local authority social services department, an Area Child Protection Committee or other party contacted by an investigator during the investigation;

- material relating to the private life of a witness.

6.15 In exceptional circumstances, where an investigator considers that material is so sensitive that its revelation to the prosecutor by means of an entry on the sensitive schedule is inappropriate, the existence of the material must be revealed to the prosecutor separately. This will apply only where compromising the material would be likely to lead directly to the loss of life, or directly threaten national security.

6.16 In such circumstances, the responsibility for informing the prosecutor lies with the investigator who knows the detail of the sensitive material. The investigator should act as soon as is reasonably practicable after the file containing the prosecution case is sent to the prosecutor. The investigator must also ensure that the prosecutor is able to inspect the material so that they can assess whether it is disclosable and, if so, whether it needs to be brought before a court for a ruling on disclosure.

REVELATION OF MATERIAL TO PROSECUTOR

7.1 Where cases have been charged on the Full Code Test and it is anticipated that the defendant will plead not guilty, the disclosure officer should provide the schedules concerning unused material to the prosecutor at the same time as submitting the case file.

7.2 In all other cases the disclosure officer must provide the schedules as soon as possible after a not guilty plea has been either indicated or entered.

7.3 The disclosure officer should draw the attention of the prosecutor to any material an investigator has retained (including material to which paragraph 6.15 applies) which it is considered may satisfy the test for prosecution disclosure in the Act, explaining the reasons for coming to that view.

7.4 The disclosure officer must give the prosecutor a copy of any such material (unless it has already been supplied as part of the file containing the material for the prosecution case), together with any material which falls into the following categories:

- information provided by an accused person which indicates an explanation for the offence with which they has been charged;
- any material casting doubt on the reliability of a confession;
- any material casting doubt on the reliability of a prosecution witness.

7.5 The disclosure officer must give the prosecutor a copy of any material which has been scheduled in accordance with paragraph 6.6, indicating whether it is, or is not, considered to satisfy the test for prosecution disclosure, and in either case explaining the reasons for coming to that view.

7.6 The disclosure officer must comply with a request from the prosecutor to be allowed to inspect material which has not already been copied to them. If the prosecutor asks to be provided with a copy of such material it should be provided, except where (having consulted the officer in charge of the investigation) the disclosure officer believes that the material is too sensitive to be copied and can only be inspected.

7.7 If material consists of information which is recorded other than in writing, whether it should be given to the prosecutor in its original form as a whole, or by way of relevant extracts recorded in the same form, or in the form of a transcript, is a matter for agreement between the disclosure officer and the prosecutor.

SUBSEQUENT ACTION BY DISCLOSURE OFFICER

8.1 At the time when a schedule of non-sensitive material is prepared, the disclosure officer may not know exactly what material will form the case against the accused. In addition, the prosecutor may not have given advice about the likely relevance of particular items of material. Once these matters have been determined, the disclosure officer must give the prosecutor, where necessary, an amended schedule listing any additional material:

- which may be relevant to the investigation,
- which does not form part of the case against the accused,
- which is not already listed on the schedule, and
- which they believe is not sensitive,

unless they are informed in writing by the prosecutor that the prosecutor intends to disclose the material to the defence.

8.2 Section 7A of the Act imposes a continuing duty on the prosecutor, for the duration of criminal proceedings against the accused, to disclose material which satisfies the test for disclosure (subject to public interest considerations). To enable this to be done, any new material coming to light should be treated in the same way as the earlier material.

8.3 In particular, after a defence statement has been given, or details of the issues in dispute have been recorded on the Preparation for Effective Trial form or the Plea and Trial Preparation Hearing form, the disclosure officer must look again at the material which has been retained and must draw the attention of the prosecutor to any material which might reasonably be considered capable of undermining the case for the prosecution against the accused or of assisting the case for the accused; and must reveal it to them in accordance with paragraphs 7.4 and 7.5 above.

CERTIFICATION BY DISCLOSURE OFFICER

9.1 The disclosure officer must certify to the prosecutor that, to the best of their knowledge and belief, all relevant material which has been retained and made available to them has been revealed to the prosecutor in accordance with this code. They must sign and date the disclosure officer certificate. It will be necessary to certify not only at the time when the schedule and accompanying material is submitted to the prosecutor, and when relevant material which has been retained is reconsidered after the accused has given a defence statement, but also whenever a schedule is otherwise given or material is otherwise revealed to the prosecutor.

DISCLOSURE OF MATERIAL TO ACCUSED

10.1 A prosecutor must review the schedules of unused material provided by the disclosure officer and endorse the schedule to indicate whether each item of material does or does not meet the test for disclosure. If any of the material does meet the test for disclosure, the prosecutor should record the reason for this decision.

10.2 A prosecutor must additionally review any material provided by the disclosure officer under paragraph 6.6 (*material likely to meet the test for disclosure*). The prosecutor must endorse the schedule to indicate whether the material does or does not meet the test for disclosure, and must record the reason for the decision.

10.3 When a prosecutor provides material to the defence in accordance with the obligation under section 3 or section 7A of the Criminal Procedure and Investigations Act 1996, the prosecutor must at the same time provide the schedule of non-sensitive material to the defence.

10.4 Other than early disclosure under Common Law, in the magistrates' court the schedule (and any relevant unused material to be disclosed under it) must be disclosed to the accused either:

- at the hearing where a not guilty plea is entered, or
- as soon as possible following a formal indication from the accused or representative that a not guilty plea will be entered at the hearing.

In the Crown Court, initial disclosure should if possible be served prior to the Plea and Trial Preparation Hearing (PTPH). Where this has not been done, it should be served as soon as possible after that hearing and in accordance with any direction made by the Court.

10.5 If material has been copied to the prosecutor, and it is to be disclosed, whether it is disclosed by the prosecutor or the disclosure officer is a matter of agreement between the two of them.

10.6 If material has not already been copied to the prosecutor, and they request its disclosure to the accused on the ground that:

- it satisfies the test for prosecution disclosure, **or**

- the court has ordered its disclosure after considering an application from the accused,

the disclosure officer must disclose it to the accused.

10.7 The disclosure officer must disclose material to the accused either by giving them a copy or by allowing them to inspect it. If the accused person asks for a copy of any material which they have been allowed to inspect, the disclosure officer must supply it, unless in the opinion of the disclosure officer that is either not practicable (for example because the material consists of an object which cannot be copied, or because the volume of material is so great), or not desirable (for example because the material is a statement by a child witness in relation to a sexual offence).

10.8 If material which the accused has been allowed to inspect consists of information which is recorded other than in writing, whether it should be given to the accused in its original form or in the form of a transcript is a matter for the discretion of the disclosure officer. If the material is transcribed, the disclosure officer must ensure that the transcript is certified to the accused as a true record of the material which has been transcribed.

10.9 If a court concludes that an item of sensitive material satisfies the prosecution disclosure test and that the interests of the defence outweigh the public interest in withholding disclosure, it will be necessary to disclose the material if the case is to proceed. This does not mean that sensitive documents must always be disclosed in their original form: for example, the court may agree that sensitive details still requiring protection should be blocked out, or that documents may be summarised, or that the prosecutor may make an admission about the substance of the material under section 10 of the Criminal Justice Act 1967.

Appendix D

Judicial Protocol on the Disclosure of Unused Material in Criminal Cases

FOREWORD

We are pleased to publish a revised judicial protocol and revised guidance on the disclosure of unused material in criminal cases. Proper disclosure of unused material, made through a rigorous and carefully considered application of the law, remains a crucial part of a fair trial, and essential to avoiding miscarriages of justice. These new documents are intended to clarify the procedures to be followed and to encourage the active participation of all parties.

They have been prepared following the recommendations of Lord Justice Gross in his September 2011 'Review of Disclosure in Criminal Proceedings' and take account of Lord Justice Gross and Lord Justice Treacy's 'Further review of disclosure in criminal proceedings: sanctions for disclosure failure', published in November 2012.

There are important roles for the prosecution, the defence and the court in ensuring that disclosure is conducted properly, including on the part of the investigating, case progression and disclosure officers, as well as the lawyers and advocates. Lord Justice Gross particularly recommended that the guidance on disclosure of unused material in criminal cases should be consolidated and abbreviated. Given all of those involved in this process have separate constitutional roles, the judiciary and the Attorney-General have worked together to produce complementary guidance that is shorter than the previous iterations, but remains comprehensive. The two documents are similarly structured for ease of reference and should be read together.

The Rt. Hon. The Lord Thomas Lord Chief Justice of England and

The Rt. Hon. Dominic Grieve QC MP Attorney General

INTRODUCTION

This protocol is prescribed for use by CPD IV Disclosure 22A: Disclosure of Unused Material. It is applicable in all the criminal courts of England and Wales, including the Crown Court, the Court Martial[1] and the magistrates'

1 The timetables given here may vary in the Court Martial and reference should be made to the Criminal Procedure and Investigations Act 1996 (Application to the Armed Forces) Order 2009 and to any practice note issued by the Judge Advocate General.

courts. It replaces the previous judicial document 'Disclosure: a Protocol for the Control and Management of Unused Material in the Crown Court'[2] and it also replaces section 4 'Disclosure' of the Lord Chief Justice's Protocol on the Control and Management of Heavy Fraud and Other Complex Criminal Cases, dated 22 March 2005.[3]

This protocol is intended to provide a central source of guidance for the judiciary, although that produced by the Attorney General also requires attention.

In summary, this judicial protocol sets out the principles to be applied to, and the importance of, disclosure; the expectations of the court and its role in disclosure, in particular in relation to case management; and the consequences if there is a failure by the prosecution or defence to comply with their obligations.

Readers should note that a review of disclosure in the magistrates' courts is currently being undertaken by HHJ Kinch QC and the Chief Magistrate, on behalf of Lord Justice Gross, the Senior Presiding Judge. Amendments may therefore be made following the recommendations of that review, and in accordance with other forthcoming changes to the criminal justice system.

THE IMPORTANCE OF DISCLOSURE FOR FAIR TRIALS

1. Disclosure remains one of the most important – as well as one of the most misunderstood and abused – of the procedures relating to criminal trials. Lord Justice Gross' review has re-emphasised the need for all those involved to understand the statutory requirements and to undertake their roles with rigour, in a timely manner.

2. The House of Lords stated in *R v H and C* [2004] UKHL 3; [2004] 2 AC 134; [2004] 2 Cr App R 10:

> "*Fairness ordinarily requires that any material held by the prosecution which weakens its case or strengthens that of the defendant, if not relied on as part of its formal case against the defendant, should be disclosed to the defence. Bitter experience has shown that miscarriages of justice may occur where such material is withheld from disclosure. The golden rule is that full disclosure of such material should be made.*" *([2004] 2 AC 134, at 147)*

The Criminal Cases Review Commission has recently noted that failure to disclose material to the defence to which they were entitled remains the biggest single cause of miscarriages of justice.

3. However, it is also essential that the trial process is not overburdened or diverted by erroneous and inappropriate disclosure of unused prosecution material or by misconceived applications. Although the drafters of the Criminal

2 The previous judicial protocol was endorsed by the Court of Appeal in *R v K* [2006] EWCA Crim 724; [2006] 2 All ER 552 (Note); [2006] Crim LR 1012.

3 This protocol also replaces the Protocol for the Provision of Advance Information, Prosecution Evidence and Disclosure of Unused Material in the Magistrates' Courts, dated 12 May 2006, which was adopted as part of the Stop Delaying Justice initiative.

Procedure and Investigations Act 1996 ('CPIA 1996') cannot have anticipated the vast increase in the amount of electronic material that has been generated in recent years, nevertheless the principles of that Act still hold true. Applications by the parties or decisions by judges based on misconceptions of the law or a general laxity of approach (however well-intentioned) which result in an improper application of the disclosure regime have, time and again, proved unnecessarily costly and have obstructed justice. As Lord Justice Gross noted, the burden of disclosure must not be allowed to render the prosecution of cases impracticable.

4. The overarching principle is that unused prosecution material will fall to be disclosed if, and only if, it satisfies the test for disclosure applicable to the proceedings in question, subject to any overriding public interest considerations. The test for disclosure will depend on the date the criminal investigation in question commenced, as this will determine whether the common law disclosure regime applies, or either of the two disclosure regimes under the CPIA 1996.

5. The test for disclosure under section 3 of the CPIA 1996 as amended will be applicable in nearly every case and all those involved in the process will need to be familiar with it. Material fulfils the test if – but only if – it 'might reasonably be considered capable of undermining the case for the prosecution … or of assisting the case for the accused.'

6. The disclosure process must be led by the prosecution so as to trigger comprehensive defence engagement, supported by robust judicial case management. Active participation by the court in the disclosure process is a critical means of ensuring that delays and adjournments are avoided, given failures by the parties to comply with their obligations may disrupt and (in some cases) frustrate the course of justice.

DISCLOSURE OF UNUSED MATERIAL IN CRIMINAL CASES

7. The court should keep the timetable for prosecution and defence disclosure under review from the first hearing. Judges should as a matter of course ask the parties to identify the issues in the case, and invite the parties to indicate whether further disclosure is sought, and on what topics. For example, it is not enough for the judge to rely on the content of the PCMH form. Proper completion of the disclosure process is a vital part of case preparation, and it may well affect the progress of the case. The court will expect disclosure to have been considered from the outset; the prosecution and defence advocates need to be aware of any potential problems and substantive difficulties should be explained to the judge; and the parties should propose a sensible timetable. Realism is preferable to optimistic but unachievable deadlines which may dislocate the court schedule and imperil the date of trial. It follows that judges should not impose deadlines for service of the case papers or disclosure until they are confident that the prosecution advocate has taken instructions from the individuals who are best placed to evaluate the work to be undertaken.

8. The advocates – both prosecution and defence – must be kept fully informed throughout the course of the proceedings as to any difficulties which may prevent them from complying with their disclosure obligations. When problems arise or come to light after directions have been given, the advocates should notify the court and the other party (or parties) immediately rather than waiting until the date set by the court for the service of the material is imminent or has passed, and they must provide the court with a suggested timetable in order to resolve the problem. The progress of the disclosure process should be reviewed at every hearing. There remains no basis in practice or law for Counsel to Counsel disclosure.

9. If there is a preliminary hearing the judge should seize the opportunity to impose an early timetable for disclosure and to identify any likely problems including as regards third party material and material that will require an application to the Family Court. In an appropriate case the court should consider holding a Joint Criminal/Care Directions Hearing. See Material held by Third Parties, from paragraph 44 below.

10. For the PCMH to be effective, the defence must have a proper opportunity to review the case papers and consider initial disclosure, with a view to preparing a properly completed defence statement which will inform the judge's conduct of the PCMH, and inform the prosecution of the matters required by sections 5, 6A and 6C of the CPIA. As the Court of Appeal noted in *R v Newell* [2012] EWCA Crim 650; [2012] 2 Cr App R 10, "a typed defence statement must be provided before the PCMH. If there is no defence statement by the time of the PCMH, then a judge will usually require the trial advocate to see that such a statement is provided and not proceed with the PCMH until that is done. In the ordinary case the trial advocate will be required to do that at the court and the PCMH resumed later in the day to avoid delay". There may be some instances when there will be a well-founded defence application to extend the 28-day time limit for serving a proper defence statement. In a proper case (but never routinely), it may be appropriate to put the PCMH back by a week or more, to enable an appropriate defence statement to be filed.

11. The defence statement can be admitted into evidence under section 6E(4) of the CPIA 1996. However, information included on the PCMH form (which is primarily an administrative form) will not usually be admitted in evidence when the defence advocate has complied with the letter and the spirit of the Criminal Procedure Rules.[4] Introducing the PCMH form (or part of it) during the trial is likely to be an exceptional event. The status of the trial preparation form in the magistrates' court is somewhat different, as discussed below.

12. The court should not extend time lightly or as a matter of course. If an extension is sought, it ought to be accompanied by an appropriate explanation. For instance, it is not sufficient for the prosecutor merely to say that the investigator has delivered the papers late: the underlying reasons are to

4 *R v Newell* [2012] EWCA Crim 650; [2012] 2 Cr App R 10.

be provided to the court. The same applies if the defence statement is delayed. Whichever party is at fault, realistic proposals for service are to be set out.

13. Judges should not allow the prosecution to avoid their statutory responsibility for reviewing the unused material by the expedient of permitting the defence to have access to (or providing the defence with copies of) the material listed in the schedules of non-sensitive unused prosecution material irrespective of whether it satisfies, wholly or in part, the relevant test for disclosure. Additionally, it is for the prosecutor to decide on the manner of disclosure, and it does not have to mirror the form in which the information was originally recorded. Rose LJ gave guidance on case management issues in this context in *R v CPS* (Interlocutory Application under sections 35/36 CPIA) [2005] EWCA Crim 2342. Allowing the defence to inspect items that fulfil the disclosure test is also a valid means of providing disclosure.

14. The larger and more complex the case, the more important it is for the prosecution to adhere to the overarching principle and ensure that sufficient prosecution attention and resources are allocated to the task. Handing the defendant the "keys to the warehouse" has been the cause of many gross abuses in the past, resulting in considerable expenditure by the defence without any material benefit to the course of justice. The circumstances relating to large and complex cases are outlined below.

15. The court will require the defence to engage and assist in the early identification of the real issues in the case and, particularly in the larger and more complex cases, to contribute to the search terms to be used for, and the parameters of, the review of any electronically held material (which can be very considerable). Any defence criticisms of the prosecution approach to disclosure should be timely and reasoned; there is no place for disclosure "ambushes" or for late or uninformative defence statements. Admissions should be used so far as possible to narrow the real issues in dispute.

16. A constructive approach to disclosure is a necessary part of professional best practice, for the defence and prosecution. This does not undermine the defendant's legitimate interests, it accords with his or her obligations under the Rules and it ensures that all the relevant material is provided. Delays and failures by the prosecution and the defence are equally damaging to a timely, fair and efficient trial, and judges should be vigilant in preventing and addressing abuses. Accordingly, whenever there are potential failings by either the defence or the prosecution, judges, in exercising appropriate oversight of disclosure, should carefully investigate the suggested default and give timely directions.

17. In the Crown Court, the defence statement is to be served within 28 days of the date when the prosecution complies with its duty of initial disclosure (or purports to do so) and whenever section 5(5) of the CPIA applies to the proceedings, and the defence statement must comply with section 6A of the CPIA. Service of the defence statement is a most important stage in the disclosure process, and timely service is necessary to facilitate proper consideration of the disclosure issues well in advance of the trial date. Judges expect a defence statement to contain a clear and detailed exposition of the

issues of fact and law. Defence statements that merely rehearse the suggestion that the defendant is innocent do not comply with the requirements of the CPIA.

18. The prosecutor should consider the defence statement carefully and promptly provide a copy to the disclosure officer, to assist the prosecution in its continuing disclosure obligations. The court expects the Crown to identify any suggested deficiencies in the defence statement, and to draw these to the attention of the defence and the court; in particular in large and complex cases, it will assist the court if this is in writing. Although the prosecution's ability to request, and the court's jurisdiction to give, an adverse inference direction under section 11 of CPIA is not contingent on the prosecution having earlier identified any suggested deficiencies, nevertheless the prosecutor must provide a timely written explanation of its position.

19. Judges should examine the defence statement with care to ensure that it complies with the formalities required by the CPIA. As stated in *R v H and C* (supra) (paragraph 35):

> *"If material does not weaken the prosecution case or strengthen that of the defendant, there is no requirement to disclose it. For this purpose the parties' respective cases should not be restrictively analysed. But they must be carefully analysed, to ascertain the specific facts the prosecution seek to establish and the specific grounds on which the charges are resisted. The trial process is not well served if the defence are permitted to make general and unspecified allegations and then seek far-reaching disclosure in the hope that material may turn up to make them good. Neutral material or material damaging to the defendant need not be disclosed and should not be brought to the attention of the court."*

20. If no defence statement – or an inadequate defence statement – is served within the relevant time limits, the judge should investigate the position. At every PCMH where there is no defence statement, including those where an extension has been given, or the time for filing has not yet expired, the defence should be warned in appropriate terms that pursuant to section 6E(2) of the CPIA an adverse inference may be drawn during the trial, and this result is likely if there is no justification for the deficiency. The fact that a warning has been given should be noted.

21. An adverse inference may be drawn under section 11 of the CPIA if the accused fails to discharge his or her disclosure obligations. Whenever the amended CPIA regime applies, the prosecution may comment on any failure in defence disclosure (except where the failure relates to a point of law) without leave of the court, but counsel should use a measure of judgment as to whether it is wise to embark on cross-examination about such a failure.[5] If the accused is cross-examined about discrepancies between his evidence and his defence statement, or if adverse comment is made, the judge must give appropriate guidance to the jury.[6]

5 *R v Essa* [2009] EWCA Crim 43, paragraph 22.
6 *R v Hanyes* [2011] EWCA Crim 3281.

22. In order to secure a fair trial, it is vital that the prosecution is mindful of its continuing duty of disclosure. Once the defence statement has been received, the Crown must review disclosure in the light of the issues identified in the defence statement. In cases of complexity, the following steps are then likely to be necessary:

i. Service by the prosecution of any further material due to the defence following receipt of the defence statement.

ii. Any defence request to the prosecution for service of additional specific items. As discussed below, these requests must be justified by reference to the defence statement and they should be submitted on the section 8 form.

iii. Prosecution response to the defence request.

iv. If the defence considers that disclosable items are still outstanding, a section 8 application should be made using the appropriate form.

23. It follows that all requests by the defence to the prosecution for disclosure should be made on the section 8 application form, even if no hearing is sought in the first instance. Discussion and co-operation between the parties outside of court is encouraged in order to ensure that the court is only asked to issue a ruling when strictly necessary. However, use of the section 8 form will ensure that focussed requests are clearly set out in one place.

24. The judge should set a date as part of the timetabling exercise by which any application under section 8 is to be made, if this appears to be a likely eventuality.

25. The Court will require the section 8 application to be served on the prosecution well in advance of the hearing – indeed, prior to requesting the hearing – to enable the Crown to identify and serve any items that meet the test for disclosure.

26. Service of a defence statement is an essential precondition for an application under section 8, and applications should not be heard or directions for disclosure issued in the absence of a properly completed statement (see Part 22 of the Criminal Procedure Rules). In particular, blanket orders in this context are inconsistent with the statutory framework for disclosure laid down by the CPIA and the decision of the House of Lords in *R v H and C* (supra). It follows that defence requests for disclosure of particular pieces of unused prosecution material which are not referable to any issue in the case identified in the defence statement should be rejected.

27. Judges must ensure that defendants are not prejudiced on account of the failures of their lawyers, and, when necessary, the professions should be reminded that if justice is to be done, and if disclosure is to be dealt with fairly in accordance with the law, a full and careful defence statement and a reasoned approach to section 8 applications are essential. In exploring the adequacy of the defence statement, a judge should always ask what the issues are and upon what matters of fact the defendant intends to rely[7] and on what matters of fact the defendant takes issue.

7 *R v Rochford* [2010] EWCA Crim 1928; [2011] 1 Cr App R 11.

Listing

28. Sufficient time is necessary for the judge properly to undertake the PCMH, and this is a paramount consideration when listing cases. Unless the court is able to sit early, judges who are part heard on trials are probably not best placed to conduct PCMHs.

29. Cases that raise particularly difficult issues of disclosure should be referred to the Resident Judge for directions (unless a trial judge has been allocated) and, for trials of real complexity, the trial judge should be identified at an early stage, prior to the PCMH if possible. Listing officers, working in consultation with the Resident Judge and, if allocated, the trial judge, should ensure that sufficient time is allowed for judges to prepare and deal with prosecution and defence applications relating to disclosure, particularly in the more complex cases.

Magistrates' Courts (including the Youth Court)

30. The principles relating to disclosure apply equally in the magistrates' courts. It follows that whilst disclosure of unused material in compliance with the statutory test is undoubtedly essential in order to achieve justice, it is critical that summary trials are not delayed or made over-complicated by misconceived applications for, or inappropriate disclosure of, prosecution material.

31. Magistrates will rely on their legal advisers for guidance, and the latter should draw the attention of the parties and the court to the statutory provisions and the applicable case law. Cases raising disclosure issues of particular complexity should be referred to a District Judge (Magistrates' Courts), if available.

32. Although service of a defence statement is voluntary for summary trials (section 6 CPIA), the defendant cannot make an application for specific disclosure under section 8 CPIA, and the court cannot make any orders in this regard, unless a proper defence statement has been provided. It follows that although providing a defence statement is not mandatory, it remains a critical stage in the disclosure process. If disclosure issues are to be raised by the defence, a defence statement must be served well in advance of the trial date. Any section 8 application must be made in strict compliance with the Rules.

33. The case-management forms used in the magistrates' courts fulfil some of the functions of a defence statement, and the prosecution must take into account the information provided as to the defence case when conducting its on-going review of unused material. As the Court of Appeal noted in *R v Newell* (supra), admissions can be made in the Trial Preparation Form and the defence is able to identify the matters that are not in issue. Admissions made in these circumstances may be admissible during the trial. However, other information on the form that does not come within the section relating to admissions should be treated in the same way as the contents of a PCMH form in the Crown Court and it should not generally be introduced as part of the evidence at trial. However, the contents of the Trial Preparation Form do not replace the need to serve a defence statement if the defendant seeks to apply for disclosure under section 8 CPIA.

34. The standard directions require that any defence statement is to be served within 14 days of the date upon which the prosecution has complied with, or purported to comply with, the duty to provide initial disclosure. There may be some instances when there will be a well-founded defence application to extend the 14-day time limit for serving the defence statement. These applications must be made in accordance with the Criminal Procedure Rules, in writing and before the time limit expires.

35. Although CCTV footage frequently causes difficulties, it is to be treated as any other category of unused material and it should only be disclosed if the material meets the appropriate test for disclosure under the CPIA. The defence should either be provided with copies of the sections of the CCTV or afforded an opportunity to view them. If the prosecution refuses to disclose CCTV material that the defence considers to be discloseable, the courts should not make standard or general directions requiring the prosecutor to disclose material of this kind in the absence of an application under section 8. When potentially relevant CCTV footage is not in the possession of the police, the guidance in relation to third party material will apply, although the police remain under a duty to pursue all reasonable lines of inquiry, including those leading away from a suspect, whether or not defence requests are made.

36. The previous convictions of witnesses and any disciplinary findings against officers in the case are frequently discloseable and care should be taken to disclose them as appropriate. Documents such as crime reports or records of emergency calls should not be provided on a routine basis, for instance as part of a bundle of disclosed documents, irrespective of whether the material satisfies the appropriate test for disclosure. Defence advocates should not request this material in standard or routine correspondence, and instead focussed consideration should be given to the circumstances of the particular case. Unjustified requests for disclosure of material of this kind are routinely made, frequently leading to unnecessary delays and adjournments. The prosecution should always consider whether the request is properly made out.

37. The supervisory role of the courts is critical in this context, and magistrates must guard against granting unnecessary adjournments and issuing unjustified directions.

Large and complex cases in the Crown Court

38. Disclosure is a particular problem with the larger and more complex cases, which require a scrupulous approach by the parties and robust case management by the judiciary. If possible, the trial judge should be identified at the outset.

39. The legal representatives need to fulfil their duties in this context with care and efficiency; they should co-operate with the other party (or parties) and the court; and the judge and the other party (or parties) are to be informed of any difficulties, as soon as they arise. The court should be provided with an up-to-date timetable for disclosure whenever there are material changes in this regard. A disclosure-management document, or similar, prepared by the

prosecution will be of particular assistance to the court in large and complex cases.

40. Judges should be prepared to give early guidance as to the prosecution's approach to disclosure, thereby ensuring early engagement by the defence.

41. Cases of this nature frequently include large volumes of digitally stored material. The Attorney General's 2011 guidance (now included as an annex to the Attorney General's Guidelines on Disclosure 2013) is of particular relevance and assistance in this context.

42. Applications for witness anonymity orders require particular attention; as the Court of Appeal noted in *R v Mayers and Others* [2008] EWCA Crim 2989; [2009] 1 Cr App R 30, in making such an application, the prosecution's obligations of disclosure "go much further than the ordinary duties of disclosure".

43. If the judge considers that there are reasonable grounds to doubt the good faith of the investigation, he or she will be concerned to see that there has been independent and effective appraisal of the documents contained in the disclosure schedule and that its contents are adequate. In appropriate cases where this issue has arisen and there are grounds which show there is a real issue, consideration should be given to receiving evidence on oath from the senior investigating officer at an early case management hearing.

Material held by Third Parties

44. Where material is held by a third party such as a local authority, a social services department, hospital or business, the investigators and the prosecution may need to make enquiries of the third party, with a view to inspecting the material and assessing whether the relevant test for disclosure is met and determining whether any or all of the material should be retained, recorded and, in due course, disclosed to the accused. If access by the prosecution is granted, the investigators and the prosecution will need to establish whether the custodian of the material intends to raise PII issues, as a result of which the material may have to be placed before the court for a decision. This does not obviate the need for the defence to conduct its own enquiries as appropriate. Speculative enquiries without any proper basis in relation to third party material – whether by the prosecution or the defence – are to be discouraged, and, in appropriate cases, the court will consider making an order for costs where an application is clearly unmeritorious and misconceived.

45. The 2013 Protocol and Good Practice Model on Disclosure of Information in Cases of Alleged Child Abuse and Linked Criminal and Care Directions Hearings has recently been published. It provides a framework and timetable for the police and CPS to obtain discloseable material from local authorities, and for applications to be made to the Family Court. It is applicable to all cases of alleged child abuse where the child is aged 17 years or under. It is not binding on local authorities, but it does represent best practice and therefore should be consulted in all such cases. Delays in obtaining this type of material have led to unacceptable delays to trials involving particularly vulnerable

witnesses and every effort must be made to ensure that all discloseable material is identified at an early stage so that any necessary applications can be made and the defence receive material to which they are entitled in good time.

46. There is no specific procedure for disclosure of material held by third parties in criminal proceedings, although the procedure established under section 2 of the Criminal Procedure (Attendance of Witnesses) Act 1965 or section 97 of the Magistrates' Courts Act 1980 is often used for this purpose. Where the third party in question declines to allow inspection of the material, or requires the prosecution to obtain an order before providing copies, the prosecutor will need to consider whether it is appropriate to obtain a witness summons under either section 2 of the Criminal Procedure (Attendance of Witnesses) Act 1965 or section 97 of the Magistrates' Court Act 1980. Part 28 of the Criminal Procedure Rules and paragraphs 3.5 and 3.6 of the Code of Practice under the CPIA 1996 should be followed.

47. Applications for third party disclosure must identify the documents that are sought and provide full details of why they are discloseable. This is particularly relevant when access is sought to the medical records of those who allege they are victims of crime. It should be appreciated that a duty to assert confidentiality may arise when a third party receives a request for disclosure, or the right to privacy may be claimed under article 8 of the ECHR (see in particular Crim PR Part 28.6). Victims do not waive the confidentiality of their medical records, or their right to privacy under article 8 of the ECHR, by making a complaint against the accused. The court, as a public authority, must ensure that any interference with the right to privacy under article 8 is in accordance with the law, and is necessary in pursuit of a legitimate public interest. General and unspecified requests to trawl through such records should be refused. Confidentiality rests with the subject of the material, not with the authority holding it. The subject is entitled to service of the application and has the right to make representations: Criminal Procedure Rule 22.3 and *R (on the application of B) v Stafford Combined Court* [2006] EWHC 1645 (Admin); [2006] 2 Cr App R 34. The 2013 Protocol and Good Practice Model at paragraph 13 should be followed. It is likely that the judge will need to issue directions when issues of this kind are raised (e.g. whether enquiries with the third party are likely to be appropriate; who is to make the request; what material is to be sought, and from whom; and a timetable should be set).

48. The judge should consider whether to take any steps if a third party fails, or refuses, to comply with a request for disclosure, including suggesting that either of the parties pursue the request and, if necessary, make an application for a witness summons. In these circumstances, the court will need to set an appropriate timetable for compliance with Part 28 of the Rules. Any failure to comply with the timetable must immediately be referred back to the court for further directions, although a hearing will not always be necessary. Generally, it may be appropriate for the defence to pursue requests of this kind when the prosecution, for good reason, decline to do so and the court will need to ensure that this procedure does not delay the trial.

49. There are very limited circumstances in which information relating to Family Court proceedings (e.g. where there have been care proceedings in

relation to a child who has complained to the police of mistreatment) may be communicated without a court order: see the Family Procedure Rules 12.73. Reference should be made to the 2013 Protocol and Good Practice Model. In most circumstances, a court order will be required and paragraph 11 of the Protocol which sets out how an application should be made should be followed.

Other Government Departments

50. Material held by other government departments or other Crown agencies will not be prosecution material for the purposes of section 3(2) or section 8(4) of the CPIA if it has not been inspected, recorded and retained during the course of the relevant criminal investigation. The CPIA Code of Practice and the Attorney General's Guidelines on Disclosure, however, impose a duty upon the investigators and the prosecution to pursue all reasonable lines of inquiry and that may involve seeking disclosure from the relevant body.

International matters

51. The obligations of the Crown in relation to relevant third-party material held overseas are as set out in *R v Flook* [2009] EWCA Crim 682; [2010] 1 Cr App R 30: the Crown must pursue reasonable lines of enquiry and if it appears there is relevant material, all reasonable steps must be taken to obtain it, whether formally or otherwise. To a great extent, the success of these enquiries will depend on the laws of the country where the material is held and the facts of the individual case. It needs to be recognised that when the material is held in a country outside of the European Union, the power of the Crown and the courts of England and Wales to obtain third-party material may well be limited. If informal requests are unsuccessful, the avenues are limited to the Crime (International Co-operation) Act 2003 and any applicable international conventions. It cannot, in any sense, be guaranteed that a request to a foreign government, court or body will produce the material sought. Additionally, some foreign authorities may be prepared to show the material in question to the investigating officers, whilst refusing to allow the material to be copied or otherwise made available.

52. As the Court of Appeal observed in *R v Khyam* [2008] EWCA Crim 1612; [2009] 1 Cr App R (S) 77:

> *"The prosecuting authorities in this jurisdiction simply cannot compel authorities in a foreign country to acknowledge, let alone comply with, our disclosure principles." ([2008] EWCA Crim 1612, at paragraph 37)*

The obligation is therefore to take reasonable steps. Whether the Crown has complied with that obligation is for the courts to judge in each case.

53. It is, therefore, important that the prosecution sets out the position clearly in writing, including any inability to inspect or retrieve any material that potentially ought to be disclosed, along with the steps that have been taken.

Applications for Non-Disclosure in the Public Interest

54. Applications in this context, whenever possible, should be considered by the trial judge. The House of Lords in *R v H and C* (supra) has provided useful guidance as to the proper approach to be applied (paragraph 36):

> *"When any issue of derogation from the golden rule of full disclosure comes before it, the court must address a series of questions:*
>
> *(1) What is the material which the prosecution seek to withhold? This must be considered by the court in detail.*
>
> *(2) Is the material such as may weaken the prosecution case or strengthen that of the defence? If No, disclosure should not be ordered. If Yes, full disclosure should (subject to (3), (4) and (5) below) be ordered.*
>
> *(3) Is there a real risk of serious prejudice to an important public interest (and, if so, what) if full disclosure of the material is ordered? If No, full disclosure should be ordered.*
>
> *(4) If the answer to (2) and (3) is Yes, can the defendant's interest be protected without disclosure or disclosure be ordered to an extent or in a way which will give adequate protection to the public interest in question and also afford adequate protection to the interests of the defence?*
>
> *This question requires the court to consider, with specific reference to the material which the prosecution seek to withhold and the facts of the case and the defence as disclosed, whether the prosecution should formally admit what the defence seek to establish or whether disclosure short of full disclosure may be ordered. This may be done in appropriate cases by the preparation of summaries or extracts of evidence, or the provision of documents in an edited or anonymised form, provided the documents supplied are in each instance approved by the judge. In appropriate cases the appointment of special counsel may be a necessary step to ensure that the contentions of the prosecution are tested and the interests of the defendant protected (see para 22 above). In cases of exceptional difficulty the court may require the appointment of special counsel to ensure a correct answer to questions (2) and (3) as well as (4).*
>
> *(5) Do the measures proposed in answer to (4) represent the minimum derogation necessary to protect the public interest in question? If No, the court should order such greater disclosure as will represent the minimum derogation from the golden rule of full disclosure.*
>
> *(6) If limited disclosure is ordered pursuant to (4) or (5), may the effect be to render the trial process, viewed as a whole, unfair to the defendant? If Yes, then fuller disclosure should be ordered even if this leads or may lead the prosecution to discontinue the proceedings so as to avoid having to make disclosure.*
>
> *(7) If the answer to (6) when first given is No, does that remain the correct answer as the trial unfolds, evidence is adduced and the defence advanced?*

It is important that the answer to (6) should not be treated as a final, once-and-for-all, answer but as a provisional answer which the court must keep under review." ([2004] 2 AC 134, at 155-156)

55. In this context, the following matters are to be emphasised:

a. The procedure for making applications to the court is set out in the Criminal Procedure Rules, Part 22;

b. When the PII application is a Type 1 or Type 2 application, proper notice to the defence is necessary to enable the accused to make focused submissions to the court and the notice should be as specific as the nature of the material allows. It is appreciated that in some cases only the generic nature of the material can be identified. In some wholly exceptional cases (Type 3 cases) it may be justified to give no notice at all. The judge should always ask the prosecution to justify the form of notice (or the decision to give no notice at all).

c. The prosecution should be alert to the possibility of disclosing a statement in a redacted form by, for example, simply removing personal details. This may obviate the need for a PII application, unless the redacted material satisfies the test for disclosure.

d. Except when the material is very short (for instance only a few sheets), or for reasons of sensitivity, the prosecution should supply securely sealed copies to the judge in advance, together with a short statement explaining the relevance of each document, how it satisfies the disclosure test and why it is suggested that disclosure would result in a real risk of serious prejudice to an important public interest; in undertaking this task, the use of merely formulaic expressions is to be discouraged. In any case of complexity a schedule of the material should be provided, identifying the particular objection to disclosure in relation to each item, and leaving a space for the judge's decision.

e. The application, even if held in private or in secret, should be recorded. The judge should give some short statement of reasons; this is often best done document by document as the hearing proceeds.

f. The recording, copies of the judge's orders (and any copies of the material retained by the court) should be clearly identified, securely sealed and kept in the court building in a safe or locked cabinet consistent with its security classification, and there should be a proper register of the contents. Arrangements should be made for the return of the material to the prosecution once the case is concluded and the time for an appeal has elapsed.

CONCLUSION

56. Historically, disclosure was viewed essentially as being a matter to be resolved between the parties, and the court only became engaged if a particular issue or complaint was raised. That perception is now wholly out

of date. The regime established under the Criminal Justice Act 2003 and the Criminal Procedure Rules gives judges the power – indeed, it imposes a duty on the judiciary – actively to manage disclosure in every case. The efficient, effective and timely resolution of these issues is a critical element in meeting the overriding objective of the Criminal Procedure Rules of dealing with cases justly.

Index

[All references are to paragraph number]

www.ingramcontent.com/pod-product-compliance
Lightning Source LLC
LaVergne TN
LVHW052205200926
848481LV00001B/35
9781526515162